Encyclopedia of Women and Sport in America

Edited by
Carole A. Oglesby
with
Doreen L. Greenberg, Ruth Louise Hall, Karen L. Hill, Frances Johnston, and Sheila Easterby Ridley

Oryx Press
1998

The rare Arabian Oryx is believed to have inspired the myth of the unicorn. This desert antelope became virtually extinct in the early 1960s. At that time several groups of international conservationists arranged to have 9 animals sent to the Phoenix Zoo to be the nucleus of a captive breeding herd. Today the Oryx population is over 1,000 and over 500 have been returned to the Middle East.

© 1998 by The Oryx Press
4041 North Central at Indian School Road
Phoenix, Arizona 85012-3397

Published simultaneously in Canada
Printed and Bound in the United States of America

Cover photo courtesy of Allsport Photography, Inc., Al Bello, "Lisa Leslie/USA, 1996 Olympic Games"

∞ The paper used in this publication meets the minimum requirements of American National Standard for Information Science—Permanence of Paper for Printed Library Materials, ANSI Z39.48, 1984.

Library of Congress Cataloging-in-Publication Data

Encyclopedia of women and sport in America / edited by Carole A.
  Oglesby . . . [et al.].
    p. cm.
  Includes bibliographical references and index.
  ISBN 0-89774-993-6 (alk. paper) √
  1. Women athletes—United States—Encyclopedias. 2. Sports for
women—United States—Encyclopedias. I. Oglesby, Carole A.
GV709.E53 1998
796'.082—dc21   97-52787
                                                     CIP

Contents

Contents

Contents

Foreword

by Mariah Burton Nelson

A few years ago, while coaching high school basketball, I noticed something odd about our best player, a six-foot sophomore guard named Michelle. She was agile and selfless, averaging six assists and six steals per game. Yet when her name was announced, she would shuffle onto the court hunched over like an old woman with osteoporosis.

"Why do you walk like that?" I asked.

"I'm embarrassed," she admitted. She felt shy about being a star. Athletic excellence just didn't seem right—in a girl.

Oh dear, I thought. This was 1994. It was not the 1950s. I wanted to lecture her: "Have you no idea how many women over the years have worked hard to get you to this position, where you can develop your talent, where you can play each week in front of hundreds of adoring parents and peers, where you can work toward a full athletic scholarship at a major university? Embarrassed by success? Michelle, it is *good* to be successful! It is good for girls to be successful! You're 15 years old. Hasn't anyone told you that yet?"

Somehow I managed to skip the lecture. Instead I asked, "Who do you look up to?"

"Sheryl Swoopes," she answered immediately. Swoopes had scored 47 points for Texas Tech in the National Collegiate Athletic Association (NCAA) championship game the previous season.

"How does she carry herself?" I asked.

"She looks proud," said Michelle, lifting her chin.

Two years later, Sheryl Swoopes and the national women's basketball team toured the country, winning 60 games en route to an Olympic gold medal. Michelle attended one of their games. By then Michelle had come to resemble Sheryl, walking with an air of confidence that inspired younger teammates. She had come to understand that "little girls need big girls to look up to," as basketball star Teresa Edwards put it.

The need for role models became a sort of theme song for the American women in the 1996 Olympic Games. Lisa Leslie, the starting center on the basketball team, said, "You recognize that you're representing your country—especially the little girls who hopefully will follow in our footsteps."

Mariah Burton Nelson is an award-winning journalist and author.

Gold-medal-winning tennis player Lindsay Davenport said, "These Olympics, probably more than any before, are showing a lot of little girls it's okay to sweat; it's okay to play hard; it's okay to be an athlete."

Swimmer Amy Van Dyken said after winning four gold medals, "Growing up, we didn't have as many role models as the boys did. Girls need to understand it's cool to be athletic."

It's definitely cool to be athletic. Role models surely make life easier.

Yet American women did not achieve their unprecedented success in the 1996 Olympic Games because little girls had big girls to look up to. They were successful because of Title IX, the 1972 federal law that prohibits sex discrimination in high school and college, including in athletic activities. They were successful because after athletic directors dragged their feet about enforcing the law for the first decade, and after the Supreme Court weakened the law in 1984, Olympian Flo Hyman and others in the feminist sports movement lobbied Congress to pass the 1988 "Civil Rights Restoration Act" (enacted over President Reagan's veto), which clarified that Title IX applies to athletic programs. American Olympians were successful because, 24 years after the passage of Title IX, schools and universities were finally giving women a chance to compete.

Despite these successes, discrimination remains the norm: men receive two-thirds of all athletic scholarships; male coaches are paid more than women for coaching women's teams; men coach more than half of all women's teams, while women coach fewer than 1 percent of men's teams. But in response to frequent lawsuits, high schools and universities are gradually (albeit begrudgingly) coming into compliance with the law.

Michelle and my other high school players had never heard of Title IX. When I talk to college students today, few know who Billie Jean King is. Young women today have little sense of their own history or their legal rights. Many still believe the myth that football "makes money for the school" (80 percent of football programs lose money) or that women "deserve" fewer opportunities because their sports are rarely revenue-producing (courts have consistently ruled that financial considerations are irrelevant in Title IX cases) or that women are just not as interested as men are in receiving $100,000 athletic scholarships (yeah, right).

So little girls need heroes, sure, but they also need information about who female athletes were in the past and who they could be in the future. They need to know about athletes and also about coaches, commentators, administrators, officials, sponsors, and scholars. What was the Association of Intercollegiate Athletics for Women (AIAW), and what was its philosophy? Why are female gymnasts so often injured? How many golf courses still discriminate against women? Which companies design sports clothing and equipment based on women's bodies? Why are African American women successful in track and basketball, but rarely in golf or swimming? Why is less than 5 percent of sports media coverage devoted to women? In which sports careers have women made the greatest strides?

Carole Oglesby, who wrote *Women and Sport: From Myth to Reality* in 1978, is a pioneering athlete, professor, and political organizer who has been helping the rest of us distinguish myth from reality for more than three decades. We can trust her to tell us the truth. This book is full of role models, but it's also overflowing with useful and accurate information about women's rights, women's experiences, and the history and culture of women's sports. It will show proud readers their place in a long line of impressive and devoted sportswomen. It will take us one step closer to a world in which athletic girls and women need never apologize for their own success.

Foreword

by Marilyn Oshman

When I was growing up, I was not a great athlete, but I loved sports. As one of two daughters in a family whose business was the major sporting goods store in Houston, I was exposed to more athletes, athletics, and outdoor experiences than most of my friends. Sports and the outdoors were a natural part of our family life. You didn't need to be the best at sports, but somehow its very existence made life better and more interesting.

In our house, it seemed that if you worked hard, believed in yourself, and did your best—somehow you would succeed in your endeavor, whether it was academic, sports, or business. Because I was not an elite athlete, I was completely unaware of the intense struggle for funding, participation, and recognition in women's sports. When I became involved with my family's sporting goods business in 1990, all that changed within months.

I am grateful for the *Encyclopedia of Women and Sport in America* because it explains the scope and complexity of the issues facing females interested in any career in athletics, whether on the field or in the office. The importance of listing and telling the individual stories in this book cannot be overstated. In our culture, written records provide a reference that creates the legacy these achievements so richly deserve. Books make things more real. Understanding the history of women's sports gives all of women's recent achievements a historical context and even gives perspective to other women's issues.

In addition to being a registry, this collection of material serves as an inspiration. I see it as a spiritual guide for the elite athlete as well as for the girls who are playing and reaping the benefits of Title IX. As a businesswoman, I am moved by the courage, fortitude, and persistence of these heroines as they attacked their own field of interest. As we all know, when we are in the midst of a struggle, there is a strange sort of relief in hearing other stories and great comfort in discovering we are not alone.

Another important aspect of the *Encyclopedia* is the inclusion of women like Jody Conradt, Val Ackerman, and Ann Meyers-Drysdale, who have established sports-related careers for themselves. Their successes have helped expand the range of careers in sports available to interested women. Elite athletes are few and far between; that is why their stories are so intriguing. The great majority of us love

Marilyn Oshman is chair of the board of Oshman's Sporting Goods.

sports and have longed for the opportunity to work in our chosen field, not necessarily on the court or the playing field, but in something related to sports. Today major American companies are acknowledging the emerging women's market. This development is creating a demand for women in decision-making capacities (to help explain and service this market). Carole Oglesby and her co-authors have not neglected these professional breakthroughs and in describing them here, they have created even more opportunities for all of us.

The book is enriched by the consideration of so many of the issues that relate to women's involvement with sports. The encyclopedic reach of Oglesby's and her co-authors' research is a great contribution to all of us who care to know what is going on today.

Finally, in contemplating the long-range value of this book, I wonder "What do all these women have in common?" Their vision, their perseverance, their steadfastness, and their belief in themselves seems to be a thread that runs through all the unique stories. The lessons from the field, the value of teamwork, and the belief in yourself are all the qualities that are required to have a successful life, on the field or off. Each woman faced challenges, some of them seemingly insurmountable. Each woman conquered those circumstances. Just as it is fun to read a favorite old story over and over again, these stories will provide endless inspiration to succeeding generations of women, young and old alike. Today, in my role as chair of the board of Oshman's Sporting Goods, these stories renew my fortitude and courage as I face personal business challenges of great magnitude. They serve as a reminder to me of our family values and regenerate my energy to do my best.

Preface

At the launch of this reference work, perceptions of a variety of complications beset the editorial team. First, the hope that the work would be widely read became palpable. The awareness that an "encyclopedia" is generally approached for a particular answer to a particular question brought the accompanying realization that few will take on the book "cover to cover." This realization quickly gave rise to yet another consideration that such use will diminish the work's comprehensibility in its conceived wholeness. The preface material is intended to supply a framework so that these considerations will be obviated.

We set out to tell the story of women and sport in America in true A to Z fashion. Because this book attempts to address this subject in a single volume, we cannot do full justice to the topic. To each and every person whose story we have failed to tell, we offer regrets. It is our belief and hope that this encyclopedia will spawn a hundred other such projects (possibly an "encyclopedia" on women in each specific sport, for example) and that the omissions will be corrected in the great order of time.

Any A to Z encyclopedia of women's sports, in our view, should cover the full meaning and place of sport in the life of every woman. It should deal with what Mariah Burton Nelson has called the "courage to compete." It should point out the void that can result from a woman's limited sense of self when opportunities are denied her. This examination of the meaning of sport thus takes into account the *absence* of sport and active lifestyle in the lives of many women, long excluded from the fruits of a powerful and pervasive element of American society. As we read, for example, the entry "Elderly Women and Exercise," we are reading mostly of women whose childhoods (in the early decades of this century) were marked by severely limited access to sport. We see in this one essay the potential place of sport and exercise in the cycle of women's lives. The frail elderly woman is advantaged in her senior years if the fun and challenge of play, games, and sport are present in any measure in her life. Her condition, weakened as it may be, has been worsened because of a lifetime of social and institutional limits on her "athletic self." But as the reader will see, opportunities have changed for the better. We can project years ahead and ask ourselves what will be the condition of today's young American woman in 2050 or 2070? Will today's high school athlete be a strong and vital masters competitor? We think yes.

The encyclopedia has, at its core, over 140 biographies of great American women athletes and descriptions of the sports with which they are associated. The same theme is repeated over and over again. Women of uncommon courage simply refused to take "no" for an answer when it made no sense to do so and persisted in the passionate pursuit of a sport in which mastery was within their grasp. In choosing the women and the sports to include, we aimed for diversity. In sports that have been little pursued by women, or that are very new to women, we have sought to present a role model. Her story might seem somewhat modest when compared to someone we have omitted in a "mighty sport" for women. We had to make painful choices, but we aimed to have as full a range as possible of the activities in which women have made a contribution.

We believe that women's "place" in sport is not only as a competitor. Thus, we have included entries on many of the career options within sport. We describe the field generally and then emphasize the special steps a woman can take to maximize the possibility of a successful career in that field as well as any special gifts or qualities a woman would particularly bring to that career.

Many of the entries describe what we know about women and sport from the various disciplines of sport science. Exercise physiologists, biomechanists, physicians, fitness experts, historians, sport psychologists, sport sociologists, and physical educators all illuminate the challenges and benefits for women following the path of the sportswoman. There is not unanimity of view across the scientific spectrum. The variations in interpretations are both interesting and exciting in the way new, and better, methods and designs are suggested. Some of the entries are designated as "essays" and are marked by a shaded background to distinguish them from the other encyclopedia entries. These essays may favor a point of view or offer a personal narrative.

Some of the essays in sport psychology, imagery and mental practice, and the basic mechanics of performance aim to inform girls and women whose store of information on the rudiments of sport may be lacking. Plain "how to" talk can benefit both the reader and, in the case of a mother or mentor, her children as she functions as their first coach.

An important contribution in this book is the addition of voices seldom heard in published accounts of women and sport. Women who may be considered "minorities" put forward their stories. African American, Asian, Latina, and Native American women's views are described from their unique vantage points on sport. The high-level sport and cultural participation of Jewish women in the Macabbiah Games is also presented. The participation and records of women with disabilities are catalogued, as are considerations of lesbian women. Finally, a "nontraditional" group in an encyclopedia of women and sport is *men*. One essay specifically credits the strong and brave stances of many men who have advocated in their life work on behalf of women in sport. These men join, of course, the fathers, husbands, brothers, and male coaches who have prominent places in many biographies throughout the book.

As we neared the end of this publication process, we observed, perhaps not surprisingly, that the accurate, comprehensive *record* of women's participation in sport is woeful. We had great difficulty in finding, and obtaining permission to use pictures (of even the most famous). Locating *action* pictures and action pictures of "historic moments" were particularly challenging. Any approximation of the "true record" is largely still in people's attics, notebooks of faded clippings, or uncatalogued boxes of mementos. All of us who have acted in an editorial capacity would plead with readers to take notice of any woman in your family, community, school, or favorite sport, who has excelled. While she is still available to you, or at least while people who have seen her perform firsthand may be available to you, catalogue her formative years, exploits, and contributions. Then make sure that someone—in your community or your sport, a women's sports organization like Women's Sports Foundation or the National Association of Girls and Women in Sport, or one of our editorial staff—receives information concerning this record. It is a gift to our mutual posterity. To preserve this kind of information and to make any additions or modifications to our text, contact us through our publisher at 4041 N. Central Ave., Phoenix, AZ 85012 or through info@oryxpress.com.

As readers are beginning to make their way through the *Encyclopedia*, a few pointers are in order. Some entries are designated by a special "boundary breaker" symbol ( ). This symbol signifies that the women so noted accomplished a task or feat for the first time and in such a way that public perceptions of women were altered. The decision on the boundary breaker designation was made by the editorial team. As mentioned earlier, entries marked by a shaded background are designated as essays, which may favor a point of view or offer a personal narrative.

We were fortunate, as the editorial team, to have had the assistance of over 70 contributors. Entries from contributors are noted with the individual's initials at the conclusion of the entry. Any entry without initials was a composite effort of the editorial team.

This encyclopedia provides a comprehensive record of how far women have come in sport and how far they have yet to go. For me, the journey of women and sport is not complete until every woman experiences, as her birthright, the full potential of her body. She must believe with perfect confidence in her right to pursue healthy activities that develop this potential through joy and challenge. This perception of birthright will open nursing homes and nursery schools, school yards and recreation areas, and health clubs and Olympian fields for girls' and women's sport experiences.

Fostering this perception means continuing to change and enhance the opportunities for girls and women in the world around us. We all have little girls, or younger protégés, in our lives who still harbor fears and perceptions of their own limitations. We have daughters, sisters, and nieces who may (with a bit more encouragement and a generous measure of institutional resources) graduate from being enthusiasts of "gym class" to a life of joy and satisfaction with their own embodiment. You can "catch the spirit" in the voices of two girls telling it their own way. *CAO*

Sarah Oglesby
8 years

Question: What do you like most about school?

"I like recess because you get to play. My favorite thing to play is punchball. In PE (physical education), you get to run and that is very fun. It is also more organized into games like dodgeball, kickball, and relay races. My teacher is not a PE teacher, but she still makes it fun.

PE is more fun than recess because you don't get hurt in PE. In recess, you might get hurt because you run more and you might run into somebody. PE and recess are my favorite classes."

Molly Oglesby
12 years

Question: Do you learn things in physical education class?

"The two most important things I have gained from being in physical education in middle school are getting fit and becoming more flexible. In elementary school, we mostly just played games and had recess. I have the opportunity in middle school to work with a lot of people and gain trust from them. I'm also learning new games and how to play the old ones better. We run more in middle school so I've learned to breathe when I'm running longer distances. Listening and following directions are very important in PE, so I must be sure I do that. My favorite thing in PE is that I get the opportunity to do Project Adventure, which is very challenging. But the thing I like the least is dressing out because I'm always hurried and if I get a tardy, my grade will be lowered."

Acknowledgments

Our thanks for manuscript preparation go to Patrick Auerbach, Kathy Davis, Cathy Finney, Shawn Gomer, Linda Muraresku, Mariah Burton Nelson, and Brian Walker and to Sean Tape, Anne Thompson, and Natalie Lang from Oryx Press.

Contributors

R. VIVIAN ACOSTA

Dr. R. Vivian Acosta, a professor at Brooklyn College of the City University of New York, serves as the senior associate athletic director and the senior women's administrator as well as the chair of the graduate program within the Department of Physical Education and Exercise Science. She received her B.S. and M.S. degrees from Brigham Young University and her Ph.D. from the University of Southern California. Her areas of specialization are women in sport and sport administration.

MARLENE ADRIAN

Dr. Adrian is a renowned researcher in biomechanics and sport medicine, focusing on aging and movement challenges of the disabled. Member of U.S. Olympic Committee's Science and Technology Committee and champion fencer, she recently founded Women of Diversity Productions, Inc. http://www.womenofdiversity.org.

ALPHA ALEXANDER

Since 1992, Dr. Alexander has been the director of Health and Sports Advocacy for the Young Women's Christian Association (YWCA) of the USA. She serves as vice president of the Black Women in Sport Foundation and as a member of the board of directors of the U.S. Olympic Committee, the New York City Sports Commission, and the advisory board of the Women's Sports Foundation.

EVA AUCHINCLOSS

The founding executive director of the Women's Sports Foundation (1976-1986), Eva Auchincloss has been a national consultant for the United States Olympic Committee, Girls Incorporated, Girl Scouts, Explorer Scouts, and the Young Women's Christian Association (YWCA) of America. She currently manages a sports marketing firm for women and sports—Principal, Auchincloss & Turner, Inc.

GORDON BAKOULIS

Gordon Bakoulis is the editor of *Running Times* magazine. Prior to this, she was the health editor of *Women's Day*. She is also the author of *Cross Training* and *How to Train for and Run Your Best Marathon* (both by Fireside). As a national-class marathon runner for 11 years, Bakoulis competed in the 1988 and 1996 United States Olympic Women's Marathon Trials and represented the United States in world cup and world championship marathons.

Contributors

BRENDA LIGHT BREDEMEIER

Dr. Bredemeier is an associate professor at the University of California, Berkeley, whose research and publication have defined current work in moral behavior and sport. Deeply involved with her church, community, and family, Dr. Bredemeier has served in leadership capacities in the Association for Advancement of Applied Sport Psychology and in the administration of the Arts and Science College at Berkeley.

LINDA BUNKER

Formerly the associate dean for academic and student affairs at the University of Virginia, Dr. Bunker is internationally renowned for her work in sport psychology with professional golfers and tennis players. Noted for her dedication to girls and women in sport, she is on the advisory boards of the Women's Sports Foundation, Melpomene Institute, and *Shape Magazine*.

CARRIE BURROUS

Carrie Burrous, M.A., has been an ultrarunner since 1992. In 1995, she ran her first 100-mile ultra marathon and was the only woman under 30 years old to finish. She is a registered psychotherapist intern planning to work with female athletes and body image issues.

HOLLY CADWALLADER

Holly Cadwallader earned a master's degree in psychology of human movement at Temple University and is a doctoral candidate at this time. She is applying her expertise in exercise psychology, nutrition, and meditation in the area of holistic health.

ELLEN CARLTON (EC1)

Dr. Ellen Carlton is an associate professor in the Department of Kinesiology at Sonoma State University. Her current research is the "Strength of Character" project, a collaborative investigation of identity and moral development in lesbian sportswomen.

LINDA JEAN CARPENTER

Linda Jean Carpenter is a professor in the Department of Physical Education and Exercise Science at Brooklyn College of the City University of New York. She received her B.S. and M.S. from Brigham Young University, her Ph.D. from the University of Southern California, and her J.D. from Fordham Law School. Her area of research is women in sport, and she frequently writes in the area of sport law. She has been named a Tow Professor at Brooklyn College.

NICHOLE S. CHO

Nichole S. Cho is a program specialist in the Health and Sports Advocacy Department at the Young Women's Christian Association (YWCA) of the USA. Previously, Cho was an intern at the Women's Sports Foundation in the Grants and Awards Department. At Wesleyan University, she was captain of the varsity field hockey and lacrosse teams.

REBECCA A. CLARK

Dr. Rebecca Clark is a three-time participant with the USA Deaf Olympic Women's Volleyball Team, earning one gold and two silver medals. She presently works as a freelance writer and sport psychology consultant and maintains a private clinical social work practice.

EMILY CLASPELL (EC2)

Dr. Emily Claspell is a licensed psychologist. She is certified through the Association for Advancement of Applied Sport Psychology and is on the registry of the U.S. Olympic Committee. Dr. Claspell is a Korean-American living in Hawaii.

ROBERT (BOB) CLOTWORTHY

Olympic diver Bob Clotworthy was a national champion diver at Ohio State University in the early 1950s. At the 1952 Olympic Games in Helsinki, he won a bronze medal in springboard diving. He capped his career by winning the gold at the 1956 Olympic Games in Melbourne. Recently retired after 40 years of coaching/teaching, he is writing a book about the history of diving.

GERTRUDE COPPERMAN

Gertrude Copperman, M.D., has been practicing general medicine since 1952. She earned her medical degree from Pennsylvania's Women's Medical College in 1949. She is a consultant at St. Luke's Hospital. She enjoyed sports as a child and has been an exercise enthusiast all her adult life.

ELEANOR DAVIS

Eleanor Davis is a graduate of the University of Pennsylvania, receiving a master's degree from the School of Nursing. A community leader, she is on the board of trustees of Philadelphia's University of the Arts, on the board of the School of Nursing at the University of Pennsylvania, and in 1996 received the Wilma Rudolph Courage Award from the Philadelphia Awards and Grants Committee of the Women's Sports Foundation.

KATHY DAVIS

An associate professor of physical education at North Carolina State University, Kathy Davis has over 20 years of volleyball officiating experience. She was a National Association for Girls and Women in Sport (NAGWS) nationally rated volleyball official and a member of the NAGWS National Rating Team for volleyball.

KAREN P. DEPAUW

Dr. DePauw is an internationally recognized scholar and leader in adapted physical activity and disability sport. She recently co-authored *Disability and Sport* with Sue Gavron. Dr. DePauw is a professor of kinesiology and dean of the Graduate School at Washington State University.

BARBARA DRINKWATER

Dr. Drinkwater is a research physiologist in the Department of Medicine at the Pacific Medical Center in Seattle, WA. Her research focuses on women and exercise, and more recently on osteoporosis. Fellow and past president of the American College of Sports Medicine (ACSM), she received the 1996 ACSM Honor Award.

CARA DUNNE

Part of the national champion tandem cycling team of the United States Disabled Cycling Team, Cara Dunne lost her eyesight at the age of five. She and partner Scott Evans won silver and bronze medals in the Paralympic Games in Atlanta. From 1982 to 1989, Dunne competed, and medaled, as a member of the United States Disabled Alpine Ski Team. A graduate of Harvard University, Dunne recently graduated from the University of California at Los Angeles Law School.

DIANA EVERETT

Dr. Everett is the executive director of the National Association for Girls and Women in Sport (NAGWS). She was assistant athletic director at Texas Women's University. She has coached volleyball and track for 14 years. Her honors include *Who's Who Among American Women* and *Who's Who Among American Educators*.

SARAH FEYERHERM

Sarah Feyerherm is the former sports information director at Washington College in Chestertown, MD, where she currently serves as head field hockey coach and coordinator of student-athlete services and sports information. With a bachelor's degree from Hamilton College and a master's of science degree from the University of Massachusetts, Feyerherm was also a sports writer for the *Courier Post* in Cherry Hill, NJ.

DAVID GARBER

David Garber is the executive director of U.S.A. Curling. He has been curling since 1966 (age 12) and for many years was a competitive curler.

EVAN GOLDMAN

Evan Goldman is pursuing a doctorate in exercise science at Temple University. He regularly races keel boats and conducts sailing clinics for elite junior female sailors. He has coached women's sailing at a U.S. Olympic Sports Festival.

Contributors

JOY GORDON (JG1)

Joy Gordon was the director of public relations for Maccabi USA/Sports for Israel in Philadelphia for seven years. She has authored a number of articles on the Maccabiah Games and the Maccabi experience. She is currently the director of sponsorship development for Educational Marketing Concepts in Wayne, PA.

DOREEN L. GREENBERG

Doreen L. Greenberg, Ph.D., is an adjunct professor in the Department of Psychology at West Chester University, PA. She is an Association for the Advancement of Applied Sport Psychology (AAASP) certified sport psychology consultant and a member of the U.S. Olympic Committee Sport Psychology Registry.

SUSAN L. GREENDORFER

Dr. Susan Greendorfer is a sociologist of sport, recognized for her studies of women and gender relations in sport/physical activity. Noted for her research on female socialization into sport, sex differences in children's sport socialization, and female sport retirement, her current research focuses on ethnic differences in disordered eating among college women.

JOY GRIFFIN (JG2)

Joy Griffin, Ed.D., is an associate professor specializing in sport psychology/sociology at the University of New Mexico. She has published many books and presented numerous papers regarding Native Americans and physical activity. Dr. Griffin serves on many national committees committed to diversity issues.

PAT GRIFFIN

Dr. Pat Griffin is professor in social justice education at the University of Massachusetts and a former coach and athlete. Her main research focus is gay, lesbian, bisexual, and transgender issues in sport. Griffin has recently written a book entitled *Strong Women, Deep Closets: Lesbians and Homophobia in Sport.*

RUTH LOUISE HALL

Ruth Louise Hall, Ph.D., is an associate professor of psychology at the College of New Jersey. She is a licensed psychologist and also has a master's degree in sport psychology. She is a member of the Women's Sports Foundation Advisory Board.

MEREDITH HANSEN (MH1)

Meredith Hansen is an adjunct professor at South Puget Sound Community College. She completed a bachelor's degree at Springfield College and a master's degree at Smith College. She has coached swimming and was a member of 1996 Summer Biathlon Team.

MARCIA HELFANT (MH2)

Marcia Helfant, an administrator in long-term care facilities, has worked with the geriatric population for the last 20 years. She has been a nursing home ombudsperson and director of older adult services at a community center. An enthusiastic tennis player and hiker, Helfant has long been a proponent of exercise for older adults.

KAREN L. HILL

Karen L. Hill, Ph.D., is an associate professor in the Department of Kinesiology at Penn State University, Delaware County. She is an AAASP certified sport psychology consultant and a member of the U.S. Olympic Committee Sport Psychology Registry.

JACKIE HUDSON

Dr. Hudson is a tenured associate professor in biomechanics at California State University at Chico. Her research focuses on women in sport and skillful movement. Hudson played basketball at the University of Texas. She received her Ph.D. in biomechanics from Temple University.

ARLENE IGNICO

Dr. Arlene Ignico is a professor of physical education at Ball State University in Muncie, IN. She earned her doctorate at the University of Tennessee, Knoxville.

YOLANDA L. JACKSON

Yolanda L. Jackson is director of athlete services for the Women's Sports Foundation. She is responsible for all activities involving champion, elite, and Olympic female athletes and the WSF.

KATHERINE M. JAMIESON

Katherine Jamieson is a doctoral candidate in the Department of Physical Education and Exercise Science at Michigan State University. She completed her undergraduate and master's degrees at California State University at Fullerton. Her research interests include women of color in sport, with a specific focus on Latinas in United States sport.

MICHAEL JANES

Michael Janes is media relations manager for Special Olympics International in Washington, D.C.

FRANCES JOHNSTON

Frances Johnston, Ph.D., is president of Management and Organization Development Learning Systems (MODLS), a consulting firm specializing in individual and organization growth and development. She coaches rugby and tries to bridge the sport and business worlds in creative and healthy ways.

RUSTY KANOKOGI

Rusty Kanokogi is a trustee of the Women's Sports Foundation and an inductee into their International Women Athletes Hall of Fame. She is a historic figure in the sport of judo. (See "Judo and Women," p. 150).

ELLYN KESTNBAUM

Ellyn Kestnbaum is a Ph.D. candidate in the Department of Theater and Drama at the University of Wisconsin. A recreational figure skater, she is writing her doctoral dissertation about cultural meanings of figure skating.

SUSAN A. KOHLER

Susan A. Kohler earned a B.A. in psychology with an emphasis in physical education. She is pursuing a graduate degree in sport psychology, specializing in coaching behavior, motivation, and eating disorders.

PIRO KRAMÁR

Piro Kramár, M.D., has been an ophthalmic surgeon at Pacific Medical Center in Seattle, Washington, since 1970. She received her medical degree from Creighton University. She began mountain climbing during her internship—primarily in the Northwest. She was a member of the Annapurna (1978) and Brigupanth (1980) expeditions.

SHAWN LADDA

Dr. Ladda is an assistant professor in the Department of Physical Education and Human Performance at Manhattan College. Previously, Ladda was the woman's soccer coach at Columbia University for six years. Her doctoral dissertation was entitled *The History of Intercollegiate Women's Soccer in the United States*.

DEBORAH SLANER LARKIN

Deborah Larkin, a management consultant, is a member of the President's Council on Physical Fitness and Sports and chairs its National Task Force on Females and Minorities. A former executive director of the Women's Sports Foundation, she serves on many boards, including the National Women's Law Center, Girls' Inc., the Center for Sport in Society, and the Women's Basketball Coaches Association.

NANCY LEVIN

Nancy Levin is founder, editor, and publisher of the *Women's Sports Connection*, a multisport publication devoted to female sports (http://www.well.com/user/wsports). She co-founded and was captain of the Harvard University Women's Soccer Team and went on to receive her master's degree from Yale University's School of Management. Levin can be reached at P.O. Box 31580, San Francisco, CA 94131-0580, 415-241-8879 (voice), 415-586-4114 (fax), Wmnsports@aol.com.

GRACE LICHTENSTEIN

Grace Lichtenstein is a former *New York Times* reporter and a former executive editor of *World Tennis* magazine. She is the author of *A Long Way, Baby: Behind the Scenes in*

Women's Pro Tennis (Fawcitt, 1975; Morrow, 1974). She was recently editor of the Web site, "Just Sports for Women." http://www.justwomen.com.

JUDY MAHLE LUTTER

As president and founder of the Melpomene Institute, Judy Mahle Lutter researches, writes, and speaks on physical activity and health issues for females. Co-author of *The Bodywise Woman*, 2nd ed. (1996) and author of *Of Heroes, Hopes, and Level Playing Fields* (1996), she writes a biweekly column for the St. Paul, Minnesota, *Pioneer Press*.

PAT LYONS

Pat Lyons is co-author of *Great Shape: The First Fitness Guide for Large Women* and directs the "Connections—Women's Health Consulting Network." She is a program development specialist and speaks on issues of weight discrimination in health care and of promotion of access to sport and fitness for girls and women of all sizes.

BARBARA MEAD

Dr. Mead is a retired professor of physical education at the University of Tennessee. An athlete in her youth, Dr. Mead spent her career in developmental movement programs for preschoolers.

JAN MEYER

Jan Meyer is an avid skydiver with more than 3,500 jumps. She participated in the world's largest skydiving formation: 297 people in Anapa, Russia, on September 29, 1996. Meyer has B.S. and M.S. degrees in physics. She owns her own business, specializing in Internet sites and software development. She can be reached at aerosoftware@makeithappen.com.

ERNESTINE MILLER

Dr. Ernestine Miller is a writer and sports historian. Miller received her doctorate in education and communication from American University in 1981. Charter member and secretary of Women in Sports and Events (WISE), Miller is also on the board of directors of the Babe Ruth Museum. Her

Sportswomen Daybook features reproductions from her collection of American magazine covers (circa 1860-1940) of women in sport.

KAREN MONICO

Dr. Karen Monico is a National Archery Association certified instructor and has taught archery at Penn State for almost 25 years. Currently, she is teaching at Cabrini College, Radnor, PA.

SHARON MONPLAISIR

Sharon Monplaisir is a three-time member of the U.S. Olympic team in Fencing (1984, 1988, 1992). She won gold medals in the 1987 and 1991 Pan American Games. Sharon currently owns her own business as an athletic personal trainer.

CAMERON "CAMMY" MYLER

An eight-time U.S.A. Luge Female Athlete of the Year, Cammy Myler carried the U.S. flag at opening ceremonies of the 1994 Olympic Games. Myler graduated cum laude from Dartmouth College and is a member of the USOC Board of Directors.

KATHY NEAL

Currently a public school physical education teacher and coach in Amherst, Massachusetts, Kathy Neal has coached collegiate softball and volleyball. An athlete in her own right, she has played collegiate volleyball, basketball, field hockey, track and field, and professional women's softball with the World Champion Connecticut Falcons.

RUTH N. NELSON

Ruth Nelson has been an outstanding athlete, coach, and athletic administrator. She was asked to coach the women's volleyball team at the World University Games in Mexico City, 1979. Recently, she began a new career in nonprofit organization fundraising, working with the Special Olympics for several years.

CAROLE A. OGLESBY

Carole A. Oglesby is a professor at Temple University and a sport psychology consultant. Author, researcher, and athlete, Oglesby participated in three Amateur Softball Association (ASA) National Championships (1962, 1963, and 1965).

ALBERT M. PAOLONE

Albert M. Paolone, Ed.D., is a professor in the Department of Physical Education at Temple University. He is a fellow in the American College of Sports Medicine and a member of the board of directors of Ursinus College, Collegeville, PA. Dr. Paolone's research emphasis has been environmental exercise physiology and exercise and pregnancy. He is married and the father of four children and a former successful wrestling coach.

JOAN PAUL

Dr. Joan Paul is a noted sport historian. She is professor and former chair of the Department of Physical Education at the University of Tennessee. Her current academic appointment is in cultural studies. She is a former president of the North American Society for Sport History (NASSH).

LUAN PESZEK

Luan Peszek is a staff member of USA Gymnastics. She edits *USA Gymnastics* magazine.

KRISTINE PLEIMANN

Kristine Pleimann is manager of media and public relations for USA Hockey in Colorado Springs, CO. She earned a bachelor's degree in journalism from Colorado State University and worked at Princeton and California State at Fresno. She is the press officer for her sport at the 1998 Olympic Games in Nagano, Japan.

MARCELLA RIDENOUR (MR1)

Dr. Marcella Ridenour is a professor, Temple University, specializing in motor development across the life span. She has been actively racing sailboats for the past 15 years and is a member of the U.S. Sailing Women's Committee. She is the mother of Mary Ridenour, a champion young yachtswoman.

MARY RIDENOUR (MR2)

Mary Ridenour is an academically talented student from Wyncote, PA. Mary has been ranked third among USA junior women sailors and also excels in ice hockey.

SHEILA E. RIDLEY

Dr. Sheila E. Ridley is a faculty member at Penn State University, Berks Lehigh Valley, and a sport psychology consultant. She has coached internationally (lacrosse and volleyball). Her doctoral degree is in sport psychology and her master's degree is in history.

KRISTENNE ROBISON

Kristenne Robison is near completion of an M.A. degree in exercise and sport studies at Ohio State University. Additionally, she is assistant volleyball and track coach at Denison University, Granville, OH. She received her B.A. from Baldwin-Wallace, Berea, OH, in 1996 and hopes to pursue a career as head coach and educator at the collegiate level.

DON SABO

Dr. Don Sabo is a professor of sociology at D'Youville College, Buffalo, NY, and a trustee of the Women's Sports Foundation. He is a prolific researcher and author in the areas of gender and health and equity issues.

MICHAEL SACHS (MS1)

Michael Sachs, Ph.D., a professor at Temple University, is a former president of the Association for Advancement of Applied Sports Psychology. An avid runner and father of two daughters, he is a prolific author/researcher.

PATRICK SCANNELL

Patrick Scannell is the program director for the Winter Sports Foundation. He has also been a ski competitor, ski shop manager, and head university ski coach. He is a doctoral candidate in policy analysis at the University of Colorado, Boulder.

GRETCHEN SCHMELZER

Gretchen Schmelzer received a master's degree in counseling athletes from Springfield

College and is currently completing a doctorate in counseling psychology at Northeastern University. She is a therapist working with children and families in the Boston area. Her interest in aviation was inspired by her father's love of flying.

SUE SCHOOLEY

Sue Schooley is a successful lacrosse coach in Cherry Hill, NJ. She was an outstanding player, has coached the USA Women's Lacrosse team, and is an inductee to the National Lacrosse Hall of Fame.

CHRISTINE SHELTON

Christine Shelton is an associate professor of exercise and sport studies at Smith College. She is vice president of the International Association of Physical Education and Sport for Girls and Women (IAPESGW).

MARJ SNYDER (MS2)

Associate executive director of the Women's Sports Foundation, Marj Snyder earned a doctorate in psychology of human movement at Temple University after a successful career in collegiate coaching.

ELLEN J. STAUROWSKY

Dr. Staurowsky is an associate professor in the Department of Exercise and Sport Sciences at Ithaca College. A former head coach of field hockey and lacrosse at Oberlin College and men's soccer at Daniel Webster College, Staurowsky was an athletic director at three colleges. Staurowsky has served on the Women's Sports Foundation's Advisory Board, and the professional development board of the National Association for Girls and Women in Sport.

KATHRINE SWITZER

Noted for breaking the gender barrier in the once all-male Boston Marathon in 1967, Kathrine Switzer went on to win the New York Marathon and to help make the women's marathon an Olympic event. Now a television sports commentator and contributor to many publications, including a fitness column for *Women Today*, she is the owner of an events management company, AT-A-Lanta Sports Promotions, Inc.

KELLY TIBBETTS

Sadly, after making her contribution to this book, Kelly Tibbetts died in January 1998. The U.S.A. Badminton Federation stated that Helen Noble "Kelly" Tibbetts gave 61 years of love and service to badminton in the United States. Kelly held the 1952 and 1971 National Adult Mixed Doubles title and was 1968 U.S. Ladies Doubles champion.

LOUISE TRICARD

Louise Tricard began her involvement in track and field in the track club of the Police Athletic League, Bronx, NY. She was a member of the 1959 Pan American team in the 200-meter race and set an American indoor record for the 400-meter. She earned bachelor's and master's of science degrees from Hunter College and a master's of education from Columbia University and completed her book *American Women's Track and Field: A History 1895–1980* in 1996.

SUSAN TRUE

Dr. True is the assistant director of the National Federation of State High School Associations, a Women's Sports Foundation trustee, and a member of the Executive Board of U.S. Gymnastics Federation and the U.S. Volleyball Association.

M. ELIZABETH VERNER

Dr. Verner is an associate professor at Illinois State University, teaching sport and fitness management. She coordinates professional practice programs and supervises interns. Her scholarly focus is on experiential learning and athletic donor motivation. She has participated in and coached both swimming and volleyball.

ANDREA N. WHITTAKER

Andrea N. Whittaker is a reporter for *Sports Illustrated for Kids*. She was a contributing researcher for the Black Women Sports Foundation manual that aims to increase girls' participation in sports. Whittaker earned her M.A. degree in journalism from New York University and also writes for MSNBC's online news service.

MAXINE BACA ZINN

Dr. Maxine Baca Zinn is a professor of sociology and senior research associate at Julian Samora Research Institute, Michigan State University. She is co-editor of *Through the Prism of Difference: A Sex and Gender Reader* (Needham Heights, MA: Allyn & Bacon, 1977), the co-author with D. Stanley Etizen of *Diversity in Families* (New York: HarperCollins, 1996), and the co-editor of *Women of Color in U.S. Society* (Philadelphia: Temple University Press, 1994).

A

Valerie Ackerman

Born on November 7, 1959, in Lakewood, New Jersey, Ackerman attended the University of Virginia from 1977 to 1981. She was a four-year starter for the women's basketball team, captain for three years, and an Academic All-American her final two years.

Ackerman went on to play with a semi-professional team in Cosne-sur-Loire, France. In 1982, she entered the School of Law at the University of California, Los Angeles. Following graduation, she worked for a law firm and then joined the National Basketball Association (NBA) as a staff attorney.

As the NBA's vice president of business affairs, she was responsible for the league's relationship with USA Basketball and for the NBA's efforts to support USA Basketball's men's and women's teams. This responsibility included supervising the 1996 Dream Team and the 1995-96 United States Women's National Basketball Team, both of which competed in the 1996 Olympic Games in Atlanta, Georgia.

Ackerman is a member of the USA Basketball Executive Board and the Naismith Memorial Basketball Hall of Fame Board of Trustees. She is currently the president of the Women's National Basketball Association (WNBA).

Aconcagua Mountain: The Climb for Life

 In February 1995, 17 women climbed the highest mountain in the Western Hemisphere. Located on the border of Argentina and Chile in South America, Aconcagua is 23,085 feet above sea level. These women, ranging in age from 22 to 62, had an important commonality that brought them together: they all had breast cancer.

The project was conceived by Laura Evans of Sun Valley, Idaho. Laura, an avid hiker and sportswear designer, was a healthy 40 year old. She did not worry about her burgeoning career and looked forward to longer and harder business journeys all over the world. Her life changed quickly and dramatically, as it does for all women, when she was diagnosed with breast cancer.

Laura was given a 15 percent chance of survival. Isolated from her family, she underwent months of chemotherapy and a bone marrow transplant. Her dream of hiking and climbing gave her hope while she worked on regaining her strength. Because Laura wanted to share her dream and hope with other cancer patients, she launched "Expedition Inspiration" with the help of her friend, climbing expert Peter Whittaker.

Three hundred breast cancer survivors submitted applications to join Laura on her climb in South America. Of these women, 16 were chosen. The team was divided into two groups. The six members of the summit team would attempt to reach the top of Aconcagua at 23,085 feet. These women were more experienced climbers. As team doctor Kathleen Grant stated, "they were the body of Expedition Inspiration." The 11 other women comprised the trek team. Their goal was to reach base camp at 14,500 feet. They brought their energy and support to the summit team. Dr. Grant referred to the trek team as the "spirit" of the expedition.

Each of these women was active in her community, helped to raise funds for cancer programs, and was well informed and willing to share her cancer experience in a supportive way. What was new, for many of the trek team, was camping and climbing an enormous mountain. For each woman, the mountain became a metaphor for her cancer experience. Just as each woman had struggled to overcome her fear of death and made the journey to regain her health, each now joined to train, to climb a mountain, and to bring the message of hope to other cancer patients. "If we can do this so can you; understanding that the mountain climbed to regain your health is different for each individual, it still begins with the first step."

In July 1994, the team met for the first time on Mt. Rainer in Washington to practice climbing on snow. The experience was both physically demanding and psychologically rewarding. The women helped each other, they shared their cancer experiences, and they vowed to bring the message of hope and wellness to others—they became a team.

During the next six months they trained diligently. They lifted weights, filled their backpacks with weights, and walked hundreds of miles up and down the hills of their hometowns to prepare for the journey up Aconcagua. No one wanted to be a weak link, and all were full of anxiety, worrying whether they could accomplish their goal.

Three members of the summit team reached the top of the mountain on February 4, 1995. They, along with the other members of the team, helped to realize Laura's dream. Expedition Inspiration raised $1.5 million for cancer research. The team's message to all cancer patients is the following: "Although you are frightened, do not give up; continue to focus on a helpful future. Take charge of your health and well-being, and remember, do not ever be afraid to ask for help along your journey." *ED*

See also **Annapurna I**

R. Vivian Acosta, Ph.D., and Linda Jean Carpenter, Ph.D., J.D.

Drs. R. Vivian Acosta and Linda Jean Carpenter have conducted some of the most cited research in women's intercollegiate sport. Acosta and Carpenter have both served on the faculty of Brooklyn College since 1967. Their longitudinal research on "Women in Intercollegiate Sport" documents the decline in the number of women in collegiate coaching and sport administration from the early 1970s to the present. The different perspectives of males and females regarding this decline is the topic of a recent, related study by Carpenter and Acosta. Their documentation of the decline of women in intercollegiate sport leadership positions has provided the driving force for programs designed to prepare women for these positions in sport organizations around the nation.

In addition to their research, both Drs. Carpenter and Acosta have firsthand experience in women's sport governance. Dr. Carpenter has served as a member and chair of the Women's Sports Foundation's (WSF) Coaches Advisory Roundtable, and Dr. Acosta has served as president of the National Association for Girls and Women in Sport, as well as serving as a member of the WSF Advisory Board. In 1991, Acosta and Carpenter were recipients of the WSF Billie Jean King Contribution Award, given to the corporations, organizations, or individuals who are deemed to have contributed most significantly to the advancement of women in sport.

Adventure Experiences and Outdoor Pursuits

Adventure experiences and outdoor activities are sought by millions of Americans. Outdoor adventure usually implies a recreational or educational setting that is both exciting and physically challenging, with the opportunity to take risks. These risks may be physical, mental, or emotional. It is the risk taking that gives "adventure" to the outdoor activities. Outdoor adventure pursuits include an interaction with the environment and a sense of uncertainty about the outcome that can be influenced by the environmental circumstances and the individuals involved.

Almost any outdoor activity may be included in outdoor adventure and many groups and companies in all states offer this type of activity. Perhaps the most widely known is Outward Bound, founded in England and now international. They offer courses ranging from one week to more that one month in activities as diverse as alpine mountaineering, winter ski expeditions, desert and canyon exploration, white water rafting and canoeing, sailing, and expeditions to specific parts of the country.

Not all adventure projects stand alone. One such aspect is Project Adventure, originating at Hamilton, Massachusetts, and funded by a Title III grant in the 1970s. Project Adventure has developed into a school curriculum based upon the philosophy of adventure education. It draws upon risk taking

in order to help towards the total development of each student socially, physically, and emotionally with the stated object of producing effective citizens.

The Association for Experiential Education is another professional organization with its roots in adventure education. They offer courses for leaders in adventure education to teach them to help people to blend together from a shared experience in the outdoors—from a local ropes course to high-risk adventure expeditions. The thrust is to teach fitness of body and mind, to enhance self-esteem and teamwork through shared experiences. This international organization publishes articles, has conferences for leaders in outdoor education, and publishes an annual directory where many of the adventure center addresses can be found.

Most centers cater to both girls and boys, women and men. The Woodswomen organization, however, is an example of a center catering only to girls and women. They started in 1977 to fulfill the particular needs of women and to offer adventure and expedition for women only. Their expeditions have included trips to Nepal, climbing Mt. McKinley, river trips, and biking and climbing expeditions. They train other leaders and guides and have leadership

White water challenge.

programs. They challenge women to face new experiences and possibilities through challenges in the outdoors.

Outward Bound National Office
Route 9D
R2 Box 280
Garrison, NY 10524
1-800-243-8520

Association for Experiential Education
2305 Canyon Road, Suite 100
Boulder, Colorado 80302

Woodswomen
25 W. Diamond Lake Road
Minneapolis, MN 55419

African American Women and Sport

Many people first became aware of African American women athletes through the accomplishments of Olympic star Wilma Rudolph or of tennis great Althea Gibson. African American women, however, were athletes and were participating in sport years before the accomplishments of these two African American women. Unfortunately, many of the pioneers' accomplishments were not documented and are lost to history.

The ability to pursue athletic careers was frequently compromised for African American women, then and now. As African Americans and as women, their opportunities in athletics (as in other careers and vocations) were often limited by sexism and racism. Many sports were denied to women (e.g., men-only facilities) and to people of color (e.g., golf course membership restrictions). Even though Title IX, which was supposed to guarantee equal funding for men's and women's educational activities, relatively recently opened the doors of opportunity for college women, it provided no automatic legal protection, especially for African Americans. Despite these odds, African American women still have made their marks in athletics, coaching, administration, sportscasting, and sports marketing. Without the barriers of gender, race, and

socioeconomic status, their impact might have been even greater.

Barriers and Visibility

The barriers for African American women in pursuit of an athletic career are both overt and covert. The early invisibility of the pioneers in sport is a result, to an unknown extent, of racism and sexism. Even today, successful African American female athletes do not receive as many product endorsements as White women or African American men. Furthermore, most of the literature on women athletes focuses on White women, while the literature on African Americans focuses on African American males (Birrell, 1989; Hall, 1995). According to Birrell (1989), there is a "growing criticism of sport as a sexist, racist, and classist institution, as a site for the reproduction of relations of privilege and oppression, and the dominance and subordination structured along gender, race, and class lines" (p. 213).

The history of discrimination against African American women based on race and gender is extensive. For example, Bessie Coleman (1893-1926) was unable to obtain flying lessons due to her gender and race. Her desire for a pilot's license was so great that she went to France to obtain her training and license and then became the first licensed African American pilot in any country!

Class Issues

Smith (1992) suggested that socioeconomic status must also be taken into account when discussing African American female athletes since a disproportionate number of African Americans are from low-income households. Athletic opportunities for girls and young women from families with limited means are restricted to those primarily supported by public facilities (recreational departments or schools), track and field and basketball for example (Green, 1981; Smith, 1992). These activities require the least number of participants and the least amount of equipment as well. In addition, African American girls and women with limited income cannot afford private coaches or lessons and may not have access to other types of facilities necessary to develop athletic interests (e.g., tennis courts, swimming pools, golf courses, rowing clubs, skating rinks, and the like). Thus, both the opportunities and the most numerous and visible role models for African American girls and young women are in track and field and basketball. Many African American girls may erroneously conclude that track and field or basketball are the only avenues to success open to them as athletes.

Additionally, many African American girls and women must work to contribute to the family's income and to help make ends meet. Working after school compromises the time available to participate in extracurricular activities in high school or college (Davis, 1983; Green, Oglesby, Alexander, & Franke, 1981; Smith , 1992). Both accessibility and availability curtail the opportunity for many African American girls and young women to pursue athletics.

Cultural Strengths

One of the many strengths of the African American community is an intrinsic support for the athletic endeavors of African American girls and women. Since African American culture appreciates a greater flexibility of gender roles and accepts a broader range of gender appropriate behaviors, African American women are not as bound as White women by gender role stereotypes (Hall & Bowers, 1994; Smith, 1992). Athletics for girls and women is not perceived as antithetical to an African American female's gender role. Hall and Bower's qualitative study of African American females found that African American women defined themselves as "softly strong"—owning both strength and femininity without conflict. Welcome support from the African American community has energized many African American girls and women to participate in sports.

Representation

African American women who enter sport, particularly a predominantly "White" sport, find themselves under a lot of pressure because of their visibility as African American women. In addition, cultural differences come into play and may make an African American female feel isolated or lead her to believe that she is given accolades more for being "an exception" than for being a talented athlete. Race, rather than ability, often becomes the most salient issue, to account for the success of an African American woman athlete. She may also feel that she has to represent an entire community rather than only herself in her athletic endeavors. This type of stress is not consistently experienced by White female athletes, but it is akin to what Billie Jean King felt when she represented "all womanhood" in her match with Bobby Riggs in 1973. For African American women, this scenario is oft-repeated.

Community Support

Like many other college athletes, African American women have used scholarships to procure an education and continue their athletic careers after high school. Historically Black colleges were central in the athletic careers of several African American women pioneers. Many of the most gifted track and field stars attended Black colleges like Tuskegee Institute, Tennessee State University, and Florida A & M (Ashe, 1988a; Smith, 1992), including May Faggs, Mildred McDaniel, Wilma Rudolph, Lucinda Williams, and Willye White, to name but a few. The financial and emotional support provided by historically Black colleges and universities, and the encouragement and skills of their coaches, created an environment that promoted African American women's athletics.

Trail Blazers

Even though African American women have had their greatest number of successes in track and field and basketball, they have succeeded in other sports as well. In 1950, Althea Gibson became the first African American accepted into "mainstream" tennis competition. In 1957, she became the first African American woman to win Wimbledon (singles and doubles) and the United States Open, and in 1963, she was the only African

American woman to play in the Ladies Professional Golf Association (LPGA) Tour. In 1968, Tina Sloan Green became the first African American member of the United States Lacrosse Team. She was also on the national field hockey team at one time. Nikki Franke, a two-time Olympian and two-time national fencing champion, was ranked as the number one foil fencer in 1980. In 1986, Debi Thomas became the first African American woman to win the United States Figure Skating Championship and the first person of color to win the Women's World Figure Skating Championship. Flo Hyman, a renowned African American volleyball player, was struck down with Marfan's Syndrome and died in 1986, but because of her acknowledged contributions to women's sport, an award was created in her honor. The Flo Hyman Award is given annually to the nation's outstanding female athlete on National Girls and Women in Sports Day. Wendy Hilliard was another pioneer, becoming the first African American Olympian in the sport of rhythmic gymnastics and also the first African American president of the Women's Sports Foundation (1994-96).

In track and field and basketball, African American stars reign as well. In 1948, Alice Coachman became the first African American woman to win an Olympic medal in track and field. She won the high jump with a leap of five feet six and one half inches, an Olympic record.

Two of the best known African American women basketball players are Cheryl Miller, 1984 National Collegiate Athletic Association (NCAA) Most Valuable Player (and a member of the University of Southern California basketball team that won the NCAA title), and Lynette Woodard, 1984 Olympian and all-time Big Eight scorer (among men or women). Lynette was also the first woman to play for the Harlem Globetrotters. Lucy Harris, a 1976 Olympian, was the first African American female to be drafted by an NBA basketball team. Sheryl Swoopes holds the all-time NCAA scoring record for women or men in a NCAA

Basketball championship game with her 47-point performance in the 1993 championship contest. Clearly, the successes of African American women have been substantial, and the potential for other African American girls and women to succeed is clear.

Coaches and Administrators

The number of African American coaches and administrators is low but has been growing since the 1980s (Corbett, 1995; Smith, 1995). In basketball, then Iowa coach Vivian Stringer was named *Sports Illustrated* 1993 Coach of the Year and has coached teams from two different institutions in the NCAA Final Four. Cheryl Miller was the head coach of the USC women's basketball team, and is now the head coach of the Phoenix Mercury of the new WNBA (Women's National Basketball Association). Tina Sloan Green led the Temple University women's lacrosse team to three national championships and was named Lacrosse Coach of the Year in 1988.

In administration, Doris Corbett became the first African American woman president of the American Association of Health, Physical Education, Recreation and Dance (AAHPERD) in 1990. Two-time Olympian Anita DeFrantz was the first African American woman on the International Olympic Committee. Dr. Nell Jackson (1929-88), a track and field star in the 1948 Olympic Games, was the first African American female to coach the Women's Olympic Track and Field Team in 1956. She was an administrator as well, demonstrating that her talent went beyond the event and that her impact on sport was greater than her athletic prowess alone.

An exciting affirmative program was launched in 1992 when Tina Sloan-Green, championship lacrosse player and coach, founded the "Black Women's Sport Foundation." The BWSF is a nonprofit organization dedicated to increasing the involvement of Black women and girls in all aspects of sport. Currently, the BWSF is distributing an excellent video on the contributions of African American women to sport.

The contributions of African American women to athletics have been outstanding and the talent stream seems endless. The greatest remaining challenge is to make all sports accessible for African American women. *RLH*

References

Amazing Grace (video) (1993). Black Women's Sport Foundation, 712 N. 23rd St., Philadelphia, PA 19130.

Althouse, R., and Brooks, D. (1993). *Racism in college athletics: The African American athlete.* Morgantown, WV: Fitness Information Technology.

Ashe, A. R. (1988). *A hard road to glory: 1619-1918.* New York: Warner Books.

———. (1988). *A hard road to glory: 1919-1945.* New York: Warner Books.

Birrell, S. (1989). Women of color, critical autobiography, and sport. Sport, men, and the gender order. *Critical feminist perspectives* (pp. 185-99). Champaign, IL: Human Kinetics.

———. (1990). Racial relations theories and sport: Suggestions for a more critical analysis. *Sociology of Sport Journal*, 6(3), 212-27.

Duda, J. L., and Allison, M. T. (1990). Cross-cultural analysis in exercise and sport psychology: A void in the field. *Journal of Sport and Exercise Psychology*, 12, 114-31.

Hall, R L. (1995). Sweating it out: Women and sport. In J. C. Chrisler, C. Golden, and P. D. Rozee (eds.), *Lectures on the psychology of women* (pp. 74-89). New York: McGraw-Hill.

Hall, R. L. and Bowers, C. D. (1994). *Self definition and African American womanhood.* Presentation at the Black Women in the Academy: Defending our Name, 1894-1994. Sponsored by MIT and Radcliffe College. Cambridge, MA.

Oglesby, C. (1993). Issues of sport and racism: Where is the White in the rainbow coalition? In D. D. Brooks, and R. C. Althouse (Eds.), *Racism in college athletics* (pp. 252-67). Morgantown, VA: Fitness Information Technology.

Smith, J. C. (ed.). (1992). *Notable Black American women.* Detroit: Gale Research.

Smith, Y. R. (1992). Women of color in society and sport. *Quest*, 44. 228-50.

Tenley Albright

Tenley Albright (Blakely), an American figure skater, was born on July 18, 1935, in Newton Center, Massachusetts. At the 1952 Winter Olympic Games in Oslo, Norway, she won a silver medal when she was 16, only the second silver medal won by an American female skater. But she is best known for

Tenley Albright.
Photo courtesy of the World Figure Skating Museum.

winning a gold medal in women's skating in the 1956 Winter Olympic Games in Cortina d'Ampezzo, Italy, the first gold medal in this event for an American woman.

Albright overcame leg problems associated with polio to become a figure skater. When she was nine years old, her parents bought her a pair of white hockey skates for a Christmas present. To try out the skates that year, she persuaded her father to flood the backyard with water so it would freeze into a thick piece of ice, suitable for skating. She joined a skating club the next year, but at age 11 she was afflicted with a condition then known as infantile paralysis. Her doctor suggested that she continue to skate for therapeutic reasons and for pleasure.

Albright's skating career involved more than just Olympic success. In 1953, Albright became the first American to win a world skating championship, and she recaptured the title in 1955. During this time, she also won five straight United States titles.

Albright attended Radcliffe College and graduated from Harvard Medical School in

1960. She is now a successful surgeon and resides in Boston, Massachusetts.

Annapurna I: A Vertical Breakthrough

"Goddess of the Harvest," better known as Annapurna, is a huge massif in the Nepali Himalayan chain, and its highest peak, Annapurna I at 8,091 meters above sea level (26,504 ft), is the 10th highest mountain in the world. It consists of four distinct peaks several miles apart. One of only 14 peaks over 8,000 meters, Annapurna was one of the great unrealized prizes of mountaineers until 1950 when Annapurna I was finally climbed by a French team, the first successful ascent of an "eight thousander." Maurice Herzog, the expedition leader, and fellow climber Louis Lachenal, reached the summit without extra oxygen, but suffered severe frostbite injuries during their descent. Over the next 28 years, four of the 13 attempts to climb the peak were successful, each placing two climbers on the summit. The first ascent by Americans occurred in the fall of 1978, when two American women and two Sherpas reached the top.

Women mountaineers were no novelty, but in 1972 no woman had ever climbed to or above 8,000 meters. In that year, the idea of an all-women's expedition to an eight thousander was conceived by a group of women climbers. All were climbing big mountains but, as women, found various difficulties in being invited and accepted as equal climbing partners in a mixed group.

One of these women was Arlene Blum, a 25-year-old biochemist from California. Arlene became the leader of the 1978 expedition.

Initially, the prime motivating force for organizing an all-women's expedition was to give women a chance to climb a Himalayan peak, where gender in itself would not be a prohibitive factor. The women wished to be an integral part of the organizing, the fundraising (collecting $80,000), and the equipment and food gathering. Later, because of some doubters, an element of "we'll show you" crept in, but it was a wish not to disappoint the many helpers and supporters that became one of the prime motivations to succeed.

There were considerable difficulties in obtaining the permit for the climb. The Foreign Ministry in Kathmandu, Nepal, granted the permit, but it was contingent on the American Alpine Club's (AAC) formal approval. Never having approved an all-women's expedition before, the AAC was apparently reluctant to establish a precedent. However, after lengthy negotiations, mostly on the part of one of the climbers, Vera Watson, the approval and the permit were received for the postmonsoon season of 1978.

Route up Annapurna.
Photo courtesy of Piro Kramár.

The team of 10 climbers that gathered in Kathmandu in early August 1978 consisted of Arlene Blum, Vera Watson, Irene Miller, Alison Chadwick-Onyszkiewicz, Elizabeth Klobusicky-Mailaender, Vera Komarkova, Joan Firey, Annie Whitehouse, Margie Rusmore, and myself, Piro Kramár. Christy Tews was the base camp manager. Two young film makers, Dyanna Taylor and Marie Ashton, also joined us. While in Kathmandu, we met our six Sherpas, sirdar (foreman), liaison officer, kitchen crew, and special porters. On buses we proceeded to Pokhara, where 200 porters were hired (10 of them women) for the 80-mile trek to base camp at 14,500 feet. (I should note here that, as the author of this essay, I have tried to keep the factual material accurate. As for the subjective portions involving motives, thoughts, and interpretations of actions, I speak strictly for myself.)

The planned route up the mountain traversed below the Sickle Glacier of the 1950 expedition and climbed the adjacent Dutch Rib. This route would

Piro Kramár.
Photo courtesy of Piro Kramár.

decrease the exposure to the worst avalanche danger from a period of days to less than one hour. The style chosen for the climb was that of the classic pyramidal expedition (i.e., establish a chain of fixed camps, usually about 2,000 vertical feet apart). We would have five camps above base camp, with the last one at 24,000 feet. The logistic complexity of organizing an expedition of this size was enormous. This complexity continued up the mountain, compounded by unexpected developments—both man-made and acts of God—requiring quick adjustments. The ultimate goal of the expedition was "flexible stability." This pyramid style is safer, albeit significantly slower and less elegant, than the rapid alpine style, which requires the climbers to carry all their gear while moving their camp successively up the mountain. Safety was also the dominant factor in deciding to take enough oxygen for the final summit push, despite the extra weight involved.

This emphasis on safety vs. speed was chosen for obvious reasons. First, none of us underestimated the seriousness of the mountain. Second, only two or three of the 10 climbers had ever been on any climb remotely similar in scope. Coincidentally, as the preparations for the climb were intensifying, so was the accompanying, mostly unsolicited, publicity. A freer, alpine-style climb would have invited more doubt and criticism, and we courted neither notoriety nor controversy.

Once base camp was established and the loads downsized for higher carries, rising excitement and anticipation were palpable. The summit was often visible from our tents a mere two miles away, vertically and horizontally. We all realized that the next several weeks would involve much "grunt" work, but any chance for leading and route finding with light packs to establish the next camp was considered a plum and eagerly sought. After all, it was for this we had really come.

Because every climber's ambition is to lead, it is somewhat surprising in retrospect that there was never any sign of hostile competitiveness. In fact, any disagreements or arguments were usually not on a personal level but tended to focus on the ethics and style of climbing. This relative harmony was due in great part to the intelligent leadership of Arlene. After one false move involving a decision-making technique, Arlene hit the correct and delicate balance between allowing freedom for 10 diverse and rather strong personalities and making authoritative decisions when needed.

The other explanation may well involve some basic differences between most Western men and women. I refer here to the well-known need and facility of many women to express and discuss their thoughts, feelings, and fears in some detail. And discuss we did at several meetings during which all had the opportunity for soul baring. I believe that these meetings, although not my personal favorite pastime, were constructive and helpful. They helped highlight the differences in personalities and temperaments and enabled us to modify our own idiosyncrasies for the good of the team. We were thus able to form a fairly comfortable and cohesive working unit with one major goal—climb the mountain, safely if possible, but enjoy it all even if we failed to reach the top.

Aside from some early skirmishes between Arlene and Joan, both experienced climbers with definite opinions, it is noteworthy that the only acrimonious conflicts arose between management and employees—between the two leaders (Arlene and Lopsang, the sirdar) on the one hand and the Sherpas on the other. During one of several storms, which essentially paralyzed the expedition for days, the team was strung out over three camps. The Sherpas, apparently for many reasons accumulating over the days, decided to abandon the expedition and retreated en masse to base camp. A frantic Arlene followed and, together with Lopsang, tried to explain, mollify, and negotiate. It turned out that all would be forgiven and forgotten if we gave them additional gear, duplicating equipment that they had already received and that we literally did not have. Gradually, it emerged that an equivalent amount of money would also be acceptable. In short, we had a Sherpa strike, not unknown on these expeditions. The language barrier certainly played a role in the strike, but basic "cultural" differences were predominant. Whereas a promise or contract to most Westerners is considered as absolute and unvarying, it seemed that for Sherpas, as well as for porters, a contract is open to interpretation, depending on any number of conditions. By and large, however, I found that when working and climbing with Sherpas on equal terms (e.g., switching leads) they were delightful and usually very skillful and strong.

The Sherpas were originally included to function as high-altitude porters and for them to climb the summit was not necessarily in the picture. The Sherpas, however, were just as eager to try for the top as the women. Several of us, especially after the strike, felt that we should continue and finish the climb without the Sherpas. Alison, except for Arlene the most experienced expedition climber in the team, was adamant about continuing as a purely women's team. Although very safety conscious, Alison's climbing style was tough, uncompromising, and verging on the Spartan. She was also strongly of the opinion that all the members should have a chance at the summit and not just the first team. This arrangement would entail more carries to the highest camps and would take more time. These divergent views had come up before. As a leader, Arlene had both the capacity and the opportunity to assess the whole picture much better than the rest of us who were more involved with our individual tasks. She was better able to weigh the margin of safety. Although the climb was feasible without Sherpas, it was undoubtedly safer and faster with them. The window for climbable weather was rapidly closing. A compromise was reached and both Alison and Arlene agreed that one Sherpa would accompany each summit team. Little did Arlene know that the Sherpas later decided that three of them would accompany the first team. This decision may have had a seminal effect on events to come.

The direct courting of danger is not a desirable quality in a climber, and certainly none of us suffered from this malady. Still, we had all come to this mountain voluntarily, fully aware of the statistic that 1 out of 10 expedition climbers does not return home. The avalanche danger was very high at any time of the day and at almost any spot on the mountain. The previous 13 expeditions lost nine of their members, seven of them to avalanches. During our climb, an avalanche came close to base camp, the first known time that this had occurred. The danger was especially intense between camp II and the base of the Dutch Rib, traversing below the Sickle Glacier. Each traverse required a conscious effort, and there were many traverses.

In climbing, as in any human activity, natural selection plays a decisive role in determining who will be attracted to this happy marriage of the physical and the intellectual. Some common characteristics that supposedly describe climbers are aggressive, competitive, and introspective. Be that as it may and regardless of gender, I believe that the ability to compartmentalize is essential for effective climbing in the face of danger. Climbers first analyze the degree of potential danger and its consequences. If the decision then is made to climb, we have learned, or are innately able, to lock all thoughts of this analysis in a recess of our minds and throw the key away. Without this conscious mental maneuver, serious climbing is impossible because concentration and focus must be absolute.

Women, no less than men, leave family and friends behind and must deal with the essential egoism of expedition climbing. Ironically, it is even harder for their families to come to terms with the same trait. Irene, with two young children at home, agonized about her climbing on Annapurna. Yet once she made the decision, she went on to the top. I think that for Irene any personal ambition for summiting was overshadowed by a deep sense of responsibility and gratitude to the expedition's numerous volunteers and supporters, many of whom were her friends.

The motives for climbing this mountain (or for climbing at all) are many-faceted, even in the same individual climber, but a common thread coursed through all of us: for someone, anyone, to reach the top safely and return. Layered on top of this group goal were individual motivations, some shared with others, others unique to the individual. These specific driving forces would come into dominating focus at different times, depending on the mountain's and climber's condition. Joan Firey, for example, a very strong and determined climber, was the only one I really knew before Annapurna. She was, in fact, responsible for my acceptance into the team. We had shared many good climbs and "epics" in the Washington Cascades and Canada. She was a highly imaginative climber, always brimming with new ideas. Regrettably, she became seriously ill and was slowly recuperating from pneumonia while we were already establishing the two camps on the rib. It was obvious to all, including Joan, that she would not be on a summit team. Setting summit aspirations aside, Joan proceeded with perseverance to regain her strength and actually carried support loads to camp III at 21,000 feet. This elevation was the highest she had ever reached, and so a modified personal ambition was satisfied by helping the team.

Several of the climbers felt that even if we failed to reach the top, the coveted leads, especially the more difficult ones, were so fulfilling that they would have few regrets. Each day of leading, like a chapter in a book, became a self-contained, circumscribed unit, a part of the whole yet complete in itself. Most climbers are reluctant to answer when asked the inevitable "why do you climb" question, but they will eventually mumble something about testing one's limits, self-conquest, and self-knowledge. Certainly one has ample opportunity for self-analysis, especially while trudging with heavy loads between camps. Even with others around, a feeling of isolation is common while climbing and thoughts turn inward. The emerging self-portrait is not always flattering.

Besides these various motivations, there are more immediate and obvious pleasures. On my climbs before Annapurna, I had seen some spectacular scenery. But never had I been immersed in and surrounded by beauty so intense and concentrated that it brought tears to my eyes. Only later, "recollecting in tranquility," was I able to assimilate the spectacles to some extent. This overwhelming sense of beauty was with me on the way to camp V, one day before the first summit attempt.

The first team consisted of Irene Miller, Vera Komarkova, myself, and three Sherpas; two of them self-appointed. The Sherpas were Mingma Tsering, Chewang Rinjing, and Lakpa Norbu. The following morning, through an undiscovered hole in my glove, I froze my right index finger on my camera casing. I did not realize it for several minutes until I finally noticed my completely white and immovable finger poking out through the hole. There was no dithering or agonizing or even conscious decision making. I simply announced to the others that I would not go for the summit and went back to our tent. It was my fastest bit of action above 18,000 feet. Lakpa had a headache and spent the day in the Sherpa tent. The other four continued, and at 3:30 P.M. on October 15, Irene, Vera K., Mingma, and Chewang stood on the highest summit of Annapurna I.

In this instance, my own fear (the possible loss of a digit) outweighed the team motivation. Perhaps the knowledge that the others had a good chance of reaching the summit had some influence on my rapid and seemingly subconscious decision. I often wonder if, for some reason, both women were unable to climb that day, would I have had the determination and strength (some would claim the stupidity) to completely embrace the team's motivation and make the attempt with the two Sherpas? I shall always wonder.

On our descent, we met the ascending second team, Alison Chadwick-Onyszkiewicz, Vera Watson, and their Sherpa, Wangel, at camp IV. This planned Sherpa support evaporated the next day when Wangel had to descend because of altitude sickness. In spite of this reduction of strength and in spite of the summit having been climbed, both Vera and Alison were determined to make another attempt. Arlene, at camp II seeing the overall picture literally as well as figuratively, was appalled. She tried to dissuade them, and after much to-and-fro radio discussion, she was promised that they would only go above camp V if conditions were favorable. Options included an attempt at a first ascent of the closer and lower Central summit. (Annapurna I has two additional peaks, a previously climbed East summit and the unclimbed Central summit. The North summit just climbed is the highest of the three.) If all else failed, they would carry down the gear left at camp V specifically for the second team.

We five, in our cramped tent at camp IV, not only had no view of the whole picture but relative hypoxia (lack of oxygen) probably clouded our judgment as well. We assured Vera and Alison that there were no technical difficulties ahead, except for one short icy section, which we climbed without any problems. Alison and Vera also decided that they would be prepared to bivouac (camp out with minimal equipment) if necessary to climb the central peak. This decision we found eminently reasonable, whereas Arlene was horrified when she heard about these plans much later. A bivouac at 25,000 feet is no light matter.

As it was, we never discovered what happened to Alison and Vera. They were seen the following day near dusk approaching camp V and only 200 feet from the tent. Although the Central peak was not visible from below, the entire route between camp IV and the North summit was exposed to those watching from below in camp III. Neither of the two women was seen ascending or descending over the next two days. On the third day, two of the Sherpas spotted Alison's red jacket below camp IV and well to the east of our ascending route. Due to the extreme nature of the intervening terrain, it was not possible to reach them safely, and no attempt was made to retrieve their bodies. The only conclusion we could draw was that they fell or were swept to their deaths before reaching camp V that first evening. At base camp, Vera's and Alison's names were carved into a memorial boulder, adding them to the other nine names already there. For our team, two members would not return home.

As with many expeditions, whether all male, female, or both, the final assessment of success is a mixed bag. We succeeded in climbing the world's 10th highest mountain safely, but we failed by leaving two of our own behind. We, too, paid the price for daring. Proving that "women can do it" may not have been our original agenda, but it became a natural consequence of our climb. Recommended Reading: *Annapurna, A Woman's Place* by Arlene Blum, Sierra Club (1980). **PK**

See also Aconcagua Mountain: The Climb for Life

Constance M.K. Applebee

Constance Applebee (June 4, 1873, to January 26, 1981) was a British physical educator who founded field hockey in the United States. In 1901, she attended a summer course at Harvard. In a class discussion of women's exercise, the Americans mentioned the game "musical chairs." Applebee commented that people in Britain "play those games at parties; for exercise, we play hockey." Her demonstration with makeshift equipment led to an invitation to teach the game to Vassar College students. A lifelong mission to spread the game began, as she started field hockey at Vassar and at many other colleges.

Applebee became the director of health education at Bryn Mawr College in 1904 and continued to coach their field hockey team until 1967. She founded an annual hockey camp in Pennsylvania, which she ran from 1923 through 1965, coaching virtually every top field hockey player in America. She also founded the United States Field Hockey Association (USFHA) in 1922 and published *Sportswomen* magazine for 10 years. She was inducted into the International Women's Sports Hall of Fame in 1991.

Archery

Cave drawings in Spain depict the use of the bow and arrow for hunting as early as the Stone Age. The bow and arrow has also been used as a weapon of war by many people. Today, the bow and arrow is used by millions of archers throughout the world for hunting, target archery, field archery, and other forms of archery. Archery can be enjoyed by everyone: young and old, men and women, and the disabled.

Archery can be done for recreation and for competition. Bowhunting is extremely popular in the United States and Canada. Bowfishing, a combination of bowhunting and fishing, is becoming increasingly popular in many areas. Target archery is perhaps the best-known competitive format. This form of

Celebrating field hockey, the game Constance Applebee introduced to the U.S.
Photo courtesy of the *Camden Courier Post.*

competition, which was first promoted by King Henry VIII of England, requires the archer to shoot a set number of arrows accurately over long distances on flat, open terrain. A five-colored target face with 10 scoring rings, ranging from 10 points in the center to 1 point for the outermost ring, is used. The archer with the highest point total wins. Another competitive form of archery, field archery, involves shooting four arrows at each of 28 targets that vary in distance. The targets are positioned along a trail in natural terrain ranging from open fields to open woods. Points are awarded for hitting target areas and highest point total determines the winner. Other forms of archery include flight (shooting for distance), clout (shooting at a large target on the ground), archery golf, and crossbow shooting. Men and women compete separately in most competitions.

Archer shooting a modern bow.

Anne Boleyn and Elizabeth I, both queens of England, were two early accomplished woman archers. Women, however, were not admitted to archery societies or allowed to compete until the late 1700s. Despite these early restrictions, women have made their mark on archery. Two women, Dorothy Smith Cummings and Ann Weber-Hoyt, have been inducted into the Archery Hall of Fame in Grayling, Michigan. Between 1919 and 1931, Smith Cummings won 7 National Archery Association (NAA) Championships and 11 Eastern Archery Association Championships. From 1940 to 1959, Weber-Hoyt dominated archery in the United States. She won five NAA Championships, a National Field Archery Association Championship, and an international target and field championship.

Women first competed in Olympic Archery competitions in the 1904 and the 1908 Olympics. After 1908 archery was cancelled as an Olympic sport due to inconsistancies in international rules and competition format. Archery was reintroduced in 1972 and has been in the Games ever since. Three American Olympian archers of note are Doreen Wilber, who won a gold medal in the 1972 Games; Luann Ryon, who won a gold medal in the 1976 Games; and Denise Parker, a likely Hall of Fame inductee, who won a bronze medal at the 1988 Games. Parker's other accomplishments include a bronze medal at the 1989 world championships; gold medals at the Pan American Games in 1987 and 1991; national championships in 1990 and 1991; indoor national championships seven of the last eight years; United States Olympic Committee Athlete of the Year award, 1992; and four gold medals and one silver medal at the 1995 Pan American Games.

A number of organizations regulate the sport of archery. The National Archery Association is responsible for selecting and training teams for the Olympic Games, world championships, and Pan American Games. The NAA also conducts annual national championships. Training and practice for young people is provided by the

Junior Olympic Archery Development (JOAD) program. The Federation Internationale de tir al'Arc (FITA) promotes archery worldwide and conducts world and regional championships. The National Field Archery Association is the governing body for field archery in the United States and also organizes championship tournaments every two years. The Professional Archers Association (PAA) is responsible for promoting and educating people about professional archery and for conducting indoor and outdoor competitions for prize money.

Many archers get started at local archery clubs and organizations, which provide year-round training and competition. Commercial indoor archery ranges and archery tackle shops are also important resources for the would-be archer. More information on archery can be obtained by contacting the National Archery Association, One Olympic Plaza, Colorado Springs, CO 80909. *KM*

Evelyn Ashford

Evelyn Ashford, "The Queen of American Sprinters," was born in Shreveport, Louisiana, on April 15, 1957. She overcame a series of injuries to win four gold medals and one silver medal in her Olympic career, which lasted for 16 years from 1976 to 1992. After an outstanding career as a high school sprinter on the boys' track team, she was one of the first females to earn an athletic scholarship at the University of California, Los Angeles (UCLA). By her sophomore year, she was an Olympic veteran, having been a member of the 1976 United States Olympic Track and Field Team. She placed fifth in the 100-meter dash at the 1976 Games in Montreal, Canada.

In 1977 and 1978, Ashford won the Association of Intercollegiate Athletics for Women (AIAW) Championships in both the 100- and 200-meter dashes. The following year, she defeated two East German world record holders to capture first place at the 1979 World Cup Championships. In 1980, (when she was favored to win her first Olympic gold medal), the United States

boycotted the Games in Moscow, Russia (then part of the Soviet Union).

Ashford then focused her energy on the 1984 Olympic Games in Los Angeles, California. Despite a hamstring injury, she won gold medals in the 100-meter dash and as a member of the 4 x 100-meter relay team. In 1985, Ashford took time off to start a family, but a year later she returned to earn top honors at the Goodwill Games. At the 1988 Olympic Games in Seoul, South Korea, she took a silver medal in the 100-meter dash and anchored the gold medal 4 x 100-meter relay team. At the age of 35, Ashford closed her career at the 1992 Olympic Games in Barcelona, Spain, with a gold medal in the 4 x 100-meter relay, making her the oldest American woman to earn an Olympic track and field medal.

In 1993, Ashford was honored by the United States Olympic Committee and received the Robert J. Kane Award for her consistent excellence in American amateur sport. She is now an early morning walker who resides in California.

Asian American Women in Sport

With the recent spotlight on Amy Chow, who won the silver medal on the uneven bars and a gold medal as part of the Olympic Gymnastics Team at the 1996 Summer Olympic Games in Atlanta, Georgia, it is difficult to imagine sport without Asian American women athletes. Despite recent gains in visibility, little research and professional exposure has been devoted to this group. There may be several reasons for this state of affairs.

The first reason, which largely complicates obtaining accurate information about Asian American women, involves the very definition of "Asian." Asian American women do not share a common culture, language, physique, or color (Ligutom-Kimura, 1995). The 1990 United States Census Bureau acknowledged that the Chinese, Filipinos, and Japanese make up the largest Asian American groups in the United States, followed by Southeast Asians and Koreans. Without an accurate portrayal depicting distinctions between Asian American groups, generalizations about Asian American women's participation in sports can be biased and incomplete.

The second reason, which can confuse the issues associated with Asian American women's participation in sport, is that studies tend to incorporate the "minority" experience group together, creating categories that include all women, or women *and* men, who share a similar ethnic background. Inaccuracies thus can evolve which preclude the understanding of the experience of Asian American women, whose unique culture and individual portrait can be overshadowed by studying these broader groups.

For example, studies of enforced leisure and recreation in Japanese internment camps during 1942 and 1945 showed that men, women, and children participated in organized and unorganized athletic events. These events helped unify Japanese Americans, in that many found an opportunity to sustain their culture, but these recreational programs also created tension between the *issei* (the first generation, immigrant Japanese) and the *nisei* (children of the *issei*, born in America). Not everyone enjoyed the recreational activities because they disrupted patterns in family life, a value greatly embraced by the Japanese (Wrynn, 1994). When reflecting on this example, one wonders about the Japanese woman's experience as it relates to participation in sport in this context, and the consequences of her actions on the evolution of her role outside the family. Did these internment camp experiences support or hinder her motivation for athleticism? It is difficult to answer these questions without exploring the Japanese American woman's unique experience. In the same vein, it would be inappropriate to apply these Japanese American women's experiences to all Asian American women.

In the 1800s, thousands of immigrants from China, Japan, and Korea came to Hawaii and the United States mainland to work in the plantations, railroads, and

mines. For many Asian women, this immigration meant being cut off from their families, suffering hardships and alienation, even from each other. Women remained in these difficult situations for fear of dishonor and from economic necessity. Physical activity took the form of work, with little time for recreation. As Asian American women became acculturated, and as Asian American families began establishing themselves in the larger social community, barriers to recreation and sports began to come down. This process was gradual, as education and financial success were priorities to most early immigrants, values that continue to be emphasized today. Thus, young girls could become involved in sport through a church, community center, or an Asian recreation program, if it did not interfere with academic success. Sport was a way to find acceptance in a new culture and a means for accomplishment within the family, but only if it didn't conflict with family goals.

Family approval is a large factor for Asian American females participating in sport. In many Asian cultures, physical exercise or movement-related activities were historically linked to the support of cultural traditions, such as dance and drama. In many Asian cultures, it is the role of the female to hold on to these cultural values and traditions and to carry them through to the next generation. Activities outside this context may be difficult for families to embrace, particularly if they are perceived to be at odds with the family's cultural worldview. There may be additional conflicts in the family associated with the physicality of the sport, the type of clothing and equipment used, and the relationship to authority figures, like coaches. All these factors may have contributed to restricting the range and visibility of sports participation among Asian American females. Any study of the Asian American female athlete would have to explore family structure and expectations, as these are so related to determining the freedom of choice and commitment toward an opportunity for participating in sport.

Despite these limitations, Asian American women have made their mark on sports. In the 1990s, Asian American women are participating in a wide variety of sport activities. The recent focus on multiculturalism in sport is a positive one. The stereotype of the Asian American female as submissive and domestic is changing. Asian American women are speaking out and developing an identity that is a blending of the sociological and historical experiences that they have had in Hawaii and on the United States mainland and the personal values that have emerged through their evolution toward independence and equality.

Asian American women continue to strive for acceptance in the sporting arena by participating in sports and by taking on leadership roles. Throughout the 1980s, one of the most dominant players on the United States Volleyball Team was setter Debbie Green. Other role models such as Michelle Kwan, Kristi Yamaguchi (who won the gold medal in figure skating at the 1992 Winter Olympic Games), and Amy Chow demonstrate the strength and power of the Asian American competitor and the ability of the Asian female to excel in her sport. The explosion of Asian women in sport influences the visibility of all women in sport. *EC2*

References

Ligutom-Kimura, D. (1995). "The invisible women", *Journal of Physical Education, Recreation and Dance*, 66, 7, 34–41.

Wrynn, A. (1994). "The recreational and leisure pursuits of Japanese-American Women in World War II internment camps." In Eisen, G. and Wiggins, D. (eds.) *Ethnicity and Sport in North America*, Greenwood Press, Westport, CT.

The Association for Intercollegiate Athletics for Women (AIAW)

The Association for Intercollegiate Athletics for Women (AIAW) was established to govern women's athletic competition at the college level in both two- and four-year institutions. The AIAW was a comprehensive organization that controlled all aspects of governance of women's intercollegiate sport for member institutions. The AIAW originated in the Division for Girls and Women's Sport (DGWS) under the auspices of a physical education professional association, the Alliance for Health, Physical Education and Recreation (AAHPER). In addition to its ties with the DGWS and AAHPER, the AIAW worked with amateur sports organizations, the U.S. Olympic Committee, sport governing organizations, and other scholastic sports organizations to expand athletic opportunities for women and to assure them equal opportunity in collegiate athletic programs.

Established in 1971, the AIAW succeeded the DGWS's Commission on Intercollegiate Athletics for Women (CIAW) as the governing organization for women's intercollegiate sport. Prior to the founding of the AIAW, intercollegiate sport for women depended on volunteer efforts of individuals, usually university women and physical education faculty, to organize and fund competitions between institutions. These competitions were sporadic, underfunded, and often organized as "play days" emphasizing the educational value of sport.

The first president of the AIAW was Dr. Carole Oglesby, then at the University of Massachusetts. Initially the organization included a paid executive director, shared with the DGWS, an elected Executive Board, national commissioners for sport championships, and nine elected regional representatives. Each member had one representative in the Delegates Assembly, giving all member institutions an equal vote in the organization. Soon after its inception, the AIAW also added student representatives to most of its major committees, giving student athletes a voice in their own governance.

The philosophy, structure, rules and regulations of the AIAW reflected its roots in the physical education profession, as well as one of the major social movements of that era, feminism. While men's sport celebrated the elite athlete, professionalism, and a "win-oriented" philosophy, women's sport emphasized universal participation, amateurism, and an "athlete-oriented" philosophy. The AIAW reflected the feminism of the time in its leadership (all Executive Board members and the majority of delegates were women) and in its efforts to keep women's sport separate from men's sport and under the control of women.

The goals of the AIAW included:

1. To foster broad programs of women's intercollegiate athletics which are consistent with the educational aims and objectives of the member schools.
2. To assist member schools in the extension and enrichment of their programs of intercollegiate athletics for women.
3. To stimulate the development of quality leadership among persons responsible for women's intercollegiate athletic programs.
4. To encourage excellence in performance of participants in women's intercollegiate athletics.

The education-oriented philosophy of the AIAW translated into some unique and controversial governance regulations for women's intercollegiate sports. Observing the abuses in men's sport attributed to the primacy of economic factors, the AIAW initially forbade the granting of athletic scholarships and excluded institutions that provided scholarships for women athletes from AIAW national competitions. In 1971, scholarship athletes from Marymount College in Florida challenged this rule in court (the *Kellmayer* case). The AIAW subsequently changed its position on athletic scholarships, clearing the path for increased financial aid for women athletes. As a result of this policy change, financial aid for women athletes rose to an estimated 32 million dollars by 1981.

The scholarship policy was not the only unique and controversial governance philosophy of the AIAW. Self-policing of infractions by the institutions themselves, liberal "waivers" from eligibility requirements for student athletes, and appeals through due process procedures, also emanated from the student-centered, education-oriented philosophy of the organization.

Central to the educationally oriented philosophy of the AIAW was the principle that women should be student-athletes, with the emphasis on being students first and athletes second. This principle resulted in rules and regulations designed to assure that the female athlete maintained all of the privileges of other students and did not enjoy additional privileges just because she was an athlete. Consequently, the AIAW allowed women student-athletes to transfer from one institution to another without eligibility penalties, ensuring that athletes had the same transfer options as other students, and it imposed strict rules against recruiting women solely for athletic talent by member institutions because that would be an additional privilege.

In the early 1970s, the AIAW supported passage of Title IX of the Educational Amendments of 1972, which forbade discrimination in any educational program or activity receiving federal financial assistance. The primary governing organization of men's intercollegiate sport, the National Collegiate Athletic Association (NCAA), opposed the passage of Title IX and its provisions of equal athletic opportunities for members of both sexes. The passage of Title IX was a victory for women's sports and the AIAW, but it ultimately led to the demise of the organization. The ideal of "equal athletic opportunity" legislated by Title IX became synonymous with the male model of athletics. Becoming "equal" to men's athletics was interpreted as being "like" men's athletics, and the female model of athletics promoted by the AIAW was subsumed by the male model. In the early 1980s, the NCAA expanded its governance into women's athletics by offering national championships for women in competition with the AIAW national championships. Quickly, larger institutions moved their membership from the AIAW to the NCAA, and the AIAW suspended operations in 1982.

While the AIAW did not survive the challenge from the NCAA, it succeeded in promoting the growth of intercollegiate sport for women. During the 10 years of its operation, the AIAW provided female student-athletes with the opportunity to compete against each other in over 750 state, regional, and national championships.

Funding for women's athletic programs increased along with public attention through corporate sponsorship and television contracts. Most importantly, the philosophy that athletics exists for the betterment of the student-athlete and that the welfare of the student-athlete is primary, dominated the "childhood" of women's intercollegiate sports. *KLH*

References

Hult, J.S. (1991). "The Legacy of AIAW." In Hult & Trekell (eds.) *A century of women's basketball.* Reston, VA: National Association for Girls and Women in Sport.

Spears, B. & Swanson, R. (1988). *History of sport and physical education in the United States.* Dubuque, IA: Wm. C. Brown Publishers.

Tracy Austin

Tracy Austin was born into one of California's top tennis families on December 12, 1962. All her brothers and her sister played tennis competitively, and three of her siblings played professional tennis. As a junior player, Austin's strong baseline game and powerful two-handed backhand catapulted her to the top of the junior rankings. Austin dominated the national girls tennis scene, winning 25 age-group titles between 1972 and 1978. She turned professional in October 1978, just before her 16th birthday. She immediately established herself as the teenage phenomenon of the tennis world. By 1980 she was ranked number one in women's professional tennis—the youngest woman to obtain the ranking at the time. She also set records as the youngest professional tennis player to earn $1 million in prize money, the youngest player to win the United States Open, and the youngest player to win the Filderstadt tournament.

Her records against Chris Evert and Martina Navratilova, the dominant players of the time, were equally impressive. She defeated Evert in the semifinals of the 1980 Italian Open to end Evert's 125-match clay-court winning streak. She won the U.S. Open in 1979 and 1981, defeating Navratilova in the final in 1981. She scored victories in the 1979 Filderstadt, 1980

Virginia Slims, 1981 Canadian Open, and 1981 Toyota Championships. During the same period, she and her brother, Jeff, became the only brother/sister team to win the Wimbledon mixed doubles title. Honors from the sport world followed these impressive accomplishments. Austin was the Associated Press Female Athlete of the year in both 1979 and 1981, and she was the recipient of the 1980 Women's Sports Foundation Sportswoman of the Year award.

After 1983, Austin's career was severely disrupted by a chronic back injury. Though she attempted to return to the pro tour in 1988, the long lay-off for recovery and a subsequent car accident in 1989 severely hampered her return to professional tennis. Off the court, Austin has enjoyed success in many endeavors. She has worked as a television tennis commentator for NBC and ABC, written an autobiography, and volunteered her talents in service of many charitable causes. She was elected to the International Tennis Hall of Fame in 1992.

Auto Racing. *See* Motor Sports Racing

Aviation and Women

Women's aviation history began with a balloon flight made by a 14-year-old French teenager as a passenger. This first female balloon passenger, Sophie Blanchard, was dubbed the official Aeronaut of the French Empire by Napoleon. In the beginning days of aeronautical history, women were considered pioneers by simply agreeing to be passengers on these "dangerous voyages."

However, in 1910, tired of being a passenger, Raymond de Laroche, a French woman, became the first woman in the world to be issued a pilot's licence. Harriet Quimby, an American, quickly followed suit, and became the first woman to cross the English Channel by plane.

Despite the fact that women's flying records were recorded as "Miscellaneous Air Performances" until 1929, women were undaunted in pursuit of records. Ruth Law set numerous altitude records for women in her flying career, but in 1916 she set a distance record for all pilots, flying nonstop from Chicago to New York.

In 1919, the first competitive cross-country event for women was held, the Women's Air Derby. The race, which started in Santa Monica and finished in Cleveland, carried a $2,500 prize. It took a week with the 40 competitors flying solo over 300 miles a day. Louise Thaden, age 23, won the inaugural competition. Louise went on to win the Bendix race, a race for male pilots, from Los Angeles to Cleveland.

Almost all early women pilots suffered from the sexist attitudes of the time. In addition to sexism experienced by women pilots of their era, Bessie Coleman, Willa Brown Chappell, and Janet Harmon Bragg also had to battle racism to become pilots. Bessie Coleman was the first African American woman to earn a pilot's license. She could not find anyone in the United States who would teach her to fly, and so in 1920 she went to France to learn. In doing so, she became the first African American to earn an international pilot's license. She planned to open a flying school for African Americans, but, she tragically died in a plane crash during a fundraising stunt show with her mechanic in the pilot's seat.

Willa Brown Chappell opened a pilot's training center for African American pilots. She and her husband trained many pilots including the Tuskegee Airmen. Janet Harmon Bragg had to go to two air schools during the 1930s before someone would issue her a license. She later opened the first African American-owned airport.

In October 1929, a club of licensed women pilots was formed. There were 99 original members, and thus the club was called the "Ninety-Nines." Amelia Earhart was the first president. This worldwide organization now has over 7,000 members and continues to be a source of strength, support, and information for women in the world of aviation. The Ninety-Nines sponsor air derbies and act as judges for the National Intercollegiate Flying Association Competitions.

One of the best-known female pilots, Amelia Earhart was born in 1897 in Atchinson, Kansas. She was known to be a tomboy and was the first girl in her town to wear a gymsuit to play in, rather than a dress. In high school, her heroines were women who succeeded at being first in their field—first bank president, first forestry worker—and she kept newspaper clippings of these pioneers in her schoolbooks.

Amelia Earhart began to fly at age 23. Her first flying instructor was a woman, and in 1933, she made her first solo flight. Soon thereafter she set a new women's altitude record in a open cockpit plane.

In 1932, she planned the first woman's Trans-Atlantic flight from Newfoundland to Paris. During the flight she experienced some severe engine trouble and chose to land in a pasture in Ireland instead of in Paris. Yet, even with these setbacks, her flight was a success. She became the first woman to pilot a plane across the Atlantic, the first woman to fly solo across the Atlantic, and her flight was the fastest Trans-Atlantic flight by anyone. Amelia Earhart disappeared on July 2, 1937, during an attempt to fly around the globe.

The dream to be the first woman to fly around the world was fulfilled by Geraldine Mock in 1964. She flew a single-engine Cessna. Then, in May 1997, Linda Finch completed a 10-week, 26,000-mile reenactment of Amelia Earhart's journey using a fully restored Lockheed Electra, the same type of plane flown by Amelia Earhart. Ms. Finch, however, used modern navigational aids and had another plane trailing her.

Young women have also been inspired to pursue dreams in the sky. At the age of 12, Victoria Van Meter, from Meadesville, Pennsylvania became the youngest girl to have completed a Trans-Atlantic flight in her plane *Harmony*. Another young pilot, Jessica Dubroff, age 8, had set out to become the youngest person to fly a plane across the United States. She was known for wearing a baseball cap with the motto "Women fly" on it. Jessica's plane crashed in Cheyenne, Wyoming, during the second leg of her journey. Jessica, her father, and her flight instructor were killed.

Long-distance flight has taken on a new meaning with advances for women in aviation. In more recent times, with women being trained as naval combat pilots, women have had opportunities for both combat flights and space flight. On February 5, 1995, Lt. Colonel Eileen Collins was the first woman in the pilot's seat in NASA's history, the copilot of the Space Shuttle *Discovery*.
GS

References

Bragg, J. (1996). *Soaring above setbacks: Autobiography of Janet Harmon Bragg, African American aviator.* Washington, DC: Smithsonian Institution Press.

Jaros, D. (1993). *Heroes without legacy: American airwomen 1912-1944.* Niwot, CO: University Press of Colorado.

Lomax, J. (1987). *Women of the air.* New York: Dodd, Mead & Company.

B

Shirley Babashoff

Shirley Babashoff, born in Vernon, California, on January 31, 1957, is the all-time Olympic medal leader among United States women, having earned eight gold and silver medals in swimming. In the 1972 Olympic Games in Munich, Germany, she earned one gold and two silver medals. The gold medal was for a relay, and the silver medals came from the 200-meter and 400-meter freestyle races. In the 1976 Olympic Games in Montreal, Canada, she won one gold medal in a relay race, and four silver medals, one for a relay and the other three for individual freestyle events. In five of her silver medal races, she was defeated four times by performers who set world records and once by a competitor setting an Olympic record.

During her career, Babashoff set 11 world records, 17 United States records, and 6 individual records. In addition to her Olympic success, she won gold medals in the 200- and 400-meter freestyle races at the world championships in 1973. Because of her excellence in swimming, she was named the AP 1974 Sportswoman of the Year. In 1987, she was inducted into the United States Olympic Committee (USOC) Hall of Fame.

Sharron Backus

On May 2, 1993, softball coach Sharron Backus reached the 700-win level, giving her more wins than any other active Division I softball coach in the National Collegiate Athletic Association (NCAA). In her years with the UCLA Bruins, Backus had a record of 707-136-3 (.836), including a postseason record of 99-26 (.792). The Bruins went to the College World Series 12 out of 14 years. They captured 7 of the first 11 NCAA Softball Championship titles contested. UCLA did not commit a single error in College World Series play during the 1978, 1982, and 1988 seasons. Backus's teams have included 48 All-American players.

Backus was named Diamond National Coach of the Year in 1984 and 1985 and was inducted as a coach into the Amateur Softball Association (ASA) Hall of Fame in 1996. A star shortstop herself, Backus was inducted as a player into the ASA Hall of Fame in 1985. She was instrumental in winning seven ASA Championships and two amateur international world championships. She also played professional softball for the Connecticut Falcons, winning three world championships.

Badminton and Women

Badminton is a racquet sport in which a unique cork-and-feather projectile, called a shuttlecock, is hit back and forth over a five-foot net. Women's singles games are played to 11 points; doubles and mixed doubles games are played to 15 points. Two out of three games constitutes a match. In 1992, it became an Olympic medal sport, with medals being awarded in four events: men's and women's singles, and men's and women's doubles. The Olympic Games in 1996 saw the addition of a fifth event, mixed doubles, making badminton the only Olympic sport with a mixed event. The sport enjoys great popularity worldwide, especially in Asian and Pacific-rim countries where it is one of the top three sports.

Often thought of as a party or lawn game, badminton is fast and strenuous when played at the top levels. Shuttlecocks can travel at speeds up to 200 miles per hour when coming off the racquet of an experienced player. The game demands agility and quick reflexes, in addition to the stamina needed for completing the multiple games making up a match. At lower levels of play, the game offers opportunity for fun and exercise.

The first notable United States woman in badminton was Bertha Barkhuff, who swept the first United States Nationals to include women in 1937, winning the singles, doubles, and mixed titles. The following year she won the women's singles and mixed titles before retiring from the game. She was followed by Thelma Kingsbury, a successful professional badminton player during the late 1930s and early 1940s. Kingsbury used professional competitions to advance United States badminton, but there were not enough professional exhibitions to support her financially or to keep her playing on a regular basis. She decided she wanted more opportunities to compete and participate in national tournaments, so she went through the process of regaining her amateur status. In 1941, she won the singles and doubles titles at the United States Nationals. After World War II, she won four more doubles titles.

The United States National Championships were suspended for World War II. In 1947, the first postwar women's singles title was won by Ethel Marshall. She won titles the next six years before she retired from singles play. Her participation in doubles continued, however, and she won two additional women's doubles crowns.

Marshall's seven singles titles in a row seemed to be a record that would last forever, but in 1954, Judy Devlin won the first of her 12 singles titles to go with her 12 doubles titles, and seven mixed doubles titles. Devlin's record of 31 national titles has never been surpassed by an American woman. In 1967, she became the first United States woman to win the All-England Championship. She continued to play internationally, winning 10 singles crowns and seven doubles crowns in the All-England Championships, which were considered to be the world championships of the time.

International team competition for women began with the creation of the Uber Cup in 1957. The Uber Cup was played every three years, and the United States women's team won the first three meets in 1957, 1960, and 1963. It is now played every other year and is called the Thomas Cup Championships. The results of all international tournaments are used to determine world rankings in singles, doubles, and mixed doubles badminton.

As the century draws to a close, the number of women playing badminton is increasing. Opportunities for women in badminton have expanded with the establishment of a number of badminton training centers throughout the United States, offering excellent coaching, training, and playing conditions. Information regarding badminton training centers may be obtained by contacting the national governing body in the USA, the United States Badminton Association, One Olympic Plaza, Colorado Springs, CO 80909. This organization establishes the rules of the game, sanctions tournaments, and regulates badminton in the USA. *KT*

Baseball and Women

Baseball originated in the United States in the 1800s. The game is a team sport in which two teams of nine players each compete to score "runs" by batting the ball and running around four bases in a game that typically consists of nine innings. Batting, catching, and throwing skills are required of every player, but which skill is emphasized varies with the position played in the field. Typically, the pitcher must excel at throwing skills and fielders at catching skills. All players have a chance "at bat," so hitting skills are important for all players. The ball used in baseball is smaller than the ball used in the similar sport of softball, and although it is called a "hardball," it is not much harder than a regulation softball. Because the ball is smaller, it is more easily gripped by a child's smaller hands, making baseball a good sport for developing biomechanically correct throwing motions.

The first women's baseball team in the United States was organized by Harry Freeman in the 1880s. While some women played in amateur leagues and as part of physical education programs at women's colleges, the first professional baseball leagues were all male. During World War II, the All American Girls Baseball League offered professional opportunities to women, but the league disappeared in the years after the war. Advocacy efforts on behalf of women in sport opened the door for women to participate in baseball in the 1970s. As the national governing body of amateur baseball in the

Hardball is easier for small hands to grip.
Photo courtesy of Gini Alvord.

United States, and seeking to bring baseball into the Olympic family, USA Baseball met its obligations in regard to the Amateur Sport Act of 1978 and provided women the opportunity to participate in baseball.

In an effort to increase baseball opportunities for women, USA Baseball, in conjunction with one of its national member groups, the American Amateur Baseball Congress (AABC), developed a pilot women's program in 1996. This program began with a five-team league in the Midwest (Chicago, Illinois; Lansing, Michigan; Battle Creek, Michigan; Grand Rapids, Michigan; and South Bend, Indiana). In addition, an invitational women's baseball championship was conducted from August 16 to 18, 1996, in Battle Creek as part of the Stan Musial (unlimited age) Division of the AABC. Teams from Los Angeles, Phoenix, Philadelphia, Chicago, Lansing, and Battle Creek participated in the tournament. Los Angeles emerged victorious by posting a 13-3 win over Philadelphia.

At the professional level, the Colorado Silver Bullets began operating in 1994 and recently became a USA Baseball member organization. The Silver Bullets have been designated as the United States' first women's national team. The team is sanctioned to represent the United States in tournaments, playing against men's and women's international baseball teams.

There have been some well-known individual female baseball players. Mildred "Babe" Didrikson toured with her "All Americans" team in the early 1930s. In 1931, Jackie Mitchell pitched in an exhibition game between the New York Yankees and the amateur Chattanooga Lookouts. She struck out Babe Ruth and Lou Gehrig. A modern-day player of note is Silver Bullet's pitcher Pamela Davis. In 1996, she pitched an inning in an exhibition game for the Jacksonville Suns and became the first woman to pitch for a male professional baseball team.

Several baseball training programs are available for youths, with the largest being Little League baseball. Little League baseball was opened to girls in 1974, and today girls and boys play in the same leagues and on the same teams. Little League instructional programs begin for children at the age of five with T-ball, and progress to higher levels of competition, including international competition for older age groups. Young girls interested in playing baseball will find the local Little League organization a good place to begin their skill training. Further information may be obtained from USA Baseball, 2160 Greenwood Avenue, Trenton, NJ 08609. USA Baseball is currently in the process of building a database of baseball contacts and is developing a "starter kit" for individuals interested in playing baseball. *KLH*

Basketball and Women

Basketball was created in the United States in December 1891 by James Naismith for his students at the Young Men's Christian Association (YMCA) Training School in Springfield, Massachusetts. Today, basketball is a team sport in which two teams of five players each compete against each other to score field goals or free throws. Shooting the basketball through an iron hoop (basket) is how a team scores points: three points for a successful shot outside of the 3-point arc, two points for a field goal (shot taken from anywhere inside the 3-point arc), and one point

for a free throw (shot awarded after a foul is committed by the opposing team). The basketball may be passed between teammates, or dribbled (bounced) by an individual player while moving, but the ball cannot be advanced without passing or dribbling. The basketball used in the current women's game is smaller than the ball used for the men's game, thus more easily gripped by women's (on average) smaller hands.

In 1892, a physical education instructor named Senda Berenson introduced basketball to her Smith College students. She transformed the 13 original rules of James Naismith's game into a divided court game, which was considered more suitable for women. She created five additional rules that would make the game more "womanly and vigorous":

1. The court was divided into three equal parts

The game has changed since the early days.
Photo courtesy of the *Camden Courier Post.*

2. Batting or stealing the ball was illegal
3. Holding the ball longer than three seconds was a foul
4. Only a three-bounce dribble was allowed
5. Five to 10 players were allowed on the team.

Berenson, like Naismith, used peach baskets for goals and a soccer ball as a basketball, and the Smith College women played the first recorded game of basketball for women in 1892.

Another early rules developer, Clara Gregory Baer, invented another set of more stringent rules. These rules were published in 1895 in the first women's basketball rule book. Baer's rules had one unique feature: the one-handed push shot was mandatory. Ironically, this one-handed shot became popular in men's basketball more than 40 years later and is currently favored by both men and women.

In 1899, a committee of four women (including Berenson) was formed to study the problems of women's "basket ball." (The game had a two-word name at that time). Too many different sets of rules had been developed, which was confusing when schools began to compete. This committee created a common set of rules for women. These rules were published in 1901 by Spalding's Athletic Library, and Senda Berenson was the editor. This committee was the first to organize athletics for girls and women, and through a series of name changes, evolved into the present National Association for Girls and Women in Sport (NAGWS).

In the 1938 season, the rules were changed to a two-court game, with three players limited to offense only and three players limited to defense. (The three players on offense had to stay in the frontcourt, and the three on defense had to stay in the backcourt.) In the early 1960s, two roving players (one defensive, one offensive per team) were permitted to move across the center line and around the entire court. All players, however, were still limited to a three-bounce dribble. The continuous dribble was added to the rules in 1966. In 1971, the women's game was completely changed to a five-player game with a 30-second shot clock. The shot clock was used in women's basketball at least a decade before the men's rules adopted a similar time clock. Extensive research and experimentation, by the (then) Division of Girls and Women in Sport (DGWS), preceded every significant change in rules.

Senda Berenson.
Photo courtesy of the Smith College Archives.

The first intercollegiate women's basketball game was played in San Francisco on April 4, 1896, between California and Stanford. The game was played before a crowd of approximately 700 women. By 1911, there was a noticeable decline in enthusiasm for women's basketball, probably due to several reported injuries. By 1925, however, 37 states had varsity basketball and/or state tournaments for women. Many industrial leagues for women were formed, and the Amateur Athletic Union (AAU) started a national women's tournament in 1926. Mildred "Babe" Didrickson played for a Dallas insurance company team that won

Basketball is one of the most popular sports in high school.
Photo courtesy of the *Camden Courier Post.*

the 1931 AAU Championship. She later became a star performer in track and golf.

In 1953, a world championship for women's basketball was held for the first time, with the United States team winning the gold medal. Two years later, women's

basketball was introduced to the Pan American Games, and the United States won the gold medal with an 8-0 record. The first National Collegiate Invitational Tournament was played in West Chester, Pennsylvania, in 1969, again under the general auspices of DGWS. This tournament continued for two more years, until the Association of Intercollegiate Athletics for Women (AIAW of DGWS) developed the first National Collegiate Women's Basketball Championship in 1971. Women's basketball became an official Olympic sport at the 1976 Games in Montreal, Canada. In 1981, the National Collegiate Athletic Association (NCAA) took over the governance of women's athletics, and the first NCAA Women's Basketball Championship was played in 1982.

At the professional level, the All-American Red Heads Team was formed in 1936 in Crossville, Missouri, and it lasted longer than any other women's professional team. The Red Heads teams toured and competed for more than 50 years. They won 85 to 90 percent of their games, playing by men's rules and competing against men's teams. Throughout their history, the Red Heads were featured in such magazines as *Life*, *Colliers*, *Sports Illustrated*, and *Women's Sports*. They were also guests on several television shows such as *What's My Line* and *Real People*. In the 1980s, a professional league for women's basketball was formed, known as the Liberty League, but it lasted less than two years. Currently, there are two professional women's basketball leagues in the United States, the Women's National Basketball Association (WNBA) sponsored by the National Basketball Association (NBA), and the American Basketball League (ABL).

Many individual female basketball players, officials, and coaches have made contributions to women's basketball. Babe Didrickson was a three-time AAU All-American. Denise Long, of Union-Whitten High School in Iowa, finished her career with 6,260 points and was drafted by the NBA's Golden State Warriors. Coach Cathy Rush of Immaculata College (Philadelphia, Pennsylvania) led her team to three national championships from 1972 to 1974. Margaret Wade also coached her Delta State University team to three national championships from 1975 to 1977. The Wade Trophy is now given in her honor to the outstanding women's collegiate basketball player every year. Carol Blazejowski of Montclair State won the first Wade Trophy given in 1978. Lynette Woodard of Kansas joins a list of 71 players who have scored over 2,000 career points, and was the first woman to play for the Harlem Globetrotters. University of California at Los Angeles' Ann Meyers, Old Dominion's Nancy Lieberman, and Delta State's Luisa Harris all played on the first United States Women's Olympic Basketball Team in the 1976 Montreal Games, winning the silver medal. Cheryl Miller from the University of Southern California, led the 1984 gold-medal-winning Olympic team in scoring, rebounding, steals, and assists. Darlene May was the first woman to be chosen as an Olympic basketball official for the 1984 Olympic Games in Los Angeles, California. May was also the first woman to referee an international men's game at the World University Games in 1977 in Bulgaria. In 1994, Charlotte Smith made a three-point shot with less than one second left on the clock to win the NCAA National Championship for the University of North Carolina. Teresa Edwards, from the University of Georgia, has played on four United States Women's Olympic Basketball Teams from 1984 to 1996. Sheryl Swoopes scored a stunning 47 points in an NCAA 1993 championship game, a record for collegiate women and men.

Many opportunities for youth to train in basketball are available. Most of these opportunities come from schools, but other organizations such as the YMCA and Young Women's Christian Association (YWCA) offer youth leagues. The national governing body for basketball in the United States is USA Basketball. It is responsible for the selection and training of all the teams that represent the United States in international basketball competition. USA Basketball fields teams, variously composed of professional, collegiate, and high school players, for such competitions as the Olympic Games, the world championships, the Pan American Games, the Goodwill Games, the World University Games, and the World Games for the Deaf. They also send United States teams to several international wheelchair events. Further information may be obtained from USA Basketball, 5465 Mark Dabling Boulevard, Colorado Springs, CO 80918-3842 (or online at www.usabasketball.com). *KD*

Joan Benoit

Joan Benoit (Samuelson), born on May 16, 1957, in Cape Elizabeth, Maine, won the first women's Olympic Marathon in the 1984 Los Angeles, California, Games in a time of 2:24:52. The road to this finish had been considerably longer than the 26 plus miles Benoit ran. In 1928, Olympic officials decided to prohibit women from competing in races over 200 meters because the longer distances might be "too strenuous." In the 1960s, women were again allowed to compete in races over 200 meters, but the longest race was still only 800 meters. In 1984, the women's marathon was finally added to the Olympic events, after Kathrine Switzer and a generation of women marathoners had lobbied the International Olympic Committee to include it.

Benoit originally wanted to be a professional skier. At the age of 15, a broken leg suffered while skiing a slalom course shattered those dreams. Throughout high school, she participated in both field hockey and track. After realizing that field hockey held no future for her, she concentrated on a successful career in track. At North Carolina State University, she spent two semesters on an athletic scholarship. During this time, she began to enter and win 10 K (kilometer) races, moving on to marathons. In 1979, she placed second in the Bermuda marathon, which qualified her for the Boston Marathon in the same year.

In 1983, Benoit set a world, course, and United States record by winning the Boston Marathon with a time of 2:22:43. The year before the 1984 Olympic marathon trials, she had recovered from double Achilles tendon surgery. Just 17 days before the trials began, another injury requiring arthroscopic knee surgery occurred. Five days after that operation, she pulled a hamstring muscle, which interfered further with her preparation for the trials. She surprised everyone by not only finishing the race, but by winning the Olympic marathon trials in 1984. En route to winning the gold medal in 1984, she skipped the first water station and broke away from the other runners after just three miles. Her lead was never threatened, and she entered the Los Angeles Coliseum alone to win the first women's Olympic marathon.

Benoit retired from racing and now lives in New England.

Biathlon—Summer and Winter

Summer Biathlon

Summer biathlon is a relatively new sport that involves cross-country running and shooting. It was developed to keep Olympic-level winter biathletes (cross-country skiers and shooters) competition-ready during the summer months. Summer biathlon is governed by the United States Biathlon Association (also the national governing body for the Olympic sport of winter bi–athlon) and in 1997 celebrated its 10th year as an organized sport. Summer biathlon has grown from one race in 1987 to 100 races across the United States in 1996. More then 7,000 people participate in summer biathlon events annually and 25 percent of all partici-pants are women.

The running distance for summer biathlon is five kilometers (3.1 miles) and is typically run on a fun and challenging cross-country course, which is split into three segments. The shooting distance is 25 meters using summer targets, or 50 meters using winter targets (which are a little larger).

Shooting distance is determined by the race director and usually depends on the size of the range and the number of participants. Racers begin by running a mile loop, then shooting five shots in the prone position (lying down), running another mile loop (usually a different loop), shooting five more shots standing, and then running a final loop to bring the total run to 5 kilometers or 3.1 miles.

Summer biathlon is scored by combining the total race time and number of targets hit on the range. A time deduction is awarded for each target hit. In the prone position, 15 seconds are deducted from the total time for each hit, and in the standing position, 30 seconds are deducted for each hit. The clock remains running while the competitor is at the range, so the object is to run fast and shoot straight. The average time spent on the range is one minute for each shooting segment. The average competitor hits five targets: three in the prone and two while standing.

Summer biathlon differs from winter biathlon in that the rifle is left at the range while the competitor is out running. In winter biathlon, the rifle is carried on the back like a backpack. In summer biathlon, the competitor runs a loop, walks onto the range, picks up the rifle, inserts a five shot clip, fires five shots, empties the clip from the rifle, places the rifle back on the rifle rack (or on a mat), walks off the range, and begins running again.

The strategy involved with a successful race is very important. Summer biathlon provides a unique challenge because the competitor wants to run fast and shoot well. Shooting well is difficult when the heart rate is elevated from strenuous exercise. The first loop should be run fairly aggressively because the first bout of shooting is in the prone position and the ground supports the competitor's body weight and most of the rifle weight. The second loop should be run much more conservatively because the second round of shooting is done while standing, and it is very difficult to shoot in this position when the body is tired. Holding the rifle steady is a chore with a high heart rate and high rate of breathing. After the final shooting bout, the final loop is a sprint to the finish. Summer biathlon is fun because each course is different and involves an adjustment of strategy depending on the difficulty of the running course. While a competitor wants to run very fast, it is advantageous to have a slow heart beat and relaxed breathing rhythm when shooting. A competitor should slow her running pace for 200 to 400 meters prior to each shooting bout to ensure a decreased heart rate, which usually improves shooting accuracy.

Equipment is provided at each race site. The .22 caliber biathlon rifles are used with federal standard velocity ammunition. Summer biathlon metal knockdown targets are utilized and each target is a round plate 3.5 inches in diameter. Personal rifles are allowed, but must be .22 caliber, bolt or lever action, and magazine-fed with a five shot clip. First-time participants must attend a prerace clinic that covers range safety, proper use of the rifle, race strategy, and shooting technique tips.

Between 80 and 100 summer biathlon races are scheduled from April through October and are held nationwide. A 23-person national team competes at summer biathlons across the country. Prize money for both men and women is awarded at all National Series races and the national championships offer a $10,000 prize purse. To be eligible for the purse, a competitor must race in a minimum of two summer biathlons, including at least one National Series race. Summer biathlon is taking the necessary steps to become an Olympic sport as early as the 2000 Games in Sydney, Australia.

For more information or a race schedule contact Jerry Kokesh at the Summer Biathlon office 314-434-9577. *MH1*

Winter Biathlon

The Greek name *biathlon*, meaning dual test, has been given to the exciting Olympic sport that combines cross-country (Nordic) skiing with precision rifle shooting. This unusual combination of skills has its origin in Scandinavia. Rock carvings dating from over 4,000 years ago have been found in Norway, depicting two men on skis stalking animals. Biathlon has evolved from a means of survival, to a system of national defense, and finally to a highly technical and competitive Olympic sport.

The first international competition in biathlon for men came during the Winter Olympic Games in Chamonix, France, in 1924. During these Games, the Military Patrol was included as a demonstration event, and was continued in the Winter Olympic Games of 1928, 1936, and 1948. After 1948, the Military Patrol was dropped from the Olympic Games because of the antimilitary feelings following World War II.

The United States reintroduced what is now the sport of biathlon to the Winter Olympic Games in Squaw Valley, California, in 1960. At this time there were still only men's events, and women's biathlon had not yet emerged. These competitions differed significantly from today's events. Competitors used a NATO 3.08 caliber and then a large bore .223, until the .22 caliber rifle was made standard in 1978, just prior to the 1980 Olympic Games at Lake Placid, New York. Today, the rifle target and range are the same for men and women. Women's distances are 7.5 km for the sprint (10 for men) and 15 km for the individual competition (20 for men).

In the fall of 1978, Holly Beattie made her mark in the sport of biathlon. Beattie appeared at the Men's National Biathlon Training Camp in Squaw Valley and quickly took an active interest in the sport. She was well known for her accomplishments in endurance sports, and the men's biathlon team was eager to offer help and to teach her to shoot. The sport had just changed from large bore rifles to small bore weapons, whose smaller size facilitated movement towards mass participation. After an introduction to the sport, Beattie began to show up regularly, intrigued by the biathlon challenges.

Although there was no program for women anywhere in the sport, national team coaches, Art Stegan and Bill Spencer, were very supportive and encouraged Beattie's training. She eventually expressed a desire to compete despite the nonexistence of a separate class for women. In light of the growing concerns for equal opportunities in sports for women, Stegan and Spencer contemplated the prospects and took the opportunity to promote her desires. The fact that both Stegan and Spencer felt strongly about equal opportunity and that both have daughters increased their support. In addition, the public relations benefit that could be gained was obvious since shooting sports had a negative image during the post-Vietnam era. The national governing body at the time, United States Modern Pentathlon and Biathlon Association (USMPBA), did not oppose her participating and supported the coaches' decision.

Holly Beattie tried a few of the early races during the start of the 1978–79 winter season. These events were all held at Jackson Hole, Wyoming. During the preseason training and racing there, another successful endurance athlete, Pam Weiss, observed Beattie and quickly became interested. However, without any real racing opportunity, nothing more occurred that season. During the next season, 1979–80, things really began to develop.

In the fall of 1979, Beattie took a much more committed approach to biathlon and became a regular at the training camp at Squaw Valley. During that year also, Julie Newman from Washington developed an interest in the sport when her college ski team went to Squaw Valley and she saw Beattie training. When the training moved to Jackson, Wyoming, Beattie followed. Pam Weiss had maintained her interest so a women's class was added to the early season races. The women's class attracted the attention of Betty Stroock, a Dartmouth ski team graduate living there.

These women were invited to race in a competition in Bozeman, Montana, that the Canadians were also attending. The Cana-

dian coach, Kosti Unsitarkano, was surprised to see the women racing and expressed interest in getting a Finnish/Canadian woman, Karina Englebrecht, started in biathlon. The first international women's biathlon event would be held shortly afterwards at the United States Olympic trials in Valcartier, Quebec. (The United States Olympic trials had been moved north to Canada due to a lack of snowfall that year.) The Canadian coach brought Englebrecht to participate in the trials. He was disappointed to learn that no American women had come to race. Stegan quickly telephoned Beattie and Weiss and proposed they fly to Valcartier. They would be included on the start list, although there would be no official Olympic team for women. Beattie came and raced against Englebrecht who won all the races. This competition presented a real opportunity and opened the door to women's participation. At the 1980 Olympic Games, Stegan mentioned to several foreign coaches that women were competing in North America. Unfortunately, they were not interested in promoting the sport among women at that time.

In the spring of 1980, Stegan and Spencer invited women to attend the spring training camp at Squaw Valley. Due to worries about using the Olympic training facilities for women who were not included in the Olympic events, the invitation was extended to women quietly through the regional coaches. Several women attended, including Pam Nordheim and Patrice Anderson from Minnesota. Both Nordheim and Anderson would later go on to be named to the first women's Olympic team in 1992.

During the winter of 1981, a women's class was included for most of the races and participation grew dramatically. Howard Buxton, the first president of the new national governing body, United States Biathlon Association, was extremely supportive and encouraged women's events in the national championships. The women's distances were the same as junior men, and each regional relay team included a woman team member.

During the mid-1980s, a regular group of women biathletes competed across the country. Laura Freeman was encouraged by her father, a National Guard racer from Vermont, to take up the sport. She joined the National Guard and earned All-Guard honors even though there was no separate class for women.

Also during the mid-1980s, some nations in Europe began to open their races to women competitors. The Czechs, Poles, and French were among the first. By 1984, the first Women's World Biathlon Championship was held in Chamonix, France. The United States women were immediately successful when Kari Swenson became the first American athlete to win a world championship biathlon bronze medal. Other medals included a gold in 1988 when Nancy Bell-Johnstone, Patrice Anderson, and Pam Nordheim won the relay in Antholtz, Italy. That same year, Mary Ostergren, Joan Smith, and Patrice Anderson earned a relay bronze medal in Ruhpolding, Germany. Anna Sommerup would add to the medal count in 1991 when she placed second in a World Cup race.

Women's biathlon was finally granted full medal status in the 1992 Olympic Games held in Albertville, France. Members of the seven-member U.S. team included Patrice Anderson, Nancy Johnstone-Bell, Beth Coats, Joan Guetschow, Mary Ostergren, Pam Nordheim, and Joan Smith. The 1994 Olympic team in Lillehammer, Norway, included Coats, Guetschon, Ostergren, and Smith (1992 team) and newcomers Laurie Tavares and Ntala Skinner. Participants are presently in training for the 1998 Games in Nagano, Japan. *PS*

Black Women and Sport. *See* **African American Women and Sport**

Bonnie Blair

Speedskater Bonnie Blair was born on May 18, 1964, in Cornwall, New York. After winning her sixth career Olympic medal at the 1994 Winter Olymic Games in Lillehammer, Norway, Blair emerged as the most decorated United States athlete in Winter Olympics history. In 1994, Blair's Olympic gold medal count rose to five, the most won by any American woman in any sport. The only woman to ever win consecutive gold medals in the 500-meter speedskating event, Blair won the event with a time of 39.25 seconds at the 1994 Games. Blair also entered the record books as the only United States athlete to win a gold medal in the same event (500-meters) in three consecutive Winter Olympic Games. She also earned a gold medal for her spectacular performance in the 1,000 meter race with a time of 1:18.74 at the 1994 Games.

After her remarkable Olympic performances, Blair won two more gold medals in

Bonnie Blair.

both the 500-meter and 1,000-meter races at the world sprint championships. She set the world record in the 500-meter (38.99 seconds) in March at the 1994 world championship in Calgary. Blair, the 1994 United States National Sprint Champion, has held this title since 1985. She broke the world record for overall points at the 1994 World Sprint Speed Skating Championship in Calgary, a record she first set in 1989.

Blair has received many honors for her outstanding achievements. She was voted the 1994 Women's Sports Foundation Individual Sportswoman of the Year. Her other 1994 honors include being named *Sports Illustrated's* Sportswoman of the Year, the Associated Press Female Athlete of the Year, the ESPY Female Athlete of the Year, the United States Olympic Committee's Sportswoman of the Year from 1992 to 1994, and *Glamour* magazine's Woman of the Year. Blair is now focused on coaching as a career.

Tenley Albright Blakely. *See* Tenley Albright

Theresa Weld Blanchard. *See* Theresa Weld

Bobsledding and Women

The use of bobsleds in the United States dates back to 1839, when they were used to carry wood. Competitive bobsledding originated in Davos, Switzerland, during the winter of 1888, when an Englishman connected two toboggans together and attached a rake for a brake. Steering was done with ropes. The sport, which got its name from the bobbing motion riders made to hasten the sled's progress, caught on quickly with the wealthy. Clubs formed and money was contributed to build race courses. During the winter of 1889, the first steel bobsled was used, a two-seater or multi-seater. The list of winners in that first St. Moritz, Switzerland, race showed that there were no separate categories; three-man to six-man teams competed against each other. At the first Winter Olympic Games in 1924, five-man bobsledding was included.

Bobsledding took a firm hold in the United States when a bobsled run was built at Lake Placid, New York, for the 1932 Winter Olympic Games.

Originally, bobsledding was a mixed sport that required women team members. A five-person bobsled team had to have at least one woman, adorned in heavy petticoats. Yet, as early as 1924, women began to be banned from competition because bobsledding was considered too dangerous for women. In 1940, the Amateur Athletic Union reopened the sport to women. Days later, Katharine Dewey (granddaughter of Melvil Dewey, creator of the Dewey Decimal library catalog system) was on a team that won the United States National Four-Man Bobsled Championship, becoming the only woman in the history of bobsledding to win a national championship in open competition against men. The Amateur Athletic Union quickly reversed its decision and ruled that women could compete only against other women, a move that primarily served to ban Dewey from the sport.

But the spirit and determination of Dewey lives on in others. Julie Walzak of Lake Placid, New York, was the first woman since the Dewey race to frequent the Mt. Hovenberg bobsled run in her hometown, the only bobsled run in the United States during the 1980s. For years, Walzak was the only woman sledding, facing the adversity often associated with pioneers.

In 1994, the first United States Women's Bobsled Team was named, with Walzak cheering them on. Pushing a 325-lb, two-person sled down a 55-meter railed summer track testing facility, Jill Bakken, Patty Driscoll, Nancy Lang, Laurie Millett, Liz Parr-Smestad, Alexandra Powe-Allred, Michelle Powe and Sharon Slader competed in the first Women's National Push Track Championship. Powe-Allred won the gold medal, with Parr-Smestad taking the silver medal.

In the winter of 1994, Powe-Allred and Bakken competed in St. Moritz, becoming the first United States female pilots to compete in international bobsled competition. Later that same winter, Powe-Allred and

Sharon Slader competed head to head against other United States women, claiming the first national champion honor.

By 1996, only four of the original crew, Bakken, Michelle Powe, Parr-Smestad, and Powe-Allred, remained actively competing. With new, young talent, the United States Women's Bobsled Team is capable of being a top competitor against strong competition. At this time, however, their biggest struggle is financial. At each race they have to rent sleds and runners (blades) from whatever host country they are visiting. While traditional powers in the sport like the German, Swiss, British, Latvian, Austrian, and Canadian women's teams own their own equipment, the United States women must spend several days repairing and adjusting to their new sleds before each race. The United States Women's Bobsled Team has been self-taught, quickly learning how to drive, repair, and move the 400-lb sleds by themselves.

To date, bobsledding is not an Olympic event for women, although there are indications that it will be included at the 2002 Olympic Games. Obstacles still exist, however. Some still believe that bobsledding is not a sport for women. Without the promise of an Olympic event, sponsors have been hard to find. American Skandia Life Assurance Corporation has become the chief supporter of the women's program, making international competition possible for the team. It is only with the backing of a corporation like American Skandia, and with the determination and grit of the women bobsledders, that the United States program and the dream of having women's bobsledding be an Olympic event lives on. With the help of American Skandia, team manager Stewart Flaherty and team members are purchasing sleds and the equipment necessary to be a strong competitive force. The national governing body is U.S. Bobsled and Skeleton Federation, PO Box 828, Lake Placid, NY 12946. (518-523-1842). *PS*

Bowling and Women

Bowling is an ancient sport that can be traced to the training and practice exercises of primitive hunters who depended on their skill to knock down objects with stones. The first acknowledged evidence of a game similar to bowling was discovered by British anthropologist Finder Petrie who found three stone balls, nine cone-shaped stones, and a piece of marble with three arches in an Egyptian child's grave, dating back to around 5200 B.C. Petrie believed the artifacts were game pieces, speculating that the balls were pitched through the marble arches before knocking down cone pins. Ancient games from other cultures also resemble bowling. Among them are the Polynesian game of *ula maika*, the Italian game of bocci, and the many forms of "ninepins" played throughout Europe, often under different rules and conditions.

Ninepins probably originated in Germany, possibly as early as the third century A.D., not as a sport, but as a religious ceremony. Reports describe religious ceremonies in which a man could prove that he was leading a pure life by attempting to knock over his *kagel*, a clublike weapon with a stone ball, thrown from one end of the building to the other. If the man was successful at knocking down the kagel, he was deemed to be living a clean life. If unsuccessful, he needed to attend church more often and mend his ways. The religious ceremony gradually changed to a game as more kagels (or pins) were added, and men played for secular rather than religious reasons. Martin Luther is credited with establishing the number of pins for the game at nine, resulting in the name "ninepins."

Bowling came to America with the colonists, and despite the negative Puritan attitudes toward play, the game became popular. As early as 1626, a bowling green for playing the Dutch version of ninepins was established in New York City. One of the earliest American literary references to bowling is found in Washington Irving's 1819 work, *Rip Van Winkle*. By 1840, many bowling lanes were established in New York

City, but the game of ninepins was associated with vice and gambling and was outlawed in many places. A crafty, but unknown individual added a 10th pin to the game and changed the configuration from the ninepins diamond set-up to the current 10-pin, triangular set-up, perhaps to circumvent laws against playing ninepins.

The first national organization to standardize the rules of bowling was the National Bowling Association, founded in 1875. It was followed by the American Amateur Bowling Union and then the American Bowling Congress (ABC) in the 1890s. The American Bowling Congress was so successful at promoting the sport that it became one of the largest sports organizations in the world. Because ABC was a male organization, women bowlers established the Women's International Bowling Congress (WIBC) in 1916, which continues to support and promote women's bowling today.

The modern sport of bowling involves rolling a large, heavy ball down a 60-foot, lane to knock down 10 pins set up in a triangular pattern. All the elements of the game—weight, and size of the ball, dimensions of the pins, the finish used on the lanes—are set by parameters established by the ABC. A game consists of 10 frames, with the possibility of adding 1 frame with a strike in the 10th frame, and a perfect game score is 300. Competition rules and tournament events are governed by the ABC and WIBC. Youth bowling is governed by the Youth Bowling Congress. The game is popular with all ages and can be modified in various ways to allow disabled athletes to compete.

Bowling was an Olympic exhibition sport at the 1988 Summer Games in Seoul, South Korea, but has not attained permanent status in spite of efforts to make it so. Team USA is the national team that represents the United States in international competitions such as the Pan American Games and the Federation Internationale des Quilleurs (FIQ) Championships (FIQ is the international governing body of bowling).

Many notable American women bowlers have graced the sport. Among the early women bowlers was Floretta McCutcheon, known as the "Pied Piper of Bowling" because she brought so many women into the game. McCutcheon started bowling in 1923 and amazed the bowling world by defeating the reigning male world bowling champion, Jimmy Smith. By the age of 50, McCutcheon was the best woman bowler in the world and its most ardent supporter. McCutcheon retired in the mid 1950s, and her position as the first lady of bowling was passed on to Marion Ladewig. Ladewig won the All Star Championship eight times, won the first women's professional bowling tournament, was named WIBC Woman Bowler of the Year nine times, and was the first woman elected to the WIBC Hall of Fame. In the 1970s, Patty Costello and Paula Sperber-Carter were among the female bowling elite. Costello won 25 professional titles during her career and was named bowler of the year in 1972 and 1976. Sperber-Carter won the United States Open Championship in 1971 and 1974 and brought more attention to bowling with her guest spots on the *Tonight Show*, and a feature article in *Sports Illustrated*, which publicized women's bowling and added to its popularity.

The Women's Pro Tour was established in 1959. In 1981, it was replaced by the Ladies Pro Bowlers Tour which grew into a major event during the 1980s with Lisa Wagner becoming the first woman to earn over $100,000 a year on the tour. Wagner also won 28 professional titles and was named bowler of the year four times and bowler of the decade for the 1980s. Current female bowling greats include Aleta Sill, Tish Johnson, Anne Marie Duggan, and Liz Johnson. At the age of 19, Johnson became the youngest national amateur champion ever. She also won gold and silver medals at the 1995 Pan American Games.

The various bowling membership organizations, among them the ABC, WIBC, and the American Junior Bowling Congress (AJBC), sponsor many programs that promote bowling. Competition at all levels is provided by bowling leagues located at bowling centers around the United States. In addition to competitive tournaments and leagues, these organizations offer instructional guides and publications about bowling. For further information about bowling, contact USA Bowling, 5301 South 76th St., Greendale, WI 53129-0500.

Boxing

Boxing is an ancient sport that has its roots in fighting skills used in war. The sport consists of two opponents exchanging fist punches aimed at the front of the upper body, head, and face. The contest takes place in a square, rope-enclosed area that is called the ring. Punches that land in the target areas score points, and the winner of the bout is the person with the most points as determined by a panel of judges. The contest can also be won by one opponent knocking the other unconscious or by disabling them such that the referee determines that the contest cannot continue. Contests are conducted between opponents in the same weight class and weight classes range from heavyweight to flyweight.

Women have participated in boxing events for several centuries, but most of the bouts were novelty events associated with fairs and circuses rather than sport. London newspaper reports detail boxing tournaments involving women in the early 1700s and similar reports can be found in United States newspapers from the late 1800s. Female pugilists (fighters) were an anomaly, however, in a sport often referred to as the "manly art of self-defense."

Today, female membership in USA Boxing, the national governing body for boxing, remains very small in relation to male membership. In 1996, 574 women held membership in USA Boxing, compared with 21,990 men. The number of women interested in boxing as a fitness regimen, however, has increased recently because of its excellence as a vehicle for physical training. Many women have joined gyms to train for the physical benefits, without an initial interest in competing in the ring. This demanding sport requires strength, stamina, and agility. Training for boxing improves both cardiovascular capacity and upper and lower body muscle strength and stamina. An additional benefit reported by women is an increased sense of control and security as they become proficient in the skills of boxing.

Some women do choose to compete in the ring, but few local amateur events have been held. The primary obstacle to local and national development of boxing for women is that the lack of competitors in each weight division makes it difficult to organize matches for competitive female amateur boxers. Therefore, opportunities for women competitors are quite limited. In the Olympic Games, boxing is strictly a male event, but 1995 saw the debut of the first women's bracket in the 69-year history of the New York Golden Gloves amateur boxing tournament.

In the professional arena, the presence of professional women boxers Christy Salters Martin and Deidre Gogarty is increasing popular interest in women's professional matches. Martin, in particular, has received media attention from *Sports Illustrated*, *Time* magazine, and many national newspapers for her skills in the ring. Her outstanding record—currently 35-2-2, with 25 knockouts—has made her one of the most highly paid and renowned women boxers in modern history.

Local boxing gyms provide the best places to start training for boxing. Some local gyms offer admission and training for females who want to begin boxing. The organization that sets the rules and regulations for international amateur boxing is the Association Internationale de Boxe Amateur (AIBA). In the United States, the governing organization for boxing is USA Boxing. Information about the sport can be obtained by writing to USA Boxing, 1520 N. Union Blvd., Suite B, Colorado Springs, CO 80909.

Pat Bradley

Pat Bradley, an American golfer, was born on March 24, 1951, in Westford, Massachusetts. Since joining the Ladies Professional

Golf Association (LPGA) Tour in 1974, she has participated in 581 tournaments, with 301 "top-10" finishes. She has won six major championship titles, including the 1986 LPGA Championship, the 1986 Nabisco Dinah Shore Tournament, and the 1981 United States Women's Open. She has won a total of 31 victories on the tour. Her most recent win came at the HEALTHSOUTH Inaugural Tournament in 1995. She was the fourth player in LPGA history to reach the $1 million mark in earnings but became the first player to reach the $2, $3, and $4 million marks. In 1992, she won the JC Penney/LPGA Skins Game, earning $200,000. Bradley was inducted into the LPGA Hall of Fame on January 18, 1992, in Boston, Massachusetts.

Bradley started playing golf when she was 11 years old under the tutelage of John Wirbal of Nashua Country Club in Nashua, New Hampshire. She graduated from Florida International University (FIU) in 1974 and is a member of the FIU Hall of Fame. A member of the FIU golf team, she was named an All-American in 1970. She credits her instructor, Gail Davis, with much of her success and states that her career was influenced greatly by her late father. After each tournament Bradley wins, her mother rings a bell on the family back porch, no matter what the time of day.

In addition to golf, Bradley has interests in other areas. She was a former skiing instructor and skied in the Gerald Ford Invitational at Vail, Colorado, from 1981 to 1983. In 1988, she was diagnosed with hyperthyroidism (Graves' Disease) and took time off from the LPGA tour. She returned to the tour in 1989 and won the All Star/ Centinela Hospital Classic, her first victory since 1987.

Bradley has been honored many times for her talent in golf. She was the recipient of the 1992 Samaritan Award, the 1991 William and Mousie Powell Award, and the 1989 Jack Nicklaus Family of the Year Award given by the National Golf Foundation. She is the honorary director of the Thyroid Foundation of America at Massachusetts General Hospital in Boston, Massachusetts. Bradley was a member of the LPGA Executive Committee from 1993 to 1995. She continues to play professionally and is endorsed and financially supported by Yamaha Golf.

Valerie Brisco-Hooks

Valerie Brisco-Hooks was born on July 6, 1960, in Greenwood, Mississippi, but grew up in Los Angeles, California. As a resident of Los Angeles, it was particularly fitting that she should be the track and field star of the 1984 Olympic Games in Los Angeles, California. Her triple gold medal accomplishments in those games, (200-meter, 400-meter, and 4 x 400-meter relay races) included becoming the first Olympian to win both the 200- and 400-meter races within the same Olympic Games, over a decade before Michael Johnson achieved the same feat at the 1995 world championships and the 1996 Olympic Games. Her time of 48.83 seconds in the 400-meter race still stands as the United States record.

Brisco-Hooks raised her gold medal count when she ran on the winning 4 x 400-meter relay team in the 1988 Olympic Games in Seoul, South Korea. That year, she became the only American woman to achieve world ranking in all three sprint races (100-meter, 200-meter, and 400-meter races) within the same year. She was also outstanding at the Pan American Games, winning gold medals in 1979 and in 1987. She won a bronze medal at the 1987 world championships in Rome.

Brisco-Hooks credits much of her success to her late brother, who was a hurdler in high school. She has dedicated her career to him, using his abilities as her inspiration.

Earlene Brown

For Earlene Brown, born in Los Angeles in 1936, the Police Athletic League was the place where she received guidance and encouragement for her abilities in track and field. A natural athlete, Brown participated in running events and basketball and baseball throws. She was also a catcher for an elite-level softball team. In 1956, she joined the Amateur Athletic Union (AAU) and not only won her events, the shot put and the discus, but also became the record holder in these events as well. In the 1959 Pan American Games, Brown won the shot put and the discus, with meet records in both. She continued to break records with her throws and was the first woman to put the shot over 50 feet. Because she had to work and support a child, Brown was not able to train as much as other competitors, but she continued to place in several competitions including the Commonwealth Games and AAU Outdoor Nationals. Brown is the only woman shot-putter who competed in three consecutive Olympic Games, 1956, 1960, and 1964. In the 1960 Games, she won the bronze medal in the shot put.

Karin Buchholz

The United States Olympic Committee has named Karin Buchholz as the first director of its innovative development program that seeks to use urban areas as "micro-Olympic Training Centers." Buchholz was awarded this responsibility because of her success as national coordinator of the United States Tennis Association (USTA) Junior Recreational Tennis Program. She was responsible for coordinating the USTA Junior Team Tennis leagues and was staff liaison for the National Junior Recreational Tennis Committee. She was formerly the executive director and head tennis professional of the Harlem Junior Tennis Program. From her background as an exceptional tennis athlete, Buchholz often gives motivational speeches in the areas of inner-city recreational and educational programming and women and youth in sport.

Susan Butcher

When Susan Butcher won the Iditarod Sled Dog Race in 1988, she became the first person ever to win this grueling 1,158-mile race three times. The Iditarod, held in Alaska, starts at Anchorage and finishes in Nome, taking approximately 11

days to complete. Butcher has now won the race four times. Her success elevated the race to new levels of public awareness.

Born on December 26, 1954, in Cambridge, Massachusetts, Butcher grew up a very determined and independent person, two attributes that were to help her as she became a musher, the name for a person who races dogsleds. As a musher, she displayed women's endurance and stamina capabilities in one of the toughest sports in the world. To take part, she had to plan races from a tactical point of view, train her dogs to optimal performance levels, and endure the isolation and loneliness of the Alaskan wilderness.

Butcher entered her first Iditarod in 1978 and finished 19th. In 1979 she was ninth. For the next six years she trained thousands of miles every year in her attempt to win. In 1985, she was leading the race, when a moose killed two of her dogs. That same year Libby Riddles became the first woman to win the race. But Butcher did not give up her quest and was determined to become the first woman to win more than one race, which she did with wins in 1986, 1987, 1988, and 1990. In the 14 Iditarod races in which she has competed, Butcher has finished in the "top 10" 11 times. She attributes her success to her ability to train her dogs and to her skill and experience in determining which trails to take during the

Susan Butcher.
Photo courtesy of Jim Brown photo.

race, for there is no set route for the Iditarod race.

Susan Butcher has twice been named Women's Sports Foundation's Professional Sportswoman of the Year (1987-88). In 1990, she was awarded one of the Amateur Athletic Foundation's six regional trophies. With these, and other sled dog successes, Susan Butcher helped to eradicate any myth that portrayed women as the weaker sex. Indeed, Riddles and Butcher were the basis for a humorous new mythology: "Alaska, where men are men and women win the Iditarod."

Robin Byrd-Goad

Born on January 17, 1970, Robin Byrd-Goad is one of America's best weightlifters. In 1994, she became the second United States woman to win the world championship in weightlifting, competing in the 114-pound division. That same year she set 10 United States records and two world records (one official and one unofficial) and was named the United States Weightlifting Foundation (USWF) 1994 Woman Athlete of the Year.

Another great year for Byrd-Goad was 1991. She was named United States Weightlifting Foundation Woman Athlete of the Year and set the world record in the snatch (weight moves in one continuous motion into the held position) and finished second in the world championships in this event. She was the only weightlifter from the Unites States invited to the World Cup Gala in Barcelona, Spain, in 1991. Only weightlifters capable of setting a world record were invited to this event, and Byrd-Goad did just that. She currently lives in Auburn, Washington.

C

Canoe-Kayak and Women

Like cycling, running, and some other sports, canoeing and kayaking were originally methods of transportation that evolved into sports and recreational pursuits. The kayak originated among the Eskimo groups in Arctic waters and canoes were used by various Native American tribes. Recreational canoeing includes touring, wilderness exploration, and wild-water (white-water) paddling. These canoeing activities are also associated with other outdoor sports like fishing or camping. Competitive canoeing involves racing, head-to-head or timed trials. Canoe polo and canoe surfing are other related sports.

The modern founder of recreational and sport canoeing is John MacGregor of Great Britain, who invented the Rob Roy type of canoe in 1865 and popularized recreational canoeing through his canoe travelogues describing trips through Europe and the Middle East. The Rob Roy was a decked canoe patterned along the lines of the kayak. It was an exemplar of the transitional canoes, moving from birchbark to those made of modern material like canvas. Also in 1865, MacGregor was influential in establishing the first canoe club—The Royal Canoe Club of London.

The first canoe club in the United States was established in New York in 1871 by William Alden and M. Schuyler. Other canoe clubs were soon organized in New York, New Jersey, and Pennsylvania. In 1880, the American Canoe Association (ACA) was created, with William Alden serving as its first commodore. The founding of the ACA immediately increased the number of permanent canoeing competitions offered in the United States. The ACA remains the governing body of United States canoeing and is responsible for selecting the United States Olympic Team. The most influential committee of the ACA is the National Paddling Committee, which sets all the rules and regulations of the sport and sponsors national championships.

The International Representation for the Canoeing Sport (IRK) was the first organization to govern the sport of canoeing internationally. The IRK successfully applied to have canoeing accepted as an Olympic sport. Canoeing was a demonstration sport at the 1924 Olympic Games in Paris, France, and became a permanent event at the 1936 Olympic Games in Berlin, Germany. After World War II, the IRK was reorganized into the Federation International de Canoe (FIC), which is currently located in Budapest, Hungary.

Canoeing and kayaking are paddling sports, with the canoeist using a single-bladed paddle and the kayaker employing a double-bladed paddle. Another difference between the two types of crafts is that a canoeist kneels while a kayaker sits with her feet in front of her. There are many types of canoes and kayaks, but all are essentially small, lightweight shells that are pointed at both ends. The FIC specifies kayak and canoe lengths and weights for various events. Single-seat kayaks are referred to as K-1 and two-people kayaks as K-2. The same indicators exist for canoes with the number of paddlers ranging from one (C-1) to seven (C-7). Kayaks, and some canoes, are covered by decks.

There are three types of canoe competitions for women. The first, and oldest, is the 500-meter flat water race. In this race, canoes race in lanes. The short duration of the race requires great strength and anaerobic power from competitors, much like a sprint event in running or swimming. The other two categories of competition are white-water, or wild-water, races, and slalom competitions, which are races through gated courses. Slalom events were added to the Olympic competitions in 1972 at the Games in Munich, Germany.

Women did not compete in the first canoe competitions in the 1936 Berlin Games. The first women's Olympic event was a 500-meter kayak singles (K-1) competition at the 1948 Games on the River Thames, London, England. A 500-meter pairs event was added in 1960.

Canoe and kayak events in both men and women's divisions have been dominated by Western European, Soviet, and Eastern European competitors. United States women did not medal in Olympic canoeing events until 1964, when Marcia Jones won a bronze medal in the singles race (K-1) and Francine Fox and Gloriane Perrier won a silver in the pairs competitions (K-2).

National championships for women were established in 1959. In that year, Mary Ann Duchai became the first national women's champion in the single kayak, and she teamed with Diane Jerome to win the K-2 title as well. A women's national championship in the four-women kayak (K-4) was established in 1962, with members of the Niles Kayak and Canoe Club taking the first title. Contemporary United States canoeing women champions are Dana Chladek and Cathy Hearn. Chladek, a kayak slalom competitor, was ranked ninth in the 1994 World Cup standings and won a bronze medal in the 1992 Olympic Games in Barcelona, Spain. Cathy Hearn was ranked 14th in the 1995 slalom World Cup standings.

Requests for information on recreational canoeing and kayak programs should be addressed to the America Canoe Association, 7432 Alban Station Boulevard, Suite B-226, Springfield, VA 22150. For information on Olympic canoe and kayak programs, contact the United States Canoe and Kayak Team, Pan-American Plaza, Suite 610, 201 South Capitol Avenue, Indianapolis, IN 46225.

Cappy Productions

Winner of the 1994 Women's Sports Foundation (WSF) Billie Jean King Contribution Award, Cappy Productions is known as the primary producer of sports documentaries and films worldwide. For many years, Bud Greenspan and his wife Cappy (for whom Cappy Productions was named) received six Emmy nominations through the course of their work together. After his wife's death, Greenspan and Nancy Beffa have continued the commitment to portraying male and female athletes in their productions. Many Cappy films have documented the Olympic Games and include "16 Days to Glory," and "Women Gold Medal Winners," a 10-hour series on women in the Olympic Games. Cappy Productions won two Emmys for its series on women Olympians, which has now been expanded into 22 one-hour shows. In 1977, Cappy produced the NBC movie, *Wilma*, based on the life of Wilma Rudolph. Cappy Productions has over 21 different topical films and continues to provide a forum for displaying the accomplishments of women athletes.

Jennifer Capriati

Jennifer Capriati was born on March 29, 1976, in Long Island, New York. Her father, Stefano Capriati, is a professional tennis instructor. Capriati picked up a tennis racket for the first time when she was three years old. At the age of four, she began hitting tennis balls on a regular basis. The family then moved to Florida to be in a year-round tennis environment. Stefano asked Jimmy Evert, father of Chris Evert, to coach Jennifer, and Evert coached her for five years. During this time, Capriati became friends with Chris Evert and practiced with her often.

At the age of 12, Capriati began winning many amateur tournaments, defeating girls much older than herself and many hometown players, male and female. In 1988, she won both the National 18-and-under Clay Court and the Hard Court Tennis Championships, as well as the junior championships at the French and the United States Open tournaments. The International Tennis Federation ranked her second among 18-and-under players.

In 1990, the Women's International Tennis Federation ruled that the earliest a player could become professional was in the month the player would become 14 years old. Ostensibly, the rule was made to protect players from injuring themselves physically at a young age.

On March 6, 1990, in the month of her 14th birthday, Jennifer made her debut as a professional in the Virginia Slims Tournament in Boca Raton, Florida. She defeated four seeded players before losing to Gabriela Sabatini in the finals. The media was enthralled with Capriati, calling her the "Eighth Grade Wonder" and the "Next Chris Evert." She also played doubles in the same tournament with the all-time great, Billie Jean King, but they lost in the second round of doubles competition. She won her first professional tournament in October, the Puerto Rican Open, and was ranked eighth in the world by the end of her first year as a professional. *Tennis Magazine* named her 1990 Rookie of the Year.

In the preseason of 1991, Capriati began to work more with weights. Building upper body strength gave her a more powerful serve and lower body strength enabled her to improve footspeed. In the 1991 quarterfinals at Wimbledon, she beat Martina Navratilova in two sets (6-4, 7-5) to advance to the semifinals against Sabatini. Although she lost in the semifinals, Capriati became the youngest player to reach the semifinals in Wimbledon history. In August of that year, she won the Mazda Classic, beating Monica Seles in the finals. A week later, she won the Player's Challenge over Katrina Maleeva. By the end of this impressive year, Capriati was ranked sixth in the world (her highest singles ranking).

To date, Capriati has won six titles and $1.4 million. The highlight of her career was winning the gold medal for the United States in women's tennis at the 1992 Olympic Games in Barcelona, Spain, defeating Steffi Graf, 3-6, 6-3, 6-4.

Several years after her initial successes, Capriati experienced a great deal of personal difficulty. Many believe the constant attention and pressure to win became unbearable, and she exhibited some negative behaviors in her efforts to "escape." Allegations were made concerning drug use and shoplifting, but her level of personal involvement in these matters was not entirely clear. She dropped off the professional tennis tour in 1993. After an ill-fated return in 1995, she began anew in 1996, competing again as an unranked player. There is great hope that she will find a way to remain connected to a sport in which she was so successful.

Car Racing. *See* **Motor Sports Racing**

Careers in Sport: Agent

In 1974, when Ellen Zavian entered the sixth grade, she had already been recognized in the top 10 percent of her class, starred in a school play, and was halfway through her 14 years of ballet. She seemed an unlikely woman sports "pioneer," but Zavian is one of the first female sports agents in the United States. She "cut her teeth" professionally as an intern with the National Football League Players Association during law school. As happens with so many young people, a paid position opened to Ms. Zavian when the internship was completed.

At present, Ms. Zavian is a practicing attorney, an agent representing over 30 professional athletes and entertainers, a law school professor, and "recreationally," a full-time advocate for women in sport. Her deep commitment to women's sport did not evolve from the grandstand, either, as she has been a competitive body builder, runner, and triathlete and continues a rigorous training regimen today.

According to Zavian, an agent functions for her client (a hypothetical professional athlete) on at least three levels. At a most basic level, the agent negotiates the client's employment contract with the owner/management of the team. When a deeper and more complex relationship evolves, an agent manages the business affairs of a client, such as financial planning, preparation of wills, setting up budgets, and tax matters. At the deepest level, the agent may even select and manage the purchase of homes, represent the client to the press on delicate matters, or represent clients who find themselves in trouble of all kinds. Recently, Ms. Zavian even acted as the legal representative for two women's gold-medal-winning Olympic teams; both the United States Soccer and Softball Teams had disputes with their respective national governing bodies, which were, fortunately, amicably settled before the 1996 Atlanta, Georgia, Games began.

Asked if a sports agent must be a lawyer, Ms. Zavian answered, in effect, "only if you are a woman." Her meaning, in this context, was that if one is to be first (a pioneer in new territory), it is necessary to be extraordinarily qualified and to do all tasks with impeccable competence.

In addition to the "ordinary" skills and knowledge that every sport agent must possess—business media awareness and contacts, legal expertise, and negotiation skills—Ms. Zavian recommended several special additional qualities that will stand women in good stead in this vocation. In Zavian terms,

the female sports agent will need to cultivate "chutzpah and moxie" (both boldness and a keen insight into the inner workings of an organizational framework). Additionally, at a personal interaction level, a woman must be careful to set her moral values (her compass) early on and refrain from "adjusting them" in moments of stress. She must work extra hard to set professional boundaries and maintain those boundaries even when that means passing up a social "night on the town" at a convention or meeting. Until she has established her reputation as "agent first and foremost," she will probably need to avoid even the appearance of using her job as a social vehicle. Linked with this discretion is the capacity to deal with many people as "business partners, not friends," realizing that trust between individuals and corporations must be earned in a professional context, not automatically granted to all.

If a girl or women is interested in becoming a sports agent, Zavian suggests several helpful steps: obtain an appropriate sports education background; cover sports in a school or local newspaper; manage a team or be an athlete; run a charitable event; and follow through on internships or other volunteer apprenticeship opportunities. There is no one "surefire" route to this career. An MBA degree, law degree, or sport management background may be useful, but the best asset is a willingness to learn and work hard. *CAO*

Careers in Sport: Athletic Director

Connee Zotos loved sport. She was an athlete, and it seemed natural for her to go on from high school to earn a bachelor's degree in physical education at Glassboro State College in New Jersey. After graduation in 1975, it also seemed natural, and ordinary, to go directly to a position at a high school in New Jersey to teach physical education and coach. Her career became extraordinary soon after and has continued in that vein ever since.

Connee Zotos began her career coaching in three sports: field hockey, basketball, and softball. She was a high school coach for two years and a college coach for seven years. She left coaching in 1982 to accept a faculty position at the University of Texas at Austin where she worked with undergraduate and graduate students who were pursuing careers linked to professional sports franchises, Olympic development programs, or high school and university athletic departments. During her 10 years at Texas, she directed national sports camps and coaching clinics and worked as a television color commentator for Home Sports Entertainment.

Zotos is presently the director of athletics at Drew University in New Jersey. She has a master's degree in sport management from the University of Colorado and a Ph.D. in educational administration from the University of Texas at Austin.

When asked what qualities and skills are necessary for an athletic director in today's world of sport, Dr. Zotos identified several large categories of "necessities." The athletic program, at most colleges and universities in the United States, is one part educational and one part business. The director is responsible for a range of activities from counseling and care of athletes to raising thousands (or millions) of dollars to subsidize the athletic enterprise. The director must be able to communicate effectively with publics ranging from alumni (whose zealous attempts to aid recruiting can court ethical disaster) to faculty whose views may question the very existence of athletics on the campus. Truly, this line of work is a complex vocation.

An athletic director, thus, must have an advanced ability to perform what leadership theory refers to as task (instrumental) functions and people (expressive) functions. An effective director will fully understand structural (or bureaucratic) aspects of her own institution and all other conference/governing body affiliations involved in the program. The director, like a good coach, must be able to motivate her staff and must possess a willingness to confront problems while maintaining an endless capacity for conflict resolution.

Athletics today is beset by many ethical challenges. Many of these challenges revolve around core dilemmas such as recruiting top level athletes and top level students; running a program that is high in athletic success (wins), in profitability, in academic success of student-athletes, and that is ethically sound; and hiring coaches who are highly successful and caring mentors of athletes and who lead balanced personal lives. Many maintain that these diverse goals cannot be achieved, but the athletic director strives to meet them. Thus Dr. Zotos's advice regarding the ideal personal qualities of an athletic director focuses on both high, and well-developed, personal ethical standards and impeccable credentials. She particularly emphasizes that a woman will need a doctorate and faculty experience as well as business acumen and a good background in sport to earn a director's position at an institution of higher learning. A well-rounded vitae (resume) with these types of degrees and experiences will provide a snapshot of the applicant's vital skills and knowledge and the valuable "credibility" aspect, which initially opens the door.

Regarding the possibilities for women in the role of collegiate athletic director, implementation of Title IX and the Civil Rights Restoration Act has opened doors as never before. Because women do not have a history and tradition of simple "apprenticeship" into athletic administration, they tend to ascend to these positions with more "formal training" than men. They are more likely to come with a Ph.D. or M.B.A. in hand. This trend may create a new standard of competency for the athletic director role generally. It is hoped that the expansion of the role of women in athletics will bring a greater emphasis on "sanity in sport" as distinct from a "win at all costs" approach. No one suggests that women have some "biogenetic basis" for their traditional inclination towards building educational, as well as profitable, athletic programs. In earlier times, no one expected that women's athletics could be profitable. Thus, women athletic administrators were able to spend their formative years in the "luxury" of programs that focused on student growth and now may be able to spread such orientations in more profit-dependent environments.

For Connee Zotos, and other women like her, the main reward for taking on the exacting role of athletic director is the opportunity to "pass it on." She emphasizes the critical importance of sport in the success of her own life, and she wants more of the youth of today to grow as she did. If one is interested in pursuing this career, Dr. Zotos suggests that the first priority is to dedicate yourself to the pursuit of all the needed educational degrees and credentials. She personally believes that a doctorate in higher education administration or sport management is needed, and an MBA (en route) is a good step as well. To have experience coaching, in programs at varying levels, is also highly desirable. Lastly, she recommends a great deal of hands-on experience along the way in internships or other volunteer settings. *CAO*

Careers in Sport: Coaching

As long as there have been organized women's teams, there have been women coaches willing to give teams leadership and direction. Most of the early women coaches were volunteers, but their dedication matched or exceeded any coach of today. Lack of pay did not keep them from coaching. Rewards and satisfaction came from working with the girls and women, rather than money, news coverage, or other outside influences that women's athletics enjoy today.

Before Title IX passed in 1972, aimed at ending gender-based discrimination, high-school-level girls' sports teams were fortunate if they had uniforms. They often competed in gym clothes and wore pinnies with numbers. The travel budget was zero, and so mothers and coaches were the volunteer drivers. The schedule only included a few nearby schools, and most leagues were not yet established.

In colleges at this time, punch, cookies, and orange slices were served after the game,

and this social ritual was just as important as the competition. If a team traveled to a faraway school, players packed their lunches and sleeping bags because they would rarely get money for food and would sleep on the gym floor. Women athletes, despite these circumstances, felt fortunate to have a team to play against, even at the collegiate level. Most women coaches were graduates of physical education programs, which had given them the training to understand, teach, and get the most from their athletes both physically and mentally. By the 1950s and 1960s, many women believed they had come a long way, even though women's sports were still far behind the men's programs in terms of resources.

In 1972, Title IX was passed, outlawing sex discrimination in educational programs (including athletics) if the institution or district received federal money. Despite the boost this law gave to women's athletics, Title IX did not overcome all the obstacles facing women. Administrators of many programs did not try very hard to implement Title IX, and even today there are schools that are not in compliance with it.

There were few role models for women as athletes or coaches, and the jobs that supported women's athletics were scarce. The more "feminine" sports received the most publicity. Olympic coverage focused on gymnastics, figure skating, swimming, and diving. Even though women's sport has taken great strides, these individual sports still receive the most media coverage. For the majority of team-sport-oriented women athletes, there have been few publicized role models competing at international or national levels, although the media coverage and fan support of the women's soccer, softball, and basketball teams at the 1996 Olympic Games is a big step in the right direction.

Coaches and athletes who served as role models were there, inside the sport, but very little media attention was paid to these women. Young people looked up to the women who were their coaches, their own teammates, or known stars of the game, but the athletes had to wait until they were in the sport to know these people. These familiar figures became the role models for each team that passed through each community's program.

Today, women have more opportunities and career paths in sports to choose. Coaches are not only getting paid, but they are also getting paid more and finding more coaching jobs from which to choose. The women taking these new careers paths are becoming the role models of the future. Women such as basektball coaches Pat Summitt and Vivian Stringer are the pioneers laying the foundation for the next generation. This expansion in programs created several new career paths for women who are interested in a job in athletics. Women can choose areas of study in administration of athletics, athletic training or sports medicine, sports information, journalism, communications, biomechanics and movement design, per-

Coaching brings many rewards.
Photo courtesy of the *Camden Courier Post.*

sonal training in fitness and nutrition, physiology of exercise, and psychology of sport.

What does a woman need to become a coach? A passion and commitment to a sport is a basic prerequisite to becoming a coach. Depending on the level of competition, the needed qualifications will vary. At the least, one must possess a basic knowledge of the game and a desire to coach and work with young people. At the college level, the needed qualifications increase. Usually a master's degree is required, although it may be in any one of a variety of majors. A coach need not

have been an athlete in the sport, although it helps. She must, however, be an avid student of the sport. Most college coaches played at a high level of competition, either in college or through other amateur sports organizations. Other important coaching qualities are fairness, honesty, integrity, and motivational skills. Educational training often comes through a physical education program at a college, where there is specialized training in coaching.

Many programs at colleges give graduate assistantships, and a woman can get her degree while she is one of the school's assistant coaches. An assistant coach takes classes toward her master's degree and assists the head coach in areas such as recruiting, budget planning, fund raising, purchasing equipment, running tournaments, scheduling and maintaining facilities, selecting teams, and working with the athletes preseason, off-season, and in-season. The graduate assistant may also monitor study sessions and make sure the student-athlete is keeping her grades up. By being involved with a program at the college level, the graduate assistant receives the bonus of having a mentor and of doing the networking that may help in getting a job after the degree has been earned.

Classes usually offered in a program geared toward coaching include kinesiology (science of movement), psychology, sociology, philosophy of sport, athletic training, nutrition, administration, and core courses in research design. Each college that offers an M.A. or M.S. with emphasis in coaching may have some unique requirements as well.

The rewards and drawbacks in coaching should be weighed before a commitment is made. One of the best rewards is seeing the athletes doing their best and peaking during competition. This moment is when all the long hours of sweat and hard work pay off for everyone. The rewards are not necessarily measured in the win-loss column. At the beginning of a season, a team usually sets several goals, agreed upon by all, and achievement of these goals is the big reward. Athletic programs have different philosophies about winning, losing, and goal achievement that need to be considered when looking for a coaching job. The demands to win at the high school level are often a lot less than at the college level. Additionally, the high school coach does not need to recruit, the season is shorter, and the fund raising is on a smaller scale. No matter what level a coach chooses, the drawbacks are few compared to the rewards. Sometimes the salaries are very low, demands in recruiting can be intense, and getting positive media coverage for your sport can be trying, but all in all it is a most satisfying profession. *KN*

Careers in Sport: Color Analyst

In 1995, Mimi Griffin teamed up with Robin Roberts for ESPN's inaugural coverage of the Women's National Collegiate Athletic Association (NCAA) Basketball Championships. Griffin was the color analyst. The color analyst assists the play-by-play announcer, providing expert commentary on game situations and highlighting interesting facts about players. Griffin spends hours preparing for every telecast, even after 13 years on the job. The color analyst has to work very hard to get as much information as possible, knowing that she will never use it all, but not knowing in advance exactly what may be needed. In basketball, Griffin researches the starting five and speaks to players, coaches, and bystanders. She has to know player statistics, their records, biographies, schedules, and likes and dislikes.

The extensive pregame preparation is only part of the job. Once the telecast has started, the toughest part of the job begins. Almost everything the color analyst says must be in 30-second sound bytes that don't interrupt the flow of the game or the play-by-play announcer. Everything that is said "on-air" has to be factually accurate. A color analyst has to keep a balance between using the jargon of the expert and the language of the casual fan. Mimi thinks that John Madden, the football color analyst, is the best at this job.

Color analysts have to know their sports, and Mimi Griffin knows basketball. Her grandmother played, her mother played in the 1940s in the Philadelphia Catholic League, and Griffin and her three sisters played for Lancaster Catholic High School in Pennsylvania. At one time her team was so good, they were barred from the state competition!

Griffin started her career with an interest in business and says she grew up reading *Sports Illustrated* and *Forbes* magazines. To succeed in sports marketing (Griffin's "real job"), one has to get a lot of experience, and there are not many openings. The few entry-level positions that do exist usually go to someone who "knows someone." Often, women find that it is necessary to volunteer or intern with sport organizations so that people will remember them when an opportunity arises. Griffin, for example, was an "above and beyond" contributor to the Women's Basketball Coaching Association (WBCA) and this experience helped her earn the ESPN position.

She got her break as a color analyst for ESPN's coverage of Women's NCAA Basketball Championships. At first, Mimi Griffin got just a few games, but now, because she is good at her job, she gets many games. The key to her success is her genuine interest in the game of basketball, her deep knowledge of the game, and her hard work to continually get the facts.

Other women who have provided color commentary over many years include Donna de Varona (swimming and women's sports generally), Kathrine Switzer (marathon events), Diana Nyad (Olympic water sports), Cheryl Miller (basketball), and Mary Carillo (tennis). *NL*

Careers in Sport: Owning a Sports Business—Moving Comfort

Described as a "powerful proponent of women's sport," Ellen Wessel is the founder of Moving Comfort, manufacturers of women's high performance athletic wear. A pioneer in the development of running apparel for women in 1977, Wessel, as president, primarily focuses attention on the company's marketing and communications efforts. The following is her account of how she got started in a sports-oriented business, including the challenges of being such a business owner and some of the necessary characteristics needed to own a business that focuses on women and sports.

"Yes, I had a clear idea about what I was going to do when I grew up. Inconveniently, that idea changed frequently. The fact that I ended up in my own business had nothing to do with fulfilling a lifelong dream.

"When I was a senior in high school, I was going to be a psychologist. On the last day of college, I was quite anxious to be a wife. My second choice that day was going to paralegal school. After I got kicked out of paralegal school for an inappropriate attitude, I refocused on an earlier passion, politics. My first postcollege job (1973) was in Washington, D.C. I was a 'Girl Friday' for the Washington Bureau of the *Philadelphia Bulletin*, a now defunct city newspaper.

"Three and a half years later, and a few 'career changes' in between, another woman and I started a business called Moving Comfort. At the time, we were marathon training together, running 70 miles a week. Over hill and dale, we had lots of time to brainstorm and to notice that our clothes were not working correctly. When we stopped thinking it was because our bodies needed to be leaner, we realized it was because we were shaped like women but the clothes were not. That was 1977. In 1997, we celebrated our twentieth anniversary in business, making high performance athletic wear for women.

"I started running in 1974 so I could quit being a smoker and become an athlete. As I got more and more obsessed with my running, I became increasingly eager to control how I spent my time. I found it increasingly difficult to have a boss. I combined this 'itchiness to be in charge' with the observation that no one was making running clothes that fit women, and a business was born. I was young, 26, had no one financially dependent on me, had few fixed expenses, and was too naive to know that the garment industry can

be brutal. Ignorance was truly a blessing in those first few years. Knowing much more than nothing would have left me paralyzed with fear. Instead, I was joyfully persistent about clearing one hurdle after another.

"It's remarkable how many different careers you can have when you own your own business. Over the past 20 years, I have been a fabric cutter, graphic designer, copy writer, production coordinator, sales person, sales manager, business manager, and bill collector. I was pretty bad at a lot of these jobs, but what an opportunity to get to know yourself and your business really well!

"So what are the gender-free characteristics essential to growing a sports business? Persistence, tenacity, a deep emotional belief in the value of your product or service, adaptability, ability to inspire others to work with you, willingness to be objective about your strengths and shortcomings, eagerness to learn new things all the time, humility, self-confidence, honesty, integrity, trustworthiness, and trusting other people all play an important role. Above all, you need to have a fierce drive to be independent and a vehement belief in what you are doing to sustain the massive commitment to owning your own business. The lows are very scary. The highs are in the stratosphere."

Wessel's record backs up her words of advice. To further her company's goal of promoting increased participation and gender equity for women and girls in sports and fitness activities, Wessel is actively involved with both industry and consumer-oriented organizations, including the following:

Board of Trustees, Sporting Goods Manufacturers Association (SGMA); Board of Directors, Outdoor Recreation Coalition of America (ORCA); Executive Committee, Outdoor Products Council, SGMA; Executive Committee, Sports Apparel Products Council, SGMA; Advisory Board, Women's Sports Foundation; Advisory Board, Melpomene Institute for Women's Health Research; Advisory Board, Continental Divide Trail Association; and Advisory Board, Road Runners Club of America.

In 1996, Wessel was voted "Woman of the Year in Sports" in the Supplier category. The award program is sponsored by the sporting goods industry trade publication, *Sporting Goods Business*, and the *New York Times*.

Today Wessel is a retired marathoner (a veteran of nine races, including the Boston and New York Marathons). She continues to run and weight train to maintain fitness for horseback riding, hiking, and working. *CAO*

Careers in Sports: Sport Information

Sports information exists as a vital arm of a college or university's athletic department. Charged with media and public relations responsibilities, the sports information office acts as a liaison between the athletic department, its teams and coaches, and various media outlets and other interested parties. The sports information director (or SID) must perform a wide variety of functions, including, but not limited to, the writing of press releases, brochures, feature stories, game programs, publicity posters, schedule cards, and other publications. She serves as a departmental spokesperson, scheduling interviews between the press and athletes or coaches and dispersing other information as needed. The sports information office is also responsible for keeping updated and accurate statistics and records of the school's athletic teams. An SID must be adept with verbal skills, have the ability to think and speak clearly and to communicate effectively with a diverse group of people, including athletic department personnel, media representatives, conference and National Collegiate Athletic Association (NCAA) staffers, as well as the general public.

Sports information, also known as athletic communications and as sports media relations, is a growing and changing field that has been forced to adjust to the increasing demands of the print and broadcast media over the past few decades. The growing number of local and national cable networks has increased the number of televised college athletic contests, which, in turn, has in-creased the need for timely statistics, player and coach information, and other support services. An increasing interest in women's sports, particularly basketball and soccer, has placed even more demands on the sports information offices, which until recently spent much of their efforts on the "high profile" sports of football and men's basketball. The impact of Title IX, providing equal opportunities for women in education, including athletics, has been felt in the sports information field, which now spends an increasing amount of time promoting and publicizing women's sports.

Sports information offices range in size and complexity, depending upon the nature of the athletic program at the college or university, the numbers of varsity athletic teams, the level of competition, the success of the programs, and the subsequent media interest in the programs. The sports information office at a small NCAA Division III school may be staffed by just one person, while a Division I school with one or more sports that regularly receive national attention may have more than five full-time workers in the sports information office, including (in addition to the SID) publications manager, office manager, assistant sports information directors, interns, and student workers.

Many large universities have also expanded their sports information offices to include staffers who have specific responsibilities for marketing and promoting athletic events, particularly at schools where there is a serious interest in gaining greater fan support and media coverage for their "marquee" sports, such as women's and men's basketball and football. These marketing directors have fewer responsibilities in the actual day-to-day production of press releases and other publications but spend most of their time coming up with ideas to draw more people to their athletic contests, such as developing "giveaway" days at games, "meet the player" days, selling advertisements for game programs, and other methods of increasing revenue for the athletic department.

While the sports information field was once largely dominated by men, a large number of women are now entering the field and moving up in the ranks. Most people working in the field earned their undergraduate degrees in communications, journalism, or a related field such as English. However, a number of people working in the sports media relations field gained experience working in their school's sports information office as an undergraduate but majored in an unrelated field.

Opportunities in the field include employment at a college or university, as well as at a conference office (Pacific 10, Big 10). Conference offices perform sport information functions for several schools, supporting individual school promotional efforts through the production of conference statistics, players of the week, and all-conference teams. An entry-level position at a Division I school or conference would often come in the form of an internship or a graduate assistantship, while at a Division II or III school or conference, someone with little experience may be able to step into a sports information director position immediately.

Career growth in the sports information field can take one of several directions, including promotion within the athletic department to "Assistant Athletic Director for Media Relations," or outside the department into the print or broadcast media departments. Sports information directors sometimes move on to positions in media relations for professional sport teams or organizations, while some prefer to remain in the education setting, sometimes moving into the general public relations office of the college or university.

Anyone who wishes to enter the field of sports information should have solid writing skills, a high interest in sports and athletes, an ability to work with a variety of personalities, a capacity for working well under extreme time demands, and good organizational skills. Being a sport information director involves juggling demands of many people, many sports, and many projects at one time, but it also involves working in the exhilarating atmosphere of college sports. As long as Americans and the media continue their love affair with athletics, the opportunities in sports information will continue to grow and change. *SF*

Careers in Sport: Sport Medicine Physician

A sport medicine physician is a doctor who treats athletes and active people. Sports physicians treat a variety of athletes. Whether they are male or female, young or old, recreational or professional players, they are all motivated patients who want to get well and return to sport. This profession is very satisfying because the sports medicine doctor helps people get back to what they love—back to the action.

While the personal and professional rewards for this profession are great, the train-

Sport medicine physicians treat athletic injuries.
Photo courtesy of *Camden Courier Post.*

ing required for entry into the profession is substantial. Training includes four years of college followed by medical school. After medical school, physicians do a residency in one of several specialities such as family medicine, internal medicine, pediatrics, emergency or rehabilitation medicine. The residency is followed by a one- or two-year fellowship in sports medicine, which must be completed before one can qualify for membership in the American Medical Society for Sports Medicine (AMSSM). After completing this extensive training program, sports medicine doctors can then become board certified by passing a special examination given by the American Board of Medical Specialists. Passing this examination gives the physician an added credential called a Certificate of Added Qualification or CAQ in sport medicine.

A qualified primary care sports medicine doctor can treat about 85 percent of all injuries that occur during exercise and sports participation, according to the AMSSM. Sport medicine doctors do not do specialized surgeries like orthopedic surgeons, but they assist in many surgical procedures that patients may require. They also perform a wide variety of medical activities. For example, primary care sports medicine doctors act as team physicians and provide coverage at community, high school, college, and professional sporting events. They perform preparticipation physicals, evaluate and treat sports injuries, advise the public about exercise and physical fitness plans, and teach their patients about nutrition, diet supplementation, exercise prescriptions, and exercise limits for safety. Sports medicine doctors understand the trauma and frustrations of athletes who have been injured. They help them deal with the injury and return to active participation as quickly as possible. They also provide the recovered athlete with advice so that the athlete can avoid a recurrence of the injury.

For further information about primary care sports medicine physicians write to the American Medical Society for Sports Medicine, 7611 Elmwood Avenue, Suite 203, Middleton, WI 53562. The AMSSM can also be contacted by phone, fax, or email. Their numbers are 608-831-4484 (phone), 608-831-5122 (fax), and AMSSM@ AOL.COM (email). *KLH*

Careers in Sport: Sport Psychology

Sport psychology is an exciting area that integrates the academic discipline of psychology with exercise and sport. Sport psychology has a long history that goes back to one of the earliest experiments in social psychology with cyclists (Triplett in 1896). Even earlier, the ancient Greeks acknowledged the importance of a sound mind in a sound body. The 1920s saw particular advances in sport psychology here and abroad, but the past 15 to 20 years have seen amazing increases in our knowledge about psychology and how to apply this knowledge with athletes and recreational sport participants. For example, knowledge regarding effective implementation of goal setting, imagery, and self-talk has expanded due to recent research advances.

Sport psychology attempts to enhance integration of the mind and body in one cohesive unit. Individuals with expertise in exercise and sport psychology (many in the field define *sport psychology* as focusing upon elite athletes and *exercise psychology* as focusing upon recreational sport participants) work in a variety of settings, mainly in educational or clinical roles. Educational sport psychology focuses upon psychological skills training, wherein psychological skills such as arousal control (stress management, relaxation training), imagery, concentration, self-talk, and goal setting are taught to athletes. The focus is on education because these are skills that can be learned. Team building is also included in this educational endeavor. Clinical sport psychology addresses issues that are in the domain of clinical and counseling psychologists, such as generalized anxiety and phobias (e.g., fear of flying, fear of losing), substance abuse (steroids), and eating disorders (anorexia nervosa and bulimia nervosa). Some sport psychologists have expertise in both educational and clinical sport psychology; others have expertise in only one of the two areas.

Sport psychology consultants work with athletes ranging from neighborhood youth sport participants in a soccer or softball league to international competitors in sports such as track and field (Jackie Joyner Kersee), basketball (Rebecca Lobo), or tennis (Steffi Graf). Athletes and coaches seek out sport psychologists for a number of reasons. They may want to learn to relax before competitive events, to improve their concentration during matches, or to set more effective goals. Recreational sport participants may have problems with motivation or even addiction to exercise.

Employment opportunities for sport psychologists are available in academic settings (as university professors), in counseling and clinical settings (in private practice or in university counseling centers and athletic departments), in academic advising at the university level, and in other diverse settings such as sports medicine centers. Although these job opportunities are not plentiful (especially in settings such as sports medicine centers), the positions that are available provide the opportunity for the integration of the academic disciplines of psychology and the exercise and sport sciences.

Women have excelled in each of these settings and have demonstrated they are competent to do any of the jobs within sport psychology. Five women have been elected as president of the Association for the Advancement of Applied Sport Psychology (AAASP)—Jean Williams, Tara Scanlan, Penny McCullagh, Maureen Weiss, and Robin Vealey. Others, such as Linda Bunker, Diane Gill, Dorothy Harris, Mimi Murray, and Carole Oglesby, have been "foremothers" in the field—instrumental in the development of sport psychology as an academic discipline and in the application of this knowledge with athletes and recreational sport participants. *MS1*

See also **Imagery: Using Your Mind's Eye for Success**

Joanne Carner

Joanne Carner, an American golfer, was born on April 4, 1939, in Kirkland, Washington. After joining the Ladies Professional Golf Association (LPGA) in 1970, Carner won 42 LPGA events. She is the only woman to have won the United States Golf Association Girls' Junior, United States Women's Amateur, and the United States Women's Open titles. She is also the last amateur player to win an LPGA event, winning the 1969 Burdine's Invitational in Miami, Florida. In addition to these achievements, Carner won the United States Amateur golf title five times and competed on four Curtis Cup teams (competitions against England, a historic power in women's golf).

Carner holds the record for receiving the Vare Trophy (for the LPGA Tour's lowest scoring average) five times. She was the 10th woman inducted into the LPGA Hall of Fame in 1982, after she had won her 35th LPGA title at the Chevrolet World Championship of Women's Golf. Her last tour victory came in 1985, when she won the Elizabeth Arden Classic. In 1985, she became the 10th woman to be inducted into the World Golf Hall of Fame. In 1986, she was the second woman player to reach the $2 million mark in earnings.

Carner has been recognized throughout her career with many awards and honors. In 1994, she served as the United States' Solheim Cup captain. She received the Golf Writers' Association of America Player of the Year Award in 1981, 1982, and 1983. For her consistent excellence, she was also named the 1982 and 1983 Seagram's Seven "Crowns of Sport" Award winner and won the 1981 Bob Jones Award for her contributions to the game of golf. After winning her first LPGA tournament in 1970, she won the rookie of the year award. Outgoing and popular with the crowds, "Big Momma" Carner still finds time to encourage and support rising talent from the gallery.

Connie Carpenter-Phinney

Connie Carpenter-Phinney, an American cyclist, was born on February 26, 1957, in Madison, Wisconsin. She won the gold medal in the first Olympic women's cycling road race in 1984. Her first love, however, was speedskating. At the age of 14, she was an Olympic speedskater, finishing seventh in the 1,500 meters at the 1972 Winter Games in Sapporo, Japan. Her speedskating career ended with an ankle injury just a week before the 1976 Olympic trials, but her athletic career was far from over as she became interested in the sport of cycling.

Her switch to cycling was very successful. She won a silver medal in the 1977 world championship road race. By the opening of the 1984 Olympic Games, she had earned three more world championship medals, including a gold medal in the 3,000-meter pursuit in 1983.

Halfway through the 1984 inaugural Olympic race, 79.2 kilometers in length, six women broke away from the other competitors. Carpenter-Phinney and fellow U.S. cyclist Rebecca Twigg, winner of the 1982 world championship pursuit title, were among this leader group. With 200 meters to go, the first Olympic cycling race for women was between these two competitors. Twigg had the lead with less than 100 meters left, but Carpenter-Phinney caught her and won the race by less than half a wheel length.

In her career as a cyclist, Carpenter-Phinney has won more titles than any other United States cyclist, male or female. She won 12 national titles, including three wins in the Coors International Classic. She also is one of the few athletes to compete in both the Summer and the Winter Olympic Games. Carpenter-Phinney is currently a journalist, television commentator, and coach, and she runs an annual cycling camp in Copper Mountain, Colorado.

Florence Chadwick

Florence Chadwick (1918-95) who entered her first swimming race at the age of six, had a long-distance swimming career that spanned over 40 years. Born on November 9, 1918, in San Diego, California, Chadwick was inspired as a youngster by Gertrude Ederle's record-breaking 20-mile swim across the English Channel. Determined to make a name for herself, Chadwick set out to match that accomplishment.

During the next 25 years, Chadwick swam competitively in shorter ocean races. She took on various jobs to support herself, even working with the Arabian-American Oil Company in Saudi Arabia, so that she could train in the rough waters of the Persian Gulf.

In June 1950, Chadwick's hard work paid off. She broke Ederle's 24-year-old women's record swimming the English Channel in 13 hours, 20 minutes, eclipsing Ederle's time by more than an hour.

Following her 1950 record swim, Chadwick toured the country. As a lifelong

Florence Chadwick.
Photo courtesty of The International Swimming Hall of Fame.

53

advocate of swimming, she took time out to teach children how to swim and promoted the benefits of sports and fitness. In 1952, Chadwick's triumphs in long-distance swimming continued when she became the first woman to swim the 26-mile Catalina Channel between San Diego and Catalina island. She swam through various bodies of water in 1953, including the English Channel, the straits of Gibraltar, and a round-trip swim between Europe and Asia and the Turkish Dardanelles—all in record times. Chadwick continued to dominate the swimming world, setting a new record of 13 hours, 55 minutes for the more difficult England to France route of the English Channel in 1955.

In 1960, Chadwick shared her passion with others when she opened the Florence Chadwick Swimming Schools in New York and New Jersey. At the age of 51, Chadwick entered rougher waters when she began a new career as a stockbroker. Even with her career on Wall Street, the swimming legend continued to coach young long-distance swimmers and to promote sports for women so that others following in her footsteps could have opportunities to live an active lifestyle.

Alice Coachman

Alice Coachman, the fifth of 10 children, was born on November 9, 1923, in Albany, Georgia. In the 1948 Olympic Games in London, England, she became the first African American woman ever to win an Olympic gold medal. She won it in the high jump, clearing the bar at the height of five feet, six inches, an Olympic record that stood for eight years. Throughout her career, she broke athletic records and cleared racial barriers, paving the way for later African American Olympic stars like Wilma Rudolph, Evelyn Ashford, and Jackie Joyner-Kersee.

As a child, Coachman imitated boys who ran down roads and jumped over ropes in her hometown. She first high jumped on a dare that she could not beat the local boys, but she did. Her father thought that running and jumping were not "ladylike" for girls. Nonetheless, she continued to compete and after an appearance in the United States Track and Field Championships when she was in high school, she was invited to enroll in the Tuskegee Institute. Tuskegee was famous for its women's college track programs. She received a "working" scholarship to attend, which meant she had to clean the gym and the pool, sew football uniforms, and roll the clay tennis courts. In addition to her work and track practice, she sang in the school choir and was a member of the drill team. Coachman also participated recreationally in soccer, field hockey, volleyball, swimming, and tennis.

Coachman's successes in track and field were many. At the age of 15 Coachman broke the high school and collegiate high jump records (without wearing shoes) at a meet in Tuskegee, Alabama. She won the national Amateur Athletic Union high jump competition every year from 1939 to 1948, still the record for the most consecutive victories. By the age of 25, she had won 31 national high jump and track titles.

Coachman had never been outside the United States before her trip to the 1948 Olympic Games in London. To get to the Games, she had a difficult, seven-day ocean crossing, suffering from seasickness throughout most of the journey. She qualified for the 1948 Olympic Track and Field Team with a five-foot, four-inch jump, breaking the United States record set in 1932. This qualifying competition was held on an unlighted field in Providence, Rhode Island, where she and her closest rival competed in the high jump into twilight. Qualifying for the Olympics was especially rewarding for Coachman because during her peak years the 1940 and 1944 Olympic Games were canceled due to World War II.

After her Olympic success, Coachman became the first African American woman to endorse an international product, Coca-Cola, appearing on billboards across the country with Jesse Owens, the 1936 Olympic hero. In her later years, she founded the Alice Coachman Track and Field Foundation, which helps young and retired athletes; currently she maintains an active schedule encouraging young athletes.

Bessie Coleman

In the early part of the twentieth century, neither women nor African Americans had many rights or opportunities in this country. The fledgling field of aviation was certainly not an exception to the ordinary social rules of exclusion. Coleman was born on January 20, 1893, and raised near Dallas in Waxachie, Texas. She did not let closed doors stop her. She read about the air war in Europe during World War I and became convinced that she needed to be a pilot. In the United States at that time, however, being a woman and African American were two things standing in the way of her dream. Because flying in America was impossible, Coleman learned French and earned enough money to go to France for flight lessons in 1921. In 1922, she became the first woman to earn an international aviation license from the prestigious Federation Aeronautique Internationale. She was also the world's first licensed pilot of color from any country.

Returning to the United States, Coleman gave flight lessons to other African American women. She also gave lectures and performed flying exhibitions to raise funds to start her own flight school for African Americans, which was her dream. In preparing for an exhibition show in Orlando, Florida, the controls jammed on her plane, and Coleman crashed to her death on April 30, 1936. Despite her untimely death, her example in taking to the skies has since inspired women aviators from every walk of life.

Nadia Comaneci

Born on November 12, 1961, in Onesti, Romania, Nadia Comaneci will always be associated with the number 10—for the first perfect score awarded in Olympic gymnastics competition. On the first day of competition at the 1976 Games in Montreal, Canada,

Nadia's routine on the uneven bars earned a score of 10.0. Perfect scores were so unexpected in Olympic competition that the scoring system at the venue had not been programmed to register a "10" for a perfect score, and so the number "1" was posted on the scoreboard instead. The audience was in shock until the stadium announcer cleared up the confusion: Nadia Comaneci had been awarded a perfect score. Comaneci achieved six more scores of 10 in the uneven bars, the balance beam, and the individual all-around events. She won three gold medals, including the all-around, and a silver and a bronze medal.

Comaneci's Olympic success came only one year after she won the first of her three consecutive European championships, defeating five-time champion Ludmila Tourischeva of the Soviet Union. Comaneci was only 13 years old then, the youngest European champion ever.

At the next Olympic Games in Moscow, Russia (then part of the Soviet Union), Comaneci needed a 9.9 on the balance beam to tie Yelena Davydova of the Soviet Union for the gold medal in the all-around. After her routine, judges argued for 28 minutes over her score. The score was 9.85, thanks to

Nadia Comaneci.

two 9.8 scores from Soviet and Polish judges. Despite this huge disappointment, Comaneci came back to win gold medals in the balance beam and floor exercise.

After defecting to the United States from Romania in 1989, she moved to Oklahoma. She and her husband, Bart Conner (a United States Olympic gymnast), built a gymnasium in Norman, Oklahoma, and began a professional career of gymnastics training.

Competing with Boys: A Girl's View

"Being a woman is a terribly difficult trade, since it consists principally of dealing with men" (Joseph Conrad). One area of life in which Conrad's quote is especially true is in sports.

The one sport in which I have competed my best is one in which males and females compete head-to-head—sailing. By ranking third overall in the nation and by being the best girl in the Western Hemisphere for my age group, and the only girl to make the world team in nine years, I have proven that girls can compete at the same level as boys, and beat them. It was not easy getting to their sailing level, but I achieved it with hard work.

Initially, I was intimidated by the boys, but once I obtained the confidence to accomplish my goals, I began to defeat them and continue to do so. Early on, the boys often became vindictive after I won sailing competitions. To deal with their anger, they would sail up to my boat after races pretending they were my friends, but instead they would board my boat and capsize it. After the award ceremony, the boys would hunt me down, take me to the dock, and then throw me in the freezing salt water as my punishment for winning. Later, as they came to accept the fact that I was competing at their level and with their skills, the boys gradually began to accept and welcome me as a new challenge, not as a threat.

At first I thought it was unfair that girls had to compete against the boys in sailing. I felt that they were far superior to girls. But then I realized, it was more unfair for girls not to compete against the boys and not have the opportunity to show that they can be better. As *Optinews*, a sailing magazine, said in a September 1996 article "Mary Ridenour has made an invaluable point; that girls can compete with and beat the boys, even at the top of the sailing world."

On my way to the top, I had many sailors that influenced me. One particular sailor, Tine Moberg-Parker, a 1996 Olympian, encouraged me by saying "If they can do it, you can do it." Tine was the only female coach that I have had in sailing, and she had the biggest impact on my life. She provided a model for me to look up to because she is an accomplished female sailor. She also influenced me by reminding me that, "You can't get anywhere without working with your team." This quote caught my attention early in my sailing life. Because of her words, I

Sailing is a sport where women and men compete head-to-head.
Photo courtesy of Kelly O'Neill.

took my team very seriously. Having to travel almost every weekend to another state, just for a two-day practice, seemed like nothing compared to what I got out of it. Through practicing and learning from the techniques of the boys' sailing, I developed a technique of my own that was unbeatable. "She (Mary Ridenour) has the speed and grit to compete at the top of any fleet" (*Optinews*, October, 1996).

I used to succumb to my fears, letting my fears have power over me. I sometimes did not sail because of strong winds, and at times I did not compete because I felt I would lose. Eventually I came to the conclusion that I would not let my insecurities take control of me. I forced myself to feel that I could always do better next time, and instead of regretting an experience, I found I could learn from it. Facing my fears and learning not to fear failure made all the difference in my life.

From what I learned, the advice that I would give other girls is, don't let the boys intimidate you. They are flesh and bone just like you. Girls can be just as strong as boys. "If I have to, I can do anything. I am strong, I am invincible, I am woman" (Helen Reddy). *MR2*

See also **Sailing and Women**

Maureen Connolly

Though her playing days were cut short, Maureen Connolly, known as "Little Mo," was one of the most outstanding players tennis has ever seen. Born on September 17, 1934, Connolly entered the professional tennis circuit at the age of 14 and won 56 straight matches. In 1953, at the age of 19, Connolly became the first woman to win the Grand Slam in tennis, which consists of winning the Australian Open, the French Open, Wimbledon, and the United States Open in a calendar year. Connolly was forced to retire in 1954 after a horseback-riding accident. She devoted the rest of her short life to supporting and promoting junior tennis, dying of cancer on June 21, 1969, at 34 years of age.

Jody Conradt

Born on May 13, 1941, in Goldwaithe, Texas, Jody Conradt is the winningest women's basketball coach in history and the second winningest active Division I coach, men or women. She holds a career record of 697 wins and 198 losses in her 26-year career. Conradt's University of Texas teams averaged 29 victories per season in her 19 years coaching at Texas. Her teams dominated the basketball courts in the Southwest Conference from January 1978 through January 1991, winning 183 consecutive conference games. Overall, Conradt's teams have appeared in 14 National Collegiate Athletic Association (NCAA) postseason tournaments, including two Final Four finishes and one national championship, and 15 finishes among the top 20 in the Associated Press final poll.

With Conradt at the helm, her team became the first NCAA women's team to complete a season undefeated (34-0) in 1986.

Maureen Connolly.
Photo courtesy of Maureen Connolly Brinker Tennis Foundation.

She also coached teams that were ranked number one at one time or another from 1984 to 1987. Conradt led the United States National Women's Basketball Team to a gold medal at the 1987 Pan American Games. Conradt's program has produced four United States Olympic Team members, one Broderick Award winner (given to the outstanding collegiate athlete), two Wade Trophy Award winners (given to the outstanding collegiate woman basketball player), and 19 All-Americans. Her teams also have a strong graduation rate, in excess of 90 percent. While Conradt coached at Texas, the Lady Longhorns led the nation in attendance average for six consecutive years (1985-1986 through 1990-1991), averaging 5,740 fans per game in the 1991-92 season.

Conradt was voted National Coach of the Year four times (1979-1980, 1983-1984, 1985-1986, 1996-1997). This award, given by her peers, is regarded as one of the highest honors in her profession. She was also honored as the Southwest Coach of the Year in 1984, 1985, 1987, and 1988. The Women's Basketball Coaches Association bestowed their highest honor, the Carol Eckman Award, on Conradt in 1987. She was inducted into the International Women's Sports Hall of Fame in 1995. In 1998, Conradt is to be inducted into the Texas Sports Hall of Fame.

In addition to her present duties as athletic director at Texas since 1992, she helped to establish the Neighborhood Longhorn program that encourages Austin's youth to excel academically, offering basketball as an incentive. She also created her own fantasy basketball camp called "If I Only Had a Chance Camp," in which she coaches women between the ages of 35 and 65.

Willa McGuire Cook. *See* **Willa McGuire**

Julie Croteau

Julie Croteau is the first and thus far, the only woman to play National Collegiate Athletic Association (NCAA) baseball and the first woman to coach NCAA baseball. In 1994, she was one of the first women to break into Major League Baseball, a historically male organization, when she was invited to play for the Maui Stingrays in a sanctioned winter league. She also played first base for the inaugural women's baseball team to play against men, known as the Colorado Silver Bullets. Based in Atlanta, Georgia, the first Silver Bullets team played exhibition matches against professional men's teams at double- and triple-A levels. In addition to her on-field duties, Croteau also served as spokesperson for the team until injuries forced her from active play.

At Saint Mary's College in Maryland, Croteau played three years of varsity baseball on the men's team. On an internship from Smith College's masters program in coaching, Julie was the assistant baseball coach for the University of Massachusetts in Amherst, a Division I NCAA institution; Croteau helped coach her team to two Atlantic 10 Conference Championships and one undefeated conference record (10-0).

Croteau's baseball abilities have opened doors to other career opportunities. She got a taste of the film world when she was a consultant to director Penny Marshall to ensure an accurate portrayal of the athletes who appeared in the movie *A League of Their Own*, which was based on the All American Girls Professional Baseball League that operated from 1943 to 1954. Her most recent work experience has been as a baseball analyst for Liberty Sports television network. She provided the color commentary and analysis during the live national coverage of the Colorado Silver Bullets baseball games. She also covered the 1995 Fast Pitch Softball Junior Olympic Games.

Croteau has won many honors and awards. Her glove and photo are on display at the Baseball Hall of Fame in Cooperstown, New York. In 1994, *Mirabella* gave her its Leading Women of the Nineties Award. The American Association of University Women presented her with the Margaret Brent Award in 1992 for contributions to women in higher education. In that same year, she received an award on the National Girls and

Women in Sport Day in Washington, DC, for her contributions to women's sports. In 1991, she was the keynote speaker for the All-American Girls Professional Baseball League's 50th Reunion.

Curling and Women

The ice sport of curling has evolved from a source of casual recreation in sixteenth-century Scotland to a full-medal Olympic sport that will make its Winter Games debut in Japan in 1998. Originally played outdoors with smooth stones found near Scottish lochs (long, narrow lakes), the sport is now enjoyed in modern, climate-controlled arenas where the players use specialized equipment. Modern curling is a team sport with four players to a side. The players slide a granite stone along a 146-foot sheet of ice (approx. 14 feet wide) with two concentric circle targets at each end (the "house"). The center of the "house" is called the "tee," and it is what players try to hit. While one person "shoots," two players follow the stone ready to "sweep" the ice in front of the stone if the stone needs to go farther. The fourth player, the "skip," holds her broom by the tee as a target for the shooter. One point is given to the team/player whose stone is closest to the tee.

Until relatively recent times, women were "second class" citizens in the curling world, even though they had participated in the sport for many years. Curling clubs were historically controlled by men, although 40 percent of all curlers in the United States are women. The typical United States curling club had a women's "club-within-a-club," subservient to the club board of directors. Women were allocated less ice time, usually during the day, or if at night, only in mixed leagues playing with their spouses. Starting in the late 1940s, United States women's roles in the curling establishment, and as curler athletes, began to develop steadily. By the late 1980s, women were full members of the United States curling clubs, and today women are fully represented on curling organizations from local to national levels.

The United States Women's Curling Association (USWCA), which has 2,969 members in 25 states, was formed in 1947, making it the oldest United States national curling organization. (The United States Men's Curling Association [USMCA] was formed in 1958.) Bernie Roth of Wauwatosa, Wisconsin, was the first USWCA president. The USWCA established the Women's National Curling Championship in 1977.

The World Curling Federation (WCF) was founded in 1968. The WCF established an annual women's world championship in 1979 and the junior women's world championship in 1988. The WCF originally accommodated women through its "Ladies Branch." Today, women are fully integrated into the WCF, although women have yet to serve at the highest officer levels.

The United States Olympic movement provided a major catalyst for increasing women's representation at the national level in curling. In 1986, the United States Curling Association (USCA) joined the United States Olympic Committee (USOC). The USCA succeeded the USMCA, which removed the "M" in the late 1970s. As of 1986, however, most USCA directors were male. Then a USCA president, Robert Hardy of Seattle, spearheaded a by-law change to double the size of the board and to make all the new directors women. This move accomplished two purposes: the USOC then recognized the USCA as the sole governing body of curling in the United States of America, and the USCA could stake a legitimate claim to represent all American curlers.

In 1987, the USWCA turned over the women's national championship to the USCA, and the USCA initiated a junior women's national championship (21 years and under). Today, the USWCA, an affiliate USCA member, operates several national events for women curlers and promotes women's curling in the United States. The USWCA and its legacy are alive and well.

Women are now prominent in the national governance of curling. Since 1991, three of the six USCA presidents have been women: Ann Brown, Evelyn Nostrand, and Winifred Bloomquist. In this same time period, three women have been inducted into the USCA American Curling Hall of Fame: Mary Van Ess (a pioneer in the WCF Ladies Branch), Ann Brown, and Bernie Roth, the USWCA's first president.

Female curlers compete on near-equal terms with men, as strength is only a minimal factor in the sport. Men's teams usually have a slight advantage in "take-out" (hits that dislodge others' stones) shots and in sweeping, but top women's teams can beat top men's teams in a given game. There are annual national curling championships for women, men, juniors, and for mixed teams (two men, two women), with world championships in all but mixed teams.

Since 1990, the women's team headed by Lisa Schoeneberg and Bev Behnke has won three national championships. In the 1997 World Curling Championship, the U.S. team tied for sixth place. The members were Patti Lank, Analissa Johnson, Joni Cotton, Tracy Sachtjen, and Alison Darragh.

Today over 15,000 curlers belong to more than 135 clubs in the United States. Many Unites States curlers have Scottish roots, but curling club membership rosters tend to reflect an ethnic cross-section of their communities, primarily small towns and rural communities. The sport is often passed down through families. Like the other Scottish sport, golf, curling is both a recreational and an athletic pastime, marked by a strong code of fair play and courtesy. About 1.5 million people, from ages 8 to 80, in over 33 countries, curl.

Getting started in curling is easy if there is a curling club in the area. Curling is most common in Wisconsin, Minnesota, North Dakota, New York, and Massachusetts, but clubs are scattered throughout 21 other states. The dues are usually nominal ($100 to $300 for a five-month season) and include free instruction. About 30 colleges in the Midwest offer curling as a club sport. Serious athletes interested in curling should contact the USCA for a list of certified coaches in their area (PO Box 866, Stevens Point, WI 54481). *DG*

References

Kerr, J. (1890). *A history of curling*. Edinburgh, Scotland: David Douglas.

Murray, W.J. (1981). *The curling companion*. Glasgow, Scotland: Richard Drew.

Smith, D.B. (1981). *Curling: An illustrated history*. Edinburgh, Scotland: John Donald.

United States Curling News (USCA). Published seven times per year since 1945.

Cycling and Women

Cycling is a diverse sport with not one, but many competitive events. These events include road racing, which involves competing with multigeared bicycles on roadways; mountain biking in which competitors race across rough terrain on fat-tire bikes, and track cycling, where sleek, gearless, brakeless cycles race in special cycling venues called velodromes.

In the late 1890s, generally considered to be the golden age of cycling, women's cycling competitions in the United States consisted of grueling six-day races emphasizing endurance and determination. As the bike was displaced by automobiles, these cycling competitions for women faded. Even though cycling has been an Olympic event since the first modern Olympic Games in 1896, it was not until the 1980s that women's cycling events were incorporated into Olympic competitions.

Within the three general cycling categories (mountain, road, and track), different events emphasize specialized skills, but all events emphasize speed. In mountain biking, for example, athletes compete in cross-country, downhill, and slalom races. In cross-country races, the competition is usually against other competitors who are trying to be the first to complete the course. As the name suggests, mountain biking courses usually have several steep grades over unpaved trails. Considerable endurance and strength is required to climb the hills, and skill, with a large dose of courage, is required on the descent.

Mountain biking is the fastest growing segment of cycling, and it was a medal sport (with both men's and women's division) for the first time in the 1996 Olympic Games in

Atlanta, Georgia. United States cyclist Susan Demattel won the bronze medal at this inaugural event. Jacquie Phelan, a pioneer in the United States mountain biking, was the first women inducted into the recently established Mountain Bike Hall of Fame in Crested Butte, Colorado.

Road racing events include team and individual time trials and the criterium. Team time trials are usually 50-kilometer events in which teams of four riders each work together to beat the clock. The criterium is a popular event in which riders race head-to-head on a tight multilap course trying to be the first rider to cross the finish line. Beth Heiden, a speed skater turned cyclist, became the first woman to complete a 25-mile time trial in less than an hour in 1979. A year later she won the world road championship. Women's road racing was included as an Olympic event for the first time in 1984 at Los Angeles. The gold medal was won by Connie Carpenter-Phinney, another former speed skater, who completed the 79-kilometer course by lunging across the finish line seconds before fellow United States cyclist, Rebecca Twigg.

Track cycling events include time trials, pursuits, and sprints. The pursuits are particularly exciting: two cyclists line up on opposite ends of the track and "pursue" each other while trying to finish first. Events are held indoors on wooden banked tracks, called velodromes. Competitors use lightweight bicycles without gears or brakes. These events require speed, power, skill, and tactical acumen. In 1973, Sheila Young became the first United States woman since 1912 to win the world track sprint title. She won a total of five world cycling medals, including three championships. Sue Novara-Reber holds more world cycling medals than any other United States cyclist. She won seven consecutive world medals including two gold medals in 1975 and 1980. Jane Eichhoff Quigley, a model of hard work and consistency in track cycling, has been named the United States Cycling Federation Female Athlete of the Year three times.

Amateur cycling is governed by the United States Cycling Federation (USCF) and the American Bicycle Association (ABA), both of whom issue racing licenses. These organizations sponsor competitions divided into age and sex divisions with each division separated into skill categories ranging from novice (CAT IV) to national, international, and Olympic levels (CAT I). Mountain biking is sanctioned by the National Off-Road Bicycling Association (NORBA), which is affiliated with the USCF. The United States Professional Cycling Federation governs professional bike racing in the United States. Local bike clubs and professional bike shops are the best starting points for local information regarding competitive or recreational cycling.

Cycling and Women with Disabilities: Faster, Higher, Stronger

Certius, *altius*, *fortius* (faster, higher, stronger) is the Olympic motto and every athlete's endeavor throughout training, whether the athlete is male or female. Yet, when a United States team official at the 1996 Paralympic Games in Atlanta, Georgia, was asked which teams were expected to excel, she responded "Track cycling is a testosterone-driven sport. Watch our men's teams."

On August 17, 1996, at the Paralympic Games, where athletes with disabilities from around the world competed, the six women of the 33-member United States Disabled Cycling Team were not concerned with lipstick or hairdos. We were preoccupied with chain lube, disk wheels, and water consumption. Ask one of us our measurements, and we'd spit out our seat heights, our cardiovascular efficiency ratings, and flying 200-meter sprint times. Mental images of our desired physical appearance for the day featured sharply sculpted calf muscles against madly churning bicycle wheels and our obsessive conceptualizations were of optimal cardiovascular fitness, muscle strength, and leg speed. None of us cared if someone gawked at our skin-tight lycra. It would be the record-breaking times splashed across the scoreboard upon which we wanted all to feast their eyes. The flutter of star-spangled banners above medal stands was what we yearned to hear. The only male to whom we were "attached" in this moment was our coach doling out those impossible times we were supposed to "just go out there and hit." Personally, the only male I planned on taking second seat to was my sighted tandem pilot, and that was only a matter of necessity!

We may have been testosterone deficient, but we were adrenaline-saturated. As the three days of tandem track racing progressed, it would be the men's team who watched each and every American female tandem cyclist collect a Paralympic medal. Like our male bike partners, many of whom were nationally ranked and incredibly accomplished single bike racers in their own right, we were living the dream of competing with the best, but such achievement didn't come without sacrifice. We'd all stumbled miserably as our oxygen-starved bodies betrayed us, and dragged ourselves across finish lines with battered muscles and broken hearts, wondering if we'd ever finish a race without having first been lapped by the leaders. We'd all forced ourselves through the days, months, and years of brutal training while simultaneously juggling work or school. We all had crumpled, agonizing moments when lung-pounding, thigh-busting, uphill sprints culminated in hairbreadth defeats, leaving us to rack our brains for defects in strategy. We all knew how to grit our teeth while gravel was scraped from road rash or broken bones were set. It must also be said that we had been buoyed up on clouds of joy after winning that first race, eclipsing personal records, and rising beyond wildest expectations. Like our female Olympic counterparts, we all knew how to transform gracefully from civilians in off-cycle society to teeth-baring, glazed-eyed maniacs in the world where "winning wasn't everything; it was the only thing."

But unlike many of our female Olympic counterparts, the six women on the disabled cycling team had crashed through additional obstacles along the road to the summit. One woman lost her eyesight to diabetes as a young adult, received a kidney transplant, and dealt daily with the challenges of monitoring blood sugar and administering insulin. Another mysteriously lost both hearing and eyesight during her twenties, after a distinguished career as an equestrian athlete. Another team member lost her eyesight at age five to a rare form of retinal cancer and suffered a recurrence just three years ago. She commenced her bike racing career three months after finishing chemotherapy. One cyclist faces continual vision loss and copes with severe domestic discord. Her bike-partner is neither disabled nor male but a nationally ranked cyclist who has competed in the Tour de France-Feminine. Together, they represented the United States (the only women's tandem team in an open tandem competition) and garnered two of the 13 cycling medals for our country.

Blind tandems "going at it," pretraining at 1996 Paralympic Games in Atlanta.

Like the male paralympians who compete tandem, we had mucked through training, constrained by limited opportunities to recruit talented partners willing to commit time and energy to the Paralympic effort. We'd battled the frustration of having to resort to stationary trainers when partners could not be found. We'd confronted skeptical and discouraging coaches who could not possibly fathom that a disabled athlete could display the same talent, determination, or discipline as her able-bodied counterparts. All of us had spent hours and hours drafting proposals to convince sponsors that endorsing a disabled athlete could blossom into a mutually beneficial arrangement. For the 1996 Games, we experienced the shock and disillusionment that resulted from learning that the substantial stipend awarded by the United States Olympic Committee to United States Olympic medal winners would not be showing up on our balance sheets. European Paralympic athletes received this benefit, along with their Olympic compatriots.

And yet, the women's and mixed tandem teams spent their time in the Atlanta Games absorbing the "dream" and memorializing themselves in Paralympic history. For the first time ever, the Paralympic cycling program consisted of three events. In addition to two events on the 250-meter, 44-foot sloped Olympic velodrome, there was a 40-mile road race. The only disabled single-bike female racer has cerebral palsy and competes in the track division for which there is no separate category for women.

The tandems raced for separate medals in different events while the single-bike racers received a composite point total for all the events and one medal. The men's, women's, and mixed tandem teams competed in pursuit and kilometer time trial. Only the men competed in the one-on-one matched sprints. Reasons given for this prohibition seemed to center on perceived lack of aggressiveness in women drivers and the extreme bike handling skills thought needed for this breathtaking event. Ironically, the gold and silver medal winning mixed tandem sprinters were captained by female drivers! This Paralympic Games was the first time that the cycling event boasted a separate category for women's teams.

Success shimmered all around our Paralympic Women's Cycling Team in Atlanta, Georgia, in 1996. Julie Haft and sighted partner Tiffany Treschock earned the silver medal in the road race and the bronze medal in the pursuit. Kathy Urschel and Mike Hopper took a silver medal in the mixed tandem pursuit, setting a United States record. Pam Fernandez and Mike Rosenberg took a bronze medal in the kilometer time trial after smashing the old world record by over two seconds. (Their "new" record was later eclipsed by other racers in the same competition.) Scott Evans and Cara Dunne took silver medal in the kilometer setting both a personal record and a new United States record. These two also set a Paralympic and American record in the flying 200-meter qualifying sprint only to suffer a later loss to the Australians. This loss bumped them from the gold-medal round and into a comfortable, but less satisfying, bronze-medal victory.

Medals and world records may be what people remember of the disabled cycling team's Atlanta experience but hopefully much more memorable will be the message that neither gender nor disability are measuring sticks of ability and athletic and personal worthiness. We send this message from a world where slamming elbows with the racer on a bike just inches from you must be a signal to push harder rather than flinch, where one leans forward on the starting line, realizing that a current "personal" best may not even put you in the top 10 today. *CD*

See also **Disabled Women and Sport**

Isabelle Daniel

Isabelle Daniel's first international success came when she and her teammates won a bronze medal for the United States 4 x 100-meter relay at the 1956 Olympic Games in Melbourne, Australia. Daniel was born on July 31, 1937, in Jakin, Georgia. Even as a child, she was recognized for her athletic ability and practiced by running to school—a 13-mile trek! After high school in 1953, Isabelle attended Tennessee State University (a member of the noted "Tigerbelles") on an athletic scholarship and was a member of the winning 4 x 200-meter relay team at the Amateur Athletic Union (AAU) Women's Track and Field National Championships in 1954. She was an AAU All-American in 1957, 1958, and 1959, frequently setting new meet records. In 1960 Daniel and her teammates on the 4 x 100-meter relay set a world record and won the gold medal at the Olympic Games in Rome, Italy.

In total, Daniel won more than 100 awards and participated in more than 25 international meets. In 1985, she was honored as the Track Coach of the Year by the National High School Athletic Coaches Association. She was inducted into the Georgia Hall of Fame in 1987.

Deaf Women in Sport

Organized sports for deaf athletes were formally established in 1924 with the inception of the International Committee of Sports of the Deaf (CISS). The first World Games for the Deaf (WGD), affectionately known as the Deaf Olympic Games, were held in the summer of 1924 in Paris, France. The first winter WGD were held in Seefeld, Austria, in 1949. The United States has participated in these Games, which are contested every four years, since 1935. The United States team, however, did not enter its first deaf women athletes until the summer 1957 Games in Milan, Italy.

The American Athletic Association of the Deaf (AAAD) was established in 1945 and serves as the national governing body of all deaf sport programs in the United States today. It works closely with the United States Olympic Committee and the CISS to promote various levels of competition (Olympic, international, national, regional, and local) for deaf athletes in the United States and throughout the world. Women who have a hearing loss of 55 decibels or more in their better ear are eligible for participation in deaf sport organizations in the United States and around the world.

Deaf women participate in all levels of sport from club teams to Olympic squads. As is the case with other women in sport, there is a dearth of published information (compared to their male counterparts) about their achievements and accomplishments as athletes.

Before discussing deaf women's achievements in deaf-sporting events, it is important to note, however, that not all deaf and hard-of-hearing female athletes participate in the "known-deaf" sports world. They may elect to play in mainstream athletic programs from the club to university to Olympic levels. These athletes go unnoticed and undetected, unless they perform at the higher echelon of their sport. More often than not, these mainstream athletes find themselves the lone deaf or hard-of-hearing player on their teams. They often experience the loneliness, isolation, and frustration of playing on a team that most often communicates differently than they do. It is especially difficult for them to succeed in team sports with athletes who have normal hearing. Deaf athletes in mainstream programs may find better opportunities and success competing in individual sports (i.e., cross country, golf, or swimming).

Many of these mainstream athletes make the crossover into deaf sports organizations, where they find a new sense of belonging and camaraderie among other deaf athletes. Because of the lack of development programs and trained coaches who are fluent in sign language and knowledgeable about deaf culture, deaf women have lagged behind their hearing counterparts in opportunities to develop and hone their athletics skills. There has been significant progress in the last 10 years, however, as AAAD received more funding to develop training programs for deaf athletes and to hire coaches at the grassroots level to improve skills and to prepare for higher levels of competition.

AAAD made history in 1990, when it appointed Shirley Hortie Platt as its first executive director. Ms. Platt was active in club and regional sport administrations before taking the reins of the AAAD. According to Ms. Platt, deaf women athletes and leaders have had a difficult time breaking through the "glass ceiling" in the male-dominated AAAD. Presently, there are only 2 deaf female officers at the regional level,

compared to 38 positions at the same level held by deaf men. The numbers are even lower at the club level, even though deaf women athletes make up approximately 25 percent of the AAAD membership. Ms. Platt emphasizes that AAAD is committed to providing equal opportunities for deaf women athletes and coaches in leadership positions as AAAD moves into the twenty-first century. Ms. Platt also serves as a member of the National Advisory Board of the Women's Sports Foundation.

Prior to the establishment of AAAD, the first known organization of a deaf women's athletic team in the United States was women's basketball at Gallaudet College in Washington, DC, in 1896. (Gallaudet College, now known as Gallaudet University, is the only four-year liberal arts educational institution for deaf people in the world.) The Lady Bisonettes posted a winning record (3-0) in their first season of play.

Gallaudet currently offers seven sports (basketball, cross country, softball, swimming, tennis, track and field, and volleyball) for females competing in Division III of the National Collegiate Athletic Association (NCAA) and one club team (soccer). The volleyball program has enjoyed the most success at Gallaudet University as a member of the Capital Athletic Conference (CAC). Peg Worthington has coached the squad for 26 years (excluding a two-year hiatus). Coach Worthington, who is not deaf but is fluent in sign language and knowledgeable of deaf culture, is closing in on 600 wins. Her career record in 1998 stands at 619-315 with a winning percentage of .663. Under her leadership, Gallaudet produced the first deaf Association of Intercollegiate Athletics for Women (AIAW) (1981) All-American, middle blocker Nancy Mumme. Ms. Mumme also played on three World Games for the Deaf teams that produced two silver medals and one gold medal for the United States. Coach Worthington has served as coach of five WGD women's volleyball teams.

Luanne Barron Ward played for the Gallaudet University volleyball team for four years (1978–1982) as an outside hitter. She competed on four WGD teams (two silver and two gold medals), served as assistant volleyball coach at Gallaudet University for five years, was an assistant coach for the 1991 Deaf National Women's Volleyball Team that competed in the United States Olympic Festival for the first time as a demonstration (onetime experiment) sport, and finally, served as the first deaf women's assistant volleyball coach on the 1993 WGD team that won the gold medal.

Another three-time World Games for the Deaf athlete and former Gallaudet volleyball player, Vicki Kitsembel Grossinger, was appointed the first team director (male or female) of the American Deaf Volleyball Association (ADVBA) in 1987. Besides the women mentioned so far, a number of deaf women in sports have performed amazing feats, broken Olympic and world records, and are recognized for their accomplishments. It is beyond the scope of this article to list everyone, but a small selection of these deaf women and coaches are listed below:

Gertrude Ederle was hearing impaired the rest of her life after she became the first woman to swim the English Channel in 1926, breaking all the men's records for the swim.

Helen Thomas, a skeet shooter, was named the first Deaf Athlete of the Year by AAAD in 1955. In that year, as a 15 year old, she became the youngest national trapshooting champion of the North American Women's Clay Target event. According to *Deaf Women—A Parade through the Decades*, she shot down 197 out of 200 clay birds. Ms. Thomas was inducted into the AAAD Hall of Fame in 1987.

Ruth Seeger was the United States' first deaf woman to participate in the WGD in 1957. She competed in the high jump in track and field and placed sixth. Ms. Seeger, a retired physical education teacher at the Texas School for the Deaf (TSD) in Austin, was the first deaf woman to be inducted into the AAAD Hall of Fame in 1975. She was also one of six females, and the first deaf woman, inducted into the Texas Hall of Fame in the athletes category in 1988. Not only was she an outstanding athlete in her own right, Ms. Seeger also coached girls track and field at TSD (four national championships) and was a coach for the United States' deaf women's track and field teams in six WGD.

Donalda Ammons was the first deaf vice-chairperson of the United States' WGD committee from 1982 to 1986.

Carol Billone served as the first deaf director and vice chairperson of the XVth WGD in Los Angeles, California.

Dr. Judith Pachciarz (the only known deaf person with a Ph.D. and an M.D.) served as the medical director of the XVth WGD.

Connie Johnson Ruberry, considered the deaf women's version of Jackie Joyner-Kersee, established Olympic and world records in the heptathlon in two WGD (1985 and 1989). She also excels in volleyball.

Betsy Batchel won All-American honors in 1986 in the NCAA Division III National Cross Country Championships.

Laurie Barber won 10 gold medals in swimming at the 1977 WGD in Bucharest, Romania.

Carrie Miller shattered WGD swimming records at the 1989 games.

The United States' Deaf Women's Basketball team has won gold medals at every WGD since their first competition in 1981.

Becky Clark, WGD medal winner in volleyball, also was the first deaf person to earn a doctorate in sport psychology.

Shelly Beattie, professional bodybuilder, also known as "Siren" on the television program *American Gladiators*, was chosen Female Athlete of Year in 1995 by AAAD.

Gwen Rocque was the first deaf woman flag-bearer for the United States' team in the 1977 WGD. She won eight medals in tennis during three WGD.

The list of outstanding deaf women in sport is endless. It is an impossible task to name all the female athletes and coaches who have made and continue to make important and lasting contributions to deaf sport. Deaf women in sport have come a long way since their first organized team started play in the late 1800s. *RAC*

***See also* Disabled Women and Sport**

References

Byrd, T. (1992). Let the games begin! *Gallaudet Today*, Winter, 10-21.

Clark, R. A., and Sachs, M. L. (1991). Challenges and opportunities in psychological skills training in deaf athletes. *The Sport Psychologist*, 5(4), 392-98.

Holcomb, M., and Wood, S. (1989). *Deaf women: A parade through the decades*. Berkeley, CA: Dawn Sign Press.

Ivey, L. (1995). Shellie Beattie and John Funk names 1995 AAAD athletes of the year. *Deaf Sports Review*, Winter, 13, 16.

Ruth Seeger named to Texas Hall of Fame. (1989). *Silent News*, July, 36.

Anita DeFrantz

Anita DeFrantz was born on October 4, 1952, in Philadelphia, Pennsylvania and trained on the Schuylkill River in single sculls. Olympic medalist, attorney, and executive member of the International Olympic Committee, one of the most powerful organizations in sport, Anita DeFrantz is an example of the message she sends: sports help us learn skills that are important in life. At only 45 years of age, DeFrantz has already been recognized as one of the 100 Most Powerful People in Sports by The *Sporting News*, one of the 100 Most Important Women in America by *Ladies Home Journal*, and one of the 10 Outstanding Women of the Year by the *Los Angeles Sentinel*.

As an African American child growing up in the 1960s, DeFrantz was not given the same opportunities to participate in sport as many White children. It was not until she entered college that she began her formal involvement in sports. As a first-year student at Connecticut College, she joined the rowing team. She graduated with honors from Connecticut and received a law degree from the University of Pennsylvania in 1974. During that period, she continued her intensive athletic training at the prestigious Vesper Boat Club in Philadelphia. DeFrantz and her teammates won an Olympic bronze medal in the women's eight at the 1976 Olympic Games, just six years after she had been introduced to the sport of rowing.

From 1975 to 1980, she was a member of the United States Rowing Team. In addition to her bronze medal, DeFrantz and her teammates went on to capture the National Rowing title six times, and she was a five-time finalist in World Rowing Championships. At the 1978 World Rowing Championship, DeFrantz won a silver medal. As a member of the 1980 Olympic Team, she hoped to improve her third-place finish to first. Instead, she found herself leading the protest against the United States boycott of the 1980 Olympic Games in Moscow and the entire United States Olympic Committee (USOC). DeFrantz was so persuasive that President Jimmy Carter sent Vice President Walter Mondale to the April meeting of the United States Olympic Committee House of Delegates, where the delegates were to vote on the boycott (the boycott was not overturned). In recognition of her enormous contributions, she was awarded the Medal of the Olympic Order by the International Olympic Committee (IOC).

In 1986, DeFrantz attained lifelong membership status in one of the most exclusive and prestigious organizations in sport, the International Olympic Committee. As a member of IOC's Executive Committee, DeFrantz also serves on its Program Commission, Eligibility Commission, and Judicial Commission. She has used her influence in the passage of legislation ensuring that women make up at least 10 percent of the IOC, as well as 10 percent of the leadership of all 197 national Olympic committees by the year 2000. Later, she was instrumental in the movement to further increase the target to 20 percent by the year 2005.

From 1981 to 1984, DeFrantz was the vice president of the Los Angeles Olympic Organizing Committee. Her success with the committee led her to be named the president of the Amateur Athletic Foundation, an organization responsible for the distribution of a $90 million surplus from the 1984 Olympic Games in Los Angeles, California. The money has been used to help transform impoverished communities of Los Angeles into places where sports clubs thrive and have a positive impact. Looking to give back to others and serving girls and women in sports and fitness has always been one of DeFrantz's goals. She is currently a member of the Women's Sports Foundation's Board of Stewards and has held office on its Board of Trustees. Today, the strength of spirit and presence of mind of Anita DeFrantz continues to grace the world of sports as she remains a guiding light for the entire amateur athletic community.

Donna de Varona

Donna de Varona, who was born on April 20, 1947, in San Diego, California, won two gold medals in swimming at the 1964 Olympic Games in Tokyo, Japan—one for the 400-meter individual medley and one for the 4 x 100-meter freestyle relay. The freestyle relay team set a world record of 4:03.8 minutes. Prior to joining the United States Olympic Swimming Team in 1960, she had broken 18 world records and 10 American records, and she had collected scores of United States National Swimming Championship wins. In

Donna de Varona.
Photo courtesy of Preston Levi.

1964, she was voted AP/UP Outstanding Woman Athlete and the Outstanding American Female Swimmer.

After her swimming career ended, de Varona worked for the passage of Title IX of the Education Act of 1972 and the Amateur Sports Act of 1978. One effect of Title IX was to make training facilities and money more available to minorities and women. She was given the 1996 Flo Hyman Award at the 10th annual National Girls and Women in Sport Day. This award is annually given to a female athlete who exemplifies the dignity and excellence of the late Flo Hyman. Besides these awards and lobbying activities, de Varona was also instrumental in the founding of the Women's Sport Foundation.

De Varona has been a pioneer in other areas as well. She became the first woman to work as a sports broadcaster on network television when she joined ABC Sports as a commentator in 1965. She is also a member of the International Women's Sports Hall of Fame and the International Swimming Hall of Fame. At present, de Varona continues her broadcast career, and is an executive board member for the 1998 Soccer World Cup event in the United States.

Gail Devers

Gail Devers is one of the most successful sprinters and hurdlers in American sports, but her road to stardom was a hard one. Devers was a distance runner in high school and did not even begin to focus on the 100-meter run and 100-meter hurdles until she started at the University of California, Los Angeles (UCLA).Initially, Devers was a hurdler in the 1988 Olympic Games but did not perform to her own expectations. Diagnosed with Graves' disease (a thyroid problem) in 1990, Devers decided not to take the prescribed medication because it was on the banned substance list of the Olympic Medical Commission She accepted radiation treatment but her reaction to the radiation caused severe problems including intense pain and fluid build up in her feet. Amputation was even considered for a time. Once the etiology (causes) of the complications was discovered, Devers' medication was changed, and she was able to walk, and then to run and win. Devers is an athlete who truly overcame adversity of the most trying kind. In 1992 at the Barcelona Olympics, Devers completed her comeback by winning the 100 meters and may have won a second gold but for stumbling and falling while leading the 100-meter

Gail Devers (left) and Gwen Torrence.
© Allsport USA/Gary Mortimore.

hurdles. In 1993, Devers was named Athlete of the Year by the United States Olympic Committee as she won the gold medal for her performance in the 1992 100-meter run. At the Atlanta Olympic Games, she successfully defended her 100-meter title and helped the United States win the 4 x 100-meter relay.

Judy Devlin

Judy Devlin (Hashman), whose name is synonymous with the sport of badminton, is touted as the best female player in the history of the sport. An American citizen, she became the most accomplished player ever, holding the record for singles victories in the All-England Club Championship with 10 wins. Born in Winnipeg, Canada, on October 22, 1935, Devlin was first given a racquet and a shuttlecock when she was 7 years old and had won every junior U.S. badminton title by the age of 13. She won six consecutive junior singles titles from 1949 to 1954. Devlin captured the junior, senior, and world titles within a month of each other in 1954, and with her sister, Susan, took the All-England doubles and United States doubles crowns for the second time.

At the age of 14, Devlin earned her first adult title by defeating Ruth Jett and Patsey Stephens in the Mason Dixon Tournament. Three years later, she played in her first national championship in Boston, losing in the singles finals and winning the doubles

match with her sister, Susan. Overall, Devlin won 31 national women's singles and doubles championship titles from 1953 to 1967. The holder of 12 United States Open Women's Singles Championship titles and 11 United States Open Women's Doubles Championship titles (including 10 paired with her sister, Susan), Devlin also earned 17 titles at the All-England Women's Singles and Doubles Championships from 1954 to 1967. Devlin's last All-England title came in 1966 at the age of 31.

Devlin was inducted into the Helms National Badminton Hall of Fame in 1963. She was a member of the World Championship National United States Uber Cup team from 1957 to 1969. She was awarded the International Badminton Federation Distinguished Service Award and the National Ken Davis Sportsmanship Award from the American Badminton Association in 1966. During the course of her career she lived in England periodically and thus captained both the United States and English national teams. During the 1960s, Devlin coached several Thomas Cup (men's competition) and Uber Cup (women's competition) Championship teams. She continues to coach junior entry-level badminton in England as well as tennis and squash.

Devlin also excelled in the sport of lacrosse as a member of the United States team for five years, was nationally ranked in tennis, and played field hockey and basketball with skill. She credits her father, Frank Devlin, for her success with his unassertive and gentle coaching, practice techniques, and advice.

Mildred "Babe" Didrikson

Mildred Didrikson (Zaharias) was one of the greatest athletes of all time. She won more medals (setting more records) in more sports than any other athlete in the twentieth century. She first played basketball, then went on to track and field in the Olympic Games, and finished with a professional golf career. She also mastered tennis, played organized softball and baseball, and was an expert bowler, diver, and roller skater. She became so famous that she was known by one name, "Babe"—the first American woman athlete to receive such adulation.

She was born Mildred Ella Didriksen on June 26, 1911, in Port Arthur, Texas. As an adult, she changed the spelling of her last name by replacing the "e" with an "o" (Didrikson). She grew up in Beaumont, Texas, and later married professional wrestler George Zaharias in 1938. Didrikson earned her nickname, Babe, after hitting five home runs in a baseball game when she was young, much like Babe Ruth.

Didrikson's early sports success came in basketball. She played for a Dallas insurance company team that won the Amateur Athletic Union (AAU) National Basketball Tournament in 1931. She was a three-time AAU All-American in basketball.

Babe Didrikson gained world fame in track and field at the 1932 Olympic Games in Los Angeles, California, as she won two gold medals and a silver medal. She won the gold medals in the javelin, setting an Olympic record, and in the 80-meter hurdles, setting a world record. She also shared the world record in the high jump as she won the silver medal. (She didn't win the gold because the judges ruled that her jumping style was illegal.) Earlier in 1932, she won 8 of 10 events in the AAU National Women's Track and Field Championships.

Didrikson took up golf in 1935. Before turning professional, she won 17 amateur tournaments in a row, including the 1946 United States Women's Amateur and the 1947 British Amateur. She was the first American to win the British Amateur since it was founded in 1893. As a professional, she won 31 tournaments in a span of eight years, including three United States Women's Open Tournaments.

Didrikson was a founder and charter member of the Ladies Professional Golf Association (LPGA), which began play in 1949. She was one of the four original inductees into the LPGA Hall of Fame in

Mildred "Babe" Didrikson.
Photo courtesy of the Babe Didrikson Museum.

1951. The Associated Press honored Didrikson by naming her as the Woman Athlete of the Year five times and by choosing her as the Greatest Woman Athlete of the First Half of the Twentieth Century. Her play brought new meaning to the word "competitor," but her toughest battle was not on the golf course, track, or court.

In 1953, while in her early 40s, Babe Didrikson was stricken with cancer. Despite being in pain after the first of two major cancer surgeries, she returned to the Tour the following year to win five LPGA tournaments, including her third United States Women's Open Tournament.

Babe Didrikson Zaharias died of cancer on September 27, 1956, at the age of 45. She fought the disease with the same determination she had used in the sports she played. The Babe Zaharias Foundation, founded in her memory, continues to raise funds for cancer research.

Disabled Women and Sport

Females with disabilities entered the competitive sporting arena in the early to mid-twentieth century. Women with hearing impairments competed at the first World Games for the Deaf in Paris, France, in 1924.

Three women and 13 men competed in wheelchair archery at the Stoke Mandeville Hospital in England, a competition that marked the beginning of wheelchair sport. In 1952, Liz Hartel (postpolio) won a silver medal in dressage in the Equestrian event at the summer Olympic Games in Helsinki, Finland.

Despite these notable exceptions, it was not until the 1960s that women with disabilities truly began to gain access to the world of sport. Special Olympic Games were founded in 1968, and females with mental retardation were able to compete at the first International Special Olympic Games that year. Also in 1968, at the Paralympics in Tel Aviv, Israel, women's wheelchair basketball was introduced. The United States National Wheelchair Basketball Association (NWBA) held the first women's national wheelchair basketball tournament in 1975. Since the 1970s, girls and women with disabilities have been active participants in sport at all levels. Additional milestones and accomplishments are highlighted in exhibit 1.

International and National Competitions

Women with disabilities have participated as fully accepted Olympians, both in the Summer and Winter Olympic Games. Two notable examples are Liz Hartel and Nerol Fairhall, who represented New Zealand, competing in archery from her wheelchair during the 1984 Olympic Games in Los Angeles, California.

In addition to these women, male and female athletes with disabilities have competed in exhibition events at the Olympic Games since 1984. These events included downhill (Alpine) skiing and Nordic (cross-country) skiing events in Sarajevo, Yugoslavia (1984), Calgary, Canada (1988), and Albertville, France (1992); 800-meter wheelchair race for women and 1,500-meter wheelchair race for men in Los Angeles (1984), Seoul, South Korea (1988), Barcelona, Spain (1992), and Atlanta, Georgia (1996).

Athletes with disabilities regularly compete in marathons around the world. Most notable of these is the Boston Marathon, which included wheelchair athletes as early as 1974 (male competitors). The first female wheelchair athlete to compete, Sharon Rahn (Hedrick), entered the race in 1977 and won with a time of 3:48.51. Since then, the winning times for men and women has dramatically decreased; wheelchair men often finish under 1:30 and women under 1:45. Because of the Boston Marathon, wheelchair divisions (for men and for women) are frequently included at major marathons and road races.

Because of increased visibility and acceptance, athletes with disabilities are increasingly able to pursue athletic careers. Wheelchair divisions in major road races allow wheelchair athletes to compete professionally for substantial prize money. Athletes with disabilities are also now able to attract major corporate sponsors to assist with their careers (e.g., Diana Golden, skier; Jean Driscoll, seven-time winner of the Boston Marathon). Additionally, selected colleges and universities currently offer intercollegiate athletics and athletic scholarships for individuals with disabilities. (See *Sports n' Spokes* magazine for more information.)

Disability Sport Organizations

By the 1960s, women with disabilities had already broken through the barrier to sport. As a result of this breakthrough, international disability sport organizations formed after the 1960s, such as International Sport Organization for the Disabled (ISOD), Cerebral Palsy-International Sports and Recreation Association (CP-ISRA), International Blind Sports Association (IBSA), International Sports Federation for Persons with Mental Handicap (INAS-FMH), and International Paralympic Committee (IPC). These organizations provided opportunities for both men and women from the outset.

In the United States, most of the existing disability sport organizations were also formed during or after the 1960s. These organizations currently provide access to sport opportunities for both males and females with disabilities. A partial list of these organizations, also members of the United States Olympic Committee, is shown in exhibit 2.

Date	Event
1924	First International Silent Games (Paris, France); women among competitors
1952	Liz Hartel (postpolio) won silver medal in dressage (an equestrian event) at Summer Olympic Games (Helsinki, Finland)
1957	First United States National Wheelchair Games (New York) to include women
1960	First International Games for Disabled (Paralympics) in Rome, Italy; women included among the competitors
1968	International Special Olympic Games founded by Eunice Kennedy Shriver; first competition held in Chicago, Illinois
1974	First Women's National Wheelchair Basketball Tournament
1976	UNESCO conference established right of individuals with disabilities to participate in physical education and sport; rights secured for females as well as males
1977	First female wheelchair entrant to the women's division of Boston Marathon
1982	Karen Farmer, a single leg amputee, attends college on Athletic Scholarship for Women's Track at Eastern Washington University
	Blind women compete for the first time in the World Goal Ball Championships at Butler University
1984	Nerol Fairhall is first wheelchair athlete to meet eligibility and compete in Olympic Games; competed in women's archery
	First wheelchair races as Exhibition events for 1984 Olympic Games (1,500-meter won by Paul Van Winkle at Belgium in 3:58.50; 800-meter is won by Sharon Rahn Hedrick in 2:15.50)
1987	Candace Cable (wheelchair athlete) won the Boston Marathon for the fifth time
1988	Winter Olympic Games in Calgary include exhibition events (three-track Alpine, Blind Nordic) for males and females
	Summer Olympic Games (South Korea) include wheelchair races as exhibition events (1,500 meter for men; 800-meter for females); Sharon Hedrick wins second gold medal in Olympic Wheelchair 800-meter (2:11.49)
1990	Dr. Donalda Ammons appointed the first deaf female director of the World Games for the Deaf United States Team
	Diana Golden, disabled skier, signs sponsorship agreement with Subaru and also as Official Spokesperson for ChapStick Challenge for Disabled Skiers
1991	Jean Driscoll becomes the first athlete with a disability to win the WSF Sudafed Female Athlete of the Year Award
	Sue Moucha attends as the first athlete with a disability at the International Olympic Academy (IOA) in Greece
	Jan Wilson named the first coordinator, Disabled Sport Programs, United States Olympic Committee (USOC)
1992	Connie Hansen and Candace Cable become the only two women to compete in all Summer Olympic exhibition events to date
1996	Jean Driscoll becomes the first seven-time wheelchair athlete winner of the Boston Marathon

HIGHLIGHTS OF MILESTONES FOR WOMEN WITH DISABILITIES IN SPORT

EXHIBIT 1

American Athletic Association for the Deaf (AAAD)
c/o Martin Belsky
1134 Davenport Drive
Burton, MI 48529

Committee on Sports for the Disabled
Mark Shepherd, Manager
Disabled Sports Services
One Olympic Plaza
Colorado Springs, CO 80909

Disabled Sports USA
Kirk Bauer, Executive Director
451 Hungerford Dr.
Suite 100
Rockville, MD 20850

Special Olympic Games International (SOI)
1350 New York Ave., NW
Suite 500
Washington, DC 20005

United States Association for Blind Athletes (USABA)
33 N. Institute St.
Brown Hall. Suite 015
Colorado Springs, CO 80903

United States Cerebral Palsy Athletic Association (USCPAA)
34518 Warren Rd.
Suite 264
Westland, MI 48185

Wheelchair Sports USA
3595 East Fountain Boulevard
Suite L-10
Colorado Springs, CO 80910

ADDRESSES FOR DISABILITY SPORT ORGANIZATIONS

EXHIBIT 2

These disability sport organizations, and others around the world, provide a valuable resource for girls and women with disabilities who wish to participate in sport. They often provide educational and training programs for athletes and coaches, training tips, sports medicine information, nutrition counseling, assisted technology training, and the like. Through these organizations, girls and women with disabilities can gain access to state, regional, national, and international competitions. Among these events are Summer and Winter Paralympic Games, Summer and Winter World Games for the Deaf, International Special Olympic Games, and numerous world championships (e.g., skiing, goal ball, swimming).

The Paralympic Games, Summer and Winter, provide international competition for athletes with disabilities. Since the first Games in Rome in 1960, the Paralympics have grown into one of the major international sporting events in the world. For example, the Summer 1996 Paralympic Games in Atlanta included 4,000 plus athletes (amputees, blind, cerebral palsy, dwarf, and spinal-cord injured) from more than 100 countries competing in 16 sports. In addition to the Paralympic Games, the World Games for the Deaf are held every four years as a celebration of community along with athletic competition in numerous sports, including basketball, team handball, water polo, wrestling, and many more.

Concluding Comment

Sport and physical activity can be an integral part of the lives of girls and women with disabilities, and there are virtually no limits on the extent to which girls and women can participate in sport and physical activity. In addition to competitive sport experiences offered, numerous recreation and physical activity opportunities are available as well. Many of these can be found through the local school district, through intramural programs at colleges and universities, and at local parks and recreation centers, health/fitness/wellness clubs, and community centers. By contacting the available agencies in the local area or by contacting the national disability sport organizations, the journey into physical activity and sporting lifestyle can begin. *KPD*

Selected Readings

DePauw, K.P., & Gavron, S.J. (1995). *Disability and sport*. Champaign, IL: Human Kinetics

Palaestra. Forum for sport, physical education, and recreation for those with disabilities, magazine available from Challenge Publications, PO Box 508, Macomb, IL.

Sports n' Spokes magazine available from PVA, 2111 East Highland Ave., Suite 180, Phoenix, AZ 85016-4702.

Diving and Women

There is evidence that people were diving as far back as the sixth century B.C., while diving from heights dates back hundreds of years. Olympic diving, however, did not start until 1904, and women were not allowed to compete until 1912, when Greta Johansson of Sweden won the first women's platform event.

Since the turn of the century, changes in the sport have been significant. In the 1912 Olympic Games, women wore knee-length bathing suits with wide shoulder straps or partial sleeves. Prior to that, women divers were required to wear ankle-length suits, some of which had stockings that covered the feet. Thankfully, modern suits have a trim cut that allows the freedom of movement so necessary to execute the more difficult dives performed today.

Early diving was always done outdoors, frequently in lakes, rivers, bays, or (as in the 1920 Olympic Games in Antwerp, Belgium) in a moat, or canal, which surrounded the city. There was no control over the weather, nor the temperature of the water, which was sometimes in the 50-degree range. Occasionally the movement of the tide changed the height of the diving board or platform. The well-designed and regulated modern pools, many indoors, and most with hot tubs, are a far cry from the diving environments of the early days of the sport.

American women did not compete in Olympic diving until 1920 when the women's three-meter springboard was added to the Olympic program. In that event, three Americans, Aileen Riggin, Helen Wainwright, and Thelma Payne, won the first three places. Since then, American women have established a remarkable record. In 17 Olympic three-meter springboard events, American divers have won 33 of 51 medals—11 gold, 10 silver, and 12 bronze. Of the 17 Olympic 10-meter platform contests, United States divers have won 27 of the 51 medals—8 gold, 10 silver, and 9 bronze. This domination has slipped somewhat in recent years. Because of the spread of information about diving and the standardization of equipment worldwide in the past two decades, women from China and other countries have improved, challenging the United States' women divers in the Olympic Games.

Perhaps the most important improvement has been the development of superior diving equipment. Originally, the springboards were made of wood and sometimes covered with cocoa matting, but there was no standardization of the springboards. Moveable fulcrums were nonexistent, and so divers couldn't adjust the board to fit their body type or diving style. The early boards were frequently so stiff that they barely bent, minimizing the height the diver could achieve and her ability to perform difficult dives. Fourteen-year-old Aileen Riggin, for example, weighed only 65 pounds when she won the gold medal in Antwerp in 1920 and found it difficult to get much spring from the inferior wooden board. Beginning in the mid-1940s, manufacturers experimented with fiberglass and metal and created boards that made wooden springboards obsolete. Now, Duraflex's high tech Maxiflex "B," which weighs less than half of what the old-time boards weighed, can be bent as much as three feet. This flex, plus the tremendous thrust created by this aluminum-alloy board, makes it possible for the modern diver to achieve dives that were not dreamed of in the early days.

Divers have several important international diving competitions at which to display their skills. The Pan American Games (a competition among the countries of North and South America), began in 1951 and is held the year before the Olympic Games. The World Diving Championships started in 1973 and are held approximately every three years, around the time of the Olympic Games. Because the world championships are exclusively for diving, new events were added to the competition which enhance the sport and allow more divers from each country to compete. The one-meter springboard and the new synchronized diving events, which are not Olympic events, have proven to be extremely popular among divers and spectators alike. The Diving World Cup, started in 1979, brings together the top divers of the world every two years, and other international meets created in the past decade make it possible for modern divers to compete internationally every year.

As important as these meets are, the Olympic Games remain the ultimate goal and the primary focus of the world's top divers for two reasons. First, the Olympic Games are held once every four years, less than any other world competition. Second, modern Olympic diving has a tradition dating back to 1904. In addition, there is the prestige of competing in an event associated with the Olympic Games of ancient Greece.

Top United States Women Divers

The following list includes some of the top United States women divers. Although 10 American women have won the springboard and the platform in Olympic competitions, other divers are mentioned in this honor roll, along with the gold medalists.

Aileen Riggin-Soule: The pioneer of American Olympic diving, Aileen won the first women's Olympic springboard event in the 1920 Games in Antwerp, Belgium, when she was 14 years old; she placed fifth in the platform event. In 1924, she took second in the springboard, but also won a bronze medal in the 100-meter backstroke. At the age of 90, she was a world record holder in her age group in several swimming events.

Betty Becker-Pinkston: She won the springboard and was second in the platform in 1924, and she won the platform in 1928. Caroline Smith won the platform in 1924 and Caroline Fletcher was third in the springboard. The springboard champion of 1928 was Helen Meany.

Dorothy Poynton-Hill: She was on three Olympic teams and was a four-time Olympic medalist, winning the platform in 1932 and 1936. She may well have been on a fourth team if the Games of 1940 had not been canceled due to World War II. Velma Dunn was second to her on the platform at the Berlin Games in 1936.

Georgia Coleman: Another four-time medalist, Coleman was on two Olympic teams and won the springboard event in 1932. Her coach, Fred Cady, said that she was the first woman with enough strength to do the dives having a higher degree of difficulty rating; until that time these dives were only performed by men. Jane Fauntz was third to Georgia in the springboard in 1932 and Marion Roper placed third in the platform. Tragically, Georgia Coleman died at the age of 29.

Marjorie Gestring: The youngest Olympic winner, she was 13 years old when she won the springboard event at the Berlin Olympic Games in 1936. Although she remained a prominent American diver, cancellation of the Games in 1940 and 1944 because of World War II denied her additional Olympic accomplishments. Her attempt to make the team in 1948 at the age of 25 failed as she took fourth in the springboard by a fraction of a point. Katherine Rawls, second in the springboard in 1932 and 1936, also came close, placing fifth in the trials of 1948. Two other diving greats who were deprived of the Olympic Games by World War II were Helen Crelenkovich Morgan and Anne Ross, both of whom won numerous national titles in the late 1930s and early 1940s.

Vicki Manalo Draves: Her mother was English and her father Filipino. She overcame bigotry to win both the springboard and platform titles in 1948. In these Games, Pat Elsener won the bronze medal in the springboard and the silver medal in the platform while Zoe Ann Olsen placed second in the springboard. This competition was also the first Olympic Games for Juno Stover Irwin, who medaled twice while competing in the platform event in every Olympic Games from 1948 through 1960.

Pat McCormick: She has been America's most successful woman diver, winning four Olympic gold medals, springboard and platform in 1952 and 1956, plus three Pan American Championships. With 27 titles, McCormick was the holder of the most American titles and remained so for 23 years. Her daughter, Kelly, medaled in the 1984 and 1988 Games. Paula Jean Myers Pope was a four-time medalist as a member of the 1952, 1956, and 1960 teams, finishing in second place in each event she entered. Jeanne Collier and Patsy Willard took second and third in the springboard in 1964. Defending champion Kramer Engle of Germany was upset by 17-year-old Lesley Busch in the 10-meter platform in 1964, the last time an American has won this event. Michelle Mitchell, however, placed second in 1984 and 1988 while bronze medals were won by Ann Peterson in 1968, Deborah Wilson in 1976, Wendy Wyland in 1984 and

1988, and Mary Ellen Clark in 1992 and 1996.

Mary Ellen Clark: Mary Ellen Clark was a bronze medalist in diving at the 1992 Summer Olympic Games in Barcelona, Spain. She was also the 1987 and 1992 10-meter national champion and a member of the Pan American Teams in 1987 and 1991. She was a member of the United States National Team seven times. As a motivational speaker, Clark often talks to organizations about the mental aspects of sports, teamwork, goal-setting, and women in sport. She was widely acclaimed for re-turning to successful diving, in the 1996 Olympic Games in Atlanta, Georgia, after a devastating illness and injury.

Americans won the three-meter springboard from 1968 through 1976. Sue Gossick, who was fourth in 1964, won in 1968; Micky King, who hit the board and broke her arm on her next-to-the-last dive while leading the competition in 1968, placed fourth and won the event in 1972. Teenager Jennifer Chandler won in 1976, the last time the United States won a gold medal in this event. In the springboard, Keala O'Sullivan placed third in 1968, Cynthia Potter was third in 1976, and Chris Seufert won the bronze in 1984. Kelly McCormick was second in 1984 and third in 1988. Special mention should be made of Cynthia Potter who was on three Olympic teams and broke Pat McCormick's long-standing record of 27 national titles by winning her 28th national championship in 1979.

For more than a decade now, the Chinese women have dominated the medals at both the Olympic Games and the world championships. The rest of the world has caught up to the United States women divers. The competition is intense and women's diving is gaining popularity worldwide.

For more information contact the national governing body of Diving: United States Diving Inc.; Pan American Plaza, Suite 430; 201 S. Capitol Ave.; Indianapolis, Indiana 46225; 317-237-5252. *RC*

Anne Donovan

Anne Donovan, a three-time All-American and Olympic basketball player, was born in Ridgewood, New Jersey, on November 1, 1961. She was a member of the United States Olympic Basketball Team in 1980, 1984, and 1988, leading the United States to gold medals in the 1984 and 1988 Olympic Games. In the 1988 Games in Seoul, South Korea, she served as team captain. She was also a member of the United States National Basketball Team for seven seasons between 1977 and 1988.

A 1983 graduate of Old Dominion University, Donovan was the Wade Trophy recipient in 1983 and a member of the Lady Monarch national championship squads in 1979 and 1980. She ended her playing career at Old Dominion as the all-time NCAA leading scorer, rebounder, and shot blocker. Her 801 career blocks still stands as the National Collegiate Athletic Association (NCAA) record. Donovan was also recognized as a two-time Academic All-American and was inducted into the Academic All-American Hall of Fame in 1994.

From 1983 to 1988, Donovan played semi-professional basketball in Japan, and then she played in Italy during 1989. She accepted the position of assistant basketball coach at Old Dominion in 1989.

A 1995 inductee into the National Basketball Hall of Fame, Donovan was hired as the sixth head coach of the East Carolina University Women's Basketball Team. In addition to her coaching duties, she serves as a representative on the Board of Directors of USA Basketball. Donovan was also a representative to the organizing committee for the 1996 Olympic Games in Atlanta, Georgia.

Jean Driscoll

Jean Driscoll, a marathon racer born on November 18, 1966, in Milwaukee, Wisconsin, has had spina bifida (an opening in the spine) since birth and has never had the use of her legs. She began her marathon career like many runners, experiencing difficulty in her first road race, a five-miler in her hometown of Milwaukee, Wisconsin. She competed for the wheelchair track and field and basketball teams at the University of Illinois, where she now is the assistant coach. She began marathon racing in 1990, when she won her first Boston Marathon.

Nine days before the 1991 Boston Marathon, Driscoll was not able to get in her usual practices on the roads. She was too busy helping the University of Illinois women's wheelchair basketball team defend their national collegiate title. After being named Second Team All Tournament, Driscoll headed to Boston to defend her marathon title.

She won the 1991 Boston Marathon in world-record time. Driscoll and University of Illinois teammate Ann Cody-Morris broke away from the others 11 miles into the race. Six miles later, Driscoll left her teammate behind on a downhill roll. She pushed her way across the finish line in one hour, 42 minutes, and 42 seconds, 35 seconds faster than her 1990 world mark. Driscoll later set a world record for the 10 kilometer race, as well as setting United States records in the 400-meter, 800-meter, 1,500-meter, and 5,000-meter races.

Driscoll won the 100th Boston Marathon in 1996, her seventh consecutive win. With this victory, she tied Clarence DeMar for the most Boston Marathon victories in any division.

Drug Testing

Two types of drug abuse concern women athletes: use of performance-enhancing drugs and use of so-called recreational drugs. Performance-enhancing drugs are used to improve performance. There are six primary categories of such drugs: anabolic steroids, pain suppressants, stimulants, beta blockers, diuretics, and peptide hormones. Anabolic steroids make athletes stronger, help them recover more quickly from fatigue, and enhance activation levels. Pain suppressants reduce awareness of pain while stimulants make an athlete more alert and increase endurance (and possibly aggression as well). Beta blockers aid in decreasing anxiety and decrease an athlete's blood pressure and heartrate. Diuretics increase the elimination of fluids and result in a temporary loss of weight, while peptide hormones increase endurance and strength.

The use of such performance-enhancing drugs is illegal in athletics. Besides giving athletes an unfair advantage, these drugs also have long-term negative side effects including heart and liver problems. In addition, the use of performance-enhancing drugs may become addictive.

Besides pharmacological performance enhancement, other prohibited methods of performance enhancement include blood doping, and chemical and physical manipulation. Blood doping is introducing more blood, particularly red blood cells, into the athlete's blood stream to enhance performance. Chemical and physical manipulation involves, for example, substituting someone else's urine sample for one's own.

Recreational drugs that are prohibited by various governing bodies include both legal and illegal substances: alcohol, marijuana, cocaine/crack, and heroin. Although not prohibited, the use of tobacco, especially smokeless products, is discouraged.

The International Olympic Committee (IOC) has banned some substances (stimulants, narcotics, anabolic agents, diuretics, peptide and glycoprotein hormones, and analogues) and places certain restrictions on other drugs (alcohol, marijuana, local anaesthetics, corticosteriods, and beta-blockers). Caffeine is included under the restrictions of stimulants.

Random drug testing, via blood and urine samples from athletes, is done to ensure that drugs do not play a role in any athlete's performance. Other than for performance enhancement, Weinberg and Gould (1995) suggest that athletes' use of drugs is influenced by peer pressure, curiosity, and self-esteem issues. Peer pressure, the desire to fit in with colleagues, is a process that can exacerbate an athlete's natural curiosity about the effects of different drugs. This process may provide a false boost of an athlete's self-confidence and self-esteem.

Regardless of their intent, all athletes should be fully informed on restricted drug use in sports. Ignorance is no excuse if a positive drug test results. *RLH*

References:

http://www.firstlab.com/sports.html (October 29, 1997)

http://www.olympic.org/medical/emedch2.html (October 29, 1997)

http://www.olympic.org/medical/emedch9.html (October 29, 1997)

Weinberg, R.S., & Gould, D. (1995). *Foundations of sport and exercise psychology*. Champaign, IL: Human Kinetics.

Ann Meyers-Drysdale. *See* **Ann Meyers**

Camille Duvall

With parents who were both competitive water skiers, Camille Duvall was destined to be great on water. Growing up near a lake in Greenville, South Carolina, where she was born on July 11, 1961, was ideal for the budding young athlete who learned how to water ski at four years of age.

Five-time World Professional Slalom Water Skiing and United States Overall Water Skiing Champion, Duvall won the United States water ski title 13 times. At one time she held the triple crown (titles in slalom, trick, and jump). She was a member of the United States Water Ski Team that was undefeated in the world from 1975 to 1978 and from 1983 to 1987.

Now known as Camille Duvall-Hero, she currently is the editor of *Competitor for Women* magazine. She became the first water skier to be honored by the Women's Sports Foundation when she was nominated in 1985, 1986, and 1987 as their Professional Sportswoman of the Year. She is on the Board of Directors of the New York City Sports Development Corporation and Big Brothers/Big Sisters of America. Duvall-Hero is also on the Board of Trustees of the American Sports Medicine Institute and the Women's Sports Foundation. She is the author of the *Camille Duvall Instructional Guide to Water Skiing* (Simon & Schuster, 1992).

E

Amelia Earhart

Amelia Millie Earhart is not only a famous woman of sport; she is an internationally recognized aviator who became a true American heroine. Born in Atchison, Kansas on July 24, 1897 to Amy and Edwin Earhart, Amelia and her sister Muriel enjoyed a life of comfort and privilege provided by their grandparents. Amelia's grandfather, Alfred Otis, was a prominent citizen of Atchison. Amelia and Muriel lived in Atchison with their grandparents for the first 10 years of Amelia's life, while their parents tried to establish themselves in Des Moines, Iowa.

At the age of 10, shortly after being reunited with her parents in Iowa, Earhart saw her first airplane on a family outing to the Iowa State Fair. She was not impressed and showed little interest in the new flying machines. The family fell on hard times and moved to Chicago. A trust fund provided by her grandparents financed preparatory school for Earhart. During World War I, she worked as a nurses's aide in Toronto, Canada. Her experience in the military hospital led to enrollment in Columbia University's pre-medicine program. She abandoned medicine after a year and headed to California to join her parents who had settled there. It was in California, at the age of 23, that she had her first experience flying in an open cockpit. A passion for flying dominated the rest of her life.

Earhart started taking flying lessons from Anita Snook and, by 1922, she began challenging the flying records set by other women. The thrill of breaking records and pushing herself to the limit suited her adventurous spirit. In 1925 she moved to Boston to work for Kinner Airplanes. She gained media attention as she promoted women's flying. In 1928, she was tapped by New York publishing giant, George Palmer Putnam, to be the first woman to fly across the Atlantic in a plane piloted by Wilmer Stultz and Louis Gordon. Upon returning to the United States, Earhart became a popular and well-known supporter of women's place in the emerging field of aviation. Even though she did not pilot her first trans-Atlantic flight, she attained celebrity status. During the course of her career, she became a consultant for Trans World Airlines, organized a coast-to-coast air race for women pilots known as the "Powder Puff Derby," and founded the women's pilot organization called the Ninety-Nines.

In 1932, after marrying her supporter, George Putnam, Earhart became the first woman, and the first person since Lindbergh, to successfully solo pilot a trans-Atlantic flight. She flew from Harbour Grace, Newfoundland, to Londonderry, Ireland, setting a new time record for the trans-Atlantic crossing. She continued to seek new challenges and in 1935, she successfully flew from Hawaii to California. With flights over the Atlantic and Pacific under her belt, Earhart began thinking about an around-the-world flight. On May 21, 1937, her plans to circumnavigate the world on the longest' flight ever attempted became a reality. With her navigator, Fred Noonan, Earhart took off east from Los Angeles for her last and most daring flight. After making it virtually around the world, their Lockheed Electra mysteriously disappeared over the Pacific Ocean on July 2, 1937. Despite intensive search efforts, the plane was never recovered. This mysterious and tragic end to Amelia Earhart's story has fascinated the American public for decades, contributing to her celebrity status as one of America's great heroines.

See also **Aviation and Women**

Eating Disorders. *See* **Female Athlete Triad**

Gertrude Ederle

Gertrude Caroline Ederle, born in New York City on October 23, 1906, was the first woman to swim across the English Channel. She accomplished this feat in 1926. To put this feat into the perspective of the times, remember that the XIX Amendment giving women the vote had been ratified only six years prior to her accomplishment. Ederle was pulled off course by storm currents, adding 14 miles to the 21 mile route from Cape Gris-Nez, France, to Dover, England. Her world record time of 14 hours, 31 minutes was almost 2 hours faster than the men's channel record of 16 hours, 23 minutes.

Ederle learned to swim at a young age and began competing as a teenager, joining a local swim club at 13 so that she could swim all year. From the time she was 15 until she reached 19, she broke 29 United States and world swimming records. She was the youngest woman ever to set a world record in the 880-yard freestyle, which is now a discontinued event. As an Olympian at the 1924 Games in Paris, France, Ederle won a gold medal as a member of the 4 x 100-meter freestyle relay team and two bronze medals in the individual 100- and 400-meter freestyle events. She broke a total of nine world records during her career.

After her success in the 1924 Olympic Games, Ederle turned professional in 1925. Her goal, however, was to be the first woman to swim the English Channel. At 16, she won a 3-mile ocean race, and at 18, she was the first female entrant in the 21-mile Battery to Sandy Hook race in New York, breaking the men's record in the process. Like other competitors of the time, Ederle failed in her first attempt to swim the Channel. She continued to train and was successful on August 6, 1926.

Gertrude Ederle.
Photo courtesy of the International Swimming Hall of Fame.

The cold water of the English Channel permanently damaged Ederle's inner ear, resulting in deafness. She later became a swimming instructor, focusing on teaching deaf children to swim. In 1965 Ederle was inducted into the Swimming Hall of Fame and in 1980 into the International Women's Sports Hall of Fame.

Swimming the English Channel propelled her to stardom in the United States. Because of her fame, she went on to star with Johnny Weissmuller in the Tarzan movie series. Ederle, along with Glenna Collett (golf) and Helen Wills (tennis), were major players in the 1920s Golden Age of American Sport. She currently lives in Flushing, New York.

Teresa Edwards

To qualify for an Olympic team is a sign of an athlete's dedication and hard work. To be a part of four consecutive Olympic basketball teams is a feat achieved by no other United States basketball player, male or female. To be asked to take the athlete's oath for all the athletes at the Centennial Olympic Games in Atlanta is an once-in-a-lifetime honor. For Teresa Edwards, these are just a small portion of a spectacular sport resume.

Edwards, born July 19, 1964, in Cairo, Georgia, began her Olympic basketball career by winning gold medals in both the 1984 Games in Los Angeles, California, and the 1988 Games in Seoul, South Korea. She was also the co-captain of the 1992 United States Olympic Basketball Team, which earned a bronze medal.

As co-captain, Edwards led the 1996 United States Olympic Basketball Team to a gold medal and helped to revolutionize the sport of women's basketball in the United States. During those Centennial Games, Edwards scored a total of 55 points and dished out 64 assists. She averaged seven points per game, and a team-high eight assists per game. In the game against Australia she set an Olympic record with 15 assists.

Edwards, or "T" as she is known to friends, was one of the first women named to the 1995-1996 United States Women's Basketball National Team, a standing national team that trained and competed on tour as a unit for two years prior to the Olympic Games. During the tour, the team posted a 52-0 record. Edwards was the team assists leader, averaging 5.1 assists per game and 6.4 points per game while shooting 52 percent from the field. In her best game on the national tour, she recorded a game high of 17 points, 12 assists, 7 rebounds, and 5 steals, playing a total of 40 minutes.

A graduate of the University of Georgia with a degree in recreation, Edwards was a two-time All-American in basketball. During her four years at Georgia, the team compiled a 116-17 record and participated in four National Collegiate Athletic Association (NCAA) Women's Basketball Tournaments. She was one of only three Georgia women's basketball players to have her number (#5) retired.

In addition to basketball, Edwards enjoys football, track and field, and volleyball. Edwards credits Ann Meyers and Lynette Woodard as her basketball role models. She hopes to emulate these women as a member and coach of the Atlanta Glory of the American Basketball League, one of two women's professional basketball leagues that formed in the wake of the 1996 team's success.

Janie Eichkoff

When track cycling coaches are looking for a name athlete who will personify "work ethic" in the young or developing athlete's mind, the ready choice is Janie Eichkoff (Quigley). With a longevity of 12 years in racing that belies her own youthful appearance, Janie sets the standard of excellence within this rigorous and punishing sport. Proof of this standing can be found in her many records, but perhaps most telling is that Janie Eichkoff was the 1996 United States Cycling Federation Female Athlete of the Year, the third time she has been awarded this honor. She is also a two-time nominee for the Sullivan Award, which honors the nation's top amateur athlete across all sports.

Eichkoff's specialties were individual pursuit (two cyclists line up on opposite ends of a banked track and "pursue" each other while trying to finish first), 3000 meter timed races (against the clock and other contestants) and points (races where riders sprint for points on designated laps of the race).

Born on June 15, 1970, in Wilmington, Delaware, Eichkoff began bike racing at the urging of her father who later enjoyed watching the event at the 1984 Olympics. Among the many high–lights of Janie Eichkoff's track cycling career are the following: 17-time national champion, 7-time world championship medalist; 9-time medalist at World Cup Competition, Goodwill Games Pursuit Champion, Pan American Games Pursuit and Points Race Champion, Pan American Games record holder in the 3000-meter pursuit, and former world record holder in the 1,000-meter time trial.

Equestrian Events

Equestrian sports, which are not one but several events for horses and riders, have been in the modern Olympic Games since the nineteenth century. The three modern events of dressage, show jumping, and three-day eventing have comprised the equestrian events at the Olympic Games since 1912. There is no distinction between male and female riders in the Olympic Program. Since 1912, the United States has won over 30 medals, with women being an integral part of many teams. Other non-Olympic equestrian competitions include driving, hunter class, jumpers, parade horses, vaulting equitation, and endurance events. Although the modern equestrian events evolved relatively recently, competing on horseback has existed since people tamed horses to ride, and existing evidence shows that women, as well as men, have always ridden horses.

Dressage is French for "training," and the event displays the horse's three natural gaits: walk, trot, and canter. Required movements are scored from 0–10 each, and these scores are combined with scores for such characteristics as horse's submission, effortlessness of rider control, and rider seat and position. Highest total score wins the event. It is a very demanding discipline requiring years of training for both horse and rider. Horses must be at least 7 years of age to compete and riders at least 16 years. Most riders and horses are much older. Women of 70 have competed in dressage, and horses are often 12 or 13 years old. All riders wear a special uniform of top hat, white breeches (pants), black boots, and black or dark blue tail coat. Riders also wear white gloves and spurs on their boots.

In show jumping, also known as grand prix jumping, the horse and rider jump a series of obstacles to gain a "clear round." A clean round is scored when the horse and rider complete the course without knocking down any obstacles, or exceeding a given

Horse and rider clearing a jump.

time period. Riders must be at least 18 years old to compete, but most are much older.

Three-day eventing is perhaps the most exciting and demanding of the three Olympic equestrian sports for both horse and rider.

The history of this event goes back to the days of cavalries. To be successful in the cavalry, the horse and rider needed to be brave, athletic, and fit. The horse had to be well-trained, and both horse and rider had to be able to withstand long, grueling rides. Today, these aspects are tested over three days. Day one is dressage, which emphasizes obedience and is similar to the single dressage event mentioned earlier. Day two is a four-phased endurance and jumping test. The cross-country event is perhaps the toughest of the four phases. Fixed obstacles on this course are often large; the horse and rider must negotiate water jumps and ditches and go down and up banks as quickly as possible. Before the cross-country section, the horse and rider compete in two sets of "roads and tracks," which involve a number of miles of trotting and slow cantering, and one phase of a steeple chase where horses and riders manage various barriers and water hazards. The horse and rider have to complete all courses in a given time, although extra points are not awarded for going faster than the time specified. At each stage, the horses are examined by a veterinarian to make sure they are fit enough to continue competing. Day three involves a show-jumping competition similar to the single-day jumping event.

All events feature four-person teams with the highest three scores being combined to arrive at the team score. The highest scores by individuals are used to determine winners of individual championships. There is no separately contested "individual" event.

The United States teams have had several noted women riders. Most recently, Michelle Gibson from Roswell, Georgia, was a member of the United States bronze-medal-winning dressage team at the 1996 Olympic Games in Atlanta, Georgia, and Carol Lavell of Fairfax, Virginia, was a member of the bronze medal team at the 1992 Olympic Games in Barcelona, Spain, and her team also won the 1987 silver medal at the Pan American Games.

Anne Kursinski won an individual gold medal in show jumping at the 1988 Olympic Games in Seoul, South Korea, and a team silver medal at the 1996 Olympic Games in Atlanta in show jumping. She also won gold medals at the Pan American Games of 1983 and 1993 in the same events.

In three-day eventing, Kerry Millikin of Westport, Massachusetts, won the individual bronze medal for the United States at the 1996 Olympic Games, and Karen Lende O'Connor from The Plains, Virginia, was a member of the 1996 Olympic Games silver medal three-day eventing team.

Information for all events and the sport in general can be obtained from the national governing body: American Horse Shows Association (AHSA) 220 East 42nd Street New York, NY 10017-5876, which is the governing body of all equestrian events.

Janet Evans

Swimmer Janet Evans was born on August 28, 1971, in Placentia, California. Although her straight-armed, choppy swim stroke looks better suited to sprints, Evans owns the world record for three of the longer freestyle swimming events. At the 1988 Summer Olympic Games in Seoul, South Korea, 17-

Janet Evans.
© Daniel Kron.

year-old Evans captured three gold medals and set a record in each event: a world record in the 400-meter freestyle, an Olympic record in the 800-meter freestyle, and a United States record in the 400-meter individual medley. She is the only female swimmer to hold three world records at the same time, in the 400-, 800-, and 1,500-meter freestyle races.

In the 1992 Olympic Games in Barcelona, Spain, Evans won a gold medal in the 800-meter freestyle, as well as a silver medal in the 400-meter freestyle. Upon returning home to the United States, she retired from swimming. Her "retirement" lasted for only a short time. Evans qualified for her third United States Olympic Swim Team in 1996. She did not win any medals in Atlanta.

Evans is the only female swimmer to capture four Olympic individual gold medals in her career. In 1989, she was the recipient of the Sullivan Award as the outstanding amateur female athlete of the year. She holds six United States records and has won 42 United States titles.

Chris Evert

Chris Evert, one of the most decorated players in tennis, has won 18 Grand Slam (Wimbledon and Australian, French, and United States Open) singles titles, 157 professional tennis titles, and 1,309 matches. She won the French Open seven times, the United States Open six times, Wimbledon three times, and the Australian Open twice. She was one of the first top tennis players to rely on a two-handed backhand.

Born on December 21, 1954, in Fort Lauderdale, Florida, Christine Marie Evert owns the highest winning percentage in tennis history (.900). As an amateur player,

she received recognition by defeating such tennis legends as Margaret Court, Virginia Wade, and Billie Jean King. Her father, Jimmy, taught her to play tennis and coached her from the time she was five years old.

Chris Evert quickly became a favorite with the spectators and the media as she had a poised and intensely concentrated style of play. Evert turned professional in 1972 at the age of 17. Her popularity helped attract larger audiences and significantly higher prize money to women's professional tennis. In 1984, she became the first player to win 1,000 singles matches. Evert owns the best record on clay of any player, setting a 125-match winning streak on clay courts from 1973 to 1979. She reached the semifinals or better in 52 of the 56 Grand Slam events she entered. Her record of 157 singles titles, more than any other male or female tennis player at the time, remained intact for many years until Martina Navratilova broke it by earning her 158th singles title in 1992. Evert

Chris Evert.
Photo courtest of International Tennis Hall of Fame.

was ranked number one eight times between 1975 and 1985.

Evert retired from professional tennis in 1989, after losing to Zina Garrison in the quarterfinals of the United States Open. She was the president of the Women's Tennis Association (WTA) from 1975 to 1976 and from 1983 to 1991. She is currently a color commentator for NBC television for major tennis tournaments.

Evert has won a number of honors and awards throughout her career. In 1981, she was named the Women's Sports Foundation Professional Sportswoman of the Year and was inducted into their International Women's Sports Hall of Fame. She was also named the Greatest Woman Athlete of the Last 25 Years by the Women's Sports Foundation in 1985. Evert received the Flo Hyman Award from President George Bush in 1990 for the outstanding athlete of the year. In July 1995, she was inducted into the International Tennis Hall of Fame by a unanimous vote.

Evert and her husband, Olympic skier Andy Mill, host the Annual Chris Evert Pro/Celebrity Tennis Classic, which raises money for hurricane relief and for the fight against drug abuse. In the 1994 event, they raised a record $850,000 for substance abuse programs in South Florida.

Exercise and Elderly Women

As the number of elderly citizens surges in the United States, our national health care policy must be prepared to serve an increasingly older population. A few statistics illuminate the situation. While approximately 13 percent of the population was 65 years old or over in 1995, the United States census figures project that by the year 2050, 24 percent or almost one out of every 4 people, will be 65 or older. Within that group, approximately 24 percent will be 85 years old or older. Given these demographic trends and the soaring costs of health care for the elderly, the United States must increasingly look for ways to improve well-being and the quality of life for the elderly.

The health of this aging population is of particular interest to women because women live longer and therefore make up a large percentage of the elderly population. Aging is also a women's issue because it is primarily women who care for the aged both at home and in institutions.

Exercise and the Healthy Senior

The importance of exercise for improving the well being of both men and women throughout the lifespan has been well documented. Research on the efficacy of training programs for the elderly has shown that older adults do experience a training effect as a result of exercise. Furthermore, when measured as a percent of initial conditions, this training effect equals and in some cases exceeds the positive training effects experienced by younger individuals.

Research studies have shown that physical training increases physical work capacity (VO^2 Max or the amount of oxygen the body can use per kilogram of weight per minute) in women, including women over 60 years of age. Other positive cardiorespiratory improvements related to exercise for elderly women are an increase in oxygen pulse and improvement in electrocardiogram abnormalities. Lowered heart rates, which indicate increased economy of effort with physical work, are an additional benefit of exercise training programs for older women.

In addition to these favorable cardiorespiratory changes, exercise also produces desirable changes in body composition and bones. Exercise programs have been shown to increase muscle mass and decrease body fat in postmenopausal women. The increased strength resulting from increased muscle mass allows elderly women to do more without becoming fatigued, and exercise helps avoid obesity and its associated diseases like diabetes and high blood pressure. Exercise is also recommended as a preventative measure for osteoporosis (thinning of the bones) because weight-bearing exercise retards bone mineral loss associated with aging. For example, one study showed that 20 women with a mean age of 82 gained 4.2 percent in bone mineral composition as a result of exercise compared with members of the control group who lost 2.5 percent over the same 36-month period.

It is generally recommended that healthy elderly individuals engage in an exercise program that includes: 1) three, 30-minute weekly sessions of cardiovascular exercises, such as walking and swimming; 2) three weekly sessions of strength or resistance training exercises, such as weight lifting and; 3) daily flexibility exercises such as static stretching. In addition to all the physical benefits of exercises, older adults often enjoy psychological benefits such as the elevation of mood and the pleasures associated with socializing with others while engaging in exercise. Many seniors also enjoy exercise in the form of athletic competitions such as the Senior Games sponsored by the United States Olympic Committee.

Exercise and the Frail Senior

The positive aspects of exercise for healthy senior citizens have been well demonstrated. Until recently, however, such activity has not been considered appropriate for those frail elderly who, because of either chronic disease, decreased muscle strength, or impaired gait or balance, have limited ability to perform the activities of daily living (ADL), such as walking, bathing, or dressing.

In 1993, the National Institute on Aging and the National Institute for Nursing Research jointly sponsored a multisite study called "Frailty and Injuries: Cooperative Studies of Intervention Techniques (FICSIT)," a collection of eight independent clinical trials that assessed the effectiveness of a variety of exercise intervention strategies in reducing falls in the frail elderly. The focus of the research resulted from earlier findings that falls, and their resulting injuries, affect approximately 30 percent of people over 65 years of age. In deaths caused by unintentional injury, the majority are caused by falls, especially for those aged 85 years and older. Moreover, fall survivors experience greater declines in their ability to function independently, and are thus at greater risk of a lessening quality of life and institutionalization. If falls often occur because of declining

muscle strength and deterioration in gait and balance, it seems reasonable to study whether exercise designed to improve these functions would result in fewer falls and prevent loss of life and the declining ability to function in the activities of daily life.

Participants in the studies lived in the community, retirement homes, and nursing homes, and ranged in age from 65 to over 90 years old. The various studies included elderly people who were ambulatory (able to walk unassisted) and those using canes, walkers, and wheelchairs for assistance; those who were functionally dependent in two or more activities of daily living (ADL); and those with balance deficits, lower extremity weakness, or deemed to be at high risk of falling. Within each study, the exercise and control groups were matched for physical conditions.

The types of exercise ranged from high- to low-level resistance training (depending on the frailty of the population), endurance training, flexibility exercises, static balance training on a balance platform, and tai chi for dynamic balance. The trial interventions lasted from 10 weeks to nine months, with follow-up continuing for two to four years. In each study, the primary care physician approved the individual's participation in the exercise program.

In the results to date, published in 1995, the researchers concluded that overall treatments including exercise for elderly adults did indeed reduce the risk of falls. It is less clear which type of exercise was most effective since the health conditions of groups differed, even though matched control and treatment groups were used within each study.

The community-dwelling group, using balance training on a balance platform and tai chi, showed significant decreases in falling, as did a group using balance and resistance training. Near significant decreases in falls were noted in two other groups using balance and resistance training and low-level endurance training followed by flexibility exercises.

Most encouraging of all are studies on the use of exercise with the most frail elderly population, those residing in nursing homes. Studies conducted as part of the FICST group, as well as independent studies in the United States, Australia, and New Zealand, have all shown that exercise improved muscle strength, muscle size, and flexibility. Additionally, the level of spontaneous physical activity increased in the test groups as compared to control groups (who were given other recreational activities). The exercise groups were conducted two to three times a week for an average of 45 minutes and included range of motion exercises, mildly progressive resistance exercises using ankle and wrist weights, or high-intensity progressive resistance training of hip and knee extensors. Besides the more obvious health benefits, the Australian study also noted a reduction in depression that was greater in the exercising group than in the control group, who had been involved in a reminiscing class, always a favorite activity in long-term care facilities.

While it is still not yet clear exactly what kind of exercise is most effective with the frail elderly population, much evidence shows that exercise of some kind is important in the later decades of life for maintaining muscle strength and functional mobility. Years of working with frail elderly people, living in both the community and long-term care facilities, have shown that the ability to be functionally independent is more than a health issue. It is an issue that is intimately related to one's self-esteem and the social and psychological quality of life one is able to have in these later years. Exercise, then, is an essential for maintaining health and well-being in the later decades of life as it is in the earlier ones. *MH2*

References

deVries, H. A. (1980). *Physiology of exercise.* Dubuque, IA: Wm. C. Brown Co. Publishers.

Wells, C. (1985). *Women, sport and performance: A physiological perspective.* Champaign, IL: Human Kinetics Press.

Exercise and Women's Health: A Physician's View

Exercise is one of the best prescriptions in medicine for all ages. Human beings thrive on movement, which produces pleasure and stimulates creativity. Aerobic exercise stimulates blood flow and growth of skeletal muscle. It also eases the fatigue of nervous tension and sedentary behavior and potentially prevents disease.

Benjamin Franklin said, "Be careful in preserving health by exercise and great temperance, for in sickness the imagination is disturbed and disagreeable and sometimes terrible ideas are apt to present themselves." Today, psychotherapists appreciate the interaction of the mind and physiology and encourage exercise for their depressed patients. The release of endorphins following physical activity is thought to produce the "good feeling," but until the 1960s, women were conditioned never to exert enough effort to reach this state. Heavy aerobic activity was unfeminine; women could "glisten," but not "sweat"! Fortunately, it is no longer frowned upon for young girls and women to participate in heavy sports activity. A decrease in cancer, particularly breast cancer, has been correlated with exercise starting in early teen years and continuing into adulthood.

Each year lack of physical activity is a contributing factor in more than 250,000 deaths in the United States. Only 22 percent of adults are physically active at the recommended levels for health benefits, and 24 percent are completely sedentary (inactive). The United States Public Health Service has finally recognized that exercise is an important component of a healthy lifestyle and has set a goal of increased physical activity for "Healthy People" for the year 2000.

Exercise has been shown to help in the prevention of disease, in the treatment of disease, and in the process of rehabilitation. Exercise not only prolongs life, but it also produces a healthier and more enjoyable old age. The following paragraphs outline some of the benefits of exercise as well as some of the diseases it helps prevent.

Emotional Health

Recent studies showed that a group of healthy, middle-aged adults who exercised regularly exhibited less anxiety, tension, depression, and fatigue than their sedentary counterparts. Researchers using Beck's Depression Inventory, a depression measuring system, found that depressed women who did strenuous exercise had a significantly greater decrease in depression than those who did relaxation exercises, or none at all.

Aerobically fit subjects had a reduced psychosocial stress response when compared with a control group, regardless of the psychological measures used. These beneficial effects have been attributed to hemodynamic changes, sympathetic nervous system activity, baro-receptor function changes, and release of endogenous opiates (endorphins) that all occur during strenuous exercise.

Menopause

Menopause occurs, on the average, at about the age of 52 years. Specific types of exercise ("stress" exercise or high-impact aerobics) ease the various symptoms experienced by this age group. Vasomotor complaints (hot flashes), which lead to sleeplessness and irritability, have been shown to be less common in physically active women. Cardiovascular disease, degenerative disease, and osteoporosis (thinning of bone tissue) in the aging woman are affected by obesity and decreased aerobic activity as well. "Stress" exercise combats these changes. The short-term goal of exercise is minimizing menopausal symptoms. The longer-term goal is enabling women to remain well and self-sufficient throughout their older years.

Chronic Obstructive Pulmonary Disease (Emphysema)

Emphysema is the fourth-leading cause of death in the United States. Patients suffering from this disease show greater improvement in breathing capacity with increased exercise. Exercise increases lung capacity and improves oxygen exchange, thus improving endurance and the extent and quality of life.

Benefit can be achieved even in those who have severe airflow obstruction. Even contracting and relaxing muscle groups while sitting can prove to be therapeutic.

Exercise for the Third Stage, or Maturity

Whether a person is 30 or 90, weak or strong, strength training may be the single most important way to improve life and to thrive as the years accumulate. To halt the "flab for muscle exchange" requires not only the aerobic activities like walking, running, and biking, but also weightlifting to preserve muscle strength.

Reduced skeletal muscle strength in the elderly is a major cause of increasing disability. It causes walking impairment and higher incidence of falls. Skeletal muscle plays a role, not only in preserving strength, but also in increasing energy metabolism, contributing to reduction in insulin sensitivity, and adding aerobic capacity. Therefore, preserving and increasing muscle mass and strength in the sedentary elderly can increase independence and decrease aging associated with the chronic diseases, such as diabetes, cardiovascular pathology, obesity, and senility.

For persons between 65 and 70 years of age, on the average, 38 percent of their remaining years will be spent dependent on others. Nursing home residents classified as "fallers" are shown to be significantly weaker in all muscle groups of the knees and the ankles. Dramatic increase in strength, using progressive resistance training, has demonstrated an improvement in bone density, perceptions of vitality, and weight control. Exercise increases metabolism, with relief of such problems as constipation and urinary incontinence. Increased circulatory flow produces increased oxygenation of vital organs and the brain. This oxygenation leads to better functioning, reduction in confusion and memory loss, and improvement in cognitive functioning.

Osteoporosis

Osteoporosis, or thinning of the bones, results in weakening of the skeleton and frequent fractures with minimal trauma. Risk factors are very lean body weight, cigarette smoking, lack of calcium and/or Vitamin-D, little exposure to the sun, and aging. After age 50, bone loss is one to six percent per year. Therefore, exercise, which helps to preserve bone density, is even more important as one ages.

Sarcopenia

Sarcopenia (the loss of skeletal muscle with advancing age) results in lower basal metabolism, weakness, reduced activity levels, decreased bone density, and lower caloric needs. Related increase in body fat is linked to high blood pressure and abnormal glucose tolerance (diabetes). To remain independent in function and vital in cognitive ability, and to gain pleasure in life, aerobic exercise is important at any age but even more important in the "Third Stage—the mature years."

Cardiovascular (Heart) Disease

Studies have shown that physical activity delays the onset of cardiovascular disease and strokes, and helps to reverse established cardiovascular disease. In a study of 2,200 men and women, subclinical cardiovascular disease was less prevalent among physically active older people who engaged in moderate or high intensity physical activity. Inactive persons had higher blood pressure, serum glucose, hematocrit (potentially leading to stroke), and uric acid (gout) levels.

Not too many years ago a heart attack patient was treated with complete bed rest for weeks. Today, early ambulation (walking and moving about) helps to repair the pathology of disease as well as improving the psychologic components of stress that heart attack victims often feel.

Peripheral Vascular Disease

Claudication (leg pain) is caused by insufficient oxygen being delivered to the muscles as a result of decreased quality of the blood vessels (i.e., peripheral vascular disease). Factors contributing to this condition, and to aging, are smoking, high blood pressure, high blood lipids (cholesterol, etc.), diabetes, and obesity. "Stress" exercise, walking, and biking help the body form new collateral blood vessels, thus increasing the volume of blood and oxygen being delivered and relieving the disease process. Exercise can produce a dramatic effect even in advanced stages of the disease.

Cancer

Exercise reduces the risk of breast and colon cancer. Over 182,000 cases of breast cancer occur each year. This figure can be reduced by as much as one-third through exercise. A study of 500 women in their 30s, showed that active women had almost half the breast cancer risk as the least active women. As little exercise as 30 to 40 minutes per day can be effective.

To remain independent in function, vital in cognitive ability, and to obtain pleasure in life, aerobic exercise is important at every age, but it is even more important as one ages. Because of the longer lifespan of women, these medical recommendations need to be widely promulgated among women. *GC*

Expedition Inspiration. *See* Aconcagua Mountain

Aeriwentha Mae Faggs

Aeriwentha Mae Faggs (Starr) began her track career as a member of the Police Athletic League (PAL). She later became a member of an Amateur Athletic Union (AAU) team started by PAL, and soon afterward made the United States Olympic Track and Field Team. Faggs entered Tennessee State University (TSU) and was a star there before the Tigerbelles became a powerhouse in women's track and field.

Born on April 10, 1932, in Mays Landing, New Jersey, Faggs made her first Olympic track team in 1948 when she was 16 years old, the team's youngest member. She was the first African American woman to participate in three Olympic Games: 1948, 1952, and 1956. In 1952, Faggs won a gold medal in the 4 x 100-meter relay and a bronze medal for the same event in 1956. Faggs competed for 10 years, mostly in relay and 100-meter sprints, and won 100 medals, 26 trophies, and 3 plaques in national and international competitions. An accomplished runner, Faggs has held every indoor and outdoor sprint record and has contributed to the success of several relay teams. Faggs is a member of the International Women's Sport Hall of Fame, Pioneer Category. She was also inducted into the National Track and Field Hall of Fame in 1975.

Female Athlete Triad

Under intense pressure from coaches, parents, teammates—often even from themselves—to lose weight, many young athletes slip into disordered eating, which in turn often leads to serious eating disorders such as anorexia or bulimia and related conditions: amenorrhea (absence of menses) and osteoporosis (bone loss). Although any one of these conditions can occur in isolation, the emphasis on weight loss often begins a cycle in which all three occur in sequence—hence the term "Female Athlete Triad."

Weight loss does not necessarily ensure improvement in athletic performance. Muscle mass, as well as fat, is lost during extreme dieting, and performance may actually deteriorate. Other side effects of poor nutrition, such as fatigue, anemia, electrolyte abnormalities, and depression, can also contribute to a poor performance. Although many coaches now realize that body composition measurements provide better information than body weight alone, most do not realize that these measures are far from precise and that holding all athletes to a single standard for body fat can have serious repercussions. Pressuring athletes to achieve an unrealistic weight loss or percent body fat

Barbara Drinkwater, leading research physiologist.

ignores individual variability in body build and often leads to disordered eating.

Disordered eating can range from poor nutrition and/or inadequate caloric intake to meet the energy demands of the sport to a serious eating disorder such as anorexia or bulimia. All forms of disordered eating are likely to diminish athletic performance and increase the athlete's risk of developing serious medical problems. Everyone personally involved with the athlete—the parents, coach, trainers, and team physician—should be alert to the following signs of an eating disorder.

Anorexia Nervosa

1. Weight 15 percent below normal weight for age and height.
2. Intense fear of gaining weight even though underweight.
3. Weight or body shape determines self-esteem.
4. Denial of reality concerning body and/or weight.
5. Amenorrhea.

Bulimia

1. Episodes of binge eating accompanied by a feeling of lack of control over what and how much is eaten.
2. Purging behavior (self-induced vomiting, laxatives, excessive exercise, diuretics) follows bingeing. Episodes occur at least twice a week for three months.
3. Self-esteem unduly influenced by body shape or weight.

Although the actual number of athletes at risk for the Triad is unknown, among those affected there appears to be a continuum of disordered eating ranging from poor nutrition to anorexia and/or bulimia. A number of serious medical complications result from the Female Athlete Triad. Some of these complications are reversible, but others permanently impair the major organ systems, including the kidneys, heart, gastrointestinal tract, and skeleton. In addition, the complications from eating disorders can cause problems with fluid and electrolyte balance, central nervous system, and endocrine function. The final outcome for some young athletes is death.

Amenorrhea

The absence of menses, amenorrhea, is the most common symptom of eating disorders in women. Menstrual irregularities, however, can occur in the absence of an eating disorder. As a result of the high energy demands of exercise, athletes may be energy deficient even while consuming meals considered normal for healthy nonathletes. While the precise etiology of amenorrhea and oligomenorrhea (irregular menses) has yet to be determined, it is possible that even seemingly minor deficits between caloric expenditure and caloric intake may play a role. Stress, such as the pressure to meet impossible weight standards, may also be a factor. What is certain is that the prevalence of amenorrhea among athletes is high, ranging from 10 to 45 percent depending on the sport. The above conditions are especially common among those athletes who participate in sports where a low body weight is presumed to improve performance or where the body shape may influence judges' scoring. The incidence of amenorrhea is high in gymnastics, distance running, ballet, and figure skating, but it can occur in any sport where the athlete is pressured to lose weight. Amenorrhea is usually an overt sign of a decrease in estrogen production. In most amenorrheic athletes, estrogen levels drop to postmenopausal levels, and bone mass decreases significantly.

Osteoporosis

The third point of the Female Athlete Triad is a disease characterized by low bone mass and microarchitectural deterioration of the bone tissue leading to increased bone fragility and an increased risk of fractures. In the female athlete, this condition can result from inadequate bone formation during the critical growth years and/or a premature loss of bone mass in the young adult years. This loss of bone mineral density (BMD) is usually first observed in the spine, but if the amenorrhea is prolonged, bone loss can occur in other parts of the skeleton as well. Early studies suggested that with the resumption of menses, some of the bone could be regained, but more recent studies report that recovery of bone is limited and that some of the loss may be irreversible. The spinal density of some young athletes has been observed to be similar to that of women in their 70s and 80s and may never return to normal. Evidence is mounting that these athletes are at increased risk for stress fractures and more serious fractures of the pelvis, hip, and spine. What the future holds for these women is uncertain, but there is great concern about the potential for premature osteoporotic fractures as these women age.

Preventing the Female Athlete Triad involves educating athletes, parents, coaches, health professionals, and athletic administrators about the seriousness of the problem and how to recognize the warning signs. Standards of conduct for coaches which prohibit the type of behaviors that encourage disordered eating should be established. In sports such as gymnastics and figure skating where success depends upon judges' ratings,

less emphasis must be placed on body shape and more on the actual execution of the skill. Finally, the positive aspects of sport, the enjoyment of the athlete, and the physical, social, and psychological benefits should always remain the first priority in any sport program. *BD*

Fencing and Women

Fencing was one of the 10 original sports of the modern Olympic Games of 1896. Within the sport of fencing are three events: epee, foil, and sabre. Generally, individuals specialize in only one of the three events because the technique required of each one is extremely difficult to master. The differences between each event are the target area and scoring. In epee, the entire body is the target, points are scored with the tip of the weapon only, and both opponents can score simultaneously. In foil, only the torso is the target, and once again points are scored with the tip of the weapon only; however, only one opponent can score at a time. In sabre, everything from the waist up is the target including the head and arms. Points are scored with the side of the blade as well as the tip, and (as in foil) only one opponent can score at a time. In all three events, a referee controls the matches and awards the points.

The heat of competition.
Photo courtesy of Gini Alvord.

Fencing has a long history.

Women fencers first appeared in the Olympic Games in 1924. Unlike men, at that time women could only compete in foil. The 1996 Olympic Games in Atlanta, Georgia, were the first in which epee competition was added to the foil event for women.

Until the 1970s, there were no organized women's epee or sabre competitions in the world. In the United States, the university and high school fencing teams consisted of women's foil, men's foil, men's epee, and men's sabre members. Numerous reasons have been given for this state of affairs. The most popular reasons were the following: (a) foil fencing develops grace and beauty, desirable qualities for women, while the epee is too heavy, stiff, and dangerous a weapon for women; and (b) the sabre is too aggressive and athletic for women. Financial considerations were also involved. Teaching techniques in the use of weapons that would not be used in competition was deemed imprudent. The money available, beyond foil fencing support, was to be used for those who could benefit from international competition in epee and sabre, i.e., men.

Despite the lack of opportunities in two of the events, women fencers have left their mark. Throughout the years, women foil fencers have participated in the university intercollegiate women's national competition, in Amateur Fencing League of America (ALFA)

competitions, and in the United States Fencing Association competions. Internationally, women foilists participated in world cups, University Games, Maccabiah Games, Pan American Games, and Olympic Games. Janice Romary participated in six Olympic Games. She carried the USA flag in her last Games in 1968. Throughout the years of women's foil fencing, no United States Olympians have won medals, but three women have placed in the top ten: Maria Cerra Tishman, 1948, placed fourth (if she had scored one more touch—to win a close bout she lost—she would have won a gold medal). In 1996 Marion Lloyd Vince placed ninth and Ann Marsh placed seventh.

Some women of color have also made their mark in fencing. Ruth White was the first African American national champion. Nikki Franke, however, truly became the role model for African American women. She won a national championship, fenced internationally, and is a nationally recognized outstanding university coach at Temple University.

Other greats in the history of women's fencing are Denise O'Conner, Maxine Mitchell, and Vincent Bradford. Maxine is especially noteworthy for her longevity, being in the top 24 women foilists until the age of 60 years.

Despite this long history of successful women participating in foil fencing, the other areas of fencing remained closed to women. The Women's Movement in the 1970s brought a surge of interest in equality for women. In the fencing world at this time, women began to demand, organize, and petition for competitions in epee and sabre. These women were found primarily in the Midwest and in California. Responding to this pressure, Canadian fencing leaders sponsored a women's epee and sabre competition in London, Ontario. A "Western Women's Classic" also emerged in San Francisco. Women saw no reason for restrictions on the use of epee and sabre, and many had informally been working with those weapons in their clubs.

Even though such events and competitions represent progress, there is still no sabre for women at elite levels. Unofficial competitions in individual and team epee were held at the USFA National Tournament in the 1970s, and, in 1982, USFA sanctioned an official women's individual epee event. Susan Badders finished first, Marlene Adrian was second, and Anne Klinger third, in this competition. At the time, all were over 35 years of age. All had been foil fencers, and Badders had been on the Olympic foil team four years earlier. Adrian also won the Gilman Tournament in Cleveland, an interesting tournament in which each fencer fenced with a foil and then fenced every person in her pool with an epee. Advancement to the next round was based on the record with both weapons. The top two fencers then fenced each other again, first with one weapon and then with the other. In 1986, Vincent Bradford won a gold medal in epee in the Pan American Games.

Unlike the situation of fencers in countries that fully fund their athletes, the fencers of the United States had to carry the burden of expenses by themselves until 1993. This funding deficit placed the United States fencers at a disadvantage. It was very difficult to get the international experience needed to become one of the best in the world without the money to pay for all the travel and competition expenses. Despite the lack of funding, the U.S. team has had some successes. In 1988, Catlin Bilodeau placed ninth in foil fencing at the Olympic Games, and the United States team finished sixth, making the first breakthrough to the "top 10" in 60 years. This finish was a very important occurrence for the United States. Bilodeau's record led the way for others to believe that they could beat the professionals of other countries on an amateur budget.

Presently, the United States Fencing Association (USFA) provides $10,000 grants (plus placement bonuses) per year to individual competitors if they meet specific performance standards from the previous year. Under this new system of funding, the U.S. has seen the emergence of such wonderful talented women fencers as the Zimmerman sisters, Felicia and Irish, and Ann Marsh.

In 1995, Felicia Zimmerman gave the United States its first ever World Cup Under 20 Champion in women's foil. The world cup champion is a prestigious title awarded to the individual who was ranked in the greatest number of the many world cup events held around the world in a single year. In the same year, Felicia continued her progress by being one of only two United States women in the last three decades to make the finals of the adult world championships. The only other United States woman to make the finals in the world championship was Donna Stone, in 1989, in women's epee.

In 1995 and 1996, the United States women continued to improve. The Under 17 World Champion was Irish Zimmerman, a 14 year old with astonishing talent and capability. In 1996, Irish Zimmerman also placed third in the "Under 20 World Championships," competing with older and more experienced fencers. Another outstanding young fencer is Ann Marsh. Marsh did what no United States woman has done since the 1930s when she made the finals of the Olympic Games in 1996 in women's foil.

Fencing has also been popular with older athletes. For more than 20 years, Senior fencing (over 50) has taken place, primarily at national championships. Women fencing all three weapons, and taking first place in one or more events, have included Marlene Adrian, Anne Klinger, and Cynthia Carter. This veteran group has a quarterly newsletter, officers, and a circuit of national and international competitions. The foil and epee women representing the United States at the first such international competition for seniors, held in Germany in 1996, earned second places in foil (Cynthia Carter) and epee (Veronica Morrison).

Other women in the USFA who devoted their energy to promoting fencing were Colleen Olney, Eleanor Turney, and Emily Johnson. All have been active in creating opportunities in epee and sabre for women. The present director of programs for USFA, Carla Richards, has had significant impact on the direction of fencing in the United States in her position of executive director of AFLA/USFA for 11 years. The talent of these women and many others has helped bring respect and recognition to the United States in the sport of fencing. The future of American fencing is looking brighter every day with the present and upcoming talent—women who have the potential to excel in fencing.

The national governing body for fencing is the U.S. Fencing Association; One Olympic Plaza; Colorado Springs, Colorado 80909-5774; 719-578-4511. *MA & SM*

Lisa Fernandez

The old softball adage has always been "pitching wins games." This is often the case when Lisa Fernandez, one of the sport's most dominating and successful pitchers, takes the mound. Fernandez, born on February 22, 1971, in Long Beach, California, has shown her dominance in softball in the 1990s. As a member of the United States Olympic Softball Team, she won a gold medal in the 1996 Games in Atlanta, Georgia. She was also a member of the USA softball team that won the gold medal at the 1995 Superball Classic in Columbus, Georgia. In the 1995 Pan American zone qualifying games in Guatemala, she pitched a perfect game (no hits and no walks). Fernandez also batted .511 during this event. In the 1994 South Pacific Classic in Australia, Fernandez dominated with a 3-0 record, 0.00 earned run average (ERA), and an amazing 24 strikeouts and was named to the First Team All-Tournament. In the 1993 Inter–continental Cup, Fernandez's 3-0 record and 0.00 ERA helped the United States team clinch the gold medal. When she was not pitching, the multitalented athlete played third base flawlessly.

Fernandez has won many honors in her successful career. She was named Sudafed Sportswoman of the Year by the Women's Sports Foundation in 1994. Her former coach at the University of California, Los Angeles (UCLA), Women's Sports Foundation Hall of Famer Sharron Backus, said that Fernandez was a tireless worker and a perfect student athlete. While at UCLA from 1989 to 1993, Fernandez was a four-time All-American, compiling a 93-7 won-loss record. In 1993, she was named the National Collegiate Athletic Association (NCAA) Woman Athlete of the Year, and she received a UCLA Post-Graduate Scholarship Award.

Two more prestigious awards were given to Fernandez for her accomplishments in 1993. She was honored with the Amoco/USA Softball Leadership Award, given to America's outstanding softball athlete. She also received the Honda-Broderick Cup, given to America's outstanding collegiate woman athlete. Fernandez has received much news media attention and has been

Lisa Fernandez.

featured in *Sports Illustrated*, *USA Today*, and on the *Today Show*.

Barbara Ferrell

Born on July 28, 1947, in Los Angeles, California, Ferrell was a track and field star whose specialties were the 4 x 100-meter relay and the 100-meter sprint. In Mexico City (1968), Barbara won a silver medal in the 100-meter dash, and her 4 x 100-meter relay team set the world record for the event. She won the 100-meter events in both the 1967 Pan American Games and the Amateur Athletic Association (AAU) Championships of the same year. She was the top-ranked United States sprinter in 1967 and 1969. Ferrell is a 1969 graduate of California State University, where she competed on the track and field team.

Field Hockey and Women

Constance M. K. Applebee, affectionately known as the "Apple," brought field hockey to the United States from England in 1901. She popularized the women's game by establishing clubs in major cities, primarily in the north-eastern part of the country. Applebee, who taught at Bryn Mawr College near Philadel-phia, also established a famous hockey camp, Camp Tegawitha, in the Pennsylvania Poconos. She organized the American Field Hockey Association, predecessor to the United States Field Hockey Association (USFHA), to codify the official rules of the game. By 1924, Applebee felt she had enough skilled players to form a team to

play against European clubs, and the United States women got their first taste of international competition that year. In the years following Applebee's introduction, women's field hockey continued to grow and develop. Men's field hockey developed more slowly and under a different governing body, the Field Hockey Association of America (FHAA). Part of the reason for this uneven development is that field hockey was not publicly perceived as a "men's game" in the United States until the sport was added to the Olympic program in 1980.

In 1993, the FHAA merged with the USFHA, making it the sole governing body of field hockey in the United States and a member of the United States Olympic Committee (USOC). The goals of the USFHA are to foster and promote amateur field hockey, to provide opportunities for play, and to prepare teams to represent the

Field hockey has been popular since its introduction to this country.
Photo courtesy of the *Camden Courier Post*.

United States in the Olympic Games, Pan American Games, and other international competitions. The USFHA sponsors many programs to implement these goals. Among these programs are the USA Junior Hockey Program for boys and girls from 8 to 13 years old, the National Indoor Hockey Tournament, the National Hockey Festival, the extensive adult club hockey programs, the various clinics and educational outreach efforts, and the publication of *Hockey News* and *The Eagle* to keep its members informed about opportunities and developments in field hockey.

Field hockey is a team sport in which two teams of 11 players each attempt to score points by shooting a solid plastic ball into the goal of the opposing team. The field is 100 yards by 60 yards with a goal at each end of the field. Play begins with a pass back at the center of the field. From that point, teams try to drive the ball toward their opponent's goal by dribbling and passing the ball using the flat side of the curved hardwood stick. One point is awarded for successfully shooting the ball into the opponent's goal. A game consists of two 35-minute halves, and the team with the most goals at the end of the second half wins. In case of a tie score at the end of regulation, the game is decided by a shoot-out.

Due to the boycott of the 1980 Olympic Games, American women first competed in the 1984 games, taking a bronze medal. In 1996 at the Olympic Games in Atlanta, Georgia, the United States women entered the competition ranked number three in the world, but failed to medal by placing fourth in the round-robin competition. Pam Bustin, Kris Fillat, Tracey Fuchs, Kelli James, Katie Kauffman, Antoinette Lucas, Leslie Lyness, Diane Madl, Barb Marois, Laurel Martin, Marcia Pankratz, Jill Reeve, Patty Shea, Liz Tchou, Cindy Werley, and Andrea Wieland were the members of the 1996 United States Women's Olympic Field Hockey Team.

Information about educational programs and playing opportunities can be obtained by writing to the United States Field Hockey Association, One Olympic Plaza, Colorado Springs, CO 80909-5773. *SER*

Figure Skating and Women

Figure skating at the international level consists of four major disciplines—men and women's singles, pairs skating, and ice dancing. Singles skating competition began in the 1880s, with official world championships sponsored by the International Skating Union (ISU) in 1896. In 1902, Madge Syers of Great Britain entered this competition and placed second, prompting the ISU to forbid women from competing against men and to institute a separate "ladies' championship" in 1906.

Pairs skating is performed by a team of one male and one female skater doing side-by-side freestyle moves as well as lifts, death spirals, and other athletic pair moves. Pairs have been a part of the ISU competition since 1908. Ice dance, also performed by male-female teams, originated as ballroom dancing on ice and emphasized close partner positions and complex footwork. The first world championship in ice dance was held in 1952 and the first Olympic competition in 1976. Thus, female skaters were among the first women to participate in the modern Olympic Games, competing in singles and pairs skating since 1908, when winter sports were first included in the Olympic Games. Women also competed in the first unofficial winter competitions in 1920 and have competed since the Winter Games were established in 1924.

Originally the emphasis of the sport for singles skaters was on tracing precise patterns (or figures) on the ice using the two edges of each blade going forward and backward and the various methods of turning from one edge and direction to another. Freeskating developed from the special figures, incorporating showy athletic moves such as jumps and spins, connected by edges and turns and performed to music. This expressive side of skating, seen in ice shows as well as athletic competition, has made figure skating increasingly popular as a spectator sport. Until 1972, figures constituted 60 percent of a singles skater's score and freeskating only 40 percent. In the 1972-1973 season, a "short program" of compulsory freeskating moves was introduced, and in the 1990–1991 season the ISU eliminated figures from international competition, although the United States Figure Skating Association (USFSA) continues to offer separate figures tests and competitions.

The sport has come a long ways from its beginnings to the athleticism of today's skaters. In the 1920 Games, American Theresa (Tee) Weld (Blanchard), who participated in both ladies' single and pairs, received a reprimand for daring to execute a simple salchow jump. Beatrix Loughran became the first American woman to win an Olympic medal (silver) in any winter sport when she finished second in the skating competition in 1924. Maribel Vinson (Owen) represented the United States in international competition in the late 1920s and early 1930s, and later became a prominent coach. With their writings about skating in books and magazines (Blanchard was the first, and long-time, editor of the USFSA's *Skating Magazine*), Blanchard and Owen did much to introduce skating technique to American audiences.

Athleticism in female skating took a big leap forward with the arrival of 11-year-old Sonja Henie of Norway at the 1924 Olympic Winter Games in Chamonix, France. Henie's youth and short skirt allowed her to perform the single jumps and flying sitspins that longer-skirted contemporaries dared not attempt. As her figures were not yet up to the standards of the older competitors, she finished eighth out of eight competitors, but her exciting freeskating program provided a glimpse of the future. In 1927, Henie won her first world championship at the age of 14, still the youngest ever to do so, and went on to dominate ladies' figure skating and win a total of 10 world championships and three Olympic gold medals before retiring from amateur competition in 1936. She then starred in a series of touring ice shows and popular Hollywood movies. Henie's success introduced skating to a much wider audience in the United States and Canada, firmly associating figure skating with glamour and femininity in the popular imagination ever since that time. In addition to her introduc-

tion of short skirts and a number of athletic moves, Henie is responsible for introducing fashions such as white, and later beige, skates for female skaters (who had previously worn black skates) and ballet-inspired movements on the ice.

Henie is also credited as the first woman to perform a one-and-a-half-revolution axel jump. Cecilia Colledge of Great Britain, Henie's contemporary and successor as world champion in the 1930s, was the first woman to execute double (salchow) jumps in competition. Colledge also invented the layback spin and camel spin.

World War II prevented many European skaters, and many male skaters in North America, from continuing their skating careers, further establishing skating as a predominantly female sport on this continent. In the immediate postwar generation, Dick Button of the United States and Barbara Ann Scott of Canada ruled in international competition, winning every competition they entered. Double jumps were now becoming the norm for both sexes. Button introduced the first double axel in 1948 and the first triple jump (a triple loop) in 1952. Tenley Albright became the first United States woman to win the world championships in 1953 and 1955, and she won the gold medal at the Olympic Games in 1956, closely followed by fellow American Carol Heiss, who won five world championships from 1956 (defeating Albright) to 1960, when she also won an Olympic gold medal. A decade after Button, Heiss was the first woman to perform the double axel jump in competition.

American dominance of international skating was tragically interrupted when the plane carrying the entire American team for the 1961 world championships crashed, prompting the cancellation of that year's world championships. By 1964, however, the United States had a new star with 15-year-old champion Peggy Fleming, who went on to win the world championships in 1966 and 1967 and the gold medal at the 1968 Olympic Games. She set new standards for combining flowing edges, athletic jumps, and graceful arm movements. Fleming went on to a professional skating career that made her the highest-paid female athlete of her day. As a junior skater in the 1960s, Janet Lynn, United States champion from 1969 through 1973, was one of the first women to perform a triple jump. Known for the transcendent quality of her freeskating, Lynn won the freeskating portion of the world championships but at the 1972 Olympic Games, due to the untouchable superiority of Austrian Trixi Schuba in figures, and mistakes in the newly introduced short program, Lynn had to settle for an overall bronze instead of a gold medal. Dorothy Hamill, another strong freeskater, reached her peak in the 1976 season, winning gold medals at both the Olympic Games and the world championships. Besides her prowess on the ice, Hamill inspired many American women and girls to emulate her sporty, elegant hairstyle.

By the late 1970s and early 1980s, triple jumps were becoming more common among the top female competitors. American women in the forefront of this movement included Linda Fratianne (1977 and 1979 world champion and 1980 Olympic silver medalist), Elaine Zayak (world champion in 1982), and Debi Thomas (world champion in 1986 and Olympic bronze medalist in 1988). Throughout this period, it was common for the top female competitors to perform triple loops and salchows, with the best jumpers also including the more difficult triples: flip or lutz. Zayak did triple toe loops (and toe walleys, which are practically the same jump) so easily that she would include up to five of these jumps in her free programs, along with a triple salchow (or two). This practice inspired the ISU to institute a limitation familiarly known as "the Zayak rule," permitting skaters to repeat only two different triple jumps, and to repeat them only once, to prevent skaters from performing the same move over and over again in the same program. Successful American skaters of the 1980s, who performed enough triple jumps to be competitive but were known more for well-rounded skating, include

Rosalynn Sumners (world champion in 1983 and Olympic silver medalist in 1984) and Jill Trenary (world champion in 1990).

In 1989, Midori Ito of Japan won the world championship with a free program that demonstrated all six of the possible triple jumps, including the first triple axel ever landed in competition by a woman. It was only a poor showing in the figures that kept her behind Trenary in 1990. Ito and Tonya Harding remain the only two women to have landed the triple axel in competition.

The elimination of figures in 1991 had the effect of favoring strong freeskaters and encouraging skaters, especially female skaters, to perform more and more triple jumps. Injuries and nerves kept Ito from taking full advantage of this change; she finished fourth at the 1991 world championships and second at the 1992 Olympic Games. The beneficiaries, taking the other top spots at these events, were Americans Kristi Yamaguchi, Tonya Harding (who also completed triple axels to win the 1991 United States championship and world silver medal), and Nancy Kerrigan. These three swept the medals in the 1991 world championships. Close behind was Surya Bonaly of France, who, like Yamaguchi and Kerrigan, had five triple jumps in her repertoire. Bonaly has attempted quadruple toe loops and salchows in competition, although never hitting them with clean enough landings to be officially recognized by the ISU.

As younger skaters, such as 1998 United States champion Michelle Kwan, and Tara Lipinski, 1997 United States and world champion, enter international competition, more and more of the top ladies are doing all five of the three-revolution jumps, so that just the ability to do a triple lutz is no longer enough to put a skater in reach of a medal. Triple jumps are needed, but so are strong edges and flow across the ice, good spins, intricate footwork, and good artistry and presentation skills.

Most rinks in the United States offer classes in basic skating technique and, depending on demand, in the various disciplines of figure skating. The classes operate under the auspices of either the ISI (an association of rink owners) or the USFSA's "Skate with US" program. The ISI programs are geared toward the recreational skater who may prefer group lessons and less stressful competitive formats throughout their skating careers. The USFSA classes do not go as far as higher-level skills, such as double jumps, but serve as a foundation in basic skills, after which a skater would be prepared to join a USFSA-affiliated skating club and prepare for more advanced tests and competitions.

Skaters aiming at the top competitive levels must devote large amounts of time and money to training. World-class skaters usually begin skating well before the age of 10, and one must spend several hours a day in practice with a private coach for many years before reaching the elite levels. Many recreational skaters, adults and children, enjoy participating in local competitions even without the prospect of reaching the elite competitive levels. Others prefer to measure their progress by testing without competing or simply by increasing their repertoire of skills. Depending on the skating culture in your area, there may be opportunities to join a precision team, participate in ice dance sessions or "dance weekends" with a social emphasis, or perform in a club or skating-school show. Club members, mostly the parents of young skaters, adult skaters, and former skaters, provide the volunteer labor necessary to organize and run local competitions, test sessions, shows, and other club activities. Judges and competition accountants are also volunteers, but most go through ongoing training to qualify for these positions. The national governing body of figure skating is U.S. Figure Skating Association, which can be contacted at 20 First St., Colorado Springs, Colorado 80906-3697, 719-635-5200. *EK*

Fit and Fat: An Idea Whose Time Has Come

The front-page newspaper photos of Lisa Fernandez jumping into the air to celebrate pitching the gold-medal softball game at the 1996 Olympic Games caused other women to jump into the air, too, and not just because United States women had won a gold medal in a sport that didn't require sequins. In their comments, Lisa and her teammates talked about how they were "just regular women who weighed between 90 and 200 pounds." There was a place on the gold medal team for all of them.

In a report about Fernandez a couple of years ago when she was having great success at UCLA, the reporter couldn't help but mention that she was a "big girl." Well, hooray for Lisa Fernandez and every other large female athlete who has decided to be healthy and strong and fit and not let the world's limited view about their size, or their readiness for the mantle of "fitness," interfere with their attaining even the highest sporting goal. With pixie gymnasts receiving most of the Olympic media attention, and given the concerns of sports writers and even the *New England Journal of Medicine* about the gymnasts' potential eating disorders, girls and women need role models like Lisa Fernandez more than ever.

Every woman has a great deal to gain from living an active life, and what she has to gain in well-being far outweighs any pounds she may lose. But the pressure on women to be thin is greater today than ever before. In virtually every women's magazine and every ad, waif models sport a "heroin chic" look, or they alternate with the "lean and aerobicized" look of 12-year-old boys. A student reviewed 40 recent copies of a popular women's magazine and found only 10 photos of large women, out of hundreds of photos. All 10 were pictures of women taken in the "before" body; before they had made changes to lose weight and to be deemed "successful."

Other than Rosie O'Donnell, there are virtually no large women in the public eye who are not trying to remake themselves with weight loss or plastic surgery. It is no wonder that women who do not meet the thin social ideal still struggle with their weight and self-esteem. It is no wonder that we have an ever-increasing epidemic of chronic dieting and eating disorders.

Add to this cultural soup the articles quoting obesity researchers in *Readers's Digest, Family Circle,* and other mainstream magazines that promote so-called new diet pills as a miracle for weight loss, and you have a serious problem on your hands. Weight loss clinics have sprung up on street corners all over America; a woman of any size who can produce the money can obtain a prescription for diet pills, despite the absence of long-term safety and efficacy data on these drugs. All of this cultural baggage has given even the most stalwart believer in size acceptance a moment's pause.

Despite all the cultural pressures against it, size acceptance is not a new concept. In 1988, in the first chapter of *Great Shape: The First Fitness Guide for Large Women,* Debby Burgard and I said the time for "Fat and Fit" had arrived. We were ahead of our time, but the principles of size acceptance are needed now more than ever.

Redefining the Issues: Healing vs. Curing

"Healing" means inspiring the will to live, in ourselves and others. For healing to occur, a trusting relationship has to be established within one's body, mind, spirit, and social surroundings. Learning to care for oneself, by learning to trust one's body and one's own experience, is a fundamental shift in view and can help people better take charge of their health. But that doesn't mean it's easy to make this shift, especially when it relates to fatness.

The truth is, there is no "cure" for obesity. Without even entering into the debate about whether people can be defined as "diseased" simply by the physical characteristic of body size, the fact is that safe, effective treatment to sustain significant weight loss (long-term) does not exist. While there is no doubt that people of all sizes could benefit from eating a high quality, nutritious diet,

this maxim does not mean that people who are already fat will be able to become thin by making these dietary changes. Research shows that once people are fat, they will likely remain so (Garner & Wooley, 1991; NIH, 1993; Leibel et al., 1995).

But people can become healthier, regardless of their size, and increasing physical activity is a primary way to do so. Eating well and exercising may result in a small amount of weight loss for some people, but this weight loss is a by-product of changes that must be maintained for the benefits to be maintained. The most significant predictor of long-term weight maintenance is exercise (Kayman, 1990). But unless dramatic change is undertaken (as television personality Oprah Winfrey has done) and sustained for life (which Winfrey is now having trouble doing), a dramatic change in weight is unlikely to be maintained. People whose genetics and dieting history predispose them to greater body weight can improve their overall health with moderate lifestyle change, but they will probably remain at a weight higher than the culture rewards. That is why self-acceptance and size acceptance are such critical parts of a new approach to health and weight.

Why Bother If I Don't Lose Weight?

This view is probably held by the majority of the 60 percent of inactive Americans. Until medical treatment and health education focus on reducing the stigma against fatness, few large people will feel welcome in the traditional "fit = thin" exercise arena. Without a shift away from weight loss as the purpose, people who are able to begin activity will continue to feel like failures or give up when they do not lose weight for their efforts. In the words of one woman, "I walked for an hour every day for a month and felt terrific. But my schedule changed and it became more difficult to fit walking in. Besides, I hadn't lost any weight, so I figured 'why bother.'"

Another woman sought help from a fitness program because she wanted to run a marathon. Her body fat was tested at 35 percent, and she was told to focus on reducing that percentage rather than her weight per se. She trained for six months and completed the marathon, running more than six hours to do so. When she returned to have her body fat tested, it had not changed at all. She was devastated. Although her trainer tried to convince her that she'd made incredible progress by just being able to do the run, it was too late. She'd counted on reducing her body fat and was inconsolable when she hadn't.

Many people have had experiences such as these. Some of these people have returned to a life of inactivity. If we are interested in improving health, we must help individuals of all sizes answer the "why bother" question in a way that will inspire them to continue being active for the inherent pleasure and the health benefits of exercise, even in the absence of weight or body fat reduction. We must focus on helping people see what they have to gain from a more active life, rather than on what they must lose to feel successful.

Making the Shift

A primary task in implementing the shift away from exercising only for the purpose of weight loss is reducing the social stigma against fatness, particularly as it affects people's willingness and ability to begin and stay with activity. In addition, we have to restore the attitude of play from childhood (when we ran outside to play because it was fun, not because it was "good for us") and stop promoting the no pain/no gain ethic that has so dominated the fitness industry. Reducing cultural barriers and promoting the inherent pleasure of activity have to become primary focuses in developing health programs for women. One such program is the Great Shape Program for Large Women at Kaiser Permanente in Northern California.

The Great Shape Program creates an environment that welcomes large women as they are, and allows them to obtain the health benefits of a more physically active life without increasing shame or guilt for failing to attain a smaller body size as a result

of their efforts. The participants reported many benefits, but perhaps the most telling statistic from the program so far is that 67 percent of the participants responding to the one-year follow-up survey had not dieted in the year following program completion. These results, and others, encourage continued effort and additional research to see if these strategies will improve women's health status long-term. It is very clear that large women need and deserve the compassion and respect offered in programs such as Great Shape.

Conclusion

The strongest resource we can encourage in people is the ability to respect themselves and believe in themselves regardless of their size. When we reduce the stigma against fatness, we reduce a primary barrier to participation in the healing power of sport and physical activity. When we acknowledge that differences in body size are strongly related to genetic heritage, we can affirm the right of all people to compassionate and respectful treatment by society and by health professionals.

In making playing fields and dance floors more accessible to the fattest woman, we make them more accessible to anyone who is embarrassed about weight or being out of shape. We need commitment, patience, and perseverance to make this happen. On the other hand, we often believe that it takes a long time and a great deal of investment of resources to help people shift attitudes. Instead, sometimes it can happen very quickly.

One woman came up after a two-hour introductory Great Shape session saying she'd come "wanting to do something about my weight before my son's wedding in three weeks." Everyone laughed knowingly; what can you really do about your weight in three weeks? She said she'd learned in the session to wear the beautiful dress she'd bought and to smile and dance at her son's wedding because she deserved to do so. That's really what size acceptance is all about: loving yourself and living a great life, regardless of your size. Now *that's* an idea that's long overdue. *PL*

References

Barlow, C., Kohl, H. Gibbons, L., and Blair, S. N. (1995). Physical fitness, mortality and obesity. *International Journal of Obesity, 4*, S41-S44.

Garner, D., & Wooley, S. (1991). Confronting the failure of behavioral and dietary treatments for obesity. *Clinical Physiology Reviews, 11*, 729-80.

Kayman, S., Bruvold, W., and Stern, J. S. (1990). Maintenance and relapse after weight loss in women; behavioral aspects. *American Journal of Clinicians, 52*, 800-07.

Leibel, R. L., Rosenbaum, M., and Hirsch, J. (1995). Changes in energy expenditure resulting from altered body weight. *New England Journal of Medicine, 332*, 621-28.

Lutter, J. M., and Jaffee, L. (1996). *The bodywise woman* (2nd ed.). Human Kinetics Press. (612) 641-1951.

Lyons, P. and Burgard, D. (1990). *Great Shape: The First Fitness Guide for Large Woman.* Bull Publishing. (800) 676- 2855.

NIH Technology Assessment Conference Panel. (1993). Methods for voluntary eight loss and control. *Annals of International Medicine, 119–21.*

Fitness and Women

Today it is taken for granted that the well-known benefits of a fit, healthy body apply to both sexes, but such was not always the case. For much of the nineteenth century, Victorian ideals of feminine beauty and passivity barred women from vigorous physical activity, at least among the upper classes (for slave and working-class women, "fitness" meant back-breaking labor in fields and factories). Victorian-era "ladies" were expected to stay indoors, cultivating frailty to the point of sickliness. Fainting was considered a sign of good breeding. Women's clothing—waist-cinching whalebone corsets; full, heavy, ankle-length skirts; high necks; and full sleeves—sent a clear message: Don't exert yourself!

Restricting women's physical activity was thought to be necessary to protect their supreme function, childbearing. Upper-class women were confined to the home for the entire nine months of pregnancy and expected to "recuperate" in bed for many months afterward. No physical activity was permitted during pregnancy, and activity was restricted even during the monthly menstrual period.

Things began to change in the 1870s and 1880s with the opening of women's colleges, most of which required physical education classes in sports such as archery, croquet, golf, gymnastics, rowing, swimming, and tennis. All activity, however, was performed in a restrained, "lady-like" manner that discouraged physical contact and exertion. In particular, competition, aggressiveness, and individual excellence were felt to be out of line with women's "innate" modesty.

In the early twentieth century, a number of events and historical strands combined to challenge the ideas that a lady should not sweat: (1) The suffragette movement empowered women politically, (2) the popularity of bicycling lent great visibility to physically active upper-class women, and (3) World War I drew women into factory jobs to support the war effort. Women's clothing and the ideal of female beauty changed radically in the 1920s. The "flapper," with her short skirts, daring ways, and boyish figure and hair style, idealized a fit, athletic female

Today women enjoy a wide variety of fitness activities.
Photo courtesy of Gini Alvord.

body. Women joined in both team and individual sports in record levels. In the 1932 Olympic Games in Los Angeles, California, Mildred "Babe" Didrikson set world records in track and field, a sport in which very few American women even dreamed of competing.

Many barriers remained along women's path toward equality with men in the sports and fitness realm. Didrikson, for example, was reviled for her "manliness," and until 1960, no woman was allowed to run distances longer than 200 meters in the Olympic Games. Although World War II brought even more women into construction and manufacturing jobs and into the armed forces, society took a step backward in the postwar years, when women were expected to stay home raising children and playing a supportive role to their breadwinning husbands.

In the 1960s a few talented African-American athletes, notably Wilma Rudolph and Willye White, encouraged girls and women to spread their wings in sports requiring strength and endurance. The work of women's sports advocates to give females equal opportunities in school-based sports led, in 1972, to the passage of Title IX, which prohibited discrimination on the basis of gender in federally funded educational programs, including sports. Although Title IX has been challenged over the years, its overwhelming effect has been to vastly increase the participation of girls and women in sports. According to the National Federation of State High School Associations, 2,310,315 high school girls played sports from 1993 to 1994, a 400 percent increase in 20 years.

Women's gains in fitness since the early 1970s have been phenomenal as well. The American running boom, ignited by Frank Shorter's marathon gold medal at the 1972 Olympic Games in West Germany, and propelled by the Avon running events staged by Kathrine Switzer, drew thousands of women into fitness running, right alongside men. Pioneer women runners faced some ridicule, a lack of appropriate clothing, and significant barriers to competitive equality.

(There was no Olympic marathon for women until 1984, no 10,000-meter contest until 1988, and no 5,000-meter event until 1996.) By and large, however, women were welcomed into the fitness-running movement, and indeed, have become leaders as organizers, officials, and race directors. More important, the reality of a woman running for health and fitness is now unquestioned.

Other fitness activities followed the lead of running. In the 1980s, women created the aerobic-fitness movement, comprising 80 to 90 percent of aerobics participants and instructors. Today, women get fit and stay fit in every way imaginable, from windsurfing to rock climbing to in-line skating. Role models abound in every pursuit. Women are celebrated for having muscles, for sweating, and for giving their all to fitness pursuits.

At the same time, study after study on women has shown that fitness extends life and reduces the risk of major, life-threatening diseases—heart disease, diabetes, perhaps even cancer. Research has shown that women can exercise safely throughout the menstrual cycle and during a healthy pregnancy. It seems unlikely that American society will ever return to the Victorian ideal of female "unfitness." The fit, powerful woman is here to stay. *GB*

See Also **Exercise and Health: A Physician's View**

Benita Fitzgerald

Benita Fitzgerald is a three-time Olympian who won a gold medal in the 100-meter hurdles at the 1984 Olympic Games in Los Angeles, California. She was named Hurdler of the Decade for the 1980s by *Track and Field News*. Born on July 6, 1961, in Dale City, Virginia, Fitzgerald has a street named after her in her hometown: "Benita Fitzgerald Drive."

Fitzgerald's involvement with sports did not stop when her hurdling career came to an end. She currently serves as the director of the United States Olympic Committee's training facility at Colorado Springs, Colorado. The Unified States Olympic Committee's training centers in Lake Placid, San Diego and Colorado Springs give America's athletes places to develop their athletic prowess.

Having graduated with a degree in industrial engineering, Fitzgerald believes that experience is helping her in the management and marketing aspects of her job. Her previous position was program director with the Atlanta Committee for the Olympic Games, helping national governing bodies, such as the United States Track and Field Association, market themselves. She also served as a member of the Women's Sports Foundation's Board of Trustees and was a president of that organization. She is often asked to give motivational lectures on such topics as relating hurdling to life's obstacles, motivating people to reach their dreams, and the 1996 Atlanta Centennial Olympic Games. Fitzgerald focuses steadily on the future, in which she will be helping other American athletes experience their own Olympic dreams.

Peggy Fleming

Peggy Gale Fleming (Jenkins) was born in San Jose, California, in 1948. One of America's finest figure skaters, she won the ladies' figure skating gold medal at the 1968 Winter Olympic Games in Grenoble, France. The ABC network televised the 1968 Winter Games live and in color for the first time, and the most enduring image of that coverage will always be of Fleming's freeskating program, as she performed in a light green outfit. That performance won her the gold medal by 88.2 points over her closest competitor—the only gold medal the United States brought home from Grenoble.

Fleming's childhood passions were baseball and tree climbing, which were soon replaced the first time she put on a pair of figure skates at the age of nine. Her memory of that first day on the ice is one of quiet, effortless movement. At that time, she did not know she would soon

shoulder much of the responsibility for keeping the sport of figure skating alive in the United States.

Fleming was 12 years old when her coach was killed, along with the entire United States Figure Skating Team, in a plane crash. The plane was en route to Prague and the world championships in 1961. With all her role models gone, it would be up to Fleming to create an image of style and grace that would lead her to five United States titles, three world titles, and an Olympic gold medal in 1968.

The Olympic image of Fleming fulfilling her dream, televised live by satellite in 1968, was the beginning of a long and mutually satisfying relationship between skating and television. After her victory at the 1968 world championships, she retired from competitive skating. Six months after the Olympic Games in Grenoble, Fleming would

Peggy Fleming.
Photo courtesy of the World Figure Skating Museum.

star in the first of five television specials that highlighted her skating talent. Her Sun Valley Special won two Emmy Awards. Her fourth special became the first joint production by Soviets and Americans, filmed entirely in the USSR in 1973.

Fleming has been invited to the White House by four different presidents, and in 1980, she was the first skater ever invited to perform there. At the 1986 unveiling of the refurbished Statue of Liberty, she was also asked to perform. Her 13 years as an on-air analyst for ABC Sports have taken her to both the Sarajevo and Calgary Olympic Games. She continues to provide commentary for both national and international skating competitions.

Peggy Fleming has always regarded her place in sports history as an honor, and from this perspective she has made her career choices. She was inducted into the World Figure Skating Hall of Fame in 1976. Today, her interests are focused on health issues as well as fitness. Because of this interest, she has served on several community project boards, such as the San Jose Sports Authority and as honorary chairperson for Easter Seals and the National Parent Teacher Association. She has also been honored by organizations such as Youth Sports for Understanding, the Girl Scouts, Special Olympic Games, and the Children's Miracle Network.

Fleming lives in the San Francisco Bay area, and she continues her role as a professional television commentator for ABC Sports.

Julie Foudy

Julie Foudy was the co-captain of the United States Women's Olympic Soccer Team that won the gold medal in the 1996 Olympic Games in Atlanta, Georgia. Foudy was born on January 23, 1971. Her home is in Mission Viejo, California, where she played high school soccer. While at Mission Viejo High School, she was named first-team All-American twice and was voted Player of the Year for Southern California for three straight years, from 1987 to 1989, as well as

being named the *Los Angeles Times'* Soccer Player of the Decade.

Foudy continued her brilliant play at Stanford University, where she collected a long list of awards and honors. She was voted Stanford's Freshman Athlete of the Year in 1989 and named the teams' Most Valuable Player for three consecutive years from 1989 to 1991. In 1991, she was named Soccer America Player of the Year, and the National Soccer Coaches Association of America elected her as an All-American four times. Foudy graduated from Stanford with a bachelor of science degree in biology, finishing her college career having scored 52 goals and 32 assists for a total of 136 points. In 1991 and 1992, she led the Stanford Cardinal to National Collegiate Athletic Association (NCAA) tournament berths.

Foudy played for the Tyreso Football Club in Sweden in 1994. It was her illustrious play with the United States National Women's Soccer Team, however, that brought her to national prominence. She made her first appearance on the United States team in 1988 when she was just 16 years old. As a member of the national team, she was instrumental in helping the team win the inaugural Federation Internationale de Football Association (FIFA) Women's World Championship in China, capture a silver medal at the 1993 World University Games, earn a third place finish at the 1995 world championships, and win the gold medal at the 1996 Atlanta Summer Olympic Games.

Fundraising and Women's Sport

Nonprofit fundraising, simply put, consists of a set of strategies that not-for-profit organizations employ to raise funds to financially support their work. Traditionally, women's sport programs were "nonprofit-based" activities, although, as we enter the twenty-first century, this seems to be changing to some degree. One strategy is to encourage corporations to take part in a "cause" (i.e., opening sport opportunities for girls and women), forming a cause-marketing partnership with the nonprofit organization.

Corporate sponsorships and partnerships take the form of money, in-kind contributions (e.g., shoe company donates athletic shoes), pro bono consulting, offering knowledge of other corporations that might help, or a combination of all the above.

More and more corporations are adding so-called 'cause-marketing' to their general marketing programs. Carol Cone, CEO of Cone Communications, cited why companies were engaging in cause-marketing in the August 26, 1996, issue of *Marketing News*. Some reasons included building deeper relationships with customers (93 percent), enhancing corporate image and reputation (89 percent), creating or maintaining a compelling corporate purpose (59 percent), and increasing sales (50 percent). As Cone said, "The fact that 90 percent of the executives reported being satisfied with their cause-marketing efforts shows that companies see the value of such marketing in helping them earn their customer's trust and their business."

Why do sports organizations have to raise money in the first place? In sport, at the least, it takes money to buy uniforms and equipment. It also takes money to travel to and from practice and competition. But where does this money come from? Who is doing nonprofit fundraising to foster the financial support and growth of sports for girls and women?

At the national level, several different groups are involved in nonprofit fundraising to support and grow sports programs for girls and women. A few of these groups are the United States Olympic Committee (USOC), Special Olympic Games International, and the Women's Sports Foundation.

The USOC oversees the national sports governing bodies and acknowledges several affiliated sports organizations in the United States. The USOC is a nonprofit organization that fundraises through direct mail, donations, and corporate sponsorships. One of the USOC's initiatives is to provide grants to its national sports governing bodies and affiliate sports organizations to develop and sustain the growth of sport programs for girls and women.

Special Olympic Games International provides sports training and competition in a variety of Olympic-type sports for individuals with mental retardation. It is a nonprofit organization and a charity that fundraises through direct mail, donations, and corporate sponsorships to support its Special Olympic Games athletes and programs nationally and globally. One of the Special Olympic Games International's current initiatives is to provide grants to the United States and other nations' Special Olympic Games programs in order to initiate, develop, and sustain team sport programs for girls and women with mental retardation.

The Women's Sports Foundation (WSF) is a nonprofit educational organization that is dedicated to promoting and enhancing the sports and fitness experience for all girls and women. The WSF fundraises through direct mail, donations, and corporate sponsorships to support its four program areas: education, opportunity, advocacy, and recognition. One of its major initiates is the Grants for Girls Sports (GFG) Program (for girls 9 to 14 years of age) as part of its National Grant Programs. Working with Tambrands Inc as its "partner", the WSF GFG program awards funds on a competitive basis to local groups which design and model girls sports programs for communities across the nation.

On the local level, girls and women's sports programs, in and out of schools, have traditionally held bake sales, candy sales, raffles, car washes, and the like to raise money for their own programs. While upgrading women's sports has been touted as "going beyond bake sales," fundraising remains a fact of life in almost all of sport. One new nonprofit fundraising opportunity involves telecommunications and the sale of prepaid phone cards. A nonprofit organization can earn up to 60 percent of the purchase price of the prepaid phone card on an initial sale. In addition, it can earn residuals from card renewals.

What are the steps in nonprofit fund–raising to financially support and expand girls and women's sports programs? The following list provides some basic guidelines:

1. Develop a resource team of people who are interested in the same goals or program and who have connections in the community. Create a fundraising plan together. Divide the responsibilities among team members to maximize resources and efforts.

2. Contact the appropriate organizations to see if your group is, or could be, eligible for monies through already existing grant programs.

   • If you are eligible, submit a proposal to qualify for such funds.
   • Identify the amount of the grant.
   • Identify what contingencies go along with receiving the funds.
   • Determine the length of time that the grant covers.
   • Determine if the grant can be extended or renewed.

3. Decide what fundraising opportunities best fit one's needs, interests, and efforts.

   • Research local corporations. Try to link with a corporation that has been, or may be, open and able to take part in cause-marketing in support of sports programs for girls and women.
   • Decide whether the fundraising efforts will be through one major activity or through a variety of smaller, similar, or diverse activities.
   • Research the use of prepaid phonecards as a viable opportunity for your efforts.

4. Consider potential obstacles and plan for them. We all know that not everything will be successful. Car washes may have to be postponed because of rainy weather. Some companies may not be open to cause-marketing in providing funds to support and grow girls and women's sports programs. But the "yes" will eventually be there.

5. Take action and keep a record of your efforts. Identify the what and the who of both the successful and the not-so-successful ventures. Use them as a guide for future plans and actions.

6. Follow up and thank others for their time and consideration. You never know when a previous "loss" may become a potential success. Also thank those that provide the needed funds for help. Efforts to retain those who have been supportive is just as important as the efforts to gain new support.

All strategies listed above are successful, only in varying degrees and within differing time frames. The challenge lies in developing a variety of strategies that fit the organization's needs and goals, in acknowledging the "no," and in raising enough money to move beyond the obstacles and to enable more girls and women to participate in sports. *RNN*

Fundraising Organizations

United States Olympic Committee
One Olympic Plaza
Colorado Springs, CO 80909-5670
Phone: 719-578-4622
Fax: 719-632-5352

Special Olympics International
1325 G Street, NW, Suite 500
Washington, DC 20005
Phone: 202-628-3630
Fax: 202-824-0200

Women's Sports Foundation
Eisenhower Park
East Meadow, NY 11554
Phone: 516-542-4700
Fax: 516-542-4716
E-mail: wosport@aol.com
Web: http://www.lifetimetv.com/wosport

G

Zina Garrison

Zina Garrison (Jackson) was born the youngest of seven children on November 16, 1963, in Houston, Texas. Having learned tennis in the public parks system in Houston, she earned the gold medal in doubles (with her partner Pam Shriver) and the bronze medal in singles at the 1988 Olympic Games in Seoul, South Korea. In 1989, she defeated tennis legend Chris Evert in the United States Open quarterfinals, Evert's final career match. In the 1990 Wimbledon tournament, she became the first African American woman to reach the finals of a Grand Slam (Wimbledon and the Australian, French, and United States Open) event since Althea Gibson won at Wimbledon in 1957 and 1958. After that 1990 Wimbledon appearance, Garrison signed three major advertising endorsements with manufactures of shoes, clothes, and tennis racquets. In 1993, she received the Tennis Educational Merit Award from the International Tennis Hall of Fame. Garrison turned professional in 1982, and in her career has won 14 professional singles titles and 20 professional doubles titles in major competitions.

Garrison's work extends far beyond the tennis courts. She has worked for charity groups to raise money, and she often makes appearances at schools to give motivational talks to young people. In 1988, she founded the Zina Garrison Foundation to provide funds and support for the homeless, youth organizations, anti-drug groups, and other charitable organizations. In the summer of 1992, she started the Zina Garrison All-Court Tennis Program to give inner-city youth the opportunity to build self-esteem and to learn about themselves through tennis. That same year, she received the first-ever *Family Circle* magazine Player Who Makes a Difference Award, with *Family Circle* and Hormel each donating $10,000 to the charities of her choice. Garrison also received the 1992 Sports Illustrated for Kids Good Sport Award. In 1990, she was named the national spokeswoman for the Young Woman's Christian Association (YWCA) tennis program. After she retires, she wants to open a homeless shelter and start junior tennis programs all across the state of Texas.

Gender Differences and Performance

Are there differences between a beautifully developed and conditioned female athlete and her male counterpart? Obviously there are morphological (structural), physiological, and psychological differences, as there are between any two individuals of the same gender. But are there differences between male and female athletes that are related solely to the fact that one is a female and one is a male?

The answer is yes, and these differences are related to the only function which, so far, cannot be reversed across men and women, and that is their role in the reproductive process. Since there are reproductive differences that cannot be ignored and that are related to the respective reproductive roles of males and females, are there jobs or societal roles that must be exclusively male and exclusively female? To ovulate is distinctly and exclusively female and to fertilize is distinctly and exclusively male. These biological functions ensure continuation of the species. However, no other roles, be they traditionally male or female, are beyond the capabilities of all men or all women.

With the understanding that all male-female differences, morphological and physiological, stem initially from the reproductive function, as modified by sociocultural influences, let us examine these differences and their implications for performance in athletics and in occupational tasks. We can then examine some societal issues of the 1990s which grow out of questions concerning gender and performance.

Differences

What are the morphological, or structural, differences?

On the average, adult men are 7 to 10 percent taller than women and weigh 15 to 20 percent more. On average, women have proportionately wider hips than men. Males have a greater body density than women at all ages, and consequently a lower percentage of their body weight is fat. The average percent of fat for adult males is 15 percent, while the average for females is 27 percent. This difference, of course, is a factor that is potentially affected by sociocultural considerations. For example, a social prohibition on athletic participation among women would tend to result in inactivity and higher fat values among women.

Forty-five percent of the weight of the average adult male is muscle; while for the female 36 percent of body weight is muscle. Distribution of the total muscle mass is gender related, with the male having proportionately more muscle mass in the upper body. The adult female also has a smaller body surface area than her male counterpart.

Center of mass (or center of gravity), which may be defined as the point of intersection of the various planes used to divide the body into equal weighted halves, is approximately 1 to 6 percent lower in women. This difference reflects the differential distribution of body weight in men and women, in which women carry proportionately more weight in the lower body. However, some researchers suggest that the center of gravity is determined more by the individual's height and body type than by gender.

Christine Wells (1991), a noted exercise physiologist, has presented some of the physiological gender differences and their relationships to exercise performance. The following is drawn from the body of her work.

On average, the adult female has a smaller total blood volume, 6 percent fewer red blood cells and 15 percent less hemoglobin than the adult male, and consequently, she has a lower total oxygen-carrying capacity. The adult female has a smaller heart volume and her heart weight to body weight ratio is 85 to 90 percent of the same ratio for the adult male. There is, however, less difference in heart volume between trained men and women than between untrained subjects, particularly when heart volume is expressed in milliliters per unit of body weight (e.g., milliliters per kilogram). Stroke volume, the amount of blood circulated in one contraction of the heart, is smaller in the female, resulting in a heart rate that is five to eight beats per minute higher than males at the same exercise intensity and cardiac output.

The female has approximately 30 percent lower maximum cardiac output than the male and a 40 to 60 percent lower maximal oxygen consumption expressed in liters per minute. This discrepancy is largely a reflection of the difference in body size between males and females. P. O. Astrand and E.H. Christensen's research (1964) showed that beyond age 12 or 13, male maximal oxygen consumption values exceed female values and remain higher throughout adult life. This difference is associated with the 10-fold increase in testosterone in pubescent males, which causes a large increase in muscle mass. When oxygen consumption is expressed per unit of body weight, the average difference between genders is reduced to 20 to 25 percent, and when expressed per unit of fat-free weight, the difference is further reduced to 15 percent. The adult female has a lower vital lung capacity (3,200 milliliters compared to 4,800 milliliters for men) and a lower maximum ventilatory volume.

Women have approximately 33 percent less total body strength than men, 40 to 60 percent less in the upper body and 25 percent less in the lower body. When strength is expressed relative to lean body mass (that portion of body weight distinct from fat weight), the difference is reduced and even eliminated in some muscle groups. J. H. Wilmore's research (1974) on male and female strength in specific muscle groups shows that 1) absolute strength is greater for males, 2) but normalizing for body weight and for lean body weight reduces the difference, with women actually having greater leg strength per unit of lean tissue, and 3) the greatest difference between men and women is in upper body muscle groups.

When strength differences between males and females are examined over the lifespan, a similar pattern to the maximum oxygen consumption pattern is seen, with the first strength differences showing up at ages 12 to 15 when male testosterone levels increase 10-fold. On the average, strength for females is 50 percent that of males and hand-grip strength of females is 45 percent that of males throughout adult life. Strength continues to increase in a women until she reaches 30 years of age, but peaks at age 25 for men.

As previously indicated, the morphological and physiological differences are based on average values from populations of adult males and adult females. It must be recognized, however, that there is overlap of the male and female distributions. For most variables, the distribution of the male and female populations overlap to the degree that some individuals in the female population fall above the mean for the male population. For many variables, the differences between two individuals of the same sex are greater than the differences between two individuals of the different sex. This phenomenon was recognized by researchers at least 50 years ago, but then seemed to get lost for some 30 years, only to resurface when attention was refocused on gender differences in the 1970s.

In 1942, Eleanor Metheny and associates (1942) compared 17 healthy women hygiene and physical education majors from Wellesley College to 30 nonathlete male subjects from a population being studied at the Harvard Fatigue Laboratory. Measurements were taken in response to moderate exercise of 15 minutes duration and to strenuous exercise to exhaustion. Metheny concluded that the means of data for all 17 women and 30 men prompt the generalization that the women as a group are the "weaker sex," being less fit for both the moderate and strenuous exertion. However, comparisons of the data for the 8 best women and the 10 poorest men indicates that this generalization may be made only about the average performance of the two groups. The responses of the 8 best women closely approximate those of the 10 poorest men. For the best half of the women and the poorest third of the men studied, the overlap is complete.

The overlap of distributions is also evident in Wilmore's research comparing maximal oxygen uptake (VO^{2}max) values for male and female athletes in various sports. While the male cross-country skiers, runners, and rowers in this study have higher VO^2 max than the female athletes of the same sports, the data show that females who train for endurance events have maximal values that are higher than males who do not train for such events.

In summary, some women are stronger than some men, and some women have larger hearts than some men, higher maximum cardiac outputs than some men, and higher maximum oxygen consumption values than some men. We must keep these facts in mind as we discuss performance in athletic events, in occupational tasks, and opportunities for improvement in performance.

Performance

Given the morphological and physiological differences between men and women, one would expect differences in performance, and we typically use athletic performance as objective measures of physical prowess. Research from the Nike Sport Research Laboratory (*Information please sports almanac*, 1989; Senior world championships, 1989) examined the percentage by which male performance was better than female performance based on world records as of October 1,1989, in running, jumping ,and freestyle swimming; and in world and national events in speed skating, rowing, and cycling from 1988 to 1990. The study showed that in absolute terms, male performances surpassed female performances.

But things are changing. Improvement data from Hult (1989) and the Sports Almanac (1989) show greater improvement by women in most events when 1990 performance is compared to the year of first performance of the event. Analysis of improvement data shows that only in the 1,500-meter run, 400-meter swim, and 100-meter swim has improvement been greater for men. In all other areas, improvement has been better for women. For example, Florence Griffith Joyner's 1988 record in the track 200-meter race reduced the difference between male and female performance in that event to 7.59 percent. To what can we attribute the greater improvement in the performance of women in athletic events? Part of the percentage gains in performance may be due to the ceiling effect for men. The ceiling effect refers to the fact that once a high level of performance has been achieved by an individual or group, it is more difficult to improve, and improvement mea-

sured as a percentage of previous best performance tends to decrease.

Cultural acceptability for women athletes and opportunity for women in sport, however, have provided the greatest impetus for the improvement of women's sport performance. Title IX of the educational amendments of 1972 to Public Law 92-318 mandated equality in educational programs receiving federal financial assistance and opened the door of opportunity for women. In the academic year 1971-1972, 77 high schools provided cross-country teams for young women. In 1981-1982, the number was 7,475, a 100-fold increase. During the same time period, the number of high school track and field teams for young women increased from 2,992 to 13,925, a number which was comparable to that for young men. At the college level, the number of women's track and field teams increased from 95 to almost 500 during the same decade. These new opportunities for participating, with improved equipment, facilities, and improved training methods, resulted in the fulfillment of athletic potential for a great number of women for whom the opportunities did not exist prior to 1972.

The record is clear that improved performance follows greater opportunity. In the years from 1973 to 1982 (post-Title IX), American women broke 31 United States national records in running distances between 1,500 meters and the marathon. American men broke 15 national records in this area in the same period.

If opportunity and quality of performance are so inextricably related in athletic events, then why not in occupational tasks? Of over 243,000 career fire fighters nationwide, why in 1990, were only 200 women? Why were only 2.1 percent of the nation's construction workers women (scarcely higher than the proportion in the late 1970s when feminists and federal regulators set ambitious goals to help women get good paying jobs in the construction trades)?

One reason for the gap in male and female hiring for good paying jobs that seem to require a substantial amount of physical prowess is, of course, discriminatory hiring practices. These discriminatory practices have persisted in spite of court rulings such as *Griggs v. Duke Power Company* (1971) in which the United States Supreme Court ruled that a business could set requirements for hiring and promoting certain workers if it could prove a clear business necessity.

Under the *Griggs v. Duke Power* decision, a company had to prove that its survival depended on being able to hire certain types of workers. If it could make the case, a company could hire, for example, only tall, muscular workers because the job routinely involved lifting heavy objects.

The burden for proving the necessity of such hiring clearly rested with the company. But in 1989, the conservative U.S. Supreme Court effectively overturned the Griggs standard. In its ruling in *Wards Cove Packing Company v. Atonio*, the Court made it more difficult for a worker to prove that he or she had been discriminated against by an employer. In that decision, the court shifted the burden of proving discrimination to the worker, and a company no longer had to prove that its business survival depends on being able to hire only certain types of workers.

A second reason for the gender hiring gap is physical performance testing standards, which have had an adverse impact on the hiring of women. The experience of the Los Angeles Fire Department, however, indicates that it is not necessary to lower standards to narrow the gap, but rather to provide the opportunity for women to train to meet the standards. Fourteen of 15 women who initially failed the Los Angeles Fire Department's physical performance test, passed it after completing task-specific training programs. Given this experience, one might ask, can we afford to invest the resources required to raise the level of performance of women applicants to required standards? When one considers the number of single-parent families headed by women and the cost of entitlement pro-

grams, the more appropriate question might be, can we afford *not* to invest these resources? Furthermore, the issue is more than just an economic one. It is an issue of maximization of human potential.

It is not likely that female athletic performance or physical prowess in occupational tasks can be raised to the level of males, but we can certainly expect the degree of overlap to increase. It is also unlikely that the time will come when men and women will be competing against each other on a large scale in the athletic arena, but it is right and moral to provide the opportunity for all people to be all that they can and want to be.

How far have women come in gaining the opportunities to perform in what have been thought to be traditionally male jobs? The gender barrier has been broken in admitting women to the service academies. The barrier has been broken in firefighting, police work, and the construction trades. Astronaut Sally Ride has been in space, Eileen Collins recently became the first woman pilot of the space shuttle, and Shannon Lucid has set records for time in space. Geraldine Ferraro has run for vice president on a national ticket, and the numbers of women in Congress have increased, although the perception of women as national political leaders has not taken hold in the United States. Women have been involved in combat action with the military in Panama and the Persian Gulf, and most women Army officers polled believe that women should have the right to assume combat roles if they choose. Progress in the military realm continues, although at slower pace than many would like. Recently, an Army project was completed involving 40 civilian women volunteers who trained for six months at the U.S. Army Research Institute of Environmental Medicine, Natick, Massachusetts. After participating in a program to increase their strength to perform heavy military tasks typically assigned to men, 75 percent of the women qualified for the "very heavy" job classification after training (Hult, 1989).

When we assess how well women have done in male-dominated occupations requiring a substantial amount of physical prowess, the record shows that they have performed admirably. Of course, the ability to think, reason, and be creative may reduce the reliance on physical prowess alone in many of these situations. For example, in 1994 an all-female crew competed in the male-dominated America's Cup sailing races. Although the average strength of the male crews exceeded the average strength of the women's crew, they managed to defeat the all-male crew, skippered by America's Cup Veteran captain Dennis Connor, twice in the Defenders Challenge series. The successes of the all-female crew support the contention that, on at least two occasions, the strength of the women's crew was enough for the task. The point is that women do not have to be as strong as men to accomplish the task; they just need to be strong enough to do the job. Beyond that, competitive performance often depends on nonphysical parameters, like skill, intelligence, and creativity.

The change credited to the women's movement, like all change, is difficult and disruptive. But is this difficulty any reason to stop the movement toward equal opportunity for women to be all that they can be and want to be, and to invest economically, socially, spiritually, and emotionally in the effort? The answer is no, of course not. We must simply find new ways to cope with and to accommodate women's progress. *AMP*

References

Astrand, P.O., and Christensen, E.H. (1964) "Aerobic work capacity," In F. Kickens, E. Neil, and W.F. Widdas (eds.), *Oxygen in the animal organism*, New York: Pergamon Press, p. 295.

Hammel, S. (1996) Basic training experiment tests: How strong a woman can really get. *SHAPE*, Oct., 69–71, 138–40.

Hult, J.S. (1989) In *Female Endurance Athletes*, Champaigne, IL: Human Kinetics Publishers, Inc. pp. 1–3.

Information Please Sports Almanac. (1989) Boston, MA: Houghton Mifflin Co., pp. 446–76.

Metheny, E.L., Brouha, L., Johnson, R.E., and Forbes, W.H. (1942). Some physiologic responses of women and men to moderate and strenuous exercise: A comparative study. *Am. J. Physiol. 137*: 318.

Senior world championships. (1989) *American Rowing*. 25–27.

Wells, C.L. (1991) *Women, sport, and performance: A physiological perspective*, 2nd ed. Champaigne, IL: Human Kinetics Publishers Inc., pp. 19–34.

Wilmore, J.H. (1974) Alterations in strength, body composition, and anthropometric measurements consequent to 10-week weight training program. *Medicine and Science in Sports & Exercise. 6*: 133–38.

Gender Stereotypical Play: Consider the Consequences

A cross culturally observed phenomenon associated with children's play is that increasingly, from early through middle childhood, same-sex playmates are preferred. Developmentalists explain this preference variously, but a popular hypothesis is that this phenomenon results from the ways children form their gender identity and from their concurrent and subsequent socialization into stereotypical gender roles. This socialization from the gender-based blue or pink color coding of newborns and their sex-differentiated handling by adults to their continued socialization by the media, parents, peers, and teachers. These messages push children into gender-stereotypical roles with associated rewards and punishments for compliance or violation. Children thus, form their gender identity based on the gender roles that their culture assigns to their biological sex. Childhood gender role prescriptions regulate play styles as well as activity and toy preferences, factors that directly contribute to sex-segregated, gender-stereotypical play.

If this is such a universal phenomenon, why are some concerned that children play in same-sex groups and play in gender-stereotypical ways? Because play of this sort produces outcomes that differ by sex, resulting in unequal benefits. Since research confirms that play contributes to development, the outcomes, or consequences, of the play behavior are far-reaching. Parents and educators in the United States and other countries (e.g., Italy, Japan, Taiwan), value the contribution play can make to the intellectual, creative, social, and/or physical development of children. Yet, despite the near universal recognition of the value of play, gender-based play roles continue to be the norm.

The outcomes of play can be logically categorized as occurring in three domains: cognitive (in thought), affective (in emotions), and psychomotor (in bodily movement). One frequently cited cognitive outcome of gender-stereotypical play is that boys' historically heavy participation in ball game sports helps develop their visuospatial skills. These skills are believed to contribute to better performances in mathematics, statistics, and physics; thus, the traditional play of males gives them advantages in some measures of academic performance, as well as in related career opportunities.

In the affective domain, sociologists and developmentalists have discovered contrasts in stereotypical boy and girl play which result in socialization and social skill differences that also impact future roles and career success. For example, compared to girls play patterns, studies show that boys more often tend to play outdoors, farther from home, and in larger, same age groups. Boys play also tends to be more competitive and complex, having explicit goals and rules, and is engaged in for longer periods of time. Girls, on the other hand, generally engage in less physically active play, characterized by cooperation, turn-taking, smaller numbers of players, and loose, fluid structures.

The social skills that boys' play develops include independence but also the ability to function interdependently; interpersonal skills and adaptability; and the ability to comply with rules, resolve conflicts, and play different roles within complex, hierarchical, and authoritarian social structures. By contrast, the stereotypical play of girls is conducive to the development of socio-emotional skills, sensitivity to and nurturance of others, self-expression, and cooperative behavior. This differential socialization of males and females through play is thought to predispose them toward success in different adult roles. The skills typically developed by males through play prepare them for adaptability and success in the complex, interpersonal world of business and industry where historically the management model has been authoritarian and hierarchical. Girls, through their play and gender-role stereotyping, are better prepared for working cooperatively; for serving others, especially on a one-to-one or small group basis; and for self-expression through communication and creativity.

When considering whether males or females are better off by virtue of their socialization through play, it should be noted that in forecasting for the 1990s and beyond, futurists predict a business/industry leadership model of cooperation and a management trend away from hierarchies to networking. They believe that in terms of business leadership, males are no longer advantaged by their socialization. Indeed, while females may appear to have some advantage if this holds true, it can be argued that each sex would benefit by the development of certain abilities typically resulting from the play of the opposite, regardless of future developments in business and industry.

From the standpoint of the psychomotor domain, that area pertaining directly to sport, few sex differences have been noted in the motor performance of preschool children and only slight differences are evident in childhood. In mid-adolescence, however, the time by which frequent, vigorous play, and goal-directed practice of motor skills should lead to increasingly higher levels of skill performance, as is true for males, girls' performance reaches a plateau or even regresses. Most motor developmentalists believe that the contrasting sport socialization of males and females, the resultant play/practice differences, the gender-biased wish fulfillment seeking, the related motivation attempts, and the sport skill competency notions of parents lead to this performance differential. Research of the late 1980s and the 1990s has added empirical support to the notion that sex differences in performance of a perceptual-motor task are negated when prior experience with open-task sports and video-games is taken into account. In other words, girls' motor skills develop just as well as boys' when they have the same play experiences. When gender-role adherence and stereotypical play have limited sport skill experience, females are clearly disadvantaged in their motor development and therefore limited in sport opportunities. *BM*

See Also **Socialization Influences: Girls and Women in Sport; Teacher Influences on Girls' Play**

References

Beitel, P. A., and Kuhlman, J. S. (1992). Relationships among age, sex, and depth of sport experience with initial open-task performance by 4- to 10-year-old children. *Perceptual and Motor Skills, 74,* 387-96.

Geadelmann, P. L. (1985). Sex equity in physical education and athletics. In S. S. Klein (ed.), *Handbook for achieving sex equity through education* (pp. 319-37). Baltimore, MD: John Hopkins University Press.

Maccoby, E. E. (1988). Gender as a social category. *Developmental Psychology, 24,* 755-65.

———. (1987). Gender segregation in childhood. In H.W. Reese (ed.), *Advances in child development and behavior* (Vol. 20, pp. 239-87). Orlando, FL: Academic Press.

Mead, B. J., and Ignico, A. A. (1992). Children's gender-typed perceptions of physical activity: Consequences and implications. *Perceptual and Motor Skills, 75,* 1035-42.

Roopnarine, J. L., Johnson, J. E., and Hooper, F. H. (eds.). (1994). *Children's play in diverse cultures.* Albany, NY: State University of New York Press.

Gender Verification

In the 1930s, many male sport leaders involved in women's athletic events felt that women who excelled in athletics were risking their femininity, their attractiveness to men, their childbearing abilities, and their heterosexuality. In fact, some held the belief that women who performed well in athletics were not women at all but were genetically males and that "normal" women could not perform to the standards set by many outstanding female athletes. Gender verification, which refers to the practice of testing women to validate their biological sex, began in this time. This practice is exclusively used with women to ensure that no male competes in women's events, which would, it is believed, result in unfair competition in those events.

In 1960, the International Amateur Athletics Federation (IAAF) began to assess female athletes for gender verification to determine their eligibility to participate in IAAF events. Physical examinations were the initial means by which gender was verified. This was replaced by buccal smears (a scraping from inside the cheek) to determine the chromosome makeup of each female athlete, a practice still used today by the International Olympic Committee (IOC). In 1967, the IOC instituted mandatory testing of female athletes for the 1968 Mexico Olympics. There were several problems with the buccal approach, including false positives (testing as male due to poor laboratory methods). Another complicating factor is a congenital chromosomal condition which leads to a false positive (and disqualification). These conditions are, in fact, anomalies creating no athletic advantage for the female competitor. Having to participate in such testing was (and still is) uncomfortable for female athletes, particularly if the results—whether a false positive or a chromosomal anomaly—challenge their biological sex for reasons that have nothing to do with athletic performance. Chromosome testing excluded other important issues, such as the levels of estrogen and testosterone and other hormones as well as the psychosocial experiences of a female athlete.

Since an official observes the voiding (urine samples) of each athlete for drug screening, the IAAF determined that male/female distinctions could be made by the official and discontinued the buccal smears for gender verification in 1992. A growing consensus among the women's sport medicine community is that gender verification is not necessary. The IOC still maintains the practice, and "a valid certificate of femininity is issued" (http://www.olympic.org/medical/emedch3.html) by the IOC for every female athlete who passes the screening. Some measure of protection is provided to the athlete since the results are not made public.

The only verifiable incident of a male passing as a female was in the 1936 Olympics in Berlin, Germany, and it was not revealed until 1957. Hermann Ratjent, a German, stated that he was ordered by the Nazi Party to pose as a woman athlete to compete in the 1936 Olympics (Cahn, 1994). *RLH*

References

Cahn, S.K. (1994). *Coming on strong: Gender and sexuality in twentieth-century women's sport.* Cambridge, MA: Harvard University Press.

http://www.olympic.org/medical/emedch3.html (October 29, 1997)

Althea Gibson

Althea Gibson, an African American tennis player and golfer, was born on August 25, 1927, in Silver, South Carolina. She is best known as the winner of two Wimbledon singles titles, two United States Open titles, and one French Open title. In doubles, she won the 1956 French Open women's title with Angela Buxton, the 1957 United States Open mixed title with Kurt Nielsen, and the 1957 Australian Open women's title with S. Fry. Gibson has won at least one championship in each of the four Grand Slam events: the Australian Open, the French Open, Wimbledon, and the United States Open.

At the age of three, Gibson was sent to New York City by her parents, Daniel and Annie Gibson, to live with her Aunt Sally. Gibson grew up in Harlem, and was given a tennis racquet by a recreation director named Buddy Walker at age 13. Walker told her to go take tennis lessons from the legendary, one-armed coach Fred Johnson. The Cosmopolitan Tennis Club, where Johnson coached, was so impressed with her ability, they asked Gibson to become an honorary member. After finishing high school, she received a tennis and basketball scholarship from the Florida Agricultural and Mechanical University, a historically Black college.

Gibson first made her presence known in the tennis world through the American Tennis Association (ATA). Founded in 1916, the ATA was the African American counterpart to the all-White United States Tennis Association (USTA). At the age of 15, Gibson won the singles event in the New York State "Black Girls' Tennis Championships." She won the ATA Women's singles title every year from 1947 to 1956. Despite her success in the ATA, Gibson was not allowed to play in many USTA events and had to rely on the African American community to support her career financially because she was only approached by two companies about endorsing products. Boxer Sugar Ray Robinson and his wife helped pay for her travel to tournaments. Other people who helped her career are R.W. Johnson, a North Carolina doctor who gave Gibson a place to live as she attended a local high school, and Hubert Eaton, another doctor who coached her in the 1940s.

In 1950, Gibson walked onto the courts at the United States Open with tennis legend Alice Marble to become the first African American to play at Forest Hills. Alice Marble had played a key role in this drama by writing a guest editorial in a tennis magazine condemning the exclusion of players based on race, but it was Althea Gibson who paved the way for so many athletes and African Americans to achieve

Althea Gibson.
Photo courtesy of the International Tennis Hall of Fame.

great success, as she carried tennis out of segregation.

In 1957, Gibson was named Woman Athlete of the Year by the Associated Press because of her singles wins at the All-England Championships at Wimbledon, at the United States Women's Clay Court Championships, and at the United States Open. Gibson was an aggressive player who charged the net and reached for impossible shots, acquiring a serve-and-volley style of play that is often found in today's professional tennis competition.

After retiring from amateur competition (the Grand Slam events were not professional events until the 1970s), Gibson played professional exhibition tennis during 1959 and 1960 before Harlem Globetrotter basketball games, making approximately $100,000. In 1960, she decided to learn another "country club" sport. After Gibson qualified for the Ladies Professional Golf Association (LPGA) Tour, she played from 1963 to 1977, making a small sum of money. Again she broke new ground as the first African American member of the LPGA, often being the first African American woman to compete at many country clubs. She opened the doors for many women, regardless of color, to be accepted as strong athletic competitors.

Althea Gibson eventually became the athletic commissioner for the state of New Jersey. She was also a community-relations liaison for the city of Orange, New Jersey. She was named to the National Tennis Hall of Fame in 1971.

Girl Scouts of the United States of America

Girl Scouts of the United States of America (GSUSA) is building on its partnerships in the National Girls and Women in Sports Day (NGWSD). In 1996, the organization launched its first nationally based sports initiative for members called "Girls and Sports = A Winning Team." This national sport project aims to teach sport skills, promote fair play and teamwork, foster leadership skills, develop health and fitness ideals and behaviors, and educate both girls and women on how to combine sports into lifelong fitness activities.

Of the organization's 331 councils, 17 were chosen to participate in the pilot project that allowed girls to plan and implement a variety of sports programs. Girls developed their skills in either tennis, softball, golf, swimming, soccer, volleyball, or basketball. On the basis of the pilot, GSUSA will develop resources for girls, leaders, and councils to make the project available nationwide in late 1997.

Girl Scouts membership is open to girls ages five to 17 years or to those who are in kindergarten through grade 12. Members must follow the Girl Scout Promise and Law that includes serving her God and her country, having self-respect, and showing respect to others. GSUSA is the largest voluntary organization for girls in the world. It has approximately 3.5 million members, including 2,613,000 girls and 827,000 adult female and male volunteers.

GSUSA was founded March 21, 1912, in Savannah, Georgia, by a skilled painter and sculptor named Juliette Gordon Lowe. Lowe brought together 18 girls to form the first two "American Girl Guide" troops, modeled after the Girl Guides in England. In 1913, the name Girl Guides was changed to Girl Scouts. (It is still called Girl Guides in England.) Lowe introduced girls to the outdoors and gave them the chance to learn about nature and how to be confident and inventive. Lowe invited girls of all ethnicities to look behind traditional homemaking roles for professional careers in the arts, sciences, and business and at roles as leading citizens. Eighty-five years later, sport has become another means for Girl Scouts to achieve their goals, make new friends, and develop leadership skills in a positive and nurturing atmosphere.

In addition to "Girls and Sports = A Winning Team," GSUSA publishes literature on general health and fitness including: *Developing Health and Fitness: Be Your Best!*, which discusses nutrition, physical exercise, stress reduction, avoidance of harmful substances, good grooming/personal hygiene, and environmental health; and *Girls Scouts, Be Your Best!*, a colorful poster that illustrates the path to health and fitness. Furthermore, GSUSA offers the *Be Your Best* video, a 32-minute health and fitness video for girls ages nine to 17 years, hosted by Olympic swimmer Janet Evans. GSUSA also challenges players eight years and up to reach the "Good Health Zone" in the board game *Highway to Health*.

For more information about Girl Scouting and GSUSA resources, contact Girl Scouts of the United States of America, 420 Fifth Avenue, New York, NY 10018-2702 or call 212-852-8000 or fax 212-852-6509. *ANW*

See also **National Girls and Women in Sports Day.**

Girls Incorporated

Girls Incorporated is a national nonprofit organization dedicated to helping girls ages six to 18 years become strong, smart, and responsible women. Girls Inc. has 136 affiliates in 35 states and serves 350,000 young people in over 900 local sites across the United States. To build upon its partnership in the National Girls and Women in Sports Day (NGWSD), Girls Inc. created the three-part "Sporting Chance" series to teach girls about competition, cooperation, risk taking, and teamwork.

"Steppingstones," the first program in the series, concentrates on motor-skill development. Girls ages six to eight engage in running, jumping, leaping, twisting, bending, and balancing. They learn to move confidently, to become familiar with physical activity, and to understand that sports are for everyone.

"Bridges," the next program, teaches nine to 11 year old girls about organized sports and educational and career opportunities in sports. Girls Inc. focuses on four team sports while continuing motor-skill activities: soft-

ball (throwing, catching, and hitting), soccer (kicking and agility), basketball (shooting and teamwork), and tennis (striking and individual ability).

"Sports Unlimited" is the final part of the series. Girls ages 12 to 14 explore all individual and team sports. They visit community athletic facilities for instruction and participation. They develop an understanding about their own skill levels, the physical and emotional benefits of different sports, the importance of nutrition, and how they can pursue their own sports and fitness goals.

In addition to "Sporting Chance," Girls Inc. created a "Sports Resource Kit" for anyone interested in organizing local sports programs for girls. The kit includes a *Sports Resource Guide*; *On Your Mark: A Complete Guide to Developing Sports Programs for Girls*; *Ten Principles of Girls' Sports Participation*; *Sports Beyond Winning*, a video promoting sports involvement to teenaged girls; and more. The kit costs $45.00.

For further information about Girls Incorporated programs and resources, contact Girls Incorporated, 30 East 33rd Street, New York, NY 10016-5394 or call 212-689-3700, fax 212-683-1253, or email HN3578Ahandsnet.org. *ANW*

See also **National Girls and Women in Sports Day.**

Goal-Setting and Women

Sport psychologists have found that the way in which people define, or measure, success influences the types of goals that are set and the perceived purpose of the activity. Achievement motivation theory (attempting to explain why individuals behave as they do in performance settings) divides individual goal orientations into two broad categories: Task-oriented and ego-oriented. Task-oriented individuals set goals about improving their performance based on past accomplishments. They use a self-referenced standard to measure the success of a performance. They perceive the purpose of sports as an opportunity to improve self. Ego-oriented individuals use an other-based-referenced standard. They set goals primarily based on winning and defeating others in the process. A successful performance is defined by how it ranks with the competition. Sport is seen by these individuals as a way to advance the social status of the individual or team.

Research in this area by Duda, White, Kohler, and others has revealed that female athletes tend to participate in athletics for task-oriented reasons while males often have more ego-oriented goals. Women set goals primarily about improving performance levels. Research also suggests that female athletes tend to define success as meeting goals of skill mastery and increased effort levels. They see the purpose of sport as improving one's character, self-esteem, and ability to work well with others, and as being part of an active lifestyle.

While female athletes are generally more task-oriented, male athletes are more likely to be motivated by ego-oriented goals. Men primarily set goals regarding the win/loss record. Success is determined by beating the competition. Therefore, the purpose of sport, in the eyes of ego-oriented athletes, is to achieve a high status through defeating or overcoming challenging competition.

Athletes who are ego-oriented do not face the challenges that task-oriented athletes face in an athletic realm traditionally dominated by the ego-oriented ethic. While the lower levels of sport encourage athletes to have fun playing, the higher levels of competition foster ego-oriented goals where the focus is on winning. Although task-orientation is more strongly related to higher confidence levels and more enjoyable experiences than ego-orientation, coaches often, unintentionally, discourage the task-orientation. As a result, many female athletes experience a decrease in performance levels, self-esteem, and satisfaction as their athletic careers progress to more elite level competition.

Coaches need to understand how female task-oriented athletes differ from ego-oriented males in how they set goals, define success, and view the purpose of sports. By understanding that one's gender and com-

petitive level influence goal orientation, coaches can work more effectively with their athletes to develop a more enjoyable athletic program in which everyone can feel successful. *SAK*

Diana Golden

Born on March 20, 1963, in Cambridge, Massachusetts, Diana Golden was an avid skier as a child. One night in 1975, when she was just 12 years old, Golden's leg collapsed beneath her. The diagnosis was bone cancer. A short time later, doctors told her that her right leg would have to be amputated. Despite this crushing setback, she went on to dominate the sport of disabled skiing, skiing on standard poles and thrilling fans with 65-mile-per-hour downhill runs and winning nearly every competition.

Golden won a gold medal in disabled skiing in the 1988 Winter Olympic Games. She has also won 29 national and international disabled skiing competitions. In 1991, she was the recipient of the Women's Sports Foundation's prestigious Flo Hyman Award given to the year's outstanding athlete. She also won the 1986 United States Ski Writers' Association's Outstanding Competitor

Diana Golden.

Award. The United States Olympic Committee (USOC) chose Golden as the United States Female Skier of the Year.

Today, retired from ski racing, Golden often gives speeches to various audiences about facing fears and overcoming obstacles. Her spectacular successes, on and off the ski slopes, have earned her a well-deserved place in sports history and the admiration of fans around the world.

Golf and Women

It is said that the world's first known woman golfer was Mary, Queen of Scots. The first women's golf organization, the Ladies Golf Union, was formed in England in 1893.

In the game of golf, the player hits a small, hard ball toward a target hole using a variety of metal-bladed or wooden-bladed sticks, called clubs. Players compete either individually, in pairs, or in teams. A standard golf course has 18 different holes. The object of the game is to get the ball into each hole with the fewest number of strokes. Men and women play the same rules, although many women may play from shorter tee distances (the smooth, level area from which a player makes the first stroke).

The Illustrated History of Women's Golf (Glenn, 1991) notes that the first golf course designated for women only was built in 1892 at Shinnacock Hills, New Jersey. In 1893, the Morris County Golf Club in New Jersey was the first all-women's club. The first United States Women's Amateur Championship was held in 1895 and featured 11 contestants. Beatrix Hoyt was the first American woman golf star, winning three consecutive national championships from 1896 to 1898.

In the early years of women's golf, there seemed to have been an intrinsic appeal and rivalry between England and the United States. An informal "America vs. England" competition was played in England in 1905. Two American sisters, Margaret and Harriet Curtis, were influential in the increasing formalization of this rivalry, which in 1932 finally culminated in the "Curtis Cup," a team competition between American and

Golf is now enjoyed by women of all ages and backgrounds.
Photo courtesy of Gini Alvord.

European women golfers. Glenna Collett Vare was another early pioneer in women's golf, winning her first national championship in 1922 at 19 years of age. Her record in the United States Women's Amateur was remarkable, as she won in 1922, 1925, 1928, 1929, 1930, and 1935. In 1953 the LPGA created the Vare trophy in her honor. The award is given annually to the woman with the lowest score on the tour.

Two of the greatest players in the era from 1930 to 1950 were also influential in the beginnings and growth of the Ladies Professional Golf Association (LPGA)—Patty Berg and Babe Didrikson Zaharias. Patty Berg's career spanned generations of players. In 1935, as a teen, Berg was beaten in the final of the United States Women's Amateur by Glenna Collett Vare. As an amateur, Berg won 29 tournaments, and she was the Associated Press's "Woman Athlete of the Year" in 1938.

Babe Didrikson Zaharias.
Photo courtesy of the Babe Didrikson Zaharias Museum.

Babe Didrikson Zaharias, a one-woman track team and storied athlete in many disciplines, was an amazing golfer. She won her first golf championship, the Women's Texas Golf Association Championship, in 1935. Her career was interrupted for several years when she lost her amateur status. After regaining her amateur status, Zaharias won 13 straight tournaments in 1946 and 1947 before officially becoming a professional in 1947. In 1950, Babe Didrikson Zaharias won five of 11 LPGA tournaments, and in 1951, she won seven of 16 tournaments. Though she suffered through cancer treatment and a colostomy in 1953, she returned to play and won the United States Women's Open in 1954.

The LPGA was born in 1949. Along with Didrikson Zaharias and Berg, 11 other women founded the tour. Other consistent winners were Louise Suggs, Betsy Rawls, and Betty Jameson. By 1954, the United States Golf Association assumed sponsorship of the United States Women's Open, which made a strong statement about the credibility of the founding women's efforts. In 1975, Betsy Rawls became the LPGA's first paid tournament director and for years headed a premier

event of the men's and women's tours, the McDonald's Championships.

Another notable event in the history of women's golfing heritage is the 1956 tee-off of Ann Gregory, the first African American woman to play in the United States Women's Amateur Championship, held in Indianapolis. Other outstanding African American women players were Eoline Thornton, Renee Powell, and Althea Gibson. Ms. Gregory continued to play the game throughout her life and her last competitive appearance was in the 1988 Senior Women's Amateur Championships.

The great stars like Berg and Didrikson Zaharias were succeeded by another generation of equally impressive golfers. Kathy Whitworth was named Player of the Year seven times, was the leading money winner eight times, and was elected president of the LPGA three times before 1980. Another entry in golf's great women's tradition is Mickey Wright. She was the only woman to have held four major titles at one time. She won United States Open titles in 1958, 1959, 1961, and 1964. She won the LPGA four times, the Titleholder's twice, and the Western Women's Open three times. Her two consecutive rounds of 62 remained an LPGA record for more than 25 years. The main tournaments (Grand Slams) in Women's Golf today include the *U.S. Open Championship* (1946–), the *LPGA Championship* (1955), *The Nabisco-Dinah Shore Winners Circle* (1972–), and the *du Maurier Classic* (1973–).

Reference

Glenn, R. (1991). *The illustrated history of women's golf.* Dallas, TX: Taylor.

Christine Grant

Christine Grant, born on May 27, 1936, in Scotland, became a pioneer in the work to pass the Title IX legislation, which outlawed gender-based discrimination in education, including sports. Dr. Christine Grant has been the athletic director for women since 1973 at the University of Iowa, which has one of the top sports programs in the country. Through her work as a consultant for various gender equity issues, she continues to be a visible champion for women's rights in athletics.

In 1995 alone, Grant was selected as an expert witness in sport discrimination cases against Louisiana State, Virginia Tech, and Drake Universities. She testified before the United States House of Representatives Subcommittee on Postsecondary Education, Training and Lifelong Learning on Title IX, and was one of three collegiate athletic administrators selected to meet with Richard Riley, secretary of the United States Department of Education, and nine senior staff members from the Department of Education regarding Title IX. She has also been responsible for Title IX activities on behalf of the National Association of Collegiate Women Athletic Administrators (NACWAA).

Prior to 1995, Grant testified before the United States House of Representatives Subcommittee on Commerce, Consumer Protection, and Competitiveness regarding sport discrimination. She was also an expert witness in cases involving Brown University, Indiana University of Pennsylvania, University of Texas at Austin, Washington State University, and Temple University.

In 1992, with Grant's influence, the University of Iowa became the first university voluntarily to set as its goal a male-female student-athlete participant and athletic scholarship ratio reflective of the male-female undergraduate population. This commitment was strongly and unanimously reaffirmed by the University of Iowa Board in Control of Athletics in June 1995.

Grant has also served on the Board of Directors of NACWAA, as well as being elected its president in 1987. In 1993, Grant was selected as the NACWAA Administrator of the Year. She also served as the president of the Association of Intercollegiate Athletics for Women (AIAW) from 1980 to 1981.

A Women's Sports Foundation Advisory Board member since 1988, Grant played an integral role on the Coaches Advisory Roundtable (CAR) the organization's body that provides the coach's perspective to the WSF. She was also a speaker at the Foundation's New Agenda Conference in 1983, and at many other WSF events.

Muriel Grossfeld

Born in Indianapolis, Indiana, in 1941, Muriel Davis Grossfeld, a national champion gymnast herself, began coaching well before her final Olympic appearance in 1964. She began her career at age 14, and won her first event in the 1956 Amatuer Athletic Union Championship in floor exercise. She won 18 national titles in eight years. At the Olympic Games in 1968, she was the head coach of the United States Women's Gymnastics Team. Her team finished in sixth place. By the 1972 Olympic Games in Munich, Germany, the United States team had improved to fourth place, with Grossfeld again coaching. She also coached the United States women's teams in three world championships and two Pan American Games.

Grossfeld began coaching in 1962 and started her own gymnastics school in 1968, where up to 100 elite gymnasts trained each year. One of those athletes was Marcia Frederick, whom Grossfeld coached to a gold medal at the world championships, the first-ever gold medal for an American woman gymnast. Grossfeld was voted Coach of the Year for 1979. During her career, Grossfeld coached 17 Olympians and 15 national champions.

Janet Guthrie

The first woman to ever compete in the Indianapolis 500, Janet Guthrie has a diversified background. Besides being a race car driver, she has also been a pilot and flight instructor, an aerospace engineer, a technical editor, and a public representative for some of the country's major corporations.

Born in Iowa City, Iowa, on March 7, 1938, Guthrie had 13 years of experience on sports car road racing circuits before being invited to test a car for the Indianapolis 500 in 1976. That same year, she also became the first woman to compete in a NASCAR Winston Cup superspeedway stock car (3500 lbs. vehicles) race at Grand National Speedway and was 15th of 27 drivers. In 1977, she made her milestone appearance in the Indianapolis 500, qualifying with an average speed of 168.403 mph and reaching speeds above 190 mph during the race. She was also voted the top rookie at the Daytona 500 that same year. Her best finish at the Indianapolis 500 was in 1978, when she finished ninth, racing with a wrist she had broken just days before.

Before Guthrie began racing, women had not been allowed in the pit area (where cars are refueled during a race and repairs are made), and no one thought that a woman could handle a 1,500 lb. racing car. She came into the Indy 500 having won the 1962 Gymkhana (low speed) Women's Championship and nine endurance races. Guthrie was not well received at Indianapolis, and many did not want her to race. However, given a chance to drive in A.J. Foyt's backup car in 1976, she passed the rookie qualifying test, although she didn't have a car to drive in the race.

Guthrie has received many honors for her pioneering efforts. Her helmet and driver's suit are on display in the Smithsonian Institute in Washington. She was also one of the first athletes to be named to the Women's International Sports Hall of Fame.

Gymnastics: Artistic and Rhythmic

The sport of gymnastics has existed for more than 2,000 years; the Greek translation of gymnasium is "a place to exercise naked." Its development as a competitive sport began a little more than 100 years ago, based on the German system that used apparatus such as parallel bars. In the mid-nineteenth century, Germans who immigrated to America formed gymnastics societies, which served as focal points for the sport. Women, however, weren't allowed to be full members of these societies until 1904. The first class in women's gymnastics was held in Mt. Holyoke, Massachusetts, in 1862, but gymnastics was not emphasized for girls and women in schools. Sports that were considered more natural were favored, and as late as the 1920s, gymnastics was rarely part of a physical education program.

In 1897, the Amateur Athletic Union (AAU) became the governing body of the sport, and the first national championships were held in 1931. The AAU continued to be the governing body until 1963 when the United States Gymnastics Federation (USGF) was created. That same year the sport received another boost when the United Olympic Committee (USOC) and the Division of Girls and Women in Sport (DGWS) targeted gymnastics as a sport to develop.

Although women's gymnastics is often associated with the Olympics, it was not one of the original sports contested. The 1928 Olympic Games witnessed the debut of the first women's event, the team combined exercise, won by the Netherlands. The United States women have come a long way from their first Olympic appearance in 1936 to winning the team gold medal at the 1996 Olympic Games. The 1936 events were the horse, uneven bars, and the balance beam. Floor exercise has since been added and is now standard for all gymnastics.

The sport of gymnastics is actually divided into two separate disciplines, rhythmic and artistic gymnastics. Women's artistic gymnastics is composed of four events: vault, uneven bars, balance beam, and floor exercise. The winner of the all-around competition is determined by adding the gymnasts' scores on each of the four events. The scoring is very complicated and varies by level of qualification. The best score a gymnast can score on any apparatus is 10. Below are brief descriptions of each of the four events.

The vault is a power event. A successful vault begins with a strong and accelerated run. At the end of her run, the vaulter explodes off the springboard, raising her feet up over her head with tremendous quickness during the preflight phase of the vault from the springboard to contact with the horse. During the support phase (when the gymnast pushes off the horse), the judges are looking for proper body alignment, shoulder, and hand position, and an instantaneous propulsion off the horse. The second flight phase and the landing are critical areas as well. Judges watch for the height and distance traveled, as well as the number of saltos (forward or backward somersaults completed in the air) and twists. The gymnast must "stick her landing" by not taking extra steps.

Uneven bars are probably the most spectacular of the women's events. The bars demand strength as well as concentration, courage, coordination, precision, and split-second timing. Spectators and judges watch for the big swings that begin on the high bar, incorporating multiple hand changes, pirouettes, and release elements. The routine must move from the low bar to high bar, incorporating many grip changes, releases and regrasps, flight elements, changes of direction, saltos, and circle swings through the handstand position. The entire routine should flow from one movement to the next, without pauses or extra swings. The last element is the flying dismount, with the landing being a critical part of the gymnast's score.

Balance beam is probably the most difficult event in women's gymnastics. It requires intense concentration and nerves of steel to perform difficult stunts on a four-inch-wide beam. The routine must last between 70 and 90 seconds and cover the entire length of the beam. The gymnast must use acrobatic, gymnastic, and dance movements to create high points or peaks in the exercise. The gymnast must also include an element or maneuver close to the beam and has to finish the routine with a dismount, which of course, needs to be stuck. The best gymnasts look as if they are performing their beam routines on the floor.

The floor exercise allows the gymnast to show off her personality. The floor routine must be choreographed to music, last between 70 and 90 seconds, and cover the entire area of the floor. Again, the gymnast must harmoniously blend acrobatic, dance, and gymnastics elements in the exercise while making

versatile use of floor space, changing both the direction and the level of movement. Look for the gymnast's dancer-like command of music, rhythm, and space. The gymnastic elements should flow freely into each other while the leaps cover impressive distances and the pirouettes and turns add excitement to the music. The floor exercise mat is 40 feet by 40 feet, and athletes are penalized for stepping out of bounds.

Many United States athletes have been standouts in the sport of artistic gymnastics. Mary Lou Retton won the all-around title at the 1984 Olympic Games and became a household name. Kim Zmeskal won the 1991 World Gymnastics Championships all-around title and was a member of the bronze-medal team at the 1992 Olympic Games. Shannon Miller has won more world and Olympic medals than any other United States gymnast, including a total of seven Olympic medals and two world championship all-around titles. Shannon and her teammates, Amanda Borden, Amy Chow, Dominique Dawes, Dominique Moceanu, Jaycie Phelps, and Kerri Strug won the first-ever Olympic team gold medal for the United States at the 1996 Olympic Games in Atlanta, Georgia.

Rhythmic gymnastics first became an Olympic event in 1948. The event was dropped in 1956 and did not return in the Olympics until 1984. It has two divisions—individual and group competition. Each movement of a rhythmic gymnastics routine involves a high degree of athletic skill and coordination. Physical abilities needed by a rhythmic gymnast include strength, power, flexibility, agility, dexterity, and endurance. In the group event, athletes need to develop teamwork, sensitivity, quick adaptation, and anticipation, in addition to the skills listed above. Rhythmic gymnastics uses five types of hand apparatus: rope, hoop, ball, clubs, and ribbon.

Each apparatus has its own unique features. During a rope routine, the gymnast must swing, circle, wrap, unwrap, toss, and catch the apparatus. In the hoop event, the athlete must swing, roll, toss, catch, spin, pass through, and rotate the hoop. The ball event requires gymnasts to wave, circle, toss and catch, bounce, and roll the ball. In the club event, the gymnast uses swings, tosses, catches, and utilizes small mill circles. (A forward circle around a horizontal or an uneven bar. The bar is grasped at hip level with legs and arms extended straight.) During the ribbon event, the gymnast must use the ribbon to perform snakes, spirals, swings, circles, tosses, and figure-eight movements. Athletes are judged in all five events by how well their routines flow, and gymnasts are penalized for any drops and slips during their highly complex and difficult routines.

In the group event, five athletes work together as one cohesive unit. The group is judged on the ability of the athletes to demonstrate mastery of body and apparatus in a synchronized, harmonious manner. A group exercise must include difficulties from the same body movement categories that apply to the individual competition and characteristic movements from the appara-

tus. In addition, the group athletes must execute elements involving both large and small exchanges of equipment between gymnasts. The more interaction between the athletes, the better the group exercise.

The 1984 Olympic Games in Los Angeles, California, was the inaugural Games for the sport of individual rhythmic gymnastics. The 1996 Olympic Games in Atlanta, Georgia, was the inaugural Games for group rhythmic gymnastics.

The sport of rhythmic gymnastics is young in the United States and, therefore, has not produced a medalist from the United States in its four Olympic Games appearances. However, the sport is growing strong, and the United States is hopeful that it will be competitive in future Olympic Games. Some of the stars in rythmic gymnastics include Ellie Takahachi, Meaghan Miller, and Natalie Lacuera, all winners in the 1997 Rhythmic National Championship. Up-and-coming stars include Kate Jeffress who won first place in the all-around, rope, hoop, ball, and ribbon in the 1997 Rhythmic National Championships Junior Division. *LP*

Halls of Fame

Halls of fame and museums have been established to recognize people who have excelled in or given an outstanding contribution to their sport in some manner. To be a "Hall of Famer" is the highest honor an athlete has bestowed upon them in the United States. An athlete is inducted into a hall of fame at a ceremony and is usually given a commemorative plaque. Most, but not all, halls of fame are established in a building that is open to the general public. They contain memorabilia of the sport, photographs, film, video, and artifacts from famous athletes of the particular sport for which the hall of fame was established. Many colleges and universities have their own sports hall of fame for athletes from that institution. The Women's Sports Foundation has a hall of fame devoted to famous athletes from many sports. Some halls of fame, e.g., the National Women's Hall of Fame, are not dedicated to athletes but include some athletes. Criteria for inclusion in a hall of fame vary a great deal. Some sports only induct former players, while others include coaches and those who have made a significant contribution to the development of the sport, e.g., the Lacrosse Foundation Hall of Fame and the Figure Skating Hall of Fame. In some halls of fame, entrance is gained by

a points system, as is required, for example, by the Women's Field Hockey Hall of Fame. In others, the person has to have represented her country in that sport. Many halls of fame have different categories. In the National Motorcycle Hall of Fame, for example, there is a promotion category, a category for leadership, and also a category for honorary inductees who may have helped establish the sport. The International Tennis Hall of Fame inducts players from all over the world.

One of the oldest halls of fame for women (started in 1951), and possibly the most difficult hall of fame in which to be inducted, is the Ladies Professional Golf Association (LPGA) Hall of Fame. The prerequisites for the LPGA are that a member has to have been a player in the Association for at least 10 consecutive years and have won at least 30 official events, including two major championships, or won 35 official events, with one major championship title, or 40 official events with no major championship.

Besides honoring individual athletes of extraordinary note, several halls of fame also have exhibitions that chronicle the development of the sport and the developing technology in the sport, as do, for example, the Bicycling Hall of Fame and the Ski Hall of Fame. The Bowling Hall of Fame inducts both amateur and professional bowlers. It has a category for international bowlers as well as Americans. Babe Didrikson Zaharias has a Hall of Fame and Museum devoted just to her. The Babe Ruth Baseball Center at Camden Station, Baltimore, has a Women Sports Center that highlights the role women have played in United States sports history.

Listed below are addresses of many of the halls of fame of sports included in this encyclopedia. Halls of fame are constantly being added or changing their venue, and some halls of fame exist but as yet do not have a building, e.g., the Track and Field Hall of Fame and the Women's Sports Foundation Hall of Fame. Many halls of fame issue lists of their inductees upon request.

A useful directory of halls of fame is *The Volvo Guide to Halls of Fame* (Washington, DC: Living Planet Press, 1995) by Paul Dickson and Robert Skole. *SER*

African American Athletes
International Afro-American Sports Hall of Fame and Gallery
Old Wayne County Building
600 Randolph
Detroit, Michigan 48227

Aviation
National Aviation Hall of Fame
Dayton Convention and Exhibition Center
Dayton, Ohio 45402

Baseball
Babe Ruth Baseball Center
Camden Station
216 Emory Street
Baltimore, MD 21230

Basketball
Naismith Memorial Basketball Hall of Fame
1150 West Columbus Avenue
Springfield, Massachusetts 01101
Women's Basketball Hall of Fame (being built)
P.O. Box 1331
Jackson, Tennessee 38302

Bicycling
The U.S.Bicycling Hall of Fame
166 West Maine Street
Somerville, NJ 08876

Bowling
National Bowling Hall of Fame
111 Stadium Plaza
St. Louis, Missouri 63102

Dog Mushing
The Dog Mushers Hall of Fame
Mile 13.9 Knik road
Knik, Alaska 99687

Field Hockey
The United States Field Hockey Association Hall of Fame
Hilfferich Hall
Ursinus College
Collegeville, Pennsylvania 19426

Figure Skating
The World Figure Skating Hall of Fame and Museum
20 First Street
Colorado Springs, Colorado 80906

Golf
Ladies Professional Golf Association
100 International Golf Drive
Daytona Beach, Florida 32124-1092

Gymnastics
The International Gymnastics Hall of Fame
227 Brooks Street
Oceanside, California 92054

Indianapolis Motor Speedway
The Indianapolis Motor Speedway Hall of Fame Museum
4790 West 16th Street
Indianapolis, Indiana 46222

Lacrosse
The Lacrosse Hall of Fame
113 West University Parkway
Baltimore, Maryland 21210-3300

Motorcycling
National Motorcycle Museum and Hall of Fame
2438 South Junction Avenue
Sturgis, South Dakota 57785

Mountain Biking
Mountain Bike Hall of Fame
126 Elk Avenue
P.O. Box 845
Crested Butte, Colorado 81224

Racquetball
Americal Amateur Racquetball Association Hall of Fame
1685 Unitah
Colorado Springs, Colorado 80904

Roller Skating
National Museum of Roller Skating and Roller Skating Amateur Athletic Hall of Fame
4730 South Street
Lincoln, Nebraska 68506

Show Jumping
Show Jumping Hall of Fame and Museum
3104 Cherry Palm Drive
Suite 220
Tampa, Florida 33619

Skiing
The United States National Ski Hall of Fame
610 Palms Avenue
P.O. Box 191
Ishpeming, Michigan 49849

Soccer
The National Soccer Hall of Fame
5-11 Ford Avenue
Oneonta, New York 13820

Softball
Amateur Softball Association
2801 Northeast 50th Street
Oklahoma City, Oklahoma 73111

Swimming
The International Swimming Hall of Fame
One Hall of Fame Drive
Ft. Lauderdale, Florida 33316

Tennis
Collegiate Tennis Hall of Fame
Henry Field Tennis Stadium
Athens, Georgia 30612
International Tennis Hall of Fame
Newport Casino
194 Bellevue Avenue
Newport, Rhode Island 02840-3586

Track and Field
National Track and Field Hall of Fame
No Building. For information call
Indianapolis City Center (317) 237-5200

Volleyball
Volleyball Hall of Fame
444 Dwight Street
Holyoke, Massachusetts 01041

Water Skiing
The Water Ski Museum/Hall of Fame
799 Overlook Drive, SE
Winter Haven, Florida 33884

Women's Sports
International Women's Sports Hall of Fame
Women's Sports Foundation (Call 1-900-227-3988)
National Women's Hall of Fame
76 Fall Street
Seneca Falls, New York 13148
The Babe Didrikson Zaharias Museum and Visitors Center
1750-10 East
Beaumont, Texas 77704

Dorothy Hamill

Dorothy Stuart Hamill, an American figure skater, was born on July 26, 1956, in Chicago, Illinois. She is best known for winning a gold medal for ladies' figure skating at the 1976 Winter Olympic Games in Innsbruck, Austria. She captivated the audience and the judges, who voted unanimously in awarding her the gold medal. Shortly after Hamill won the world championship for the first time.

Hamill began skating at the age of six. In 1969, she won the national novice title, and in 1970, the national junior silver medal at the United States Figure Skating Championships. From 1973 to 1976, she won several

Dorothy Hamill.
Photo courtesy of the World Figure Skating Museum.

international competitions and finished second in two world championships.

Hamill turned professional in 1976 after her Olympic success. She became one of the most popular performers in the United States, starring in numerous touring ice shows and television specials. One of Hamill's skating spins on the ice, named the "Hamill Camel," became one of her trademarks. The other trademark was her hairstyle; *Life* magazine called her "wedge" haircut a fashion statement, one that thousands of girls emulated.

In 1993, she bought the Ice Capades, a large touring ice show in which she had been regularly performing . She was the art director for the show and a star performer in the Ice Capades' productions of Cinderella (1993) and Hansel and Gretel (1994). She and her husband sold the Ice Capades in 1994, and she performed for the last time in December of that year.

Despite the years that have passed since her Olympic success, Hamill has remained popular. In a 1992 poll, Americans said Hamill represents an all-American, honest image. She was elected to the United States Olympic Hall

of Fame in 1991 and to the United States Figure Skating Hall of Fame in 1992. Hamill recently returned to skating to compete in the ESPN "Legends" figure skating competition.

Mia Hamm

Mia Hamm has emerged from the competitive world of United States soccer as one of the greatest contemporary female athletes in the world. Born on March 17, 1972, Hamm made the United States Women's Soccer Team at age 15 and contributed to their winning the first Women's World Championship of Soccer. She did this by starting five of the six games and scoring a pair of goals against China in the final game. Hamm was named Most Valuable Player of the United States Women's Cup in 1995.

Hamm is known as a versatile and intensely competitive player. She played forward, midfield, and even goalkeeper at the second International Federation of Football Associations (FIFA) Women's World Championship in Sweden in 1995. She was named United States Soccer's 1995 Female Athlete of the Year, becoming only the second player ever to be so honored in consecutive years. She also led the United States Women's Soccer Team to the gold medal at the 1996 Olympic Games, playing before 80,000 fans, the largest crowd ever to watch women play.

Hamm is a formidable presence on the United States team. She has grown to dominate the sport and now plays primarily on the front line, where she commands the respect and attention, and all the pressure, of a clutch scorer. She relishes the pressure of being the most dangerous forward on the field. "That's always the player I wanted to become . . . the one the opposition is worried about."

Mia Hamm played collegiate soccer for the University of North Carolina and is the all-time leading scorer in National Collegiate Athletic Association (NCAA) women's soccer competition, with 103 goals and 72 assists and a combined total

Mia Hamm (middle).
© Daniel Kron.

of 278 points over 91 games. Hamm scored a goal once in every 4.1 shots during her college career, with an average of 1.12 goals per game. She is a three-time All-American, a three-time Atlantic Coast Conference (ACC) Player of the Year (1990, 1991, 1992), as well as a three-time National Player of the Year. Hamm's success comes from her quickness, speed, and will to succeed. She hates losing and is quick to compliment and acknowledge the contributions of her teammates. Hamm grew up in Virginia and Texas and earned a bachelor's degree in political science in 1994.

Judy Devlin Hashman. *See* **Judy Devlin**

Sandra Haynie

Born in Fort Worth, Texas, on June 4, 1943, Sandra Haynie began playing golf when she was 11 years old and had a successful amateur career in her home state. In 1957 and 1958, Haynie won the Texas State Publinx, and in 1958 and 1959, she won the Texas Amateur. Sandra Haynie joined the

Ladies Professional Golf Association (LPGA) in 1961 and won 42 LPGA titles and four championship titles during her career. In 1970, Haynie was named Player of the Year, and in 1974, she became the second woman to win the LPGA Championship and the United States Women's Open in the same season. Haynie's career was interrupted by injuries and surgeries on two occasions, which only motivated her to return and win. Haynie competed in her last full season in 1989, but she has competed in the Sprint Senior Challenge since 1993. Haynie was inducted into the LPGA Hall of Fame in 1977.

Carol Heiss

Carol Elizabeth Heiss (Jenkins) was born in Queens, New York on January 20, 1940. A gifted skater, she won her first national championship (ladies' novice division) at the age of 11. When she was 12 years old, she added the junior title. She was the youngest skater at that time to win the novice and junior championships consecutively. By the

Carol Heiss.
Photo courtesy of the World Figure Skating Museum.

age of 13, Heiss was a top international competitor, finishing fourth at the world championships in 1953. In 1955, she moved up to second place in the world champion- ships, finishing behind American Tenley Albright.

When she was 14, Heiss suffered a severed tendon in her lower leg after colliding on the ice with her sister Nancy. She over- came this career-threatening injury within a year. When she was 15, she earned a silver medal at the 1956 Olympic Games in Cortina d'Ampezzo, Italy, again behind Tenley Albright. Two weeks later, they switched places when Heiss won the world championships, with Albright taking second place. Heiss won the world championships every year from 1956 through 1960. She finished her amateur career with a gold medal at the 1960 Olympics in Squaw Valley, California. Before turning professional after the 1960 Games, Heiss won more interna- tional skating titles than any other North American skater.

Heiss's athletic and dynamic freeskating program included a double axel. She was one of the first women to master this jump. She now gives back to her sport as a coach. Because of her extraordinary talent at skating, Heiss was named to the Interna- tional Women's Sports Hall of Fame.

Betty Hicks

Best known as a crusader for women's golf, Betty Hicks helped launch the Women's Professional Golf Association, the predeces- sor to the Ladies Professional Golf Associa- tion (LPGA). Hicks was born on November 16, 1920, in Long Beach, California. Her career on the links began in 1937 as a member of a freshman golf class at Long Beach City College. She won her first tournament in 1938 at the Long Beach City Championship, just one year after taking up the sport. With her first win under her belt, Hicks won the Palm Springs Invitational, Western Medal Play, and the Southern California Championship in 1939 and 1940.

In 1941, she won the United States National Championship, the Miami-

Biltmore Invitational, and the "California State." That same year, she was named Woman Athlete of the Year by the Associated Press. Hicks also won at the All-American Open and Chicago Open in 1943, and then in 1944, she won the Portland Open. Hicks was the runner-up to Babe Didrikson Zaharias in both the 1947 and 1954 United States Open Tournaments. Her success on the links ranked her sixth in the 1954 LPGA Leading Money Winners with $7,054.84, and eighth in the 1955 LPGA Leading Money Winners with $8,334.92, a far cry from the winning's of today's golfers!

Hicks shot her best round (68) at the Spartanburg Open in 1957. Forty-eight years after winning her first golf tournament, Hicks won the Seniors Division in the LPGA Teaching Division, Western Section, in 1986.

Hicks moved to the administrative side of golf in 1944 when she served as the first president of the Women's Professional Golf Association. Hicks worked as tournament director of the LPGA from 1954 to 1955 and was the first teaching chairperson from 1959 to 1960. With her expansive knowledge of all aspects of the sport of golf, Hicks lent her expertise as a member of the Golf Advisory Staff for Wilson Sporting Goods from 1955 through 1992. She was awarded an Honorary Lifetime Membership to the LPGA Teaching Division. Hicks has written more than 400 articles on golf for such publications as *Golf for Women, Today's Woman, Sports Illus- trated, Sport, Golf Digest, The Saturday Evening Post, Atlantic Monthly,* and *Golf Illustrated.*

Golf is not the only area of Hick's expertise. Flying became Hick's passion in 1958, when she took it up to avoid driving from tournament to tournament. She was named "Flight Instructor of the Year" in 1979 by the San Jose Federal Aviation Administration General Aviation District Office. Hicks retired in 1993 as chair of the Aviation Department at Foothill College, a position she held for 21 years. Hicks has written extensively on aviation for magazines and instructional textbooks, as well as for television and instructional videos.

History: Girls and Women in Sport, 1890 to 1972

Through the ages, activities that appeared to be associated with danger, that called for vigorous activity, that required special costumes, and that elicited a competitive nature were seen as more appropriate for boys and men than for women. Two examples of this attitude are war and sports. Only in the latter part of the past half-century have females been seen as serious, capable, and important influences in either. Growing up in the 1940s, many little girls tried to kiss their elbows, believing the old wives' tale that this feat would turn them into a boy. Why would a little girl even choose to change her sex? Because in that era girls who loved sport and had a deep-seated desire to be an athlete did not have access to competitive sports.

Even when opportunities were granted to women, their acceptance as viable athletes was limited. When the All American Girls Professional Baseball League was formed in 1943, the first professional sports opportunity for women, it received limited attention. The majority of the public only considered it a novel attraction. This opportunity was further limited to a handful of young women. Most girls and women were barred from competitive sports until Title IX legislation (designed to end discrimination based on sex in education programs) was passed in 1972. During most of the previous 80 years, public opinion was mostly nonsupportive of female athletes, sometimes to the point of condemning the girls and women who defied societal norms and competed in "boyish" sports. The various forms of physical education for girls and the women's sports organizations of the time (National Section for Girls and Women's Sport [NSGWS], Division of Girls and Women's Sport [DGWS], National Association of Girls and Women's Sport [NAGWS]) seem very conservative by contemporary standards. These professional women, however, were seeking to protect and preserve a place for

women's sport and exercise during this restrictive era, and much of what they were doing was considered radical at the time.

A few pioneer sportswomen excelled in sport before Title IX made it a guaranteed right. Prior to the 1890s, women's role in sport was primarily as spectators in all but the most passive of games. Bicycling, croquet, archery, and swimming were the main sports in which women engaged, and even swimming was often criticized as being inappropriate because of the costume required and because women could develop undesirable muscles by participating. Women wishing to engage in sport (with any degree of public acceptance) in the late nineteenth and early twentieth centuries had to meet these conditions: (1) the activity had to be considered healthful; (2) it had to be mild enough to allow participation in street clothes; (3) the activity had to provide for social interaction; and (4) winning had to be of little consequence. When women were introduced to competitive sport in the 1890s, great precautions were taken by those in control to make certain that these unwritten rules of acceptability were adhered to by students in schools and colleges. While sport for women was taught as mild educational games, boys and men's sports developed inside and outside the schools as highly competitive activities.

The first team games, volleyball, basketball (and the closely related southern version—Newcomb ball), were taught to college women in the 1890s. Team sports for women quickly became controversial because they were vigorous and promoted more serious competitive attitudes. Basketball became the most controversial because it demanded vigorous play that was considered more appropriate for boys. However, the first set of women's rules, published in 1895 by Clara Gregory Baer (of Newcomb College in New Orleans, for which Newcomb ball was named) attempted to alleviate contact and undesirable vigor. Her set of rules made falling down a foul, allowed no movement by players except when the ball was in the air, and disallowed guarding a player. When Senda Berenson of Smith College, who was one of the first to bring the game to women, published the first official basketball rules for women in 1901, the rules were less restrictive but still prohibited physical contact and limited running, jumping, and dribbling.

From the earliest period of college women playing these sports until the 1960s, most physical educators accepted sport for health and social reasons while frowning on the idea of girls and women's teams competing against each other. During the first half of the twentieth century, individual and dual sports were seen as more appropriate for females because costumes were more feminine without being revealing, and no

Senda Berenson.
Photo courtesy of the Smith College Archives.

physical contact could occur. From childhood, girls and women were conditioned in these sexist attitudes which prohibited their engagement in highly competitive activities. Most people accepted the notion that such restrictions were in keeping with "appropriate differences" between males and females in sport. However, as women continued to work for political freedom through suffrage (the right to vote), they began to challenge gender restriction in many other areas of life, including competitive sporting opportunities.

While male athletic stars of the past are well known from the publicity they received for their accomplishments, many of the early outstanding women athletes remain relatively obscure. One of these brave women was blue blood Eleanora Sears who thumbed her nose at Boston society by playing sports from polo to squash with abandon. Sears wore boyish clothes so that she could play these games and is noted as the first woman in the United States to publicly ride a horse astride, not the traditional sidesaddle. Although she was a debutante and voted the best dressed in Boston for social events, her brazen entry into the male sports world caused a California "Mothers' Club" in 1912 to pass a resolution against her conduct. Despite such reactions, this great-great-granddaughter of Thomas Jefferson continued to compete in national tennis and squash tournaments until she was 70 years old, and she remained a horsewoman until her death in 1968 at the age of 86 years. "Eleo" Sears was one of the earliest emancipators of athletic girls and women.

Other outstanding women in early twentieth century sport were Glenna Collett (Vare) and Helen Wills (Moody), who exemplified "the lady sportswoman" and were truly great athletes. Collett was a remarkable amateur golfer who played from 1917 through the 1930s, winning many tournaments including the United States Women's Amateur Championship six times between 1922 and 1935. The Vare Trophy, given for the lowest average score on the Ladies Professional Golf Association (LPGA) Tour, was inaugurated under her married name in 1953. Helen Wills dominated women's tennis in the 1920s and 1930s. She won eight Wimbledon singles titles between 1927 and 1938, won eight United States National titles between 1923 and 1931, and won every set she played between 1927 and

1932. She was ranked number one in tennis for seven years.

Other women athletes who broke barriers during this time were Mildred "Babe" Didrikson (Zaharias), Gertrude Ederle, and Althea Gibson. Ederle was the first woman to swim the English Channel (20.6 miles) from France to England. Only five men had accomplished this feat, and her record-breaking swim in 1926 beat the men's record by two hours. In the 1932 Olympic Games in Los Angeles, California, Babe Didrikson won two gold medals and a silver medal in track and field. (She actually qualified for more events, but Olympic rules at the time limited her to three events.) As an amateur, and later as a professional golfer, she dominated golf from the 1930s until her premature death in 1956. In 1950, she was voted the Greatest Woman Athlete of the First Half of the Twentieth Century. At a time when prejudice against women athletes was more palpable than racial prejudice, Althea Gibson defeated them both. She was the first African American to hurdle the racial barriers in Whites-only tennis tournaments. In 1956, she became the first African American to win the French National Championship and in 1957 she was the first African American to win both Wimbledon and the U.S. Open. She repeated both victories in 1958 and was the first African American to be named Associated Press Woman Athlete of the Year.

Besides these women, there were other pioneers. Margaret Abbot, in 1900 at the Olympic Games in Paris, France, became the first woman to win a gold medal in the Olympics, and May Sutton won the Wimbledon singles title in 1905, becoming the first American to do so. Constance Applebee, from England, is credited with introducing field hockey to her American sisters in 1901. She coached the sport at summer camps until she was 95 years old. Other deserving women athletes of the pre-Title IX era whose lives should be further explored by historians are the Curtis sisters (Harriet and Margaret), Patty Berg, Betty Hicks, Mickey Wright, and Louise Suggs in golf; Bertha Ragen Tickey and Joan Joyce in

softball; Mary Outerbridge, Hazel Hotchkiss Wightman, Alice Marble, Helen Jacobs, and Maureen Connolly in tennis; Tenley Albright, Carol Heiss, and Peggy Fleming in figure skating; Nera White in basketball and softball; and Stella Walsh, Alice Coachman, Wyomia Tyus, and Wilma Rudolph in track and field. It was these many women, and so many more unnamed and some even unknown women, who pushed open the doors for girls and women in sport. *JP*

See also Association of Intercollegiate Athletics for Women; National Association for Girls and Women in Sport; Olympic Games and Women

Hockey. *See* Field Hockey and Women; Ice Hockey for Women

Nancy Hogshead

Nancy Hogshead was born on April 17, 1962, in Iowa City, Iowa. Nancy was raised in Jacksonville, Florida, in a warm and supportive family environment that encouraged achievement in all endeavors—athletic or academic.

Nancy's affinity for the water became apparent early. In 1975, she was the second youngest person to compete in the Amateur Athletic Union (AAU) Indoor National Championship. At age 14, she set U.S. records in the 100- and 200- meter butterfly events.

Through the late 1970s, Nancy Hogshead (like so many USA athletes) devoted herself to preparation for the 1980 Olympic Games. She was known for her grueling training regime but what was *not* known throughout almost all of her swimming career was that she suffered from asthma. She kept that suffering to herself.

The boycott of the Moscow Olympics ended Hogshead's Olympic dream, and she entered Duke University, swimming varsity one year and retiring from the sport. The retirement lasted two years, but Nancy Hogshead knew that her swimming career was not yet over. In 1983, she left Duke to focus again on swimming. She used a private coach and, unusual for the time, her own sport psychologist. In the 1984 Games, she won gold in the 100-meter freestyle, 4 x 100 medley relay, and 4 x 100 freestyle relay. She won a silver in the 200-meter individual medley and was going for her fifth medal when she almost collapsed on the course, fading to fourth place. It was only in the aftermath that her asthma was diagnosed for the first time.

Hogshead retired from swimming after the 1984 Games, returned to Duke where she graduated with honors. Recently, she completed a law degree as well. She is a frequent motivational speaker, was national spokesperson for the American Lung Association, and served as president of the Women's Sports Foundation. In 1994, she was inducted into the International Swimming Hall of Fame.

Dianne Holum

Dianne Holum, born in Northbrook, Illinois, on May 19, 1951, set the standard for the many athletes she would coach, when she became the first United States woman to win an Olympic gold medal in speedskating at the 1972 Olympic Games in Sapporo, Japan, winning the 1,500-meter race. Showing her dominance both on and off the ice, Holum helped speedskating's contemporary superstars such as Bonnie Blair, Mary and Sarah Doctor, and Eric and Beth Heiden to numerous national and international championship titles.

Before the 1980 Olympics, Holum, who at the time was the only woman coach of world-class speedskaters, devised a training program for the Heidens (Eric and Beth) stressing dry-land training, bicycling, weightlifting, and a series of exercises meant to imitate proper skating technique. Since 1973, Holum has coached at numerous high schools, clubs, and colleges in swimming, skating, track and field, and cycling. These programs included coaching some of the members of the world-caliber "Seven-Eleven Cycling Team" from 1982 to 1984.

Holum coached the United States National Speedskating Team from 1975 to 1980 and from 1983 to 1985. She personally coached 14 skaters to 120 medals in the world championships, 13 world titles, and 7 world records. As the United States Olympic Speedskating coach, her teams won a total of 13 Olympic medals in the 1976, 1980, and 1984 Olympic Games.

In addition to her own gold medal and Olympic record (2:20.85) performance in the 1,500-meter race in 1972, Holum clinched a silver medal in the 3,000-meter race at the same Games. At the 1968 Olympic Games, she skated to silver and bronze medal finishes in the 500- and 1,000-meter races, respectively.

She currently coaches the West Allis Speedskating Club in Wisconsin. During her "spare time," Holum has served on the Sports Medicine Committee of the United States International Speedskating Association, published several papers and books on speedskating and conditioning, and developed off-season conditioning programs for various sports. Holum feels her greatest contribution to sports has been the development of young skaters into international caliber athletes.

Homophobia in Women's Sport

Throughout the history of women's sports, critics have tried to discourage individual women from pursuing their sport interests and sought to limit their opportunities. One of the consistent concerns raised by these critics has been the perceived appropriateness (or lack thereof) of women's sport participation. Early in the twentieth century, critics of women's sports raised health concerns and warned about the potential for damage to women's reproductive organs and the "masculinizing" effects of strenuous physical activity.

By the mid-twentieth century, as women's increasing sport participation had proved that the earlier concerns were unwarranted, new issues were raised about the social appropriateness of sport and about the possibility that women athletes were vulnerable to the development of "deviant" sexual interests, either uncontrolled heterosexual promiscuity or a preference for women as sexual partners. In response, supporters of women's sports adopted a strategy of "denial to all charges" to defend women's sports against these concerns. Advocates promoted women's sport as a "wholesome" pursuit that was entirely consistent with prevailing social norms of femininity and chaste heterosexuality.

Despite the consistent denials through the years, the general public remained suspicious of women athletes, and little attention or resources were given to women's sports programs. An association between lesbianism and sport was "whispered but not spoken" in the public mind. The general perception was that sport was a male domain, and the prevailing stereotype of lesbians was one of masculine women interested in male pursuits, and therefore, women's sports were seen as a lesbian activity. As a result, until relatively recently, some women and girls chose not to pursue their sport interests to avoid association with an unsavory image.

In the 1970s, with the enactment of Title IX (federal legislation to end sex discrimination in education) and the support of a burgeoning feminist movement, women's sports participation increased tremendously. As a result, being an athlete became a more accepted, and even admired, role for women. Yet, even with increased participation and acceptance of women as athletes, the fear of lesbians, the discrimination against lesbians in sport, and the use of the lesbian label to intimidate all women in sport, persisted then and persists still.

Despite this hostile climate, lesbians have played important leadership roles in the development of women's sports throughout the twentieth century. They are athletes, teachers, coaches, leaders of women's sports advocacy groups, fans, and role models for other women and girls. Unfortunately, with the exception of a small minority of courageous women, lesbians have made their contributions to sport while hiding their sexual orientation from all but the most trusted friends and colleagues. This secrecy is prompted by numerous incidents of discrimination and prejudice against lesbians in sport. Even today, women in sport presumed to be lesbians are fired from coaching jobs or not hired in the first place, dismissed or banned from teams, assumed to be unfit coaches or role models, ostracized by colleagues or teammates, blamed for a team conflict, used in negative recruiting by college coaches to dissuade athletes from attending rival schools, pressured to keep their sexual orientation secret to "protect" women's sports image, and, among professional athletes, shunned by commercial sponsors looking for athletes to endorse their products. Typically, lesbians in sport who are targeted by anti-lesbian discrimination have not violated any ethical or professional standards. Their sexual orientation, and the stereotypes and assumptions made about lesbians, are enough to provoke discrimination.

In this silence, stereotypes about lesbians thrive and can be used against not only lesbians but any woman in sport who challenges the status quo. For example, women who file Title IX suits protesting the unequal distribution of resources in men's and women's sport are sometimes called lesbians as a way to discourage them from continuing their legal challenge. Any woman who challenges sexism, does not live up to traditional expectations of physical appearance and demeanor, or who can not or will not demonstrate her heterosexuality with the presence of a boyfriend or husband in her life is vulnerable to anti-lesbian attacks.

This "lesbian-baiting" in women's sports discourages many girls and women from active sports participation and affects the ability of women to develop strong social and political ties with colleagues or teammates out of fear of being associated with lesbians or being perceived as a lesbian. Anti-lesbian bias also takes the form of blaming lesbians for other important problems in women's sport, such as sexual harassment of athletes or sexual relationships between coaches and athletes. Despite evidence that women athletes are at greater risk of being sexually harassed or attacked by male athletes and coaches than by lesbian teammates and coaches and that male coaches are at least as likely to become sexually involved with women athletes as are their lesbian counterparts, framing these problems as a lesbian issue has complicated addressing these real issues in more effective and comprehensive ways.

As we move to the twenty-first century, it is clear that change is coming. Women's sports leaders are beginning to address anti-lesbian discrimination through educational seminars for coaches and athletes. Articles about homophobia in sport, gay and lesbian athletes, and discrimination against lesbians in sport now appear in both professional journals and mainstream newspapers. In addition, some sport governing bodies are beginning to take a stand against discrimination based on sexual orientation. Moreover, as lesbian athletes and coaches, such as tennis player Martina Navratilova and golfer Muffin Spencer-Devlin, become more open about their identities, destructive stereotypes will lose their power to incite fear and prejudice.

Discrimination against groups of women based on stereotypical assumptions or fears, without regard for individual character or accomplishment, diminishes women's sport by limiting opportunities and overlooking the contributions made by women from many diverse groups. As this discrimination in regard to lesbians diminishes, other prejudices born of ignorance and fear will lose their power to intimidate and limit women in sport. *PG*

Flo Hyman

Flora Jean Hyman was born on July 29, 1954, in Los Angeles, California. She grew up in the nearby town of Inglewood, California, near the beach community of South Bay, California, where volleyball was the fad. When she was young, Hyman was much taller than the other children her age. When her schoolmates were four feet tall, she was one foot taller. She had the nickname "Jolly Green Giant" because of her height.

Hyman also had two older sisters who played volleyball with her at Inglewood's Morningside High School. The Morningside High School varsity team was Hyman's first volleyball team. As a freshman, she was allowed to play on the varsity team. She did not learn to spike until her senior year, when she was also voted the team's most valuable player.

From the day Hyman first learned that volleyball was an Olympic sport, she knew exactly where she was going. She always wanted to be on the national women's volleyball team and to play in the Olympic Games. Beth DiStefano, her coach in high school, took Hyman and her teammates to United States Volleyball Association (USVBA, now called USAV) tournaments on Saturdays. Hyman and her teammates were all searching for a club team where they could gain some playing experience. Hyman first chose the Long Beach Hangers, based on their teamwork and stylish uniforms. She then moved up to play for the South Bay Spikers, who became the USVBA champions in 1977.

In 1974, the citizens of Pasadena, Texas, began providing homes, jobs, and scholarships at the University of Houston for invited volleyball champions to train for the 1980 Olympic Games. Hyman was asked to join the national team. She was All-American for four years at the University of Houston, where she studied mathematics on her volleyball scholarship, graduating in 1980.

In 1979, the women's national team qualified for the Olympic Games in a regional contest against Cuba. Hyman was voted the most valuable player for the tournament. The team was favored to win an Olympic medal in 1980, but the U.S. boycott of the Moscow Games postponed that dream. Before Hyman joined the national team, they had performed terribly in the 1964 and 1968 Olympic Games, and they had failed to even qualify for the 1972 Olympic Games.

After the boycott, Hyman was one of seven players who dedicated four more years to the pursuit of an Olympic medal in volleyball. Under the guidance of Coach Arie Selinger, the team trained six to eight hours a day for the 1984 Olympic Games in Los Angeles, California. Hyman was the team leader and spokesperson. If she played well, so did the team. She was the oldest female volleyball player in the 1984 Olympic Games, turning 30 years old on the first day of competition. The women's team won the silver medal at Los Angeles, losing to a talented team from China in the finals. Hyman's leadership on the Olympic team has inspired more female African American athletes to play volleyball.

Flo Hyman was a major force in turning the women's national team from a "would be" team to a respected international power. Many athletes would be disappointed with winning a silver medal instead of a gold medal, but Hyman was proud of her silver medal. The license tag rims on her car read "1984 Olympian: A Silver Lined with Gold." She set a goal to win an Olympic medal and worked for 10 years in pursuit of it.

Hyman retired from the national team in 1985, but she was not satisfied with her accomplishments in volleyball. She tried a brief acting career, and then she decided to play volleyball professionally in Japan for a year.

On January 24, 1986, Hyman's Japanese team, Daiei, was playing a match against Hitachi in Matsue City, Japan. In the third game, she came out of the game during a regular substitution. She sat down on the bench and started cheering for her team. In a few moments, she collapsed and fell to the floor. She was taken to the Red Cross Hospital where she was pronounced dead.

Hyman died of a rare disease known as Marfan's syndrome, which commonly affects tall, slender people. (She was six feet five inches tall and weighed 180 pounds.) With Marfan's syndrome, a person's heart enlarges and forces weak spots in the aorta to burst. Because of Hyman's death, awareness of the symptoms of Marfan's syndrome has increased.

Flo Hyman will always be considered one of the best female volleyball players in the world. She was also an advocate for creating opportunities for women athletes and was especially involved with having the Civil Rights Restoration Act passed—an act that ensured that girls and women would not be discriminated against in high school and college athletic programs. She always represented a dedication to excellence. Several awards and scholarships have been given to female athletes in memory of Hyman's determination, work ethic, and will to succeed. The National Girls and Women in Sport Day was launched, in no small measure as a tribute to Flo Hyman's memory. In addition, the Flo Hyman award is given annually by the Women's Sports Foundation to a U.S. athlete who exhibits Hyman's "dignity, spirit and commitment to excellence."

Ice Hockey for Women

Most people are surprised to learn that women's ice hockey has a history that dates back to 1892, when the first organized and recorded all-female ice hockey game was played in Ontario, Canada. Over the span of more than a century, girls and women have pursued the sport, clearly reflected today by their increasing membership in USA Hockey. USA Hockey is the national governing body for ice hockey in the United States. It is responsible for organizing and training teams for such international tournaments as the International Ice Hockey Federation World Championships and the Olympic Winter Games, which will include women's hockey as a full medal sport for the 2002 Games. A look back at the last several years reveals greater changes and growth in women's ice hockey, with the best yet to come.

Ice hockey is a high-speed game that is played on an ice rink by two opposing teams of skaters. Players use curved sticks to drive a puck (a hard rubber disk) into the opponent's netted goal. Six players are allowed on the ice at a time, including a goalkeeper. Points are scored for goals and assists, and the winning team is the one that has scored the most points in the three 20-minute periods of a game. The rules for ice hockey are the same for men and women, except that girls/women's ice hockey has no checking (not even in world or Olympic championships). This rule is different from the male verion, which allows checking at the high school, college, and professional levels.

During the 1990-1991 season, 5,533 female ice hockey players registered with USA Hockey. In 1996, that number had increased nearly 400 percent with more than 20,555 registered girls and women playing ice hockey across the United States. While the number of girls and women's teams has grown from 149 in 1990 to 710 in 1995, the majority of females continue to play on mixed teams. Approximately half of all females registered with USA Hockey currently play on boys' or men's teams.

In 1993, a survey was conducted by the Minnesota State High School League to assess which sports held the most interest for the girls in Minnesota. More than 8,000 females expressed interest in ice hockey. On March 21, 1994, the Minnesota State High School League sanctioned girls' ice hockey as a varsity sport, making Minnesota the first state to do so.

In the inaugural 1994 season, 24 schools formed girls' varsity teams, and on March 25, 1995, Apple Valley became the first Minnesota girls' state high school champion, defeating the South St. Paul Packers by a score of 2-0. The league grew to 47 teams in its second season, and 67 teams registered for the 1996 season, with no signs that the league's growth is slowing.

With the support and approval of the National Collegiate Athletic Association (which has designated women's ice hockey as an emerging sport and thus, earmarked for support), the Eastern College Athletic Conference (ECAC) now sponsors two leagues for women. Those leagues are known as the ECAC Women's Hockey League, a Division I-level league composed strictly of varsity teams, and the ECAC Women's Hockey Alliance, a Division III-level league composed of both varsity and club teams.

The state of Minnesota continues to lead the Midwestern interest in women's ice hockey. In 1995, Augsburg College in Minneapolis became the first college in the state to fully fund women's varsity ice hockey. The University of Minnesota quickly followed suit with the decision to upgrade its club team to varsity status beginning in 1997.

In the eastern United States, considered the hotbed of women's college hockey, more and more colleges and universities are viewing women's ice hockey as a solution for meeting Title IX requirements that guarantee equal funding for women's sports. Beginning in 1996, Hamilton College, New York, upgraded its women's ice hockey program to varsity status after 21 years as a club team.

Women's hockey has a surprisingly long history of international competition. As far back as 1916, women's ice hockey teams from Canada and the United States competed against each other. In the 1980s, however, women's ice hockey experienced explosive growth. In April 1987, the Ontario Women's Hockey Association hosted the first world invitational tournament, which was a resounding success, with

Canadian teams dominating. During that tournament, representatives from participating nations met to discuss the future of women's ice hockey. They also established a strategy to lobby the International Ice Hockey Federation (IIHF) for the creation of a women's world championship.

Those discussions led to the first IIHF Women's World Championship, which was held in March 1990, in Ottawa, Ontario. Canada won the gold medal at that historic event and repeated as champion at the next two IIHF Women's World Championships (1992 in Tampere, Finland, and 1994 in Lake Placid, New York). In these same years, the United States took the silver medal, and Finland the bronze medal.

Women's ice hockey received its most prestigious acknowledgment in 1992 when the International Olympic Committee (IOC) voted to include women's ice hockey as an Olympic medal sport beginning in the year 2002. The IOC gave the organizers of the 1994 Games in Lillehammer, Norway, and the 1998 Games in Nagano, Japan, the option of including women's ice hockey on their programs. While Norway declined, Japan accepted and debuted women's ice hockey at the 1998 Olympic Winter Games as a demonstration sport, with the United States winning the gold.

Kitchener, Ontario, served as the host for the 1997 IIHF Women's World Championship. National teams from Canada, China, Finland, Norway, Russia, Sweden, Switzerland, and the United States participated in the international tournament that served as the qualifier for the 1998 Olympic Winter Games. Canada won its fourth world's championship, with the United States finishing second. The top five teams, Canada, USA, Finland, China, and Sweden, along with the host team from Japan, competed in the 1998 Winter Olympics.

In April 1995, the first IIHF Pacific Women's Hockey Championship was held in San Jose, California, with teams competing from the United States, Canada, China, and Japan. Vancouver, British Columbia, served as the site for the 1996 IIHF Pacific

Women's Hockey Championship, where Canada, the United States, and China triumphed as gold, silver, and bronze medalists respectively.

The IIHF Women's World Championship, the IIHF Pacific Women's Hockey Championship, and the IIHF European Championship have allowed elite-level women's ice hockey players to display their talent at the highest level available to women in sport. The 1998 Olympic Winter Games in Nagano, Japan, allowed these same athletes to strive for the highest honor in all of amateur sports, an Olympic medal. The history and contemporary accomplishments of women's ice hockey bear witness to its rightful place among women's competitive sports and for the future of the game for women and girls. The national governing body of hockey is USA Hockey Inc, which can be reached at 4965 N. 30th St., Colorado Springs, CO 80919, (719) 599-5500. *KP*

Imagery: Using the Mind's Eye for Success

Almost all great performers—musicians, actors, and athletes—use their minds to imagine their performances before they ever occur. Like a dream, imagery mimics real-life perceptual experiences, except imagery occurs voluntarily when someone tries to remember or create the feelings, smells, and visions of an experience. These images differ from dreaming or daydreaming because the individual is consciously aware of the experience and has been actively involved in creating it.

Great athletes can often be seen preparing for a performance by closing their eyes and "going through the action" without even moving. During this covert practice, they are sensing their muscles, feeling their body positions, and seeing themselves perform. It takes place without any known sensory antecedent or stimulus to cause the image, only the desire of the individual. For example, no tennis court, racket, or ball is necessary for a tennis player to experience the sensations of hitting a great serve through her imagery.

Imagery and mental practice can be effectively used to help learn a new skill or to rehearse an already learned skill just before performing it. People have often assumed that the only way to learn a skill is to repeat it overtly hundreds of times. Research, however, has shown that learning is improved when cognitive (thinking) aspects of practice are included and that insight is gained about how a skill is performed by merely imagining its performance. In addition, imagery is often combined with other forms of mental practice such as reading about a skill, watching a video, or observing highly talented models perform the skill. For any girl or woman who is seeking to improve her skill, looking for an "edge," or wanting to improve more quickly than others around her, the use of imagery training, and other psychological skills training, can be very useful.

Using imagery before a race.

Imagery can take place in every sensory system. For example, imagine a bright, yellow lemon being sliced in your hand. Can you feel the texture of the wax-like peel on the lemon, sense the sticky juice on your hands, feel the knife in your other hand as you cut into the peel, smell and taste the lemon sensation, and see the yellow color? The vividness of these sensations is directly related to the strength of your image of that lemon. Similarly, if you were using imagery to practice skiing down a long hill, you would feel your toes and shins in your ski boots, sense the icy spot you just hit as you tried to turn, and feel the cold air rushing by your cheeks and the grips of the poles in your hands.

When using imagery to learn a new skill, it is important to create images that are as realistic as possible. If a gymnast is imagining performing a back handspring in gymnastics, she should be sure to image it with full speed, with great extension in her legs and back, and with firm contact on her hands as they spring her body back off the mat. If she imagines such skills in slow motion, her muscles cannot sense the actual feel of the real movement. The real timing of images is also important because some research has shown that during imagery the nerves of the body are actually generating small signals to the same muscles that will perform the actual skill. It is, therefore, important that these impulses are properly timed and given the appropriate relative force during the imaging process.

Visual imagery is only one form of imagery, but it can be quite powerful because of the mind's ability to manipulate the images. For example, a tennis player might imagine herself hitting a tennis ball overhead as if she were watching herself on a video-taped playback. From that external, third-person perspective, she can easily see the ball toss, her body rotate, back extend, and racket arm reach high in the air to contact the ball. This view can be a good perspective from which to get the idea of a skill or to refine subtle biomechanical aspects of the skill. As

an alternative, she can imagine her serve from inside her own head, looking out her own eyes. From this internal perspective, she can see all the things she would actually see if she were executing the skill. She is looking up at the ball and seeing her forearm as it comes from behind her to extend up toward the ball. From this internal perspective, she can most closely approximate what the actual serve will look and feel like.

Because imagery can be used for two different purposes (to learn a new skill or to rehearse an already learned skill), it can be created in two different ways: mastery images or coping images. When rehearsing a skill just before performing it in competition, the image should be of a perfect performance. This visualization of the best technique is called mastery imagery and is used to build confidence, control arousal levels, and rehearse just before performing.

Another use of imagery is to prepare for decisions that must be made, a process known as coping imagery. For example, if a "hitter" is practicing during the weeks before a volleyball tournament, she might want to rehearse how she will compensate for sets that are too low or too far behind her. Using coping imagery, she could practice how she would handle each of the potential problems that might come up during the volleyball match. In this fashion, she is practicing making decisions and varying her skill to match unpredictable situations. Then, when these situations come up in the game, she has already had experience with them and will be able to make a better, quicker decision. This form of imagery practice is especially important in open skills and sports or those that have a lot of variability.

Imagery can also be used to control pain and direct attention. Runners often describe the phenomenon of "hitting the wall" when they have been running long distances and it seems they cannot run any farther. When this happens, many runners use imagery to focus on a positive experience (perhaps a beach scene) or to imagine a little engine kicking in to help them keep going. Similarly, injured athletes sometimes use imagery to help tolerate pain or to imagine continuing to practice while they are in rehabilitation.

Both negative and positive images work—but they produce opposite results. To be successful, you must imagine success. If you create negative images, such as missing the target when throwing darts, you will likely miss it when you actually throw them. Similarly, if a golfer sees a large water hazard in front of the green, reaches for an old beat-up ball, and imagines the shot going in the water, it likely will go there. All women athletes, presently training or "wannabees," should remember this motto that many athletes have hung in their lockers to remind them of the importance of positive images: "Winners imagine what they want to happen; losers imagine what they fear might happen." *LB*

Suggested Reading

Bunker, L.K. (1995). The mind's "I": Imagery for performance and health enhancement. *Proceedings: ICHPER-SD*, 3-23. International Council for Health, Physical Education and Recreation—Sport and Dance.

The Internet and Women in Sport

Anyone who is interested in women's sports will find extensive information on the Internet (specifically, the World Wide Web). One method of finding information about women's sports on the Internet is simply to search through a search engine like Yahoo (http://www.yahoo.com) or Lycos (http://www.lycos.com), using the key words "women in sport." (If this search brings up too many "hits," refine the search with more specific terms, such as the name of the sport.) Several specific Web sites, however, provide interesting information on the issues, resources, and athletes involved with women's sports.

Women's Sports—General Information

The following is a list of just a few of the home pages related to women's sports: WWW Women's Sport Page http://fiat.gslis.utexas.edu/~lewisa/womsprt.html (June 11, 1997)

Written, compiled, and copyrighted by Amy Lewis, this Web site is an excellent place to begin searching for information on all of women's sports and female athletes. This site contains links to women's sports Web pages in approximately 30 different sports. It also presents many biographies of accomplished female athletes and their personal stories about their sport experiences. Women's sports organizations, resources, and issues such as gender equity and media coverage are also presented in this home page, which is continually updated.

Women in Sport

http://www.makeithappen.com/wis/ (August 7, 1997)

This Web page is dedicated to providing role models of women athletes that confirm women's accomplishments and to sustaining a new vision of women's abilities. It provides a reading list of resources about women's sports, displays posters of women athletes, and gives information about how to fund a women's sport team. Women athletes are indexed both by name and by sport. Sections called "Women in Sports Business" and "Women's Record" are also included. This unique resource in compiled by Jan Meyer.

WomenSport International

http://www.per.ualberta.ca/wsi/ (August 7, 1997)

Assembled by Ann Hall for WomenSport International (WSI), this home page is for an organization dedicated to creating positive change for women and girls in sport and to encouraging physical activity at all levels of involvement. It contains general information about the WSI organization, task forces working for the advocacy of women's sports, international contacts, new sections on the "latest news" in women's sports, and an organizational online newsletter. Perhaps the best resource of the site is the segment entitled "Women's Sport on the Web," which provides links to 10 related sites about women's sports.

Women's Sport Foundation

http://www.lifetimetv.com/wosport/ default.htm (June 11, 1997)

Visitors to this site can find 150 documents on topics and issues in women's sports, information on over 70 different sports, and biographies of over 100 champion female athletes. It also outlines how to apply for the organization's grants, which fund team projects, and describes individual athletes related to women's sports. This "WSF Information Center for Women's Sports and Fitness" site also lists televised women's sporting events, links to other women's sports sites, topics and issues including fitness and training, and resources available in the foundation's library collection.

Feminist Majority Foundation (FMF) Internet Gateway: Women's Sports

http://www.feminist.org/gateway/ sp_exec2.html (June 11, 1997)

This section of the FMF Internet Gateway contains links and summaries of Web sites dealing with women and girls in sport. An executive summary of women's sports is presented, along with a representative sample of Internet resources pertaining to the topic of women's sports. The Feminist Majority also provides a home page (http://www.feminist.org/other/olympic/ ir.html) that lists the Internet resources to be found in three major areas: women's sports general information sites, women in the Olympic Games sites, and specific sports sites.

Gender Equity in Sport

http://www.arcade.uiowa.edu/proj/ge/ resources.html#400 (June 11, 1997)

This text-based Web site provides a thorough examination of Title IX. It includes documents relating to that legislation, as well as links to Web sites and other resources for anyone searching for information about interscholastic or intercollegiate sport. This site is maintained by Mary C. Curtis and Dr. Christine Grant at The University of Iowa. It also contains information for students and coaches, and it lists several organizations and contact people involved in women's sports.

Women in the Olympic Games

The following are Web sites that contain information about past and present women Olympians:

http://www.netsrq.com/~dbois/sports.html (June 11, 1997)—offers a name index of a sampling of biographies about former and current women Olympians that can be accessed through links to other sites; site is copyrighted by Microsoft (R) Encarta.

http://www.olympics.nbc.com (June 11, 1997)—operated by the National Broadcasting Company (NBC), this site contains short biographies of female and male Olympians from the United States Olympic Committee's Hall of Fame.

Women in Specific Sports

Several national governing bodies (NGBs) in the United States provide information on the Internet about women athletes in their specific sports. Here are just a few samples:

http://www.usabasketball.com (June 11, 1997)—United States Basketball

http://www.volleyball.org/usav (June 11, 1997)—United States Volleyball

http://www.usswim.org (June 11, 1997)— United States Swimming, Inc.

http://www.usa-gymnastics.org (June 11, 1997)—United States Gymnastics

http://www.golf.com (June 11, 1997)—LPGA biographies

The Internet and Women in Sport

Women in Sport Listserv

Women in Sports, Health, Physical Education, Recreation and Dance (WISHPERD)—LISTSERV@jsuvml.sjsu.edu (type "SUBSCRIBE WISHPERD")

This site is the only known "listserv" involving women's sports. After subscribing to this no-cost listserv, you will be able to converse with all of the other subscribers about issues in women's sports through an e-mail format. *KD*

J

Barbara Jacket

Barbara Jacket has established herself as one of the top women's track and field coaches. In her 27 years at Prairie View A & M University, she has coached her team to 19 conference championships. During her tenure, Prairie View captured the National Association of Intercollegiate Athletics (NAIA) National Indoor Championship in 1984, 1987, and 1991. More impressive, Prairie View collected the National Association for Intercollegiate Athletics (NAIA) Outdoor Championship for nine consecutive years, from 1982 to 1990.

Born on December 26, 1935, in Port Arthur, Texas, Jacket began her career at Prairie View in 1964 as the physical education teacher and swimming instructor. She did not begin coaching until 1966, when she started the track program. Prior to becoming a coach, she competed for the Tuskegee Institute. In the 1970s, Jacket was an assistant coach for the United States Junior Amateur Athletic Union (AAU) Team and also lent her expertise during the World University Games and the Pan American Games. She was named head manager for the 1981 World University Games and head coach for the Pacific Conference Games.

Jacket excelled as head coach for several teams during the 1980s and 1990s, including the South Team at the 1983 National Sports Festival and the track and field contigent at the 1985 and 1991 World University Games, and the U.S. national team at the 1987 World Track and Field Championships. She retired as head coach of Prairie View in 1991 to devote her time and energy to coach the 1992 Olympic team. As a result of Jacket's desire and dedication to get the most out of her athletes, the Women's Olympic Track and Field Team captured four gold medals, three silver medals, and three bronze medals. She continued her commitment to Prairie View by serving as its athletic director after retiring as coach of the school's track and field teams.

Throughout Jacket's tenure, 27 of her athletes achieved All-American status. Jacket was honored as the NAIA Coach of the Year six times between 1983 and 1991. Because of her guidance on the field, Jacket was inducted into the Tuskegee Athletic Hall of Fame in 1987, the Prairie View A & M University Sports Hall of Fame in 1992, and the Southwestern Athletic Conference Hall of Fame in 1993. A 1958 graduate of Tuskegee Institute in Alabama, Jacket currently resides in Prairie View, Texas.

Nell Jackson

Nell Jackson had a remarkable track and field career, both as an athlete and as a coach. Jackson was born on July 1, 1929, in Athens, Georgia. In 1949, she set the American record in the 200-meter dash. Jackson was a member of the Tuskegee Institute track team in Alabama and a 1948 Olympian. Her record in the 200-meter stood for six years, and by that time Jackson was coaching at Tuskegee Institute. In 1956, Jackson, who was then only 27 years old, became the coach of the 1956 United States Women's Olympic Track and Field Team. The first African American coach of an Olympic team, Jackson coached the Women's Olympic Track and Field Team again in 1972. In 1968, she became one of the first two women, and the first African American, to serve on the Board of Directors of the United States Olympic Committee (USOC).

Jackson was successful outside of the Olympic arena as well. After earning her doctorate in physical education at the University of Iowa, Jackson coached and taught at Illinois State University and the University of Illinois. She moved into athletic administration at Michigan State University. In 1981, she became director of intercollegiate athletics (for men's and women's programs) at the State University of New York at Binghamton, becoming one of the first women to serve in that position. She remained in this job until her untimely death in 1988. The National Association of Girls and Women in Sport annually gives a Nell Jackson Award to honor this outstanding advocate of women's sport. This award recognizes outstanding minority women athletes in track and field and is also awarded to outstanding minority women coaches, leaders, or mentors in track and field.

Zina Garrison Jackson. *See* **Zina Garrison**

Betty Jameson

Betty Jameson, born on May 19, 1919, in Norman, Oklahoma, was a founder and charter member of the Women's Professional Golf Association (1944) which later (1949) became the Ladies Professional Golf Association (LPGA). Early tour members included "Babe" Zaharias, Patty Berg, Betty Jameson, Bettye Danoff, and Helen Hicks. Her first successes in golf came early. Jameson won the Texas Publinx title in 1932 when she was 13 years old and the Southern Championship when she was 15. In 1939 and 1940, Jameson won the United States Amateur Championships, and in 1942, she became the first player to win the Western Open and the Western Amateur in the same season.

Jameson won 14 championships before turning professional in 1945. In 1947, Jameson won the Women's United States Open, and she won the Western Open (a major championship at the time) for a second time in 1954. In total, she won 10 LPGA events. In 1955 alone, she won the Sarasota Open, Babe Zaharias Open, White Mountains Open, and Richmond Open. Jameson was one of the first four inductees into the LPGA Hall of Fame.

Carol Heiss Jenkins. *See* **Carol Heiss**

Peggy Fleming Jenkins. *See* **Peggy Fleming**

Barbara Jones

Born on March 26, 1937, Barbara Jones won her first gold medal at age 15, as a member of her 4 x 100-meter relay team. She repeated this accomplishment at the 1960 Olympic Games, helping her team set an Olympic record. Before participating in the 1960 Olympic Games, and while attending Tennessee State University, Jones won five gold medals at the National Amateur Athletic Union (AAU) Championships (1952, 1954, 1955, 1958). She was an AAU All-American in 1958 and in 1959. She went on to win several more events, including the 1959 Pan American Games 100-meter dash, in which she set a Pan American record. She returned to the Pan American Games in 1960 and was a member of the gold-medal-winning 4 x 100-meter relay team.

Joan Joyce

At the 1958 National Fast Pitch Softball Championships, 18-year-old first baseman Joan Joyce, already a two-year veteran with the Raybestos Brakettes softball team, relieved injured star pitcher Bertha Regan Tickey. Joyce pitched a no-hitter for the national championship title, one of 15 titles over the course of her career.

Joyce went on to compile an amateur career record of 509-33, with 105 no-hitters, 33 perfect games (no hits or walks), an ERA (Earned Run Average) of 0.21, and a batting average of .327. Her record in the International Women's Professional Softball League (which she helped found in 1975) included 34 no-hitters, 8 perfect games, and a batting average of .290. She still holds nine Brakette pitching and hitting records. Named to 18 Amateur Softball Association (ASA) All-American Teams, Joyce was the most valuable player eight times. She was runner-up for the 1976 Women Sports Magazine Athlete of the Year Award. She was inducted into the International Women's Sports Hall of Fame in 1989.

Joyce was born on August 1, 1940, in Waterbury, Connecticut. Besides her prowess in softball, Joyce was also a champion basketball and volleyball player and a bowler. In 1977, at the age of 37, Joyce qualified for the Ladies Professional Golf Association (LPGA) tour.

In May 1994 she returned to coaching softball and guided Florida Atlantic University (FAU) to a 33-18 record. She also coaches the FAU golf team, and in January 1996 assumed senior women's administrator duties.

Florence Griffith Joyner

Delorez Florence Griffith Joyner was born on December 21, 1959, in Los Angeles, California. Her nickname "Flo-Jo" has come to represent blazing speed, grace, and talent. Having grown up in Los Angeles, she began running track at the age of 7. At 14, she was a champion runner at the Jesse Owens National Youth Games. In 1979, she en-rolled at California State University to train with the famous coach, Bob Kersee. She then transferred to UCLA when he went there to coach.

After winning a silver medal in the 200-meter dash at the 1984 Olympic Games in Los Angeles, California, Griffith went into semi-retirement. She returned to competition in 1987 at the world championships in Rome, taking the silver medal in the 200-meter dash and a gold medal as part of the 4 x 100-meter relay team. That same year, she married championship triple-jumper Al Joyner (Jackie Joyner-Kersee's brother), who was Griffith Joyner's coach until her retirement from track in 1989.

It was at the 1988 Olympic trials and the 1988 Olympic Games in Seoul, South Korea, that her talent was most visible. The records she set during 1988 will probably prevail into the twenty-first century. She still holds the women's world records of 10.49 seconds for the 100-meter dash and 21.34 seconds for the 200-meter dash. Her time of 10.49 seconds in the 100-meter race at the 1988 Olympic trials in Indianapolis was one of the most spectacular performances in track and field history, breaking the world records by .27 seconds (a huge amount of time for a short sprint). At the Seoul Olympic Games, she won three gold medals in the 100-meter, the 200-meter, and the 4 x 100-meter relay races, setting a world record in the 200-meters. She also received a silver medal as a member of the 4 x 400-meter relay team.

After the Seoul Olympics, Florence Griffith-Joyner became a media sensation and one of the highest paid sports figures in the world with her glamour, style, and elegant clothes. Since her retirement, she has devoted much of her time to commercial enterprises, writing, and modeling. In 1988, she received the Sullivan Award, which is the nation's highest amateur sports honor.

Jackie Joyner-Kersee

Jackie Joyner-Kersee was born on March 3, 1962, in East St. Louis, Illinois. Many believe that she is the world's greatest all-around female athlete since "Babe"

Didrikson. Throughout her career, she has portrayed what is great about sports—dedication, discipline, and a true sense of fair play. Joyner-Kersee has won three Olympic gold medals, one silver medal, and two bronze medals in track and field.

At the age of 14, she won the first of four consecutive United States pentathlon (five track and field events, now the heptathlon, a seven-event competition) championships. After graduating from high school, she accepted a basketball scholarship at the University of California at Los Angeles (UCLA). However, the track and field coach (and her future husband), Bob Kersee, encouraged her to train in track and field events. In 1983, Joyner-Kersee and her brother, Al Joyner, represented the United States in Helsinki, Finland, for the world championships. They both participated in the 1984 Olympic Games in Los Angeles, California, where Joyner-Kersee won a silver medal in the heptathlon, only a few years after beginning the sport. Al won a gold medal in the triple jump.

The heptathlon, Joyner-Kersee's specialty, is a two-day event in which track and field athletes compete in the high jump, the 100-meter hurdles, the shot put, and the 200-meter race on the first day. On the second day, they compete in the long jump, the 800-meter race, and the javelin.

Joyner-Kersee graduated with a history degree from UCLA in 1985. In the summer of 1986, she set the United States record in the heptathlon with 6,841 points. In the Goodwill Games in Moscow (1987), she broke the world record and became the first athlete to score more than 7,000 points in the heptathlon. In the 1988 Olympic Games in Seoul, South Korea, she won two more gold medals. One came in the long jump, where she set an Olympic record. The other gold medal came in the heptathlon where she scored 7,291 points, setting new world, Olympic, and United States records in the process. In the 1992 Games in Barcelona, Spain, she won a gold medal in the heptathlon and a bronze medal in the long jump. In the 1996 Olympic Games in Atlanta, Georgia, she won a bronze medal in the long jump, after withdrawing from the heptathlon competition due to an injury.

In addition to Joyner-Kersee's Olympic accomplishments, she has been the recipient of numerous general athletic honors. She was named the 1994 International Amateur Athletic Federation (IAAF) Female Athlete of the Year. She was the 1996 Sullivan Award winner (the nation's highest amateur sports honor) for outstanding amateur athletic performance. She is a two-time recipient of the Jesse Owens Award in 1986 and 1987, becoming the first athlete to win this award twice. In 1992, she was named the Women's Sports Foundation Amateur Athlete of the Year for the third time, becoming the only athlete so honored.

Even though being an athlete has been important to Joyner-Kersee, she has always remembered to give back to her community. She created the JJK Community Foundation, which develops leadership programs for youth in urban areas across the country. In addition to being a motivational speaker, she is president and founder of JJK & Associates, a sports marketing business.

Judo and Women

The sport of judo is derived from *jutisu*, the art of bare-handed fighting that was popular from the twelfth to the sixteenth centuries in feudal Japan. Judo can be practiced as a form of self-defense, as free play, or as actual combative tournament competition. Much of the Japanese terminology is still used for judo competition.

The training hall for judo is called the *dojo*. Judo competition takes place between two competitors on a mat. A judo competitor wears a uniform of white or off-white jacket and pants, called the *judogi*. The judo teacher is called the *sensei*. There are seven weight classes from the lightest (under 48 kilograms) to the heaviest (72 kilograms). A competitor initially attempts to throw her opponent to the mat and then engage in ground work. Besides judo competition, individuals can earn grade levels through points and testing, yielding different color belts from the white belt (beginner) to the five levels of black belt.

Men's and women's judo differs significantly, particularly in *randori*, or free form fighting, and in *kata*, the repitition of basic forms of judo exercises. The emphasis, traditionally, has been on randori for men and a balance of randori and kata for women. Olympic competition for women focuses on fighting. In judo, a match consists of a four-minute maximum contest for women while men have a five-minute maximum period. The match ends if a competitor wins a full point with a move or the winner may be declared by the earning of the highest fractions of points in a period. If by no other means, the judge will declare a winner if the score is tied at the end of the period. The jackets worn are often pulled open or askew, thus the only difference in the competition rules is that women wear an under "T-shirt". Women were not allowed to do randori until 1974 because fighting was considered dangerous. In competition, each athlete fights a match in a particular weight division against a similarly sized opponent. There are seven weight divisions for women and the open division. The most difficult competition is in the open division, where anyone, regardless of weight class, competes. Usually the best competitors from the other weight classes fight in the open division.

The history of women's judo in the United States is a story of perserverances, courage, and strong advocacy. Phyllis Harper began practicing judo in 1952 in Chicago at the Jujitsu Institute. In the 1960s, she developed a newsletter called the *Willow in the Wind*, to communicate with other women in judo around the United States. The newsletter incorporated training tips and judo anecdotes, but it was primarily used to vent the complaints of unfairness and discrimination against girls and women in judo. Harper unsuccessfully petitioned the Amateur Athletic Union (AAU), which controlled judo at the time, to allow women to compete.

Meanwhile, in New York, Rusty Steward Kanokogi was training at the YMCA, the only place to train in judo. She was the lone woman in a class of 40 men. Kanokogi objected to the fact that women were not allowed to complete in this ancient martial art. With her hair cut short, no make-up, and bound breasts, she competed as a man in an event. She won her final match and the championship, but one official guessed that she was female and threatened to disqualify the entire team if she did not give back her medal.

Kanokogi also started petitioning the AAU for women's participation in judo, but the AAU still would not sanction girls' and women's competitions. Because women were such a minority in judo, they had no political power, even though more and more girls and women were practicing judo throughout the country.

In 1967, as a competitor and coach of a small women's team, Kanokogi pushed to host the first national championships for women. The AAU countered by offering a women's competition, but with severe restrictions. There were certain moves and mat work that the AAU would not allow in sanctioned women's events. Harper agreed with this ruling (believing it at last allowed women to compete), but Kanogkogi said, "No" to any concessions. She was determined to have "women's judo" be traditional judo, and her position was supported.

Meanwhile, a fellow New Yorker, Maureen Braziel, won a silver medal at an international competition in England. Kanokogi used this achievement by an American female competitor at an international competition to demonstrate that it made no sense to keep women out a national competitions. At last, the first National Judo Championship for Women was held in Phoenix, Arizona, in 1974. There were six weight divisions in the event.

The first Grand Champion (as the national title is named in Judo) of the United States was Maureen Braziel. In 1975, Braziel received the Outstanding Player Award from the AAU, for both men and women. This award was ironic in that, five years before, the AAU would not even recognize judo as a woman's sport, and now they recognized a woman as the top judo athlete! With this success, Kanokogi was now more determined than ever before that women compete in world and Olympic championships in the sport of judo.

In 1977, in conjunction with the national championships, the first Women's Pan American Judo Union Championships were held. Such events were prerequisites for establishing a women's world championship. Kanokogi convinced the AAU to bid, successfully, for the United States to host the first world championship for women in 1980. Twenty-seven countries participated.

After United States Judo, Inc., became the national governing body for judo competition, the battle was on, to get women's judo into the Olympic program. To be eligible for travel and training reimbursements, to be allowed to train at the Olympic Training Center in Colorado Springs, Colorado, and to have her sport be recognized as a sport at the Olympic Sports Festival, Kanokogi had to file a 1980 lawsuit with the Division of Human Rights in New York and the American Civil Liberties Union in California.

In 1981, opportunities began to expand for women's judo. The top female competi-tors in each weight division competed at the 1981 Olympic Sports Festival in Syracuse, New York. In 1984, Kanokogi threatened another lawsuit to get women's judo into the Olympic Games. With the threat of pending litigation, and the support of the International Judo Federation (IJF), the International Olympic Committee (IOC) voted to include women's judo as a demonstration sport at the 1988 Games in Seoul, South Korea. At the 1992 Olympic Games in Barcelona, Spain, women's judo became a full medal sport

In 1988, when judo was a demonstration sport, three USA women qualified to compete and two won medals: Margaret Cástro-Gomez (Bronze), Lynn Rothke (Silver), and Eve Trivella. No medals were won in 1992 and 1996 by USA women, and the USA is focusing on the top world competitors: Cuba, France, and Japan.

Some of the prominent women in the sport include Maureen Braziel, Diane Pierce and Margaret Castro (Gomez) in the 1970s; Eve Aronoff Trivella, Jean Kanokogi, Diane Bridges, Susan Alexander in the 1980s; and Sandra Becker, Naomi Peters, Liliko Ogasawara, Hannelori Brown in the 1990s.

Additionally it should be noted that Yolanda Mack was the first nationally ranked African American woman in judo. *RK & HC*

Rusty Kanokogi

Born on July 30, 1935, in Brooklyn, New York, Rusty Kanokogi is a trailblazer in the world of women's judo. In 1962, she became the first woman ever invited to train in the main *dojo* (training hall) of the Kodokan in Tokyo. After her squads won the 1977 Pan American Championships and the 1977 and 1979 British Open Championships, Kanokogi was granted the British Judo Association's Dame Enid Russell Award in 1979. This award is presented to an outstanding judo coach.

In 1980, she received a special Gratitude Award from the Women's World Judo Championship Organizing Committee. Additionally, she received the Dr. Matsumae Sports Award from Tokai University in Japan. This award honored her pioneering efforts in women's judo competition. The first world championship judo tournament for women was created by Kanokogi in 1980. This tournament brought together 149 athletes from 27 countries at Madison Square Garden in New York City.

Kanokogi mentored the United States delegation through numerous tours to judo competitions from 1985 to 1988, including the Austrian Open (1985), German Open (1986), Pan American Games (1986), world championships (1986), Dutch Open (1987), and the Poland Open (1988). She led the effort to establish women's judo as an Olympic event and finally saw her efforts come to fruition in 1988, when the sport became a demonstration event. She coached the 1988 U.S. Women's Olympic Judo Team in Seoul, South Korea. The sport then became a full-fledged medal sport for the 1992 Summer Games in Barcelona, Spain.

Throughout her coaching career, Kanokogi has received numerous awards for her dedication to judo. In 1985, United States Judo, Inc., honored Kanokogi for her outstanding contribution to women's judo, and in 1989, she received the Andrea Bergman Memorial Award. The Women's Sports Foundation recognized Kanokogi with its 1991 President's Award for her contributions to the foundation and women's sports. She was also a 1994 inductee into the Women's Sports Foundation International Women's Sports Hall of Fame.

Currently, Kanokogi is the highest-ranking American woman in judo with a fifth-degree black belt. She teaches judo at 14 independent schools and colleges to approximately 400 people per week. She was appointed Judo Commissioner for the 1998 Goodwill Games in New York.

Pat McCormick Keller. *See* **Pat McCormick**

Betsy King

Betsy King, Ladies Professional Golf Association (LPGA) Hall of Famer, was born in Reading, Pennsylvania, on August 13, 1955. As an amateur, King was a member of Furman University's 1976 Association for Intercollegiate Athletics for Women (AIAW) Championship Team. She joined the LPGA in 1977 but did not win an event until the 1984 Women's Kemper Open. That win was the first of 20 tournament titles won by King between 1984 and 1989, a mark that made her the winningest professional woman golfer of that era. Among women golfers, King is number one in career earnings with total winnings of over five million dollars. She was inducted into the LPGA Hall of Fame in 1995 with 30 career victories and is still an active player on the tour.

Billie Jean King

Billie Jean Moffat King, born on November 22, 1943, in Long Beach, California, is so well known in the world of sport that, like "Babe" Didrickson before her, she is usually referred to by her first names only, "Billie Jean." King was involved in sports from an early age, often playing baseball and football with her father and brother. At the age of 10, she played on a championship softball team. At age 11, her parents encouraged her to play tennis, and she was enrolled at the local municipal courts. She wrote in her autobiography, *Billie Jean*, that she told her mother "I want to play tennis forever. I am going to be the number one tennis player." And that is exactly what she became.

In 1960, Billie Jean and Karen Hantz became the youngest women ever to win the doubles title at Wimbledon. In 1962, she won the Wimbledon singles title for the first time, beating number one seed Margaret Smith of Australia. This win established Billie Jean King as a world-class tennis player and was the beginning of numerous championship wins all over the world. King still holds the record for the most championship wins at Wimbledon, with 20 singles, doubles, and mixed doubles titles. She is the only woman to win the United States Open singles titles on four surfaces (grass, clay, carpet, hard court). She was ranked number one in the world five times between 1966 and 1972. King's tennis records would take pages to list and can be found in many accounts of the history of tennis. She was a phenomenal player and was inducted into the International Tennis Hall of Fame in 1987.

One of Billie Jean King's most notable attributes was not simply her prowess as a tennis player but what she gave back to tennis and the world, and to women's sport in general. King is an outspoken proponent for women's rights. As the top tennis player in the world at the time, she spearheaded

Billie Jean King.

and encouraged the formation of a group of women players who would play a professional circuit. With the sponsorship of Virginia Slims cigarettes, this became known as the Virginia Slims Tournament. Tournament games were played in several cities, with players gathering points for wins. The players with the most points played in a final tournament.

The era in which Billie Jean King played was a time of much discussion concerning equal rights for women and debates about whether men or women were better at tennis. Bobby Riggs, a former Wimbledon Champion, challenged King to a five-set tennis match in 1973, which became known as the "Battle of the Sexes." King played Riggs in the Houston Astrodome before a crowd of 30,472 spectators, the largest paying crowd in tennis history. The game was also televised to millions of viewers. She won easily, 6-4, 6-3, 6-3. This win helped to advance the notion that a woman has the right to participate in sports on her own terms—and be successful.

In 1973, King founded the Women's Tennis Association (WTA). She served as its president from June 1973 to September 1975, and again from September 1980 to September 1981. She did much to advance the cause of equal opportunity for women in tennis, particularly professional women tennis players, who until this time received considerably less prize money than men professionals.

To give women in sport visibility and a platform to discuss their issues, Billie Jean King also founded (1981) a magazine, *womenSports*, which was a forerunner to *Women's Sports and Fitness*. She was also a founding member and prime mover of the Women's Sports Foundation (WSF), a foundation she helped establish with a $5,000 check presented by Bob Hope on behalf of the Gillette Cavalcade of Sports. A trustee of the WSF, King served on its board from 1983 to 1987 and began her second tenure with the WSF's Board of Trustees in 1996. She also helped establish the International Women's Professional Softball Association with Joan Joyce. King was a former softball player and was convinced that team sports are of great benefit for women.

The impact of Billie Jean King on the advancement of opportunities for women in sport was exemplified in 1990 when *Life* magazine declared her one of the "100 Most Important Americans of the Twentieth Century," taking her place alongside the only other athletes on the list—Babe Ruth, Muhammad Ali, and Jackie Robinson. *Life* called King the "winningest woman for equal rights." She was inducted into the WSF International Women's Hall of Fame as a charter member in 1980. Billie Jean King has received numerous accolades from people and organizations around the world. She is both an outstanding tennis player, and an outstanding promoter for equal opportunity for women in sports. No matter the age, or the sport, King champions the breaking of barriers that would deny these opportunities to women. She is still actively involved in championing the right for women to succeed in sport, at all levels.

Marilyn King

Born May 21, 1949, in Boston, Massachusetts, Marilyn King is a two-time Olympic champion, and the University of California's first women's track and field coach. Her 20-year athletic career includes five national titles and a world record. As a child, she was an ordinary athlete, not particularly strong, fast, or quick to learn. She began training as a pentathlete during high school and decided that one day she would compete in the Olympic Games.

In 1972, she qualified in the pentathlon (five track and field events, now known as the heptathlon) for the United States Women's Olympic Track and Field Team, and in 1976, she placed 13th in the event at the Olympic Games in Montreal, Canada. At that point, she decided she would go for the gold medal in the next Olympic Games and would devote the entire year of 1979 to training. In November of that year, however, she was injured in a head-on collision and suffered a serious spinal injury that left her temporarily unable to walk. Despite this setback, she decided not to give up on her Olympic dream.

For the next few months, she was unable to do the physical training required of a pentathlete, so she decided to use mental rehearsal skills. From her bed, she watched films, projected onto the ceiling, of the world-record holders in all five of the pentathalon events. She made mental images of herself performing, and when she was able to walk again, she would painfully walk the course as she imaged herself performing.

Amazingly, with practically no "traditional" physical training, she qualified for the 1980 Games in Moscow, then part of the Soviet Union, by placing second in the Olympic trials. Unfortunately, 1980 was the year of the Olympic boycott by the U.S. Olympic team. Something positive, however, did come out of King's efforts. Her experience prompted her to research the use of imagery in sport. Recognizing that many Olympians used these skills to become champions, she noted that many of them did not continue to use the skills throughout their lives. This realization led to the formation of the Olympic Peace Team, sponsored by the United Nations, to engage former Olympians to teach mental imagery skills to young people. Marilyn King has become an internationally recognized expert on exceptional human performance in the fields of business and education.

Maxine "Micki" King

Maxine "Micki" King, an American diver born on July 26, 1944, in Pontiac, Michigan, won a gold medal in springboard diving at the 1972 Olympic Games in Munich, Germany. Her success in Munich helped redeem an earlier Olympic disappointment. At the 1968 Summer Olympic Games in Mexico City, Mexico, King was leading the springboard diving competition after eight dives when she shattered her left arm by hitting the diving board on her ninth dive. She bravely finished the competition, placing fourth, just out of the medals. King initially retired after the 1968 Games, but soon

returned to competive diving. Her determination paid off four years later when she won the Olympic gold medal. King is a retired colonel from the United States Air Force.

Kodak All America Women's Basketball Team

One of the most significant sponsors of women's collegiate basketball is the Kodak Corporation. In 1973, Kodak began its relationship with women's basketball by sponsoring the Poconos Invitational Girls' Basketball Camps in Pennsylvania. One of the camp coaches, Cathy Rush, was a coach at an Association of Intercollegiate Athletics for Women (AIAW) member school and an informal dialogue began. Kodak was interested in getting the AIAW to use Kodak film for their events and promotional materials. In 1975 Kodak, in concert with the AIAW, sponsored the first All-America Women's College Basketball Team. Ten outstanding women's Division I basketball players were selected to be on the team. The Kodak All-America Women's College Basketball Team joined the Kodak All-America Football Team (1960-93) and the Kodak Men's Basketball Player of the Year (1975-94).

The publicity for women's basketball was the incentive for the AIAW to team up with Kodak. The AIAW (1971-82) was also committed to getting exposure for women's basketball, but they were concerned that corporate sponsorship would compromise their commitment to working with women athletes, to educating young women, and to building women's skills in teamwork. Kodak supported the goals of the AIAW, and both ultimately agreed that teams and individuals could be highlighted without diminishing those goals. Although Kodak was not a sponsor of the AIAW when the first women's Kodak All-America Team was named in 1975, Kodak and the AIAW worked closely together. The next year, 1976, Kodak became a sponsor for the AIAW, and the first Kodak-AIAW National Basketball Championship Trophy was awarded to the winner that year. Tel-Ra Productions produced a video series on the Kodak All-America Team and a promotions package (including posters) was developed. In addition, the AIAW was responsible for getting the first AIAW Championship aired on NBC in 1978, which offered much desired media exposure for women's collegiate basketball.

As the years passed, the position of the AIAW became more and more precarious. The National Collegiate Athletic Association (NCAA), which was larger and more powerful, was pushing to integrate women's programs into its own organization. Kodak was concerned because the NCAA did not endorse sponsored teams, which clearly jeopardized the Kodak All-America Team. Kodak decided to sponsor the newly forming Women's Basketball Coaches Association (WBCA), feeling that the coaches association was a perfect place to house an All-America team. In 1981, Pat Head Summit and her colleagues received $10,000 seed money from Kodak, and the WBCA became a reality. The WBCA held its first national convention in 1992. One problem remained, the AIAW would not release Kodak from its contract with them. With the vigorous persuasion of Merrily Dean Baker, president of the AIAW in 1981, Kodak's contract with the AIAW was terminated, and the Kodak All-America Team was able to continue its relationship with the WBCA.

The All-America team concept grew as a result of the partnership between the WBCA and Kodak. In 1982, All-America teams were identified for the first time in Division II and III schools, in the National Association for Intercollegiate Athletics (NAIA) schools, and in junior/community colleges. In 1992, the girls High School All-America Game and Summer Camps program began, with Kodak as its sponsor.

The Kodak teams have highlighted oustanding sports participation. They have given women's basketball players the recognition they deserve and have helped raise the visibility of women's sports in general. *CS*

Division I

1975

Carolyn Busch	Wayland Baptist College
Marianne Crawford	Immaculata College
Nancy Dunkle	Cal State-Fullerton
Luisa Harris	Delta State College
Jan Irby	William Penn College
Ann Meyers	UCLA
Brenda Moeller	Wayland Baptist College
Debbie Oing	Indiana University
Sue Rojcewicz	Southern Connecticut
Susan Yow	Elon College

1976

Carol Blazejowski	Montclair State University
Cindy Brogdon	Mercer University
Nancy Dunkle	Cal State-Fullerton
Doris Federhoff	Stephen F. Austin University
Luisa Harris	Delta State College
Susie Kudrna	William Penn College
Ann Meyers	UCLA
Marianne Crawford Stanley	Immaculata College
Perl Worrell	Wayland Baptist College
Susan Yow	North Carolina State University

ALL-TIME KODAK ALL-AMERICA ROSTERS

EXHIBIT 1

1977

Carol Blazejowski	Montclair State University
Nancy Dunkle	Cal-State-Fullerton
Rita Easterling	Mississippi College
Suzie Snider Eppers	Baylor University
Doris Federhoff	Stephen F. Austin University
Luisa Harris	Delta State College
Charlotte Lewis	Illinois State University
Ann Meyers	UCLA
Patricia Roberts	University of Tennessee
Mary Scharff	Immaculata College

1978

Genia Beasley	North Carolina State University
Carol Blazejowski	Montclair State University
Debbie Brock	Delta State College
Cindy Brogdon	University of Tennessee
Julie Gross	Louisiana State University
Althea Gayn	Queens College
Kathy Harston	Wayland Baptist College
Nancy Lieberman	Old Dominion University
Ann Meyers	UCLA
Lynette Woodard	University of Kansas

1979

Cindy Brogdon	University of Tennessee
Carol Chason	Valdosta State University
Pat Colasardo	Montclair State University
Denise Curry	UCLA
Nancy Lieberman	Old Dominion University
Jill Rankin	Wayland Baptist College
Susan Taylor	Valdosta State University
Rosie Walker	Stephen F. Austin University
Franci Washington	Ohio State University
Lynette Woodard	University of Kansas

1980

Denise Curry	UCLA
Tina Gunn	Brigham Young University
Pam Kelly	Louisiana Tech University
Nancy Lieberman	Old Dominion University
Inga Nissen	Old Dominion University
Jill Rankin	University of Tennessee
Susan Taylor	Valdosta State University
Rosie Walker	Stephen F. Austin University
Holly Warlick	University of Tennessee
Lynette Woodard	University of Kansas

1981

Denise Curry	UCLA
Anne Donovan	Old Dominion University

EXHIBIT 1 (continued)

Pam Kelly	Louisiana Tech University
Kris Kirchner	Rutgers University
Carol Menken	Oregon State University
Cindy Moble	University of Tennessee
LaTaunya Pollard	Long Beach State University
Bev Smith	University of Oregon
Valerie Walker	Cheyney State University
Lynette Woodard	University of Kansas

1982

Jerilynn Harper	Tennessee Tech University
Janet Harris	University of Georgia
Pam Kelly	Louisiana Tech University
Barbara Kennedy	Clemson University
June Olkowski	Rutgers University
Mary Ostrowski	University of Tennessee
Bev Smith	University of Oregon
Valerie Still	University of Kentucky
Angela Turner	Louisiana Tech University
Valerie Walker	Cheyney State University

1983

Anne Donovan	Old Dominion University
Priscilla Gary	Kansas State University
Tanya Haave	University of Tennessee
Janice Lawrence	Louisiana Tech University
Paula McGee	University of Southern California
Cheryl Miller	University of Southern California
Jasmina Perazic	University of Maryland
LaTaunya Pollard	Long Beach State University
Valerie Still	University of Kentucky
Joyce Walker	Louisiana State University

1984

Teresa Brown	University of North Carolina
Janet Harris	University of Georgia
Becky Jackson	Auburn University
Yolanda Laney	Cheyney State University
Janice Lawrence	Louisiana Tech University
Pam McGee	University of Southern California
Cheryl Miller	University of Southern California
Annette Smith	University of Texas
Marilyn Stephens	Temple University
Joyce Walker	Louisiana State University

1985

Anucha Browne	Northwestern University
Sheila Collins	University of Tennessee
Kirsten Cummings	Long Beach State University
Medina Dixon	Old Dominion University
Teresa Edwards	University of Georgia

EXHIBIT 1 (continued)

Kamie Ethridge	University of Texas
Pam Gant	Louisiana Tech University
Janet Harris	University of Georgia
Eun Jung Lee	Northeast Louisiana University
Cheryl Miller	University of Southern California

1986

Cindy Brown	Long Beach State University
Teresa Edwards	University of Georgia
Kamie Ethridge	University of Texas
Wanda Ford	Drake University
Jennifer Gillom	University of Mississippi
Pam Leake	University of North Carolina
Lilie Mason	Western Kentucky University
Katrina McClain	University of Georgia
Cheryl Miller	University of Southern California
Sue Wicks	Rutgers University

1987

Cindy Brown	Long Beach State University
Clarissa Davis	University of Texas
Tracey Hall	Ohio State University
Donna Holt	University of Virginia
Andrea Lloyd	University of Texas
Katrina McClain	University of Georgia
Vickie Orr	Auburn University
Shelly Pennefather	Villanova University
Teresa Weatherspoon	Louisiana Tech University
Sue Wicks	Rutgers University

1988

Michelle Edwards	University of Iowa
Bridgett Gordon	University of Texas
Tracey Hall	Ohio State University
Donna Holt	University of Virginia
Suzie McConnell	Penn State University
Vickie Orr	Auburn University
Penny Toler	Long Beach State University
Teresa Weatherspoon	Louisiana Tech University
Sue Wicks	Rutgers University
Beverly Williams	University of Texas

1989

Jennifer Azzi	Stanford University
Vicky Bullett	University of Maryland
Clarissa Davis	University of Texas
Bridgette Gordon	University of Tennessee
Nora Lewis	Louisiana Tech University
Nikita Lowry	Ohio State University
Vickie Orr	Auburn University
Chana Perry	San Diego State University

EXHIBIT 1 (continued)

Deanna Tate	University of Maryland
Penny Toler	Long Beach State University

1990

Jennifer Azzi	Stanford University
Daedra Charles	University of Tennessee
Portia Hill	Stephen F. Austin University
Dale Hodges	St. Joseph's University
Carolyn Jones	Auburn University
Venus Lacy	Louisiana Tech University
Franthea Price	University of Iowa
Wendy Scholtens	Vanderbilt University
Dawn Staley	University of Virginia
Andrea Stinson	North Carolina State University

1991

Kerry Bascom	University of Connecticut
Daedra Charles	University of Tennessee
Dana Chatman	Louisiana State University
Delmonica DeHorney	University of Arkansas
Sonia Henning	Stanford University
Joy Holmes	Purdue University
Carolyn Jones	Auburn University
Genia Miller	Cal State-Fullerton
Dawn Staley	University of Virginia
Andrea Stinson	North Carolina State University

1992

Shannon Cate	University of Montana
Dena Head	University of Tennessee
MaChelle Joseph	Purdue University
Rosemary Kosiorek	West Virginia University
Tammi Reiss	University of Virginia
Susan Robinson	Penn State University
Frances Savage	University of Miami
Dawn Staley	University of Virginia
Sheryl Swoopes	Texas Tech University
Val Whiting	Stanford University

1993

Andrea Congreaves	Mercer University
Toni Foster	University of Iowa
Mauretta Freeman	Auburn University
Heidi Gillingham	Vanderbilt University
Lisa Harrison	University of Tennessee
Karen Jennings	University of Nebraska
Katie Smith	Ohio State University
Sheryl Swoopes	Texas Tech University
Val Whiting	Stanford University

EXHIBIT 1 (continued)

1994

Jessica Barr	Clemson University
Janice Felder	University of Southern Mississippi
Niesa Johnson	University of Alabama
Lisa Leslie	University of Southern California
Rebecca Lobo	University of Connecticut
Nikki McCray	University of Tennessee
Andrea Nagy	Florida International University
Tonya Sampson	University of North Carolina
Carol Ann Shudlick	University of Minnesota
Natalie Williams	UCLA

1995

Angela Aycock	University of Kansas
Niesa Johnson	University of Alabama
Vickie Johnson	Louisiana Tech University
Stacey Lovelace	Purdue University
Rebecca Lobo	University of Connecticut
Nikki McCray	University of Tennessee
Wendy Palmer	University of Virginia
Jennifer Rizzotti	University of Connecticut
Shelley Sheetz	University of Colorado
Charlotte Smith	University of North Carolina

1996

Shalonda Enis	University of Alabama
Chamique Holdsclaw	Univeristy of Tennessee
Vickie Johnson	Louisiana Tech University
Wendy Palmer	University of Virginia
Jennifer Rizzotti	Univeristy of Connecticut
Saudia Roundtree	University of Georgia
Sheri Sam	Vanderbilt Universitiy
Katie Smith	Ohio State University
Kate Starbird	Stanford University
Debra Williams	Louisiana Tech University

Division II

1983

Donna Burks	Dayton
Beth Couture	Erskine
Candy Crosby	Northeast Illinois
Stacey Cunningham	Shippensburg State University
Carla Eades	Central Missouri State
Kelli Kitsch	SW Oklahoma State
Lorena Legarde	University of Portland
Francine Perry	Quinnipiac College
Claudia Schleyer	Abilene Christian
Janice Washington	Valdosta State

EXHIBIT 1 (continued)

1984

Mary Beasley	Barry
Regina Brown	College of Charleston
Daphne Donnelly	Francis Marion
Carla Eades	Central Missouri State
Alison Fay	Bentley College
Linda Krawford	Oakland University
Kelli Litsch	SW Oklahoma State
Robin Mortensen	St. John Fisher
Carol Welch	Cal Poly-Pomona
Jackie White	Cal Poly-Pomona

1985

Darlene Chaney	Hampton Institute
Anita Cooper	Hampton Institute
Julie Fruendt	Lewis University
Rosie Jones	Central Missouri State
Rachel Jackson	St. Anselm College
Sharon Lyke	Utica
Vincene Morris	Philadelphia Textile
Francine Perry	Quinnipiac College
Lynette Richardson	Florida International
Claudia Schleyer	Abilene Christian

1986

Von Fulmore	North Carolina Central
Jackie Harris	Central Missouri State
Hope Linthicum	Central Connecticut State
Vickie Mitchell	Cal Poly-Pomona
Vincene Morris	Philadelphia Textile
Leone Patterson	Chapman
Delinda Samuel	Delta State
Claudia Schleyer	Abilene Christian
Diane Walker	Slippery Rock University
Lisa Walters	Mankato State

1987

Laura J. Anderson	Nebraska-Omaha
Kim Disbro	Florida Southern
Jennifer DiMaggio	Pace
Jackie Dolberry	Hampton
Candace Fincher	Valdosta State
Joy Jeter	New Haven
Debra Larsen	Cal Poly-Pomona
Michelle McCoy	Cal Poly-Pomona
Lisa Walters	Mankato State
Vanissa Wells	West Texas State

1988

Jennifer Dimaggio	Pace
Jackie Dolberry	Hampton

EXHIBIT 1 (continued)

Cathy Gooden	Cal Poly-Ponoma
Jill Halapin	Pittsburgh-Johnstown
Joy Jeter	New Haven
Mary Naughton	Stonehill College
Julie Wells	Northern Kentucky
Vanessa Wells	West Texas State
Shannon Williams	Valdosta State
Tammy Wilson	Central Missouri State

1989

Sonja "Niki" Bracken	Cal Poly-Pomona
Jackie Dolberry	Hampton
Cathy Gooden	Cal Poly-Pomona
Joy Jeter	New Haven
Velisa Levett	West Georgia College
Pat Smykowski	North Dakota State
Charlene Taylor	New Haven
Teresa Tinner	West Texas State
Shannon Williams	Valdosta State
Tammy Wilson	Central Missouri State

1990

Carmille Barnette	Longwood College
Sonja "Niki" Bracken	Cal Poly-Pomona
Kammy Brown	Virginia State
Julie Dabrowski	New Hampshire College
Debbie Delle	Oakland University
Bridget Hale	Pittsburgh-Johnstown
Crystal Hardy	Delta State
Durene Hesler	North Dakota
Shannon Williams	Valdosta State
Jeanette Yeoman	St. Joseph's (Ind.)

1991

Joy Barry	Assumption College
Dana Bright	Jacksonville State
Stephanie Coons	Cal Poly-Ponoma
Jackie Givens	Fort Valley State
Pat McDonald	West Texas State
Whitney Meier	North Dakota
Sharonda O'Bannon	Bellarmine College
Kim Penwell	Bentley College
Tracy Saunders	Norfolk State
Jerri Wiley	Southeast Missouri State

1992

Pat McDonald	West Texas State
Lisa Miller	Indiana/Purdue-Fort Wayne
Dana Jo Neilsen	Augustana College
Laurie Northrop	Portland State
Latanya Patty	Delta State
Kim Penwell	Bentley College
Nadine Schmidt	North Dakota State
Tracie Seymour	Bentley College

EXHIBIT 1 (continued)

Tammy Walker-Strode	Edinboro
Mindy Young	Pittsburg-Johnstown

1993

Carolyn Brown	St. Augustine's College
Jody Buck	North Dakota State
Shelly Foster	Washburn University
Yolanda Griffith	Florida Atlantic
Jeannine Jean-Pierre	Edinboro
Amy Molina	St. Michael's
Dana Jo Neilsen	Augustana College
Latanya Patty	Delta State University
Rachel Rosario	California, Riverside
Courtney Sands	University of Indianapolis

1994

Rozetha Burrow	West Georgia State
Nicole Collins	Angelo State
Michelle Doonan	Stonehill College
Kristi Greene	Norfolk State
Tammy Greene	Philadelphia Textile
Carlita Jones	Clarion University
Sheri Kleinsassar	North Dakota
Kathy Lauck	Southern Indiana
Darlene Orlando-Garcia	Massachusetts-Lowell
Darci Steeve	North Dakota State

1995

Jennifer Clarkson	Abilene Christian University
Michelle Doonon	Stonehill College
LeAnn Freeland	Southern Indiana
Kristi Greene	Norfolk State
Carlita Jones	Clarion University
Sheri Kleinsasser	North Dakota
Kim Manifesto	Portland State
Kasey Morlock	North Dakota State
Kristi Smith	Portland State
Teresa Szumigala	Mercyhurst
Dawn Wynn	Valdosta State

1996

Jennifer Clarkson	Abilene Christian
Kim Cummings	Bentley College
LeAnn Freeland	Southern Indiana
Faye Hogan	Cal-State-Dominquez Hills
Susie Hopson	Mars Hill
Stacy Johnson	Delta State
Kim Manifesto	Portland State
Kasey Morlock	North Dakota State
Suzanne Patchett	Stonehill College
Kristi Smith	Portland State

EXHIBIT 1 (continued)

Division III

1983

Michelle Blazevich	UNC-Greenville
Maureen Burchill	South Maine
Carol Ferren	Pomona-Pitzer
Fran Harkins	Scranton
Jody Imbrie	Grove City
Betty Jackson	Lynchburg
Bonnie Jansen	North Central College
Margie O'Brien	Clark University
Laurie Sankey	Simpson
Leslie Spencer	William Penn

1984

Kaye Cross	Colby
Salley Gangell	Hartwick
Sherri Kinsey	Elizabethtown
Deanna Kyle	Wilkes
Page Lutz	Elizabethtown
Sallie Maxwell	Kean
Evelyn Oquendo	Salem State
Eva Marie Pittman	St. Andrews
Lois Salto	College of New Rochelle
Lauri Sankey	Simpson

1985

Maureen Burchill	Southern Maine
Dawn Cillo	College of New Rochelle
Jeannie Demers	Buena Vista
Wendy Engelmann	North Carolina-Greensboro
Ann Fitzpatrick	College of New Rochelle
Deanna Kyle	Scranton
Evelyn Oquendo	Salem State
Terri Schumacher	Wisconsin-Oshkosh
Shontel Sherwood	Pomona-Pitzer-Claremont
Tracy Weaver	Muskingum

1986

Jeannie Demers	Buena Vista
Una Expenkotter	Scranton
Cathy Lanni	Rhode Island
Rinny Lesane	SUNY-Albany
Jane Meyer	Elizabethtown
Evelyn Oquendo	Salem State
Amy Proctor	St. Norbert
Connie Sanford	Heidelberg
Mary Schultz	St. Mary's, Maryland
Pam Stewart	Christopher Newport

EXHIBIT 1 (continued)

1987

Jessica Beachy	Concordia (Minn.)
Robin Brooks	North Carolina Wesleyan
Jeannie Demers	Buena Vista (Iowa)
Alfredia Gibbs	Cabrini
Becky Inman	William Penn
Trish Neary	Western Connecticut St.
Shelly Parks	Scranton
Torrie Rumph	Kean-New Jersey
Sonja Sorensen	Wisconsin-Stevens Pt.
Michele White	SUNY-Stoney Brook

1988

Jessica Beachy	Concordia-Moorehead
Catie Cleary	Pine Manor
Lesa Dennis	Emmanuel
Kimm Lacken	Trenton State
Louise MacDonald	St. John Fisher
Linda Mason	Rust
Pattie McCrudden	New York University
Angle Polk	UNC-Greensboro
Sonja Sorenson	Wisconsin-Stevens Pt.
Michelle Swantner	Elizabethtown

1989

Shannon Collins	Centre College (KY)
Diana Duff	Southern Maine
Kirsten Dumford	Cal State-Stanislaus
Susan Heidt	St. John Fisher
Mona Henriksen	Luther College
Nancy Keene	Elizabethtown
Pattie McCrudden	New York University
Tara McGuire	Clark University
Jillayn Quaschnick	Concordia (Minn.)
Joan Watza	St. Norbert

1990

Kim Beckman	Buena Vista
Cathy Clark	Marietta College
Arlene Eagan	Buffalo State
Robin R. Gaby	Eastern Connecticut St.
Ann Gilbert	Oberlin College
Anestine Hector	Clark University
Susan Heldt	St. John Fisher
Anne Kumrine	Franklin & Marshall
Michelle Thykeson	Concordia (Minn.)
Susan Yates	Centre College

1991

Kathy Beck	Moravian College
Arlene Eagean	Buffalo State

EXHIBIT 1 (continued)

Ann Gilbert	Oberlin College
Karen Hermann	Washington University
Karen Jenkins	Roanoke College
Kisa Kirchenwitz	Wisconsin-Oshkosh
Laura Pate	Southern Maine
Missy Sharer	Grinnell College
Joyce Spanier	St. Benedict
Laurie Trow	St. Thomas

1992

Kathy Beck	Moravian College
Sandy Buddelmeyer	Capital University
Donna Cogar	Roanoke College
Caryn Cranston	Pomona-Pitzer
Kristen Curtis	Western Connecticut St.
Trish Harvey	Luther College
Diane Ring	Wisconsin-Eau Claire
Kathy Roberts	Wartburg College
Stephanie Sullivan	Wisconsin-Plattville
Laurie Trow	St. Thomas

1993

Sandy Buddelmeyer	Capital University
Lynne Kempski	Scranton
Sladja Kovljanic	Middlebury College
Donna Layne	New York University
Kelly J. Mahlum	St. Benedict
Julie Maki	Wisconsin-Stout
Leah Onks	Maryville College
Kathy Roberts	Wartburg College
Laurie Trow	St. Thomas
Tracy Wilson	Central College

1994

Karen Barefoot	Christopher Newport
Amy Bot	St. Thomas
Jackie Dougherty	Scranton
Beth Green	Wittenberg University
Emilie Hanson	Central University
Elizabeth "Liza" Janssen	Wellesley College
Donna Layne	New York University
Katie Mans	Alma College
Leah Onks	Maryville
Laura Schmeltzer	Capital University

1995

Leslie Ferguson	Redlands
Emilie Hanson	Central College
Rita Hurtgen	Wisconsin-River Falls
Arlene Melnholz	Wisconsin-Eau Claire
Jennifer Nish	Scranton

EXHIBIT 1 (continued)

Jamie Parrott	Maryville College
Katie Smith	SUNY-Geneseo
B.J. Toolan	Trinity College
Kari Tuffe	Luther College
Dana Zarzycki	Mount Union College

1996

Corrine Carson	Marymount College
Amy Flory	Defiance College
Meegan Garrity	Clark University
Jennifer Goodell	William Smith College
Marsha Harris	New York University
Jamie Parrott	Maryville College
Leslee Rogers	LaVerne College
Karie Tufte	Luther College
Wendy Wangerin	Wisconsin-Oshkosh
Laura Witte	St. Thomas

NAIA

1985

Jenetta Alston	Francis Marion
Karol Busche	Wisconsin
Terry Condor	Central Arkansas
Ann Cooper	St. Mary's
Temple Elmore	College of Charleston
Lori Harris	Defiance
Kelli Kitsch	Southwestern Oklahoma
Lorena Legarde	Portland
Karne Morton	Carson-Newman
Gail Scardillo	Geordina Court

1986

Pam DeCosta	Mesa
LeAnne DeYoung	Purdue-Calumet
Karman Dolfo	Western Washington
Janice Joseph	Louisiana
Karen Morton	Carson-Newman
Sandra Tanner	Berry College
Tracy Tillman	Francis Marion
Lisa Washington	College of Charleston
Amy Wilheim	Morningside
Carmen Wynn	Wayland Baptist

1987

Jenne Barta	Wisconsin-Green Bay
LeAnn DeYoung	Purdue-Calumet
Brenda Hill	North Georgia
Demetria Lang	Xavier
Mary McCullom	William Carey
Tracy Tillman	Francis Marion

EXHIBIT 1 (continued)

Georgia Walton	Panhandle State
Tina Webb	Arkansas-Monticello
Amy Whilhelm	Morningside (Iowa)
Carmen Wynn	Wayland Baptist

1988

Cheryl Barrineau	Wingate
Donna Brunson	Arkansas Tech
LeAnn DeYoung	Purdue-Calumet
Cheryl Dreckman	Briar Cliff
Sharla Harrison	Wayland Baptist
Mary McCullom	William Carey
Miriam Samuels-Walker	Claflin College
Tracy Tilman	Francis Marion
Tina Webb	Arkansas-Monticello
Heidi Wimmer	Friends

1989

Rose Avery	Arkansas-Monticello
Robin Becker	St. Ambrose
Lanell Dawson	Arkansas Tech
Cheryl Dreckman	Briar Cliff
Sharla Harrison George	Wayland Baptist
Schironda Jones	St. Thomas Aquinas
Darla Pannier	Central Methodist
Miriam Samuels-Walker	Claflin College
Dorene Thomas	Wingate College
Tina Webb	Arkansas-Monticello

1990

Rose Avery	Arkansas-Monticello
Robin Becker	St. Ambrose
Ruby Byrd	Claflin College
Lanell Dawson	Arkansas Tech
Avrli Freeman	Southern Nazarene
Schironda Jones	St. Thomas Aquinas
Henriette Mitchell	Xavier of Louisiana
Mirian Samuels-Walker	Claflin College
Brenda Shaffer-Dahl	Washburn
Tina Webb	Arkansas-Monticello

1991

Ruby Byrd	Calflin College
Lynn Cole	Southwestern
Angela Ernst	Western Oregon State
Paula Johnson	Phillips
Schironda Jones	St. Thomas Aquinas
Dina Kangas	Minnesota-Duluth
Jill Reid	Tri-State
Checola Seals	Central Arkansas
Jackie Snodgress	SW Oklahoma State
Dorene Thomas	Wingate College

EXHIBIT 1 (continued)

1992

Carol Balley-Sessums	Wayland Baptist
Kris DeClerk	Moorhead State
Cindy Hays	Midland Lutheran
Michell Hendry	Simon Fraser
Dana Morton	Bloomfield College
Andrea Schneider	Simon Fraser
Checola Seals	Central Arkansas
Jackie Snodgrass	SW Oklahoma State
Antionette Vinson	Central State
LaShana White	Seattle University

1993

Carol Bailey-Sessums	Wayland Baptist
Kathy Comeaux	Henderson State
Kari Farstveet	Moorhead State
Julie Jensen	Northern State
Taj McWilliams	St. Edwards
Penni Pappas	University of the Ozarks
Julie Stringer	Lewis-Clark State (Idaho)
Antoinette Vinson	Central State
LaShana White	Seattle University
Beth Willis	David Lipscomb

1994

Shenna Bowling	Montevallo
Lynn Buckmaster	Midwestern State
Andrea Deaton	Campbellsville
Dawn Grell	Arkansas Tech
Julie Jensen	Northern State
Cherilyn Morris	Southern Nazarene
Stephanie Strack	Arkansas Tech
Antoinette Vinson	Central State
Emily Wetzel	Simon Fraser
LaShana White	Seattle University

1995

Nicole Cleaver	Findlay (Ohio)
Andrea Deaton	Campbellsville College
Kristina Edwards	Wayland Baptist
Carol Harrington	Arkansas-Monticello
Angie Henderson	Mount Mercy College
Julie Jensen	North State (SD)
April Kaalohelo	Oklahoma Christian
Ana Paula Monteiro	Mary Hardin-Baylor
Cherilyn Morris	Southern Nazarene
Beth Stewart	Lipscomb

1996

Joanna Cuprys	Auburn at Montgomery
Sandie Graves	Western Oregon State
Marieme Lo	Central State

EXHIBIT 1 (continued)

Mari Maaske	Doane College
Ana Paula Monteiro	Mary Hardin-Baylor
Gina Sampson	Western Washington
Brandy Scheckel	St. Ambrose
Beth Stewart	Lipscomb
Cheryl Stinchfield	McKendree College
Julia Yunusova	Southern Nazarene

JC/CC

1983

Carolyn Blair	Shelby State
Lori Carriere	North Dakota-Williamson
Tonie Edwards	Anderson Junior
Clara Faison	Louisburg
Jackie Gloseen	Moberly Junior
Nell Haskins	Howard
Sheri Hennum	Fullerton
Linda Martin	Illinois Central
LuAnn Underhill	Peace College
Mary Jo Vodenichar	Penn State University Shenango

1984

Felicia Brown	Lackawana Junior
Debra DeGrate	McClennan
Marlene Flanagan	Central Arizona
Angela Fletcher	Roane State Community
Julie Hendricksen	North Dakota-Williston
Julie Hogan	Mitchell College
Rhonda Mikes	Northwest Mississippi
Jodi Moan	Vincennes University
Carla Shuck	Worthington Community
Rhonda Smith	Conors State

1985

Miroslava Acosta	Cochise
Charlene James	Tyler Junior
Rhonda Miles	Northwest Mississippi
Kristi Moore	Illinois Central
Shamona Mosely	LA Trade Tech
Robin Parsons	Martin
Pam Pringle	Alpena Community
Angela Saunders	Mitchell College
Rhonda Smith	Connors State
Sandy Storey	Essex Community

1986

Mozell Brooks	Angelina Junior
Dorothea Conwell	Odessa Community
Lorrie Corella	Mitchell College
Carolyn Davis	Central Arizona

EXHIBIT 1 (continued)

Lorriane Frazier	Anderson
Kim Green	Lincoln
Teresa Grove	Roane State Community
Cathy Snipes	NE Oklahoma A & M
Sue Stechet	Union County
Angie Thompson	Hiwassee

1987

Valerie Avant	Florida Junior
Rose Ballard	Roane State Community
Stacy Boyle	Dodge City Community
Portia Hill	Trinity Valley Community
Tami Liekem	Central Arizona
Kariassa Moore	North Arkansas Community
Carol Poll	Lewis & Clark (IL)
Sallie Routt	Blinn Junior
Lisa Stlepler	Essex Community
Sherry Szczuka	Delaware Tech

1988

Khadljah Brown	Truman
Vanessa Foster	Trustt-McConnell
Portia Hill	Trinity Valley
Pam Hudson	Kilgore Community
Tami Morre	Kaskaskia College
Barbara Pierce	Mitchell College
Sheila Reynolds	St. Gregory
Melba Roy	Odessa
Angela Taylor	Florida Community
Evelyn Thompson	NE Mississippi Junior

1989

Dematra Adams	Florida Community
Nickey Allen	Western Texas College
Kris Collins	Mitchell College
LaWaynta Dawson	Moberty Area Junior
Nancy Foster	Union County
Debbie Johnson	Barton County Community
Paula Johnson	Paris Junior (TX)
Kristi Kincade	Central Arizona College
Jerri Wiley	Kaskaskia College

1990

Barbara Appling	Emmanuel College
Carolyn Brown	Louisburg College
Linda Burgess	John C. Calhoun Community
Kris Collins	Mitchell College
Kieishasha Garnes	Hilbert College
Sharon Hargrove	Central Arizona
Lisa Payne	Kilgore College

EXHIBIT 1 (continued)

Suzette Sargeant	Central Arizona
Sheryl Swoopes	South Plains College
LaTonya Thomas	Allen County Community

1991

Malissa Boles	Sullivan College
Shawnette Brock	Hiwassee College
Angel Henderson	Louisburg College
Leanne Hertsenberg	Mitchell College
Anne Miller	Waldorf College
Bridget Pettis	Central Arizona College
Charlotte Powell	Cuyahoga Community
Beth Salvaggio	Elgin Community
Elizabeth Sirchia	Golden West College
Jaime White	Utah Valley Community

1992

Kathy Brown	Miami-Dade Community
Daniellette Coleman	Miami-Dade Community
Jody Davis	Central Arizona College
Bonnie Dove	Central Arizona College
Sonya Harlin	Moberly College
Leanne Hertsenberg	Mitchell College
Tina Malone	Kilgore Community
Nicole McCrimmon	New Mexico Junior
Loretta Stafford	Connors State College
Shawna Tubbs	Trinity Valley Community

1993

Simone Edwards	Seminole Junior
Meghan Flynn	Frederick Community
Beth McGawan	Lackawanna Junior
Amy Nelson	Fergus Falls Community
Michelle Reed	Sulivan College
ShaRhonda Reynolds	Kilgore Community
Connie Robinson	Central Florida Community
Allegra Schell	Mitchell College
Karleen Shields	Contra Costa College
Shawna Tubbs	Trinity Valley Community

1994

Mandy Bryan	Illinois Central College
LaTisha Burnett	LA Harbor College
Sue Jones	Florida Community-Jacksonville
Keshana Ledet	Central Arizona College
Laticia Morris	Odessa College
Pam Pennon	Connors State College
Saudia Roundtree	Kilgore College
Tracy Consuela Sadler	Anderson College
Eliza Sokolowska	Independence Community
Rouzanna Vagradian	Mitchell College

EXHIBIT 1 (continued)

1995	
Tora Darden	Sullivan College
Shalonda Enis	Trinity Valley Community
Shelly Nichols	Central Florida Community
Elaine Powell	Pearl River Community
Tracy Sadler	Anderson Junior (SC)
Julia Terenjuk	Independence Community (Kansas)
Lashanda L. White	Miami-Dade CC North
Kim Williams	Westark Community
Rita Williams	Mitchell College
Jurate Zukauskalte	Merritt College
1996	
Alisa Burras	Westark Community
Monica Echeverria	Central Florida Community
Natalie Hughes	Central Arizona College
Raqia Johnson	Union County College
Deneta Joyner	Gateway Community Tech
Amy Kieckbusch	Kankakee Communicy
Ewa Laskowska	Independence Community (Kansas)
Nicole Mamula	Frederick Community
Tasha Mills	Trinity Valley Community
Terri Mitchell	Trinity Valley Community

EXHIBIT 1 (continued)

Olga Korbut

At the 1972 Olympic Games in Munich, Germany, an alternate for the Soviet team focused the world's attention on gymnastics. Substituting for an injured teammate, Olga Korbut won three gold medals and one silver medal while performing risky and innovative routines. After a disappointing performance in the all-around competition, Olga's dra–matic comeback to win three individual medals captured the imagination of the public. Born in Hrodna, on May 16, 1955, in the former Belorussian Soviet Socialist Republic (now the republic of Belarus), Korbut entered a government sports school when she was 11 years old.

After the 1972 Olympic Games, she was named Female Athlete of the Year by the Associated Press. In 1973, her presence on a Soviet gymnastics team that toured the United States attracted crowds of record size.

Competing at the 1976 Olympic Games in Montreal, Canada, at the age of 21, Korbut won a team gold medal and a silver medal in the balance beam. In addition to being inducted into the International Gymnastics Hall of Fame in 1988, she was inducted into the Women's Sports Foundation's International Women's Sports Hall of Fame in 1982.

Korbut has been involved in a number of activities since her retirement from competi-tion. She was active in the relief efforts following the Chernobyl nuclear accident in 1986, which took place in Ukraine close to her native Belarus. Korbut moved to the United States in 1991. She currently teaches gymnastics in public schools and is preparing to open an International Gymnastics Training Center near her new home in Atlanta, Georgia.

Julie Krone

Julie Krone is one of the few women compet-ing in horse racing, a sport dominated by men. In March 1988, she rode in her 1,205th winning race, passing Patricia Cooksey to become the top female rider in history. She was the first woman to capture a riding championship at a major track, and the first woman to compete at the Breeders' Cup races. She is credited with a subtle ability to motivate the horses she rides to superior performances.

Born in Benton Harbor, Michigan, on July 24, 1963, Julie Krone knew she was born to ride. At four feet, ten inches and 100 pounds, she is the daughter of a champion horse-woman. At the age of 16, she set her sights for Churchill Downs and the Kentucky Derby. Since then, Krone has become the most celebrated female jockey in the history of horse racing.

In 1992, she finished the year with 278 wins and over $9.1 million in prize money to rank ninth among all jockeys nationally. In 1993, she captured a race meet title at Gulf–stream Park Meet, taking first place in the jockey standings with a meet record 97 wins.

Krone was the first woman to ride in a Triple Crown race (Kentucky Derby, Preakness, or Belmont Stakes). In 1993, she finished "in the money" (first, second, or third) at Belmont Stakes when she rode Colonial Affair to a win. She has also won the Jersey Derby, the Fountain of Youth Stakes, the New York Handicap, and the Lexington Stakes.

Krone suffered through many injuries, but perhaps the worst was a career-threatening ankle injury suffered in a 1993 riding accident. She later wrote a book about her experiences called *Riding for My Life* (Little & Brown, 1995). Krone was named ESPN's Outstanding Female Athlete of 1993.

L

Lacrosse for Women

The game of women's lacrosse is an aesthetically beautiful game enjoyed by players and spectators around the world. A high-scoring game with no "offsides," it incorporates intricate skills with speed and freedom, as there are no boundaries within the field of play.

The playing field is 120 yards by 70 yards. The goals are 100 yards apart measured from goal line to goal line. The object of the game is to score more goals than your opponent. A goal is scored by passing the whole ball completely over the goal line and into the goal, which is six-feet wide and six-feet high. Each team has 12 players and each player plays both offense and defense. The game starts in the center of the field with a draw. In the draw, two players place the ball between the backs of their sticks. On the official's whistle, they attempt to pass the ball, through an up-and-away movement, to a teammate.

The lacrosse stick (or "crosse") has a long handle with a triangular, meshed-enclosed opening. The stick is used to keep the ball in the player's possession by "cradling" it in the "net," and to pass, shoot, and catch the ball. The team without the ball (defense) uses the crosse to steal the ball from the attacking

Women's lacrosse emphasizes free flowing action.

team by interceptions, ground-ball pick ups, or a stick check (hitting an opponent's stick to dislodge the ball and gain possession). The few rules are designed for safety and fairness. The women's game should not be confused with the rough men's game. No body contact

177

is permitted, and thus not as much equipment is needed. The only similarities to the men's game are the name, the ball, and the goal cage. In essence, the women's game is a giant game of keep away, with the object being to shoot the ball into a goal.

The exact origins of lacrosse are unknown, but it is known that Native Americans played a game called *baggataway* that was similar to the modern game of lacrosse. The French Canadians saw baggataway played near Montreal and began to take part. In 1867, the Canadian Lacrosse Association was founded and rules were written, which are similar to the rules of the women's game today. A touring team went to England and demonstrated the game before Queen Victoria in 1876. By 1912, England had formed a lacrosse association and international games commenced. In the early 1900s, British women teaching in United States schools introduced the game here. In 1926, Rosabelle Sinclair, the first woman to be inducted into the Lacrosse Hall of Fame in 1993, introduced the sport at the Bryn Mawr School in Baltimore and organized high school teams and clubs in the area. The game soon spread to Philadelphia and New York. In 1931, the United States Women's Lacrosse Association (USWLA) was founded, and the first national tournament was played at Greenwich, Connecticut, in 1933. Teams continue to be chosen by a selection committee of USWLA members.

During these early stages of development, England provided coaching, touring teams, and clinics, especially in the Merestead Camp System. When the United States women's team tied the All England team 7-7 in 1957, it became apparent that United States lacrosse was truly established and ready to take its place with the best in the world. In 1973, the United States team defeated Great Britain for the first time. In 1975, the United States touring team that went to England returned undefeated for the first time.

Because lacrosse is not an Olympic sport, the highest form of competition is the World Cup Championship. The first World Cup Tournament was held in Nottingham, England. The United States team, coached by Jackie Pitts, placed first among the six countries participating. Recently, the United States women have dominated the game, winning three of the four World Cup Championships, losing only to Australia in 1986 in the final game. The 1993 World Cup Championships consisted of teams from the United States, England, Australia, Canada, Scotland, Wales, Japan, and Czech Republic.

In the United States, lacrosse has grown from an East Coast sport to a national sport played in most states and by many Division I, II, and III colleges. If you are interested in participating in this exciting, fast-growing game, contact: USWLA Executive Director, 35 Wisconsin Circle, Suite 525, Chevy Chase, MD 20815. *SS*

Marion Ladewig

Marion Ladewig, "The Lady of the Lanes," along with Floretta McCutcheon, "The Pied Piper of Bowling," are considered the first ladies of bowling. Ladewig's record-breaking performances, lifetime accomplishments, and efforts in promoting bowling make her deserving of sharing this honorable title with McCutcheon.

Born on October 30, 1914, in Grand Rapids, Michigan, Ladewig was a self-proclaimed tomboy as a child. She loved to run, play baseball, and engage in other athletic activities not deemed "acceptable" for young girls of the time. As a teenager, she took a job working in a bowling alley, making her first connection with a sport that she would later dominate. During this period, she developed a bowling style based on accuracy and spin that put her at the top of the list of bowling champions for all time.

Ladewig won the biggest bowling title of her era—the All Star—for the first time in 1949. She went on to take this title seven more times between 1949 and 1963. Her scores in the 1951 All Star not only bested all the other women bowlers, but the men as well. Her record also includes two national doubles crowns; two Women's International Bowling Congress (WIBC) All Events; and captain of the two-time national match game team champions, the Fantorium majors. She also captured the World Invitational Championship five times.

Recognized as one of the great bowlers in history, Ladewig was selected as "Woman Bowler of the Year" nine times and named the "Greatest Woman Bowler of All Time" by the Bowling Writers Association of America in 1973. She retired in 1965 at the age of 50, but continues to serve on the Brunswick Advisory Staff of Champions promoting the sport.

Ladies Professional Golf Association: Hall of Fame

Entry into the Ladies Professional Golf Association (LPGA) Hall of Fame is a daunting challenge. An entrant must have fulfilled all of the following: (a) been a member of the LPGA for 10 consecutive years; (b) won at least 30 official events (including two major championships), or 35 official events with one major championship, or 40 official events exclusive of a major.

The LPGA Hall of Fame was established in 1967, with the initial inductees being those already entered into the Women's Golf Hall of Fame. Beginning in April 1998, the LPGA Hall of Fame will combine with the PGA (Professional Golf Association) and the World Golf Hall of Fame in the brand new World Golf Village. The World Golf Village is located just outside of St. Augustine, Florida, and is expected to be a very exciting tribute to all of golf's great stars.

The most recent inductee is Betsy King, but several active players are within reach of the requirements. (Unlike some other sports, golfers can enter the Hall of Fame while still active on the tour.) Entering the 1996 season, Amy Alcott has 29 victories and needs only one more to reach Hall of Fame status. Beth Daniel has 32 victories with one major and is another one to watch.

See also **Halls of Fame**

1951	Patty Berg	57 career victories
1951	Betty Jameson	10 career victories
1951	Louise Suggs	50 career victories
1951	Babe Didrickson Zaharias	31 career victories
1960	Betsy Rawls	55 career victories
1964	Mickey Wright	82 career victories
1975	Kathy Whitworth	88 career victories
1977	Sandra Haynie	42 career victories
1977	Carol Mann	38 career victories
1982	JoAnne Carner	42 career victories*
1987	Nancy Lopez	47 career victories*
1991	Pat Bradley	31 career victories*
1993	Patty Sheehan	34 career victories*
1995	Betsy King	30 career victories*
1994	Dinah Shore	Honorary Member

* Denotes players still on tour as of 1996

MEMBERS OF THE LPGA HALL OF FAME

EXHIBIT 1

Latinas in Sport

What do we know about racial matters in women's sports? Are women from certain racial and ethnic groups more athletic and competitive than others? How do patterns of women's sport participation compare among Latinas, African Americans, Asians, Native Americans, and Whites? While caution must be exercised when making generalizations about heterogeneous racial and ethnic groups, these are important questions in light of the United States' future as a multiracial, multicultural society. Unfortunately, despite far-reaching changes in women's sport participation and the growth and momentum of feminist sport scholarship, scant attention has been devoted to women of color in sports. Routinely we point to dramatic increases in, and general acceptance of, sport participation by women. But women are of many races and ethnic backgrounds, and such generalizations are not applicable to all. Traditional sport studies research not only makes false generalizations about women, but also masks deep racial divisions in "gender equity."

Latina Athleticism over the Years

The public knows little about Latinas' experiences in North American sport. This lack of knowledge is a troubling paradox because Latina participation in sport is not a new phenomenon. Examples of Latina athleticism date back to the 1940s, when the All American Girls Baseball League (AAGBL) began recruiting baseball players from a Cuban women's league, called Estrellas Cubanas. By 1949, Cuban women such as Eulalia Gonzales, Isabel Alvarez, Ysora del Castillo, Mirtha Marrero, and Migdalia Perez had all joined the AAGBL minor league ranks (Gregorich, 1993).

More recently, several Latinas have made names for themselves as professional and Olympic athletes. Nancy Lopez, for example, began winning prestigious golf titles at the age of 12 and was the only woman to compete on the boys' golf team at her high school. Lopez joined the Ladies Professional Golf Association (LPGA) tour in 1978 and was named LPGA Rookie of the Year. Lopez is a three-time LPGA Player of the Year and a member of the LPGA Hall of Fame. She remains the only United States Latina on the LPGA roster.

Women's professional tennis boasts a diverse field of Latina athletes. While not all United States natives, Gigi Fernandez, Mary Jo Fernandez, Aranxta Sanchez-Vicario, and Conchita Martinez, regularly compete in United States and international tennis events. In 1996, the Latina duo of Mary Jo Fernandez and Gigi Fernandez won the Olympic gold medal for the USA in the women's doubles tennis event.

Latinas have been successful in other sports as well. Lisa Fernandez dominated as a pitcher for the women's softball team at the University of California, Los Angeles. In 1993, Fernandez earned the Broderick Award, given to the top female collegiate athlete of the year. In addition to her outstanding college career, Fernandez is perhaps best known for her performance in the 1996 Olympic games, as she pitched the United States Women's Olympic Softball Team to a gold medal victory.

Despite the existence of these Latina athletes and others, Latina participation in sport remains invisible in scholarly research and popular accounts of female athleticism. At least three reasons account for this invisibility. First, it parallels the long-standing national neglect of the Latino population in general. Second, sport research has focused on women as a generic category, overlooking the different experiences of Latinas and other women of color. Third, compared to Whites and African American women, Latinas do exhibit lower rates of sport participation.

What We Know about Latinas and Sport Participation

Although Latinas have often been overlooked, they have been included in some key research attempts (Acosta & Carpenter, 1988; National Collegiate Athletic Association [NCAA], 1994; Women's Sports Foundation [WSF], 1989). This research has shown that Latinas are unequal beneficiaries of gender equity in sport.

A report by the WSF (1989) showed that even after oversampling high schools with high percentages of Latino students, Latinas accounted for only 8 percent of the female athletes in the study (as compared to 12 percent for African American females and 79 percent for White females). This result is striking in light of ever-increasing levels of participation in high school sports among African American women and White women. Even more disturbing is the fact that no attempt has been made to discern trends in preference for type of sport among Latina athletes. These data will most likely reveal a narrow scope of high school sport involvement for Latinas, in contrast to the broad range of sport involvement among White females. For Latinas in the WSF study, participation in high school athletics was positively associated with high school retention, lower drop out rates, higher achievement test scores, college attendance, and progress toward a bachelor's degree for rural Latinas. In fact, Latina athletes from rural schools were three times less likely than their nonathletic peers to drop out of school. All Latina athletes in the WSF study were two to four times more likely than Latina nonathletes to attend and to stay in college.

Acosta and Carpenter (1988) found that Latino/Latina leadership in NCAA colleges and universities was scarce at best. As part of their study, NCAA schools (N=800) that offer intercollegiate athletic programs for women were surveyed. The study revealed that significantly and disproportionately low numbers of Latinas are in positions of administrator, head coach, and assistant coach in the NCAA institutions surveyed (as compared to estimates for White women and African American women). In the same study, Latinas accounted for one percent of all female athletes among the NCAA institutions that responded, as compared with African American women who made up 10 percent and White women who accounted for 87 percent.

A 1994 report of NCAA graduation rates revealed that Latinas accounted for five percent of all female students in Division I, II, and III schools combined, but made up only

two percent of female athletes. In contrast, African American women accounted for 10 percent of female students and 15 percent of female athletes, while White women accounted for 74 percent of female students and 77 percent of female athletes.

Explaining Latinas' Low Participation Rates

Why are Latinas underrepresented in sport? Common explanations point to Latino culture. Popular and academic thinking has assumed that strong family bonds, male dominance, and traditional female expectations are the main obstacles to Latina athleticism. But while gender-role ideologies of different groups may contribute to distinctive sport participation patterns, there is no empirical evidence to substantiate the claim that a cultural emphasis on protecting women and girls makes Latinas' experiences so different from those of White and African American women.

The most plausible reasons for Latinas' underrepresentation lies in their social location. Latinos fare poorly in the social order. Many are constrained by economic marginality, which limits their educational and leisure choices. Although United States women now have new opportunities in sport, society treats Latinas very differently. The underlying racial structure acts as a barrier to Latina athleticism. Latinas' low levels of sport participation are the results of several factors:

1. Low levels of school enrollment at the secondary level and in higher education.
2. Neighborhood and school segregation.
3. Lower-than-average levels of family income.

School attendance for Latinas falls behind that of other women. They are disproportionately found in segregated, more poorly equipped and financed schools. Even the presence of recreational programs and adequate sports budgets and facilities does not guarantee equality for young Latinas. Latino families, on the average, earn less than others. Therefore, the cost of sporting equipment and transportation to and from athletic events, combined with the need for students to work at part-time jobs, deprives young Latinas of equal access to sport. Research focusing on Latina athletes holds many valuable lessons for sport studies by showing how cross-cutting structures of race, class, and gender shape sport and sport participation. *KMJ & MBZ*

References

Acosta, R.V., and Carpenter, J.J. (1988). Minority group membership in athletic leadership and athletic participation. Unpublished raw data, Brooklyn College, NY.

Gregorich, B. (1993). *Women at play: The story of women in baseball.* San Diego, CA: Harcourt & Brace.

National Collegiate Athletic Association. (June, 1994). *1994 Division I graduation rates summary* (Document #9940-6/94). Overland Park, KS: National Collegiate Athletic Association.

Women's Sports Foundation. (August, 1989). *Minorities in sport: The effect of varsity sports participation on the social, educational, and career mobility of minority students* (ISBN #89-051333). New York: Women's Sports Foundation.

Andrea Mead Lawrence

Andrea Mead Lawrence, born on April 19, 1932, in Rutland, Vermont, became the first United States skier, male or female, to win a pair of gold medals in Alpine skiing within the same Winter Olympic Games. In the 1952 Games at Oslo, Norway, Mead Lawrence won the gold medal in both the slalom and the giant slalom events. After giving birth to her third child, Mead Lawrence returned four years later to come within one-tenth of a second of capturing a bronze medal in the 1956 Winter Games at Cortina d'Ampezzo, Italy. She had the honor of carrying the Olympic Flame into the stadium at Squaw Valley, California, to open the 1960 Winter Games.

In 1958, Mead Lawrence was elected to the National Ski Hall of Fame, and she was inducted into the Women Sports Foundation (WSF) International Women's Sports Hall of Fame in 1983.

Lesbian Identity and Sport

Women who identify themselves as lesbians participate in sport, dance, and fitness activities of all types and at all levels. As in the larger society, most sporting environments include both heterosexual and homosexual women. Lesbian athletes, coaches, teachers, administrators, officials, trainers, and physicians participate in the whole spectrum of sport. Despite this legacy of participation, misconceptions about the relationship between lesbian identity and sport persist.

Some people believe that sporting environments not only attract large numbers of lesbians, but that sports experiences can actually make someone lesbian. In part, this perception relates to the legacy of viewing sport as more appropriate for men. Women who participate in sports (traditionally viewed as masculine activities), challenge gender stereotypes about what women can and cannot do.

Some people label these women lesbian, implying that by participating in sport they have crossed the boundaries of traditional expectations regarding the nature of women. Because lesbians are sometimes subject to legal and social discrimination, violence, and prejudice, many women athletes fear the lesbian label. Subsequently, there have been efforts to silence lesbians in sport. Homophobic attitudes have been used to discourage participation in sport by women and have often led to the creation of sporting environments that are hostile toward lesbians. Often, the message to lesbians is that it is acceptable to participate in sport as long as they are not obviously (or openly), lesbian. This questionable logic holds that lesbianism hurts "legitimate claims" for girls and women's sport to be recognized, accepted, and promoted. It is important to disentangle the lesbian sport experience from these homophobic attitudes and to recognize the contribution of lesbians in all aspects of sports.

Ironically, while all women who participate in sports are potentially "tainted" with the lesbian label, many lesbians live their whole lives without ever being involved in sport. Yet for those who do choose to participate, sport can be a very important aspect of their lives. Sport may provide a context for the athlete to "come out," and may provide a sense of community. However, in the cases of some professional athletes, sport may also provide the "closet" that prohibits them from coming out, for fear of losing their livelihood or extra endorsements.

Although sports does not make someone lesbian, lesbians do work together to develop affirming, celebratory, and transformative sporting environments. Lesbians working cooperatively with gay men have created sporting communities including Front Runners (a running club), the United States Gay Open (an annual tennis tournament), and the Gay and Lesbian Cloggers (a country-western dance troupe). These organizations help to strengthen and support the lesbian and gay athletic community.

In addition to organizing and participating in such sport communities, lesbians have been involved as organizers and participants in the Gay Games. The Gay Games (originally called the Gay Olympic Games before the United States Olympic Committee successfully litigated to preclude their use of the word "Olympics" in this context) is an international sport and cultural event held every four years. The first Gay Games were held in San Francisco in 1982, and the 1998 Games will be in Amsterdam, Netherlands. The goal of these Games is to promote the emancipation of gay men and lesbian women through strengthening self-respect and sense of community. By policy and tradition, the Gay Games are not restricted to gay men and lesbians; anyone who shares the belief that to do one's personal best is the ultimate goal of all human achievement, is welcome to participate. Participation in sporting events like the Gay Games provides a feeling of inclusion for gay men and lesbians. For lesbians, to move from the illegitimate status of "lesbian menace" to that of a fully valued participant, celebrating sport and experiencing the camaraderie of a community supporting every participant's efforts (whether coming in first or last in the competition), is an all too rare, wonderful, affirming experience.

Adopting an open and positive attitude toward lesbians will enhance the experience of all women who desire to participate in the world of sport. Lesbians challenging stereotypes about what it means to be women have given women of all sexualities increased opportunities to participate. It is only right that they share in this legacy they helped create. *EC1*

See Also Homophobia in Women's Sports

Lisa Leslie

Born on July 7, 1972, Lisa Leslie has been described as the quintessential California hoopster. Leslie, who is finesse personified, has great fundamental skills and athleticism and plays a dominating game. At six-feet five-inches, Leslie was encouraged by her cousin Craig to become a great player. He encouraged her to work out, including playing with boys, whenever possible. She honed her skills in Hawthorne and Inglewood, California, and as a high school senior, scored 101 points in only one half of a game. One day, after her basketball career is over, she hopes to become a model.

Leslie was a former National Player of the Year (1993 & 1994) and All-American while at the University of Southern California. She holds the PAC 10 scoring record with 2,414 points. Coming back from adversity is something Leslie knows about as she had to rehabilitate a serious knee injury. She was a member of the United States team at the 1996 Olympic Games and will go down in history as a gold medal winner. As she said of the Olympic Team, "It's a great opportunity for us to be showcased as role models not only for young girls that play basketball, but for women in general." She currently plays (1997) for the Los Angeles Sparks in the Women's National Basketball Association.

Nancy Lieberman-Cline

Born on July 1, 1958, in Brooklyn, New York, Nancy Lieberman-Cline was a 1976 Women's Olympic Basketball Team member and, at 18 years old, was the youngest basketball player in Olympic history to win a medal (silver). She was also a member of the 1980 Women's Olympic Basketball Team

Nancy Lieberman-Cline.

that didn't participate due to the United States boycott of the Moscow Olympics. In 1986, she made history by being the first woman to play in a men's professional league, the United States Basketball League.

She is currently a motivational speaker on the topics of making solid decisions, sports marketing, and why girls should be involved in sport. She is also the owner of ProMotion Events, a sports marketing company, and often serves as a television commentator. She recently returned to basketball as a professional, playing for the Phoenix Mercury of the Women's National Basketball Association (WNBA) in 1997.

Rebecca Lobo

As the most celebrated collegiate basketball player of the 1994-1995 season, Rebecca Lobo helped the University of Connecticut Huskies win the Division I National Collegiate Athletic Association (NCAA) title. She won the NCAA Women's Final Four Most Outstanding Player Award that season. With 7.1 points per game, Lobo led the Huskies to a perfect 35-0 record. Lobo also totaled 129 assists and 122 blocks. She is second all-time

for points scored (2,133) and games played (126) at the collegiate level. She led Division I in final statistics for blocked shots (3.5 per game).

Born on October 6, 1973, Lobo has a street named after her in her hometown of Southwick, Massachusetts, "Rebecca Lobo Way." In addition to being a full-time basketball star, Lobo and her mother have written an autobiography entitled *The Home Team*, which records their experiences, good and bad, including her mother's battle with cancer and Lobo's speedy rise to fame.

For all of her hard work on the court, Lobo was named the 1995 National Player of the Year by the Associated Press, the United States Basketball Writer's Association, and *College Sports* magazine. The Rawlings Women's Basketball Coaches Association Player of the Year, Lobo was also awarded the 1995 Wade Trophy, symbolizing the college senior basketball player who is viewed as the most positive role model for women in sports.

In May 1995, Lobo was named to the historic United States Women's National Basketball Team, which toured the country playing exhibition games prior to the 1996 Olympics. Her teammates gave her the nickname "Rookie," because she was the youngest member of the team. The team was a revolutionary, one-time program designed to develop the United States talent pool prior to the selection of the 1996 United States Olympic Team. The team went undefeated in their tour and went on to capture gold in Atlanta. Lobo played in most games, but as the "rookie" on the team she did not gain maximum playing time—among these women she was classed as a solid fundamental player.

Lobo continues to be motivated by a desire to excel. In the summer of 1997 she played for the New York Liberty in the Women's National Basketball Association (WNBA), and was chosen as one of the initial front women in the advertising campaign. She earned a reported $250,000 for her work with the WNBA.

Nancy Lopez

Nancy Lopez, an American golfer, is a four-time winner of the Ladies Professional Golf Association (LPGA) Player of the Year Award. Born on January 6, 1957, in Torrance, California, Lopez was only 12 years old when she won the New Mexico Women's Amateur Tournament in 1969. In 1975, she entered the United States Open as an amateur player and finished in a tie for second place. Before her professional career, Lopez attended the University of Tulsa. In 1976, she captured the Association of Intercollegiate Athletics for Women (AIAW) Championship.

Lopez left school in 1977 to become a professional, and she found immediate success, finishing second in her first three tournaments. She received the LPGA Rookie of the Year Award for her performance in that 1977 season. Her first major tournament victory came in 1978 when she won the LPGA Championship. At the age of 30, Lopez was inducted into the LPGA Hall of Fame in 1987 after winning 35 tournaments.

Lopez has now won 48 tournaments on the LPGA Tour; her success is credited to her ability to combine an unorthodox swing with excellent putting and a relaxed attitude. In 1985, she won her third Vare Trophy, given to the player with lowest scoring average. Her most successful financial season was in 1989 when she earned $487,153 and won three tournaments, including the Mazda LPGA Championship. That same year, she was inducted into the Professional Golf Association (PGA) World Golf Hall of Fame. Lopez was named Golfer of the Decade by *Golf Magazine* for the years 1978 to 1987, and she was given the Flo Hyman Award by the Women's Sports Foundation in 1992.

A role model for females in many sports, this Latina woman demonstrates how it is possible to continue to play at the very top of her sport and successfully raise a family.

Donna Lopiano

Donna Lopiano, executive director of the Women's Sports Foundation, has a passion for sport. She is on a mission to increase sporting opportunities for women and girls so others do not have to suffer the same disappointments and prejudices that she faced as a female athlete. Born in 1946 in Stamford, Connecticut, Lopiano started her athletic career by being "cut" from the local Little League team, not for lack of talent, but simply because she was female. Disappointed, but not disheartened, she looked for other opportunities to express her considerable athletic talents. She found one of those opportunities at the age of 16 with the Raybestos Brakettes, a nationally recognized women's softball team. Lopiano spent nine years playing first and second base and pitching for the Brakettes. Her pitching, fielding, and hitting skills contributed to the Brakettes' six national softball titles. Three times she was voted the most valuable player (MVP) of the softball national tournament and she was named an All-American nine times.

In between trips to Europe and Asia with the Brakettes, Lopiano earned a BA in physical education from Southern Connecticut State University, where she played softball, basketball, volleyball, and field hockey. She continued her studies, earning a master's degree and doctorate from the University of Southern California.

Brooklyn College was the next stop for Lopiano. At Brooklyn, she was an assistant athletic director and coached three sports—softball, basketball, and volleyball—before moving to Texas as director of women's athletics. As the athletic director at the University of Texas, Lopiano gained a national reputation for promoting women's athletics. Under her guidance, women's athletic programs at the University of Texas won 18 national championships and the women's athletic budget increased from $57,000 to $4 million. Her accomplishments as athletic director and her struggles to push for equity for women's athletics brought media attention from local and national sources, including a feature article in *Sports Illustrated*.

In 1992, Lopiano accepted the challenge to lead the Women's Sports Foundation in promoting women's sport on the national and international level. As executive director of the Women's Sports Foundation, Lopiano has pushed for full equity for women's sports and implementation of Title IX. She has also worked to increase corporate interests in promoting women's athletics and is a tireless advocate for women's sports.

Lynnette Love

Lynnette Love is a two-time Olympian, having won the gold medal in tae kwon do (a form of karate) at the 1988 Olympic Games in Seoul, South Korea, and a bronze medal at the 1992 Olympic Games in Barcelona, Spain. That same year, she was also nominated for the Sullivan Award, the highest award in amateur athletics. She is a 10-time national champion and a four-time world champion in Tae Kwon Do. She currently holds the distinction of being the only woman representing tae kwon do in the *Guiness Book of World Records*. She is also a motivational speaker in the areas of education, Olympic training, and goal setting.

Luge and Women

In a sport long dominated by the Alpine countries of Europe, American women have finally started challenging the best athletes in luge. Since February 12, 1883, when several Americans competed in the first organized international luge race in Switzerland, the United States program has evolved dramatically. On that day, 21 men from seven countries gathered to race down a four-kilometer trail through the woods between the towns of St. Wolfgang and Klosters. Today, both women and men from the 44 member nations of the International Luge Federation compete on highly technical, refrigerated tracks of variable length—a minimum of 800 meters and maximum of 1,050 meters for women, which is slightly shorter than men's distances. As they wind down the hillsides of countries around the globe, women lugers reach speeds approaching 80 miles per hour. The fastest total time attained in two trials wins the day in world

cup events while the Olympic format uses the fastest total of four heats over two days.

Since the second European Championship race in 1928, women have actively competed in all local, national, and international competitions. When luge made its Olympic debut in 1964 at the Winter Olympic Games in Innsbruck, Austria, only one American woman was entered on the roster, and she did not start the race. Throughout the next decade, the United States was represented in luge competition primarily by military personnel stationed in Europe. It was not until 1979, when North American's first luge track was built in Lake Placid, New York, that the United States Luge Association was formed to oversee the development of the sport in this country. The United States spent the 1980s trying to catch the leaders in the sport (Austria, Germany, and Italy) who have claimed 25 of the potential 27 Olympic medals for women in luge.

In 1985, NYNEX (a regional Bell telephone company) joined forces with the United States Luge Association (USLA) as the team's primary sponsor, and American lugers first stepped foot on the medal stand. Since then, American athletes have won over 100 medals in international competition.

One of the first American women to devote herself to the luge was Erica Terwillegar. When Terwillegar began sliding in 1977 at the age of 14 , there was no luge track in North America and certainly no junior program in this country. Like everyone else who was interested in luge at the time, she first started sliding on the bobsled run in Lake Placid. She was an alternate for both the 1980 and 1984 Olympic Luge Teams before earning a spot on the team for both the 1988 and the 1992 Olympic Games in which she finished 11th and 9th, respectively.

In 1980, a native Californian, Bonny Warner, made her way to Lake Placid as the Olympic torch bearer for her state. Although she had never before seen a luge sled, Warner was enticed by the thrill of the sport. Just four years later she earned a berth on the

1984 Olympic Luge Team. Her 15th place in Sarajevo, Yugoslavia, was the best for the American luge women at those Olympic Games. In the 1988 Games in Calgary, Canada, Warner shattered the top-ten barrier with a sixth-place finish, at the time the best ever for an American woman in Olympic luge competition. Warner went on to compete in the 1992 Olympic Games in Albertville, France. She also holds five national championship titles. In addition to her feats on the track, Warner served as luge's representative to the Athlete Advisory Council of the United States Olympic Committee, where she played a key role in promoting the sport.

In 1980, another American woman embarked on a long career in luge. Cammy Myler began sliding at the age of 11 years and won a Junior Olympic title that same year. In 1985, at the age of 16, she became the youngest person to win a Senior National Luge Championship and was subsequently named to the national team. In 1987 at Sarajevo, Yugoslavia, she was the first American, male or female, to medal in World Cup competition, bringing home a bronze medal. In the 1992 Winter Olympic Games in Albertville, France, Myler recorded a fifth-place finish, the best ever for an American woman in Olympic competition. Overall, Myler has won nine World Cup medals (including two golds), holds six national

championship titles, and has been named Luge Sportswoman of the Year for eight consecutive years. In 1994 as a high point of a long career, she had the honor of representing her country and her sport by carrying the American flag at the opening ceremonies in Lillehammer, Norway.

Future stars can already be seen on the horizon. Maryann Baribault has been setting records on the junior circuit in the sport. In 1995 at Lake Placid, New York, Baribault was the first American woman to win the World Junior Luge Championship, and she repeated the feat the following year in Calgary, Canada. In addition to holding three national junior championship titles, she was first overall in the 1994-1995 Nations Cup standings and is now climbing the ranks on the senior circuit.

Because the sport is still relatively new in the United States, there is a limited pool of athletes from which coaches could possibly emerge. To date, there have been no female coaches for either the junior or senior national teams. However, from 1985 to 1996, two women, Mary Ellen Fletcher and Claire Sherred, each served in the demanding role of team manager. The national governing body of luge is the U.S. Luge Association, which can be reached at PO Box 651, 35 Church St, Lake Placid, NY 12946, (518)523-2071. *CM*

Maccabiah Games

The Maccabiah Games is an Olympic-sanctioned and Olympic-style competition for Jewish athletes and is among the top five international athletic events in the world. Inspired by European gymnastics clubs and received with open arms by the Maccabi World Congress of 1919, the Maccabiah Games made their formal entrance into the sporting world in 1932. It was a most improbable beginning, given that the problems facing the organizers were immense. In addition to the lack of funds and athletic facilities, the world was suffering from the effects of the Depression. Israel's (then called Palestine) first sport stadium, which was also the first such structure in the Middle East, was only finished the night before opening ceremonies. The crude oval stadium was built to hold 5,000 spectators, but more than 25,000 jammed in, and thousands were turned away from the opening ceremonies. And so in March 1932, 390 athletes from 14 countries, including 13 Americans, two of whom were women, headed to Israel for the glorious beginning of the Maccabiah Games. Since its inception, the Maccabiah Games have always been held in Israel.

The brainchild of Russian-born Joseph Yekutieli, this gathering of Jewish athletes has continued to grow over the years, adding more sports, nations, and participants. The Maccabiah was a natural outgrowth of the numerous Jewish sporting clubs that sprouted up throughout Europe and the Middle East in the later part of the nineteenth century. These clubs were formed when the resurgent anti-Semitic movement forced Jewish members living in Constantinople to resign from German clubs. The first all-Jewish gymnastic club, the Israelitische Turnverein Konstantinopel (Israelite Gymnastic Association Constantinople), was founded in 1895.

Coincidentally, the first stirrings of the "collective Jewish physique" came about at the same time as the increase in speculation of a Jewish homeland and in the national "Zionistic" feeling (returning to the homeland). Philosopher/educator Theodor Herzl proclaimed to Jewish people that they should "train not only the spirit, but your muscles as well. The sons of the Maccabees will return to life!"

At the same time in Europe, pogroms (organized massacres) and the ruthless destruction of Jewish communities in Eastern Europe inspired Jewish leadership to establish and promote physical education among the young so that they might be better able to defend their communities in times of danger. These factors inspired the formation of Jewish gymnastic clubs (Die Juedische Turnerschaft) throughout Europe. These sports clubs developed rapidly, and by 1913, 29 clubs with an active membership of over 4,500, were thriving. Initially, such clubs were gymnastic-based, but they slowly expanded to include a variety of body-building and competitive sports.

By the end of World War I, the Jewish sports clubs, many with different names, joined to form the Maccabi World Union. The name Maccabi maintained the connection to Zionism and signified the ancient Maccabees' courageous fight for freedom. Today, there are over 50 Maccabi territorial organizations, including Maccabi USA/Sports for Israel, the United States sponsoring organization. The modern Maccabiah currently includes 35 sports, with separate competition for women in 14 sports. The United States Maccabiah Team brings athletes in four categories: open age, juniors age (13 to 16 years of age), masters (over 35 years of age), and physically challenged.

From its inception, women athletes and sporting events were part of Maccabiah competition. In the first Maccabiah Games, female participants competed in track and field, swimming, gymnastics, and fencing. The first women to compete for the United States were Eva Bein and Sybil Koff Cooper, who were part of the 13-member American team. Sybil Koff Cooper, a New York-born track and field athlete, was one of the outstanding participants in both the first and second competitions. In 1932, at the age of 19, Cooper earned three gold medals in the 100-meter dash, in the high jump, and in the long jump. Three years later, she returned to Eretz, Israel, and earned three additional medals. Though she earned a place on the United States Olympic Team for the 1936 Olympiad, she opted not to go to Berlin.

The first Maccabiah Games was a wonderful demonstration of youth, strength, and vibrancy, greatly encouraging the Jewish people and infusing them with a sense of confidence at the very time when dark clouds were sowing seeds of despondency and fear in Europe. The second Maccabiah, held in 1935, was dubbed the "Aliyah Games." This second edition of the Games took place during a period of harsh restrictions placed on Jewish immigration into Palestine by the British Mandate Authorities. Seventeen hundred athletes came to compete. With the climate worsening in Europe, many of the athletes from Germany and the entire Bulgarian team remained in Israel. American track athlete Lillian Copeland, a 1928 and 1932 Olympian, won gold medals in the javelin, discus, and shotput in the second Maccabiah.

The third Maccabiah, though scheduled for 1938, was delayed 12 years. When the Games were held in 1950, they were the first to be played in the sovereign State of Israel, and the first time competition was held in the new stadium in Ramat Gan. Especially poignant was the appearance of a team from West Germany, composed entirely of Holocaust survivors. All together, 19 countries and 800 athletes would share in the 1950 competition.

By 1953, the modern Maccabiah was well-established. Twenty-one countries and 890 athletes participated in the fourth Games, and a new tradition was instituted: carrying the torch from Modi (birthplace of Judah Maccabee) to the stadium to open the Maccabiah. The American athletes excelled in track and field, wrestling, springboard and high diving, gymnastics, and tennis.

In 1961, at the sixth Maccabiah, Marilyn Ramenofsky, an Olympic silver medalist (1964) and three-time world record holder, led the United States Swimming Team that won all but two events! Tennis ace Julie Heldman earned three gold medals (singles, doubles, and mixed doubles) at the eighth Games in 1969. At the same Games, diver Deborah McCormick secured a gold medal for the United States, and Mark Spitz's sister, Nancy, swam her way to four golds and two silver medals. At these Games, Maccabiah participants were able for the first time to make a pilgrimage to Jerusalem and the Western Wall. Israeli Prime Minister Golda Meir was on hand for the impressive ceremony that followed on Mt. Scopus.

The ninth Maccabiah Games, in 1973, was dedicated to the Munich 11: the 11

Israelis killed at the previous year's Olympiad in Munich, Germany. Twenty-three countries and almost 1,500 athletes participated in this Maccabiah.

At the "Jubilee Maccabiah" in 1977, 33 countries and 2,700 athletes competed in 26 sports, including two new ones, chess and bridge. Fifty-five records were shattered, 25 in swimming (22 by the United States swimmers), and a young American gymnast named Sharon Shapiro won five gymnastic gold medals.

Women's basketball and volleyball were introduced in 1981. The Americans, led by Women's Amateur Basketball Association (WABA) first-round draft pick Sherry Levin, earned a silver medal, losing to Israel in the final game. In volleyball, the United States women, having previously defeated Venezuela in the semifinal round, lost to Israel in the final game for the silver medal. American women did bring home gold medals in fencing, golf, gymnastics, swimming, tennis, and track and field.

Encouraging the next generation of Jewish athletes, the 12th Maccabiah in 1985 introduced a junior age division in swimming and gymnastics. Among the outstanding and notable performances of these Games were the American women swimmers who established 13 Maccabiah records, winning all but two events.

Dubbed the "Bar Mitzvah" Games, the 13th Maccabiah in 1989 was the first time since World War II that countries from Eastern Europe took part. Yugoslavia, Hungary, and Lithuania made appearances, as did Panama and Singapore, for a total of 45 countries and 4,500 athletes. Twenty-four countries medalled, 22 swimming records were broken, and the United States earned a record tally of 199 medals.

From the first Games to those in 1993, American women have often stood on the medal platform. Debbie Adams, a golfer from Florida established a new course record at the 1993 Games. Named Florida State Amateur Champion for several years, Adams qualified for the 1993 United States Maccabiah when she was five months pregnant. At the same

Games, rhythmic gymnast Tamara Levinson, a 1992 United States Olympian, took five out of a possible six gold medals.

These women were joined by scores of others in 1993. Swimmer Lisa Martin, who had just completed her junior year in high school, took seven gold medals, besting Mark Spitz's Maccabiah six medals earned in 1969. Other swimmers established new records, including Deborah Kory and Lisa Dubbe, who established three and four new records, respectively. Margot Lulla and Audrey Tannenbaum earned gold medals in the new sport of triathalon.

Today, Maccabiah competition for women is held in the sports of badminton, fencing, field hockey, golf, gymnastics, karate, rhythmic gymnastics, rowing, shooting, squash, tennis, track and field, triathlon, and volleyball. Maccabi United States of America/Sports for Israel is interested in expanding the role of women in the Maccabiah Games by adding additional sports to the Games roster. Field hockey for women was introduced in 1989, and the United States, fielding its first team for the 14th Maccabiah, bested Argentina to earn a bronze medal.

Several innovations of the Maccabiah Games have subsequently been adopted by other competitions. Basketball was a Maccabiah sport before it appeared at the 1936 Olympic Games, and the Maccabiah was the first major international competition to have a women light the torch at its opening ceremonies, three years before a female had the same honor in the Olympic Games. The honor to light the torch in 1965 went to track and field athlete, Deborah Turner. Also in the Maccabiah, in contrast to Olympic protocol, athletes are housed according to sport, rather than country, which provides the athletes with unique opportunities to bond cross-culturally.

Currently, physically challenged competition is held simultaneous with the other competition. Brenda Levy, who has competed in the two most recent Paralympics (1996 and 1992) was the gold medalist in the wheelchair half-marathon at the 14th

Maccabiah Games, adding to her two swimming gold medals in "physically challenged" events.

Over the years, Maccabi United States America/Sports for Israel has increased its outreach efforts. At the 14th Maccabiah in 1993, athletes represented 46 states. The last Games of the twentieth century, the 15th Maccabiah, was attended by over 5,000 athletes representing 50 countries. Like the Olympic Games, the Maccabiah was born of a wish to create a showcase for athletic prowess. There is much historical significance in the century-old Maccabiah. These Games, partially founded to battle prejudice, have grown to celebrate Jewish athletic pride. Held in the "Jewish Homeland," the Maccabiah athletes have the rare opportunity to compete among their peers, tour Israel, and bond. *JG1*

Helene Madison

Helene Madison, born on June 19, 1913, competed as an American swimmer in the 1932 Olympic Games in Los Angeles, California. Only 127 women competitors participated in these Games. Madison arrived at the Olympics holding all 17 world records in freestyle swimming. She dominated the 1932 women's swimming events by winning gold medals in the 4 x 100-meter freestyle relay and the 100- and 400-meter individual freestyle events. In the 100-meter race, she broke the Olympic record, and she broke world records in the 400-meter freestyle and in the 4 x 100-meter freestyle relay. When she retired, she held all of the Olympic, world, and national freestyle records, an accomplishment that has yet to be equaled. She was inducted into the International Swimming Hall of Fame in 1966.

Magazines: Early American Magazines and Their Role in Women's Sports History

In recent years, sport has become a part of a woman's daily life, whether for the sheer benefit of exercise, for the pleasure of recreation, or for the purpose of athletic competition. Although it has taken years for women to be widely recognized and accepted as athletes, women have been active in sports for decades.

Perhaps the main vehicle for chronicling the sports culture of women in the United States has been the monthly magazine. Throughout the late nineteenth and early twentieth century, their illustrations and articles were a record of customs and events, and they clearly played an important role in women's lives.

During the years prior to the mass media of today, the arrival of the monthly magazine was a much anticipated event in homes across the country. Serving as a main source of information, the magazine kept readers informed on politics and important news

Archery was an early sport deemed appropriate for women.
Courtesy of Ernestine G. Miller.

items; soon, the leading magazines also included serious journalism, poetry, and literary fiction. For women especially, the

Tennis was popular with the "New American Woman."
Courtesy of Ernestine G. Miller.

More than any other artistic medium, illustration communicated the most positive aspects of the sportswoman. She engaged in action without losing her femininity. Through the simplicity of a picture, illustrators attracted attention by creating covers and advertisements of sporting women with captivating style. The sportswoman image evoked an immense appeal—vibrant, fashionable, and energetic. Most of all she was fit and desirable, and appealed to a White, middle-class woman who was fast becoming the target of economic and social change.

By creating advertisements for every possible commodity, the illustrations were influencing public opinion, dress, and events. Women were encouraged to express the adventurous side of their personalities, and magazines were among their leading supporters.

magazine offered advice on the home and children, education and employment, and decoration and fashion. Above all, it connected women with each other.

This genre, usually called women's magazines, were nationally circulated monthlies that became the common domain of the masses. *Women's Home Companion*, *McCall's*, *Redbook*, *Pictorial Reviews*, and *Good Housekeeping* were a few of the popular publications that appealed to the general population and were, for the most part, designed to serve as vehicles for advertising.

With advertisers realizing that their products could be made more beautiful with the addition of art, magazines soon became the leading patrons of illustrators and the main venue for companies to communicate their message. One of the favorite subjects used by illustrators for the promotion of a wide range of products was the "symbol" for the new all-American woman—the sportswoman.

Skiing was another sporting outlet for women.
Courtesy of Ernestine G. Miller.

THE SATURDAY EVENING POST

SEPT. 22, 1923

Mary King Waddington—Kenneth L. Roberts—Alice Duer Miller—Nina Wilcox Putnam
Clarence Budington Kelland—Captain Dingle—Floyd W. Parsons—Martin B. Madden

Golf was fashionable for some women in this era.
Courtesy of Ernestine G. Miller.

Colorful, bold and imaginative, these covers and full-page advertisements were captivating in their simplicity. The artists used seductive appeal to reinforce the message that "what you see is what you want to be." Their sporty, outdoors woman was portrayed in action settings for many sports: tennis, golf, basketball, swimming, cycling, and horseback riding. The attention these illustrations received helped pave the way for the development of sport as a serious recreational interest. The covers are poignant reminders of a time in this country's history when women were finally starting to be recognized for their athletic skills. Both team and individual tournaments for women became more common in the 1920s and 1930s, and with growing exposure in the national magazines, sport for women had a new acceptance and new position in society. The sportswoman, the woman of the day, was becoming braver, stronger, and more secure.

Many of the illustrators—Maxfield Parrish, Howard Chandler Christy, James Montgomery Flagg, Cole Phillips, Charles Dana Gibson, and others—became celebrities through their constant exposure to the public. Their work was in high demand, and they enjoyed a level of popularity, wealth, and status never before imagined by artists. Each had a recognizable style, their "own girl," and, collectively, their works are now part of an era called "The Golden Age of Illustration." In essence, before the onset of photography, they were the artistic historians of their time, and their illustrations are a record of both sports and social history.

Opportunities for women to enjoy sports were slowly entering a period fostered by optimism and openness rather than by catcalls and smirks. These now highly valued images played a lasting part in shaping the way women continued to be physically active. Through images and articles in American magazines, women's sport culture had begun. *EM*

Meg Mallon

Often, an athlete who suddenly wins a big competition appears to have burst onto the scene from nowhere; however, years of work produce those results. Meg Mallon has risen steadily through the ranks since she joined the Ladies Professional Golf Association (LPGA) Tour in 1986. Once calling herself a "blue collar player," she worked hard at learning the game before her "breakout" tour victories in 1991.

Mallon, born in Natick, Massachusetts, on April 14, 1963, attended the Ohio State University, where she was the runner-up in the 1985 Big Ten Championship. In 1983, Mallon won the Michigan Amateur Championship.

By the end of 1990, Mallon was playing consistently, making the cut in every tournament. (Every tournament has four rounds, but only the top finishers from the first two rounds get to compete in the final rounds, i.e., make the cut.) Despite this consistent play, Mallon had not won a major tournament. She made a breakthrough when she won her first professional tournament at the 1991 Oldsmobile LPGA Classic. At the 1991 Mazda LPGA Championship, she began the final day tied for the lead. It came down to Mallon's 15-foot putt on the final hole; a putt she made for a birdie (one under par) earning her first major title. Mallon won her second major championship at the United States Women's Open by only two shots. Mallon was the winner of *Golf Digest*'s Most Improved Player Award in 1991. She is still active in Tour play.

Carol Mann

Born on February 3, 1941, in Buffalo, New York, Carol Mann started playing golf at nine years of age. During her 22-year career she won 38 tournaments, placing her ninth on the Ladies Professional Golf Association (LPGA) all-time victory list. She attended the University of North Carolina at Greensboro, where she was honored with a Distinguished Alumni Award. Mann joined the LPGA in 1960. Her first victory came in 1964 when she won the Western Open. She won the 1965 United States Women's Open Golf Championship.

Mann was inducted into the LPGA Hall of Fame in 1977 and into the WSF International Women's Sports Hall of Fame in 1982. Mann won the Vare Trophy in 1968 for achieving the lowest LPGA scoring average, 72 strokes. She also received the 1976 Babe Didrikson Zaharias Award.

Mann was a key figure in the LPGA and served as its president from 1974 to 1975. She was the president of the Women's Sports Foundation from 1985 to 1990 and is a current member of the foundation's Board of Stewards. Mann is also a former television golf analyst for the ABC, ESPN, and NBC networks.

Currently, Mann owns and operates Carol Mann, Inc., which provides unique corporate golf programs at LPGA Tour sites for many corporations. She is also president of Carol Mann Golf Services, the first woman-owned and operated golf course design and management firm.

Madeline Manning Mims

Born on January 11, 1948, in Cleveland, Ohio, Madeline Manning Mims won a gold medal in the 800-meter run at the 1968 Olympic Games, setting new United States, Olympic, and world records. Manning Mims won a total of seven national outdoor and five national indoor titles in the 800-meter race. In 1976, she was the first American woman to break two minutes in this demanding event.

Manning Mims's Olympic experiences went far beyond her 1968 victory. She won a silver medal at the 1972 Games in Munich, Germany, as a member of the 4 x 400-meter relay, and captained the United States Women's Olympic Track Teams in 1972, 1976, and 1980. In 1984, she was inducted into the Ohio and the Olympic Halls of Fame. In 1987, she was inducted into the Women's Sports Foundation's International Women's Sports Hall of Fame.

After her retirement, she founded the Sweet Pride Gymnastics Team for the Salvation Army. An ordained minister, she has served as a Protestant chaplain at the 1988 Seoul, South Korea, Olympic Games; the 1992 Barcelona, Spain, Olympic Games; the 1993 World University Games; and both the 1993 and 1995 World Track and Field Championships. Today, Manning Mims devotes herself to her ministry and to her career as a gospel singer.

Marathon for Women

The history of the woman's marathon is one of struggle, hope, and determination. In 1896, a woman named Melpomene ran in the first modern Olympic marathon in Athens, although she was not permitted in the race as an official entrant. In fact, women were barred from participating in any

Olympic running event longer than 200 meters until 1960 due at least in part to an 800-meter run held in the 1928 Games. In this event, women were reported to have collapsed at the finish line (not an unusual sight among men and women runners today), and so races over 200 meters were forbidden. The men in Olympic leadership felt that "distance running" would overtax the female body. It was not until 1984, after intense worldwide lobbying of the International Amateur Athletic Foundation (the world governing body of track and field) and the International Olympic Committee, that women finally were allowed to run in the Olympic Marathon. Joan Benoit of the United States won the inaugural 26-mile, 385-yard event in Los Angeles in 2 hours, 24 minutes, 52 seconds.

The first woman known to complete the famed Boston Marathon, Roberta (Bobbi) Gibb, had to hide in the bushes at the start, then jump onto the course without a number in the 1966 race. Gibb later set the American marathon record. In 1967, Kathrine Switzer entered the Boston Marathon as K.V. Switzer and was almost dragged off the course at four miles by an enraged race official. Switzer went on to complete the marathon in four hours, 20 minutes. The first New York City Marathon in 1970 had only one female entrant, Nina Kucscik, who suffering from a virus dropped out after 15 miles. Kucscik went on to win the 1972 and 1973 New York City Marathons.

The early pioneers of women's marathoning now admit that as much as they loved their sport, and as passionately as they believed that women had a place in it, training and racing in those early days was tough. They speak of sneaking out before dawn and after dark to train, training by running in place, and having virtually no role models, coaching guidelines, or team support.

Today, women make up about 20 to 25 percent of entrants in American marathons, according to the United States Road Running Information Center. In most races, women receive equal prize money with men, and more or less equal media recognition. Will women ever comprise 50 percent of mara-

thon participants, as they now do in shorter road races, such as 5 kilometer and 10 kilometer races? Observers believe this level of participation unlikely because of the formidable time commitment involved in training for a marathon. Women, who still tend to assume primary child care and housework responsibilities, and who may have a full-time or part-time job as well, simply do not have the time to put in all those training miles.

The current women's world record for the marathon is 2 hours, 21 minutes, 6 seconds, set in 1985 by Ingrid Kristiansen of Norway. When examining marathon records, it is clear that women's social acceptance in distance running has translated directly into a dramatic improvement in performance. In 1926, Violete Piercy of Great Britain set a world record in the marathon of 3:40:22. This mark stood until 1964, when Dale Greig, also of Britain, ran 3:27:45. The mark fell another hour and six minutes over the next 21 years, until Kristiansen's record time. During that same time period, the men's marathon world record fell just under seven minutes, from 2:13:55 to 2:07:12.

Many observers believe that the breaking of Kristiansen's record is long overdue. Two other women have run 2:21: Benoit in 1985 and Uta Pipping of Germany in 1994. There is much speculation about when the 2:20 time barrier will be broken and by whom. The 1996 Olympic Marathon in Atlanta, Georgia, was won by an unheralded 22-year-old Ethiopian, Fatima Roba, in 2:26:05 over a hilly course on a humid summer day. Will Roba, or another woman now training and dreaming in obscurity, take the marathon to another level and inspire the next generation of women marathoners? *GB*

Anne Marden

Anne Marden is one of the most successful rowers ever to have competed for the United States. She dominated United States Women's Rowing from the late 1970s, when she made her first national team while still an undergraduate at Princeton University. In 1992, she made the finals of the Olympic Games in Barcelona, Spain, as the United

States women's single sculler. During this remarkable and unmatched run at the top, Marden represented the United States in international competition as a member of both the sweep (one oar) and sculling (two oars) national teams.

Margaret Matthews

Margaret Matthews was a consummate runner and a jumper. As runner, she won the bronze medal in the 1956 Olympic Games as part of the 4 x 100-meters relay team. In the 1960 Olympic Games, Matthews jumped over 20 feet and became the first American woman to leap this distance in the long jump, setting a new American record in the process.

Born on August 5, 1935, in Griffin, Georgia, Matthews was encouraged by her elementary physical education teacher to participate in sports. Matthews was a basketball player and a long jumper in high school. She eventually attended Tennessee State University and was the first woman athlete from that storied university to hold a world track and field record. Matthews was an Amateur Athletic Union (AAU) All-American in 1957, 1958, and 1959. Matthews also ran the 100-yard dash and won the event at several international meets as well as at the United States National Women's Track and Field Championship in 1958.

Pat McCormick

Pat McCormick (Keller), born on May 12, 1930, in Lakewood, California, was an American diver who won four gold medals in two Olympic Games. She was the only female diver to ever record such a feat. In the 1952 Games in Helsinki, Finland, she won both the springboard and platform diving events, the second woman to ever accomplish a double victory in the same Olympic Games. At the 1956 Games in Melbourne, Australia, she repeated the double victory, becoming the first diver, male or female, to record consecutive double championships at the Olympics.

McCormick was the first woman to win the prestigious Sullivan Award, the highest award in amateur athletics. She had the honor of escorting the American flag into the Los Angeles Coliseum during the opening ceremonies of the 1984 Olympic Games in Los Angeles, California. During those Games, her daughter Kelly won the silver medal for springboard diving.

Mildred McDaniel

Mildred McDaniel was the first American woman to set a world and Olympic record in the high jump. Born on November 4, 1933, in Atlanta, Georgia, Mildred's high jump career began in her own backyard, where she would jump over a self-made high jump bar. In high school, McDaniel played basketball before switching to track and field. After high school, she attended the Tuskegee Institute, where she continued her outstanding career. McDaniel won the Amateur Athletic Union (AAU) Outdoor Championship in the high jump in 1953, 1955, and 1959. She won the gold medal in the high jump at the Pan American Games in 1959. Her gold medal in the 1956 Olympic Games in Melbourne, Australia, made her the only American woman to win a gold medal that year.

Edith McGuire

In the 1964 Olympic Games in Tokyo, Japan, Edith McGuire became the second African American woman to win three medals in the same Olympic Games. She won a gold medal in the 200-meter dash and two silver medals in the 100-meter dash and in the 4 x 100-meter relay.

Born on June 3, 1944, in Atlanta, Georgia, McGuire began running in the eighth grade and continued with track in high school, where she also played basketball. A member of the famous Tennessee State University track and field team that dominated women's sprinting, she was an Amateur Athletic Union (AAU) All-American in 1961, 1963, 1964, and 1966. McGuire has captured AAU, Olympic, and world records. She participated in over 50 national and international competitions.

Willa McGuire

Willa McGuire (Cook) almost joined a water ski show in 1945. Instead, she decided to compete nationally in waterskiing. A year later, she won the slalom, tricks, and overall titles in the first National Water Ski Championships. At the first World Water Ski Championships in 1949, McGuire swept all three competitions again. She repeated her "clean sweep" at two other National Water Ski Championships in 1949 and 1951. She won the overall crown in eight of the nine National Water Ski Championships she entered and in three of the four world championships she entered. McGuire joined the Cypress Gardens water show in 1948, skiing as a prima ballerina from 1948 to 1958. She pioneered many show innovations, as she was the first person to employ musical background for show skiing, and the first person to develop moves such as the swivel swan, toe 360, and the backward swan.

Mary T. Meagher

Because of its physiological demands, butterfly is not swimming's most popular stroke. Mary T. Meagher (Plant) not only chose the stroke, she dominated it, earning the nickname "Madame Butterfly." During her career, she set 7 world and 13 American records and won 21 national titles. Born on November 27, 1964, Meagher's success came early. She set a world record while winning the 200-meter butterfly at the 1979 Pan American Games as an eighth grader and made the 1980 Olympic Team, but did not compete because of the United States boycott of the Moscow Games.

At the 1981 United States Long Course Championships, when she was 16 years old, Meagher broke her own world records in the 100-meter and 200-meter butterfly races, setting marks that still stand. *Sports Illustrated* called the 100-meter record, which dropped the time from 59.26 seconds to 57.93 seconds, the fifth-greatest single event record of all time. Meagher still holds the 10 fastest 200-meter butterfly times in history.

In 1981, she was named International Swimmer of the Year.

Meagher won a gold medal in both the 100-meter and 200-meter butterfly events at the 1984 Olympic Games in Los Angeles, California, plus a gold medal in the medley relay as she swam the butterfly leg. She claimed one gold, two silver, and two bronze medals at the 1986 world championships. Meagher rounded out her career with a bronze medal in the 200-meter butterfly and a silver medal in the 4 x 100-meter medley relay at the 1988 Olympic Games in Seoul, South Korea. Meagher is a graduate of the University of California at Berkeley.

The Media and Women's Sports

The media—newspapers, magazines, television, and radio—give us an edited version of the world. The news and entertainment media's functions are to furnish information, to interpret events, and to entertain the public. Sports are a big part of the media, providing exciting entertainment, a community focus, someone to cheer for, and a team to follow.

Sports are dramatized on television with pregame analyses, slow-motion shots, and play-by-play announcers. The camera draws attention to a particular player and focuses the viewers' thoughts on the success or failure of this person. The printed words people read about athletes help determine who should be celebrated. The media identify sports heroes by shaping images of these athletes.

In the 1990s, more girls and women are playing sports than ever before, but female athletes have yet to achieve equality with men in media coverage. Until the 1996 Summer Olympic Games in Atlanta, Georgia, and the great successes of the women's basketball, soccer, and softball teams, female athletes in team sports were almost invisible in press and television reports. With the Olympic triumphs and the advent of the new professional women's basketball leagues, women's fastpitch softball league, and baseball teams, coverage is improving.

Women athletes have made progress in the media. There have been changes, not only in the amount of reporting by newspaper and television sports journalists, but also in the way in which female athletes are covered. More women can be seen as commentators and reporters, not only covering women's sporting events, but also covering men's games. Some on-air personalities are becoming highly noticeable, women such as Robin Roberts, Leslie Visser, Hannah Storm, and Mary Carillo. There are even sports channels devoted to women's sports, such as the Liberty Network, and female executives are gaining power in the media, including Ann Liquori, who runs her own television and radio production company for sports.

Recent Coverage in the Media

The recent improvements have not come without a struggle. The message used to be that girls and women's sports were not worth as much to the public as men's sports. Research findings confirm that female athletes have traditionally received much less coverage than males from sports journalists.

Coaches of women's teams have been asked why they think that so little media attention has been given to female athletes. Some have responded that the advertisers have not been interested in promoting women's sports. The advertisers are a big part of the television, magazine, and newspaper business, and so their opinions definitely hold some weight with the media. It seemed that executives of these sponsors believed that the audiences were not interested in women's sports. Other coaches noted that the people in charge at television and radio stations and print media companies were just not familiar with girls and women as athletes. They didn't grow up in a time when there were so many opportunities for girls to play sports and were not accustomed to cheering for and following females in sports. Whatever the reason, the media coverage of women athletes suffered and continued to lag behind the coverage given to men.

In 1994, the Los Angeles Amateur Athletic Foundation (LAAAF) did a follow-up study to their 1989 report on gender and televised sports (Wilson, 1994). The new study intended to discover if any progress had been made in the coverage of women's sports. Results from the second study were both positive and negative. In the four years between the reports, there had been improvement in the national broadcast coverage of prominent competitions such as the United States Open Tennis Championships and the National Collegiate Athletic Association (NCAA) Women's Basketball Tournaments. The report also found an increased level of respect for women and their sports achievements. Television announcers are now, for the most part, depicting female athletes in more favorable terms.

The technical production of women's sports' coverage also improved, with more quality slow-motion instant replays and more cameras being used (Wilson, 1994). The pregame and half-time shows for men's sporting events were still consistently longer and better, however.

Unfortunately, local sports coverage showed little improvement. The percentage of reporting on women's sports on the late local news had not changed. Sports anchors covered men's events 94 percent of the time (Wilson, 1994). There were very few interviews with female athletes and coaches and no in-depth reporting of women's sports. When women's sports were covered in the news, video clips were used much less frequently than in the men's sports coverage.

In another recent study of four newspapers, men's sports stories outnumbered women's stories by 23 to one. Only 3.5 percent of the sport coverage was of women-only sport stories (Women's Sports Foundation, 1996).

If women's sports are underreported because of a belief about the marketability of female athletes, then business executives need to pay attention to recent research findings. WSF studies have established that the numbers of women sports viewers are growing rapidly. More importantly, at least from the point of view of potential sponsors, women have become great consumers of sporting goods, purchasing more athletic shoes and apparel than men.

Future

As we approach the next century, it is predicted that women's sport coverage will increase and improve (Gould & Gould, 1995). If this prediction is to come true, television and print news need to provide more reporting on a wider variety of women's sports, especially in an in-depth and serious manner. An excellent immediate goal would be to include coverage of female athletes in every broadcast of local television news (Wilson, 1994). Such fairness in media coverage is important, not only because of the sponsorship, financial gains, and fame for participants and sponsors alike, but also because it is desirable for young girls to watch and model female athletes playing their favorite sports. More coverage in magazines, newspapers, and television may well lead to more women sports stars and heroes. *DLG*

References

Gould, D., and Gould, B. (1995). *Women's televised sports '95.* York, ME: Gould Media Services.

Wilson, W. (Ed.). (1994). *Gender stereotyping in televised sports: A follow-up to the 1989 study.* Los Angeles: Amateur Athletic Foundation.

Women's Sports Foundation. (1996). *Images of words in women's sports: Guidelines for female athletes and the media.* East Meadow, NY: Women's Sports Foundation.

Media Images of the Female Athlete: Icons in Evolution

Women's struggle for acceptance into the athletic world has been going on for over a century. Women athletes have had their highs and lows throughout the past century, and all of these experiences have molded the portrait of the female athlete in the media. However, it must be recognized that the media has also played a role in molding the image of the female athlete. The mass media has been a powerful force in shaping society's beliefs, values, and attitudes toward women athletes.

The woman as athlete was documented in the media as early as the 1830s. Bound in corsets and a dress that covered her from neck to toes, she obviously was not the woman athlete known today. These media portrayals showed women in sedate settings such as archery and equestrian events. The sporting women were featured in various journals to encourage other women to engage in sports and physical activity, not for their own physical and emotional health, but in accord with their "Christian duty" to raise physically healthy and morally sound children. In the 1860s, more feminist views started to appear in scholarly journals, in-

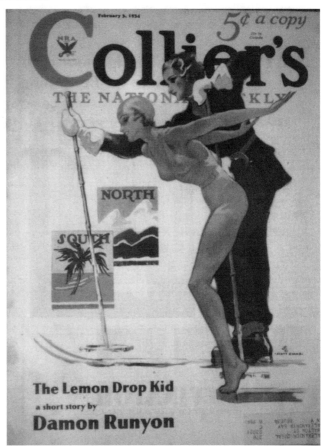

An early depiction of women athletes.
Courtesy of Ernestine G. Miller.

sisting that women needed to have increased opportunities in sport and that negative attitudes towards these females in sport had to change. These views eventually led to the image of the "New Woman" in the 1890s. This image portrayed sportswomen, not as house-bound, uninvolved with life beyond a family circle, but rather as college educated, upper class, and fully engaged in their sporting activities.

More women's magazines were launched at the start of the twentieth century, and they also began to feature sporting women. At first, the editors of these magazines featured female athletes in quiet sports such as croquet, lawn tennis, and recreational bathing. Some editors, however, began to take a progressive tack and featured women in sports such as hunting, fishing, riding, sailing, curling, golf, hockey, cricket, rowing, gymnastics, and cycling. These magazines did not focus solely on the topic of the female athlete but integrated stories on female athletes with issues on society, fashion, beauty, gardening, and the arts.

In the early 1920s, women's participation in athletics took an even greater turn. Women such as Eleanora Randolph Sears and Mildred "Babe" Didrikson Zaharias began to compete in high-profile sports championships. These women not only competed against men, but they often defeated them. Because sports had always been equated with masculinity, these female athletes started to be labeled "mannish" by the media. This sparked a negative stereotype that some elite female athletes are still trying to dispel. Females who succeeded in athletics were referred to in the media as social deviants for not following the standards of femininity that many nonathletic females displayed.

The successes of Sears and Didrickson during this period were accompanied by the phenomenon of more women being given the

chance to compete in sports. In the early 1900s, well-developed physical education programs for girls and women emerged in schools and colleges. Women, however, were still encouraged to maintain their feminin-

Another early image of the American sportswoman.
Courtesy of Ernestine G. Miller.

ity by being active in socially acceptable sports, and the media fully supported this limitation in their coverage of women as athletes.

There is no estimating how long women athletes would be hampered by these roles had society progressed without interruption. The two World Wars, however, turned society upside down. During the wars, activities that had been previously labeled masculine were now being done by women. The men marched off to war, and women took over their work on the home front, entering the work force in record numbers so that their countries could prosper.

During World War II (1939-1945), women also took over in another area, on the athletic field. The 1940s were a thriving period for the female athlete. The country was consumed with war, and the media seemed less inclined to thwart the advancement of women in sports. In fact, female involvement was encouraged. As a result, the world got its first taste of female jockeys, football coaches, umpires, horse trainers, and ball players. Most shocking of all for the times, perhaps, was the development of the All-American Girls Baseball League. This league allowed the nation to temporarily keep its mind off the war and to watch an "All-American" game of baseball with a twist, women! This league was a huge step for women athletes everywhere, but it still had its limitations. The league organizers tried to keep it within the standards of femininity by publicizing it as "femininity juxtaposed with skilled baseball ability," and by requiring the women to play in skirts.

This new acceptance of the female athlete in the media and society was short-lived, however. Soon after World War II ended, there was a backslide into stereotypic reality. Most women returned to their previous jobs as housewives, and the sports media resumed their earlier stance of supporting the female athlete in only the socially accepted sports. This negative reaction, however, was not enough to stop what had been started. Having achieved some athletic success, women were not daunted by this media reaction and used it as encouragement for future advances. Many women felt that if they had been accepted into the role of the competitive athlete once, then they could achieve this position again. For the next two decades, women fought for equality in sports, while the media continued to convey the message that competitive female athletes were too masculine and that women should have limited roles in the sports world.

The next big societal change to affect women athletes occurred during the late 1960s and the early 1970s, a period a dramatic social change for women, especially women athletes. Besides the liberating affects of the Women's Movement, the landmark passage of Title IX in 1972 prohibited sex discrimination in education, including athletic programs. Some women athletes had high hopes that with the passage of Title IX all previous social stigmas associated with women's athletics would disappear. The passage of Title IX did bring about a dramatic increase in the number of girls and women participating in athletics, but the negative image of the female athlete in the media did not wholly dissipate. Pictures of female athletes in the press, for example, were rarely action shots; instead the great athlete was shown heading out on a "date" with a gentleman friend.

Today, even with the passage of Title IX and the greater acceptance of female athletes by the public, women are still underrepresented in media coverage. Male athletes still get over three-fourths of all media coverage. The coverage that females are receiving is, in many cases, unacceptable; focusing not on being an athlete, but instead on being a "feminine woman," who also happens to be an athlete.

Some common trends have emerged in the coverage of female athletes in the media, especially local media. In coverage of female athletic contests, women were often referred to as "girls" instead of women. The commentators and anchors also called women athletes by their first names an inordinate amount of the time. Men athletes were strikingly less often referred to by first names. In interviews of female athletes, the interviewers often brought personal aspects of the female's life into the report. This type of reporting contributed to a view that the female athlete is less focused on her life as an athlete than are male athletes. One trend found on television sports programs was that men's sports were discussed first, and any leftover time would be given to women, or to sports involving both men and women. What little coverage of the women's sports events there was, often focused on scandals about women athletes. In general, the media conveyed the message that women's sports aren't as important as men's sports.

Los Angeles Amateur Athletic Foundation studies have shown that less than 1 percent of local TV sports broadcast airtime was spend on reporting women's events.

Examining visuals used by the media also reveal noticeable trends in print media coverage of male and female athletes. The text and photographs covering men's sporting events almost always appear first in the sports sections of newspapers and magazines, followed by text and photographs of women's sports. The photographs of male athletes show them in active poses (participating in their sport), while the photographs of female athletes often show them in passive poses that are sometimes not even related to sport.

Despite the negative trends that continue to this day, there have been some improvements in the depiction of the female athlete in the media. Comparatively, women athletes are being portrayed less often than before in stereotypical roles. The sports media makes fewer references to a female athlete's physical attractiveness and more references to her strength and athletic ability.

The struggle for the female athlete has been a long one, and it does not appear to be over. Female athletes are, at times, still struggling with the very problems that female athletes dealt with in the late 1800s. The media controls a major share of "stock" in the fate of the female athlete. The evolution of the image of the female athlete must continue until she is seen as an "icon" of a healthy, productive, and dedicated woman.
KR

See also **Television Docudrama: The Making of Frail Female Athletic Heroines**

Men as Advocates for Women's Sports

Historically, few men cared about the rights, abilities, and aspirations of female athletes. Political struggles over social resources and cultural recognition in sport were waged between two seemingly monolithic and separate groups—men and women. Men generally protected and hoarded resources, while women fought for access and equality. During the 1980s, however, increasing numbers of men began to realize that gender equity in sport was their issue as well as women's. Fathers expressed anger that schools did not offer the same number or quality of athletic programs to their daughters as to their sons. Some male school board members insisted that gender-equity evaluations be done in physical education and athletic programs. Male executives in the sport industry and sport media began to wake up to, and support, the growing interest of girls and women in sports and fitness activities. Some male lawyers and public policy makers worked to increase opportunities for women in sports. Political leaders such as Senator Bill Bradley (Democrat) of New Jersey, Senator Ted Stevens (Republican) of Alaska, and Tom McMillian, co-chair of The President's Council on Fitness and Sports, lobbied tirelessly on behalf of women athletes.

There also have been male coaches and administrators who have promoted the adoption of more inclusive and gender-equitable models for athletics. Indeed, some of these men paid a personal and professional price for their activism. Rudy Suwara, a former volleyball coach at San Diego State University, claimed he was fired due to his revelations concerning unequal treatment of female athletes. Jim Huffman, a coach at California State University at Fullerton, filed a lawsuit alleging that because he assisted his women's volleyball team in regaining the varsity status that was being taken away from them, he was not retained when the department restored the team.

Finally, men's support for girls and women in sport also emerged among academics and researchers during the 1980s. In addition to the growth of social scientific research on women in sports during the 1980s, scholars began to study the ways that sport enters into and reinforces male privilege, including the connections between sport and the social construction of masculinity, sexism, aggression, homophobia, men's violence against women, and sex inequality. Don Sabo and Ross Runfola

Men can support women's sports in many ways.
Photo courtesy of the *Camden Courier Post.*

efforts on behalf of gender equity. For example, from 1992 to 1996, Dr. Leroy Walker, president of the U.S. Olympic Committee, and (then) Executive Director Harvey Schiller instituted affirmative programs within the Olympic movement which were designed to increase the pool of women who would be available for leadership responsibilities.

Many male sport researchers joined female researchers in calling for an end to sex inequality and sexism in sport. Male scholars such as Jeff Benedict, Todd Crosset, Jay Coakley, Tim Curry, Eric Dunning, Jackson Katz, Bruce Kidd, Alan Klein, Richard Lapchick, Michael Messner, Brian Pronger, Don Sabo, and Phil White worked through a variety of international scholarly organizations, such as the North American Society of the Sociology of Sport and the International Committee for the Sociology of Sport, to foster research and advocacy agendas on behalf of women athletes.

published *Jock: Sports and Male Identity* in 1980, the first consciously pro-feminist collection of writings about men, sexism, and sport.

The 1990s saw the development of more nuanced and critical theories of gender in sport that opened the door to more sophisticated ways of understanding gender, men, and sport. Male scholars explored the historical relationships between masculinity and sport, contemporary constructions of men's bodies, sexualities, race and class inequalities, and violence. Michael Messner and Don Sabo published *Sport, Men and the Gender Order: Critical Feminist Perspectives* (1990), which sought to understand how the institution of sport contributes to men's collective power over women and, simultaneously, reflects the workings of intermale dominance hierarchies constructed around social class, race, ethnicity, and sexual orientation. This academic work provided a reasoned rationale which supportive male sport leaders could utilize to bolster their

In summary, gender politics in sports no longer neatly fit into the "we-men" versus "they-women" scenario. Many men who make their livelihood from traditional, male-dominated sports will continue to fight to maintain the status quo of male athletic privilege. They are angered or frightened by calls for gender equity in athletics. Other men are completely invested on behalf of women, because they feel it means fairness and a better life for themselves, the girls and women in their lives, and their institutions. **DS**

Debbie Meyer-Reyes

Debbie Meyer-Reyes, born in Annapolis, Maryland, on August 14, 1952, won three gold medals at the 1968 Olympics in swimming for the 200-meter freestyle, 400-meter freestyle, and 800-meter freestyle events. Meyer-Reyes had a distinguished swimming career before her stunning Olympic success. In 1967, the Soviet News Agency, TASS, named Debbie Meyer "Woman Athlete of the Year." It was not until 1968 that her own country honored her with the Sullivan Award, the highest award in amateur athletics. That year, she stunned the world by becoming the first swimmer ever to win three gold medals in a single Olympic competition, setting Olympic records in all three freestyle events in the Mexico City Games.

Meyer-Reyes set a career total of 24 United States and 15 world records. She was 14 years old when she set her first world record. Meyer-Reyes was inducted into the International Swimming Hall of Fame in 1977, the United States Olympic Hall of Fame in 1986, and the Women's Sports Foundation (WSF) International Sports Hall of Fame in 1987. She was also named Swimmer of the Year from 1967 to 1969 by *Swimming World* magazine. A panel of sportscasters named her the Greatest Female Swimmer of the Twentieth Century. Meyer-Reyes continues to teach young swimmers and gives numerous lectures and clinics. She owns and manages the Debbie Meyer Swim School in Sacramento, California.

Ann Meyers

Ann Meyers (-Drysdale), born on March 26, 1955, in San Diego, California, was a four-time All-American basketball player at the University of California at Los Angeles (UCLA), where she set nine school records and led her team to the Association of Intercollegiate Athletics for Women (AIAW) National Championship in 1979. In 1975, she became the first woman to attend UCLA on an athletic scholarship. Meyers played for the first United States' Women's Olympic Basketball Team in 1976, which won a silver medal. A great all-around athlete, she was also a member of the UCLA track and field and volleyball teams.

In 1979, Meyers signed a contract to play in the National Basketball Association (NBA) with the Indiana Pacers, becoming the first woman signed to a NBA basketball team. Later on, she was voted the Most Valuable Player of the Women's Basketball League (WBL), a short-lived professional league. She was inducted into the Naismith Memorial Basketball Hall of Fame in 1993. Meyers has recently been a commentator for CBS Sports at the National Collegiate Athletic Association (NCAA) Women's Basketball Tournament.

Cheryl Miller

Maybe it was the pickup games with her three brothers, or the boys' team she played on in elementary school, but by the age of 13, a determined Cheryl DeAnn Miller was already giving interviews. Born on January 3, 1964, in Riverside, California, Miller had a high school basketball career that was nothing short of spectacular. Her high school team posted a 132-4 won-loss record, and she was a four-time high school All-American. During one game, she scored 105 points.

As a University of Southern California (USC) freshman in 1983, Miller won Most Valuable Player honors in the National Collegiate Athletic Association (NCAA) National Championship as USC took the title; a title they repeated in 1984. At USC, she was named the College Player of the Year three times.

After leading the Trojans to their second straight NCAA title, Miller was the leading scorer on the gold-medal-winning 1984 United States Women's Olympic Basketball Team. As a six-foot three-inch forward, she led her teammates in scoring, rebounding, assists, steals, and blocked shots. Miller was the high scorer again in 1986 at the Goodwill Games, when the United States women defeated a Soviet team that had not lost a major international competition since 1958. The United States repeated this accomplishment at that summer's world championships. A shoo-in for the 1988 Olympic team, a knee injury kept her from participating in the Games in Seoul, Korea.

After retiring from playing, she served as the head coach at USC before becoming a television sports analyst for Turner Sports covering National Basketball Association (NBA) games. She previously worked for ABC Sports, where she covered college basketball and reported for *Wide World of Sports*.

Throughout her career, Miller has received many honors. She was the 1986 recipient of the Young Women's Christian Association (YWCA) Silver Achievement Award and was the first woman basketball player to be nominated for the Sullivan Award, the highest award in amateur athletics. She was also voted the 1984-1985 ESPN Woman Athlete of the Year. Besides these many awards and achievements, Miller has also been a spokesperson for the Los Angeles Literacy Campaign, the American Lung Association, the Diabetes and Cancer Association, and the Muscular Dystrophy Association.

She continues her involvement in women's basketball as the 1997 coach of the Phoenix Mercury of the Women's National Basketball Associations (WNBA), leading the team to the finals.

Moral Behavior in Sport: Considerations for Girls and Women

Before discussing moral behavior in girls and women's sport, it is necessary to define what is meant by "moral" behavior. Moral development theorists suggest a behavior can be considered moral if it is intentional, if it is in response to some sense of obligation, and if the obligation is a response to an ideal. It is difficult to study moral behavior because the moral meaning of an act is wedded to the intent of the actor, and an actor's intent is not directly observable. For example, a basketball coach who puts her second string in after the first-string players have built a commanding lead may be motivated by a desire to let all members of the team play, or it may be a desire to avoid the risk of injury to the best players, or perhaps, it may even be a desire to avoid humiliating the opposing team. Identical behaviors may have different meanings depending on the motivation that inspires them. Thus, the term "prosocial" behavior is used to describe action that benefits another when the actor's intentions are unknown; "moral" behavior, in contrast,

Sport can enhance moral development in the proper setting.

specifically refers to action motivated by the actor's best judgment about what is right or good.

Three major influences on moral behavior are moral reasoning and maturity, moral atmosphere, and moral identity. Most of the research examining morality in sport has focused on the development of moral reasoning. Most scholars believe that moral reasoning develops through a series of stages or levels. Though details vary, moral reasoning development is thought to progress from an initial preoccupation with self-interest to a period in which self-interest is subordinated to social norms and rules. Finally, if development continues, the interests of all parties, including the self, others, and society, are carefully balanced. While moral reasoning is an important influence on moral action in sport, it is not necessarily the most important.

A second major influence on moral conduct is moral atmosphere, a term that refers to social and environmental influences on moral thought and action. Sport groups have a moral life that is distinct from the moral life of each group member and from the moral life of groups outside sport. An athlete's moral thought and action is influenced by the importance of her team membership and by her perception of her team's behavioral norms. If she believes that her teammates condone cheating or aggressive play, for example, she will be more likely to cheat and play aggressively. In addition to collective team norms, coaches' leadership styles and relationships with team members can also influence the moral atmosphere. A coach can enhance her team's moral atmosphere by "walking the talk," embodying the values she espouses; by encouraging athletes to participate in decision-making processes based on principles of fairness; and by developing caring, mutually respectful relations with everyone associated with the team. In contrast, a coach who differentially "looks the other way" when flagrant rule violations are committed by a star player is undermining the moral atmosphere of mutual responsibility among team members.

Moral atmosphere can also be influenced by the team's motivational climate. In contexts where a task- or mastery-oriented climate prevails, team members are encouraged to define success in terms of task mastery or self-referenced goals; examples include achieving a personal best or meeting a personal goal for a particular event. In contrast, a performance-oriented climate features an emphasis on other referenced definitions of success such as winning games or outperforming a rival. Research suggests that members of mastery-oriented teams tend to chose and act on moral values more frequently than members of performance-oriented teams, who tend to endorse more cheating and aggressive behavior—win at all costs.

Moral identity is the third key influence on moral conduct. Moral identity involves both the relative importance of morality in a person's view of herself, and the prioritizing of varying moral values (compassion versus justice, for example). If morality is a central feature of a person's identity, that person sees herself as a person who holds moral values and acts according to those values. This view of oneself as a person with moral values provides motivation to act in a manner consistent with those values. If fairness, for example, is an essential and salient element in a person's moral identity, then we might anticipate that she will be highly motivated to act fairly, even when she is tempted by nonmoral values (i.e., winning at all costs). On the other hand, if moral concerns are not essential components of her sense of personal identity, she will be less motivated to act with moral fidelity.

Participation in sport has traditionally been seen as a way to "build character," implying that it enhances moral development. However, depending on whether the experience itself encourages moral reasoning and moral identity and provides a positive moral atmosphere for the athlete, it may or may not enhance moral development. In the past, women's sport has had a tradition of holding opponents in high regard; this tradition, coupled with less pressure to win at all costs, encouraged moral development of the athlete. As the stakes increase in contemporary women's sport, the challenge will be to maintain a focus on developing young athletes' moral reasoning and identity in a positive atmosphere. *BLB*

Motor Sports Racing

Motor sports racing has long been the exclusive domain of men: there have been a number of notable exceptions, however. In 1977, Janet Guthrie became the first woman to qualify and compete in the Indianapolis 500. Following in Guthrie's footsteps, Lyn St. James competed in her sixth consecutive Indy 500 in 1997. After these two women, only one other woman, Desiree Wilson, has even attempted to qualify for Indy. Women drivers have made their mark outside of the Indianapolis 500 as well. In drag racing, Shirley Muldowney not only competed, she dominated, winning numerous championships. Other women, like Kay Bignotti, worked behind the scenes as mechanics, promoters, and other support staff.

Guthrie began competing in high speed car racing in 1963 and entered endurance races a year later. She became a household name in 1977 when she became the first woman to qualify for automobile racing's most prestigious event, the Indianapolis 500. In fact she set a qualifying speed record that year. Although engine problems prevented her from completing the race in 1977, in 1978 she again qualified and finished in a strong ninth place. In all, Guthrie competed in a total of 11 Indy 500s. In 1976, she also became the first woman to compete in a Winston Cup superspeedway stock-car race. Guthrie continued to race successfully into the 1980s when she ended her career because of lack of funding. Guthrie was named to the Women's Sports Hall of Fame in 1980.

In drag racing, Shirley Muldowney crushed the gender barrier. She was the runner up in the 1996 International Hot Rod Association's (IHRA) Top Fuel Division, and is widely recognized as one of the greatest drag racers of all time. Muldowney's career has spanned three decades during which time she won three National Hot Rod

Association (NHRA) Top Fuel World Championships and one American Hot Rod Association (AHRA) World Championship. Her life and career has been documented in the 1983 film *Heart Like a Wheel*.

Perhaps one of the most interesting racing stories is Cleo Chandler. The 82-year-old great-grandmother has been a regular in the IHRA drag racing circuit for the last 15 years and races in her "Mom's Toy" a '65 Chevelle. She has earned one career national event victory (1992), and four runner-up finishes.

Women's participation in motor sports racing has not been limited to behind the wheel. Amy Faulk, a 25-year race veteran and race winner in a number of different racing categories, has earned additional respect by becoming an important figure in the business of auto racing.

Kay Bignotti, the mechanic who started Janet Guthrie's engines, is one of four women licensed by USAC as a certified mechanic. Women also work as members of the all-important support team—doctors, timers, and engineers.

Other notable women who have competed in motor racing include the "First Lady of Auto Racing" Linda Vaughn, as well as Marie Hulman-George, Betty Rutherford, and Angelle Seeling, who along with Muldowney, Guthrie, Chandler, and Faulk, were recently honored by the Speciality Equipment Market Association, an important motor sports sponsor.

Funding the expensive team it takes to race at the highest levels remains the most significant problem for women motor sports competitors. "What we really need is a woman with all the stuff that it takes to be a great driver, and be a woman with her own fortune as well," Janet Guthrie has said. "Then we'll see a woman in the victory lane."

Motorcycling and Women

Through their brief history in motorcycling, women motorcyclists have been treated inconsistently by the media and their own governing bodies. On the one hand, they have sometimes been highlighted as a refreshing antidote to the sometimes "negative image" of the reckless, wild cyclist. For example, Hazel Kolb made a solo "round the perimeter of the USA" tour in 1979 and was on the *Johnny Carson* show and received other forms of press coverage. This attention was spontaneous, as she had no formal public relations or media training. Her achievements were later recognized by the American Motorcycle Association (AMA) in the creation of the "Hazel Kolb Brighter Image Award." The first all women's national motorcycle club (Motor Maids) was formed in 1938.

Other positive examples of women motorcyclists' accomplishments are Catherine Rambeau's 1988 round trip from the USA to Tiera del Fuego aboard a Honda 250 cc cycle and the 1996 Pony Express Tour across the United States. Through that tour, the sponsor, Women's Motorcyclist Foundation, generated over $300,000 for breast cancer research. Ed Youngblood, president of the AMA, has said "Again and again it has been demonstrated that women excel at conveying the essential qualities of motorcycling, joy, adventure, self-reliance and excitement."

The other side of the coin, in which the struggle for acceptance and recognition is seen, must be faced as well. In 1907, Clare Wagner won a major endurance event but was denied her trophy and the designation of "winner" because she was a woman. Kitty Badris wanted to become the first women professional team owner and mechanic and Kerry Klied wanted to become a licensed professional racer, but, in 1971, both had to take legal action to receive their accreditations from the AMA.

While such overt discrimination took place over 25 years ago, some areas of needed change today were identified by participants in the 1996 "Women and Motorcycling National Conference." Conference attendees mentioned examples such as the image of women still being used as sex objects for marketing efforts of motorcycle companies, and that much of the current equipment is tailored to the dimensions of men. The goals set by the conference participants outline the future for women in motorcycling:

1. To identify and explore the needs and interests of women who own and ride motorcycles and those who are potential owners;

2. To bring together the richly diverse group of women who motorcycle;

3. To open all aspects of motorcycling to women;

4. To improve public understanding of motorcycling;

5. To identify areas of motorcycle product development that will enhance the motorcycling experience of women.

Margaret Thompson Murdock

When the International Shooting Union compiled its list of the 12 best shooters of all time, Margaret Murdock was sixth, and the only woman. Born on August 25, 1942, in Topeka, Kansas, Murdock has often been the only woman or the first in her sport. She was, for example, the first woman to win an open competition at the world championships, the first woman to set an individual world record in open competition, and the first woman to win an open competition at the Pan American Games. In 1976, at the Olympic Games in Montreal, Canada, the initial results showed Murdock as the winner of the small-bore rifle three-position event. Five hours of checking targets and scores revealed a tie in points between Murdock and teammate Lanny Bassham. Officially, Bassham received the gold medal based on his score on the last round, but he pulled Murdock onto the top platform with him at the awards ceremony, a memorable moment in Olympic history.

N

National Association for Girls and Women in Sport (NAGWS)

The National Association for Girls and Women in Sport (NAGWS) has existed, in different forms and under different names, since 1899. The idea for establishing a group to study the unique problems of women's physical education departments in colleges and universities seems to have come from Amy Morris Homans, a noted pioneer in physical education. Homans regularly invited other women directors of physical training from colleges in the New England area and, on occasion, student presidents of athletic associations, to join her in discussions of mutual problems. Besides these discussions, the additional purposes of the meetings were to elevate the status of women's physical education as a profession and to supervise standards of conduct for women's physical education and sports. In 1915, Homans invited the directors of all eastern colleges to meet for the purpose of creating The Association of Directors of Physical Education for Women. Several other regional associations with similar purposes were formed, all requiring membership in the American Physical Education Association (APEA), the forerunner to the present American Alliance of Health, Physical Education, Recreation, and Dance (AAHPERD). These regional groups eventually joined to form the National Association for Physical Education of College Women (NAPECW) in 1924.

At about the same time as these women's regional organizations were forming, the APEA made an attempt, in 1914, to organize a national association for women directors of physical education. The APEA had previously formed a committee in 1899 to study the different modifications of basketball rules for girls. This basketball committee was the beginning of today's National Association for Girls and Women in Sport (NAGWS). A "woman's section" was recognized on the APEA convention program in 1914, a standing committee on women's athletics was created in 1916, and the National Section of Women's Athletics (NSWA) was officially recognized by the APEA in 1932.

The NAPECW and the NSWA had many common purposes that would provide the foundation for future positions involving women in athletics. It was the belief of these women's sport leaders that only women coaches, officials, and rules should be used for women's competition. They believed in a "triangle" of physical education with instruction (first priority at the base), intramural participation (second priority), and athletic competition at the top of the triangle but last in priority.

In retrospect, many feel that the attitude of the women's sport leaders toward elite-level competition was both stifling and very rigid. Even though there seems to be a void in the literature about this issue, it is possible that some of the reluctance of early women physical education leaders to move toward elite-level athletic competition for women may have been caused by the chronically underemphasized and undersupported status of women's physical education instruction and intramural programs. The traditional women physical educators' view was that females could participate in sport without being "inappropriate," but that sport experience should be educational, safe, institutionally budgeted, and focused on maximal participation.

In 1922, women physical educators took more action to control women's competition through the NSWA. In the United States, women's sport competitions followed the rules established by the sport committees of the NSWA. In 1953, this group became the National Section of Girls and Women in Sports (NSGWS), also under the auspices of the AAHPERD forerunner, the American Association of Health, Physical Education, and Recreation (AAHPER).

In the early 1950s, the NAPECW began to conduct their meetings in conjunction with several organizations having parallel missions. There seemed to be an increasing need for cooperation between groups interested in the uniqueness of women in sport and physical education. The official position of NAPECW at that time was to be a liaison between other organizations having common problems with women's competition. In 1955, they formed a tripartite committee (the National Joint Council on Extramural Sports for College Women) with the (now) DGWS (Division of Girls and Women in Sport) and a student group, the Athletic and Recreation Federation of College Women (ARFCW), to explore the effects of intercollegiate competition for women.

In 1965, the Board of Directors of NAPECW voted to discontinue the National

Joint Council on Extramural Sports for College Women so that its function could be assumed by AAHPER's DGWS, the forerunner of NAGWS. This change was in concert with a changing philosophy of NAPECW toward the publication of scholarly studies to improve physical education. Throughout NAPECW's history, the issue of women's athletics would be a part of its proceedings. However, both the DGWS and the NAPECW had a common objective: to provide educationally sound programs for female college students.

This common objective is a key point to keep in mind when examining the evolution of the NAGWS. Women's sport programs were developed from a different philosophy than were the men's programs. The women's philosophy was intended to create a more holistic, balanced, and integrated approach than the men's approach, which they regarded as being ever-focused on the elite athlete.

One major responsibility of the DGWS was to write and publish the rules for women's sports, a duty which harkened back to the 1899 basketball rules committee. In the 1950s, these rule books took the form of Sport *Guides*. The *Guides* not only provided the rules, but they also presented articles on skills, techniques, and (later) information on the national championships for each sport. Even though the major activity of DGWS in its early years was publishing, it also governed women's intercollegiate sports and sponsored national championships for women. Rachel Bryant served as the first consultant for the DGWS. She believed in the importance of keeping women physical educators supplied with current materials. During her years of service, the DGWS sold over 3.3 million Sport *Guides*, which demonstrated the magnitude of her contributions, and those of DGWS generally.

In 1963, the DGWS co-sponsored a continuing series of "Institutes" on girls and women's sports with the United States Olympic Committee (USOC). The Institutes, under the directorship of Sara Staff Jernigan, featured top-level, national and international competition-experienced faculty who taught their skills to a selected group of participants (screened from applicants following an open, nationwide invitation). These participants then conducted local mini-workshops to spread the high-level knowledge and the latest techniques they learned.

The Institutes were widely acknowledged as successful. They created a cadre of trained professional women who were instrumental in the development of the program of invitational collegiate championships sponsored by the Commission on Intercollegiate Athletics for Women (CIAW) of DGWS from 1968 to 1971. The CIAW program's successes led directly to the formation of the Association for Intercollegiate Athletics for Women (AIAW).

In response to many internal and external influences, the DGWS created another organization in 1967 to sponsor and promote intercollegiate athletics for women, the CIAW (mentioned above). In 1971 to 1972, the AIAW replaced the CIAW, and continued to govern intercollegiate athletics for women. In their times both CIAW and AIAW sanctioned national tournaments for women's collegiate sports as the need for them became apparent. The AIAW prospered from 1971 until 1981, when the National Collegiate Athletic Association (NCAA), then the national governing body for men's sports, was successful in offering their own championship programs for women. This ended AIAW effectiveness, and the NCAA assumed the governance and control of national championships for women's collegiate athletics.

The DGWS became the National Association for Girls and Women in Sport (NAGWS) in 1974. It is now one of the structural associations of AAHPERD, with the responsibility of supporting and advocating girls and women in sport.

The tradition of NAGWS throughout the twentieth century has been to provide educational sport development in areas that have been ignored by other social institutions. Throughout the evolution of NAGWS, there has been a continuous effort to influ-

ence programs for girls and women in schools and to impact organizations that sponsored or promoted sports events nationally and internationally.

The unique purpose of NAGWS is "to develop, encourage, foster, and support programs which provide equal opportunities for females to enrich their lives through participation in sports." At no time in recent history has the need to focus on equal opportunity for women been more imperative. Despite the great advances made during the 1970s as a result of the impetus of the women's movement, Title IX of the Education Amendments of 1972, the Women's Educational Equity Act (which offered opportunity to gain funding for educational programs in nontraditional areas for women), and the Amateur Sports Act of 1978 (which re-structured the Olympic movement in the USA), the full acceptance of women in society, and in programs of sport, has not been accomplished.

As the primary professional organization for women leaders of sport for a century, NAGWS has a major role in enhancing commitment to girls and women in sport. As the twenty-first century approaches, NAGWS has begun to shed its traditional services to the world of sport. As the responsibilities for rule writing, contest regulation, and standards for participation in both secondary and post-secondary schools have been assumed by organizations once serving only males, NAGWS now moves toward other ground. NAGWS has well served the development of girls and women in sport. Current levels of programming and performance attest to the dedication, devotion, and talents of the many leaders who have gone before. NAGWS emphasis shifts now from participant to leader, as NAGWS focuses on leadership development for women in sport, and on continued advocacy for girls and women's sports and sport leaders. *KD & DE*

See Also The Association for Intercollegiate Athletics for Women (AIAW); Women's Physical Education Philosophy and Athletics: Then and Now

Term	Name	Status
1899	Alice B. Foster	Chair
1900-1901	No President/Chair	
1901-1917	Senda Berenson	Chair
1917-1921	Elizabeth Burchenal	Chair
1921-1925	Blanche W. Trilling	Chair
1925-1927	Katherine Sibley	Chair
1927-1930	Florence D. Somers	Chair
1930-1931	Helen Hazelton	Chair
1931-1932	Grace Jones	Chair
1932-1934	Grace Davies	Chair
1934-1936	Elaine vonBorries	Chair
1936-1938	Elinor M. Schreder	Chair
1938-1940	Jane W. Shurmer	Chair
1940-1942	Ruth H. Atwell	Chair
1942-1943	Alice Schriver	Chair
1943-1946	Anna S. Espenschade	Chair
1946-1948	Alfreda Mosscrop	Chair
1948-1949	Martha A. Gable	Chair
1949-1952	Laurie E. Campbell	Chair
1952-1954	Josephine Fiske	Chair
1954	Aileene Lockhart	Chair
1954-1956	Grace Fox	Chair
1956-1958	Mabel Locke	Chair
1958-1959	Jane A. Mott	Chair
1959-1960	Thelma Bishop	Chair
1960-1961	Anne Finlayson	Chair
1961-1962	Sara Staff Jernigan	Chair
1962-1963	Katherine Ley	Chair
1963-1964	Marguerite Clifton	Chair
1964-1965	Betty McCue	Chair
1965-1966	Phebe M. Scott	Chair
1966-1967	Frances McGill	Chair
1967-1968	Lucille Magnusson	Chair
1968-1969	Alyce Cheska	Chair
1969-1970	Elizabeth Ann Stitt	Chair
1970-1971	Edith Betts	Chair
1971-1972	JoAnne Thorpe	Chair
1972-1973	Betty Hartman	Chair
1973-1974	Frances B. Koenig	Chair
1974-1975	Mildred Barnes	President
1975-1976	Lou Jean Moyer	President
1976-1977	Joanne Davenport	President
1977-1978	Carole Oglesby	President
1978-1979	Leotus Morrison	President
1979-1980	Phyllis Blatz	President
1980-1981	Doris R. Corbett	President

NATIONAL ASSOCIATION FOR GIRLS AND WOMEN IN SPORT PAST PRESIDENTS

EXHIBIT 1

Term	Name	Status
1981-1982	Helen "Susie" Knierim	President
1982-1983	Bonnie Slatton	President
1983-1984	Jean Perry	President
1984-1985	Carolyn B. Mitchell	President
1985-1986	Christine Shelton	President
1986-1987	Dorothy Richey	President
1987-1988	Mimi Murray	President
1988-1989	Vivian Acosta	President
1989-1990	Laurie Priest	President
1990-1991	Darlene Kluka	President
1991-1993	Doris Hardy	President
1993-1995	Robertha Abney	President
1995-1997	Sue Durrant	President
1997–1999	Donna Pastore	President

EXHIBIT 1 (continued)

National Collegiate Athletic Association (NCAA)

The National Collegiate Athletic Association (NCAA) is the governing body for all Division I, Division II, and Division III collegiate athletics, male and female. Another similarly focused organization, the National Intercollegiate Athletic Association (NAIA), is made up of mostly smaller Midwestern colleges whose main sport is basketball. Most United States university and college athletic departments and programs, however, belong to the NCAA. This body governs, legislates, and administers its own collegiate national championships. It sets the rules regarding who may and may not compete in collegiate athletics. It provides strict sanctions for anyone who breaks rules; these sanctions can affect eligibility, recruiting, scholarships, and playing.

Players have been banned for breaking various rules, and colleges and universities have been excluded from NCAA competition for, among other things, illegal recruiting and payment of athletes. The NCAA's stated purpose is to stimulate athletic programs, to promote recreational pursuits among students, and to pursue athletic excellence. It is primarily concerned with competitive athletic championships, hence its concern with recruiting and the equal treatment of all

The NCAA sponsors championships for women in a number of different sports.

athletes so that schools can't gain an unfair advantage.

The NCAA was established as a men's association in 1905. This body was formed to standardize rules for college sports and to set policies related to eligibility, scholarships, and administration. For many years, women athletes and women's programs were not administered by the NCAA, both by choice of women (who had their own organizations, most notably the Association of Intercollegiate Athletics for Women, [AIAW]) and, early on, by choice of the NCAA, which had no interest in dealing with women's athletics. With the advent of Title IX in 1972, which required that money, personnel, facilities, and administration of athletic programs be equitably divided between men and women, it appeared that the NCAA felt obliged to exert control over women's athletics. By the late 1970s, there was considerable dispute between the AIAW and the NCAA over the latter's intent to offer its own women's championship program. In 1980, when the NCAA representatives voted to offer a program of women's national championships, the AIAW lost its member schools and soon dissolved. As the NCAA took control of women's athletics, in most cases, the two athletic programs were merged (men and women's programs had been separate), and one person was named athletic director. In the great majority of cases, the named director was a man. This situation is slowly being redressed today, but in 1997, there were still only 16 women athletic directors in the nearly 300 Division I athletic departments.

Since 1981, the NCAA has sponsored women's championships, the first being in cross-country, field hockey, and volleyball. By 1982, most collegiate women's sport national championships were sponsored by the NCAA. With the help of the NCAA's increased sponsorship and media coverage (particularly in the sport of basketball), the promotion of women's athletic championships is directed to a much wider audience. In addition to conducting the national championships, the NCAA also honors and promotes outstanding players. The NCAA

annually elects a Woman Athlete of the Year, who is awarded the Honda-Broderick Cup. Past winners have included Cheryl Miller, Jackie Joyner, and Nancy Lieberman.

The NCAA safeguards the interests of collegiate athletes, both from academic failure and from exploitation. All member colleges are subject to rulings by the NCAA, from the president of the university to the assistant coaches and the athletes themselves, so that the NCAA can attempt to make sure that all student athletes are treated fairly and equally.

National Federation of State High School Associations

The "Federation," as it often called, had its beginning in 1920, at a meeting in Chicago, Illinois. The National Federation of State High School Associations (now called National Federation of High Schools, NFHS) maintained its office in Chicago until 1979, when it was moved to Kansas City, Missouri. The primary purpose of that first meeting was to discuss problems that had resulted

Basketball is one of many sports supported by the NFHS.
Photo courtesy of the *Camden Courier Post.*

from high school contests being organized by colleges and universities and other clubs and nonschool promoters. It was the responsibility of this federation of state-focused educators to maintain the integrity and educational value of the athletic programs developing around the country. By 1969, all 50 state associations and the District of Columbia were members of the National Federation of State High School Athletic Associations. In 1970, "athletic" was removed from the name to reflect the National Federation's services in fine arts programs, speech, debate, and music. Besides the 50 states and the District of Columbia, there are about 15 affiliate members in the United States territories, Canada, and other neighboring countries that participate in meetings and activities but do not have voting privileges.

The legislative body of NFHS is its National Council, which consists of one representative from each member state association. The National Council meets twice each year. The administrative body of the National Federation is its board of directors, which is elected by the National Council. The 12-member board meets four times a year and is composed of one representative (a chief executive officer of a state association) elected from each of eight geographic sections with the remaining four members elected at-large.

Six professional organizations within the NFHS provide services and benefits to their membership. The 5,000+ members of the National Interscholastic Athletic Administrators Association (NIAAA) receive a quarterly magazine, can participate in the certified athletic administrators and/or leadership programs, and can attend the annual national conference.

The 40,000 members of the National Federation of Interscholastic Coaches Association (NFICA) and the 130,000 members of the National Federation Interscholastic Officials Association (NFIOA) receive a quarterly magazine (*Coach* and *Official*, respectively) and may participate in an annual leadership conference. The NFICA participated in the development of the National Federation Interscholastic Coaches

Education Program (NFICEP), which is recommended or required in the majority of the states.

The NFHS is also very active in supporting nonsports activities and in forming professional organizations for these activities. The National Federation Interscholastic Music Association aims to identify and meet the common needs of music educators who participate in, or sponsor, high school music activities that are an educational extension of the school music curriculum. The National Federation Interscholastic Speech and Debate Association provides in-service training and other services to high school speech and debate coaches. In addition, the NFHS is responsible for the selection of the national debate topic and the publication of materials in support of both sides of the topic.

The National Federation Interscholastic Spirit Association is the newest professional organization within the National Federation. It was formed in 1988 to identify common needs of junior high and high school spirit (cheerleaders and pom, dance, and drill team) coaches. Members receive the *Coach* publication and participate in the leadership conference along with members of the NFICA and NFIOA.

About eight million publications and materials are printed annually at the in-house printing operation of NFHS. Rules-related publications in 16 sports include rule books, case books, officials' manuals, sport handbooks, and illustrated books as well as transparencies, rule exams, meeting folders, score books, roster and line-up sheets, charts and digrams, rule videos, and many other special materials.

Other programs of the NFHS include the annual collection and publication of national high school sport records. The NFHS operates an equipment center to provide approved gear at reasonable prices to high school contest officials. Many services are provided to assist state associations, school personnel, students, and their parents to help students make healthy lifestyle choices. The NFHS's newest initiative (1997) is the "Citizenship through Sports and Fine Arts" curriculum, which will provide materials with specific examples of teachable moments for coaches and other school personnel to use to teach the general theme of respect for self and respect for others.

The NFHS conducts four conferences each year; two for its member state associations, one for high school athletic administrators, and a leadership conference for coaches and officials. In addition to these meetings, the NFHS also sponsors national rule interpreters meetings, legal seminars, and teleconferences on key issues such as healthy lifestyles; it also operates the National Collegiate Athletic Association (NCAA) Clearinghouse.

National Federation Involvement in Girls' Sports

The NFHS's record in supporting girls sports has been mixed. In 1926, the Illinois High School Association became the first state association to hire a woman administrator to be responsible for girls sports programs. The first interscholastic competition for girls golf and tennis was approved in 1927, with girls archery added in 1935; twenty-nine years later, girls badminton was added to the interscholastic competition list.

A review of regional and national meetings of the NFHS reflects a long history of consultation with the National Section on Women's Athletics (NSWA) for the American Association of Health, Physical Education, and Recreation (AAHPER). In the late 1940s, a private communication from an NSWA official to a Federation official included the quote: "It is doubtful whether the skills and mental characteristics resulting from widely publicized contests are conducive to the development of those characteristics which are associated with cultured womanhood. It is felt further that all the benefits which may be attributed to interscholastic contests for girls may be derived from games and play days which are not designed to attract a large crowd." The Federation officials were perfectly willing to accept this position.

In 1959, the National Federation established a girls basketball committee. In 1970, the Federation first published rules for girls gymnastics. All other National Federation

rule books are for boys and girls high school competition: volleyball and swimming and diving in 1973; basketball, soccer, and softball in 1976; field hockey and track and field in 1977; ice hockey in 1978; water polo in 1980; and spirit in 1988.

The NFHS began collecting participation figures for girls sports from its member state associations in 1971 with just over 290,000 participants reported. In 1972–1973, states reported just over 817,000 girls participating in interscholastic sports competition. By the 1995–1996 school year, state associations reported nearly 2,368,000 girls participating in interscholastic sports competition in addition to the thousands of girls participating on co-rec and boys teams.

The NFHS staff has had only three women sport administrators through 1997. Pam Erwin was hired in 1978 and was followed by Kristy Rowland Miskovsky, who worked for the Federation from 1979 to 1982. Susan True has been an assistant director at NFHS since the fall of 1982, responsible for the equity program as well as the rule books and related services for the sports of boys gymnastics, girls gymnastics, field hockey, spirit, swimming and diving, volleyball, and water polo.

In 1990, Dr. Sandra Scott became the first woman executive director of a state association when she was promoted to executive director of the New York State Public High School Athletic Association. Dr. Scott was also the first chair of the National Federation's Equity Committee, formed in 1993. In 1992, Becky Oakes was promoted to executive director of the Missouri State High School Activities Association and became the first woman president of NFHS in 1996.

Biographies of Important Women in the National Federation

Ola Bundy: Bundy was one of the key figures in the rise of girls high school athletics programs for 30 years. She was a member of the Illinois High School Association staff from 1967 through 1996. She had been the state's rules interpreter for the sports of volleyball, track and field, and swimming since their inception with the state association. She helped write the Illinois State Board of Education Sex Equity Rules. She is a member of three halls of fame: the Illinois Girls Coaches Association Hall of Fame, the Illinois Basketball Coaches Association Hall of Fame, and the National Federation's Sport Hall of Fame.

Dorothy McIntyre: In the 1960s, McIntyre was a physical education/social studies teacher in Minnesota. Her female students wanted more sports opportunities, and she began to conduct extramural competition with neighboring schools. Soon she had her bus driver's license, which permitted her to take girls all over the state to promote opportunities for girls. McIntyre used rhythmic gymnastics performances by her gymnasts to illustrate the values of movement and, ultimately, of competition.

McIntyre became one of the early pioneers because of her reluctance to accept the belief that females should be limited to generalized physical activity. She believed bringing people together to develop plans and to build networks would make changes happen more quickly than working alone. McIntyre was elected chair of the Minnesota Division of Girls and Women in Sport (DGWS) and appointed committees to begin developing competitive opportunities in a variety of sports. She was a member of planning committees for the early National Institute for Girls and Women in Sports sponsored in the 1960s by the DGWS of the AAHPER and by the United States Olympic Committee (USOC).

A "critical mass" was achieved when the Minnesota State High School League established a committee to prepare "Bylaws for Girls Athletics." The approval of girls athletics in 1969, as a league-sponsored program, resulted in McIntyre's employment as a member of the leagues' executive staff, one of the first three women hired by state associations to develop high school athletics. Between 1970 and 1978, high school girls sports in Minnesota grew from basically nothing to a thriving program with state tournaments and competition in 12 sports.

Since early in the 1970s, McIntyre served the National Federation of State High School Associations as a resource for information regarding gender equity by speaking at National Federation-sponsored conferences and workshops, by writing articles, and by making presentations at state association meetings across the country.

Dr. Sandra Scott: After teaching on the secondary school and collegiate levels, Dr. Scott joined the staff of the New York State Public High School Athletic Association (NYSPHSAA) in 1975. In the 1970s, she began surveying state associations regarding the involvement of women in leadership roles in their structure. The most recent survey was completed in 1992. These were the only nationwide surveys regarding women in leadership roles conducted on the scholastic level.

In 1990, Dr. Scott was selected NYSPHSAA Executive Director, becoming the first woman in the nation to assume the directorship of a state high school athletic association. In July 1993, she chaired the first forum on equity issues for the NFHS, and in 1994, she was the first chairperson for the National Federation's Equity Committee, initiated that same year.

Susan S. True: True's involvement in sports began when she became the women's gymnastics coach at Washburn University in 1972. She continued as a professor, coach, and finally women's athletic coordinator until she joined the staff of the Federation in 1982. During her tenure with the Federation, she has represented the Federation as an officer and board member of USA Volleyball, a member of the Board and Executive Committee of the USA Gymnastics Federation, a board member of the United States Field Hockey Association, an officer and member of the Board of Trustees and Executive Committee of the Women's Sports Foundation. She has also served two terms as the Federation's representative on the NCAA Competitive Safeguards and Medical Aspects of Sports Committee.

Susan True, member of executive staff of NFHS since 1982.

Sharon Wilch: Wilch is an inspiring state and national leader for improving and expanding activities and athletics for students. Her entire career has been dedicated to excellence, integrity, and equity in education. Wilch served 27 years as a Colorado High School Activities Association Assistant and Associate Commissioner. She led the sanctioning and rapid growth of girls sports over the critical period since the passage of Title IX in 1972, becoming a state and national expert on Title IX and educating schools on providing fairness and preventing litigation.

She has served on the NFHS rules committees and on the board of the United States Gymnastics Federation. Outside Colorado and nationally, she served as the National Federation's liaison with the DGWS in years past, and as a member of the Olympic Swimming Committee, the Olympic Gymnastic Committee, and the Olympic Apparel and Equipment Committee. She also served as the chair of the National Federation Girls' Gymnastic Rules Committee for 15 years.

For more information about NFHS programs contact: National Federation of State High School Associations, PO Box 20626, Kansas City, MO 64195, (816) 464-5400. *ST*

National Girls and Women in Sports Day

National Girls and Women in Sports Day (NGWSD), officially proclaimed by the Congress of the United States, is held annually on the first Thursday in February. NGWSD is a one-day celebration; a joint project of five national women's organizations with sport programs for girls and women. All five organizations have long traditions and are described in separate entries in this encyclopedia (Girls Incorporated, Girl Scouts USA, National Association for Girls and Women in Sport [NAGWS], Women's Sports Foundation [WSF], and Young Women's Christian Association [YWCA] of USA).

NGWSD began in 1987 as a day to promote girls and women's sport and particularly to commemorate Olympic volleyball legend Flo Hyman for her many athletic achievements and her work to assure equality for women's sports. On each NGWSD, the Flo Hyman Memorial Award is presented by the Women's Sports Foundation to an athlete who captures Hyman's "dignity,

National Girls and Women in Sports Day.
Photo courtesy of the *Camden Courier Post*.

spirit, and excellence." Past winners include Martina Navratilova, Jackie Joyner-Kersee, Patty Sheehan, and Mary Lou Retton. As a part of the activities of NGWSD, sports educators, coaches athletic directors, recreation directors, affiliated associations, corporations, and others, sponsor events and partake in activities that focus on the involvement of girls and women in sports.

The goal of the one-day event is to increase the visibility of women's and girls' participation and successes in sports and to remind America that the struggle for gender equity is not over. NGWSD is celebrated in many cities and towns across the nation. One can begin with a community action kit, which is free of charge. The kits can be obtained from the Women's Sports Foundation at 1-800-227-3988. This starter kit provides information about each state's coordinator of NGWSD, as well as guidelines for how to organize, host, and publicize NGWSD. All these materials are made available through the generosity of J.C. Penney, Inc., the sponsor of NGWSD.

The efforts of NGWSD-sponsoring organizations have helped to bring more girls onto basketball courts, onto baseball fields, into swimming pools, and to other sporting environments.

The five national organizers of NGWSD are committed to teaching girls that it is okay to play sports. It is healthy, it is fun, and it is not just for boys. *ANW*

National Girls and Women in Sport Symposium

The National Girls and Women in Sport Symposium (NGWSS) was founded in 1991 by Dr. Catriona T. Higgs (professor, Department of Physical Education) and Laurel Dagnon (director, Camps and Conferences) at Slippery Rock University in Pennsylvania. The purpose of the symposium was to provide an annual forum to share information pertaining to a wide variety of issues related to girls and women in sport. Each year the symposium adopts a theme and a call for papers is solicited through the mail.

Topics ranging from homophobia in sport, to gender relations, to coverage and images of women in sport, have been discussed at this conference. The symposium has attracted many of the most renowned researchers in the field including: Dr. Susan Greendorfer, Dr. Carole Oglesby, Dr. Donna Lopiano, Dr. Vivian Acosta, Dr. Linda Carpenter, and Dr. Pat Griffin.

Originally intended to celebrate National Girls and Women in Sport Day, the symposium serves to expand the examination of women's contributions to sport through presentations, panels, and workshops in an academic setting. As part of this celebration, the NGWSS instituted a Hall of Fame to honor the accomplishments of women in sport and those involved in researching this area. Amongst the inductees are Billy Jean King, Donna Lopiano, the All American Girls Professional Baseball League, Ann Bancroft, Jan Felshin, Dorothy Harris, Babe Zaharias, Nell Jackson, and Mariah Burton Nelson.

In 1994, the symposium was moved from Slippery Rock University and is now administered by an impressive advisory board that includes many of the foremost authorities in women's sports. Laurel Dagnon continues to serve as director.

National Women's Law Center

Nationally known for its advocacy role for women's rights, the National Women's Law Center (NWLC) was instrumental in the fight for implementing Title IX, winning their suit against the Department of Health, Education, and Welfare and forcing the department to enforce the law. The NWLC represented Title IX in the precedent-setting settlement in *Haffer v. Temple University* and filed friend of the court briefs for the Supreme Court rulings on *Grove City v. Bell* and *Franklin v. Gwinnett County Public Schools*. The Gwinnett County ruling established the precedent of awarding monetary damages for intentional Title IX violations. Cases that involve sex discrimination and athletes are handled by NWLC, and it is currently involved in state and federal cases. The NWLC has helped the Women's Sports Foundation develop policies to ensure that the Office of Civil Rights responds to violations of Title IX. The NWLC is the 1992 recipient of the Billie Jean King Contribution Award given by the Women's Sport's Foundation.

The NWLC is composed of a legal staff, who pursue various types of equity cases, making significant contributions of time and energy to women's sport.

Native American Women and Sport

Little research focuses on the experiences of Native American women in sport and physical activity. One problem with conducting this type of research is that Native Americans are often viewed as one large group with shared cultural and family values, even though the federal government recognizes 552 distinct tribes in the United States (Bureau of Indian Affairs [BIA], 1995). Great diversity exists among these tribes in their beliefs, languages, and cultures. Acknowledging this diversity is essential, as Native Americans are far from homogeneous.

When Native American women and girls participate in sport programs and careers, it is important to realize they bring the beliefs and values of their mother cultures (Morgan, Griffin, & Heyward, 1996). While acknowledging the diversity mentioned in the previous paragraph, some traditional beliefs and values seem to be common among many Native American peoples. Native Americans view the world as a sacred place. Everything is equal, all share the earth, and all things are mutually dependent. People are not viewed as separate from nature, and our main responsibility is to maintain harmony. Cycles represented by circles are also very important. Life is a cycle, the year is a cycle, and the universe is a cycle. Sacred practitioners attempt to maintain proper balance involving the tribe, the natural world, and the spirit world. The tribe's oral tradition serves as the foundation for their sacred way. Native American traditional culture defines success as care of the tribal group/family,

cooperation with others, and knowledge of ceremonials and tradition.

Values and skills that Native American women needed for survival were taught through games and sport. "It was through games and sports that Native Americans develop their self-esteem/worth, self-discipline, dependence, and self-reliance, and at the same time, developed skills in working cooperatively with and for the welfare of the tribe" (Schroeder, 1995, p. 50). Historically, two games were particularly widespread and played predominantly by women. Oxendine (1988) described *shinny* (also called *gugahawat*, *ohonistuts*, *kakwasethi*, and *oomatashia*) as a game quite similar to field hockey. The field was approximately one-mile long, and the manner in which the ball was decorated was of religious significance. Another game played by women was doubleball. Doubleball used two balls attached to each end of a string about one-and one-half feet long. Each woman had a short stick used to catch and throw the ball to score a goal. The goals were usually one mile or more apart, and the game was similar to lacrosse. Variations of these games are still enjoyed by Native American women.

Sport participation is imbedded in Native American tradition and is related to all aspects of life. For Native American women, there is a strong connection between sport and physical activity and social, spiritual, and economic aspects of daily life. Serious preparation of mind, body, and spirit are precursors to sport participation. The most important purposes of sport to Native Americans are to maintain kinship relations, group harmony, fair play, and consensual leadership (Cheska, 1984). Sport also develops observational skills, stamina, strength, pain tolerance, and competition required for life. Competition, however, is not viewed from a won-loss perspective. Competition for Native American women does not emphasize individual domination of an opponent but is self- and group-oriented. Competition is viewed as a way to motivate individuals and groups toward expanding self-limits and self-knowledge (Morgan et al., 1996; Schroeder, 1995).

An example of how important running is to Native American women is found in *Kinaalda*, a Navajo puberty ceremony (Begay, 1983) that has social and religious significance for girls and their families. With a girl's first menses, she "comes of age." A special four-day ceremony ushers the young woman into adult society. On the first day a medicine man, who specializes in this ceremony, is notified. A woman is also chosen to assist, and this woman dresses the girl in fine jewelry and clothing, combs and ties her hair, and molds and massages her. The girl then circles the fireplace clockwise and starts her first run. Anyone who wishes to participate follows and yells loudly for the Wind People and Holy People to witness. Participants must be careful not to compete with or run faster than the girl. She runs eastward from the hogan (a traditional Navajo, eight-sided house) and eventually circles clockwise around a plant that has not yet matured and then follows the same path back to the hogan. The girl is instructed to increase her speed as she returns. She goes through the hogan door and circles the fireplace clockwise. The girl then begins the ritual grinding of corn.

Each time she runs, the same procedure is followed, except the distance is increased. Before the sun rises on the second day, the girl and her companions run to the east to meet the sun. She is reminded to think positively that she can accomplish any goals she sets for herself. She spends the day grinding corn and runs again at noon.

On the third day, she runs farther eastward before dawn. A ceremonial cake of corn meal is prepared and cooked. At noon the girl again runs eastward with her companions. It is taboo for her to look backward during her run, for that will invite bad luck. Throughout the third night the medicine man and knowledgeable participants pray and sing over the girl from traditional Beauty Way and Blessing Way rites. Early (about 4:00 A.M.) on the fourth morning, wearing her best traditional clothes, the girl again

runs eastward. The singers begin the "Racing Songs," which continue through the run. This run is the longest, and she must again increase her pace as she returns. The medicine man ends his songs and blesses the ceremonial cake, which is shared by all. A feast then follows.

In this initiation into womanhood, running before sunrise is to strengthen the individual so she may become wealthy, healthy, wise, and strong. A Native American women's concept of health is often rooted in a sense of order and balance with a framework of family, community, and tradition. Navajo children are traditionally taught to rise early and run in the morning to develop mental, moral, and physical strength.

These cultural values may, in fortuitous circumstances, be applied to sport situations, and Native American women attach culturally specific meanings to their sport experiences (Morgan et al., 1996). Native American women are a diverse and dynamic cultural group who merit increased study that focuses on their sport and exercise experiences and meanings.

Most of all, however, Native American girls and women need opportunities to participate in sports. In the past, girls' and women's teams from reservation schools seldom competed with mainstream school sport teams. Groups like the Native American Sports Council (NASC) are only now beginning to promote sport programs for Native American girls. To contact NASC, write to 1765 S. 8th St., Suite T-6, Colorado Springs, Colorado 80906. *JG2*

References

Begay, S. (1983). *Kinaalda: A Navajo puberty ceremony*. Rough Rock, AZ: Navajo Curriculum Center.

Bureau of Indian Affairs. (1995). Indian entities recognized and eligible to receive services from the United States Bureau of Indian Affairs. *Federal Register*, 60 (32), 9250-55.

Cheska, T. A. (1984). Sport as ethnic boundary maintenance: A case of the American Indian. *International Review of Sociology of Sport*, 19, 241-55.

Morgan, L. K., Griffin, J., and Heyward, V. H. (1996). Ethnicity, gender, and experience effects on attibutional dimensions. *The Sport Psychologist*, 10, 4-16.

Oxendine, J. B. (1988). *American Indian sports heritage*. Champaign, IL: Human Kinetics.

Schroeder, J. J. (1995). Developing self-esteem and leadership skills in Native American women: The role sports and games play. *Journal of Physical Education, Recreation, and Dance, 66* (7), 48-51.

Martina Navratilova

Martina Navratilova has been called the greatest tennis player ever, and some even call her the best female athlete in the world. She is certainly one of the most famous. Born in Prague, Czechoslovakia, on October 18, 1956, Navratilova's parents and grandmother had been national team tennis players in Czechoslovakia and sports were part of her life from the beginning. (See the picture of her skiing as a child.) Naturally, Navratilova took to tennis and won her first national tournament at the age of 14. She was the Czechoslovakian national champion from 1972 to 1975. In 1973, she was the junior girls champion at Wimbledon, the international tennis championship tournament in England.

Martina Navratilova in her youth.

In 1975, at the United States Open Tournament, Navratilova decided to stay in the United States to live and play tennis. In her native country of Czechoslovakia, the communist government controlled sport, and so she defected to the United States so that she could have the freedom to plan her own career. It was not an easy decision. She was not able to see her parents or sister, who remained in Czechoslovakia, for several years. In 1975, she became a United States citizen.

Navratilova has won more singles and doubles tennis tournaments than any other female. Her accomplishments are outstanding. Her 168 singles titles are the most won by any male or female tennis player. Navratilova won a record nine Wimbledon singles titles, and many consider Wimbledon the most important tennis tournament in the world. She won 18 Grand Slam (Wimbledon and the Australian, French, and United States Open) singles titles and holds the record of 109 consecutive doubles wins with her partner Pam Shriver. At the 1987 United States Open, she completed a "triple crown," winning in singles, doubles, and mixed doubles. In all, Navratilova was ranked number one for 332 weeks.

One of the greatest rivalries in sporting history was the 10-year battle for the number one world ranking between Martina Navratilova and Chris Evert. Of the 14 Grand Slam finals in which they faced each other, Navratilova won 10.

Navratilova was a strong athlete who was known for her tough training regimen. She lifted weights, ran to increase aerobic capacity, and ate a special diet. She was also known for her forthrightness. She was open about her homosexuality and made it clear that she never thought that it was strange being gay, only strange the way the media reacted to her.

In 1986, she returned to Czechoslovakia, for the first time since her defection to the United States, to play in a tennis tournament as part of the United States Federation Cup team. She was amazed to hear the crowds cheering for her and to see them tossing flowers down on her.

In 1994, Navratilova was named president of the Women's Tennis Association. She retired from singles tennis competition later that year. At Wimbledon in 1995, she returned to win the mixed doubles championship.

With her great career success, Navratilova became one of the wealthiest women in sports, and she donates much of her money and time to charitable causes. Navratilova was honored by the Women's Sports Foundation as the Professional Sportswoman of the Year for three years (1982–1984), and she received the first Flo Hyman Award in 1987. She was named the Women's Tennis Association Player of the Year a record seven times. She was named the Female Athlete of the Decade for the 1980s by the Associated Press, United Press International, and the National Sports Review. Her autobiography, *Martina*, was published in 1985.

Navratilova lives in Aspen, Colorado and currently works as a tennis commentator for CBS and HBO television. She is co-founder of Women's Sports Legends, a sports marketing company.

Patsy E. Neal and the Wayland "Flying Queens"

Patsy Neal, a three-time Amateur Athletic Union (AAU) All-American basketball player, captained the United States women's basketball team that played in the 1964 world basketball tournament. Neal, a five-foot ten-inch forward, also was a member of the gold-medal winning 1959 Pan American women's basketball team. In the final game against Canada, which the United States won by the score of 65-28, Neal was the top scorer, and her shooting percentage for the entire Pan-Am tournament was .800.

Born in Elberton, Georgia, in 1938, Neal was an influential figure in the transition of women's sports from the low-level competition of the "play-day era" to the fast-paced, high level of competition characteristic of women's collegiate basketball today. Neal's alma mater, Wayland Baptist College, located in Texas, was one of the first schools to offer scholarships to female athletes and, beginning in the early 1950s, offered full scholarships for women's basketball. As there was no recognized women's collegiate competition at the time, the Wayland Baptist women's basketball team was known as the Hutcherson Flying Queens after the team's sponsor who flew the Queens to their away games. The Queens ran up a record that will be very difficult to match, winning 131 games in a row, including 10 AAU national titles.

Neal also was a key instructor in basketball at the United States Olympic Committee's Fourth National Institute on Girls and Women's Sport. In addition, she was an AAU member, sat on the basketball rules committee, and was professor and coach at Brevard College in North Carolina for many years. She also authored numerous books and articles on girls' and women's sport.

Mariah Burton Nelson

Mariah Burton Nelson was born in Blue Bell, Pennsylvania, in April 1954 and moved to Phoenix, Arizona, with her family when she was 16. As a high school athlete in Phoenix, she received varsity letters in five sports and played Amateur Athletic Union (AAU) basketball with the Arizona Phoenix Dusters.

A six-foot two-inch athlete, she played basketball at Stanford University where she majored in psychology. As captain of the team, she was the leading scorer and rebounder for four years at Stanford. She averaged 19 points a game, and one of her rebounding records still stands today (most rebounds in one game, 20). Nelson went on to play professional basketball in France, on the Clermont-Ferrand Team, and in the United States, with the New Jersey Gems of the shortlived Women's Professional Basketball League.

In 1983, Nelson graduated from San Jose State University with a masters degree in public health. She has dedicated her time for several years as a hospice volunteer and was a volunteer coordinator at the Hospice of Santa Cruz, California.

A prominent journalist, Nelson was the first person to write a nationally syndicated column about women and sports. Her columns appeared in over 300 newspapers. Her expertise is on sports and sexism issues. In 1988, she won the Women's Sports Foundation/Miller Lite Journalism Award. She was a finalist for this prestigious award again in 1990, 1991, and 1994. In 1995, she was honored with The National Organization for Women's award for excellence in sports writing. She has also written for *The New York Times*, *The Washington Post*, *USA Today*, *Ms.*, *Self*, *Glamour*, and others.

An influential expert on the issues of gender and sports, she has appeared on several television and radio shows. Nelson is also a consultant to The Children's Television Workshop. She is a frequent lecturer on college campuses and does presentations for various groups and organizations.

Nelson is the author of three very important books on issues concerning women and sports. Her first book, *Are We Winning Yet? How Women Are Changing Sports and Sports Are Changing Women* (Random House, 1991), received the Amateur Athletic Foundation (AAF) Book Award in 1992. Her second book is *The Stronger Women Get, The More Men Love Football* (Harcourt Brace, 1994). Her forthcoming third book, *Embracing Victory: Life Lessons in Courage and Compassion*, is to be published by William Morrow in 1998.

In 1996, Nelson received the National Association of Girls and Women in Sports (NAGWS) Guiding Woman in Sport Award and was inducted into the National Girls and Women in Sport Symposium Hall of Fame. Nelson has recently competed in the 1,500-meter freestyle event in masters swimming competitions and coached high school girls' basketball.

Paula Newby-Fraser

Paula Newby-Fraser was born in Zimbabwe (then known as Rhodesia). She lives and trains in the United States as a competitor in the triathlon. She is the leading women's champion in Ultra-Distance Triathlon.

Paula Newby-Fraser.
© Daniel Kron.

Because this demanding event requires swimming 2.4 miles, cycling 112 miles, and then running 26.2 miles, it is no wonder she has been called "The Greatest All-Around Female Athlete in the World."

Newby-Fraser has set records in winning the Japan Ironman Triathlon, the San Diego Ironman Triathlon, the Bakersfield Triathlon, the United States of America National Pro/Elite Championships, and several others. She is the only woman to win the Nice International Triathlon twice.

She is best known, however, for her accomplishments at the world-famous Hawaii Ironman Triathlon Championships. In 1996, in severe heat conditions, Newby-Fraser crossed the finish line in 9 hours, 6 minutes, and 49 seconds to win a record eighth time. No other woman has ever won more than two events. She was the first woman to break the nine-hour barrier at the Hawaii Ironman. Though she has lived and trained in the United States for some time, it wasn't until 1996 that Newby-Fraser officially became a United States citizen. She continues to compete in triathalon events.

Diana Nyad

Diana Nyad was born on August 22, 1949, in New York City, and grew up in Ft. Lauderdale, Florida, the daughter of two parents from foreign cultures (mother French, father Egyptian). Her family was decidedly nonathletic says Nyad, preferring that she pursue the piano, and horrified that she would spend hours every day engaged in an activity that built muscles and turned her hair green. Nevertheless, once Nyad discovered the sport of swimming at the age of 10, she embraced the discipline, the predawn workouts, and the long-term goals with a relentless passion.

Nyad was not a world-class sprinter, but she was a national caliber backstroker throughout her teenage years and had a long-shot chance of making her Olympic dream come true for the 1968 Games in Mexico City, Mexico. But in the summer of 1966, Nyad heard the discouraging news that she had contracted viral endocarditis. This diagnosis would mean four months of strict bed rest, a critical loss of both muscle mass and cardiovascular conditioning, and not much time to rebuild before Mexico City. By the time she began a comeback, her speed had diminished, and the Olympic Games were no longer even a distant possibility.

Shortly after the trials for the 1968 Olympic Games, Nyad was introduced to the sport of marathon swimming. The Earth is four/fifths water, and there is rich history around the world of individuals stroking across rivers, lakes, and oceans: from Byron swimming the Hellespont to Captain Matthew Webb first conquering the English Channel back in 1875, and later to Gertrude Ederle swimming the English Channel in record time. By 1969, Nyad's first year as a marathoner, tradition had made long swims in Egypt, Argentina, Italy, England, and Canada very popular. For instance, at the end of the two-week Canadian National Exhibition in Toronto each summer, the greatest distance swimmers from around the world gather to see who can swim across Lake Ontario the fastest.

For the first eight years of her decade as a marathoner, Nyad competed in these races. A hundred or so swimmers would stand on the beach on the Isle of Capri, for example, and plunge into the Bay of Naples at the sound of the gun. A few hundred yards offshore, handlers would wait in boats to pick up their respective athletes to guide them to the other shore. As a general rule, the swims would be a minimum of 25 miles, which means the winner would finish in around eight hours. With the exception of Italy and Egypt, the water was frequently cold, the currents strong, and the surface rough. It takes an iron will to persist under these conditions, and Nyad was often one of only a handful of swimmers to make it to the other shore.

Diana Nyad.

Because of her success in the competions, Nyad was named the top female distance swimmer in the world from 1969 to 1977. She also did one exceptional solo swim during this period. She was the only person to traverse Lake Ontario from north to south, fighting the powerful currents from Niagara Falls on the lake to make shore at the end.

During these years, Nyad also garnered a reputation as someone who could relate the eccentric marathon experience to the public. The extreme state of sensory deprivation (the swimmer is isolated without being able to see or hear for sometimes more than 24 hours of nonstop swimming) was a subject about which journalists interviewed Nyad extensively. She was articulate in describing each swim as worth six months on a psychiatrist's couch, because the sensory deprivation produced an alpha state that allowed the mind to free associate and reach a dream-like state of consciousness while still swimming.

Much of marathon swimming has to do with imagination, the conquering of water that means something to people who live on or by that body of water. For example, there had been a famous race for many years before World War II, in which men would race around Manhattan, and Nyad had the vision to bring the historical event back to life. Her time was a speedy 7 hours, 57 minutes, and her accomplishment, and thoughts about it, were featured on the front page of the *New York Times*, a feature article in *Sports Illustrated*, and an appearance with Johnny Carson on the *Tonight Show*.

During the prime of her career, Nyad was very outspoken about women's rights, and her athletic prowess gave her a forum to speak out just at the time the public was ripe to hear her. Billie Jean King had just beaten Bobby Riggs in a tennis match watched by millions at the Houston Astrodome in 1974, and in 1977, Janet Guthrie became the first woman to race at the Indianapolis 500. *Ms.* Magazine named Nyad their Woman of the Year in 1975 and for the next five years. Nyad was committed to making the United States a place where women could speak their minds, make the money they deserved, and chase their dreams with full societal support.

Before Nyad retired from the intense rigors of marathon swimming, she became

intrigued, almost obsessed, with the concept of swimming 100 miles in the open ocean. The world record for distance in the open sea at the time was 60 miles. In August 1978, with every news organization in the Western world reporting, Nyad boldly tried to do what no man or woman ever had: swim nonstop from Cuba to Florida. A storm system whipped up a heavy sea, but she still made it 79 miles north of Havana in a heroic effort that lasted 41 hours, 49 minutes. Weather was that project's only spoiler, and so Diana gathered her crew of personal trainers, shark experts, and navigators to mount the adventure again the next summer. The year 1979 was not an easy year for foreigners to obtain visas to Cuba, however, and Nyad's mission had to be transferred over to the Bahamas. On August 21, 1979, Diana waded into the water off the island of Bimini and power stroked her way to the Florida coast. Twenty-seven hours, 38 minutes later, on her 30th birthday, she walked, stumbled, and crawled up onto the sand at Jupiter, Florida, as several thousand fans and an enormous worldwide press contingent witnessed the completion of the longest open-water swim in history, for both men and women. The official distance was 102.5 miles, a world record.

In 1986, Nyad was inducted into the Women's Sports Foundation (WSF) International Sports Hall of Fame. She is also a hall of famer at her college (Lake Forest College) and her high school (Pine Crest Preparatory School). In 1978, she wrote her first book, *Other Shores* (Random House), which explored the physical, psychological, and emotional growth that comes from pursuing excellence. Today, Nyad works as a television correspondent and producer and comments regularly for National Public Radio, often focusing on women's courage and achievements in the world of sports.

O

Sheila Young Ochowicz. *See* **Sheila Young**

Olympic Games and Women

In the 1996 Centennial Olympic Games celebration in Atlanta, Georgia, over 3,700 women competed, 1,000 more than just four years before at Seoul, South Korea. At the first modern Olympic Games in Athens, Greece, in 1896, no women were allowed to take part. However, there is a report of a Greek woman named Melpomene running in the marathon by starting behind the 25 men competitors and completing the last lap outside the stadium. (She was not allowed in the stadium, as she was not an official runner.) She is reported to have finished in four and a half hours.

The founder of the modern Olympics, Pierre de Coubertin, and his associates who organized the revival of the Olympic Games, had lofty ideals of bringing together athletes from all over the world for a grand sporting festival that would promote international sport and bring goodwill and promote peace between nations. But this spectacle was to be for male athletes only; their reward would be the applause of women.

The nineteenth century, however, was a period of great change for women with industrialization and the rise of women's political movements, especially the fight for women's suffrage (the right to vote). It was also a time of development for women's sports influenced by the sporting craze of the time, cycling. This passion for cycling led the way for women to wear looser clothing so they could cycle and for women to begin to lead more active lives. It is interesting to see the relationship between clothing and changes in women's sporting activities.

At the dawn of the twentieth century, there was an increase in recreational sports for those woman who could afford them. Golf, sailing, and tennis were all popular. At the second Olympic Games in 1900 in Paris, France, the (unofficial) events for women were tennis and golf. Yachting was designated as an event where both men and women could compete together, but no women entered. A total of 11 women entered the 1900 Games, and Margaret Abbott became the first United States woman to win a gold medal (golf) at any Olympic Games. Her success was due to the fact that she happened to be in Paris at the time and not due to any support from the United States men who chose the male Olympic team.

The Olympic Games at the start of the twentieth century bore little resemblance to the Games at the close of the century. The events at the 1904 Olympic Games in St. Louis, Missouri, were spread over four months, and only 12 countries competed. The only event for women was archery, and Lida Howell of The United States won two team medals and one individual gold medal. This event really took place as a competition between her club, Cincinnati, and the Washington, D.C., club, which held the tournament. It was not the carefully selected women's team of future Olympic Games, but it was a start.

By 1908, the Games were more orga-nized, as nearly 2,000 men took part in the London Games, but for United States women, there was no competition. The all-male United States Olympic Committee (USOC) was opposed to women competing in events where they did not wear long skirts. But just as cycling had begun to free women from restrictive clothing, so too did the dress of women for tennis, golf, and archery contribute to the steady pace of change. The effects of the first World War also changed women's clothing, which in turn helped women in sporting activities. During the war many women took jobs in industry that had formerly been done by men, jobs that required more practical clothing. Besides affecting attitudes about dress, these war efforts also helped to build a view of women as more capable and physi-cally stronger than had been previously thought.

By the 1920 Olympic Games in Antwerp, Belgium, United States women were compet-ing in and dominating swimming events. Aileen Riggin, who was just 14 and weighed only 65 pounds, won the gold medal in springboard diving. At the 1924 Olympic Games in Paris, France, she won a silver medal in diving and a bronze medal in backstroke. The United States sent its first official team with women, including 15

swimmers and 2 figure skaters to the 1924 Games. Gertrude Ederle won two bronze medals and a gold medal in the freestyle relay. Two years later she would win acclaim for being the first woman to swim the English Channel, doing it in record time.

Throughout these early years of Olympic competion, women confronted barriers and faced struggles on many fronts. They not only had to convince the (male) International Olympic Committee (IOC) and the (male) United States Olympic Committee (USOC) of their ability to compete, but they also had to fight strong opposition from an area one might suppose they would have found help—women physical educators.

The Committee on Women's Athletics (CWA) and the American Physical Education Association (APEA) did not support women training for the Olympic Games. These two bodies were in conflict with the Amateur Athletic Union (AAU), the governing body for amateur sports in United States at the time. The CWA and APEA objected to the AAU picking the women's team because the CWA and APEA believed they, as women, should direct policies for women athletes. The APEA wanted to promote sport for all women and not focus on a few elite athletes. So it was the AAU who sanctioned women's competitions at the national and interna-tional level.

Because the CWA and APEA did not promote highly skilled girls and women athletes, United States female Olympians did not receive the training benefits in schools and colleges enjoyed by their male counter-parts. There was no special training or coaching for females, no special equipment or facilities, nor even sporting competition against other women at the same elite level. Prospective women athletes had to fund their own training and organize their own compe-titions. This situation lasted for nearly 30 years and seriously restricted opportunities for many women athletes. For those who did reach the highest levels, the AAU promoted national and international programs in basketball, gymnastics, track and field, and swimming. They provided some of the sponsorship that United States women athletes needed to compete in the Olympic Games, but it was almost exclusively up to the athlete to get herself to these elite levels of international competition.

The pioneering women who competed in the Olympic Games set the path for the many other competitors who would follow. At the 1928 Olympic Games in Amsterdam, Holland, 290 women competed, and the United States women made their debut in track and field with Elizabeth Robinson winning the first gold medal for the United States in the 100-meter dash. Since this time, many notable United States women athletes have proved themselves to be the best in the world on the track and have set many world records.

With the gains at these post-World War I Games came some setbacks. It was errone-ously reported that after the 880-yard race (now 800 meters) at the 1928 Olympic Games, exhausted women stumbled across the finish line (a common sight today for both men and women). The *New York Times* reporter wrote "The cinder track was strewn with wretched damsels in agonized distress." The *London Daily Mail* quoted a doctor declaring "women who took part in the 800 yards race . . . would become old too soon." As a result of social attitudes and responses to this type of reporting, no race longer than 200 yards (and later 200 meters) was to be permitted for women. This restriction lasted for 32 years, until the 1960 Games in Rome, Italy. The marathon for women was not added to the Olympic program until 1984 in Los Angeles, California, when American Joan Benoit won the gold medal.

Just as the experiences of World War I changed the roles of women, the experiences of World War II changed woman's image of herself. She had taken her place alongside men in the war effort, she had performed jobs previously done only by men, and she had gained new endurance and physical stamina. This new self-confidence aided the cause of women competitors as well. In 1948, at the first Olympic Games held after the war in London, England, Alice Coach-man, a high jumper, became the first African American to win a gold medal. In fact, she was the only United States track and field gold medalist at those Olympic Games.

More events were added to sports already in the Olympic Games during the 1950s and 1960s, but volleyball was the only new sport for women. In the 1950s, the socialist countries of the Soviet Union and Eastern Europe entered the world arena in sport. As part of Cold War politics, the USOC was concerned to show United States women athletes to be a match for their communist counterparts. To field such a competive team, the old conflict between the women's sports organizations and the USOC and AAU had to be resolved. The USOC set up a women's development committee with representatives from the AAU and the (now) Division of Girls and Women in Sport (DGWS) to support and develop elite sport for women. The USOC finally realized that female athletes had to be encouraged and developed in high schools and colleges, as well as in amateur programs, and people had to be trained to coach these athletes and to officiate at competitions. Philanthropist Doris Duke Cromwell donated half a million dollars to develop women's Olympic sports. This generous act and the political pressure of the Cold War, as much as any whole-hearted desire to see women compete, led to the establishment of systematic oppor-tunities for women to compete at an elite level.

The 1960 Olympic Games at Rome, Italy, were televised and broadcast worldwide for the first time. Americans saw their women athletes performing and winning gold medals. Wilma Rudolph of Tennessee State University (TSU) won three gold medals. She had polio as a young child and did not walk until she was seven years old, and now at 19 she was the fastest in the world. The Tennes-see Tigerbelles, as Rudolph and her track teammates from TSU were known, domi-nated track events during the 1960s. But more important than this domination, the success of the Tigerbelles proved the benefits of encouraging women athletes to perform at elite levels in schools and colleges.

The stories of women added new appeal to the Olympic Games. With an increase of interest in women's sports, women campaigned for more events in the Olympic Games. This broadening of the field was important, not just in terms of the Olympic Games, but also in terms of the number of competitive sporting events for women at all levels of competition, both at home and worldwide.

Eventually, more sports were added during the 1970s and 1980s. These sports included basketball, rowing, shooting, table tennis, cycling, and team handball. Not all events were competed at every Olympic Games, but opportunities for women athletes were definitely increasing. In 1996, soccer and fastpitch softball were added, and United States women won the first gold medal in both these events. There are now nearly 80 events for women at the Olympic Games.

As with the Cold War pressures mentioned above, politics have had their effect on women in the Olympic Games. In 1980, the USOC boycotted the Games in Moscow, capital of the then Soviet Union, to protest the Soviet invasion of Afghanistan, and at the 1984 Games in Los Angeles, California, the Soviet Union and other socialist countries did not attend. At these Los Angeles Games, American women took advantage of the chance to excel in events in which they had not previously been successful. Mary Lou Retton captivated audiences around the world by winning the first individual gold medal for the United States in gymnastics. This triumph heralded an increase in girls wishing to became gymnasts, and by 1996, the next time the Games were held in this country, the United States team won the team gold medal for the first time. With increased exposure of women athletes in all sports, the general effect has been to

The Philadelphia 1996 Atlanta Olympic Torch Run Ceremony.
Photo courtesy of Gini Alvord.

provide high-profile role models for girls and women in sports.

Despite the successes of the last few years, men and women still do not compete on equal terms in the Olympic Games. Men have more events, greater exposure, and greater rewards after winning. But the continued successes of women athletes help to widen the scope of women's athletic pursuits in all aspects of life.

Since 1988, the U.S. Olympic Committee has identified Task Forces (both on women and on racial minorities) to begin to address past inequities. Willie Whyte is chair of the Task Force on Women, 1996-2000.

The success of American women at the Olympic Games and the recognition they have gained in the last 20 years have shaped and extended the scope of athletics for women, not only in this country but also around the world. They have set new marks and displayed that women and sport in the United States is as natural a phenomenon as men and sport in the United States. Steps still need to be taken to realize equality of opportunity and equal representation both in sport and on governing bodies. But had it not been for the determination and success of our past women Olympians, and their coaches and supporters, many girls and women would not have the opportunities they have today to enjoy sports and feel good about themselves being involved in athletic competition and gaining recognition for outstanding feats. *SER*

Audrey "Mickey" Patterson

Audrey "Mickey" Patterson (-Tyler) became the first United States woman to run the 200-meter race in the Olympic Games, and the first African American woman to win an Olympic track medal. In the 1948 Olympic Games in London, England, she won a bronze medal in the 200-meter race. It was also one of two medals won in track and field by U.S. women at the London Olympic Games; the other, a gold, was won by Alice Coachman in the high jump. Patterson also competed in the 100-meter race and in the 4 x 100-meter relay in these Games.

"Mickey" was born in New Orleans, Louisiana, in 1927. As a child growing up in New Orleans, Patterson was a victim of segregation and discrimination. Determined to succeed, she took every opportunity to compete and excel in local and national competitions. She attended Wiley College in Marshall, Texas, in 1947, and in 1948 became one of the first successes on athletic scholarship at Tennessee State University. She became the national and international indoor-outdoor collegiate champion in the 100- and 220-yard dashes and in the 440-yard relay. In 1947, she was the national champion in the 220-yard dash. She graduated from Southern University in Baton Rouge, Louisiana, with a bachelor's degree in health and physical education.

As she competed, she came to understand that other athletes often needed help to realize their potential as athletes. To provide some of this help, Patterson led a program called "Mickey's Missiles" for 20 years, which was a national and international track team consisting of young people from all racial, economic, and social backgrounds. For this program and for many other young people, she taught, coached, and developed new sports programs. "Mickey's Missiles" reportedly helped more than 5,000 youths.

Mickey Patterson has been recognized by many groups and organizations for her community involvement. The year after she won her Olympic medal, she was honored as Woman Athlete of the Year by the Amateur Athletic Union (AAU). She was honored in 1988 at the Smithsonian Institution in Washington as part of a tribute to African American Olympians. Patterson was named the San Diego Woman of the Year by the Press Club. The National Association of Business and Professional Women gave her their Trailblazer Award, and the National Association for the Advancement of Colored People (NAACP) honored her with their Outstanding Achievement Award. She was also recognized for her service to the community by San Diego State University and by the Black Federation. Her contributions were to the thousands of young people she helped to achieve their potential.

Mickey Patterson-Tyler died at the age of 69, on August 23, 1996. One of her daughters, Cynthia, ran the 400-meter race with a time of 56.21 seconds to win the California State AAU Track Meet in 1976.

Physical Capacity of Girls and Women

Many people believe that females are physically inferior to males. They see that men run faster, jump higher and farther, and generally outperform women in the Olympic Games and in other sporting events. The typical explanation for this perfomance gap is biological. That is, the female of the species is less capable physically, and in this sense, "biology is destiny."

However, to say that biology is destiny is to say that biology is fixed. Yet, human biology changes every minute of every day. Every activity has the potential to modify our biology. Exercise, for example, seems to have a beneficial effect on the form and function of our bodies. Because many girls and women have not had long-term experience with exercise, it is too early to tell what is possible for females as a whole. But we can gain insight from those girls and women who have expended some effort in exercise.

We see, for example, that numerous young girls can compete with young boys and that female Olympians can beat many men. Some people interpret these results as evidence that females have good physical capacity. Others interpret this situation, again, as biology is destiny. They say that sex-related changes at puberty are responsible for the pre-adolescent comparability and for the post-adolescent inferiority of females. And they say that biological diversity accounts for the general inferiority of females as well as the special ability of some women to defeat many, but not all, men.

To resolve this conflict, performance comparisons should be probed more deeply. But this comparison can be more complicated than it seems. For instance, should we compare large people against small people? Historically the answer has been, "Not when it gives the large person an unfair advantage." This attitude is seen in weightlifting, wrestling, and boxing. These sports have been contested in weight classes from the earliest years of the modern Olympic Games. In fact, Naim Soleymanoglu, a 132-pound lifter, gained fame in 1988 because he lifted 419 pounds in the clean and jerk (a type of lift), three times his body weight. No lifter, before or since, has hoisted more than three times his or her body weight overhead. Even though Naim did not lift the greatest absolute weight, he was declared the best lifter because he had the best results pound for pound.

This strategy of comparing results relative to size can be used to compare females and males in other events, such as running, in which both compete. For example, we can make an inch-for-inch comparison of the Olympic performances of Gail Devers and Donovan Bailey, gold medalists in the 100-meter dash. The first step is to convert the race length into units of the runner's height by dividing 100 meters by standing height. Because Devers is five feet three inches tall, her race is 62.5 times her height. For Bailey, at six feet one inch, 100 meters is 54 times his height. The second step is to obtain relative velocity by dividing race length in heights by time. Dever's best time is 10.82 seconds, so she runs 5.78 times her height each second (i.e., 62.5 heights/10.82 seconds = 5.78 heights/seconds). Donovan tied the world record of 9.84 seconds at the 1996 Olympic Games; his velocity is 5.48 heights per second. Thus, Devers is about 5 percent faster than Donovan relative to size. This is not inferiority, and this is not unusual. Florence Griffith Joyner was about 5 percent faster than Carl Lewis in the 1988 Olympic Games, and Janet Evans, the swimmer, is comparably faster than her male counterparts. More than likely we would see similar results in most any case where individuals have full opportunity to develop their capabilities.

However, this advantage held by excellent women does not hold up when average women and girls are compared to average men and boys. In fact, average women do not compare very favorably to excellent women either. A champion miler can run her race in 39 percent of the time it takes the typical young woman to run a mile. For males, this ratio is 49 percent. Thus it seems that the average young woman is farther from her athletic potential than is the average young man. When might this phenomenon develop? The average six-year-old girl trails the average six-year-old boy by 3.5 percent in running velocity. Every year after until the age of 14, this gap widens by 2.7 percent. Half the difference is due to boys learning to run faster; the other half comes from girls "learning" to run slower. (Girls "learn" to run slower in an effort to run in a "feminine" but biomechanically inefficient manner.) Thus, it is true that average girls are slower than average boys at puberty, but this difference does not suddenly occur; it has been building progressively from the first grade, when boys and girls were relatively even.

In summary, the girls and women who have expended effort in exercise have definitely closed the gap in performance between females and males. It is only average girls and women (who have less experience with exercise) who lag behind average males and accomplished females. An unused biology may have a negative destiny, but girls and women who modify their biology through appropriate exercise should find impressive physical capability as their destiny. *JH*

Jacquelin Pitts

Jacquelin Pitts' lacrosse experience spans the entire spectrum of the sport: player, coach, educator, camp director, administrator, and pioneer of women's lacrosse in other countries. In this last role, she has been largely responsible for the growth of women's lacrosse in Japan and (what was then) Czechoslovakia. Traveling to both countries, she has coached players and organized coaches' workshops, taken players to play exhibition games, and provided the opportunity to play by forming new teams.

Born on August 18, 1937, in East Marlborough Township, Pennsylvania, Pitts began playing lacrosse at Sanford High School in Delaware. She graduated in 1959 from St. Lawrence University, where lacrosse was not offered. During this time, she played club lacrosse for the Philadelphia Bandits and the Philadelphia Women's Lacrosse Association.

An outstanding player, Pitts was a member of the United States Lacrosse Team in 1964, 1965, 1966, 1969, 1971, 1972, and 1973; and was a member of the United States Reserve Lacrosse Team in 1962, 1963, 1967, 1968, and 1974. She was also a member of the United States Touring Team in 1964, 1969, and 1970. Pitts' knowledge of the game went far beyond that of the average player. She was the head coach of the United States squad from 1979-1987, winning the first World Cup Championships of Lacrosse for the United States in 1982.

Pitts has also been a strong advocate of women's lacrosse and has supported this role as an administrator. She is a past president and vice president of the United States Women's Lacrosse Association.

Pitts has been widely honored for her contributions to the sport. She was inducted into the State of Delaware Sports Hall of Fame in 1983 and is an honorary member of the United States Women's Lacrosse Association (USWLA), International Federation of Women's Lacrosse Associations (IFWLA), and the Philadelphia Women's Lacrosse Association. Her most recent honor was to be inducted into the Lacrosse Foundation's Hall of Fame in 1994. Jackie Pitts continues to coach and provide leadership in the International Federation of Women's Lacrosse Associations.

Mary T. Meagher Plant. *See* **Mary T. Meagher**

Janie Eichkoff Quigley. *See* **Janie Eichkoff**

R

Betsy Rawls

Betsy Rawls was born on May 4, 1928, in Spartanburg, South Carolina. She achieved amateur fame by winning the 1949 Texas Amateur just four years after taking up golf. Rawls joined the Ladies Professional Golf Association (LPGA) in 1951 and has won 55 LPGA events in her career as a professional. She won eight major championships and led the Tour in wins three times—in 1952, 1957, and 1959. The year 1959 was a banner year for Rawls as she captured two titles, won the Vare Trophy (for lowest scoring average on the Tour), and set a new single-season earnings record that stood until 1963. Rawls was inducted into the LPGA Hall of Fame in 1960. She retired from professional play in 1975 but has continued to promote women's golf by serving as the LPGA's Tournament Director and the McDonald's Championships Executive Director.

Research *See* **R. Vivian Acosta, Ph.D., and Linda Jean Carpenter, Ph.D, J.D.**

Research Centers for Girls and Women in Sport

Two prominent examples of research centers for girls and women in sport are the Melpomene Institute for Women's Health Research and the Tucker Center for Research on Girls and Women in Sport. The Melpomene Center (named after the Greek woman who scandalized officials at the 1896 Olympic games by running the marathon after being told she could not enter) was established in 1982 and seeks to focus research that operates outside of academic or medical institutions. The Tucker Center (named for Dr. Dorothy Tucker, a leader in women's sport) was established in 1993 at the University of Minnesota to conduct and sponsor basic applied research on girls and women in sport.

The Melpomene Institute has a member-ship system and from these members they are able to access a population of research subjects who range in age from birth to 90 years and more. Their research has focused upon the role of physical activity in the lives of ordinary women over their lifespan. This focus includes studying physiological changes from exercise and psychological aspects impacted upon the individual as a result of exercise. Studies of body image and self-esteem are other examples of this type of research. They also conduct long-term research—one such project is the study of osteoporosis, started in 1982 with 111 women aged from 46 to 86 years; they still have 80 active participants in this research project today. The goal of the Melpomene Institute is to make their research findings accessible to a large audience. They do this through *Melpomene Journal,* published three times a year. They also publish books and individual articles on specific research topics. They have an award-winning video and accompanying curriculum that explores the relationship between physical activity and self-esteem. They are a resource center for articles and books concerning the health of women, and their Web site also provides access to information in this field.

The Tucker Center sponsors collaborative and interdisciplinary research in three major areas: psychosocial aspects of physical activity, which explores the psychological impact of role models and mentoring and the media's harmful stereotyping of female athletes; developmental aspects of sport, including the affects of play behavior on creative thinking and competence; and the impact of exercise, fitness and health on the lives of girls and women. The Center also trains and mentors graduate students and offers two research assistantships for doctoral students. The Tucker Center has an outreach and public service program and a lecture series. The chair of the center, Dr. Mary Jo Kane, invited Melpomene Institute founder Judy Mahle Lutter to be one of the distinguished speakers at their lecture series. The Tucker center provides a focus, organization, direction, and national leadership on women's sport and physical activity issues of local and national significance.

Both research centers welcome inquiries. The Melpomene Institute address is 1010 University Avenue, St. Paul, Minnesota 55104; e-mail: melpomene@skypoints.com. The Tucker Center can be contacted at the University of Minnesota, 203 Cooke Hall, 1900 University Avenue S. E., Minneapolis, Minnesota 55455. *JML & editors*

Mary Lou Retton

Mary Lou Retton was born in Fairmont, West Virginia, on January 24, 1968. At the 1984 Olympic Games in Los Angeles, California, she became the first United States woman to win a gold medal in gymnastics in the all-around competition. She also won silver medals for team competition and vault, and bronze medals for uneven bars and floor exercise. That same year, Retton was named *Sports Illustrated*'s Sportswoman of the Year, 1984 Associated Press Amateur Athlete of the Year, and became the youngest inductee into the United States Olympic Committee Hall of Fame. Retton also became the only woman to win three American Cups (1983–1985), the only American to win Japan's prestigious Chunichi Cup (1983), two United States Gymnastics Federation American Classics (1983–1984), and the all-around title at both the 1984 national championships and the Olympic trials before retiring from competitive gymnastics in 1986.

In 1993, Retton was named one of the most beloved American athletes in a survey conducted by Sports Marketing Group, a Dallas consulting firm. In 1994, the United States Olympic Committee (USOC) established the annual Mary Lou Retton Award for athletic excellence. Currently, Retton travels the country as a motivational speaker and is the new host of Intersports' syndicated show *American Sportswomen.*

Aileen Riggin

Aileen Riggin (Soule) is the pioneer of women's diving in the United States. Born on May 2, 1906, this spritely 14-year-old from New York City led an American sweep of medals in the first women's Olympic springboard event at Antwerp, Belgium, in 1920. This performance came in spite of practicing and competing in cold, rainy weather, and being forced to dive into a dark moat, with water temperature hovering in the mid 50s. Even though she and the other divers were nervous, and occasionally became disoriented in the murky water, she won the springboard and placed fifth in the platform event. Four years later in Paris, France, she placed second in the springboard at the 1924 Olympics. In a remarkable Olympic achievement, she also won a bronze medal in the 100-meter backstroke at these Paris Games.

In the earlier part of the twentieth century, few diving facilities were available, especially in the winter. Riggin, who danced with the Metropolitan Opera School of Ballet, gives considerable credit to dancing for her success in diving. "Dancing helped my diving as I had an advantage in body control, grace, pointed toes and fingers, not to mention the hurdle or takeoff."

Riggin's Olympic dream almost ended before it began. Riggin, and another 14 year old, Helen Wainwright, made the 1920 team at the Olympic trials in a tidal pool at Manhattan Beach, New York (for safety reasons, the divers could only dive at high tide!). Even though Aileen and Helen had made the team fairly through competition, the Olympic Committee, which had agreed to take women divers, now said they would not take "children." The two girls, saddened by this decision, had to unpack their steamer trunks, but quickly repacked them after a women's delegation persuaded the Olympic Committee to reinstate them as team members. After a two-week boat trip, they arrived in Belgium, where the two teenage girls proceeded to make Olympic history, taking first and second in the first women's Olympic springboard diving event.

In Antwerp, the 65-pound Riggin competed under the worst of conditions: foul weather, cold water, diving boards that hardly bent, and a scoring system so slow that the results were not known until hours later. Such deplorable conditions were not unusual at the time. Riggin and her contemporaries endured trying conditions, in many cases, practicing and competing in very shallow pools, lakes, rivers, or lagoons where the water depth and board height varied with the tides. Modern divers owe a huge debt to these Olympic forerunners. Now divers compete indoors or in warm weather outdoors. They dive from boards that weigh half

as much and flex up to three feet. They dive into deep, sanitized, heated pools, and if they are cold between dives, they can luxuriate in hot tubs on the pool deck.

After the 1924 Games, Riggin turned professional and toured for several years. She performed in Billy Rose's first Aquacade, a traveling water show. She now lives in Honolulu, and although she can no longer dive, she continues, at the age of 90, to swim in the ocean several times a week and is the holder of several world records in her age group. Riggin was a guest at the Barcelona and Atlanta Olympic Games, has been honored by the Women's Sports Foundation, and long ago was inducted into the International Swimming Hall of Fame in 1967.

Aileen Riggin Soule is perhaps diving's most important pioneer. With a sparkling personality and a sense of humor to match, she remains a vibrant and articulate spokesperson for the early years of Olympic diving.

Louise Ritter

Louise Ritter was born on February 18, 1958, in Dallas, Texas. As the premier women's high jumper in the United States for a decade, Ritter surprised the world by winning the gold medal at the 1988 Olympic Games in Seoul, South Korea. She defeated an outstanding field of competitors, but her own credentials were impressive as well. Starting in 1979, she raised the United States record from six feet four and a quarter inches to the present mark of six feet eight inches. She was on three United States Olympic Track and Field Teams and was a bronze medalist at the 1983 world championships.

Ritter's dominance of American high jumpers began early. She was one of the nation's best high school jumpers, clearing five feet eleven and a half inches for Red Oak (Texas) High School in 1976. She went on to win 10 national championships, indoors and outdoors, and was world-ranked nine times. Her second-place ranking in 1988 was her best ever. A graduate of Texas Women's University, she was the AIAW national collegiate high jump champion.

Robin Roberts

Robin Roberts teamed up with Mimi Griffin for the 1995 ESPN network's inaugural coverage of the Women's National Collegiate Athletic Association (NCAA) Basketball Championships. She is now a well-known commentator at many sporting events for both women and men. She currently anchors ESPN's *Sports Center* and hosts ABC's *Wide World of Sports*.

Born on November 23, 1960, in Alabama, Robin Roberts was an exceptional basketball player in college. She wanted to be a professional athlete, but she felt her skills were not sufficient to compete at the professional level. Even if she had wanted to play, there were few chances for women to play basketball professionally when she graduated. An older sister in television encouraged her to combine her passion for sports with her interest in journalism. Roberts listened to this advice, worked hard at her grades, and got a job right out of college, 30 hours a week as a weekend sports anchor.

Robin Roberts credits the Women's Sports Foundation, especially Executive Director Donna Lopiano, for providing role models and supporting her. Lopiano showed Roberts that to succeed as a sportscaster you have to be able to back up your comments with facts, numbers, and statistics in an interesting way. You cannot just tell funny stories; you have to know and understand the sport you are describing.

Roberts wants to bring credibility to women in sport; as part of that goal, she wants to be a good sportscaster in any sport. One of Roberts's mentors, Arthur Ashe, told her "If you are remembered for only being a sportscaster, if that is all anyone can say about you is your profession, then you haven't reached your full potential." Taking this advice to heart, she is an advocate for women in sport, encouraging women to develop through participation in sport, regardless of racial background. She is quoted as saying "I just shudder to think, if I had not been exposed to sports, I have no idea what I would have become . . . and it's not just winning and losing, but all the intangibles I learned."

To get involved in sportscasting, Robin Roberts tells people to believe in themselves. They must believe they are worthy of the job. There will be people to help them, but if they do not want it for themselves, it is not going to happen, no matter how supportive their families might be. Women have to work hard to be sportscasters. There are not many of them, although ABC Sports has been at the forefront in hiring women as sportscasters. Despite this limited success in the national arena, Roberts feels there are not enough women in sport journalism at the local level, both on television and at newspapers.

Besides the desire to become a sportscaster, Roberts believes a few other components are needed to be successful in this demanding field. A sportscaster must have a genuine interest in sport and has to be able to communicate that interest to others. She has to be able to communicate what is happening in front of her in a meaningful way, for both expert and novice in the sport. She has to be able to deal with pressure and to be flexible. She needs good grades, and in most cases, a college education. She has to be willing to break into a predominantly male world. The rewards for all this work are being able to tell people what is happening in sporting events, going to a variety of sporting events, and getting the chance to travel, even if it is often under great pressure. *NL*

See Also **Careers in Sport: Color Analyst**

Sue Rodin

Sue Rodin, born in Brooklyn, New York, on August 13, 1947, is president and founder of Stars and Strategies, Inc., a New York-based sports marketing and management agency. Her clients include *Conde' Nast Sports for Women* magazine, KidsPeace National Sports Council, Amster-Young Public Relations, and others. In addition to strategic sports marketing, Rodin represents talent, including Olympic gold medalists Julie Foudy, co-captain of the United States women's soccer team, and Julie Smith, star infielder for the United States softball team.

Prior to launching her new company, Ms. Rodin served as the in-house consultant for Avon Products Olympic Games sponsorship and licensing programs, both for domestic and global markets. Before that, Rodin was vice president, director of promotion at National Media Group (NMG), Inc., a New York-based sports marketing agency. During her six years at NMG, she created and managed national programs for clients and their sports affiliations, such as Schick Razors and Blades (NBA), Bubblicious (Little League Baseball), Tinactin (NFL), and many others. Earlier experience includes senior marketing positions at Comart-KLP, BBDO Promotion, and Don Jagoda Associates.

Besides her business, Rodin is active in other sports activities. She is the founder and president of Women in Sports and Events (WISE), a national organization for female executives. She chaired the American Marketing Association's (AMA) second annual Sports Marketing Conference and currently participates in the AMA's "Keynoters on Tour" program. In March 1997, she chaired the Strategic Research Institute's Women's Sports Marketing Conference in New York City. Ms. Rodin is a graduate of the Ohio State University and earned a master's degree from the University of Massachusetts, Amherst.

Diann Roffe-Steinrotter

Diann Roffe-Steinrotter was born on March 3, 1968, in Warsaw, New York. A world-recognized skier at the age of 17, Roffe-Steinrotter became the youngest skier ever to win a world Alpine ski championship in 1985 in the giant slalom. Plagued by a series of knee injuries, she had almost given up the sport, but she decided to fight through the injuries instead. After extensive rehabilitation, Roffe-Steinrotter came back to win two Olympic medals: the silver medal in the giant slalom at the 1992 Games in Albertville, France, and a gold medal in the super giant slalom at the 1994 Games in Lillehammer, Norway. By capturing the 1994

gold medal, she became the first American woman to bring the gold medal home in Alpine skiing. She now resides in Norwood, New York.

Rowing

Rowing is a racing sport in which a boat is propelled through water by the muscular force of one or more rowers with or without a coxswain (nonrowing member of the crew). Events for various competitions (often called regattas) vary. For example, the events for the Olympics in the year 2000 at Sidney, Australia, will differ from those run in the 1996 Atlanta Olympics. There are events based on type of boats, gender of competitors, age of rowers, weight of competitors, and skill level of competitors. Popular events are sculling (two oars for each rower) in singles, doubles, and quads, and sweep boats (one oar per rower) in pairs and eights.

There are two kinds of races in rowing: "head races," (in which each boat rows the course alone against the clock) which are three-miles long and usually happen in the fall, and the standard competitive races of 2,000 meters. The standard competitive format in crew involves preliminary heats and repechage rounds (additional heats that allow competitors to progress), which take place on the first four days of competition, with semifinal, final, A, B, and C rounds being held on the last days. Boats race six across, with the first boat to cross the finish line with its bow (front end) being declared the winner. Times are measured to the nearest .01 of a second. Competition takes place within six lanes on a 2,000-meter rowing course. Each lane is 13.5 meters wide.

Women were participating in competitive rowing events as early as the late 1880s. Amateur rowing boat clubs were established in a number of American cities. While most of the rowing participants at this time were men, there has been a steady tradition of women rowing throughout the history of the sport in America. Despite this tradition of participation, the first proposal for international races for women was turned down in 1924, but women continued to row. One of the first clubs organized for women's rowing on the East Coast of the United States was the Philadelphia Girls' Rowing Club (PGRC) formed in 1938. This club still flourishes on the banks of the Schuylkill River in Philadelphia, hosting a masters rowing program and a novice program in which they teach rowing to any interested adult woman. Until 1965, PGRC members raced among themselves, because they could find no other women's clubs against which to compete.

While PGRC and East Coast rowing were developing, on the West Coast, women's rowing had established a foothold much earlier. The ZLAC Rowing Club was organized in 1892 as an elite "athletic club for maiden ladies" in San Diego, California. ZLAC Rowing Club was not alone because between 1890 and 1915 22 afternoon tea crews were formed in San Diego. Despite the popularity of these clubs, open competitions were not held amongst them until the late 1960s.

One of the major milestones in the building of national-level rowing competitions was the formation of The National Women's Rowing Association in 1962 by Ed Lickiss, Ted Nash, Joanne Iverson (past president of PGRC), and several others. In 1964, they sponsored the first national championship race for women—a doubles race— in Philadelphia.

Women's rowing also began to grow out of some college programs. Mills College, Wellesley College, Smith College, and Princeton University are four of the earliest institutions to support women's rowing. These programs developed out of the "shell and oar" clubs, which were women's hospitality groups for college men's crews. They were often basically social clubs, similar to fraternities or sororities, but they served to introduce women to rowing and increased interest among women in rowing.

Across the ocean, a parallel growth in women's rowing was occurring. The first European women's championship was held in 1954 with four events: singles, doubles, fours, and eights.

The 1970s brought significant growth in the sport, specifically in response to the International Olympic Committee's (IOC) 1972 decision to admit women's rowing as an official sport in the next Olympiad. The 1976 Olympic Games in Montreal, Canada, marked the first year for women's rowing events at the Olympics. The 1996 Olympic Games featured 14 rowing events, 6 for women, including the first competition for lightweight women.

The United States Women's Rowing Team relocated to Chattanooga, Tennessee, from Boston, Massachusetts, during the winter of 1993. They plan to remain in the favorable weather of Tennessee at least through the year 2000. Hartmut Buschbacher, the present United States women's rowing coach, is considered the most successful women's rowing coaches in United States history. In the five years since he began coaching the United States women, 1991 to 1996, they have won two Olympic, and several world championship medals. Well-known U.S. women rowers include Anita DeFrantz, Anne Marden, and Ruth Davidon.

The members of the 1996 United States Olympic Women's Rowing Team averaged six feet one half inch in height and 166 pounds in weight. Their average age was 27 years, and their average number of years on the national team was 6. Rowers are often academically, as well as athletically, driven. Many rowers pursue graduate degrees as they train for the United States team.

At the 1996 Olympic Games in Atlanta, Georgia, the United States were guaranteed entries in 12 events by virtue of the team's finishes at the 1995 world championships, where the United States women's team gained national and international attention. At the 1995 world championships, the USA crews won five gold medals, one silver medal, and one bronze medal. All five gold medals were in sweep rowing events. This world championship performance showcased the team's strength, talent, and determination, and served as a qualification regatta for the 1996 Olympic Games in Atlanta, Georgia. The 1996 team entered the Games favored to win the women's sweep eight gold medal, having captured that title in the 1995 world championships, but Romania took the gold. Canada won the silver medal, Belarus won the bronze medal, and the Americans were fourth, once again proving that on any given day in international competition, any crew can win.

As a recreational sport, women's rowing continues to flourish as it has since the late 1880s. Many cities and towns have local "boathouses" that are usually run as private athletic clubs. Most local clubs teach beginners and sponsor competitive masters programs. Community-based rowing programs, such as the one in Boston, are growing as well, opening the sport to people of color and the not so affluent, two populations that historically have not been represented in rowing. A newcomer to rowing is considered in good shape for rowing if she is able to exercise comfortably for 11 to 12 minutes on a rowing machine and is able to run five kilometers comfortably. Most recreational rowers come to the sport long after their college days and are typically in their 40s or older.

For more information on how to participate in rowing, contact the national governing organization of rowing: United States Rowing Association, Pan American Plaza, Suite 400, 201 South Capitol Avenue, Indianapolis, IN 46225. This organization establishes rules for rowing in the United States, sanctions competitions, and selects rowers to represent the United States in international competitions. *FJ*

Rugby

Rugby is a fast-paced, full-contact game formally invented in 1871. Women first began playing rugby in the United States in the early 1970s. Inspired by the women's movement and tired of watching their boyfriends, husbands, brothers, and friends play, groups of women decided to play the game themselves.

The game was named for the English boys school where it was first played when William Webb Ellis, "with fine disregard for the rules of soccer as played in his time, first took the ball in his arms and ran with it, thus originating the distinctive features of the rugby game." For a half century, "Rugby's Game" was widely played by varying rules until 1871, when the Rugby Football Union was formed in Great Britain to codify and control the popular sport. Five years later, the United States adopted the codes of the Rugby Union of Great Britain which, due to British colonialism, had now spread throughout the world. The first recorded match played in the United States was Harvard University against McGill University of Montreal in 1874.

Since that first game in Boston, Massachusetts, rugby has enjoyed periods of popularity in the United States. In the 1920s and 1930s, national leaders advocated rugby rather than American football as the national sport. During this era, the United States won the only gold medal ever contested in rugby, and the game increased in popularity. More recently in the 1980s and 1990s, the game has enjoyed a renewed interest, especially among women. The 1990s have ushered in a period of tremendous growth in collegiate women's rugby. Currently over 20,000 college women play rugby as a club sport. As of 1996, there were 10 high school girls rugby teams.

Rugby is different from other sports in a number of ways; it has a distinct and fiercely upheld culture. Players organize themselves, raise their own funds, and schedule their own games. In other words, the administration of the game is an important part of playing the game. Rugby is also famous for its spirit of comraderie. After every match, a party ("drink-up") is hosted by the home team for the competition. The game is dissected, songs are sung, beverages and food are served, and any remaining animosity from the game is forgotten.

The game itself is played between two teams of 15 players with a ball that looks like an overinflated American football. It is a full contact sport. If a ball runner is tackled , she has to let go of the ball, after which other players may pick it up and run to score. The player can pass the ball backwards, like a lateral in football, or kick the ball down the field as in soccer. Games have two halves of 45 minutes of continuous play and very limited substitutions, also similar to soccer. "Tries," worth 5 points, are scored by running the ball past the goal line. Two points can be scored after the try with a kick through the goal posts from the spot where the try was scored. If a player successfully drop kicks the ball through the goal posts during play, three points are scored.

Women play with exactly the same rules as men and with equal gusto. In the United States, they play with significantly more success than the men. The United States women won the first-ever world cup in 1991 and have led the international community in the development of women's rugby. Notable women rugby players are Patty Jervey, Jen Crawford, and Chris Harju. Historically, most women rugby players learn to play after their collegiate sport careers have finished and they are looking for a new sport to play, although this trend is changing with the increase in collegiate women's rugby. Princeton University won the National Championship in 1995 and 1996, establishing a very high standard for collegiate women's play. They were upset in 1997 by the perennially strong Penn State University team. Most large cities have at least one women's rugby club. In some cases, both men's and women's clubs operate out of the same amateur rugby football club.

The national governing body of rugby is the United States of America Rugby Football Union, known as USARFU or USA Rugby. 3595 East Fountain Blvd; Colorado Springs, CO 80910; (719) 637-1022. This organization sets the rules and selects athletes for the national team. *FJ*

Wilma Rudolph

Wilma Rudolph's inspiring story is one of struggle, hope, and success. Rudolph was born on June 23, 1940, in Bethlehem,

Tennessee, the 20th of 22 children. She had a variety of early childhood health problems, including pneumonia and scarlet fever, that resulted in paralysis of her left leg. She struggled with braces and special shoes, first to walk and then to run. By high school, she successfully rehabilitated her leg and became an outstanding basketball player in her hometown of Clarksville, Tennessee. She became an all-state basketball player, scoring 803 points in 25 games.

Rudolph's fame was not to be in basketball, however. Her destiny would be in track. At the age of 15 years, she qualified for the 1956 Olympics in Melbourne, Australia, and brought home a bronze medal. She entered Tennessee Agricultural and Industrial State College, and under the tutelage of coach Ed Temple, developed into one of the fastest women in the history of track and field competition. She made her second appearance on the U.S. Olympic team at the 1960 Games in Rome, Italy. She won two gold medals in the 100- and 200-meter individual events, and with her teammates from Tennessee Agricultural and Industrial State College, she earned a third gold medal in the 400-meter relay. Each of her three gold medal performances also set new Olympic records. After the 1960 Olympics, she set world records in the 70-yard dash and the 100-meter race.

Rudolph retired to become a high school teacher, but continued to support and promote sports for women. She lobbied for equity for women in sport through Title IX, worked with the Women's Sports Foundation to provide opportunities for females in sport, and was a catalyst in establishing the Track and Field Hall of Fame. Rudolph was also known for her work as a champion for underprivileged children, and she established the Wilma Rudolph Foundation to support this cause. Wilma Rudolph died in 1996.

Tracie Ruiz

Tracie Ruiz (-Conforto) was born on February 4, 1963, in Honolulu, Hawaii. Credited with contributing much to the growth of the popularity of synchronized swimming as an

Olympic event, Ruiz has been said to be one of the greatest synchronized swimmers of all time. At the 1984 Olympic Games in Los Angeles, California, she won two gold medals in the inaugural solo and duet synchronized swimming events, and then followed up those victories with a silver medal in the solo competition in 1988. Ruiz also earned United States, world, and Pan American championships during her career and was ranked number one from 1981 to 1984.

S

Sailing and Women

A sailboat is propelled forward according to the aerodynamic and hydrodynamic laws of physics. The sails act like the wings of an airplane by creating negative pressures that pull the boat forward. In a sailboat, this pull is called the driving force. The hydrodynamic forces of a sailboat act in many directions, which together counteract the aerodynamic forces and aid in forcing the boat to move in a forward direction. These counteractive forces keep the boat from tipping over when the wind hits the sail. The notion of a see-saw helps in understanding this principle. Imagine a see-saw in its normal horizontal position with the wind sitting on one end, and the sailor and portions of the boat that create sideways drag in the water (center-board and rudder) on the other end.

Sailboats move in two directions as related to the direction of the wind: upwind and downwind. Upwind, also called wind-ward, refers to any heading by the boat in which the boat heads more into the direction from which the true wind is blowing. For example, if the wind were blowing directly from the top of this page towards the bottom, the boat would be sailing upwind if it were headed along any course that would eventually get it to the top of the page. Due to the limitations of sailing physics, sailboats are unable to sail directly into the wind (upwind) and will instead sail zigzag courses towards the direction of the wind. When a sailboat changes direction in this zigzag, upwind course enough to cross through the wind and the sail has crossed over the sailboat, this process of crossing through the wind is called tacking. Downwind refers to any heading in which the boat heads away from the true wind, or, in the example, the boat would be pointing more towards the bottom of the page.

Sailboats come in a variety of sizes and can be sailed by a single sailor, a pair of sailors, or a team of sailors. For recreational sailing, the size and strength of the sailor(s) are not important since sailboats designed for recreational sailing have many pulleys, winches, and cleats so that the motor skills necessary to control the sailboat are not dependent on superior strength. Some sailboats are designed for the physically challenged and have additional adjustments to control the vessel.

Racing sailboats are also available in a variety of sizes. Most racing sailboats are grouped together by size and design and must be built to conform to class rules. Groups of the same or similar sailboats race against each other. Sailboats have ideal weight ranges to maximize speed and control. "Optimists" are sailboats designed for children between 8 and 15 years of age. These boats were designed in Florida as an alternative to soap box derby, which required hills that were not available in Florida. The boat designers wanted a boat that could be successfully sailed by all sizes of children within this age range. To adapt to the wide variety of sizes of children, special sails can be purchased; lighter children would have a flatter sail, and heavier children would have a fuller sail. The Optimist sailboats are now sailed by 300,000 children around the world.

When adults select a racing sailboat, they select according to their size and sailing skill. Larger sailboats, such as the J-24, are raced by teams of four to five women. These women's teams require women of a variety of weights and physical sizes to successfully sail the boat. Some positions require placing the body near or over the edges of the boats and provide opportunities for larger women. A foredeck position requires a quick, small woman to quickly move forward to make last-minute sail adjustments without disturbing the balance of the speeding sailboat. The actual sailing or yacht racing competition involves completing a prescribed course in the shortest time possible using only sail power. The yachting events included in competition vary. In the Olympic games, events may be run for up to 10 different yachting classes. The competitions include seven timed races for each class and each yacht counts the best six results to determine the final score.

Women sailors should not underestimate their potential and should search for sailing opportunities. Great women sailors become great because they love sailing and thrive on overcoming the challenges of racing in many locations with constantly changing water and weather conditions. Women can launch an Olympic campaign and focus on becoming the best sailors in the world. Several Olympic sailboat classes are limited to only women sailors. The Europe class of boat is sailed by a single woman and the 470 class of boat is sailed by a pair of women; there is also a sailboard division limited to women. Other Olympic sailboat classes are open to men and women.

The governing body of sailing in the U.S. is the United States Sailing Association. This organization selects representatives for national teams, enforces and determines official rules, and sanctions competitions. More information on sailing can be obtained by contacting them at P.O. Box 1260, 15 Maritime D, Portsmouth, RI 02871-1260. *EG & MR1*

See also Competing with the Boys: A Girl's View

Joan Benoit Samuelson. See Joan Benoit

Patty Sheehan

Patty Sheehan was born in Middlebury, Vermont, on October 27, 1956. Sheehan joined the Ladies Professional Golf Association (LPGA) in 1980. Prior to her professional debut, she had a successful amateur career, winning the Nevada State Amateur from 1975 through 1978 and the California Amateur in 1978 and 1979. In 1980, Sheehan won the Association for Intercollegiate Athletics for Women (AIAW) National Golf Championship and was a member of the 1980 Curtis Cup Team, winning all four matches.

In 1983, Sheehan won her first LPGA Championship and three other tournaments as well. In 1984, Sheehan won another LPGA Championship and three additional tournaments. In 1986, she won three tournaments including the Sarasota Classic. In 1987, Sheehan was one of eight athletes named by *Sports Illustrated* as Sportsman of the Year. Sheehan was a member of the first United States Team for the Solheim Cup (a competition between the Women's Professional Golfers European Tour and U.S. members of the LPGA) in 1990, and she again played for the United States in 1992 and 1994. She won three titles in 1992 including the United States Women's Open. In 1993, Sheehan earned her 30th career victory and was inducted into the LPGA Hall of Fame. In 1994, Sheehan won the United States Open for a second time and was the 1994 Women's Sports Foundation's Flo Hyman Award recipient, given to the women who exemplifies the dignity and excellence of the late Flo Hyman. Sheehan has over 33 career victories and has scored three holes-in-one in competition.

Pam Shriver

Pam Shriver was born on July 4, 1963, in Baltimore, Maryland. One of the notable women's tennis players in the 1980s, she won 21 singles crowns and 93 doubles titles. She has also won 22 Grand Slam (Wimbledon and the Australian, French, and United States Opens) doubles champion-ships. In 1988, she won an Olympic gold medal in tennis doubles with her partner Zina Garrison. At the 1991 Pan American Games, she swept the gold medals in the singles, doubles, and mixed doubles.

Together with Martina Navratilova, she has won 79 doubles titles. They were named the Women's Tennis Association's (WTA) Tour Doubles Team of the Year for eight years in a row (1981–1988).

Shriver annually hosts fund-raising events for children's charities. She has served on the President's Council on Physical Fitness and Sports and is a member of the Maryland Fitness Commission. She has served as the president of the WTA Tour Players Association (1991–1994). She won the Billie Jean King Award in 1992 for her contributions to women's sport and tennis. In 1993, Shriver was the recipient of the WTA Tour Player Service Award.

Currently, Shriver serves as a vice president of the International Tennis Hall of Fame and is on the United States Tennis Association's (USTA) Executive Committee. She works as a women's tennis television analyst and is a contributing editor to *Tennis Magazine*.

Skiing and Women

The history of skiing started when the first humans had to move across snow. A pair of skis, said to be over 5,000 years old, are displayed in a museum in Stockholm, Sweden. Indeed, it was the Scandinavian countries that advanced and developed skiing as a means for travel, hunting, and even battle. In the 1590s, skiing was introduced to the central European countries through Austria, and since then has spread to every continent with snow. In the nineteenth century, fun-spirited competitions sprang up in Europe. In the 1850s, a Norwegian contest developed such a following that the king of Norway donated a trophy to what became the "Norwegian Ski Derby." Ski clubs developed across the rest of Europe over the next 75 years, and competitions became more common among them. At the birth of skiing, no distinctions existed between the different disciplines (Alpine, or downhill, skiing and Nordic, or cross-country, skiing). Athletes skied up the hill, down the hill (sometimes using the telemark technique), and jumped—all on the same equipment. At this time, it was not uncommon for women to ski.

Though no one knows exactly when the first skis were used in North America, Native Americans probably used modified snow-shoe-like skis to negotiate steep, snow-covered slopes. The immigration of Northern Europeans saw the growth of ski clubs, which developed skiing competitions in the United States, particularly in the northern Midwest. By 1904, these clubs organized together into the National Ski Association, which was concerned only with domestic competition until the advent of the modern Winter Olympic era.

Skating was a demonstration sport at some of the earlier Olympic Games, but it was not until 1924 that winter sports enthusiasts convinced the International Olympic Committee to hold a separate Games for winter sports. The first Winter Olympic Games were held in Chamonix, France, in 1924, with 16 countries represented, and skiing as the focus of the competition. The only skiing events, however, were cross-country (Nordic), jumping, and combined. Alpine, or downhill skiing, would not come to the Olympic Games until 1936. At the 1924 Games, the Scandinavians dominated skiing, with Norway winning all four skiing events. The Americans sent a team of six men, to the skiing events, which weren't open to women.

Though skiing grew over the next few years, with competitions at the 1928 Winter Olympic Games held in St. Moritz, Switzerland, and the 1932 Winter Olympic Games held in Lake Placid, New York, it was not until 1936 in Garmisch-Partenkirchen, Germany, that women first became involved in skiing at the Olympic Games. The first event for women was Alpine-combined (two races, one downhill and the other slalom), won by Cristel Cranz of Germany. Unfortunately, no United States women entered this first skiing competition.

Because of World War II, the Winter Olympic Games were suspended for the next 12 years. In the interim, winter sports continued to grow in popularity in the United States and abroad. In 1933, the first rope-ski lift was installed in Woodstock, Vermont, and a ski boom followed. This boom in winter sports lead to the United States sending a 30-member ski team to the 1948 Winter Games in St. Moritz, Switzerland, which included the first-ever United States Women's Olympic Ski Team, participating in the downhill, slalom, and alpine combined.

This team was historically important because the inclusion of United States women in the Winter Games not only led to the first-ever women's Olympic medal in skiing for the United States, but it also lead to the first-ever United States gold medal in skiing. This pioneering woman was Gretchen Fraser of Vancouver, Washington, who won the slalom event and placed second in the Alpine combined.

United States women returned to the top of the Olympic podium in the 1952 Winter Games in Oslo, Norway. Andrea Mead Lawrence, a tall 19-year-old housewife from Rutland, Vermont, won the giant slalom on the first day of the Olympic Games. Lawrence, known as Andy to her friends, beat 44 women from 15 countries. Overcoming a fall in the downhill, she came back to win another gold medal in the slalom event.

Penelope "Penny" Pitou, a New Hampshire native, starred on the 1956 United States Olympic Ski Team at the age of 15. Four years later, she was the favorite to win the downhill event at the 1960 Olympic Games in Squaw Valley, California. Nervousness, plus a near fall three gates from the finish line, cost her a gold medal, but she did win the silver medal in the downhill as well as in the giant slalom.

A young skier, who probably watched Penny compete, was Cindy Nelson. Nelson began skiing at the age of two in her home state of Minnesota. At the age of 15, she qualified for her first world cup team. Nelson went on to qualify for four Olympic Games during her 13-year career with the United States Ski Team and helped to mold the team with her leadership, consistency, and commitment. She won a bronze medal in the downhill at the 1976 Olympic Games in Innsbruck, Austria. Besides her Olympic success, she finished at the top of dozens of major international and national events, setting a high standard for future women skiers.

Among other great women skiers are 1994 gold and 1992 silver medalist Diane Roffe-Steinrotter, 1984 gold medalist Debbie Armstrong, and 1994 silver medalist and 1998 gold medalist Picabo Street. These results show a strong group of United States women skiers in Alpine skiing events and hint of many more to come. Street, in particular, with her memorable name, fun-loving and rowdy attitude, and penchant for exposure, has helped to stir the imaginations of thousands of young female skiers.

U.S. women have not fared as well in Nordic events as they have in Alpine events. Olympic Nordic events for women are races of 5, 10, 15, and 30 kilometers. U.S. women have not won any Olympic medals in these events.

The United States Ski Association, at P.O. Box 100, 1500 Keans Blvd., Park City, UT 84060, is the governing body of skiing in the United States. This organization is responsible for selecting the national team, sanctioning competitions, and regulating the rules of competition. *PS*

Skiing: Freestyle

Freestyle skiing is one sport that admirably fits the name given to it. Its 60-plus year history is marked by nonconformity, artistic expression, and rich individuality. It is second to none in pushing the abilities of the human body beyond what has been thought possible.

Even as Alpine (downhill) ski equipment was being developed, freestyle pioneers were experimenting with what could be done with this new sport. By 1930, six years before Alpine skiing would even make it into the Olympic Games, Fritz Reuel, a European, was developing pole flips and twists. He worked with gymnasts and figure skaters to develop the sport that would become the ballet discipline of freestyle skiing.

While today's athletes do many of the same ballet tricks, they do them with skis that average 150 centimeters (cm). Reuel invented these moves using the 210 cm skis that were standard at the time. Twenty years later, Stein Ericksen, the former Olympic gold medalist in downhill skiing, was pioneering another discipline of freestyle, known as aerials. A rebel who became one of the first people known to flip on skis, Ericksen performed tricks at ski shows during the 1950s in Sun Valley, Idaho. Others followed his lead and gradually increased the difficulty of the aerial maneuvers off jumps that could be accomplished on skis.

Additionally, other Alpine skiers were discovering a new technique for skiing through the moguls (bumps of snow) that form at ski areas. This technique came to be known for the terrain it covered, mogul skiing. Over the next 15 to 20 years, these three groups of creative skiers would watch, learn, and compete against each other in loose and unorganized formats.

In 1966, one of the first organized competitions, "The Masters Four," was held at the ski areas in Vermont to show off the different tricks and routines that were being developed. It was not until 1971 that the three disciples we recognize today were organized into one competition. This event,

the National Championships of Exhibition Skiing, had one difference from today's events: all of the events were combined into one run! Starting at the top of a ski run, competitors would navigate mogul fields, perform ballet maneuvers, and perform acrobatic ski jumps by the time they arrived at the bottom of the run.

Meanwhile, in the west, skiers were developing the three-separate-event format that would become the standard. The western event, Rocky Mountain Professional Freestyle Championships, also coined the eventual name for the new sport. The sport became more popular throughout the United States, as the public was attracted to the social, free-spirited mood of the sport and the daredevils who performed increasingly difficult tricks.

In the 1970s freestyle skiing really took off as an organized sport. Music was introduced to ballet by Suzy Chaffee in 1973. The United States Ski Association published a rule book for the sport, as both the professional and the amateur side of the sport grew. Freestyle truly arrived when Colgate and Midas sponsored $100,000-plus tours in 1975, and when a world cup tour was established in 1976. Unfortunately, the 1970s also saw concerns over the liability of the events, particularly aerials, and the tours were forced to move to Canada and Europe for a few years. An aerial event was held in the Pocono Mountains in 1980, and the Federation of International Skiing (FIS) approved freestyle as an official skiing sport in the 1980–1981 season. During this time, another woman skier made a dominant impact on the sport: Marion Post. Post won four out of the eight professional contests in 1978, and created the signature "Post Toastie" move still used by ballet skiers today.

Chaffee, widely known for her work with Chapstick, was also a hard worker in grassroots sports. She was one of the first women to sit on the United States Olympic Committee Board of Directors and helped form the Athletes Advisory Council of the United States Olympic Committee. Working with several other prominent women athletes, Chaffee lobbied to pass Title IX legislation and the Amateur Sports Act, which quaranteed equal funding for women's sports.

FIS approval paved the way for the formation of the United States Freestyle Ski Team, and the beginning of a strong world cup tour in North America and Europe. The United States has joined in freestyle's re-emergence with countries as far-flung as Sweden, republics of the former Soviet Union, and Australia. Freestyle has become so popular that it was a demonstration sport at the 1988 Games in Calgary, Canada, and has since received Olympic full-medal status for both aerials and moguls. Many other women have followed in the footsteps of pioneers like Chaffee and Post. Athletes such as Mary Jo Tiampo and Melanie Palenik won numerous world cup events and world championships. Palenik won the gold medal when freestyle skiing was a demonstration sport in the 1988 Games.

In ArcoSki (formerly known as ballet), Americans Ellen Breen and Jan Bucher have set the pace for the rest of the world to follow. Between the two of them, they hold over 85 world cup victories and 10 world championship titles.

This success by United States women freestylers was continued by the "Golden Girl," Donna Weinbrecht. This 1992 Olympic gold medalist (the first awarded for moguls), holds over 45 world cup victories and 5 world champion titles. Other young Americans are hot on her heels. Current United States team athletes include Olympic silver medalist Liz McIntyre for moguls, and two world champions, Nikki Stone in aerials and Kriste Porter in combined. Who knows what success the future holds for women in this sport?

Today's freestyle skiers also continue the tradition of contribution off, as well as on, the slopes. Tamara St. Germain's freestyle career was cut short by a serious skiing injury. Despite this disappointment, St. Germain founded the Winter Sports Foundation, a national nonprofit organization of athletes and coaches. With her leadership, the organization is a rapidly growing national presence. She works tirelessly supporting athletes as a member of many other boards such as the Advisory Board of the Women's Sports Foundation.

For more information, contact the governing body of skiing—the United States Ski Association, P.O. Box 100, 1500 Keans Blvd., Park City, UT 84060. *PS*

Skill in Movement

Many adult women of today feel that their opportunity to be an athlete was foreclosed long ago. Biomechanics experts assert that this assumption is not necessarily true. No matter your age or activity, you can probably learn to move more skillfully. And if you do not have access to a top-level coach? Coach yourself!

If you are a musician, you know that there are several aspects of music, such as volume, pitch, and pace, that you can adjust to improve the quality of your music. And while it might be advantageous to have your performance evaluated by a music educator, you do not have to depend on a professional before you can sing more softly or play more slowly.

Likewise, several aspects of movement can be adjusted to improve the quality of your movement. Regardless of the activities you participate in, there are about 10 things that you can change as you move. Here is a quick look at the core concepts:

1. *Range of motion* is the amount of space that you use as you move. This can apply to the whole body, as in jumping up two feet, or it can apply to a part of the body, as in taking a big backswing. Also, it can apply to an object, as in tossing a horseshoe 30 feet.

2. *Speed of motion* is how fast you move. The fastest motions use brief amounts of time to cover large ranges of motion. Again, this concept can apply to the whole body, a part of the body, or an object. For example, swimming speed can vary from a warm-up pace to a sprint, a karate chop can be fast

enough to break wood, and a racquetball can go 100 miles per hour.

3. *Number of segments* refers to how many parts of your body are active. A skilled thrower will use most segments of her body when she wishes to throw hard; a beginning thrower might not use her legs or trunk at all.

4. *Nature of segments* refers to the plane of movement. A badminton player can change planes by switching from overhead to sidearm to underhand. Another way to change planes is to incorporate more twisting motions or long-axis rotations as batters do with their trunks and forearms.

5. *Balance* means the regulation of stability and mobility. You can increase stability by centering your weight over your feet (or whatever is your base of support). You can add mobility by shifting your weight over your base of support as golfers do when they swing. If you want to be very mobile, you will need to move your weight outside your base of support, as runners do when pushing off at the start.

6. *Coordination* has many meanings in movement. Interception coordination refers to making contact with an object as in bumping a volleyball. This depends on perceptual awareness and intersegmental coordination. If the sequence of your motions is from large body segments to small and the timing of your motions is smooth rather then jerky, you are likely to have good intersegmental coordination.

7. *Extension at release or contact (strike)* is the use of leverage as you let go or strike an object. In general, you want your body stretched out at the instant you release a basketball shot or hit a serve.

8. *Compactness* refers to compressing all or part of the body into a smaller space. Divers and gymnasts make their bodies small when they want to do multiple rotational movements (flips and twists). The forward swing of a kick begins with a compact leg.

9. *Path of projection* is the arc traced by a projectile. High jumpers want high arcs for their bodies while long jumpers want flatter arcs. A volleyball spiker wants a sharp downward path of projection for the ball.

10. *Spin* refers to the revolutions taken by a person or object. A figure skater may spin around her long axis. Tennis players may hit ground strokes with topspin and serves with sidespin.

The first six concepts apply to almost every activity. If your body or a ball becomes a projectile, the last four concepts are likely to apply as well. You can think of these concepts as "knobs" (like volume control) that you can turn up or down. Some knobs are easier to turn than others: range of motion, speed of motion, and number of segments are among the easiest to adjust and improve; twisting motions, compactness, and intersegmental coordination are among the hardest. Sometimes turning one knob results in turning another knob, too. For example, increasing range of motion often leads to increasing speed of motion. On occasion, a slight turn of the knob is better than a large turn and reducing a concept may be better than increasing it. (For example, you could be using too large a range of motion in throwing.) To find out what works best for you, just pick a knob, try turning it up and down by varying amounts, and see what happens. And before long you can discover some secrets to moving skillfully. *JH*

Skydiving

Skydiving is the sport of jumping out of a perfectly good aircraft on purpose! It is exhilarating to feel the wind rush past one's entire body. Every part of the body can help direct the skydiver's motion through the air. The sport requires one to be in good physical shape to be able to wear the 35 pounds of equipment, endure 30 degree swings in temperature, have strength to maneuver the canopy, and cope with the atmospheric pressure changes from a 10,000- to 12,000- foot jump.

High-flying gymnastics.
Photo courtesy of Jan Meyer.

Women have been a part of skydiving since its inception, even though they only make up 15 percent of the jumping community. In 1908, Tiny Broadwick performed in aerial barnstorming shows when she was 15 years of age. Later, she was the first woman to jump from an airplane. Broadwick accumulated over 1,000 jumps and helped design the modern parachute pack. Women made it onto the prestigious United States Army Golden Parachute Team in 1977, when Cheryl Stearns joined the team. Dale Stuart is a pioneer in the modern discipline of freestyle, a combination of skydiving and gymnastics. Women have participated on the United States National Para-Ski, a mix of skiing and skydiving; Canopy Formation; and Style and Accuracy Teams. However, no woman has ever been on the United States National Relative Work Team.

There are various local, national, and international competitions. The competitive events include canopy formation skydiving, sometimes called canopy relative work, which involves maneuvering close to or hooking up two or more open parachute canopies during descent to create various formations; style, which is a type of freefall competition from 7000 feet where the divers execute predetermined maneuvers in the shortest possible time; and accuracy, also known as precision landing, which involves the diver trying to land on an established target. (In advanced competitions, like the Nationals, the target can be as small as 5 cm in diameter.)

Most skydivers participate in relative work, where many people join together in the air to build intricate formations. The term sequential is used when more than one formation is built. The largest all-women formation, with 100 people, was built over France in 1992.

Anyone over the age of 18 can jump. Many women start jumping in their 30s and 40s. Some women have even done their very first jump on their 50th or 60th birthday. All it takes is the courage to be in control of your own destiny. Training is required to learn how the equipment operates and how to handle emergency situations. Contact the United States Parachute Association (USPA) at 1440 Duke Street, Alexandria, VA 22314 or 703-836-3495 or uspa@uspa.org for a drop zone near you. The USPA represents skydiving before all levels of government and is an affiliate of the National Aeronautic Association. It promotes safety in skydiving, issues licenses, certifies instructors, selects the national teams, and sanctions competitions. Connections to many Internet skydiving sites may be found at http://www.afn.org/skydive/org/. *JM*

Freestyle.
Photo courtesy of Jan Meyer.

Soccer

Soccer is the most popular sport in the world as measured by the number of people of all ages who play, watch, and coach the game. While more men participate in soccer, women's participation has grown tremendously in the last 20 years. Today over 20 million girls and women play soccer in more than 100 countries.

The game is played by two teams of 11 players each. The object of the game is to put the ball into the opponent's goal without using the hands or arms. The goalkeeper is the only player permitted to play the ball with her hands. Other players use any other part of their bodies—feet, head, chest, torso—to stop, control, or advance the ball toward the opponent's goal to score. A score results in the awarding of one point, and the team with the most points at the end of 90 minutes of play (two 45 minute halves) wins the game.

It is difficult to determine the exact origins of soccer. Some believe it dates back over 2,000 years when a game called *tsu chu* or "kicking ball" was played in China. In addition, some form of soccer can be traced back to the Japanese, Greeks, Romans, and Egyptians. The first indication of women playing soccer was in sixteenth-century England. Women also played in Scotland in the 1700s as part of local festivals where the married women played against the single women. These episodes of women playing soccer, however, were quite rare.

During World War I, women factory workers in England formed company soccer teams. The most well known of these teams, the "Dick Kerr's Ladies" from Preston, staged competitions to raise money for charity. After the war, Dick Kerr's Ladies traveled to the United States in the 1920s and played a series of games against men's teams. They ended the series of games with three wins, two losses, and two ties and outscored the men's teams 35-34. Upon returning to England, the team played many more games. The games were well attended, and one game drew over 50,000 spectators. Shortly thereafter the all-male English Soccer Association banned women from using their club soccer facilities throughout the country. Without facilities, women did not participate in nearly the numbers they had previously. The English ban remained in effect for nearly 50 years. Many other countries, including France, followed England's lead in banning women from using the soccer facilities.

On the United States front, the first intercollegiate men's soccer game was played on November 6, 1869, between Princeton University and Rutgers University. Women did not participate in collegiate soccer until the early 1900s, when it was included in physical education programs. The pervasive attitude was that vigorous exercise and competition would be harmful to the female reproductive system, and thus women's soccer experiences were relegated to physical education classes and intramural activities. Once these attitudes began to change, it was a natural step for the physical education,

Only the goalie may touch the ball with her hands.
Photo courtesy of the *Camden Courier Post.*

intramural, and club activities of women's soccer at colleges to evolve into organized intercollegiate competition. But it was not until the 1960s that women were playing soccer in a more organized, competitive arena.

A group of schools in Vermont and Canada played a series of games in the 1960s, which are the first instances of women being involved in more competitive soccer games. Johnson State College, Castleton State College, and Lyndon State College were among the earliest institutions to provide women's intercollegiate competition. In addition, Brown University elevated its soccer team to varsity status in 1979, paving the way for a heightened level of play in colleges. The sport grew because more colleges and universities recognized soccer as a viable competitive activity and elevated their women's teams to varsity. With varsity status came resources for travel, recruiting, and overall respectability in the athletic community.

The University of North Carolina at Chapel Hill supported its team early in the development of women's soccer. The team achieved varsity status in 1979 and has dominated collegiate soccer for the last 15 years. Under Coach Anson Dorrance, the team has won 14 national titles and accumulated an overall record of 390-16-10. Numerous players have gone on from UNC to play on the United States National Teams that have competed in world championships and the Olympic Games.

Currently, there are over 700 intercollegiate women's soccer teams, and soccer is considered to be one of the fastest growing sports on the collegiate level. The enforcement of Title IX, guaranteeing equal funding for female athletes, has had a significant impact on colleges and universities expanding opportunities for women in soccer.

On the international front, two important events have occurred. First, two world championships have taken place (1991, China; 1995, Sweden). The United States

won the inaugural tournament in China, defeating Norway 2-1. Michelle Akers, considered to be one of the world's best players, won the Golden Boot Award as the tournament's top scorer. Carin Jennings-Gabara was recognized as the tournament's most outstanding player with the Golden Ball Award. April Heinrichs, captain of the United States team in 1991, is considered by many as the best all-around player that has played the game. The second world championship was held in Sweden in 1995. Norway won in a 2-0 final over Germany. The United States placed third.

Second, on the strength of its growing popularity, a strong United States team, and its recognized high-level of international competition, women's soccer was admitted as a medal sport for the first time in the 1996 Olympic Games in Atlanta, Georgia. The United States team beat China in the

Soccer is one of the fastest growing sports for women.
Photo courtesy of the *Camden Courier Post.*

final. Mia Hamm, a graduate of the University of North Carolina at Chapel Hill, has emerged as the recent star of the team. These events are evidence of the tremendous growth that has taken place in women's soccer, and the future looks to the establishment of a professional women's soccer league in the United States.

To get involved in the game as a coach or referee, you can contact the National Soccer Coaches Association of America (1-800-458-0678). To play soccer, contact your local United States Youth Soccer Association (1-800-4soccer). More information about women's soccer can be attained from the Women's Sports Foundation (1-800-227-3988), which provides a listing of scholarship opportunities on the collegiate level, and the National Association of Girls and Women in Sport (NAGWS) (1-800-213-7193), which can provide a variety of information for the female athlete, coach, and parent.

The governing organization for soccer in the U.S. is the United States Soccer Federation. This group is responsible for regulating and promoting soccer, and it selects the national team for Olympic and International competitions. The address for the U.S. Soccer Federation is United States Olympic Complex, 1750 East Boulder Street, Colorado Springs, CO 80909. *SL*

Socialization Influences: Girls and Women in Sport

Socialization is the social learning process that teaches us about the fabric, content, and meanings of our society and culture. Socialization orients us into particular patterns of thinking and influences our perceptions and views of activities such as sport. This process also explains how we become ingrained with deep-seated ideas and beliefs, some of which are myths. One set of beliefs, deeply ingrained in society, has promulgated ideas about female inferiority and gender equality. The most intriguing aspect of such belief systems is that they operate at an unconscious level. Often we are not aware of their presence, nor of the way that they relate to socialization.

Although socialization begins in early childhood, it influences us continuously throughout life. Essentially, everything we learn is accomplished through the process of socialization, which is one means through which we acquire the knowledge, skills, interests, dispositions, and beliefs to become culturally competent. The socialization process starts in the family and encompasses subtle daily interactions that influence what we learn about gender and the assumed link between gender and capability.

For example, all children, regardless of sex, have the capacity to crawl, run, jump, throw, catch, or slide. Yet, when it comes to critical factors that predispose children toward sport and physical activity, parents continue to be influenced by existing beliefs about motor skill, biology, and gender. These beliefs are responsible for the myth that assumes an automatic biological link exists between gender and play, games, and sport. Biology and heredity alone do not account for performance or motor skill acquisition, however. Regardless of innate motor talent, unless children are exposed to social settings that contain positive influences that reward physical activity or sport skills, they are not likely to learn physical skills. Nor are they likely to become involved in physical activity or sport or to adopt a physically active lifestyle. It is at an early crossroads that we see the first effects of this socialization process.

Who is more likely to become involved in sport and why? The answer to this question begins with parental beliefs about sons and daughters, beliefs that start a chain of events which often denies early movement and sport experiences to daughters. These beliefs influence parents to treat sons and daughters differently from birth (actually before birth if we consider how infants' rooms are furnished, decorated, and filled with toys). Despite a more enlightened consciousness and awareness of the need for equal opportunity, socialization still perpetuates many myths about sex differences and biology. For example, many parents continue to view infant females (daughters) as smaller, softer, weaker, frailer, "cuter," and more delicate than infant males, even when there are no apparent differences in physical size or dimensions. Infant males (sons) are viewed as stronger, more coordinated, and more

Sports can play a major role in socialization.
Photo courtesy of Gini Alvord.

childhood socialization, the realm of toys. Toys represent a potent mechanism for socialization, often teaching infants and toddlers about styles of play appropriate for each gender. For example, girls are given toys that encourage sedentary, quiet, and passive behavior directed toward home and caretaking; girls toys promote expressive activity. In contrast, boys are given toys that are

alert. Such descriptions are stereotypic and cannot be supported by evidence. In reality, infant females are healthier and less likely to suffer disease or infant mortality than infant males. These beliefs not only reveal assumptions about the biological inferiority of females, but such assumptions also influence child-rearing practices. One of the earliest observations that supports the existence of such socialization can be found in the way parents treat sons and daughters differently, particularly in the domain of motor skills and play. Differential treatment can be found in the way parents hold, bounce, play with, and encourage motor skills development in girls and boys.

Studies of early child-rearing practices demonstrate that parents tend to roughhouse and play more vigorously with sons than daughters and are more interested in inculcating motor skills in boys than girls. Additionally, both parents are more likely to play in physically active games with boys and have expectations for sons to be interested in learning motor skills.

Differential treatment by parents can be observed in another important domain of

more complex and promote more instrumental styles of play; boys' toys require movement and wider ranges of space (e.g., trucks, trains, steam shovels). Additional information about toys reveals that a) parents spend more time in choosing boys' toys; b) boys' toys are more expensive; and c) boys' toys are more complex and have more movable parts. Thus, beginning at a very early age, boys and girls are exposed to very different toy and play experiences. As a result of such learning experiences, accompanied by parental encouragement and reward, boys are predisposed toward rough and tumble play, large muscle activity, and a readiness to learn motor skills. Outcomes of this early socialization can be found in activities of middle and later childhood in which boys engage in vigorous outdoor activities, develop a large repertoire and wide range of motor skills, and play in competitive team games. Not only do girls not share similar socialization experiences, but the outcomes of their early socialization are quite different, particularly with respect to sport and physical activity.

Nevertheless, females do become world-class athletes and demonstrate superior skills and performance levels. For example, approximately 35 percent of high school athletes and 34 percent of college athletes are women. If these female athletes are not biologically different from their nonathletic counterparts, and there is no evidence to suggest otherwise, can these differences in skill and activity levels be explained by differences in socialization experiences, particularly during early childhood?

Why do some girls become active and involved in sports while other do not? Girls who become involved in sport or physical activity tend to be raised in a positive and supportive social milieu, one that encourages sport participation. Parents play a major role in this process by actively participating in sport themselves and by playing physically active games with their daughters. Unlike her nonathletic counterpart, the physically active female seems to have received positive reinforcement and reward for sport participation. Often becoming interested in sport at an early age (usually before the age of eight), this strong orientation toward physical activity seems to be generated within the family as part of regular family activities.

Although female nonathletes, as well as athletes, believe that their childhood was "typical," it seems that nonathletes are raised in a more traditional, gender-stereotyped environment. In contrast, active females view sport as a fundamental aspect of their lifestyle, because physical activity has been accepted and encouraged since early childhood. While the family represents a strong influence on female sport socialization, so does the peer group, particularly in early childhood. If support, reinforcement, and reward continue through elementary, high school, and college, a lifelong commitment to physical activity and an active lifestyle is established. Although this lifestyle presents quite a different pattern from that observed in inactive and nonathletic females, the difference can be attributed to very different early socialization experiences.

What does the future hold for women in sport and physical activity? While we still do not have a complete understanding of the way this dynamic and complex process of socialization works, we do know that the more the sport experience meets the expectations or satisfies reasons for participation, the more likely that females will continue to participate. The longer they participate, the better they feel about themselves. Females who participate in sport feel greater confidence in themselves, perceive themselves to be more competent, and have higher levels of self-esteem and pride. These groups have a more positive body image and experience higher states of psychological well-being than those who do not participate in sports. *SLG*

See also **Gender Stereotypical Play: Consider the Consequences; Teacher Influences on Girls' Play**

Softball and Women

When more women entered the workforce during World War II, employers began to emphasize health and fitness as necessary to the health and morale of their women workers. Women's softball, bowling, volleyball, and basketball teams and leagues emerged as a result. Of these sports, softball was one of the most popular.

The origins of softball are unclear, but it is thought to have evolved from "indoor baseball," a popular game played in the Midwest (especially Chicago and Minneapolis) during the 1880s and 1890s. The game is played by both men and women, and there are two distinct types of softball games—fastpitch (in which underhand pitching is fast and on a straight line) and slowpitch (in which the underhand pitch must have a specific arc). Other differences between fastpitch (FP) and slowpitch (SP include the distance between bases (60 feet for FP and 65 feet in SP), pitching distance (40 feet in FP and 46 feet in SP), and distance to the outfield fence (200 feet in FP and 250 in SP). The FP team is composed of nine players while the SP team fields 10 players. A game consists of seven innings, and the winning team is the one that has scored the most runs during the game.

Softball can be played in both slowpitch and fastpitch forms.
Photo courtesy of the *Camden Courier Post.*

The Amateur Softball Association (ASA), founded in 1933, is the governing body of women's softball in the United States. ASA's Major Fast Pitch Championship has been in existence since 1933 and the ASA's Major Slow Pitch Championship since 1959. The International Softball Federation (ISF) sponsors the Women's World Softball Championship and over 100 countries have national softball teams. Softball is a consistent event at the Pan American Games.

One of the "legends" of softball is Joan Joyce, whose mastery of the fastpitch changed the game forever. Her slingshot pitching style and pitching speed of 115 miles per hour made Joyce an inimitable foe. In 1975, Billie Jean King and Joyce established the International Women's Professional Softball Association (IWPSA), which lasted for four years. Besides Joyce, a number of women have made their mark in softball. Most recently, pitcher Lisa Fernandez

continues the legacy of outstanding United States softball pitchers, leading the USA Olympic team to victory in 1996.

In fact, one of the most significant events for women's softball was its inclusion as a medal sport in the 1996 Olympic Games in Atlanta, Georgia. The United States won Olympic softball's first gold medal by defeating China 3-1. This gold medal performance increased the visibility and popularity of women's softball. The International Softball Federation is encouraged by softball's inclusion as an Olympic sport, and projects a worldwide growth in softball.

From 1980 to 1990, the number of women's softball leagues in the United Stated doubled, with over 35,000 leagues nationwide. Still, the absence of sponsorship curtails the number of opportunities and leagues for women, especially on the professional level.

For more information on women's softball, contact the Amateur Softball Association, 2801 N. E. 50th Street, Oklahoma City, OK 73111.

Aileen Riggin Soule. *See* **Aileen Riggin**

Special Olympics and Women

Special Olympics is an international, year-round program of sports training and competition for individuals with mental retardation. With more than one million athletes, over a half million coaches and volunteers, and thousands of friends, supporters, and family members from around the globe, Special Olympics is one of the world's largest amateur sport organizations. By the start of the next century, thousands more from all over the world will have been touched by the Special Olympics movement.

Special Olympics was founded in 1968 by Eunice Kennedy Shriver, who felt that people with mental retardation were far more capable in athletics than most experts believed at the time. Since the first international Special Olympics that year at Chicago's Soldier Field, Special Olympics has blossomed into a worldwide movement involving 22 summer and winter sports, with accredited programs in every state and nearly 150 countries.

Special Olympics program includes the summer sports of aquatics, athletics (track and field), basketball, bowling, cycling, equestrian sports, football (soccer), golf, gymnastics, roller skating, sailing, softball, tennis, and volleyball; the winter sports of Alpine skiing, cross-country skiing, figure skating, sailing, floor hockey, and speed skating; and the demonstration sports of badminton, power lifting, table tennis, bocce, and team handball. Each of the 24 Special Olympics sports is available for female competitors. The minimum age for Special Olympics competition is eight, and there is no upper limit. Many athletes have been known to compete well into their 60s and 70s.

Special Olympics athletes compete at local, area, state, and international levels. Special Olympics World Games take place biennially (every two years), alternating between Summer and Winter Games. The 1997 Special Olympics World Winter Games were recently held in Toronto and Collingwood, Ontario, while the 1999 Special Olympics World Summer Games will be held in the triangle region of North Carolina (Raleigh, Durham, and Chapel Hill). Special Olympics has been responsible for a number of groundbreaking competitions throughout the world, including the 1996 Israel Special Olympics National Games, at which Jordanian athletes competed side-by-side with their Israeli counterparts; and the first-ever Special Olympics Asia-Pacific Games in Shanghai, China, the kick-off event to a major initiative throughout the Asian continent.

Special Olympics is unique in that it places competitors in divisions according to age, sex, and ability level, giving all athletes an equal opportunity to win. Consequently, Special Olympics competitions, featuring well-matched, similarly talented athletes and teams, often result in close, exciting con-

tests. Special Olympics events are renowned for their enthusiastic spectators, exuberant competitors, and emotionally moving moments.

Women and girls have been a substantial part of the Special Olympic movement from the beginning. Its driving force remains Mrs. Shriver, who has overseen a number of program changes, improvements, and new initiatives. Examples of these include Motor Activities Training Program, a revolutionary Special Olympic program that offers non-competitive training for individuals with severe mental retardation, and Mega-Cities, which focuses on increasing opportunities in sports and training for those individuals in large, urban regions of the world.

Another initiative currently taking form within the Special Olympics movement is an effort to increase the number of women participating in team sports. Like many women in society, women involved in Special Olympics have historically been discouraged (or not encouraged) from playing team sports. To help reverse this trend, Special Olympics International has developed a women's team sports development grant program to foster growth in this area. An increase in women's team sports involve-ment is expected both at the local level and at the World Games, where women's basket-ball, soccer, and volleyball will be showcased at future events.

Women have made an impact on the Special Olympics movement in areas such as coaching, volunteerism, and, of course, competition. Loretta Claiborne, a 42-year-old woman from York, Pennsylvania, is one of the most celebrated Special Olympics athletes in history, having gained national recognition for her impressive feats in long distance running, as well as her accomplish-ments away from the playing field. Among other highlights, Claiborne was featured on ESPN's ESPY Awards program after winning the show's prestigious Arthur Ashe Award for courage. Claiborne, a member of the Special Olympics International Board of Directors, is an advocate for the rights of individuals with mental retardation and regularly speaks to businesses and corporate leaders about her life as a Special Olympics athlete.

Women and girls who would like to get involved in the Special Olympics movement can do so in a number of ways. Schools and educational settings remain one of the most common venues for recruiting both athletes and volunteers. Girl Scouts, 4-H Clubs, and other civic groups have been involved in Special Olympics as an ongoing volunteer project, providing help with competition registration, concessions, fund-raising, officiating, coaching, and other event assistance. Professional women can help Special Olympics by donating office supplies, by providing medical or accounting services, by establishing employment programs in their workplaces involving Special Olympics athletes, or by contributing other specific skills.

Special Olympics International (SOI) located in Washington, DC, serves as the organization's global headquarters. SOI maintains a home page on the World Wide Web at http://www.specialolympics.org (June 18, 1997). Individuals wishing to become involved in Special Olympics are encouraged to contact their local Special Olympics program, listed in the phone book. *MJ*

Speedskating

Speedskating has its origins in northern Europe, where it evolved from a mode of transportation on frozen lakes and canals to a leisure activity and then to a sport. It has since grown into two different sports: long track and short track speedskating. Long track speedskating is the classic form of the sport, with a rich history. It is similar to traditional track, as it includes short sprint distances, intermediate distances, and long endurance events. All of these events are held on a 400-meter track, upon which two competitors skate at a time. The events are all individual, with distances ranging from 500 meters to 5,000 meters. Women's events are 500-meter, 1,000-meter, 1,500-meter, 3,000-meter, and 5,000-meter races. Short track speedskating takes place in standard ice

rinks that are the same size as hockey rinks, 110 to 120 meters long. Short track speedskating with its pack start (all racers starting together) originated in the U.S.

Long track speedskating is a charter event of the Winter Olympic Games, appearing at the inaugural 1924 Olympic Winter Games at Chamonix, France. Traditionally, the Europeans have been very strong in long track speedskating. The United States speedskaters, however, have won medals from the very beginning, with a gold medal in the 500-meter race at the 1924 Games.

Women first had the opportunity to participate in speedskating at the 1932 Games in Lake Placid, New York, where it was a demonstration sport for women in distances ranging from 500 to 1,500 meters. It was at this competition that the United States women provided a glimpse of their future potential, winning six of the nine available medals, including two of the three gold medals. Elizabeth DuBois of Evanston, Illinois, earned a third place in the 500-meter race and a first place in the 1,000-meter race. Kit Klein, of Buffalo, New York, double medaled with a bronze in the 500-meter and a gold in the 1,500 meters. Other pioneer stars include Helen Bina of Chicago and Dorothy Franey of St. Paul, Minnesota, who went on to become leaders of the Olympic movement.

Despite this early inclusion as a demonstration sport, it was not until the Olympic Games returned to the United States in 1960 at Squaw Valley, California, that women's speedskating earned full-medal Olympic status. Women competed in the 500-, 1,000, 1,500-, and 3,000-meter races. All of these inaugural events were won by Russia, except the 500-meter event, which was won by Helga Haase of Germany. The first official United States Olympic medal in women's speedskating was won by Jeanne Ashworth, who captured a bronze medal in the 500-meter race. At this very moment, however, two young United States women, Dianne Holum and Anne Henning, were training 1,500 miles away and were preparing for their own impact on women's speedskating.

Speedskating

In the 1964 Olympic Games in Innsbruck, Austria, the Russian speedskater Lydia Skoblikova advanced the sport by becoming the first person ever to win four gold medals in a single Winter Olympic Games. She set records in winning the 500-, 1,000-, 1,500-, and 3,000-meter races.

Holum, one of the two young Americans who were training hard during the 1960 Games, was from Northbrook, Illinois. Northbrook was known as the home of many of the United States speedskating stars. To train, Holum and other young athletes in Northbrook had to travel about 85 miles each way to the only Olympic-style speedskating rink in the United States. This dedication paid off, however, in the 1968 Games in Grenoble, France, where Holum tied for a silver medal in the 500-meter race with fellow American Jennifer Fish and won an unexpected bronze medal in the 1,000-meter race.

Holum returned to the Olympic Games four years later with another young woman from Northbrook, Anne Henning. During the 1971 world championships in Helsinki, Finland, on ice that had slowed Holum, Henning surprised everyone by winning the 500-meter race, the first American world champion in the sport. Holum came back in the 1,000-meter race to win a gold medal and took a bronze medal in the 1,500-meter race.

A year later, Henning was competing in the 1972 Winter Olympic Games in Sapparo, Japan. In her 500-meter race, she was blocked by a competitor who was disqualified. She finished under the world record time, but was given the choice to run another race by herself. Only a few other skaters had lowered their time by doing so. After all of the other racers finished, Henning was still in first place and had already won the gold medal. Surprisingly, she strapped on her skates, reraced her race by herself, and broke the world record. This was the first Olympic gold medal won by a U.S. woman in speedskating. She later competed in the 1,000-meter race, winning the bronze medal as well.

Holum also won a gold medal in 1972, in the 1,500-meter race, and captured a silver medal in the 3,000-meter race. After these Games, Holum returned to the sport as a coach and author, writing the definitive *Complete Handbook of Speedskating*. She also coached a then-unknown speedskater named Eric Heiden, who went on to win five gold medals at Lake Placid in 1980.

Skating alongside Henning in 1972, and placing fourth in the 500-meter race, was a versatile athlete named Sheila Young. A native of Birmingham, Michigan, Young trained on ponds and public rinks in the winter and on a bicycle during the summer to qualify for the 1972 Olympic Games. In 1973, however, she accomplished something no other United States athlete had ever done. She won a world championship in two completely different sports—cycling and speedskating. She then went on to another first by winning three medals at the 1976 Winter Olympic Games in Innsbruck, Austria, becoming the first American to accomplish this feat at one Winter Olympic Games. Young won the 500-meter race, an event in which she had missed winning a medal by only .08 of a second in 1972. She also took second place in the 1,500-meter race, and third in the 1,000-meter race.

A lesser known Olympic speedskater who competed in 1972 was Connie Carpenter-Phinney from Madison, Wisconsin. Carpenter-Phinney took seventh place in the 1,500-meter race. An ankle injury prevented her from competing in 1976, and she took up cycling soon after. Carpenter-Phinney went on to win many important cycling races, including the inaugural women's cycling race at 1984 Olympic Games in Los Angeles, California, becoming one of only a handful of Olympians who have competed in the Summer and Winter Games.

With pioneers like Holum, Henning, Young, and Carpenter-Phinney, it would be hard to expect that any athlete could improve on their history, but Bonnie Blair has done just that. A speedskater since the age of four, Blair has competed in four Olympic Games from 1984 to 1994. In the process, she won five gold medals, including gold medals in three successive Olympic Games. She was the first American woman, in the Summer or Winter Olympic Games, to accomplish this feat. She has won more medals in Winter Olympic Games than any American, man or woman. With perfect technique, hard work, and perseverance, Blair has inspired and set the standard for all young speedskaters to come.

Bonnie Blair (right) is America's most successful speedskater.

When short track speedskating became an official Olympic sport in 1992, United States women were waiting to compete. Cathy Turner won medals in both events available to women, winning the first-ever gold medal in the individual 500-meter race and a silver medal in the 3,000-meter relay. She returned in the 1994 Olympic Games at Lillehammer, Norway, to repeat as winner in the 500-meter race, and she earned a bronze medal in the 3,000-meter relay. Needless to say American women know how to succeed in speedskating.

For more information on speedskating contact the national governing organization,

U.S. Speedskating, P.O. Box 16157, Rocky River, Ohio 44116-6157. *PS*

Lyn St. James

Lyn St. James has set 31 national and international speed records during her professional racing career and is renowned as one of the top race car drivers in the world. As an Indianapolis 500 driver, St. James's ambition to become one of the best in her field has moved with precision, speed, determination, and focus, much like her driving.

St. James, an only child, born on March 13, 1947, in Willoughby, Ohio, developed her love for cars early, and one could say her first trainers were her parents. By spending time in her father's sheet metal shop, Lyn learned about mechanics and quickly developed a proficiency in and respect for mechanical things. Her mother, who suffered from polio as a child and was unable to walk for long distances, was completely dependent upon a car for mobility. This reliance instilled in St. James an appreciation for cars as symbols of freedom and independence.

Although her passion for cars was always there, it took years of hard work and some good luck before she was able to put her racing career on track. Following her mother's wishes that she grow up well-educated and self-sufficient, St. James attended Andrews School for Girls in Ohio, where she majored in business, played sport, and continued the piano lessons she had started at the age of six. Following high school, she went on to earn a piano-teaching certificate from the St. Louis Institute of Music and became an accomplished classical pianist.

261

During her teenage years, St. James's fascination with cars was also developing. When she was 17, she and her friends attended the drag races in Louisville, Kentucky. A male companion entered his GTO (a type of car) and lost. When St. James made a remark about her friend's driving ability, he suggested that she race it herself. She did, and won her class. In 1966, St. James went to the Indianapolis 500, where she obtained A.J. Foyt's autograph. St. James remarked "I was mesmerized, it was the most incredible experience of my life." It was also then that she realized she had to find a way to make cars her life.

At the age of 23, Lyn moved to Florida to marry John Carusso, the owner of a con-

Lyn St. James.

sumer electronics firm and later an auto parts business. Sharing a love of cars, the couple bought a Ford Pinto in 1973 to

compete in regional amateur Sports Car Club of America (SCCA) races. Carusso soon moved up to a Corvette, and the Pinto became hers. In 1976 and 1977, St. James was named the SCCA's Florida Regional Champion. In the same year, Carusso gained acclaim by finishing sixth at the 24 Hours of Daytona, the highest finish for an American car in the race. As part of her husband's crew, St. James should have been elated, but she was not. She realized then that she would not feel complete unless she was the driver.

In an attempt to carve out her own identity within their jointly owned businesses, she decided to change her last name from Carusso to St. James. Her inspiration came from watching the television show *McMillian and Wife*, starring actress Susan Saint James. From that point on, Lyn was on track to establishing herself as a successful entrepreneur and race car diver.

In 1979, her first pro season, St. James made history in the American Challenge Series with a second place finish (.079 seconds behind the winner). Shortly thereafter, she and Carusso divorced.

In 1981, the Ford Motor Company became an official backer of Lyn St. James's racing career. Although it was not until 1985 that she won her first professional race at Elkhart Lake, Wisconsin, she was winning continuous recognition in the sport. In 1984, St. James was named International Motor Sports Association (IMSA) Camel GT Rookie of the Year, and in 1985, she received the IMSA Norelco Driver of the Year honor.

After the first professional win at Elkhart Lake, St. James continued to develop name recognition, and more honors came her way. In 1987 and 1990, she was the winning GTO team driver at the 24 Hours of Daytona, and in 1991, she repeated the feat at the 24 Hours of Sebring. In 1992, Lyn raced for the first time in the Indianapolis 500. The only woman in the race, she placed 11th and was voted Rookie of the Year. She followed that accomplishment by qualifying for a position in the race each year since that time.

Her accomplishments do not all take place on the race track. In the late 1980s and early 1990s, St. James was instrumental in the establishment of Human Performance International, Inc., at Daytona Beach, Florida. She remains a minority owner and advisory board member (as well as a client) of this organization, which is devoted to personal development programs for optimizing competitive performance.

As the leading woman competing head-to-head with men in a male-dominated sport, St. James has gained renown as one of the world's top female role models. She is a woman who is as dedicated to advancing opportunities for female athletes as she is to her driving career. She served as president of the Women's Sports Foundation from 1990 to 1993. She also established the Lyn St. James Foundation in 1993, a nonprofit organization dedicated to professional race car driver development, especially for aspiring young women. It provides vision, leadership, education, and resources for these individuals; the program is also committed to promoting automotive safety in general. In 1994, St. James created the Make a Difference campaign, a program that helps girls in the Indianapolis area gain self-esteem through sports and leadership programs. She continues to stay active in auto racing and continues to successfully qualify for the Indy 500.

Dawn Staley

Dawn Staley was born in Philadelphia, Pennsylvania, on May 4, 1970. She is not only an Olympic gold medalist from the 1996 Olympic Games in Atlanta, Georgia; she is also the first woman depicted on a two-story high mural on a building in her hometown. At just five feet six inches tall, Staley is small for a guard in basketball. She developed her skills and game playing ability with men and women on the local courts in Philadelphia.

Staley was named Women's Basketball Coaches Association Player of the Year and All-American while attending the University of Virginia and is one of only three players at the university to have their playing number retired. During her four seasons at Virginia (1989–92) she made four NCAA tournament appearances, including three NCAA Final Four appearances. She ranks as the top all-time career scorer for Virginia with 2,135 points, averaging 16.3 points per game. She also holds UVA records for most points scored in a game (37) and most assists made in a season (235 in 1991).

Of playing on the 1996 United States Women's Olympic Basketball Team, she said "Now when I look back on it, making this team and opening doors for young girls is my due. I hope they realize what we are trying to do. . . . I think it's an honor playing with these women. I'll look back on this and remember the good times and the bad times and the friendships." Staley now plays on the Philadelphia Rage, a women's professional basketball team in the American Basketball League (ABL).

Aeriwentha Mae Faggs Starr. *See* **Aeriweatha Mae Faggs**

Cheryl Stearns

Cheryl Stearns was born in 1955 and grew up in Scottsdale, Arizona. She has won more skydiving championships and held more world records than anyone else, male or female. She was the first woman on the United States Army Golden Knights Parachute Team in 1977. Stearns's competitive domain in skydiving is in style and accuracy competitions. The style competition is a specific set of aerial turns, back loops, and front loops. The fastest one to complete the set, wins. Accuracy involves landing on a five-centimeter electronic disk. Dead centers, the best score, are achieved when the sky diver lands exactly at the center of the tiny disk.

Stearns has an extensive portfolio of world and United States titles. In 1990 she received the Diplome Leonardo da Vinci, the world's highest award in aerosports. At that time, she had set a total of 29 world records and at one time held four different world records simultaneously, the only person to hold four sky diving world records at one time.

In 1972 at the age of 17, Stearns started jumping in Arizona by convincing her mother to sign a consent waiver. Stearns fell in love with jumping and flying. She packed up her belongings and her dog and moved to Raeford, North Carolina, in 1975, to be coached by world-renowned skydiving coach, Gene Paul Thacker. Having received her pilot's license, she paid her way by flying jumpers and maintaining the flight line. The coaching paid off with her first national accuracy title in 1975, followed by a combined style and accuracy title in 1976. Stearns set her first world record during these competitions with a total score of 0.43 cm (average distance from the center of a 5 cm target) for 19 jumps.

In 1977, Stearns joined the United States Army and earned her way onto the Golden Knight Army Parachute Team. She took first place at all United States Nationals while in the army and set several world records in style and accuracy. Stearns was discharged in 1980 and then re-enlisted in 1982.

Stearns added more categories to her world records by performing the most jumps in a 24-hour period. In 1987, in Lodi, California, with Russell Fish, she jumped 255 times in one 24-hour period. Later she broke her own record on November 9, 1995, at Raeford, North Carolina, with 352 jumps in a 24-hour period. She also added more categories to her records at this time by scoring 188 dead centers, 104 during the daylight and 84 at night.

Currently, Stearns is an airline pilot, flying Boeing 737 300/400 series for USAir. She has over 11,000 hours in the air and nearly 16,000 landings. She continues to compete in national and international competitions. *JM*

Lydia Stephans

Lydia Stephans, a three-time national speed skating champion, was born on October 19, 1960, and was raised in Northbrook, Illinois; she started competing at the age of 12. In her skating career, she competed in the 1984 Olympic Games in Sarajevo, Yugoslavia, and also won several national and international championships. In 1994, Stephans was inducted into the Amateur Skating Union's Speed Skating Hall of Fame.

Stephans' career in sports did not end when she stopped skating competitively. After receiving a master's degree in broadcast journalism from Northwestern University in 1985, she became a production assistant at ABC Sports. In 1989, she began working as the coordinator of programming. In 1994, Stephans created the women's sport series, "A Passion to Play," in an effort to provide more television exposure for women. Since that time, five "A Passion to Play" shows have been aired with three more in production.

Today, as vice president of programming, she is the first woman in history to be made a vice president at ABC Sports. She currently oversees the *ABC Wide World of Sports* series, as well as IndyCar auto racing, Professional Golf Association Tour events, and women's sports.

Jan Stephenson

Jan Stephenson was born in Sydney, Australia on December 22, 1951. She played junior golf in New South Wales, Australia, and her amateur credentials include three Australian Junior titles. She joined the Ladies Professional Golf Association (LPGA) in 1974 and was named Rookie of the Year.

Stephenson has won 22 international ladies golf tournaments, 16 of which were LPGA events. In 1996, she reached number 10 on the all-time LPGA money winners' list. Stephenson was honored among *Golf Magazine*'s "100 Heroes" during the 1988 Centennial of Golf in America celebration. Stephenson is active outside of golf as well, acting as a representative of the Arthritis

Foundation and producing an exercise video for people who have arthritis. She lives in Forth Worth, Texas, and continues to play on the LPGA tour.

Lynne Stoessel-Ross

Lynn Stoessel-Ross was the first woman elected to the United States Weightlifting Federation (USWF) Board of Directors (1992-1994). She was re-elected as athlete's representative to the board for three more years (1994-1996) and was also elected to the Coaches Committee.

Having a woman on the USWF Board of Directors has facilitated many changes, most notably the inclusion of women in the international championships for the first time. At the 1994 International Congress, significant decisions were made regarding the future of women's weightlifting with the International Federation. The presence of Stoessel-Ross at the Congress and working as an official helped to precipitate these changes. Three of the 10 agenda items concerned women athletes.

The first of these agenda items, a motion to solidify the future of women in this international event, was passed unanimously. This motion was important because it brought the number of continental federations hosting championships for women from four to six, thus increasing opportunities for women to compete. The second item was an agreement to pursue the inclusion of women in the Pan American Games, and Lynne Stoessel-Ross was appointed to chair the International Committee established to do this. Members on the board, including representatives from Canada, Mexico, and the United States, are charged with developing and implementing a plan to advance participation of women in weightlifting. A third item, unanimously agreed upon, was to support the inclusion of women's weightlifting in the Olympic Games. USWF President Jim Schmitz recognized the importance of these events and agreed to fund Stoessel-Ross's travel to the international meetings so she can continue her advocacy for women's inclusion in Olympic weightlifting events.

Born on September 27, 1961, Stoessel-Ross has a master's degree in exercise physiology, with a specialization in strength physiology. She is certified as a strength and conditioning specialist by the National Strength and Conditioning Association (NSCA), the professional organization of strength coaches. Lynn has served on the NSCA's women's committee and has written many articles on strength training for women; she also co-authored the NSCA's position statement on strength training for women. Stoessel-Ross currently lives in Lubbock, Texas and works as an assistant strength coach at Texas Tech University she also serves as a consultant to the women's basketball team at Coronado High School.

Women are vastly underrepresented in the strength coaching profession, and Stoessel-Ross is working to develop leadership clinics for women in the strength training profession to go along with her efforts to open weightlifting competitions to women.

Toni Stone

Marcenia Lyle Alberge, who played baseball under the name of Toni Stone, was the first woman to play professional baseball in a men's league. As a child in St. Paul, Minnesota, she joined a baseball team with the help of Father Charles Keefe. Later, she persuaded former St. Louis Cardinals catcher Gabby Street to let her try out for his baseball school. She then played for an American Legion championship team in San Francisco from 1945 to 1947 and in 1947 earned a position on the semi-professional San Francisco Sea Lions, an African American barnstorming team. She drove in two runs in her first two at-bats with the Sea Lions.

On a trip through New Orleans, Stone accepted an offer from the New Orleans Black Pelicans. In 1949, Stone moved to the New Orleans Creoles, a men's Negro American League (NAL) minor league team, where she played second base and batted .265 in her final season with them. She then signed with another NAL team, the Indianapolis Clowns, in 1951. She appeared in 50 games with the Clowns, batting .243. She got a hit off the legendary pitcher Satchel Paige on Easter Sunday in 1953. Her contract was sold to the Kansas City Monarchs in 1954. At the end of the 1954 season, after nine years of playing professional baseball on men's teams, Toni Stone retired from baseball because she was disappointed with her playing time. She continued to play recreational baseball until she was 60 years old.

Vivian Stringer

Throughout her career as a women's basketball coach, Charlene Vivian Stringer has gracefully balanced career and family, making her an important role model to women interested in combining motherhood with careers. Born in Edenborn, Pennsylvania, on March 16, 1948, Stringer hoped to play basketball or run track in high school, but because there were no teams for girls, she became a cheerleader and was the first African American to make that squad. At Slippery Rock University, Stringer excelled on the basketball, field hockey, softball, and tennis teams and was later inducted into the school's Hall of Fame. In 1971, she became head basketball coach at Cheyney State University and stayed for 11 seasons. In 1981–1982 when the National Collegiate Athletic Association (NCAA) organized its first women's championship tournament, Stringer's team made the Final Four.

In 1983, Stringer moved to the University of Iowa and led the Hawkeyes to 10 straight 20-win seasons. Just before the 1991–1992 season, Stringer's husband, Bill, died of a heart attack. After nearly quitting her job to be with her three children, Stringer finished the season and became the first women's coach in the country to guide two different college teams to the NCAA Final Four. She was also named Naismith National Coach of the Year that same season. In 1995, Stringer accepted a coaching position at Rutgers University and became the highest-paid female coach in the United States at that time.

Dale Stuart

Freestyle skydiving, which combines the thrill of skydiving with the grace of gymnastics, is a relatively new discipline in skydiving. Dale Stuart is one of the pioneers in this graceful and beautiful aerial ballet performed in the skies. Stuart won the Freestyle Skydiving World Championships from 1990 to 1994. In 1995, she served as a judge, and then returned in 1996 to recapture the title. Stuart received the Outstanding Individual Freestylist Award in 1996 for her accomplishments in freestyle.

In her own words, Stuart describes how jumping has changed her life, "I've always loved flying—I learned to fly sailplanes when I was 18 years old. I also enjoyed all kinds of sports and gymnastics in particular. So freestyle skydiving was a way to bring it all together for me. It has the freedom of flying and the athleticism of gymnastics. In a new environment, I got to be a pioneer and create a lot of the sport myself as well. It's been rewarding, not only for the competition medals, but also because of the variety of people I've come in contact with, both inside and outside the sport. I love the smiles I see on people's faces when they view my performances. I love the excitement I see among the freestylists I'm coaching when they master a new move; and I love the feeling that I've made a small difference on this planet, that I've helped create something that can bring people joy, in participating or watching."

Stuart's achievements have led to movie stunts in *Terminal Velocity* and a television show called *Man and Machine*. Endorsement have come from Ellessee, Inc. and TYR Sport, Inc. Her achievements and performances have received extensive television coverage, including NBC's *I Witness Video*, ABC's *Good Morning America*, CNN's *Sporting Life*, ABC's *Prime Time Live*, ESPN's *SportsNight*, CBS *This Morning* (live), CNN *Morning News* (live), NBC's *Extra*, NBC's *Weekend Today Show*, ABC's

World News Tonight, and the syndicated *Front Runners*.

Stuart started jumping in 1986 and has accumulated over 5,000 jumps. She continues to jump and train with Greg Gusson at Skydive Arizona. *JM*

Louise Suggs

Louise Suggs was born in Atlanta, Georgia, on September 7, 1923. She holds 50 professional golfing titles, including eight major championships, and was the first woman elected to the Ladies Professional Golf Association (LPGA) Hall of Fame in 1951. Suggs had a brilliant amateur career before the LPGA was formed, winning the Georgia State Amateur Championship in 1940 and 1942, the Southern Championships in 1941 and 1947, and the North-South Championship three times (1942, 1946, and 1948). Suggs won the Titleholders in 1946, and in 1947 became the United States Women's Amateur Champion. In 1948, Suggs added the British Amateur Championship to her resume and topped off her amateur career by representing the United States on the 1948 Curtis Cup team. She turned professional on July 8, 1948. She is a founding and charter member of the LPGA and served as its president three times. She holds the fourth-highest number of career victories (50) in LPGA history.

Her professional career highlights include a 1949 United States Open victory, won by 14 strokes, setting a 72-hole scoring record of 291. In 1953, she broke her own 72-hole scoring record by shooting 288 to win the Tampa Open. In 1966, she became the first woman ever elected to the Georgia Athletic Hall of Fame.

Suggs was named as one of *Golf Magazine*'s "100 Heroes" during the 1988 Centennial of Golf in America celebration. As a measure of how golf's prize money has increased, it is interesting to note that in over 30 years in professional golf, and more than 50 career and 8 major victories, Louise Suggs earned approximately $190,475. Suggs currently lives in Delray Beach, Florida and competed in the Sprint Senior Challenge LPGA events from 1991 to 1995.

Pat Summitt

University of Tennessee head women's basketball coach Pat Summitt has not only found success on the court, but she has also used her visibility in the sports world to encourage more girls to become basketball players. In her 23rd season with the Lady Vols, Summitt is only women's coach in the National Collegiate Athletic Association (NCAA) to win four national championships (1987, 1989, 1991, and 1996). She has led Tennessee to the Final Four 13 times in 15 years, and she boasts the second-winningest record (596-33) of any active NCAA women's coach (behind Leon Barmore of Louisiana Tech).

Summitt, born on June 14, 1952, in Clarksville, Tennessee, received her bachelor's degree in 1974 from the University of Tennessee-Martin, where she played on the basketball squad for four years. In 1976, Summitt co-captained the silver-medal-winning United States Olympic Basketball Team. Eight years later she coached the USA Women's Basketball Team to its first gold medal in Olympic competition. The three-time Naismith Coach of the Year Award winner is known for her skillful recruiting, tough discipline, and dedication to her team.

Swimming and Women

Olympic women's swimming has been dominated by the United States women's swim team. The stars and personalities of women's swimming have been etched in United States sport history, with names such as Amy Van Dyken, Janet Evans, Summer Sanders, Shirley Babashoff, Tracy Caulkins, Mary T. Meagher, Ann Curtis, Donna de Varona, Debbie Meyer, Ethelda Bleibtrey, Gertrude Ederle, and Eleanor Holm.

Swim teams and clubs can be found in almost every American town and city from the recreational summer league level to the competitive year-round circuit. Swimming is

Butterfly stroke.

a varsity sport for most high schools, colleges, and universities. Girls and women of all ages compete in swimming. Swimming in the United States is a highly organized and developed sport. Girls may start swimming competitively as early as age five, and many women compete into their 70s and beyond in masters swimming programs. The organization responsible for promoting and regulating swimming in the U.S. is its governing body, United States Swimming.

Although swimming has been an event since the modern Olympic Games began in 1896, the 1912 Olympic Games in London, England, was the first time women were allowed to compete in swimming. The Women's Swimming Association of New York was formed in 1914 and offered women the opportunity to train for national and international competitions. The Olympic Games now has 32 swimming events, 16 of which are for women, including the butterfly, breaststroke, freestyle, backstroke, individual medley, 4 x 100-meter medley relay, and the 4 x 100-meter freestyle relay.

The pioneers of women's swimming emerged during the 1920s. In the 1920 Olympic Games in Antwerp, Belgium, Ethelda Bleibtrey became the first United States woman to win an Olympic medal in swimming. She was also the first woman from any country, and in any sport, to win three gold medals. Another American great was Gertrude Ederle, who in 1925 became the first woman to swim the English Chan-

nel. She completed the swim in 14 hours and 34 minutes, shattering the men's record for the crossing. Other United States swimming legends include Ann Curtis, who in 1948 became the first woman ever to win the Sullivan Award given to the nation's top amateur athlete, after winning two gold medals; Donna de Varona, who became the first woman in television sports broadcasting in 1965, after being named 1964's America's Outstanding Woman Athlete; Debbie Meyer, who became the first woman ever to win three individual gold medals in a single Olympic Games at the 1968 Games in Mexico City, Mexico, and who also won the Sullivan Award in 1969; Shirley Babashoff, who won eight Olympic medals in the 1972 and 1976 Games, the most by any United States female swimmer; Jill Sterkel, who won the Broderick Cup given to the nation's top female college athlete in 1981, and who became the first female four-time Olympian and medal winner (1976, 1980, 1984, and 1988); Tracy Caulkins, who in 1990 was named Swimmer of the Decade by *USA Today*, after becoming the only swimmer, male or female, to break United States records in every stroke, and who won the most career United States national titles with 48; Mary T. Meagher, who in 1990 was honored by *Sports Illustrated* for her 200-meter butterfly world record swim, which the magazine listed as the fifth-greatest single-event record of all sports; Janet Evans, who in 1992 joined Mark Spitz as the only American swimmers to win four individual Olympic gold medals; and Amy Van Dyken, who in 1996 became the first United States woman in any sport to win four gold medals at a single Olympic Games.

Competitive swimming has many different levels. Most swimmers become involved in competitive swimming through summer league programs. These teams may be organized and operated by city parks and recreation departments, local Young Men's and Young Women's Christian Associations (YMCA/YWCA), country clubs, or housing area pools and tennis clubs. Most swimmers have a year or two of swimming lessons before joining a swim team. Benefits of getting started through a summer league program include a short competitive season, inexpensive fees, nearby competition, and a focus on improvement and enjoyment. Ages of swimmers in summer league teams range from five to 18.

A typical second step in competitive swimming (or a first step for an exceptionally talented young person) is involvement in a year-round program. This may be with a United States Swimming organized team, or with a YMCA or a YWCA team. The year-round program is divided into two swimming seasons: a short course season that runs from September to April, and a long course season that runs from May through August. Short course is defined as competition in a 25-yard pool, and long course is defined as competition in a 50-meter pool. As the swimmers get older, stronger, and faster, most United States Swimming and YMCA/YWCA coaches will ease the athlete into twice a day practices, two to four times per week. Depending on the swimmer's ability and the coach's philosophy, strength training may be incorporated into weekly practice sessions as well. United States Swimming and YMCA/YWCA teams practice and compete frequently and may travel long distances for various competitions.

Another level of competitive swimming is at the high school level. Most high schools have varsity swim teams, and the season is usually contested during the winter months. Practices are held once every day for most high school teams, although some schools with strong swimming traditions practice two times a day.

Dramatic changes have occurred in women's swimming since the passage of Title IX and the Amateur Sports Act of 1980, which provided equal opportunities for women in education and related activities, eventually translating into college scholarships. The athlete assistance funds from the

The United States has a strong swimming history.

United States Olympic Committee (USOC) and United States Swimming lengthened many careers. Many colleges and universities now offer full or partial scholarships depending on the swimmer's ability.

The successful career of former swimmers outside of the swimming pool are also worth noting. Nancy Hogshead, a 1984 Olympic triple gold medalist, served a term as the president of the Women's Sports Foundation. Carol Zaleski, United States Swimming's president, is the first woman to chair the prestigious Technical Committee for Federation Internationale de Natation Amateur (FINA), the international governing body for swimming. Sandra Baldwin, a former United States Swimming president, is currently serving as a vice president for the United States Olympic Committee (USOC).

A fortunate cycle has developed for women in swimming in the 1990s. With each generation, new role models are produced in the sport of swimming, attracting more girls and young women to the sport. For more information about how to become involved in swimming, contact United States Swimming, One Olympic Plaza, Colorado Springs, CO 80909-5770. *MH1*

Kathrine Switzer

Kathrine Switzer epitomizes longevity and fitness in every sense: After breaking the gender barrier in the formerly all-male Boston marathon in 1967, she went on to run 35 marathons, win the 1974 New York City marathon, and lead the drive to get the women's marathon included in the Olympic Games. Now a leading expert television commentator in athletics and the owner of her own events management and sports promotions company, At-A-lanta Sports Promotions, Inc., Kathrine Switzer has broadcasted and promoted hundreds of events. For many years, Switzer combined a rigorous training schedule with successful and innovative corporate public relations and sports marketing careers for both AMF, Inc., and Avon Products Inc. In just one of her dynamic programs, the Avon Women's Sports Programs, she created opportunities in sports for over a million athletes in tennis and running, while supervising an annual budget that at times reached $7 million and a full-time staff of 14 people. She also designed all the communications around the programs as well as their organization.

Switzer was born in 1947. In 1967, as a student at Syracuse University, she ran with the men's cross-country team. The university had no women's intercollegiate sports. She persuaded her coach, Arnie Briggs, to take her to Boston for the then male-only marathon. She registered for the race as "K.V. Switzer." At 4 miles, Boston Marathon official, Jack Semple, grabbed her by the shirt to try to pull her out of the race. He was shoved away by Switzer's supporters and she finished the race. After this first Boston Marathon, Switzer ran in hundreds of competitions and eventually achieved a third all-time USA and sixth-in-the-world ranking in the marathon; in 1976 she was named "Runner of the Decade" by *Runner's World* magazine.

These athletic achievements alone would earn Switzer a place in this *Encyclopedia*, but her efforts as an advocate for women's sports and as a events and promotions consultant

Kathrine Switzer avoiding a Boston Marathon official trying to remove her from the course.
Photo courtesy of Harry Trask.

are equally worthy of mention. Switzer became internationally acclaimed as a leader in the women's sports movement when she organized the successful lobbying effort to include the women's marathon race in the Olympic Games, which until 1960 didn't include a race longer than 200 meters. Besides her advocacy work, Switzer consults on all aspects of public relations, promotions, and event tourism, and she also advises companies, teams, and athletes in self-promotion, presentation, and focusing on success.

There is still more to add to Switzer's sports resume. As a trained journalist (bachelor of arts in journalism and master of arts in communications, both from Syracuse University), Switzer has covered Olympic, Goodwill, and Asian Games; Olympic trials; national championships; and 16 Boston, 12 New York City, 11 Pittsburgh, and 4 Los Angeles Marathons among hundreds of other telecasts. She has written a monthly fitness column for *Women Today*, and is a regular contributor to *Living Fit*. Other articles of hers have appeared in the *New York Times*, the *Washington Post*, the *New York Daily News*, *Runner's World*, *Women's Sports and Fitness*, *Parade*, and others.

Numerous citations and awards for her efforts in advancing sports opportunities have been conferred on her, including the Regents Medal of Excellence from the New York State Board of Regents, the Billie Jean King Award (for outstanding individual achievement) from the Women's Sports Foundation, a Life Citation Award from the United California Bank, a Letter of Distinction Award from Syracuse University, and both an Outstanding Achievement (1984) and Healthy American Fitness Leader Award (1994) from the President's Council on Physical Fitness and Sports. In 1986, the National Association of Girls and Women in Sports named her as an Honor Fellow. For both her

organizational and sports work, she was inducted into the Halls of Fame at Syracuse University, Lynchburg College, and Roadrunners Club of America.

Although no longer a world-class athlete, she still runs seven miles a day and races in masters (veterans) competitions. She is married to Roger Robinson, professor of English at Victoria University in Wellington, New Zealand, and an author, speaker and noted world-class masters runner. Switzer resides both in the USA and in New Zealand.

Sheryl Swoopes

Sheryl Swoopes was born on March 25, 1971, and quickly developed a love for the game of basketball. It is said that Sheryl Swoopes plays basketball like nobody else. In one memorable year, Swoopes showed the world what one person can do for a basketball team. Throughout the 1992-1993 season, she showed her ability to lead the Texas Tech women's basketball team to victory. In the final game of the National

Sheryl Swoopes.
Photo courtesy of Advantage International.

Collegiate Athletic Association (NCAA) Women's Basketball Championship, Swoopes was "the game." She scored as many points in the first half (23) as most good players score in a game. In the second half, she broke the record for the most points scored in a half of the championship game by putting another 24 on the scoreboard. Her total of 47 points scored in one NCAA Championship game broke Bill Walton's record of 44 points. Swoopes also scored the most points ever in the NCAA Tournament with 177, shattering the old mark of 134 points. In the process of setting this new record for productivity, Swoopes also broke the record for most field goals (56) and free throws (57). During her collegiate career, Swoopes was named to three All-American teams and was named national player of the year by eight different organizations or publications.

Swoopes's incredible run through the NCAA tournament and her stellar career did not go unnoticed. Her spectacular style of play has inspired a whole generation of girls and has helped popularize women's basketball. With the "Air Swoopes" shoe, Sheryl Swoopes broke a sports marketing barrier by becoming the first woman athlete to have a Nike athletic shoe designed and named for her.

More recently, Swoopes was a member of the gold-medal-winning 1996 USA Women's Olympic team. She has been one of the stars used to promote the Women's National Basketball Association (WNBA), a professional women's basketball league. She started late due to her pregnancy (she has a baby boy) but played for the Houston Comets in the inaugural 1997 season.

Synchronized Swimming

Synchronized swimming began in the early 1900s. Since these early beginnings, spectators have been awed by the grace and power of this exciting sport, which requires a unique combination of overall body strength and agility, aerobic conditioning, grace and beauty, split-second timing, musical interpretation, and dramatic flair.

Synchronized swimming actually involves three disciplines—solo, duet, and team. The competitive rules and manner of judging in synchronized swimming are similar to sports such as figure skating and gymnastics. The team competition features eight women in the water at one time and is the most difficult of the three disciplines. Team members perform in nine feet of water, and without touching the bottom of the pool, use "eggbeatering" and sculling techniques to stay afloat and perform their routine. Their routines incorporate acrobatic elements such as lifts, which involve raising swimmers above the water surface using only the swimmer's body strength, and precise synchronized movements.

Synchronized swimming first became popular in 1939 when Eleanor Holm, an Olympic team member, performed at the World's Fair in New York. In 1940, Esther Williams, United States 100-meter freestyle champion and Olympic contender, further popularized synchronized swimming in the United States through her performances at the San Francisco World's Fair and in many movies.

First officially recognized as a competitive sport by the Amateur Athletic Union (AAU) in 1945, the inaugural United States National Synchronized Swimming Championships were held in 1946. A few years later, the 1955 Pan American Games included synchronized swimming events, and the World Aquatic Championships soon followed. After almost 40 years of concerted effort by individuals such as coach Mary Jo Ruggieri of the Ohio State University, synchronized swimming was included in the Olympic Games in 1984, with the United States winning the first solo (Tracie Ruiz) and duet (Ruiz and Candy Costie) Olympic gold medals. In the last 10 years, the sport has experienced unparalleled growth, culminating in the team event being introduced at the 1996 Olympic Games in Atlanta, Georgia. The United States won the gold medal in this event, which is synchronized swimming's premier competition. Team members were Suzannah Bianco, Tammy

Cleland, Becky Dyroen-Lancer, Heather Pease, Emily Porter LaSueur, Jil Savery, Nathalie Schneyder, Heather Simmons-Carrasco, Jill Sudduth, and Margot Thien.

To maintain this winning tradition, United States Synchronized Swimming, the governing body of the sport, organizes, participates in, and promotes a variety of competitive events each year. These events begin at the local level and continue in the following categories: age group, junior, and senior levels. Major national events include Olympic trials, United States National Team trials, Jantzen National Championships, United States Junior Championships, United States Collegiate Championships, United States Open Championships, United States Age Group Championships, United States Junior Olympic Championships, United States Senior Championships, and the United States Masters Championships.

World-class synchronized swimmers practice eight hours every day, six days per week. Approximately six hours are spent in the water, and an additional two hours are spent on land, with cross-training exercises such as lifting weights, biking, running, or aerobics included. An elite-level synchro-nized swimmer can swim up to 75 meters underwater without coming up for air.

Synchronized swimming has produced many outstanding athletes but one woman stands out from this impressive crowd. Becky Dyroen-Lancer, 1995 world cup solo swim-mer champion and Team USA leader, recorded her ninth consecutive "Grand Slam" by winning all the major international events in 1995. The CNN Network compared her to Wayne Gretzky and Michael Jordan in terms of her dominance of synchronized swimming.

Dyroen-Lancer has been accompanied by great teammates as well. Team USA's artistic routine for the 1995 world cup competition received a score of 99.80 out of a possible 100. This was the highest score ever achieved in world cup history. Team USA entered the 1996 Olympic competition ranked number one in the world for the previous five years and won the competition with perfect scores from 9 of the 10 judges.

For more information about synchronized swimming contact United States Synchro-nized Swimming, Pan American Plaza, 201 South Capitol Avenue, Suite 510, Indianapo-lis, IN 46225. *FJ*

T

Table Tennis and Women

Table tennis is the second most popular sport in the world, soccer being the first. Table tennis, formerly known as gossima, flim-flam, and ping pong, began in England in the late nineteenth century. In 1933, the United States Table Tennis Association was formed. Now known as USA Table Tennis, it is the governing body for the sport. Today, the sport attracts more than 40 million competitive players worldwide and unknown numbers of people who play for fun. An Olympic sport since 1988, the future of table tennis looks bright.

This Olympic sport requires concentration, touch, deception, skill, and even a bit of luck. Asian countries such as China, Japan, and Korea are the dominant forces in table tennis. These countries develop most of the top-ranked players. Table tennis at the elite level is an incredibly fast, action-packed sport. Shots include topspin shots, sidespin shots, slices, and every other type of shot players can think of to beat an opponent. With little more than a flick of the wrist, players can generate unbelievable power, propelling the ball over the net, only to see it return a split second later. This speed makes it mesmerizing to watch two competitive players rallying back and forth. Reflexes,

hand-eye coordination, and touch are essential ingredients in returning the ball.

The serve is the key to good strategy. Sometimes this means tossing the ball up to four feet overhead and hitting it over the net as it comes down, imparting sidespin, topspin, or a combination of spins. Since rallies rarely last more than 10 shots, points are fast and furious. Every 5 points, there is a change of serve, so players must take advantage of their own serve to win. The first player to score 21 points wins the game. A player, however, must win by 2 points, so a game could continue on to hundreds of points before being decided. If the score reaches 20-20, the players must then alternate serves until one has scored 2 consecutive points. Matches are decided on the best two out of three games in national competition and three out of five games in international competition.

As mentioned earlier, China has always been one of the major forces in women's table tennis. Chinese women have dominated Olympic table tennis since its inception as a medal event in 1988, winning eight of nine gold medals. Only South Korea has been able to break into the gold medal count.

The USA has had mixed results in women's table tennis. In the Olympic Games in Barcelona, Spain (1992), Lily Yip defeated Brazil's Monica Doti, a strong international player. Yip overpowered Doti, winning points on her serve 64 percent of the time and slamming 14 drives for winners. Another American, Amy Feng, was strong in the first game, but Liu Wei of China took advantage of forehand errors in the final two games to win. Neither American finished on top of her group and both failed to advance to the second round. The United States women's team is currently ranked 14th in the world.

The United States sent three performers to the 1996 Olympic Games (Yip, Feng, and Nei Wang) but again were stalled without medals. At a recent USA Table Tennis National Championship, Amy Feng completed her third "triple" (singles, doubles, and mixed doubles) as she won three championship events for a third year in a row. Feng defeated Lily Yip for the women's title.

For more information about how to participate in table tennis, contact: USA Table Tennis, One Olympic Plaza, Colorado Springs, CO 80909-5769. *FJ*

Teacher Influences on Girls' Play

It has been observed that the process of sport socialization involves several factors that differentiate girls and boys. Specifically, parents, peers, and teachers provide gender-specific information regarding the appropriateness or inappropriateness of various physical activities.

The consequences of compliance with stereotypically defined gender-role behavior are significant and impact heavily on the affective and psychomotor learning areas. Traditional "boys" activities such as team games and sports require group interaction, leadership, and assertiveness while traditional "girls" activities, such as jumping rope or playing with dolls, involve simple rules, few players, and no team strategy. These "male" activities provide boys with the opportunity to develop good leadership skills, make decisions easily, and take a stand with confidence. In contrast, the "female" activities teach girls

how to be gentle, affectionate, sympathetic, and loyal. What they do not provide is much opportunity to develop analytical skills, self-reliance, and self-confidence.

Gender-segregated play groups during childhood generally provide girls with a distinct disadvantage in the area of psycho-motor development. A large body of evidence indicates that physical activity can play a beneficial role in maintaining or enhancing physical and mental health. Prerequisite to participation in many recreational activities, however, is the mastery of basic motor skills such as ball throwing, kicking, and batting skills, which are inherent in traditional "boys" activities. When children fail to master these fundamental skills, they are faced with barriers that prevent them from participating in potentially satisfying and beneficial activities later in life.

Perhaps the most convincing research evidence of the impact of early childhood activity on development comes from the Women's Sports Foundation/Miller Lite Report on Women in Sports (1985). This survey of 7,000 females indicated that the choice of childhood playmates (according to gender) exerts an extremely powerful influence on adolescent body image, on the likelihood that girls and women will engage in or attain leadership positions, and on adult interest in sports and fitness participation.

Although children enter school with several years of gender-role socialization behind them, they learn a great deal more through their teachers' behaviors and expectations. It is apparent that two-way interactions occur between teachers and students. Both have ideas about the gender appropriateness of various activities and tend to reinforce each other. Evidence from several studies demonstrates that teachers consistently reinforce and encourage active and physical behaviors in boys and gentle and quiet behaviors in girls. In addition, teachers often criticize boys and girls for engaging in cross-gender activities and praise them for engaging in same-gender activities.

Just as parents and classroom teachers' behavior can have unintended limiting effects on children's play, physical educators also surround children with limiting "gender-appropriateness perceptions" in regard to certain games and sports. Sometimes the messages teachers give children are as blatant as segregating activities by gender, and sometimes they are as subtle as sexist posters on the gymnasium wall. Since the consequences of stereotypical gender play are potentially damaging, it is essential for all teachers to examine the setting and curricula for barriers to full development.

Attempts have been made to create educational programs that purposefully structure an environment for children that is free of stereotypical gender-role patterns. These programs have reported that distinctions on the basis of gender are lessened and mixed-sex play groups, with equal-status interactions, become common. Whether these perceptual and behavioral changes will persist over time is a question that remains to be answered. In light of the demonstrated difficulties caused by offering gender-stereotypic physical activities for children, it seems appropriate for teachers to adopt specific strategies to counteract, rather than contribute to, gender-differentiated learning experiences. *AI*

See also **Gender Stereotypical Play: Consider the Consequences; Socialization Influences: Girls and Women in Sport**

Team Handball

Although popular throughout the world, team handball is just emerging in the United States and often suffers from an identity crisis. Most of the world calls the game handball, but in the United States another sport already has that name. Because of this overlap, most Americans, hearing of team handball, envision participants on something like a racquetball court, smacking a little black ball with their hands. This vision is not accurate for, without a doubt, team handball is not "off the wall." The game is a combination of soccer and basketball, played indoors on a court slightly larger than a basketball court with soccer-like goals (protected by a keeper) at either end.

A dynamic game that is fun to play and exciting to watch, team handball had its beginnings in Europe in the late 1920s. The game originated from soccer, so first-time participants and spectators notice many similarities. In fact, many describe the game as "soccer with your hands." Each team has six court players and a goal keeper, who use their natural athletic skills of running, jumping, throwing, and catching to play the game. The ball and goals look the same as soccer, only smaller, and the court is slightly larger than a basketball court. The object is to throw the ball into the opponent's goal to score and to defend one's own goal from attack. Participants and spectators alike enjoy the continuous action, the body contact, and the spectacular goalie saves. The rules of the game are identical for men and women, except that the women's ball (at 22" circumference) is one inch smaller than the men's regulation size.

The formation of the United States Team Handball Federation (USTHF) in 1959 was the beginning of team handball in this country. The USTHF became a member of the United States Olympic Committee in 1968 and is recognized by the International Handball Federation as the governing body of the sport in the United States, conducting national and international programs. The United States women's national team competes in the Pan American Games, world championships, and Olympic Games.

Not until 1974 was a women's national squad formed, through try-outs at Iowa State University and Slippery Rock State University. The team first qualified for world championship competition in 1975. They were defeated by Japan in the Olympic Qualification Tournament and thus failed to qualify for the 1976 Olympic Games in Montreal, Canada. Because of the 1980 American boycott of the Olympic Games in Moscow, Russia (then part of the Soviet Union), the next chance for the women's national team to compete in the Olympic Games was in Los Angeles, California, in

1984. Taking advantage of the hometown support, the first U.S. women's team to qualify for Olympic competition achieved a fourth-place finish. Winning gold medals at the Pan American Championships in 1987, 1991, and 1995 qualified the team for the 1988, 1992, and 1996 Olympic Games, where they finished 6th, 7th, and 8th respectively. Bright young stars include Sharon Cain (coming from vollyball and basketball), Dawn Allinger (basketball), and Lisa Eagen (softball).

Up to the present, the USTHF's focus has been on national team programs. Teams have been fielded by recruiting graduating college athletes with a multisport background and by providing them expert European coaching and quality international competitive experiences to learn the game. The federation has given many college athletes a second athletic career and Olympic dreams, but it has not as yet directed any efforts toward the comprehensive growth and development of the sport.

Lately, however, a sense of responsibility for the sport is taking root in the federation, and the future of team handball is promising. In 1995, the USTHF adopted an additional logo and new name, USA Team Handball, and established an office and staff in Atlanta, Georgia. In 1995 to 1996, USA Team Handball, Boys and Girls Clubs, and Cumberland Mall of Atlanta, Georgia, formed a partnership and established a Team Handball Youth Development Program. Targeting 18 Cobb County, Georgia, middle schools, the program focused on education, participation, and competition. Over a nine-month period 20,000 students were introduced to team handball and participated in their school intramural programs. The program was capped off with two major competitions. Seven hundred students participated in the inaugural Cumberland Cup, and an all-star team played in the Pastille Cup in Goteborg, Sweden, the largest youth tournament in the world.

The overwhelming interest in team handball during the Olympic Games and the success of the Atlanta Youth Development Program were encouraging and inspiring. Efforts are currently underway by the USA Team Handball to develop and implement an education-based grassroots program that will provide opportunities for American young people to play and enjoy this great game on every level.

Television Docudrama: The Making of Frail Female Athletic Heroines

As the new millennium approaches, contemporary observers of sport have remarked at length upon the difference a century has made in the prospects and possibilities available for women athletes. Following a 100-year history of fitful but progressive growth, women's sport has finally realized what former Women's Sports Foundation President Wendy Hilliard described in the summer of 1996 as "a critical mass" phenomenon.

The enduring falsehood that females are naturally less interested in competing athletically, and the accompanying corollary that others are equally uninterested in watching women athletes compete, suffered deadening reality checks in the face of record numbers of female participants and spectators alike surfacing in the latter part of the twentieth century. The startling 1996 statistic that one in every three high school girls plays varsity sport (compared to a 1970 figure which showed that only one out of every 27 high school girls played varsity sport) bears resounding testament to Hilliard's notion of a critical mass effect. Further, the 76,481 enthusiastic fans who witnessed the Olympic gold medal contest in women's soccer between the United States and China may lay to rest any question as to whether or not women's athletics has the appeal to draw a crowd.

To a certain extent, the image of the female athlete as strong, competent, and independent has emerged to join such traditional and dominant icons as the fashion model, the sex kitten, and the wife and mother as symbols of female achievement.

As Holly Brubach, style editor for *NY Times Magazine* and a sports studies scholar, pointed out in her ruminations on what she called "The Athletic Esthetic," the prevailing views of women as mannequins upon which clothes are draped or fantasy women of the boudoir, contrast sharply with scenes from *Women's Sports and Fitness* magazine where female athletes, "Caught in the act of biking, rowing, jogging, training . . . look as if they refused to stop long enough to have their pictures taken."

Although the female athletic esthetic is one that has become more pronounced and more clearly defined for the American public in recent years, it is also true that another popular image, that of the female athlete as the frail and tragic heroine, has emerged in tandem with this image of female athletic strength. It is no small coincidence that as the women of the 1996 Olympiad, labeled by many as the "Games of the Woman," sped, vaulted, kicked, pushed, spiked, swam, dove, batted, and slid their way into history, the story which received the most exposure was that of Kerri Strug, a gymnast who fought through the pain of a sprained ankle to finish her vault and help secure a gold medal for the United States Women's Olympic Gymnastics Team.

In the actual moment of execution, Strug's vault was the kind of pure act of emotional will and physical strength that serves as a hallmark of superior athleticism. That act of strength, however, was quickly overpowered by the televised shot of her tiny frame being rescued by her towering, father-like coach, Bela Karoli. The meaning of NBC analyst John Tesh's description of her performance as "a piece of heroics that will always epitomize the Olympic dream" was quickly obscured by the all-too familiar image of the frail female child/woman needing the attention of a strong, male protector.

Notably, the replication of this relationship between the helpless girl and the ever-constant strong man was delivered over and over again in the aftermath of the Olympic Games. In NBC's official highlight film, entitled "America's Games: The Greatest Moments of the 1996 Centennial Olympic Games," Strug states in an interview that following her first vault, wherein she initially injured her ankle, she turned to Marta and Bela Karoli and said: "Help me out here . . . What am I supposed to do?" The camera then spans to a forceful, dynamic shot of Karoli who replies: "Listen to me. You can do this. Yes."

The so-called drama of the moment undermines the singularity of the accomplishment by representing Strug's success as a joint achievement between herself and her male coach. In effect, the message suggests that Strug could not have met the demands of the situation had it not been for the help and inspiration of Karoli. In contrast, arguably the other two most recognizable personalities from the 1996 Centennial Olympic Games, long jumper Carl Lewis and sprinter Michael Johnson, who both faced different forms of adversity and uncertainty as well, were shown in the film to take full credit for their accomplishments.

Strug, as the vulnerable female, was again revisited in a commercial made by the ESPN sports network several weeks after the Olympic Games took place. In the commercial, a parody of the "Karoli rescue" is reenacted. In this rendition of the story, Strug is transported around the ESPN *SportsCenter* stage and newsroom, being carried and then passed from one sports anchor to another, almost all of whom are male. Through the eye of the camera, Strug, a woman of certifiable athletic achievement as evidenced by her gold medal performance, is rendered helpless, an object that, incredibly, cannot even stand on her own two feet. In this particular case, the sports media neutralizes female strength by pairing it with female weakness, relying on an image that resonates with the historic and recognizable trappings of the previous century's Victorian views about women as the weaker sex.

The sport media's penchant for casting our most accomplished elite female athletes in the dual roles of brave athletes and frail and tragic heroines extends well beyond the Kerri Strug incident. Originally popularized in 1994 during the coverage of the attack on

Olympic figure skater Nancy Kerrigan, the depiction of women athletes as vulnerable females begging for protection have cropped up with disturbing frequency. From famous female "victim" athletes, including tennis player Monica Seles, tennis player Mary Pierce, and figure skater Katarina Witt, to the famous female "widowed" athlete, Ekaterina Gordeeva, their very private pain has become part of the very public marketing campaign used to "sell" women's sport.

While the notion that women's sport could actually be used as a vehicle to combat violence against women and to inspire women who struggle through personal tragedy of all sorts has some merit, to emphasize this aspect of female athletes' lives at the expense of the sheer magnitude of their athleticism both robs these women athletes individually of their personal greatness and withholds from the United States culture outright female symbols of physical strength.

As the "critical mass" phenomenon of women's sport continues to evolve into the twenty-first century, the remaining ties that bind female athletes to traditionally subservient roles can be severed permanently only if female athleticism is transmitted and translated to the United States public as a distinctive human symbol of power and strength. In the absence of such coverage, female athletes may never be free of the 100-year legacy of frailty that has served to hold women back for so long. *EJS*

Reference

Brubach, H. (1996, June 23) "The athletic esthetic" *NY Times Magazine*, 49–51.

***See Also* The Media and Women's Sports; Media Images of the Female Athlete: Icons in Evolution**

Tennis and Women: The History of Women in the Game

Almost from its inception, tennis was played by women as well as men. A game similar to tennis was enjoyed as early as the Middle Ages by the French upper classes, but it was played indoors with players using their palms, not racquets. The earliest known reference to a woman playing tennis was in 1427. Lady Margot of France was described as extremely adept at court tennis, a forerunner to the modern game.

In 1873, an Englishman, Major Walter Clopton Wingfield, took the game, by then being played by British aristocrats with a clumsy racquet, simplified the rules, and pushed it outdoors onto an hourglass-shaped court with a high net. He patented the game under the name Sphairistke.

In the modern game of tennis, a racquet is used to hit the ball back and forth across a net in a rectangular court. The ball can be hit either on the fly or after one bounce. Points are scored when a player is unable to return the ball to the opponent's court. Points, called "15", "30", "40" and "game," are scored to win a game. Six games compose a "set" but each set must be won by a margin of two games, so the set can consist of more than six games if the opponents are evenly matched. The rules in tennis are the same for men and women with the exception of the length of the match. In men's tennis, a match consists of the best three out of five sets, and women's matches consist of the best two out of three sets. The game can be played as singles (one against one), doubles (two players to a side), or mixed doubles (a man and a woman on each side).

Lawn tennis, as it came to be known, quickly grew in popularity. In 1874, an American woman from Staten Island, New York, Mary Ewing Outerbridge, noticed tennis being played by men in Bermuda. She brought the equipment back home with her, and soon Americans were swatting a ball on grass courts throughout the United States.

The year 1877 saw the first "world championships" among men played at Wimbledon, England. The progress of competitive women's tennis was initially held back by society's views of women. The first secretary of England's Lawn Tennis Association went so far as to call female athletic pursuits "unalloyed heathenism." Finally, after the rival London Athletic Club threatened to hold a ladies' championship, the All England Club held the first championship for women at Wimbledon in 1884, with 19-year-old Maud Watson beating her elder sister Lilian 6-8, 6-3, 6-3 in the finals. Three years later the United States Lawn Tennis Association followed suit with the first women's finals won by Ellen Hansell, defeating Laura Knight in 1887. In those days, the movement of women on the court was impeded by what was considered the proper attire: ankle-length skirts, petticoats, and steel-boned corsets, with a collar up to their chins and sleeves down to their wrists.

Tennis was a part of the first modern Olympic Games in 1896, only to be dropped in 1924 because of a dispute over what constituted amateur level. It did not return to the Olympic Games until 1988 in Seoul, South Korea. The amateur/professional argument was to bedevil women's tennis, as it did men's tennis, for decades.

Among those dominating the early game were English-born, California-bred May Sutton, who captured both the United States and Wimbledon singles titles; Norwegian-born Molla Bjurstedt Mallory, seven-time winner of the United States Championships and one of the originators of the baseline style of play; and Dorothy Lambert Chambers of England, considered the greatest pre-World War I female champion. Hazel Hotchkiss Wightman, a three-time American titleholder, later contributed a trophy to an annual contest between British and United States women. This contest began in 1923 and for many years was considered the women's version of the Davis Cup.

Despite the successes of these women, women's tennis was not taken very seriously in those early days. It took a French player with a hot temper, daringly short costumes, and a lethal net game to put women's tennis on the global map of sports. Many still regard Suzanne Lenglen to have been the greatest female player ever to pick up a racquet. Born in Paris, she was not only the Wimbledon singles champion every year, except one, from 1919 to 1925, but she was also a big box office draw. Her lifelong rival was an American who had a cooler, less extravagant game to go with her personality. Helen Wills (Moody), born in California, conquered most of her countrywomen with her powerful baseline play.

Strangely although Lenglen and Wills were contemporaries, they only met once. The drama was played out in Cannes, France, in 1936, when Wills was just beginning her rise to fame and Lenglen was at the peak of her game. The Frenchwoman, quaffing brandy to keep up her strength between sets, prevailed 6-3, 8-6. That match, before a sold-out crowd and observers watching from nearby roofs, had the kind of ballyhoo that was not equaled until the so-called Battle of the Sexes a half-century later (King versus Rigs, 1973).

Between them, Lenglen and Wills dominated Wimbledon for two decades. Wills won this British Championship eight times between 1927 and 1938, while claiming the trophy seven times at the United States Championships. In her later years, she was pitted against another Californian, Helen Jacobs, in what became known as the battle of the Helens. Jacobs was turned back by her older rival time after time, and when Jacobs finally prevailed, there was an asterisk after her victory; Wills retired because of back pain with Jacobs leading 3-0 in the third set of their 1933 United States Championship final at Forest Hills.

Yet another Californian, Alice Marble, began her rise in tennis in the years just before World War II. She was notable for her style of play, which was serve and volley. No player before her had employed the so-called men's style more consistently. Marble lost the chance to win more than four United States and one Wimbledon title when, in 1940, she turned professional. Pros were not allowed to compete in major tournaments until a player revolt finally persuaded tennis officialdom to usher in the overdue "open" era in 1968.

In the years just after World War II, no single player or rivalry caught the public imagination, although there were many great champions, including Pauline Betz, Louise Brough, Margaret Osborne DuPont, Doris

Hart, and for a few shining years in the early 1950s, Maureen "Little Mo" Connolly. (The nickname referred to her howlitzer-like groundstrokes: "Big Mo" was the battleship *Missouri*.) A new era of explosive strength was ushered in by Althea Gibson, a tall, South Carolina-born, Harlem-reared athlete who became the first African American to play at Forest Hills, and the first to win the championship

Maureen Connolly.
Photo courtesy of the International Tennis Hall of Fame.

there, as well as the first player of color to win at Wimbledon.

By 1968, when players were finally able to accept above-board payments (the stars had been paid under the table for years), tennis had become a worldwide phenomenon. Brazil gave the game the graceful Maria Bueno, while Australia produced long-limbed Margaret Court Smith and joyful Evonne Goolagong. Still it was another Californian, who won her first women's doubles title at Wimbledon at the age of 17

in 1961, who was destined to become a pioneer, popular star, and feminist athletic hero of the contemporary game. Her name was Billie Jean Moffit King.

A firefighter's daughter, King had no patience with the game's treatment of women as second-class players. She was the first woman of the open era to sign a professional contract, and helped lead a revolt against the lords of tennis that resulted in the creation of the Virginia Slims Tour, a separate series of events for women only. On court, she set a Wimbledon record by collecting 20 titles in singles, doubles, and mixed doubles play between 1961 and 1979.

Her most memorable victory was over a man. Angered by Margaret Court's loss in a 1973 Mother's Day exhibition match to 55-year-old hustler (and former Wimbledon champion) Bobby Riggs, King agreed to meet Riggs in the Houston Astrodome. On September 20, 1973, before a crowd of 30,472, the largest ever to witness a tennis match, and a television audience of millions, King trounced Riggs 6-4, 6-3 in what became known as "the Battle of the Sexes." She then used her fame to promote her vision of equality by starting World Team Tennis, a magazine of women's sports, and the Women's Sports Foundation.

In King's wake, two players with contrasting styles took over the pinnacle of women's tennis. They became superstars, and marched into the record books with their long rivalry. Christine Marie Evert was a Floridian with laser-like concentration and a lethal two-handed backhand. Martina Navratilova was a Czech-born lefthander who came to the net almost as much as Evert stayed pinned on the baseline. Over a span of years beginning in 1973, they met numerous times including the finals at Wimbledon in 1978, 1979, 1982, 1984, and 1985; the French Open finals in 1984, 1985, and 1986; and the United States Open finals in 1983 and 1984. Evert retired in 1989 with the highest winning percentage in professional tennis history (.900). Navratilova retired in 1994 with 167 singles titles, more than any other male or female player, and nine Wimbledon singles victories.

As tennis headed toward the millennium, German star Steffi Graf seemed on course to break many of the career records held by past champions. Unfortunately, a crazed Graf fan was responsible for sidelining her leading rival, Yugoslavia-born Monica Seles. On April 30, 1993, during a changeover at a tournament in Hamburg, Seles was stabbed in the back by German Guenter Parche. Seles, ranked Number 1 at the time, did not return to tennis for more than two years.

Despite numerous injuries and a tax scandal that landed her father, Peter, in a German jail, Graf used her crushing forehand, considered the best ever, to become the first woman to capture all four Grand Slam singles titles at least four times. With Graf leading the parade by collecting over $1 million in prize money a year, female tennis players became, by the 1990s, the highest-paid women athletes in sports.

Women's tennis in the 1990s is played by strong athletic women who earn high salaries and receive worldwide sponsorship and acclaim, a far cry from the early beginnings of a century ago. Today a host of U.S. women compete for the "Grand Slam" events (Australian Open, French Open, United States Open, and Wimbledon) and scores of other championships around the world. Lindsey Davenport, Mary Pierce, and Venus Williams are some of the rising U.S. stars on today's professional tour. In addition to the remarkable women athletes playing on the professional tour, millions of women and girls also play the sport for fun, recreation, and exercise. The governing body of tennis in the United States is the United States Tennis Association (USTA) located at 70 West Red Oak Lane, White Plains, New York, 10604-3602. **GL**

Debi Thomas

In 1986, Debi Thomas became the first African American woman to win the United States Figure Skating Championship, and the first African American to win the women's World Figure Skating Championship. Since retiring from amateur skating, Thomas has won three World Professional Figure Skating Championships. Her

Debi Thomas.
Photo courtesy of Mentor Marketing and Management.

performance in the 1988 Olympic Games earned her a bronze medal, the first and only medal won by an African American athlete in the Winter Olympic Games.

Throughout her career, Thomas has won many honors in figure skating, including being named the 1985 Figure Skater of the Year, the 1986 Amateur Female Athlete of the Year, the "Wide World of Sports" Athlete of the Year, and the Women's Sports Foundation Amateur Sportswoman of the Year. In 1997, she received her medical degree from Northwestern University.

TITLE IX: Its Effects on Women in Sport

> No person in the United States shall,
> on the basis of sex,
> be excluded from participation in,
> be denied the benefits of,
> or be subjected to discrimination under
> any education program or activity
> receiving Federal financial assistance.
>
> United States Congress
> June 23, 1972

Title IX is federal legislation that prohibits sex discrimination in any educational institution that receives federal funds. It applies to all programs within the school, not just physical education and athletics, but since its enactment, Title IX has had a particularly great impact on sports programs for women.

In the 1960s and early '70s the United States was becoming more sensitive to the need to legislate against discrimination in many areas. Although Title IX's language is similar to anti-discrimination legislation dealing with racial and religious discrimination, Title IX applies only to sex discrimination against either males or females.

The jurisdiction of Title IX is limited to educational institutions receiving federal funds, but it is highly unusual to encounter a public or a private school that does not receive some form of federal funding. Federal funding not only determines Title IX jurisdiction, but it also puts teeth into the enforcement of Title IX. An educational institution that is found to be discriminating on the basis of sex risks the loss of all its federal funding. In addition, we know from the unanimous Supreme Court decision in the 1992 *Franklin v. Gwinnett County Public Schools* that compensatory and punitive damages are also available to plaintiffs in Title IX lawsuits.

Although Title IX was enacted in 1972, schools were given six years to change their programs and thus be in compliance with the law. During the six-year period, Congress held hearings to help determine and develop regulations that would solidify the compliance process. Also during the same six-year period, groups (such as the NCAA) were trying to exempt sports programs, such as football and men's basketball, from Title IX's anti-discrimination requirements. Their efforts were unsuccessful.

By 1978, full compliance to Title IX by all educational institutions that received federal funds was mandated. At that time, however, very few educational institutions were in compliance. In effect, this meant that females were not receiving the same opportunities in sport as were males, even though these opportunities were legally guaranteed. However, some strides were made. The participation levels for females increased from 16,000 in the 1970s to over 150,000 participants on the intercollegiate level into the 1990s.

In addition to the full access to participation requirement of Title IX, (sometimes referred to as "meeting the interests and abilities of the underrepresented gender") 13 specific program areas in which discrimination is common have been identified by Congress and the Office for Civil Rights. They are the following:

- Travel and per diem allowances
- Locker rooms and other facilities
- Medical and training facilities and services
- Housing and dining facilities and services

Title IX opened many sporting opportunities for girls and women.

- Opportunity to receive coaching and academic tutoring
- Funding
- Equipment and supplies
- Tutors' pay and assignment
- Publicity
- Recruitment
- Scheduling
- Coaches' pay and assignment
- Overall equity

The United States Supreme Court's 1984 decision in the *Grove City v. Bell* case, temporarily removed intercollegiate athletics from the jurisdiction of Title IX. The case involved a number of issues but of significance was the Court's determination that only the sub-unit of an educational institution that actually received federal funding needed to comply with Title IX. For example, if the Biology department was the only sub-unit receiving federal funds, Biology was the only sub-unit on campus that had to comply with Title IX. Other departments could continue to discriminate on the basis of sex. Athletic departments usually do not receive federal funds, and so after the *Grove City* decision, Title IX, for a period of four years, could not be used to force athletic programs to offer equitable athletic programs to their women.

In 1988, Congress overrode a presidential veto to pass the Civil Rights' Restoration Act which, in effect, stated that Congress had not intended Title IX to only apply to a sub-unit of an institution but rather to the entire institution. Thus, Title IX once again applied to athletic programs.

The overall impact of Title IX on athletics programs for females has been twofold.

First, the good news: The participation levels for girls and women exploded. On all levels of education, more females are participating in sport activities than ever before in the history of sport in the United States.

Second, the bad news: Prior to Title IX, 90 percent of the coaches and administrators in female athletics programs were females. As of 1996, 47.7 percent of the coaches of intercollegiate women's teams were female and 18.5 percent of all women's intercolle-

giate programs were headed by a female administrator. The nation's secondary schools mirror these figures.

So, it could be said that although females are participating in greater numbers, the leaders of these participants are no longer female, thus the female participants are deprived of female role models.

Throughout its history, Title IX has been a controversial law as it applies to athletics. It has provided more opportunities for girls and women to participate in sport, but it has also decreased the number of female coaches and administrators. In addition, uneven compliance with Title IX provisions by some institutions has forced time-consuming, avoidable, and expensive litigation. *LJC & RVA*

Gwen Torrence

A member of three Olympic teams (1988, 1992, and 1996), Gwen Torrence won five medals—three gold, a silver, and a bronze.

Torrence was encouraged to run track in her home town high school in Decatur,

Gwen Torrence.
© Allsport USA/Jed Jacobsohn.

Georgia, and was the record holder in the 100- and 200-meter dashes for the state of Georgia. She attended the University of Georgia on an athletic scholarship and in 1987 as a senior, won the NCAA 100- and 200-meter titles Partly due to lack of international experience, Torrence did not perform well at the 1988 Seoul Olympics, but she did not give up. Prior to the 1992 Olympic Games, Torrence won a silver medal at the world championships in 1992, and won bronze, silver, and gold medals in other international competitions.

In the Barcelona Games, she won gold in the 200 meters and the 4 x 100-meter relay, and a silver in a 4 x 400-meter relay. At the 1993 world championships she won bronze in the 100 meters and silver in the 200 meters. She competed in her third Olympics at the 1996 Atlanta Games and won an individual bronze in the 100 meters and gold in the 4 x 100-meter relay.

Track and Field (Also Athletics)

In a bold and daring move on November 9, 1895, the Women's Athletic Association of Vassar College conducted the first field day for women in the United States consisting of five track and field events: the 100- and 220-yard dashes, the high jump, broad (long) jump, and the 120-yard hurdles. Prior to this time, track and field was a man's sport, even though the skills of running, jumping, and throwing are basic to all human beings.

In May 1896, Vassar's field day events doubled to 10 (100-yard dash, 220-yard dash, high jump, 120-yard hurdles, fence vault, standing broad jump, broad jump, throwing the basketball, throwing the baseball, and 300-yard relay). The Vassar women kept accurate records of their accomplishments and awarded a "V" to women who broke records. They were proud of the fact that Vassar College women held most of the world records from the start of women's track and field in 1895 through 1910. For 42 years, field day was held every May. Vassar's venture into track and field sport sparked

competition in colleges and schools throughout the country.

In 1922, the first United States international team competed in Paris, France, in the women's World Games. The women were very successful, but when they returned, Doctor Harry Eaton Stewart, the team leader and coach, was severely criticized by women physical educators. These educators took a united stand against elite competition for women and slowly, but methodically, eliminated track and field from the schools throughout the nation. Track and field struggled to survive through clubs, mainly in large cities.

The first track and field events for women in the Olympic Games were held in 1928. Five events were contested: the 100- and 800-meter runs, the high jump, discus throw, and the 400-meter relay. The first United States Olympic champion was Elizabeth Robinson, who won the 100-meter dash in world record time. But, in the 800, a furor was raised in the press over some women falling exhausted across the finish line, and as a result, no race longer than 200 meters was permitted for 32 years. The women's marathon was not added until 1984. (See the article on the marathon for additional information.)

Not until 1960, when Wilma Rudolph won three gold medals in the Olympic Games in Rome, Italy, was intense interest

Running races are the cornerstone of track and field events.
Photo courtesy of the *Camden Courier Post.*

again sparked in the United States public for women's track and field. Everyone wanted to see Rudolph, the champion of the world, run. With great publicity from the media as the winner of the 1961 Sullivan Award (the highest award given in amateur athletics), Rudolph made it acceptable again for girls to want to run, throw, and jump. Rudolph was an outstanding role model for young American women. She unfailingly exuded gentle, sincere, and captivating charm.

Because of redeveloping interest, and because of the passage in 1972 of the Title IX Act, which guaranteed equal funding in education, including sports activities, track and field was again available for girls in schools and colleges in the nation. A high school girl with an interest and talent in track and field could now receive a track scholarship to a university, an opportunity previously denied to women but awarded for years to men.

As college programs developed, additional events were added to the Olympic program. In 1984, the Olympic events were the 100-, 200-, 400-, 800-, 1,500-, 3,000-meter races; marathon; heptathlon; 100-meter and 400-meter hurdles; long jump; high hump; shot put; javelin; discus; and 400- and 1,600-meter relays.

Events for women on the national level at this time include the 100-, 200-, 400-, 800-, 1,500-, 3,000-, 5,000-, and 10,000-meter runs and the marathon, high jump, long

High jump.
Photo courtesy of the *Camden Courier Post.*

jump, triple jump, shot put, discus throw, hammer throw, pole vault, steeplechase, 100- and 400-meter hurdles, 10,000-meter walk, heptathlon, and the 400- and 1,600-meter relays.

Besides Wilma Rudolph, some of the other great female U.S track and field stars are Joan Benoit Samuelson, Florence Griffith Joyner, Gail Devers, Evelyn Ashford, and Wyomia Tyus. Biographies of these athletes can be found in this encyclopedia.

Junior and senior high schools offer track and field teams for young women interested in the sport. There are also clubs in towns and cities throughout the country. For girls who enjoy distance running, a five kilometer run (3.2 miles) is available almost every Saturday of the year in small towns and cities across the country. Check local newspapers for the schedule of races. Information on track and field can be obtained from the national governing body—U.S.A. Track & Field, P.O. Box 120, Indianapolis, IN 46206, (317) 261-0500—and in the National Scholastic Sports Foundation's *Track Digest*, *Runner's World*, and *Track and Field News*. **LT**

Monica Tranel

Monica Tranel began to row at Gonzaga University after a knee injury forced her to stop playing her first love, basketball. Born on May 4, 1966, Monica began competitive athletics at the age of 11, and so the switch to another sport was relatively painless. Her competitive record in rowing has been impressive.

Tranel has medaled in singles, doubles, quads, and the women's eight. From 1993 to 1996, Tranel won first place in at least one event in the United States National Championships (1992, senior singles; 1993, 1994, doubles; 1994, quad; and 1995, 1996, women's eight). In 1995, Tranel was part of the world championship women's eight team. Results of her 1996 competitions include first place at the Luzerne International Regatta and a fourth place finish at the Olympic Games at Atlanta in the women's eight.

Tranel is the first United States woman named as a lifetime member of the prestigious Vesper Boat Club in Philadelphia, an honor only given to world and Olympic team members. Tranel is an attorney and is presently employed in the General Counsel's Office, State of Pennsylvania, while she continues her rowing career.

Wyomia Tyus

Wyomia Tyus was the first athlete, male or female, to win an Olympic sprinting event twice in a row. She won the 100-meter race at both the 1964 Games in Tokyo, Japan, and the 1968 Games in Mexico City, Mexico. She also won a gold medal in 1968 and a silver medal in 1964 as a member of the 4 x 100-meter relay teams.

Born on August 29, 1945, in Griffin, Georgia, Tyus was a graduate of Tennessee State University. She set two world records in the 1968 Olympic Games, one in the 100 meters (11.0 seconds) and one with her teammates in the 4 x 100-meter relay (42.8 seconds). Tyus also won eight Amateur Athletic Union (AAU) National Track and Field Championships. She was inducted into the United States Olympic Hall of Fame in 1985.

UltraRunning

UltraRunning is a diverse, challenging, and unique endurance event that involves traveling on foot over distances of varying lengths on varying terrains. Technically, anything 50 kilometers (31 miles) and over is considered an "ultra," and there is no limit to the distance or the number of days over which an ultra event may be run. The most common ultra races are 50-kilometer and 50- and 100-mile races. These races may be held on roads or tracks, but most often ultra events are contested on hiking trails in mountainous areas. However, there are also stage races where runners cover a set distance for any number of days in a row (e.g., 41, 45, 52, or 61 miles), and the total time for each runner will be tallied at the end. Additionally, there are also 12-hour and 24-hour races where the distance is not set, but the time is, and the runners attempt to run as many miles as they can within the set amount of time.

To get into UltraRunning, one only needs a love of running, walking, and hiking; a mindset that comprehends the meaning of building endurance; and a willingness to take the time and commitment to the sport. Usually, UltraRunners have run in a traditional marathon and decided to take their

running in a slightly different direction. Although UltraRunning involves climbing and descending hills, peaks, and valleys, the body actually feels much less of an impact from running on dirt, compared to running on the pavement, despite the longer distances.

A common misconception is that UltraRunning always means running. Many, if not most, UltraRunners walk at various stages of the race, especially up many of the difficult climbs. To use one's body most efficiently, a common strategy is to walk uphill, run downhill, and jog the flats. Some people wear trail running shoes which are typically stiffer than a running shoe. The only other equipment needed is a water bottle(s), some energy food, and a flashlight. Many waist packs are available that carry two water bottles and some snacks.

In a typical 100-mile UltraRun, a runner is allowed to have a crew and pacers. A crew usually consists of a few people who meet the athlete at various aid stations and checkpoints to give her special food, clothes, change of shoes, and some encouragement! A pacer is a runner who is not in the race but who is there to support the racer after the 50-mile mark. There is usually a 30- or 33-hour time limit on the runs (and runners will be pulled off the course if they have not completed the run within this time). It is extremely helpful to have a pacer support a runner through the mentally difficult times and provide some companionship. Being part of the crew or a pacer is a great way to learn about UltraRunning.

People become involved in UltraRunning because they are interested in challenging themselves on a number of different levels and because they love being on the trails and out in a natural element. In general, UntraRunners are aware of the variety of physical and psychological states one can experience over the course of 100 miles. There is a saying in UltraRunning that the first 50 miles are physical (conditioning) and the second 50 miles are mental (psychological challenge).

One of the most exciting aspects of ultra-endurance sports is that the gap between men and women's performances begins to close. Additionally, the majority of women in the sport tend to be at 30, 40, and 50 years of age. Usually only a few women compete in the 20- to 30-year age group, and often many women are over 60 years. Having older women competitors may address the level of mental maturity needed to compete in UltraRunning, and reflects the fact that women's endurance strengthens with age.

Thirty-five-year-old Ann Trason is an UltraRunning legend. She has been the female winner of the Western States 100, the most prestigious ultra trail in the country, seven times. In two of these seven races, she was second among *all* competitors. In 1995, she was just five minutes behind the overall male winner with a finishing time of 18:40:01.

To find out more about UltraRunning, contact *UltraRunning* magazine, 300 N. Main St., P.O. Box 481, Sunderland, MA 01375, or call (413) 665-7573. *CB*

Amy Van Dyken

A star on the 1996 United States Olympic Swimming Team, 23-year-old Amy Van Dyken won two individual gold medals and two relay gold medals to become the first American woman ever to win four gold medals at a single Olympic Games. This feat made her the most decorated American athlete, male or female, of the 1996 Olympic Games in Atlanta, Georgia. Van Dyken's gold medal finish in the 50-meter freestyle set a new individual record with a time of 24.78 seconds and earned her the title "World's Fastest Woman" in water. With this record, Van Dyken became the first United States woman to break the 25-second mark in the 50-meter freestyle race. Her 100-meter freestyle split in the 400-meter freestyle relay (53.93 seconds) was the second-fastest split time in women's swimming history. These notable accomplishments earned Van Dyken *Swimming World* magazine's 1996 American Female Swimmer of the Year and United States Swimming's Athlete of the Year honors.

Watching Van Dyken during the 1996 Olympic Games was a dramatic ride. After her first race heat, Van Dyken collapsed because of cramps. She came back strong later that day and continued the competi-tion. Coming back from such adversity is not unusual for Van Dyken. She knows what it is like to fight against the odds. Her extraordinary success in the pool has been achieved despite her persistent challenge with asthma. In fact, Van Dyken first began swimming to relieve the persistent breathing difficulty she experienced from the asthma.

Van Dyken is not only a star performer on the United States Swim Team, but she is also a motivation for other teammates. She has been noted as a tough competitor and a warm teammate, and is known for cheering her teammates throughout the swimming and diving competition.

Born on February 16, 1973, in Cherry Creek, Colorado, Van Dyken grew up in an athletic family, as her sister Katie and brother David were high school swimmers. The United States expects Van Dyken to continue her swimming success into the 2000 Olympic Games and subsequent world championships.

Lesley Visser

Lesley Visser, a pioneer in journalism, joined ABC Sports and ESPN in September 1994. From Boston College to the sports staff of the *Boston Globe*, to CBS Sports, to ESPN/ABC Sports, she has achieved many firsts on the way to becoming a celebrated sports journalist.

Visser was born on September 11, 1959. In 1974, she came to the sports department of the *Boston Globe* on a grant from the Carnegie Foundation. While at the *Boston Globe,* she became the first female beat writer to follow a team when she covered the New England Patriots in 1986.

Joining CBS in 1988, she covered the National Basketball Association (NBA), college basketball, Major League Baseball, and college football on a full-time basis. Reporting its effect on sports, Visser also covered the fall of the Berlin Wall for CBS News in 1989. In 1992, Visser became the first woman to handle the postgame presentation ceremonies at the Super Bowl.

In the fall of 1995, Visser joined ESPN and ABC Sports to cover a wide range of events. She serves as a correspondent for ESPN's *SportsCenter* and *NFL Gameday* programs. She also reports on the Triple Crown of horse racing (Kentucky Derby, Preakness, and Belmont Stakes), college basketball and the NCAA Final Four, college football bowl games, and ABC's *Wide World of Sports*.

Visser has been recognized for her excellence in sport journalism. She received the 1983 Outstanding Woman Sportswriter in America Award and was named the New England Newswoman of the Year two times. In 1992, she received the Women's Sports Foundation's journalism award in the network television category. She received an honorary doctorate from The College of Our Lady of the Elms in Massachusetts in May of 1995.

Visser's interest in sports began well before her journalism career started. In her early years, she was named the best athlete in high school as a sophomore when she captained the basketball and field hockey teams. In 1975, she graduated cum laude from Boston College with a bachelor of arts degree in English.

Volleyball and Women

At the 1964 Olympic Games in Tokyo, Japan, a women's team sport was included in the Olympic Games for the first time. That sport was women's volleyball. The Japanese women set the tone for the future of the game with their performance at the 1964 Olympic Games. Those who saw it will not forget the images of the Japanese women rolling, diving, playing relentless defense, engaging in a superfast offense, and undergoing hours and hours of practice to win the gold medal that year. Today, women's international volleyball is a mixture of pure athleticism and sheer cunning, whereby players on the court use physical talent and intelligence to reach the final point. Although volleyball has many rules about how the ball can be hit and about players being in the net, the basics of the game are fairly simple. Six players defend a court and must return a ball across the net before it touches the ground, using only three "hits." The rules for men and women are the same—only the net height differs (7′4 1/2″ for women—7′11 5/8″ men).

Women's volleyball was not always played in today's aggressive manner. In 1895, an instructor at the Young Men's Christian Association (YMCA), William Morgan, decided to blend elements of basketball, baseball, tennis, and handball to create a game that would demand less physical contact than basketball. The YMCA took this new game around the globe and introduced this uniquely American sport to the world as volleyball.

For most of volleyball's early history, men were not very interested in women's participation. When women did play volleyball, men did not deem it worth reporting. Despite this general lack of records, there is evidence that throughout the early twentieth century, women and girls were playing and competing in volleyball on a fairly widespread and regular basis. In 1901, for example, Senda Berenson introduced volleyball as one of the activities available during Smith College's Demonstration Day. From the 1900s through the 1930s, evidence of women's participation is documented in regional Young Women's Christian Association (YWCA) leagues from Chicago, Minneapolis, Pennsylvania, California, and Quebec, Canada.

The sporadic record of women's participation changed dramatically after World War II. In the early 1960s, women's volleyball became a major team sport throughout the interscholastic and intercollegiate system. The Amateur Athletic Union (AAU) and the United States Volleyball Association (USVBA) held national championships during this period for both women and men. In 1951, the USVBA named the first women's All American team. The 1964 national championships served as tryouts for the Olympic Games of that year.

As the major national volleyball organization, and later the national governing body (NGB) of the sport, the USVBA was responsible for the development of international teams. Players on teams from California to Texas comprised most of the international teams. Unfortunately, there was no consistent training site or coaching. Texas, California, and Florida became hotbeds of competition. Finally in the late 1970s, a center was established in Southern California by a group of young volleyball players dedicated to year-round training and competition. The core of this group later formed the nucleus of the 1980 Olympic team, which was favored to win the gold medal. Unfortunately, the boycott of those Games dealt a major blow to the potential of women's volleyball in this country, as an opportunity for widespread media attention was lost.

Seven players from the 1980 team formed the core of the 1984 Olympic team. This team was led by Flo Hyman, who is possibly the best player ever to play volleyball for the United States. Her style of play and personality brought a new dimension to the women's game. Hyman was six feet five inches tall and was rated one of the best woman volleyball players in the world. Due largely to her presence, the women's volleyball team gained some of the highest television ratings of all the Olympic events in Los Angeles in their silver medal performance. Some current stars are Tara Cross-Battle, Danielle Scott, and Yoko Zetterland. Since 1984, USA Volleyball has employed full-time staff, coaches, and players to represent the United States internationally. USA Volleyball can be reached at 3595 East Fountain Blvd, Suite I-2, Colorado Springs, CO 80910-1740, (719) 637-8300. The game has grown in popularity since the 1984 Olympic Games, and the 1996 Olympic Games marked the inclusion of beach volleyball, a sport that has provided opportunities for women to make a living playing volleyball professionally.

Margaret Wade

Lily Margaret Wade played basketball for the Delta State University team until the university disbanded it in 1932 because "the game was [considered] too rough for young ladies." Forty-one years later, Wade came out of a 14-year coaching retirement to coach the new Delta State University women's basketball team in 1973. She led her team to three consecutive Association of Intercollegiate Athletics for Women (AIAW) National Championships, which is a record, and she brought national prominence to women's collegiate basketball. Wade's lifetime coaching record was 610-112-6 for a .845 winning percentage.

Margaret Wade was born on December 31, 1913. Before coaching at Delta State University, Wade coached the Cleveland (Mississippi) High School WildKittens for 17 years, advancing to the state finals for three consecutive years. In 1985, she became the first women's college basketball coach to be inducted into the National Basketball Hall of Fame. The Wade Trophy, given to the outstanding women's collegiate player of the year, is named after Margaret Wade. She died on February 16, 1995.

Grete Waitz

Grete Waitz, born on October 1, 1953, in Oslo, Norway, is one of the premier marathoners of all time. A household name in the 1980s, Waitz exploded onto the world marathon scene just as competitive women's marathon running picked up momentum. A nine-time winner of the New York City Marathon, Waitz was the first woman to break the 2:30 mark in a marathon after winning the event in 1979. A year earlier, she shocked the world by running a 2:32:30 in her first-ever marathon. Prior to concentrating on marathons, Waitz was a world-class track runner. She held the world record in the 3,000-meter race twice and was ranked number one in the mile and 1,500-meter races for a time. Waitz participated in the 1972 and 1976 Olympic Games, running the longest distance then available for women, the 1,500-meter race. She captured first place in the 1978 World Cross-Country Championships event.

In 1980, Waitz broke her own world record in the marathon, winning the New York City Marathon in 2:25:42. Waitz took first place in the 1982 and 1983 New York City Marathons, breaking another world record in the latter race, with a time of 2:25:29. Waitz took second place in the first

Women's Olympic Marathon in 1984, and later that year, won her seventh New York City Marathon. She won the 1989 London Marathon and competed in the 1988 Olympic Marathon. From 1985 to 1988, Waitz won three more New York City Marathons.

Waitz's success has brought her worldwide fame. Each year, the Grete Waitz Run, held in her hometown of Oslo, draws more than 42,000 female participants. In 1984, she was honored with a statue of her likeness outside the famous Bislett Stadium in Oslo.

With her experience as a marathon runner, Waitz develops and implements training programs emphasizing the benefits of exercise and its value in fostering self-esteem in all people. She still returns to Oslo to coach top Norwegian women runners but lives in Gainesville, Florida, since becoming a U.S. citizen.

Water Polo and Women

The year 1996 marked the 20th anniversary of the United States Women's National Water Polo Team, and the sport continues to become more and more popular among female athletes in our country. Water polo is played in a pool (no larger than 25m for women) by two teams of seven swimmers each. Players score one-point goals by propelling an inflated ball, by hand, into a cage. It is a very demanding sport as players must remain swimming at all times, and cannot touch the bottom of the pool. Before looking forward to the bright future for women's water polo in the United States and around the world, here is a look back at the history of women's water polo.

Women's water polo was played regularly in the United States, and national championships were held until 1926, when the nationals were won by the Los Angeles Athletic Club. After negative press coverage during this event, however, the sport gained a reputation of being too rough for women, and no nationals were held for the next 35 years. The Ann Arbor Swim Club, coached by Rose Mary Dawson, was particularly

successful in advocacy and were instrumental in reviving the sport. The Ann Arbor team, later coached by John Urbanchek, won the Nationals from 1961 through 1963. The goalkeeper for Ann Arbor was Micki King, later a United States Olympic diving gold medalist.

The Northern Virginia Aquatic Club won seven national titles from 1964 to 1969, although the Santa Clara Swim Club (with Pokey Watson Richardson and Claudia Kolb Thomas, both Olympic gold medalists in swimming), took two indoor titles in 1965 and 1966.

Water polo was introduced in Florida by Rob DeVust in the late 1960s, and it quickly caught on. Florida teams won the majority of the national championships from 1971 to 1975, although the Cincinnati Marlins won the indoor championship in 1974 with a team that included Deena Deardurff and Jenny Kemp, both Olympic swimmers.

Anaheim, later to become Fullerton Area Swim Team (FAST), coached by Stan Sprague, the 1978 national team coach, won the indoor nationals in 1975 and 1977, and the outdoors in 1976. Sainte Foy, from

Water polo star Maureen O'Toole Mendoza.
Photo courtesy of United States Water Polo.

Quebec, Canada, coached by Claude Lavoie, won the 1976 open indoor nationals championship event. Merced, coached by Flip Hassett, the 1979 national team coach, won the 1977 outdoors. The 1978 and 1979 indoor nationals were won by Long Beach. Kelly Kemp coached these fine players from 1976 to 1978.

Sandy Nitta's Commerce Aquatics team captured the 1978 outdoor championship and the Commerce International Women's Water Polo Championships held in Commerce, California, which was the first such tournament in the United States and the largest women's tournament in the world. Sixteen teams participated in the tournament, including 11 teams from outside the United States. Nitta, a 1964 Olympic swimmer, served as the United States Women's National Team head coach from 1980 through 1995.

During the 1978 Can-Am-Mex series in Long Beach, California, the Technical Water Polo Committee from the Federation Internationale de Natation Amateur (FINA) was able to view an exhibition game of women's water polo between the United States and Canada, with the United States winning, 3-2. As a result of viewing the strong play in this match, FINA invited five national teams to play at the third world championships in Berlin on an exhibition basis, with the United States finishing third behind Holland and Australia. After the United States earned another bronze medal in exhibition play at the 1982 world championships in Guayquil, Ecuador, women's water polo made its official world championship debut in Madrid, Spain, in 1986. The United States squads have earned bronze medals in 1986 and 1991, and finished fourth at the event. These world championships are held yearly except in the Olympic year.

In addition to the world championships, a number of other international competitions have been established. In 1979, the First International Federation World Cup for Women was organized, with the United States taking the gold medal on United States soil in Merced, California. While women do not compete in the Pan American Games, there is a junior Pan American Championship, which was won by the United States both times it was held. The most recent addition to FINA's competition schedule for women is the Junior Women's World Championship, which will be held for the second time in August 1997 in Plzen, Czech Republic.

Besides competition at the elite level, there are leagues around the United States that sponsor age-group water polo for girls. United States Water Polo hosts a National Junior Olympic tournament each summer, with divisions for girls 13 years and under, 15 years and under, and 17 years and under. Other national championships include the Junior Nationals and the Senior Nationals, both held twice yearly. Beginning in 1997, the Speedo Cup National Age Group Championships, currently a mixed tournament, will have a separate division for girls.

The United States Women's National Teams have been among the best in the world for the past 20 years, and the thousands of women playing the sport in the United States today intend to help the United States stay there.

Many water polo club teams affiliated with United States Water Polo, the national governing body of the sport, have programs for female athletes. If there is not a local girls or women's team, females can participate with males. Girls water polo is gaining popularity as a high school and collegiate sport, with many interscholastic and collegiate leagues officially sanctioning the sport and giving it varsity status. For information about water polo club programs in your area, call United States Water Polo at (719)634-0699. For information about collegiate water polo, request a Collegiate Guide by calling (610) 277-7382.

Martha Watson

An athlete who has an extended history as an Olympian, Martha Watson participated as a track and field athlete in four consecutive Olympic Games: 1964, 1968, 1972, and

1976. Her events were the long jump and the 4 x 100-meter relay. Watson was a member of the 1964 United States Track and Field Team and competed in the long jump in 1968. In 1972 she competed in the long jump and the 4 x 100-meter relay , and did the same in 1976.

Born on August 19, 1946, Watson competed in her events at the elite level for close to 20 years, winning events at many national and international meets. In 1967, she won the national title in the long jump at the indoor national championship and won three consecutive outdoor titles in the long jump from 1973 to 1975. Watson was an Amateur Athletic Union (AAU) All-American in 1967, 1968, and 1969. In 1973 and 1974, she was listed in the world's top 10 in the long jump. Watson won two gold medals at the 1975 Pan American Games in the long jump and the 4 x 100-meter relay. She is a graduate of Tennessee State University. Staying involved in track after her competitive career was over, Martha Watson was manager for the USA track and field teams in the Olympic Games of 1988, 1992, and 1996.

Weightlifting and Women

Although the early history of women weightlifters has not been well monitored, women weightlifters are gaining more visibility and more formal avenues for competition. Women's weightlifting had its formal beginning in the United States in 1980, as a team of seven women competed against the dominant women's teams in the sport: China, India, Hungary, and Korea.

In 1987, the International Weightlifting Federation (IWF) hosted the first Women's World Weightlifting Championship in Daytona Beach, Florida. Karyn Marshall won winning the first world championship for the United States that year. Seven years later, the United States celebrated its second world champion, Robin Byrd-Goad, who won the event in 1994 (114-pound division). In addition to winning the world championship, Byrd-Goad set 10 United States records and two world records (one official and one

unofficial). She was one of two United States Weightlifting Federation (USWF) 1994 Athletes of the Year.

The triumphs of the 1994 season weren't Byrd-Goad's first brush with weightlifting success. In 1991, Byrd-Goad was also named the USWF Athlete of the Year, and was the only United States weightlifter invited to the World Cup Gala in Barcelona, Spain, that year. Only weightlifters capable of setting a world record were invited to this event. Byrd-Goad set the world record in the snatch (one clean motion of the barbell from the floor to over her head) and placed second in the world championships in the snatch that same year.

Although women's weightlifting was not an event in the 1996 Olympiad, it will be a medal event in the 2000 Games at Sidney, Australia. The IWF has three women's age classes: junior (under 21) senior (open), and masters (over 35). With the visibility provided by an Olympic event, the USWF believes that there will be increased interest among women in the sport in the United States. The national governing body is the U.S. Weightlifting Federation, and it can be reached at One Olympia Plaza, Colorado Springs, CO 80909-5764, (719) 578-4508.

Theresa Weld

Born on August 21, 1893, Theresa Weld (Blanchard) was a United States figure skater. In the early 1920s, Weld's daring loops and jumps were sometimes marked down by judges for being "unladylike" at a time when other United States skaters did only a toe hop. In the first United States National Figure Skating Championship in 1914, Weld won the ladies' championship and the ice dance title with Nathaniel W. Niles. In 1920, she won the first of her five consecutive United States ladies' titles, plus the national pairs and ice dance titles. That same year, she also earned an Olympic bronze medal in the ladies' competition in the first of three Olympic Games in which she competed. (Although the first Winter Olympic Games weren't held until 1924, figure skating was an event in the 1908 and 1920 Summer

Games.) In 1923, Theresa Weld Blanchard founded *Skating* magazine, which she continued to edit for 40 years. She was also an Olympic judge who organized and conducted the nation's first judges' school.

Nera White

Nera White made the Amateur Athletic Union (AAU) All-American basketball team 15 times and was Most Valuable Player in the AAU national tournament 10 times. She was named the World's Best Player at the World Basketball Championship in 1957. Due to the nonexistence of media coverage for women's basketball in the 1950s and 1960s, and the absence of archival footage of her play, she is almost an unknown player today, despite her remarkable career. The following quote from fellow All-American Patsy Neal gives a brief verbal picture of Nera White as a player ahead of her time:

"Players who competed against Nera can tell you of feats that have not been matched even by present day all-stars. White could shoot jump shots effortlessly and accurately from center court, as well as tip balls in from five to 10 feet away from the basket. It was not unusual to see her leave the floor from the free-throw line and fly through the air for a lay-up or cover the entire court in three dribbles. Her speed and wrist strength were amazing considering the athletes of that time did not work with weights or use other modern techniques for conditioning."

Reference

Neal, P. (1991). *At the rim.* Charlottesville, VA: Tommasson Grant.

Willye B. White

Willye B. White, born on January 1, 1940, in Maney, Mississippi, burst onto the track and field scene as a 16 year old who surprised the world, and track and field experts, by capturing the silver medal in the long jump at the 1956 Olympic Games in Melbourne, Australia. This performance turned out to be a harbinger of things to come as White proceeded to make every Pan American and

Olympic team from 1956 through 1972. Three of her four Pan American performances yielded medals: bronzes in the long jump in both 1959 and 1967, and gold medals in the long jump and 4 x 100-meter relay in 1963. White won an additional Olympic silver medal in 1964 as a member of the 4 x 100-meter relay team. White is the only track athlete to compete as a member of five consecutive United States Olympic teams. (Evelyn Ashford made five consecutive teams but didn't get to compete in the 1980 Games because of the boycott.) White was named as an alternate to her sixth Olympic team in 1976, bringing to an end a 27-year, internationally competitive, track and field career.

All in all, Willye B. White was a member of 39 international teams, four Pan American teams, and five Olympic teams. In 1988, she was inducted into the Women's Sports Foundation (WSF) International Women's Sports Hall of Fame. She is past vice-president for athletes of the Women's Sports Foundation and is a current member of the WSF Advisory Board. The Willye B. White Foundation (formed in 1992) designs, implements, and funds programs that reverse the downward spiral of girls' self-esteem.

Kathy Whitworth

Kathy Whitworth, born on September 27, 1939, in Monahans, Texas, is one of the most significant women ever to have played golf. In her 32-year career, she had 88 career wins, an all-time record for both the men's and women's tours. Whitworth began playing golf at the age of 15. She attended Odessa College and joined the Ladies Professional Golf Association (LPGA) Tour in 1958. In 1981, she became the first woman on the LPGA Tour to earn more than $1 million. In 1983, she tied Sam Snead's record of 84 official professional tour victories by winning the Women's Kemper Open with a 40-foot putt on the 72nd hole.

In her career, she has been the Player of the Year seven times (1966, 1967, 1968, 1970, 1971, 1972, 1973), was a seven-time winner of the Vare Trophy for the LPGA

Tour's lowest scoring average (1965, 1966, 1967, 1969, 1970, 1971, 1972), and was the Tour's leading money winner eight times (1965, 1966, 1967, 1968, 1970, 1971, 1972, 1973). After this string of excellent years, Whitworth was elected to the LPGA Hall of Fame in 1975. Her last official victory and the 88th win of her career was recorded at the 1985 United Virginia Bank Classic.

During the 1988 Centennial of Golf in America celebration, Whitworth was named "Golfer of the Decade" by *Golf* magazine for the years 1968 to 1977. She has been inducted into the New Mexico Hall of Fame, Texas Sports and Golf Hall of Fame, World Golf Hall of Fame, and the Women's Sports Foundation (WSF) International Women's Sports Hall of Fame. In 1985, she received the William Richardson Award from the Golf Writers Association of America for consistent, outstanding contributions to golf. Whitworth represents the Wilson Sporting Goods Company, *Golf for Women* magazine, and Chateau Elan in Braselton, Georgia. Besides playing on the Sprint Senior Tour, she is currently involved in full-time business ventures and lives in Trophy Club, Texas.

Lucinda Williams

A participant in two Olympic Games, Lucinda Williams was a member of the gold-medal-winning 4 x 100-meter relay team at the 1960 Olympic Games in Rome, Italy. Born on August 10, 1937, Williams participated in track in high school and was named the outstanding senior athlete when she graduated. She attended Tennessee State University and earned a position on the United States 1956 Olympic team in her first year of college. Prior to the Olympic Games in 1956, Lucinda and her teammates set an Amateur Athletic Union (AAU) Championship record in the 1956 4 x 100-meter relay at the National AAU Women's Track and Field Championship. She was an AAU All-American in 1958 and 1959. She won the Pan American Games' 100-meter and 200-meter dashes in 1959 and set a Pan American record in the 200-meter race. She was also a member of the 4 x 100-meter relay team that won the gold medal at the 1959 Pan American Games.

Winter Sports Foundation

The Winter Sports Foundation is a national nonprofit organization of athletes and coaches in winter sports, founded by Olympic skier, Tami St. Germain, in 1992. Its mission is to promote the benefits of winter sports for all. Recognizing the importance of having healthy children in the United States, the foundation works to support grassroots, community-based programs in winter sports that help children become physically active

The Winter Sports Foundation promotes winter sports like skiing.

in sports throughout their lifetimes. It does this by holding events throughout the country that introduce children to these sports in both the summer and winter; by providing resources, advice, and information to community and sport organizations; by compiling and providing information about the sports to interested parties through a variety of communication means, in particular its Web site at www.wintersports.org (June 19, 1997); and by providing financial assistance to grassroots winter sports efforts. The Winter Sports Foundation can be reached at 905 13th Street, Boulder, CO 80302-7303, (303) 443-1839. *PS*

Women in Sports and Events (WISE)

Women in Sports and Events (WISE) held its first meeting in New York City in November, 1993. Sue Rodin, founder and president, recognized the need for women in the sport and special events industry to have a professional organization that would be a forum for networking with each other and that would offer career-related programs.

Membership consists of approximately 1,000 individuals who range from emerging professionals to key decision makers and executives. At regular meetings and workshops, members hear well-known speakers present current issues and trends as well as highlight some of the experiences that impacted their careers.

Career counseling, mentor matching, seminars, and a job board are available to serve a variety of levels and experience. Quarterly newsletters, available to all members, highlight member news and profiles, market trends, anecdotes, industry news, and survey results. WISE chapters are now operating in Washington, D.C.; Los Angeles; Chicago; New England (Boston area); and more are forming in other cities. Growth continues at an exciting pace.

An annual WISE Woman of the Year Award is given every June at a gala luncheon in New York City. The award honors an outstanding female whose accomplishments in a sport-related career have earned indus-

try-wide recognition and respect. As a visible leader who has broken down barriers, this role model has created new opportunities for women in sports and special events.

In 1995, the inaugural award was presented to Sara Levinson, president of NFL Properties, Inc. Other finalists honored included Rosa Gatti, senior vice president, Corporate Communications, ESPN; Donna Lopiano, executive director, Women's Sports Foundation; Robin Roberts, on-air personality, ABC Sports/ESPN; and Wendy Selig-Prieb, senior vice president and general counsel, Milwaukee Brewers.

In 1996, the WISE Woman of the Year was Lydia Stephans, vice president of programming, ABC Sports. Other finalists honored included Valerie B. Ackerman, vice president, Business Affairs, National Basketball Association, and now president of the Women's National Basketball Association (WNBA); Kathy Davenport, vice president, general manager, Lady Foot Locker; Anita DeFrantz, president, Amateur Athletic Foundation of Los Angeles; and Lesley Visser, correspondent, ABC Sports/ESPN. The WISE Women of the Year 1997 was Liz Dolan, VP of Marketing for Nike, Inc. *EM*

Women's International Bowling Congress

Prior to the founding of the Women's International Bowling Congress (WIBC) on November 28, 1916, women's place in bowling was on the periphery of the sport. Part of the attitude resulted from the male domination of all sports during this era and part can be attributed to the unsavory betting environment that surrounded bowling during the early twentieth century. Nevertheless, women's interest, participation, and attraction to the sport is documented as far back as the late 1800s, when women risked their reputations to enjoy a game of tenpins (an early form of bowling). The first United States women's bowling league was organized in 1907 in St. Louis by Dennis J. Sweeney, a bowling alley proprietor. In 1915, Ellen Kelly formed a women's bowling league, again in St. Louis. In 1916, Sweeney,

Kelly, and 39 other women from 11 different states formed the first national bowling organization for women, the Women's National Bowling Association (WNBA), which eventually became the WIBC. From those initial 40 members, the WIBC has grown to over four million members and is the world's largest women's sporting organization.

Catherine Menne was elected as the first president of the WNBA. A constitution was adopted that outlined the goals of the organization. Among these goals were (a) to govern and regulate the sport of American tenpins for women; (b) to promote and expand women's participation in bowling; (c) to provide rules for participation in tournaments; and (d) to establish a national tournament for women. The establishment of a national tournament was realized in 1916, when the WNBA held its first championship in St. Louis. Eight teams competed for a purse of $225. By 1997, the championship tournament had grown to include 16,704 women's teams, approximately 88,297 participants, competing in Reno, Nevada. This prestigious WIBC Tournament boasts prize funds of $2,209,748. WIBC's accomplishment of the WNBA's other charter goals has been just as impressive. Today, women participate in more than 150,000 sanctioned leagues in all parts of the nation, and the instructional and educational efforts of the WNBA (WIBC) have resulted in a variety of learning opportunities for girls and women, including the establishment of the American Junior Bowling Congress.

The strength of the WIBC is the many local volunteers who organize membership services and provide opportunities for female bowlers. The organization's success also stems from its ability to attract competent leadership at the top. Menne was succeeded by Zoe Quin and Jeannette Knepprath, who held the position for 36 years. Alberta Crowe, Helen Baker, and Gladys Banker followed. In 1992, Joyce Deitch became the sixth president of the WIBC. WIBC headquarters are located in Milwaukee, Wisconsin. WIBC can be contacted at 5301 S. 76th Street, Greendale, Wisconsin 53129-1191.

Women's Physical Education Philosophy and Athletics: Then and Now
Interview with Dr. G. Laurene (Laurie) Mabry, Former AIAW President

Reflecting on the Association of Intercollegiate Athletics for Women (AIAW) days, Laurie Mabry recalled two key issues confronting the association during her years of leadership: (1) whether to limit athletic scholarships to tuition and fees only and (2) how to create a governance structure for men's and women's athletics that provided an equal voice for all. In the interview that follows, Mabry speaks of "what was and what might have been."

Issue 1—Scholarships. Mabry supported the concept of limiting scholarship funding to tuition and fees only, no room and board or incidental expenses (i.e., a full ride). When the discussion of providing scholarships was first addressed by AIAW, there was a mixture of viewpoints among individuals associated with the organization. There were those who wanted full scholarships, some who wanted no scholarships, and the "middle of the road majority" who believed scholarships had to be considered due to gender equity considerations. Initially, AIAW had resisted scholarships. As foreign as this position is to today's thinking, it reflected a traditional women's physical education philosophy which held that 1) the cost of scholarships might force reductions in the instructional and intramural programs for all women students and that 2) subsequent external pressures might be placed on athletes as a result of participating in a revenue-producing sport. Mabry recalls the resistance to scholarships, "When cost becomes prohibitive, efforts to raise money and funds become extensive and the primary aspect of athletics *for* the participant may be lost in favor of the need to supply monies to pay for the high cost of recruitment and full ride scholarships." On the other hand, many supporting scholarships did so "because it appeared scholarships, already endorsed by the NCAA, were necessary in light of Title IX to achieve equity in funding practices."

Traditional philosophy: opponents as co-creators of the contest, not enemies.
Photo courtesy of the *Camden Courier Post.*

The first year AIAW was to allow scholarships, the issue was brought to the association's governing assembly as a motion to limit scholarships to tuition and fees only. Mabry felt such a limitation was not allowable under Title IX, because "men were not so limited." She did not foresee that AIAW could so limit women. Therefore, Mabry amended the original motion to limit scholarships to tuition and fees only by adding the statement: "providing men's organizations operated comparably." After much discussion, the motion passed as amended. Later that same day, some of the AIAW executive leadership expressed concern over the motion that had passed. They believed the motion allowed the men's governance organizations to drive AIAW's course of action regarding scholarship allocation. Specifying "providing the men operate comparably," however, could have been a way of lessening

the costs of men's athletics and of changing their programs to become more congruent with the predominate AIAW view. Following much lengthy discussion, another vote was taken and the motion, as amended, was rescinded. With this reversal, numerous member institutions threatened to immediately withdraw from AIAW. That night a subcommittee, which included Mabry as a member, was formed to resolve the issue and come back to the convention floor with a new motion. The original motion ultimately passed, thus limiting scholarships to tuition and fees only but without the crucial stipulation "providing the men operate comparably." This posture held for only one year. The next year AIAW had to reverse the decision and began to allow full scholarships.

Today Mabry believes

> AIAW might have missed the boat. We should have pushed the men's organizations to so limit scholarships. College presidents might have welcomed the lowering of costs for men's athletics, since they knew comparable programs would have to be offered for women in the very near future. If we had pushed that issue, we might have been successful. Today, with women's athletics governed by the NCAA, there is little interest in limiting scholarships to tuition and fees. It is not likely there will be such interest in the future, unless program costs become prohibitive to more collegiate institutions.

Across the nation, high cost has limited athletics opportunities for both women and men. Men's athletics teams have been dropped to cover the cost of providing athletics opportunities for women at institutions where women were previously neglected. Likewise a number of broad-based programs for both men and women have been reduced in breadth to afford higher-cost opportunities for elite-level women athletes in some of the more visible or revenue potential sports. Mabry believed cost containment in terms of offering only tuition and fee scholarships, instead of full rides, "could have reduced the cost of intercollegiate athletics in general. Instead, participation opportunities that were and/or could have been provided by broad-based programs have been reduced for both men and women."

Issue 2—Equal voice structure. According to Mabry

The AIAW, in my belief, should have fought as strongly to develop an equal voice structure for the governance of athletics for men and women as we fought to stay separate. But we never actively advanced the equal voice—equal structure concept, even though it was mentioned in many of our early materials. As an organization, we really did not fully address an effort to establish an equal voice structure to govern athletics for both men and women served by the AIAW, NCAA, NAIA, and NJCAA.

It is Mabry's view that reluctance to advance the equal voice—equal structure concept was likely grounded in the fear of some AIAW leaders that, by doing so, they would weaken the resolve of women in AIAW to remain separate and strong in support of the alternative governance pattern offered by AIAW. Mabry's interest in pursuing an equal voice—equal structure was not to weaken the position of the women who endorsed, as she did, the AIAW philosophy, but rather to "ensure the AIAW ideal would have the opportunity to thrive in a single organization if such became necessary." Mabry believed that such a development would inevitably come to pass. As she stated in her 1980 presentation during the AIAW Living History Symposium at the University of Iowa, "if the NCAA begins to offer a full complement of championships for women, the AIAW will never last in competition with them."

Mabry felt the AIAW membership should have actively pushed for an equal voice structure as strongly as they pushed to stay separate. She based this belief on the premise that college and university presidents would have had a hard time saying such a structure shouldn't exist. Mabry felt "support could have been gained from those heading higher education institutions to change the nature of the NCAA, to ensure women an equal voice and to guarantee women would be equally represented in governance positions." During her term as AIAW president, Mabry's interest in fighting for such a structure was denied. In a communication to the AIAW Executive Board, Mabry expressed the desire for the board to refer the topic, "one voice—one structure," to the general membership for discussion when assembled during her term as president, but she was unable to amass a majority to support this action. "One voice—one structure" did not emerge as an agenda item recommended by the executive board for discussion during that delegate assembly.

Later in 1980 at the AIAW Living History Symposium, Mabry urged more directly that the "one voice—one structure" concept be explored. She again expressed strong concern for the "loss of AIAW philosophy and approach to athletics which might result if women's athletics programs were to be governed by the existing men's structures." The desire by most of the AIAW members of the 1970s, including Mabry, to remain separate won out over advancing with vigor the equal voice—equal structure concept. In Mabry's opinion, "[W]e missed an opportunity possibly to change athletics in general. Women, having been incorporated into all intercollegiate governance structures established originally for men, have not been as influential as they would have been at that point in time, 20 years ago, in an equal voice structure." This, according to Mabry, "was AIAW's most consequential missed opportunity."

Mabry, in spite of reminiscing about opportunities possibly missed by AIAW, credits the AIAW, Division of Girls and Women in Sport (DGWS), and American Alliance of Health, Physical Education, Recreation, and Dance (AAHPERD) (as do most women athletic administrators), for the development of women's athletic opportunities. According to Mabry, "it is likely, without AIAW's full initiation of championship programs for women and the requirement of equal opportunity through Title IX, women's opportunities would not have blossomed as they have within the men's organizations, and the current intercollegiate athletics governance structures would not now be offering programs for both men and women."

Without the pioneer efforts of Mabry, and women like her who fought so passionately to guarantee women's access to intercollegiate sport, it is quite possible that intercollegiate athletics opportunities for women of today would have been considerably less. *MEV*

See also **Association of Intercollegiate Athletics for Women (AIAW); National Association for Girls and Women in Sport**

Women's Sports Foundation History

Part 1: The First 10 Years

A background on the times may be helpful in understanding the urgency and necessity for creating the Women's Sports Foundation (WSF). In 1973, Billie Jean King defeated Bobby Riggs in the "Battle of the Sexes" tennis match and gave the average woman a new sense of her potential ability and power. Despite this boost, women still had a long way to go to reach equality. For example, the use of "Ms" was still considered radical by a society that felt it was still necessary to describe a women's marital status in forms of address. In the same year as King's triumph, Donna de Varona and Suzie Chaffee were in Washington, D.C., lobbying hard for Title IX, the "Equal Education Act" that promised to provide girls an equal opportunity in school and, coincidentally, many more sport opportunities. The Act passed in 1972, but guidelines and enforcement did not fully take effect until 1978, after considerable pressure had been applied by the WSF and other women's sports groups.

At this time, professional women's tennis and golf were drawing credible audiences and sponsorship dollars, but the stakes were minuscule compared to the men's rewards. Once every four years, female athletes were showcased in the Olympic Games, but there were no professional opportunities for women in basketball, softball, gymnastics, or track and field. When Kathrine Switzer ran in the 1967 Boston Marathon, an official tried to run her off the course upon discovering she was a woman. The Women's

International Bowling Congress had three million members, but could not get any television time or corporate sponsorship as men's bowling had it all. Joan Joyce was the world's greatest softball pitcher, but she could not earn enough to keep body and soul together in her sport. These, and many other highly accomplished women, were frustrated by the lack of media attention, sponsorship dollars, and fans for their sports. In the early 1970s, the participation of girls and women in sports was barely tolerated, much less respected or cheered.

These talented athletes knew they were fighting and had fought, lonely uphill battles for recognition of their sports and themselves. By teaming together, under one umbrella, they hoped that they could gain a greater voice. Thus, the WSF was born, to be the collective voice of women in sports. It would be supported by those who had achieved the heights of success but who desired to change the public's attitude toward all female athletes.

The founders of the WSF, Billie Jean King, Donna de Varona, and Eva Auchincloss, organized the foundation in 1975, with $500 seed money in the accounts. The athletes supported the cause in spirit, but they had very little time or money to give to it. Additionally, they were spread all over the country. The task was formidable, but there was one great asset. Early on, the WSF saw that influential people (politicians and chief executive officers) liked to hobnob with celebrity athletes. Trading on athletes' celebrity status became the major means of raising money for the WSF. The first $10,000, for example, was raised with a write-in auction of athlete memorabilia featured in the *WomenSports* magazine. Two years later, an auction of celebrity athlete items was televised through sponsorship by Bristol Myers. These annual fundraisers sustained the organization each year, as individual donations and foundation money were proving nearly impossible to obtain at that time. During the first five years, $25,000 from Colgate was the largest single gift received. It came at a fortuitous time as the WSF was, again, down to only a few hundred dollars in the bank accounts.

In 1978, Holly Turner joined the WSF team as development director. At this time the organization developed a new approach to fund raising. The Foundation became the first nonprofit organization to "marry" sport personalities to corporate interests by designing programs that were attractive advertising and public relations vehicles for corporations. At the time, the term "sports marketing" did not exist, but that's what it was. The first major sponsorship of this type was the 1980 inaugural of the WSF Hall of Fame and Sportswomen Awards Dinner, originally underwritten by Manufacturers Hanover Trust Company and J & B Scotch. This event worked because well-known female and male athletes came to the dinner, attracting the media coverage and corporate support so badly needed. Two other key people aided the event's success: *Today* show hostess, Jane Pauley, and national sport commentator, Dick Schaap. They not only acted as emcees for the awards programs, but they also provided news coverage on national television. Other marketing vehicles such as the "Up and Coming" and "Women in the Military" awards; "Greatest Female Athlete" contest; fitness and sports medicine clinics; educational films and programs; *Women's Coaching* and other guides; and special research projects were developed for Colgate, Coca Cola, Bonne Bell, Personal Products, Ocean Spray, Miller Light, Coors, Revlon, Sugar Free Jello, Avon, M & M, Mars, and many others.

The WSF's physical location was fairly spartan in the early years. The Foundation began in a small room donated by Kingdom Inc. (Billie Jean and Larry King's company) in San Mateo, California, and the executive director, Eva Auchincloss, volunteered her time. In 1978, the WSF was well-enough established to move its headquarters to San Francisco and to feature three paid employees. From that time on, the Foundation expanded rapidly, developing, with the help of Paula Cabot and with volunteer expertise from Dr. Dorothy Harris, an education department. Small as it was, this department was a major source of information on women's sports in America. Interns were indispensable in making the organization look bigger and more powerful than it was. Voice, and indirect representation, at the United States Olympic Committee (USOC) meetings occurred under the auspices of the Boy Scouts' Explorer program; the leaders of the Explorers selected WSF representatives to join their complement to USOC House of Delegates.

The Foundation's first major advocacy effort took place over the guidelines and enforcement of Title IX. WSF put together a coalition of sport organizations, youth organizations, women's organizations, sport personalities, and other celebrities representing 50 million people to take a plea to Washington for Title IX implementation. Meetings were arranged with President Carter, Education Secretary Patricia Harris, and members of Congress. These tasks were made possible with help from Personal Products' public relations agency and the cooperation of organization leaders such as Alberta Crowe, president of the Women's International Bowling Congress (WIBC), and other members of the foundation's diverse advisory board.

In the early days, the WSF was run on passion, hard work, and the dedication of a small staff and friends. Some of the people not previously mentioned who should be acknowledged (in no particular order) are Don Sabo, who helped formulate the Miller Lite Reports; Jim and Sue Peterson, who put together a series of national women's sports and fitness clinics; Marvin Koslow, vice president of Bristol Myers, who sponsored the first televised production of the awards dinner; and Jess Bell, who sponsored the executive women's running clinics. Carole Oglesby volunteered her time as director for the highly successful New Agenda Conference co-sponsored in 1983 with the USOC; Michael Hayes and Arlene Krupinski of Personal Products backed the New Agenda Conference. Elly Lessin's creative talents developed the format for all the awards programs. Charles Shultz and Martina Navratilova gave the organization the first lead gifts of $150,000 each for the "Aspire Higher" campaign. There were many, many others. As is always the case, things do not happen in a vacuum; the support of many friends, then and now, made the success of the WSF possible. *EA*

Women's Sports Foundation History: Part 2

In 1985 and 1986, the Women's Sport Foundation (WSF) moved headquarters from California to New York City, and Deborah Anderson (Larkin) was chosen as the executive director. The move to New York signified more than a change of locale. It represented a deliberate decision to develop the Women's Sports Foundation into a significant force in women's sports and in the general sports community. The WSF needed to develop systems and hire personnel to carry out its business plan so it could enhance its funding capabilities with the corporate community and take advantage of being in the media center of the sports world.

WSF focused on the following areas:

1. Reorganizing its programs into four categories: educational services, opportunity, advocacy, and recognition. The WSF prioritized its programs based on the needs of girls and women and its ability to deliver high-quality products to more people.

2. Hiring and developing a professional, experienced staff dedicated to fulfilling the mission of the WSF and trained in their particular area of expertise.

3. Developing a national sponsorship package (with the assistance of Marty Rudolph and Paula Oyer) designed to sell major WSF programs and provide additional revenues so that the priority programs would get funded, regardless of whether they received individual sponsorship.

4. Realigning the financial structure so as not to rely so heavily on corporate sponsorship, which accounted for approximately 80 percent of the foundation's revenues. The WSF created a plan to create licensing, membership, benefi-ciary, and other revenue-generating programs that in the long term would create an endowment and financial stability.

5. Developing a public relations strategy for each program that would garner millions of media impressions and call attention to the importance of sports for females. The long-term goal was to make a WSF endorsement equivalent to a "seal of approval" that would be valued and trusted.

The WSF did not develop and start implementing this strategic plan until 1987. Instead, the WSF staff immersed themselves in the day-to-day operations of the "Aspire Higher" campaign, the program Eva Auchincloss and Holly Turner had created to "put the WSF on the map." Within one month of moving to New York, the WSF kicked off the "Aspire Higher" campaign announcing that Martina Navratilova contributed $150,000. She urged other athletes to contribute 10 percent of their salaries. Shortly thereafter, Snoopy from the Peanuts cartoon, matched her donation (through Charles Schultz). During that two-year period the Foundation developed partnerships with seven new sponsors, including an ABC televised sports tennis special; organized the first National Girls and Women in Sports Day celebrated across the country and in the White House; created a new grants program for girls; received over two billion media impressions; and established relationships with more corporations, sports, lifestyle and women's magazines, and national sports organizations.

By 1987, and for the next four years, the WSF focused on implementing the strategic plan beginning with educational services as its first priority. The foundation expanded its services each year, sending products like booklets, videos, public service announcements, and other information to individuals and youth-serving sports organizations across the country, reaching millions of individuals.

The WSF conducted, and distributed, three nationally based research studies on females in sport. It produced a quarterly newsletter, *Headway*, with a circulation of 10,000. The staff members also wrote a one-page monthly editorial in *Women's Sports and Fitness* magazine addressing women's sports and WSF issues.

In 1988, the leadership of the WSF organized the New Agenda II Conference—different from the 1983 conference in that it targeted girls issues, conducted the first national Women's Sports Foundation annual membership meeting, and attended approximately 26 conferences, seminars, and panels, reaching over 100,000 people in an effort to educate more sports and youth-serving organizations and to develop their ties to the WSF and its programs.

Additionally during this period, the internship program flourished, and a number of interns were placed in full-time sports jobs. The Foundation continued to fund the Coaches Advisory Roundtable, a group that was created to address the problem of decreasing numbers of women coaches and administrators in women's sports. The Grassroots Grants Program was born out of a philosophy to provide seed money and grants to organizations for programs that promote sports opportunities or important sport-related services for girls and women. The Travel and Training Grants program awarded grants to 279 individuals and 73 teams in over 60 sports. The Foundation also awarded leadership development grants to coaches, athletic directors, administrators, and officials.

The WSF's advocacy efforts included the annual National Girls and Women in Sports Day. Foundation members consciously included minorities in their activities and called attention to sexist behavior and made recommendations for change. In another landmark move, the WSF held a "homophobia workshop" so the staff could understand and feel more comfortable facing the wide range of homophobic issues encountered in women's sports.

Fundraising efforts continued as a major thrust of WSF. This funding was achieved primarily through the awards programs. The WSF's "A Salute to Women in Sports" awards dinner became known as the best sports dinner in New York. The WSF has held successful dinners since 1980. From 1987 to 1991, there was a doubling of attendance at the dinner, featuring over 80 athletes and 800 corporate sponsors and ticket buyers.

Other awards programs of this period include the Coaches Advisory Roundtable (CAR) Coaches Awards, the Flo Hyman Award (given at National Girls and Women in Sports Day), and the Miller Lite Journalism Awards.

In financial terms, during this period, the WSF made significant gains. By 1991, over $400,000 in travel and training, leadership development, and grassroots grants had been distributed.

A national sponsorship package was developed, and in 1991 the WSF signed its first national sponsor, Sudafed. Additionally, the foundation signed Tambrands to fund a significant grassroots sports program; L'eggs sponsored a program to benefit high school females in schools throughout the country. The foundation also signed Lily of France Sports Bras, Continental Airlines, Budget Rent-a-Car, Bike Athletics, and Trans National Financial Services to be official sponsors of the WSF. ABC sports, Olmeyer Communications, the Sporting Goods Manufacturers Association, and Danskin made the WSF beneficiaries of programs they sponsored.

The end of 1991 marked another era for the Women's Sports Foundation. The trustees decided to focus foundation efforts on grassroots grant programs, the creation of a membership organization, and the development of a hall of fame as a home for athletes and place to honor women's sports. Deborah Anderson (now Larkin) left the WSF, and Donna Lopiano was hired to replace her. *DSL*

Women's Sports Foundation: Part Three

By all measures, the Women's Sports Foundation (WSF) has in recent years, again, greatly increased its size and reach. A good deal of this growth was made possible by a committed, new national partner, Reebok, and by the fact that sports and fitness finally seems to have become a staple in the lives of girls and women. At the WSF's 20th anniversary annual dinner, a star-studded cast of champion female athletes was assembled to create "Twenty Challenges for the Next Twenty Years." This plan was a blueprint for female athletes to follow in their efforts to assure that girls tomorrow will not have to face old barriers to play sport.

The WSF produced and distributed 200,000 copies of its college women's athletic scholarship guide with funding from Ocean Spray, revised and reprinted 200,000 copies of *Playing Fair*, a Title IX handbook, and rolled out a comprehensive Speaker Service that provided over 50 champion female athlete speakers for local community events as well as corporate engagements. Reebok created two new television public service announcements and updated three others.

On the advocacy front, the Foundation led the push for Congressional hearings on the Amateur Sports Act with the Foundation's president and chair of the board of stewards (Nancy Hogshead and Donna de Varona) testifying before the Committee on Commerce, Science, and Transportation. Efforts to pass a new federal law requiring institutions to report expenditures on college sports programs and coaches salaries by gender (the Athletic Equity Disclosure Act) were successful. National Girls and Women in Sports Day regularly includes activities such as a national women's fitness walk, a Congressional luncheon, the naming of Washington, D.C., scholar-athletes, and a culminating presentation of the Flo Hyman award. The day often receives over 150 million media impressions.

The Foundation's community awards and grants programs have sprouted in 36 states, boasting 100 cities in which grants and awards recognize the achievements of girls and women of all ages from 13 to 70+. Deserving coaches in 50 cities across the nation have been honored as well.

The WSF's annual fundraising dinner has sold out for eight years in a row, providing about $700,000 annually for foundation programs. In 1996, the WSF awarded over $800,000 in grants to 716 teams and 150 individuals, the second largest grant-giving year in its history. The Reebok Girls Sports Leadership Summit kick-off in Chicago was the first of 15 leadership conferences for boys and girls in cities across the nation. An award-winning video on women's sports issues has been created for the conferences and will be available nationally to all interested junior high and high school programs. The Foundation's endowment grew by $139,000 to its current level of $800,000 in all endowed and restricted funds.

The WSF staff has grown from eight to 21 full time employees and from five to 15 interns. Financially, revenues have increased from $1.8 million in 1993 to $5 million in 1997. This staff and budgetary growth permitted the Foundation to deliver more educational and advocacy services, expand its national and international awards programs to the grassroots level, and help more girls and women with funds to provide them with the opportunity to participate.

Education

Foundation programs educate individual and organizations to expand, improve, and take advantage of opportunities for girls and women in sports and fitness through a variety of informational outlets. The Foundation's resources center, library, and toll-free number can answer most questions about women's sports. Materials that are provided include sports guides and brochures, videos, and research reports. Public service announcements, conferences, and seminars are also part of the educational efforts.

One of the ways the Foundation exchanges information is through the toll-free phone lines. The Foundation annually publishes the Ocean Spray College Athletic Scholarship Guide for Women. The Foundation created the expert packet *Coping with Homophobia: Resources for Use in Women's Sports and Fitness Settings* and teamed with Quaker Rice Cakes to create *Health Tips*, a brochure about healthy snacking for active women.

The WSF also has issued *Images and Words in Women's Sports: Guidelines for*

Female Athletes and the Media, in response to the many inquiries the Foundation received on the portrayal of women in the media.

The WSF now reaches its audience through two additional mediums, television and America Online. In 1995, for the first time, a Women's Sports Foundation event was nationally televised. Sold out for the sixth consecutive year, the Women's Sports Foundation Annual Awards Dinner, the organization's biggest fundraiser, appeared on TNT as part of a 90-minute tribute to women's sports. The Awards Dinner's copresenters, General Motors, Ocean Spray, and Reebok, agreed to support the broadcast through 1997.

During the week leading up to the Awards Dinner, the Foundation rolled out its new site on America Online (AOL). All the Foundation's resources were made available on its AOL site, Women's Sports World, and on Lifetime Television's site. World Wide Web site. Prior to, and after, the dinner, elite female athletes such as Bonnie Blair, Chris Evert, Jackie Joyner Kersee, and Kathy Smith appeared in AOL's auditorium to answer questions about issues in women's sports and fitness. In addition to these appearances, the Foundation's Awards Dinner was broadcast live from the Waldorf Astoria on AOL.

Opportunity

The Foundation offers a number of programs that provide direct opportunities for girls and women to get involved in sports. In 1996, the Foundation awarded approximately $440,000 through corporate and individual support to needy girls' sports programs, researchers, coaches, and athletes competing nationally.

On the local level, the Foundation's Community Awards and Grants Program (CAP) increased to 100 cities in 36 states. The CAP provides grants and awards on the local level to recognize the achievements of girls and women of all ages from six to 70+.

Ocean Spray teamed up with the Foundation as a national corporate partner of the organization. Since its inception in 1984, the Ocean Spray Travel and Training Fund has awarded grants to 743 individuals and 185 teams for a total of $872,345. During the first two grant periods of 1996, $98,000 was awarded to 68 individuals and 21 teams. Of the 280 women competing on the United States team in the Centennial Olympic Games in Atlanta, Georgia, 45 of them received grants through this need-based program. Twelve of those women captured 16 of the United States women's 38 medals. In addition to the Travel and Training Fund and the scholarship guide, the Foundation agreed to work with Ocean Spray to create a national consumer promotion featuring 15 champion female athletes images on over 50 million Ocean Spray bottles.

Tambrands, the manufacturers of TAMPAX tampons, continued their commitment to the Grants for Girls Program, awarding $35,000 to 70 programs, serving girls nine to 14 nationwide. Created in 1991, this program supports girls sports and fitness programs.

The Foundation also teamed up with Spalding to create the Team Ball Grants program. Annually, one hundred grants of either basketballs, volleyballs, soccer balls, or softballs are donated to girls sports programs that have the greatest need and whose members have made significant contributions through community service.

In addition to its grants programs, the Foundation seeks to empower young women and men through its internship program. In 1997, 36 interns supported the Foundation's programs and services through supervised projects and as a result, gathered the skills necessary to go out and begin careers in the sports world. Former interns have been employed by such companies as ABC Sports, ESPN, Girl Scouts of the USA, National Hockey League, New York Mets, Reebok, and Spalding. To provide financial assistance in the training of women as sports leaders, coaches, officials, and administrators of girls and women in sport, Leadership Development Grants were created. Since its inception in 1986, over $52,000 has been distributed. Two of the 1996 grants were given to the Female Basketball Coaching Mentorship Program and the American Volleyball Coaches Association/USA Volleyball Coaching Accreditation.

Recognition

The Foundation recognizes and honors the achievements of female athletes and leaders several times during the year. Athletes are honored with the Flo Hyman Award on National Girls and Women in Sports Day in Washington, D.C. During the annual summit two sets of awards are presented, the President's Awards and the Coaches Award. The President's Award is given to recognize advisory board members for outstanding contributions toward the development of women's sports and the foundation. The Coaches Award was established in 1987 to recognize the "unsung heroine" who coaches on the grassroots level.

The Foundation's largest fund-raiser was the Women's Sports Awards Dinner to Benefit the Women's Sports Foundation. At this time the Foundation announces its inductions into the International Women's Sports Hall of Fame and the Team and Individual Sportswomen of the Year. The Foundation also presents the Billie Jean King Contribution Award, which recognizes a corporation, organization, or individual who has made significant contributions to the development of women's sports. The Miller Lite Women's Sports Journalism Awards are presented to sports journalists for outstanding coverage of women's sports. In 1996, the Foundation awarded the inaugural Wilma Rudolph Courage Award to Jackie Joyner-Kersee.

Advocacy

The WSF is steadfast in its effort to ensure that athletes, coaches, parents, and concerned individuals are provided with helpful information regarding Title IX and gender equity in sports. The Foundation works with sports governing groups, governmental agencies, legislators, and other women's sports advocates to promote sports opportunities for girls and women. *MS2 & YLJ*

World Games for the Deaf. *See* **Deaf Women in Sport**

Significant Events in Women's Sports History Since the Passage of Title IX

by Women's Sports Foundation Staff

Date	Event
1972	Title IX passed, prohibiting gender discrimination in school and college sports
1973	Billie Jean King beats Bobby Riggs in "Battle of the Sexes" tennis match
1974	*Women's Sports and Fitness* magazine is founded
1976	Nadia Comaneci scores the first perfect 10 in Olympic gymnastics competition
1977	Janet Guthrie is the first woman to compete in the Indianapolis 500
1978	Amateur Sports Act passed, prohibiting gender discrimination in open amateur sport
1980	Hundreds of United States women are denied the opportunity to participate in the Summer Olympic Games when the United States decides to boycott the events
1981	AIAW ceases operation: NCAA takes over college women's sports
1984	Joan Benoit wins the first Olympic marathon for women
	The power of Title IX is limited because of the Supreme Court's ruling in *Grove City College v. Bell*

EXHIBIT 1

1988	Civil Rights Restoration Act puts the "teeth" back in Title IX
1989	Debi Thomas becomes first African American woman to win a world championship in figure skating
1991	United States women win inaugural FIFA Women's World Soccer Championship in China defeating Norway, 2-1
1992	Barbara Hedges becomes first woman to head an athletic department at a Division I school
	The Supreme Court rules that monetary damages are available under Title IX in the *Franklin v. Gwinnett County Public School* case
	Julie Krone becomes the first woman to win a Triple Crown Race (Belmont Stakes)
	Diana Golden wins her 10th world championship in disabled skiing
1994	The Colorado Silver Bullets, the first women's professional baseball team to compete against men's professional teams, holds tryouts
	Chris Kromer, Santa Maria (Texas) Junior High, starts as quarterback for her football team
	Bill Koch announces launch of *America³*, the first all-women's team to compete against men for the America's Cup
1996	United States women win inaugural Olympic gold medals in softball, soccer, and team synchronized swimming
1997	25th anniversary of Title IX

EXHIBIT 1 (continued)

Date	Event
1974	Foundation is born in San Francisco
1975	Resource Center and Library are established
	Foundation publishes the first College Athletic Scholarship Guide for Women
1976	Foundation holds its first seminars on sports and fitness for women
1977	First grant programs including summer camp scholarships are established by the foundation
1978	Wade Trophy is created to honor outstanding basketball performance by a female basketball player
1979	Speakers Bureau formed
1980	First Annual Salute to Women in Sports
	Fundraising and Awards Dinner is held
	Sportswomen of the Year and Hall of Fame awards are created to recognize excellence in women's sports competition
1981	The beginning of the toll-free information line

WOMEN'S SPORTS FOUNDATION TIME LINE

EXHIBIT 2

1982	Internship Program established
1983	New Agenda Conference brings together the leaders of women's sports to create the blueprint for the future of women's sports
1984	First "Travel and Training" Fund grants are awarded
1985	Coaches Advisory Roundtable to promote women in sports leadership is established
	Foundation conducts its first research study, the Miller Lite Report on Women in Sports
1986	First edition of the *Parent's Guide to Girls' Sports* is published
	Foundation moves to New York City and revenues top $1,000,000 for the first time
1987	First National Girls and Women in Sports Day celebration is held in Washington, DC
	Public Service Announcement Posters, Study Skills and Career Moves are produced
1988	Foundation's second major research study. The Wilson Report: Moms, Dads, Daughters, and Sport was published as the first large-scale, nationwide intergenerational study of the female sports experience
1989	*Women's Guide to Coaching* published
	Women's Sports Foundation Report: Minorities in Sports is published
	Aspire Higher: Careers in Sports for Women video produced
1990	First "Grants for Girls" grants awarded
	National partner, Sudafed, signed
1991	Winning Combination: Girls and Sports video produced
	First two college scholarships established
	First Team Dream Grants to support high school girls sports programs awarded
1992	Community Awards and Grants Programs established
	Minority Internship Program begins
	First research grants awarded
	Playing Fair: A Guide to Title IX, produced
1993	Foundation gets a "home" in Nassau County, New York
	Miller Lite Report: Sports and Fitness in the Lives of Working Women is published
	Foundation revenues top $2,000,000
	National partner, Reebok, signs on
1994	20th Anniversary of the Foundation
	Foundation passes the $2,000,000 mark in total grants awarded to grassroots girls' sports programs, schools, and elite athletes in training
	Revenues surpass $3,000,000
	200th intern passes through the Foundation doors
	71 Community Awards and Grants Programs are operating in 35 states

EXHIBIT 2 (continued)

1995	Annual Awards Dinner televised on TNT
	National partner, Ocean Spray, signs on
	Foundation launched site on America Online
	Reebok/Women's Sports Foundation Leadership Summits held in high schools through the country
	185,000 members
1996	Revenues surpass $4,000,000
1997	*Gender Equity Report Card: A Survey of Athletic Opportunity in American Higher Education* published

EXHIBIT 2 (continued)

Date	Organization	Corporation	Individual
1980	AIAW	Bonne Bell	Dr. Dorothy Harris
1981	AAU	Avon Products	Gladys Heldman
1982	NCAA	Colgate-Palmolive	Kathrine Switzer
1983	WIBC	Coca-Cola, Inc.	Dr. Christine Wells
1984	Girls Club of America	Personal Products	Fred Thompson
1985	Boy Scouts of America Exploring Division	McDonald's Corp	David Foster

Single Winners

1986	Carole Oglesby
1987	Eva Auchincloss
1988	ABC Sports
1989	A Salute to Women in Sports, volunteers, contributors, staff
1990	No Award
1991	Sara Lee Corporation Vivian Acosta & Linda Carpenter
1992	The National Women's Law Center
1993	Judy Mahle Lutter
1994	Cappy Productions
1995	Christine Grant
1996	Anita DeFrantz
1997	Alpha Alexander

WOMEN'S SPORTS FOUNDATION: BILLIE JEAN KING CONTRIBUTION AWARD WINNERS

EXHIBIT 3

Year	Athlete/Sport
	Pioneer
1980	Patty Berg—Golf
	Amelia Earhart—Aviator
	Gertrude Ederle—Swimming
	Althea Gibson—Tennis
	Eleanor Holm—Swimming
	Mildred "Babe" Didrikson Zaharias—Golf and Track and Field
1981	Glenna Collett Vare—Golf
1982	Fanny Blankers-Koen—Track and Field
	Sonja Henie—Figure Skating
1983	Tenley Albright—Figure Skating
	Andrea Mead Lawrence—Skiing
	Helen Stephens—Track and Field
1984	Marion Ladewig—Bowling
	Suzanne Lenglen—Tennis
	Pat McCormick—Diving
	Eleanora Sears—Polo, Golf, Squash
1985	Ann Curtis Cuneo—Swimming
	Larissa Latynina—Gymnastics
1986	Charlotte Dod—Tennis, Archery, Golf
	Betsy Rawls—Golf
	Hazel Wightman—Tennis
1987	Maureen Connolly—Tennis
	Marie Marvignt—Aviator, Mounteering
	Louise Suggs—Golf
1988	Aileen Riggin Soule—Diving
1989	Theresa Weld Blanchard—Figure Skating
	Ilona Schacherer-Elek—Fencing
1990	Willa McGuire Cook—Water Skiing
1991	Crystal Cranz—Alpine Skiing
	Alice Coachman Davis—Athletics (Track and Field)
1992	Bessie Coleman—Aviator
	Carol Heiss Jenkins—Figure Skating
1993	Kit Klein Outland—Speedskating
	Toni Stone—Baseball
1994	Liz Hartel—Equestrian
1995	Judy Devlin Hashman—Badminton
	Betty Hicks—Golf

WOMEN'S SPORTS FOUNDATION: INTERNATIONAL WOMEN'S SPORTS HALL OF FAME

EXHIBIT 4

1996	Florence Chadwick—Swimming
	Mae Faggs Starr—Track and Field
1997	Barbara Ann Scott-King—Figure Skating

Contemporary

1980	Janet Guthrie—Auto Racing
	Billie Jean King—Tennis
	Wilma Rudolph—Track and Field
1981	Peggy Fleming Jenkins—Figure Skating
	Chris Evert—Tennis
	Sheila Young Ochowicz—Speedskating
	Wyomia Tyus—Track and Field
	Mickey Wright—Golf
1982	Olga Korbut—Gymnastics
	Carol Mann—Golf
	Annemarie Moser-Proell—Skiing
1983	Donna de Varona—Swimming
	Col. Micki King—Diving
1984	Martina Navratilova—Tennis
	Kathy Whitworth—Golf
1985	Dawn Fraser—Swimming
	Ann Meyers—Basketball
1986	Tracy Caulkins—Swimming
	Margaret Court—Tennis
	Flo Hyman—Volleyball
1987	JoAnne Carner—Golf
	Madeline Manning Mims—Track and Field
	Debbie Meyer-Reyes—Swimming
	Ludmilla Tourischeva—Gymnastics
1988	Margaret Murdock—Shooting
	Irina Rodnina—Figure Skating
	Willye White—Track and Field
1989	Evonne Goolagong-Cawley—Tennis
	Joan Joyce—Softball
1990	Connie Carpenter-Phinney—Cycling
	Nadia Comaneci—Gymnastics
1991	Vera Caslavska—Gymnastics
	Cheryl Miller—Basketball
1992	Irena Kirszenstein Szewinska—Track and Field
	Ludmila Belousova-Protopopova—Figure Skating

EXHIBIT 4 (continued)

1993	Mary T. Meagher—Swimming
	Mary Lou Retton—Gymnastics
	Kornelia Ender—Swimming
1994	Chi Cheng—Track and Field
1995	Annichen Kringstad—Orienteering
	Grete Waitz—Marathon Running
1996	None
1997	Evelyn Ashford—Track and Field
	Diana Golden Brosnihan—Skiing

Coaches

1990	Nell Jackson—Track and Field
	Pat Head Summitt—Basketball
1991	Constance Applebee—Field Hockey
	Muriel Grossfield—Gymnastics
1992	Margaret Wade—Basketball
1993	Sharron Backus—Softball
1994	Rusty Kanokogi—Judo
1995	Jody Conradt—Basketball
	Barbara Jacket—Track and Field
1996	Dianne Holum—Speedskating
1997	Gail Emery—Synchronized Swimming

EXHIBIT 4 (continued)

Wrestling and Women

Wrestling is perhaps the oldest sport in human history, with references to the sport going back to the earliest civilizations. In recent years, women have become increasingly active in wrestling.

On the international level, women compete in freestyle wrestling. The growth of the sport at this level has been encouraging. More nations sponsor teams and competitions for women wrestlers each year. The United States has competed in the Women's Wrestling World Championship, sanctioned by FILA (the international governing body of wrestling), since 1989. The United States placed third in the 1996 world championships, its top performance to date.

Tricia Saunders of Phoenix, Arizona, became the first United States wrestler to win a gold medal at the world championships, claiming the 50 kg (110 lbs) title at the 1992 world championships held in Willeurbanne, France. Saunders added a second world gold medal at 47 kg (103.5 lbs) in 1996 and remains the only American to win this prestigious honor. The United States has claimed 16 world medals over eight years of competition. Shannon Williams of Reno, Nevada, has won three silver medals in her outstanding career, competing at 110 and 116.5 lbs.

USA Wrestling has developed a Women's Team USA program, which supports the development of the top women wrestlers in the nation. Athletes who qualify for the team receive monthly subsistence and training stipends. Each year, top United States wrestlers compete overseas against many of the best athletes in the world. Royce Oliver, USA Wrestling's National Developmental Coach, is responsible for working with the women's program. In addition, USA Wrestling also has a Women's Wrestling Committee, which makes recommendations to the USA Wrestling Board of Directors concerning the women's wrestling program.

Women's World Championships

Over 40 nations officially sanction women athletes to compete in international competitions, and more nations are getting involved each year. Japan is the reigning world champion, winning seven of the last eight world team titles. Russia won the world team title in 1995 and finished second in 1996.

Other nations with strong wrestling traditions include France, which placed third in the 1994 and 1995 world championships, and the United States, which finished third in 1996 and was fourth in the 1993, 1994, and 1995 world championships. Norway has finished second three times, including 1993 when it lost the title by one point on its home mats. Other top teams include Ukraine, Canada, Bulgaria, China, Taipei, and Venezuela.

United States Nationals and World Team Trials

Wrestlers earn their way onto the United States World Wrestling Team at the Women's World Team trials, hosted annually by USA Wrestling. In addition to the world trials, the Women's United States Nationals are held each year, featuring the best women wrestlers in the nation. In 1996, the United States Nationals were held in Las Vegas, Nevada, and for the fifth straight year, it was hosted in association with the men's national event. The Women's United States Nationals has grown rapidly in recent years. A record 120 women entered the 1995 women's nationals, almost doubling the record of 66 entrants at the 1994 event.

Age Group Programs

Women competing against other women in wrestling has been a recent phenomenom in the United States. In earlier times, young women usually competed against males on the club and high school level, often facing discrimination and harassment. The growth of women's wrestling in the United States is providing new opportunities for young women to compete in the sport against other women.

In 1995, USA Wrestling created a series of competitions for young women wrestlers, offering an exciting new opportunity for girls to compete across the nation. The 1995 Girls Freestyle Competition Series featured events for girls 16 and younger. At least one major competition was held in every region of the country as part of this series.

In 1996, USA Wrestling hosted the first age-group national tournament for women, the Cadet National Championships in Las Vegas, Nevada, which featured young women from 14 to 16 years old. New programs are added every year.

Rules

The senior-level women athletes wrestle one period of four minutes without a break. Until 1997, there were nine weight classifications for women. Unfortunately, FILA, the international wrestling federation, has reduced the number of weight classes in international competition to six. The new women's weight classes are 46 kg (101.46 lbs), 51 kg (112.43 lbs), 56 kg (123.43 lbs), 62 kg (136.69 lbs), 68 kg (149.5 lbs), and 75 kg (165.34 lbs). USA Wrestling has also developed weight divisions and age groups for youth wrestling programs for women.

Growth

The exciting thing about women's wrestling in the United States is its growing popularity among women of all ages. USA Wrestling membership for women has increased from 760 in 1994 to 1,525 in 1995, to 1,733 in 1996. According to the National Federation of State High School Athletic Associations more females are wrestling on the high school level each year. The organization reported 112 female wrestlers in 1990 and showed an annual increase through 1995, when 804 females competed in high school wrestling programs.

Wrestling for women is making progress on the college level as well. A number of college teams around the nation have female wrestlers on their rosters. In 1995, the

University of Minnesota at Morris became the first college in the nation to sponsor a varsity team for women's wrestling.

Some Outstanding American Women Freestyle Wrestlers

- Tricia McNaughton Sanders, 1992 and 1996 World Champion, 1993 World Silver Medalist (103.5/110 lbs)
- Shannon Williams, 1991, 1993, and 1994 World Silver Medalist (110/116.5 lbs)
- Marie Ziegler Prado, 1990 and 1991 World Silver Medalist (97 lbs)
- Jackie Berube, 1996 World Silver Medalist (125.5 lbs)
- Asia DeWeese, 1989 World Silver Medalist (110 lbs)
- Leia Kawaii, 1989 World Silver Medalist (154 lbs)
- Margaret LeCates, 1994 World Silver Medalist (103.5 lbs)
- Kristie Stenglein, 1996 World Silver Medalislt (165 lbs)
- Vickie Zummo, 1995 World Bronze Medalist (97 lbs)

Wrestling on the Local Level

More young women are joining their local wrestling clubs and school teams each year. In addition, women are also becoming wrestling coaches, participating in USA Wrestling's coaches education programs. For more information on women's wrestling programs, contact USA Wrestling at 6155 Leman Dr., Colorado Springs, CO 80918, or call (719) 598-8181.

Mickey Wright

Born on February 14, 1935, in San Diego, California, and widely recognized as one of the greatest players in Ladies Professional Golf Association (LPGA) history, Mickey Wright joined the LPGA Tour in 1955 and won 82 titles in a 26-year career. Two times she won four consecutive LPGA events (1962 and 1963), and in 1961, she won three of the four LPGA major tournaments. She was voted the Associate Press Woman Athlete of the Year in 1963 and 1964. Wright was inducted into the LPGA Hall of Fame in 1964 and the World Golf Hall of Fame in 1976.

Many have marveled at her longevity in the sport. Wright entered the tour in 1955 and played her last round at the Coco Cola Classic tournament in 1979, where she was tied for the lead with four other players at tourney end. In 1995, she placed third at the Spring Senior Challenge. Her 13 victories out of 32 tour events in 1963 is a record that few believe will ever be touched.

Kristi Yamaguchi

Kristi Tsuya Yamaguchi, an American figure skater, won the 1992 ladies' figure skating Olympic gold medal at the Games in Albertville, France. She was the first American woman since Dorothy Hamill in 1976 to win the individual gold medal. In that same year, she also won the World and United States Figure Skating Championships.

Yamaguchi was born on July 12, 1971, in Hayward, California, with an abnormality in her foot structure. Despite this problem, she was enrolled by her parents, Carole and Jim Yamaguchi, in ballet lessons at the age of four, and at six, she began skating lessons to strengthen her legs and improve her coordination. At the age of eight, she began a rigorous training program with her coach Christi Kjarsgaard-Ness, which included one dance class every week. This dance training proved to be helpful because of the artistry involved in women's figure skating. Dorothy Hamill, the 1976 Olympic gold medalist in ladies' figure skating, was Yamaguchi's inspiration and role model for figure skating.

Besides her success in ladies' singles, Yamaguchi was an accomplished pairs skater. In 1983, she teamed up with Rudy Galindo, and under the direction of coach Jim Hulick,

the pair enjoyed success for the first time in 1985, when they finished fifth in the United States Junior Championships. With Galindo, she won the junior pairs title at the United States Figure Skating Championships in 1986 and the 1988 World Junior Figure Skating Championships. Amazingly enough, in that same competition, she won the singles title. These wins influenced the Women's Sports Foundation's decision to name her the "Up and Coming Artistic Athlete of the Year." In 1989 at the United States Figure Skating Championships in Baltimore, Maryland, she and her partner won the pairs title, and she received a silver medal in the singles competition, becoming the first woman in 35 years to win two medals at the National Championships.

After 1990, Yamaguchi concentrated on singles competition, earning national recognition for the technical difficulty of her routines. Her performances continued to improve, and in 1992, she swept the US and world championships and won the gold medal at the 1992 Olympics. Her Olympic success led to a professional skating career and to several commercial endorsements.

Sheila Young

Sheila Young (Ochowicz), born on October 14, 1950, in Birmingham, Michigan, is one of America's greatest speedskaters and cyclists. She set world records in both speedskating and cycling and was the first female skater to win three medals in the same Olympic Games. This feat was accomplished in 1976 at the Winter Olympic Games in Innsbruck, Austria, when she won the gold medal in the 500-meter race, setting an Olympic record of 42.76 seconds; she then took second place in the 1,500-meter race, missing the gold medal by a mere eight-tenths of a second, and placed third in the 1,000-meter race.

Sheila Young burst onto the American cycling and skating circuit in 1971 when she won both the national speedskating and the national cycling titles. In 1973, she performed a rare double, bringing home gold medals in the world sprint championships in both skating and cycling. In skating, she set a world record in the 500-meter race with a time of 40.68 seconds. Unfortunately for Young, cycling was not yet an Olympic sport during the years she was competing. Following her retirement from competition in the early 1980s, Young served on the boards of directors of the United States Olympic Committee (USOC) and the United States Cycling Federation.

Young Women's Christian Association of the USA: Grassroots Programs for Girls

"I want to play [basketball] as long as I can. [When I make a basket] it feels like I just won a medal."

Jennifer Brown, eight years old, Young Women's Christian Association (YWCA) of Greenville, South Carolina, 1995

"You feel their spirit and enthusiasm. It reminds you of what you do it for. It brings you back to [the fact that] you're doing it for the pure love of the game and love of the sport."

Amy Dougherty: Volunteer Coach for the YWCA of Schenectady, New York, and Union College Player, 1995.

". . . to empower women and girls and to eliminate racism."

This phrase is a key part of the mission of the YWCA.

The YWCA envisions sport and physical education as a way to develop physical and psychological strength. Historically, the YWCA has been at the forefront in creating opportunity for girls and women to increase their power and self-esteem.

Pioneering Promotion of "Positive Health"

The YWCA has been a pioneer in promoting physical fitness and confronting issues of sexuality for girls and women. Women in the late 1800s were considered frail, unable to endure six weeks of typing lessons and certainly not strong enough for active sports. To counter this concept, the Boston YWCA offered a course in calisthenics for young women and held a women's track meet in 1877. By 1890, several YWCAs had gymnastics, and the Buffalo YWCA introduced formal swimming instruction in its pool in 1905. On a broader level, the YWCA sponsored the first International Conference for

YWCA promotes grassroots activities for girls.
Photo courtesy of Gini Alvord.

Women Physicians in 1919, making strides with their groundbreaking discussions, mainly relating to women's sexuality and mental health. Recently, for more than three decades, "positive health" has become the watchword for the YWCA, as its physical education program became an important venue for its efforts to empower women.

YWCA Current Programs

Through participation in sport and fitness, girls gain a greater sense of self-esteem and pride. Studies have shown that most women who hold leadership positions in the workplace have participated in sport at one time or another. Sport can instill a sense of discipline, teamwork and can develop strong communication and leadership skills. However, YWCA philosophy holds that, most importantly, girls should participate in sports because it is fun. Currently, YWCAs around the country provide opportunities for girls to develop their social, athletic, and leadership skills through sports and programs such as the fol-

One of many activities sponsored by the YWCA.
Photo courtesy of Gini Alvord.

lowing: The YWCA/NIKE Sports Program (for basketball and volleyball), and grassroots programs focusing on field hockey, aquatics, fencing, and rhythmic gymnastics. In 1994, the following statistics were recorded: 257 YWCAs offered activities (from aerobics to weightlifting) to over 525,000 participants; 219 YWCAs offered healthy lifestyle education (weight control workshops, blood pressure screening, and the like) to over 275,000 participants; and 180 YWCAs provided swimming instruction to over 270,000 participants.

YWCA National Initiatives

Through the support of NIKE, Inc., the YWCA of the USA has initiated two national programs: the YWCA/NIKE Sports Program and the New Face of Fitness program. The former has produced basketball and volleyball leagues throughout the country. In its first year, 26 basketball programs were funded, reaching over 1,700 girls throughout the nation. This five-year partnership with NIKE will also include a YWCA national basketball training program and the production of a basketball video. In a society that still does not provide girls and boys with comparable opportunity to participate in sports, this exciting new program is much needed. The program targets girls of diverse backgrounds who are between the ages of nine and 14 years, as girls in this age group are more likely than other girls to drop out of sports due to outside influences. The YWCA/NIKE Sports Program provides an alternative to negative influences such as gangs or drugs and to problems such as teenage pregnancy. The program has provided girls with the opportunity to discover their potential, make friends, and have fun.

The second program, called New Face of Fitness, is an innovative health and wellness training program that includes exercise, lifestyle modification, and support groups. Designed by Dee Hakala, winner of the 1994 NIKE Fitness Innovation Award, this program addresses stereotypes about fitness and body shapes by emphasizing that fitness and health comes in all shapes and sizes. These two programs are a perfect match with the YWCA mission, empowering women and girls and eliminating racism by building self-confidence and physical fitness and by promoting a healthy lifestyle.

YWCA National Collaborations

The YWCA is one of five organizations involved in a national collaboration to celebrate National Girls and Women in Sport Day (NGWSD). Along with Girls Incorporated, Girls Scouts of the USA, National Association for Girls and Women in Sport, and the Women's Sports Foundation, the YWCA helps to organize this day, which began as a commemorative to the great Olympic volleyball player, Flo Hyman. Not only was Hyman a great athlete, but she dedicated much of her time and energy to lobbying the passage of the Civil Rights Restoration Act, which restored protection against sex discrimination in high school and college athletic programs. Each year, a female athlete is awarded the Flo Hyman Memorial Award, honoring Flo Hyman's "dignity, spirit and commitment to excellence." (Community Action Kit, 1997, p. S-18.) Today, this five-organization collaboration continues the major advocacy effort to have Congress pass the resolution to make National Girls and Women in Sport Day an "official" event and to maintain and implement Title IX of the Education Act of 1972, which promotes gender equity in sports.

In keeping the tradition of being at the forefront of empowering women, the YWCA became a member of the United States Olympic Committee in 1988. To date, the YWCA is the only national women's organization to hold a seat on the USOC Board of Directors as part of the Community-based/Military Sport Council.

The YWCA also supports organizations and programs that target girls and youth of color. The YWCA collaborates with the Black Women in Sport Foundation and the Arthur Ashe Athletic Association, which offer mentoring opportunities, making efforts to provide positive role models. The Peter Westbrook Foundation and Wendy Hilliard's Rhythmic Gymnastics are pilot programs sponsored by the YWCA. These grassroots programs encourage girls and boys of color to participate in fencing and rhythmic gymnastics. The fencing program of Peter Westbrook, (a five-time Olympian) has produced participants in the 1996 junior world championships, as well as its first national champion in junior men's saber. Wendy Hilliard was the first African American Rhythmic Gymnastics National Team member in 1978. She, in turn, coached Aliane Baquerot, a 1996 Olympian. Both programs provide youth in New York City the opportunity to participate and excel in these two nontraditional sports.

The YWCA has been a major force in the world of women and sport. By creating opportunity for girls and women from diverse backgrounds, the YWCA has remained at the forefront of providing a safe haven where girls and women can go to build their self-esteem, maintain a healthy lifestyle, and play ball.

The YWCA of the USA is a national women's membership organization with community and student associations in 3,363 locations in all 50 states. *AA & NSC*

References

Guttman, A. (1991). *Women's sports: A history*. New York: Columbia University Press.

Sims, M. S. (1950). *The YWCA: An unfolding purpose*. New York: Woman's Press.

YWCA Publications:

Southard, H. (1992). The story of the YWCA. An Exhibition of YWCA Historic Photographs and Memorabilia: Women First For 135 Years 1858-1993, The Writing Supplement. Enterprise Press. *Interchange, 21*(1), 4. (1995/1996, Winter).

Z

Z-A Postscript: Freedom to Change

In 1993, at age 36, I won two national championships in skydiving. Shortly after the final scores were posted, one of my teammates said to me, "Jan you ought to get married now and have a baby. You would be good at that." I was still basking in the thrill of victory, and he judged me on my ability to bear offspring.

Incredible as this comment was, it epitomizes attitudes towards women athletes. Men are applauded and heralded when they step into the winner's circle. All too often, women are berated, and their accomplishments are trivialized. Women are perceived to be nothing until they have children.

Social customs and expectations are difficult obstacles to change. We must bring about change by encouragement, providing conducive learning environments and providing role models. We must explain the benefits of sports and physical activity and how the skills in teamwork and networking carry over into our everyday life.

Encouragement is more than a "Go get 'em" cheer. It means helping women decide on their own destiny, insisting that they not sell out their dreams for those of another because "it's expected of them." We all have made choices that have deferred our ambitions for some other pursuit. The key to these decisions is that they are made with a full knowledge of the tradeoff and the consequences. Many of us regret the things we did not do, as compared to the things we have done. Encourage people to live each day to its fullest and prepare for tomorrow.

Conducive learning environments facilitate growth and can precipitate tremendous energy. In the environment of sport, women can grow in amazing ways. Women prefer peer to peer environments in which no one is "above" anyone else, and we can create that in sports. Many women have not had the benefit of team sports as a youth, or even as an adult. A team works towards team goals, not for the glory of an individual. Women on teams can learn to describe the things "done right" during the game or the play. We can learn to compliment those who pull off a great play. We can learn to show teammates how to find a way to make a play better; what can be done differently to be faster. We can learn to acknowledge that everyone on the team flubs a play at one time or another. We need to be able to accept each teammate as an individual, regardless of strengths or weaknesses. We must ask our-

Follow your dream.
Photo courtesy of Gini Alvord.

Role models are those heroines who we admire and sometimes aspire to be like. We need to tell the story of those who helped us learn and those who inspired us. Those women who have been the first, blazing new ground, have gone unnoticed for too long. Tell their stories. Shout about their victories and explain that they did it against all odds. Tell the stories of women who pursued their dreams, determined their own destiny, and did it full of confidence because they played sport.

Physical activity and sport benefits the whole person, not just the athlete inside. The entire body feels better after exercise. The mind is awake and alive. We think better and faster when we exercise regularly. We can use the networking skills from team sports in the business world. Above all else, one's self-confidence grows tremendously.

Sport is for women. We can achieve greatness in sport. We can tell the stories of women athletes that validate women's accomplishments and perpetuate a new vision of women's abilities, autonomy, and self-determination. Here women in sport will find the courage and daring to follow their own goals. *JM*

selves, "What can I do better on the next play?" All these "team" skills learned in sport are transferable to our personal and career lives.

Mildred Didrikson Zaharias. *See* **Mildred "Babe" Didrikson**

Suggested Readings

Archery

Haywood, K.M., & Lewis, C.F. (1997). *Archery: Steps to success* (2nd ed.). Champaign, IL: Human Kinetics.

Kenny, K. (1982). The realm of sports and the athletic woman 1850-1900. In R. Howell (ed.), *Her story in sport: A historical anthology of women in sports* (pp. 107–140). West Point, NY: Leisure Press.

Badminton

Girce, T. (1996). *Badminton: Steps to success*. Champaign, IL: Human Kinetics.

Hales, D. (1992). Different beginnings: Women and men weren't equals in early days of U.S. badminton. *Badminton-U.S.A, 51*(3), 29–30.

Baseball

Berlage, G.I. (1996). *Women baseball: The forgotten history*. Westport, CT: Praeger.

Gregorich, B. (1993). *Women at play: The story of women in baseball*. New York: Harcourt, Brace, & Co.

Macy, S. (1993). *A whole new ball game: The story of the all-American girls professional baseball league*. New York: Puffin Books.

Basketball

Beran, J.A. (1993). *From six-on-six to full court press: A century of Iowa girl's basketball*. Ames, IA: Iowa State University Press.

Griffin, M. (1995). *To be the best: 1995 Kodak women's all-America basketball team*. (videocassette)

Harris, S.L. (1996). Jump-starter. The roots of women's college basketball. *Sporting News, 220*(4), 47.

Lieberman-Cline, N., & Roberts, R. (1996). *Basketball for women: Becoming a complete player*. Champaign, IL: Human Kinetics.

Biathlon

Brown, N. (1980). Basic elements of biathlon training. *Journal of the United States Ski Coaches Association, 3*(4), 220–24.

Niinimaa, V.M.J. (1988). *Biathlon handbook*. Calgary, Alberta: Biathlon Alberta.

Sisson, M. (1989). Biathlon 101: Basic run training. *Triathlete*, 26–27.

Souza, K., & Babbitt, B. (1989). *Biathlon: Training and racing techniques*. Chicago: Contemporary Books.

Bowling

Johnson, C. (1994). *Bowling (lifetime sport and fitness)*. Scottsdale, AZ: Gorsuch Scarisbrick.

Strickland, R.H. (1996). *Bowling: Steps to success* (2nd ed.). Champaign, IL: Human Kinetics.

Boxing

Collins, N. (August, 1996). No longer the weaker sex. *Ring* 75(8), 40–42,53–55.

Farhood, S., & Collins, N. (October, 1996). What's good about boxing . . . and what's bad. *Ring*, 75(10), 27–47.

USA Boxing. (1995). *Coaching Olympic style boxing*. Carmel, IN: Cooper.

Canoeing

Gullion, L. (1994). *Canoeing*. Champaign, IL: Human Kinetics

Wyatt, J. M. (1989). Women in paddling. Four women share their perspective on the sport. *Canoe*, 17(1), 32, 34–37.

Curling

Gallagher, T. (May, 1989). Ten things you never knew about curling. *Sport*, 80, 86.

Pezer, V., & Brown, M. (1982). Some psychological determinants of curling performance. *Perceptual and Motor Skills*, 55(3), 1115–27.

Cycling, Road

Albert, E. (1991). Riding a line: Competition and cooperation in the sport of bicycle racing. *Sociology of Sport Journal*, 8(4), 341–61.

Burke, E.R. (1996). *Science of cycling*. Champaign, IL: Human Kinetics

Crooks, D. (1997). Road training for women. Build endurance, strength and power—then race to get better at racing. *VeloNews*, 26(1), 53.

Grandjean, A.C., & Ruud, J. S. (1994). Nutrition for cyclists. *Clinics in Sports Medicine*, 13(1), 235–47.

Mount, G. (1993, May). Tips for beginning women racers. *VeloNews*, 22(8), 73–74

———. (1996). Basic road training. *VeloNews*, 25(1), 15.

Road racing. A beginner's guide. *Cycling Weekly*, 5258, 3–31.

Seip, T.L. (1995, March). Back in fashion: After several lean years women's racing is making a comeback. *Winning Bicycling Illustrated*, 137, 27–29.

Woods, D., & Guinness, R. (1995). *The Dean Woods manual of cycling*. Pymble, N.S.W: Angus & Robertson.

Cycling, Track

Burke, E.R. (1994). Road and track cycling. In D.R. Lamb (ed.), *Physiology and nutrition for competitive sport*. Carmel, IN: Cooper.

Foster, B. (1983, November). Foster on sprinting. *International Cycle Sport*, 186, 26-30.

Robinson, S. (1995, March). The track bike. *Cycling Weekly*, 5374, 26–27.

Diving

Boda, W. (June, 1993). Springboard diving: improving the takeoff, spin, and entry. *Strategies*, 6(8), 19, 21–22

———. (1996, May/June). Innovative springboard hurdling techniques. *Inside-USA-diving*, 4(2), 9–11

Brown, C. (July, 1995). Springboard diving on the rebound: five steps to a safe and successful program. *Parks & Recreation*, 30(7), 52–56

Darda, G.E. (1985). Springboard diving. In T.K. Cureton. (ed.), *Human performance: efficiency and improvements in sports, exercise and fitness* (pp. 460–73). Reston, VA: American Alliance for Health, Physical Education, Recreation, and Dance.

Fairbanks, A.R. (1976). Springboard and platform diving. In C.P. Yost (ed.), *Sports safety: accident prevention and injury control in physical education, athletics, and recreation* (pp. 178-85). Washington, DC: AAHPER.

Kooi, B.W., & Kuipers, M. (1994). The dynamics of springboards. *Journal of Applied Biomechanics, 10*(4), 335–51.

McCready, J. (1986). What goes up must come down: the art and mechanics of springboard diving. *New Zealand Journal of Health, Physical Education & Recreation, 19*(3), 17–24

Michales, L., & Kerr, B. (March, 1980). Mechanical principles behind springboard and platform diving. *Swimming World and Junior Swimmer, 21*(3), 20–21

Smith, C.J., & Reardon, E.V. (1978). *Springboard diving fundamentals*. Springfield, MA: Springfield Offest.

Smith, D., & Bender, J.H. (1973). *Illustrated guide to diving*. London, England: W. Luscombe.

Still, S., & Carter, C.A. (1979). *Springboard and highboard diving: training, techniques and competition*. London, England: Pelham Books.

Equestrian

Bayler-Tischler, C. (July, 1980). Start riding right. *Dressage and CT, 17*(7), 16–18.

Brande, A. (1973). *Modern riding: Walk, trot, canter, gallop*. East Ardley, England: EP.

Francis, B. (September, 1982). From trot to canter. *Horse and Rider, 33*(367), 32–33.

Hill, C. (1992, January). Establishing ground rules. *Horse and Rider*, 52–53, 69.

Trent, R.B.; Adrian, T.M.; & Burke-Trent, E. (1985). English riding as a woman's sport: The social psychology of the equestrienne. In A.L. Reeder and J.R. Fuller (eds.), *Women in sport: Sociological and historical perspectives* (pp. 55–72). Atlanta, GA: West Georgia College Studies in the Social Sciences.

Extreme Sports

Brouwer, S. (1996). *Snowboarding . . . to the extreme-rippin'*. Wordbooks.

Guthrie, R. (1992). *Hotdogging and snowboarding*. Minneapolis, MN: Capstone Press.

Gutman, B. (1997). *Skateboarding to the extreme*. New York, NY: Tor Books.

Italia, B. (1993). *Skiing on the edge*. Minneapolis, MN: Abdo and Daughters.

Schoemaker, J. (1995). *Skateboarding streetstyle*. Minneapolis, MN: Capstone Press.

Schultheis, R. (1984). *Bone games*. New York, NY: Breakaway Books.

Fencing

Curry, N.L. (1984). *Fencing book: A comprehensive manual for developing fencing skills and fundamentals*. New York: Leisure Press.

O'Connor, D.C. (1980). Fencing. *Journal of Physical Education and Recreation, 51*(1), 62–63.

Pitman, B. (1988). *Fencing techniques of foil, epee, and sabre*. Marlborough, Wilts: Crowood Press.

Rosnet, E. (1993). Psychological characteristics and performance in young women fencers. In S. Serpa (ed.), *Proceedings: VIII World Congress of Sport Psychology*, 746–49.

Field Hockey

French, L. (1991). *How to play hockey: A step-by-step guide*. Norwich, CT: Jarrold Publishers.

Gutman, B. (1990). *Field hockey: Start right and play well*. Collinwood, Ontario: Sunders Book.

Figure Skating

Bass, H. (1979). *Ice skating for pleasure*. Toronto, Canada: Gage.

Dedic, J. (1982). *Single figure skating for beginners and champions* (2nd ed.). Olympia, Prague: International Skating Union.

Kuenzle-Watson, K., & DeArmond, S.J. (1996). *Ice skating: Steps to success*. Champaign, IL: Human Kinetics.

Maier, M. (1982). *How to succeed at skating*. New York: Sterling.

Ogilvie, R.S. (1968). *Basic ice skating skills: An official handbook prepared for the United States Figure Skating Association*. Phipadephia, PA: Lippincott

Stark-Slapnik, N. (1986). *Figure it out :Think your way to skating great figures*. Cleveland, OH: Starsports.

Gymnastics, Artistic

Australian Gymnastic Federation. (1993). *Women's artistic gymnastics, levels 1–10*. Melbourne, Australia: Australian Gymnastic Federation

Turoff, F. (1991). *Artistic gymnastics: A comprehensive guide to performing and teaching skills for beginners and advanced beginners*. Dubuque, IA: William Brown.

Gymnastics, Rhythmic

Canadian Rhythmic Sportive Gymnastic Federation (1993). *Basic development program*. Gloucester, Ontario: Canadian Rhythmic Sportive Gymnastic Federation.

Jackman, J. & Currier, B. (1992). *Gymnastic skills and games*. London, England: A & C Black.

Vyse, M. & Papas, M. (1992). *An introduction to rhythmic sportive gymnastics*. Brisbane, Australia: Boolarong.

Winter, J. (1992). *Rhythmic sportive gymnastics: Conditioning manual*. Victoria, Australia: Australian Gymnastic Federation.

Ice Hockey

Belmonte, V. (1995). *USA hockey coaching education program associate level manual. Handbook I: Methods of effective coaching*. Carmel, IN: Cooper.

Howell, L. (1996). *Analysis and design of women's protective ice hockey equipment*. Proceeding of the Human Factors Society 30th Annual Meeting. Dayton, Ohio, September 29-October 3, 1986, Volume 1, 528–30.

Theberge, N. (1995). Gender, sport, and construction of community: A case study from women's ice hockey. *Sociology of Sport Journal, 12*(4), 389–402.

Twist, P. (1997). *Complete conditioning for ice hockey*. Champaign, IL: Human Kinetics.

Inline Skating (Roller Skating)

Edwards, C. (1996). *The young inline skater*. New York, NY: DK.

Nottingham, S., & Dedel, E. (1997). *Fitness in-line skating*. Champaign, IL: Human Kinetics.

Powell, M., & Svensson, J. (1993). *In-line skating*. Champaign, IL: Human Kinetics.

Werner, D. (1995). *In-line skater's start-up*. Chula Vista, CA: Tracks.

Judo

Gleeson, G. (1990). *Judo* (2nd ed). London, England: A&C Black.

Harrington, P. (1992). *Judo: a pictorial manual*. Rutland, VT: Chalres E. Tuttle.

Little, N.G. (1991). Physical performance attributes of junior and senior women, juvenile, junior and senior men judokas. *Journal of Sports Medicine and Physical Fitness, 31*(4), 510–20.

Nader, S. (1996). Female judoists: Their hormones, muscles, and bones. *Lancet, 347*, 919–20.

Seisenbacher, P., & Kerr, G. (1991). *Modern judo: Techniques of East and West*. Swindon, Wiltshire, England: Crowood Press.

Kayak

Ford, K. (1995). *Kayaking*. Champaign, IL: Human Kinetics

Hopkinson, A. (1988, August). Beginning kayaking for women. *Canoe, 16*(4), 80.

Lewis, L. (1992). *Water's edge: women who pushed the limits in rowing, kayaking & canoeing*. Seattle, WA: Seal Press.

Lacrosse

Brackenridge, C. (1978). *Women's lacrosse.* Hauppauge, NY: Barrons Educational Series.

Trafford, B., & Howarth, K. (1990). *Women's lacrosse (skills of the game series).* Ann Arbor, MI: Crowell House Publishing Company.

Luge

Bobsleigh and luge. (December, 1986). *Alberta Sport Report,* 6–7.

Rauf, W. & Way, R. (1987). *The natural luge racing, skill development model.* Vanier, Ontario: Canadian Amateur Bobsleigh and Luge Association.

Roy. B. (1992). Biomechanical aspects of some gliding sport. *Science Periodical on Research and Technology in Sport, 12*(3), 1–7.

Way, R. & Raus, W. (1990). *Level I technical.* Gloucester, Ontario: Canadian Luge Association.

Orienteering

Kjellstrom, B. (1994). *Be expert with map and compass: The complete orienteering handbook.* New York, NY: MacMillian General Reference.

Renfrew, T. (1997). *Orienteering.* Champaign, IL: Human Kinetics.

Racquetball

Khan, J. (1993). *Learn squash and racquetball in a weekend.* New York, NY: Alfred A. Knopf.

Kittleson, S. (1992). *Racquetball: Steps to success.* Champaign, IL: Human Kinetics.

Turner, E., & Clouse, W. (1996). *Winning racquetball: Skills, drills, and strategies.* Champaign, IL: Human Kinetics.

Rowing

Brown, C.P. (1990). Women sweat too: An athlete's perspective of the road to the top. In A. Fitzgerald (ed.), *Olympic education: Breaking ground for the 21st century: Proceedings of the USOA XIII,* (pp. 55–60). Colorado Springs, CO: USOC Education Council.

Korzeniowski, K. (1990, March/April). Basic rowing technique. Part I: Body positions during the rowing stroke. *American Rowing, 22*(2), 18–20.

———. (1990). Basic rowing technique. Part II: Bladework during the rowing stroke. *American Rowing, 22*(3), May/June, 1990, 20–21.

Sailing

Donaldson, S. (1994). *Basic sailing skills.* Gloucester, Ontario: Canadian Yachting Association.

Porter, M. (1995). The mermaids are out there so why aren't we? Women and sailing. *Canadian Women's Studies, 15*(4), 102–04.

Reynolds, K. (1995, April). America 3: The women's team. *Road & Track, 46,* 98–101.

Skiing, Alpine

A World Cup interview: Winning the American way. How the U.S. women became a world alpine power. (1986, Winter). *Journal of Psychological Science,* 16–20, 26–29.

Brooks, G. (1981). Women athletes, college ski coaches and the Association for Intercollegiate Athletics for Women. *Journal of the United States Ski Coaches Association, 4,* 27–28.

Gullion, L. (1990). *Ski games: A fun-filled approach to teaching Nordic and Alpine skills.* Champaign, IL: Human Kinetics.

Leach, R.E. (1994). *Alpine skiing.* Champaign, IL: Human Kinetics.

Yacenda, J. (1992). *Alpine skiing: Steps to success.* Champaign, IL: Human Kinetics.

Skiing, Artistic

Guthrie, R. (1992). *Hotdogging and snowboarding*. Minneapolis, MN: Capstone Press.

Skiing, Cross Country

Dorsen, P. J. (1993). Women in skiing. *Cross-country skier, 13*(2), November, 1993, 72–73, 75.

Gullion, L. (1993). *Nordic skiing: Steps to success*. Champaign, IL: Human Kinetics

Loewdin, I. (1991, Summer). The history of ladies cross-country. *AST Cross-Country News, 6*(3), 14–16.

Rundell, K.W., & McCarthy, J.R. (1996). Effect of kinematic variables on performance in women during a cross-country ski race. *Medicine and Science in Sports and Exercise, 28*(11), 1413–17.

Soccer

Crisfield, D. (1996). *Winning soccer for girls*. New York, NY: Facts on File.

Hanna, S. (1996). *Beyond winning: Memoir of a women's soccer coach*. Boulder, CO: University Press.

LaBlanc, M., & Henshaw, R. (1994). *The world encyclopedia of soccer*. Detroit, MI: Visible Ink Press.

Luxbacher, J.A. (1996). *Soccer: Steps to success* (2nd ed.). Champaign, IL: Human Kinetics.

Softball

Babb, R., & the Amature Softball Association. (1997). *Etched in gold: The story of America's first-ever Olympic gold medal winning softball team*. Chicago, IL: Master Publishers.

Dickson, R. (1994). *The worth book for softball: A celebration of American's true national pastime*. New York, NY: Facts on File.

Meyer, R. (1984). *The complete book of softball: The loonies' guide to playing and enjoying the game*. Champaign, IL: Human Kinetics.

Potter, D., & Brockmeyer, G.A. (1989). *Softball: Steps to success*. Champaign, IL: Human Kinetics.

Richardson, D., & Yeager, D. (1997). *Living the dream*. Kensington.

Speedskating

Breitenbucher, C. (1995). *Bonnie Blair: Golden streak*. Minneapolis, MN: Learner.

Holum, D. (1984). *Complete handbook of speed skating*. Hillside, NJ: Enslow.

Squash

Khan, J. (1993). *Learn squash and racquetball in a weekend*. New York, NY: Alfred A. Knopf.

McKay, H. (1979). *Heather McKay's complete book of squash*. New York, NY: Ballantine Books.

Yarrow, P. (1997). *Squash: Steps to success*. Champaign, IL: Human Kinetics.

Swimming

Friedman, S. (1996). *Swimming the channel: A widow's journey to life*. New York, NY: Farrar, Straus and Giroux.

Gill, J.E. (1997). *Fly 'n' free (swim team, No. 2) young adult fiction*. New York, NY: Camelot.

Laughlin, T. (1996). *Total immersion: The revolutionary way to swim better, faster, and easier*. New York, NY: Fireside Books.

Thomas, D.G. (1996). *Swimming: Steps to success*. Champaign, IL: Human Kinetics.

Swimming (Synchronized)

Gundling, B.O., & White, J.E. (1988). *Creative synchronized swimming*. Champaign, IL: Human Kinetics.

Table Tennis

Hodges, L. (1993). *Table tennis: Steps to success*. Champaign, IL: Human Kinetics.

Seemiller, D., & Clouse, W. (1997). *Winning table tennis: Skills, drills, and strategy*. Champaign, IL: Human Kinetics.

Shaw, M., ed. (1989). *How to play table tennis*. Norwich, England: Jarrod Color.

Tae Kwon Do

Lee, K.M. (1996). *Tae kwon do: Techniques and training*. New York : Sterling Press.

Park, Y.H., & Leibowitz, J. (1994). *Fighting Back: Taekwondo for women*. Boston, MA: Charles E. Tuttle.

Park, Y.H., & Seaburne, T. (1997). *Tae kwon do: Technique and tactics*. Champaign, IL: Human Kinetics.

Wiley, C.A., ed. (1992). *Women in the marital arts (Io series, No. 46)*. Berkeley, CA: North Atlantic Books.

Team Handball

Clanton R.E., & Dwight, M.D. (1997). *Team handball: Steps to success*. Champaign, IL: Human Kinetics.

Tennis

Blue, A. (1995). *Martina: The life and times of Martina Navatilova*. New York, NY: Birch Lane Press.

Brown, J. (1995). *Tennis: Steps to success* (2nd ed.). Champaign, IL: Human Kinetics.

King, B.J. (1982). *Billie Jean*. New York, NY: Viking Press.

Seles, M. (1996). *Monica: From fear to victory*. New York, NY: Harper Collins.

United States Tennis Association. (1996). *Tennis tactics: Winning patterns and play*. Champaign, IL: Human Kinetics.

Track and Field (Field)

Jacoby, E., & Fraley, R. (1995). *Complete book of jumps*. Champaign, IL: Human Kinetics.

Santos, J., & Shamon, K. (1991). *Sports illustrated track: The field events*. New York, NY: Sports Illustrated.

Track and Field (Track)

Carr, J.A. (1991). *Fundamentals of track and field*. Champaign, IL: Human Kinetics.

Tricard, L.M. (1996). *American women's track and field: A history, 1895 through 1980*. New York, NY: McFarland and Company.

Trampoline and Tumbling

Boone, W.T. (1976). *Illustrated handbook of gymnastics, tumbling and trampolining*. New York, NY: Prentice Hall.

Griswold, L. (1962). *Trampoline tumbling*. New York, NY: Barnes.

Ward, P. (1996). *Teaching tumbling*. Champaign, IL: Human Kinetics.

Triathalon

Cook, J.S. (1992). *The triathletes: A season in lives of four women in the toughest sport of all*. New York, NY: St. Martin's Press.

Piggs, M. (1997). *Triathalon bundle pack* [Computer training kit]. Champaign, IL: Human Kinetics.

Town, G., & Kearney, T. (1994). *Swim, bike, and run*. Champaign, IL: Human Kinetics.

Volleyball

Chadwin, D. (1997). *Wahine ball: The story of Hawaii's most beloved team*. Honolulu, HI: Mutual.

Crisfield, D. (1995). *Winning volleyball for girls*. New York: Facts on File.

Hastings, J. (ed.). (1996). *Karch Kiraly's championship volleyball*. New York: Fireside Books.

Herbert, M. (1991). *Insights and strategies for winning volleyball*. Champaign, IL: Human Kinetics.

Viera, B.L., & Ferguson, B.J. (1996). *Volleyball: Steps to success*. Champaign, IL: Human Kinetics.

Volleyball (Beach)

Hastings, J. ed. (1996). *Karch Kiraly's championship volleyball*. New York, NY: Fireside.

Reece, G., & Karbo, K. (1997). *Big girl in the middle*. New York, NY: Crown.

Waterskiing

Favret, B., & Benzel, D. (1997). *Complete guide to waterskiing*. Champaign, IL: Human Kinetics.

Italia, R. (1993). *Freestyle waterskiing*. Minneapolis, MN: Abdo and Daughters.

Travers, J. (1990). *Waterskiing*. East Sussex, England: Farnhurst Books.

Walker, C. (1992). *Waterskiing and kneeboarding*. Minneapolis, MN: Capstone Press.

Weightlifting

Fodor, R.V. (1983). *Winning weight lifting*. New York, NY: Sterling.

Lund, B. (1996). *Weightlifting (extreme sports)*. Minneapolis, MN: Capstone Press.

Peterson, J.A.; Bryant, C.X.; & Peterson, S. (1995). *Strength training for women*. Champaign, IL: Human Kinetics.

Roberts, S., & Weider, B. (1994). *Strength and weight training for young athletes*. Chicago, IL: Contemporary Books.

Wrestling

Mysnyk, M.; Davis, B.; & Simpson, B. (1994). *Winning wrestling moves*. Champaign, IL: Human Kinetics.

Peterson, J.A.; Bryant, C.X.; & Peterson, S. (1995). *Strength training for women*. Champaign, IL: Human Kinetics.

Savage, J. (1996). *Wrestling basics (new action sports)*. Minneapolis, MN: Capstone Press.

Sinelli, J. (1993). *There is a girl in my hammerlock* [fiction]. New York, NY: Aladdin Paperbacks.

Selected Bibliography

Atalanta, an anthology of creative work celebrating women's athletic achievements. (1996). Los Angeles, CA: Papier-Mache Press.

Bentley, K. (1983). *Going for the gold. The story of Black women in sports.* Los Angeles, CA: Carnation Co.

Birrell, S. and Cole, C. (1994). *Women, sport, and culture.* Champaign, IL: Human Kinetics.

Blue, A. (1987). *Grace under pressure: The emergence of women in sport.* London: Sidewick & Jackson.

———. (1988). *Faster, brighter, further: Women's triumphs and disasters at the Olympics.* London: Virago Press.

Boutelier, M. (1983). *The sporting woman.* Campaign, IL: Human Kinetics.

Cahn, S. (1994). *Coming on strong, gender and sexuality in twentieth-century women's sport.* New York: Maxwell MacMillan International.

Cohen, G., and Joyner-Kersee, J. (1993). *Women in sport, issues and controversies.* Newberry Park: Sage Publications.

Creedon, P. (1994). *Women, media, and sport, challenging gender values.* Thousand Oaks, CA: Sage Publications.

Darden, A. (1976). *The sports hall of fame.* New York: Drake Publishers.

Duda, J., & Allison, M. (1990). Cross cultural analysis in exercise and sport psychology: A void in the field. *Journal of Sport and Exercise Psychology, 12,* 114–31.

Duffy, T. (1983). *Winning women, the changing image of women in sports.* New York: Times Books.

Dyer, K. (1939). *Challenging the men, the social biology of female sporting achievement.* St. Lucia; New York: University of Queensland Press.

Festle, M. (1996). *Playing nice: politics and apologies in women's sports.* New York: Columbia University Press.

Foreman, L., ed. (1996). *The Olympic century. The official first century history of the modern Olympic movement. 25 volume series.* Los Angeles, CA: World Sport Research and Publications, Inc.

Fox, S. (1989). *The sporting woman. A book of days.* Boston, MA: Bullfinch Press.

Garfield, E. (1988). *The Wilson report: Moms and dads, daughters and sports.* Los Angeles: Diagnostic Research.

Geadelmann, P. (1977). *Equality in sport for women.* Washington, DC: American

Alliance for Health, Physical Education, and Recreation.

Gerber, E.; Felshin, J.; Berlan, P.; and Wyrick, W. (1974).*The American woman in sport.* MA: Addison-Wesley Publishing Co.

Gibbon, J.; Hamby, B.; & Dennis, W. (1997). Researching gender-role ideologies internationally and cross-culturally. *Psychology of Women Quarterly, 21,* 151–70.

Green, T.; Oglesby, C.; Alexander, A.; and Franke, N. (1981). *Black women in sport.* Reston, VA: American Alliance for Health, Physical Education, Recreation and Dance.

Guttmann, A. (1991). *Women's sports: A history.* New York: Columbia University Press.

Hall, M. (1942). *Feminism and sporting bodies: Essays on theory and practice.* Champaign, IL: Human Kinetics.

Hall, R. (1996). *Ethnic identity and cross racial experiences of college athletes.* Unpublished thesis, Temple University, Philadelphia, PA.

Hargreaves, J. (1937). *Sporting females, critical issues in the history and sociology of women's sports.* New York: Routledge.

Helms, J. (1991). *Black and white racial identity: Theory, research, and practice.* New York: Greenwood Press.

Hollander, P. (1972). *American women in sports.* New York: Grosset and Dunlap.

———. (1976). *100 greatest women in sports.* New York: Grosset Dunlap.

Howell, R., ed. (1982). *Her story in sport: A historical anthology of women in sports.* West Point, NY: Leisure Press.

Jacobs, H. (1964). *Famous American women athletes.* New York: Dodd, Mead & Co.

———. (1975). *Famous modern American women athletes.* New York: Dodd & Mead & Co.

Johnson, A. (1996). *Great women in sports.* Detroit, MI: Visible Ink Press.

Jordan, P. (1977). *Broken patterns.* New York: Dodd & Mead & Co.

Kaplan, J. (1979). *Women and sports: Inspiration and information for the new female athlete.* New York: Viking Press.

Lakan, C. (1980). *Golden girls.* New York: McGraw-Hill Book Co.

Legler, G. (1995). *All the powerful invisible things: A sportswoman's notebook.* Seattle, WA: Seal Press.

Lenskyj, H. (1986). *Women, sport, and sexuality.* Toronto: The Women's Press.

———. (1998). *Women, sport and physical activity, research and bibliography—La femme, le sport el l'activite physique.* Ottowa: Government of Canada, Fitness and Amateur Sport.

Lewis, P. (1997). *A qualitative analysis of perceived influences of race, gender, and class on selected African American female athletes.* Unpublished thesis, Temple University, Philadelphia, PA.

Macintosh, P. (1995). White privilege and male privilege. In M. Anderson & P. Collins (eds.) *Race, class, and gender.* Belmont, CA: Wadsworth.

Markel, R., and Markel, N. (1985). *For the record: Women in sports.* New York: World Almanac Publishers.

Mechikoff, Robert A. with Evans, V. (1949). *Sport psychology for women.* New York: Harper & Row.

Merchant, N., & Dupay, C. (1996). Multicultural counseling and qualitative research: Shared world view and skills. *Journal of Counseling and Development, 74*(6), 537–41.

Midgley, R. (1983). *The rule book.* New York: St. Martin's Press.

Nelson Burton, M. (1991). *Are we winning yet? How women are changing sports and how sports are changing women.* New York: Random House.

———. (1994). *The stronger women get, the more men love football: Sexism and the American culture of sports.* New York: Harcourt Brace.

Oglesby, C. (1978). *Women and sport: From myth to reality.* Philadelphia: Lea and Febiger.

———. (1993). Where is white in the rainbow coalition. In D. Brooks & R. Althouse (eds.), *Racism in college athletics: The African American athlete's experience*. Morgantown, WV: Fitness Information Technology.

———. (1996). *Can I trust you in the ZONE with my daughter?* Invited lecture, University of Virginia Annual Sport Psychology Conference, Charlottesville, VA.

Oglesby, C., & Shelton, C. (1992). Exercise and sport studies: Toward a fit, informed and joyful embodiment of feminism. In C. Kramare & D. Spender (eds.), *The knowledge explosion: Generations of feminist scholarship*. New York: Teachers College Press.

Phillips, L., and Markoe, K. (1979). *Women in sports: Records, stars, feats, and facts*. New York: Harcourt Brace Jovanovich.

Pollock, J. (1985). *The Miller Lite report on women in sports*. Tselin, NJ: New World Decisions.

Rapport, R. (1994). *A kind of grace: A treasury of sport writing by women*. Berkeley, CA: Zenobia Press.

Remley, M. (1991). *Women in sport, an annotated bibliography and resource guide. 1900–1990*. Boston, MA: G.K. Hall.

Ridley, C. (1995). *Overcoming unintentional racism in counseling and therapy: A practitioner's guide to intentional intervention*. Thousand Oaks, CA: Sage Publications.

Roeder, A. and Fuller, J. (1985). *Women in sport: Sociological and historical perspectives*. Carrollton, GA: West Georgia College.

Ryan, J. (1975). *Contributions of women: Sports*. Minneapolis: Dillon Press.

———. (1995) *Little girls in pretty boxes: The making and breaking of elite gymnasts and figure skaters*. New York: Doubleday.

Sabin, F. and Parkhouse, B. (1975). *Women who win*. New York: Random House.

Salter, D. (1996). *Crashing the old boys' network: The tragedies and triumphs of girls and women in sports*. Westport, CT: Praeger.

Shoebridge, M. (1987). *Women in sport, a select bibliography*. London; New York: Mansell.

Simri, U. (1925). *A concise world history of women's sports*. Jerusalem: Physical Education Authority in the Ministry of Education and Culture.

Sparhawk, R. (1989). *A 100-year chronology*. Metuchen, NJ: Scarecrow Press.

Sparhawk, R.; Leslie, M.; Turbow, P., and Rose, Z. (1989). *American women in sports, 1887–1987*. Metuchen, NJ: The Scarecrow Press.

Spirduso, W., ed. (1974). *NAGWS research committee project*. Washington: AAHPER Publication.

Sue, D., & Sue, D. (1990). *Counseling the culturally different*. New York: John Wiley & Sons.

Triandis, H. (1996). The psychological measurement of cultural syndromes. *American Psychologist, 51*, 407–15.

Twin, S. (1978). *Jack and Jill, aspects of women's sports history in America*. Ann Arbor, MI: University Microfilms International.

———. (1979). *Out of the bleachers*. Old Westbury, New York: Feminist Press.

Woolum, Janet. (1998). *Outstanding women athletes: Who they are and how they influenced sports in America* (2nd ed.). Phoenix, AZ: Oryx Press.

Working Group on Women in Sport. (1985). *Women, sport and the media, a report to the federal government from the working group on women in sport*. Canberra: Australian Government Publishing Service.

Index

by James Minkin

Index

Index

Index

Index

Index